Popular Music in America

The Beat Goes On

Fourth Edition

MICHAEL CAMPBELL

Australia • Brazil • Japan • Korea • Mexico • Singapore • Spain • United Kingdom • United States

Popular Music in America: The Beat Goes On, Fourth Edition
Michael Campbell

Publisher: Clark Baxter

Senior Development Editor: Sue Gleason Wade

Assistant Editor: Elizabeth Newell

Managing Media Editor: Kathryn Schooling

Marketing Program Manager: Gurpreet S. Saran

Senior Content Project Manager: Michael Lepera

Art Director: Faith Brosnan

Senior Print Buyer: Mary Beth Hennebury

Text Designer: Alisa Aronson Graphic Design

Photo Manager: Mandy Groszko

Photo Researcher: Abigail Baxter

Cover Designer: LMA/Leonard Massiglia

Cover Image: iStockphoto.com/Mike Bentley

Compositor: MPS Limited

Library of Congress Control Number: 2011960082

ISBN-13: 978-0-840-02976-8

ISBN-10: 0-840-02976-4

Schirmer Cengage Learning
25 Channel Center Street
Boston, MA 02210
USA

Cengage Learning is a leading provider of customized learning solutions with office locations around the globe, including Singapore, the United Kingdom, Australia, Mexico, Brazil and Japan. Locate your local office at **international.cengage.com/region.**

Cengage Learning products are represented in Canada by Nelson Education, Ltd.

For your course and learning solutions, visit **www.cengage.com.**

Purchase any of our products at your local college store or at our preferred online store **www.cengagebrain.com.**

Instructors: Please visit **login.cengage.com** and log in to access instructor-specific resources.

Printed in the United States of America
1 2 3 4 5 6 7 15 14 13 12 11

TO

J. Bunker Clark (1931–2003), who helped make the study of American music as vibrant, eclectic, and democratic as the music itself

CONTENTS

The Swing Era 81

Blues and Black Gospel Come in from the Outskirts, 1925–1950 93

Country and Folk Music Come in from the Outskirts 109

Latin Music in the United States, 1900s–1950s 133

Popular Music Matures: Musical Theater, Modern Jazz, and Song Interpretation 143

PREFACE

POPULAR MUSIC IN AMERICA: THE BEAT GOES ON, FOURTH EDITION, is an introductory survey of popular music in the United States since 1840. In its attention to the kinship among its many musical styles and its coherent account of the evolution of popular music over the past century and a half, the book retains the overall emphasis of previous editions. But this book has also had a thorough makeover—in structure, pedagogical features, and ancillaries.

A New Structure

A quick tour of the table of contents will make the structural differences clear. This new edition aims to increase its comprehensiveness, clarity, conciseness, and customizability. Although the overall sequence of materials remains much the same as in the previous edition, a major reorganization replaces long chapters with units broken into smaller chapters. Units are clearly defined by style and time frame, and chapters have more narrowly focused objectives, lending themselves to a variety of customizable solutions.

The opening unit provides a thorough definition of popular music and introduces the elements of popular music with a single, familiar example: Chuck Berry's "Maybellene." The balance of the text—nineteen chronological units—maps a historical journey that begins with a survey of its diverse roots and an account of the emergence of a distinctively American popular music in the middle of the nineteenth century. The journey continues through the end of the twentieth century and into the present. There is proportionately greater emphasis in this edition on country, Latin, world, rock-era, and late-twentieth-century music, plus more attention to female artists, rap, alternative, and electronica.

With an eye to student success, each unit begins with an introduction that addresses the significance and direction of new developments, and each unit ends with a "Looking Back, Looking Ahead" summary that both reviews the developments of that unit and anticipates those to come.

Collectively, these changes greatly facilitate customization: Instructors can easily select only those units (including unit introductions and summaries) and chapters that they wish to cover in their course.

Pedagogical Features: Learning to Listen

This book's focus on listening may be its most important feature. Virtually all of the 139 audio selections—available in the text's download album and its dedicated iTunes® and YouTube playlists—are discussed in depth.

Listening-related materials have been streamlined in this edition: performance information, style, form, style features (points to "Listen For . . ."), and key points (points to "Remember . . .") having to do with each musical example are collected in a Listening Cue box. A detailed, timed listening guide for each selection is available online as a pdf for instructors and students.

Ancillaries for Students and Instructors

CourseMate. The book's website, now called CourseMate, gives students many more opportunities to test their understanding as they move through the text. The special listening resources available in CourseMate include the following:

- A chapter-by-chapter eBook
- A download album for many selections discussed in the text
- Downloadable pdf Listening Guides for all selections
- iTunes playlists including all selections
- YouTube playlists for the entire book
- Glossary, flashcards, and quizzes

Students may access CourseMate using the passcode on the card bound into each new copy of the text, or purchase access online at www.cengagebrain.com.

CourseMate's Engagement Tracker. Instructors can use CourseMate's gradebook, Engagement Tracker, to assess student performance, preparation, and engagement. Engagement Tracker's tracking tools allow the instructor to

- Automatically record quiz scores.
- Export all grades to an instructor's own Excel spreadsheet.
- See progress for individuals or the class as a whole.
- Identify students at risk early in the course.
- Uncover which concepts are most difficult for the class and monitor time on task.

Instructor Companion Site. Instructors have access to an Instructor's Manual and Test Bank (prepared by John Irish of Angelo State University), PowerPoint presentations, the Active Listening Guide downloads from the Third Edition, and the author's iTunes Ping list. The Instructor's Manual features detailed outline-style lecture notes on every section, of every chapter, in every unit. Most of the previous edition's manual was kept and modified for inclusion in the new manual. The Test Bank has been greatly expanded, now including over 1,200 true-false, multiple-choice, and matching items, over 100 listening items, and over 100 essay/discussion questions.

Instructors who adopt the text may also receive a copy of the 3-CD set from the Third Edition for personal, library, and class use, either by itself or in combination with the interactive Active Listening Guide downloads (prepared by Thomas Smialek and L. A. Logrande) on the Instructor Companion Site. The Active Listening Guides feature a visual fever bar tracking the progress of the audio CD, as well as "Listen For . . . " and "Remember . . . " sections, which contain audio clips and popup glossary definitions.

CengageCompose. Instructors can easily create their own personalized text, selecting the elements that meet their specific learning objectives.

CengageCompose puts the power of the vast Cengage Learning library of content at instructors' fingertips, to create exactly the text they need. The all-new, web-based CengageCompose site lets them quickly scan contents and review materials to pick what they need for their text. Site tools let them easily assemble modular learning units into the order they want and immediately provide them with an online copy for review. Instructors may add their own material as well, to build ideal learning materials, even choosing from hundreds of customizable full-color covers.

Acknowledgments

It has been fifteen years since the publication of the first edition of this book. In that time, Schirmer Books' college texts have come to make up the music division of Schirmer Cengage Learning. For me, this affiliation has been a special blessing because the new Schirmer has given this project such wonderful support. It starts at the top with publisher Clark Baxter, who committed staff and resources to making the second, third, and fourth editions of this book superior to the first and who has remained unfailingly gracious, encouraging, and positive. I owe special thanks to Sue Gleason, my development editor, whose patience and good humor have made the preparation of this edition a pleasure and a learning experience. Thanks also to managing media editor Katie Schooling for her efforts on CourseMate, editorial assistant (now assistant editor) Liz Newell for her work on the ancillaries, marketing manager Gurpreet Saran, and to the production team, particularly Michael Lepera and Bill Clark.

A number of teachers of American popular music provided immeasurably helpful advice, which led to the revision that you hold in your hands. I am in debt to each and every one of them.

Mark Bergman, George Mason University

George Beyer, Cypress College

James Cunningham, Florida Atlantic University

Jim Deys, Binghamton University

Mike Dixon, East Carolina University

Kelly Eisenhour, Green River Community College

John Fremgen, University of Texas at Austin

John Irish, Angelo State University

Scott Kasun, Pima Community College

Dan Kruse, University of Arizona

Jason Lester, Wharton County Junior College

Gayle Murchison, College of William and Mary

Michael A. Murray, Missouri State University

Erik Wallack, Owens Community College

I would also like to thank the many other people to whom I am so indebted in so many different ways. I am especially grateful to the late Jan LaRue; Allen Forte, professor emeritus of music theory at Yale University; and Susan McClary, professor of music at UCLA, for their example and their support. LaRue's seminal book *Guidelines for Style Analysis* has profoundly shaped every aspect of my musical life—research, writing, performing, composing, and teaching—and his support and advice over the many years of our friendship have been of inestimable value. My work with Allen Forte has opened up new areas of inquiry; the rigor of his thinking and the clarity of his vision have provided an admirable model. Through her writings and presentations, Susan McClary has taught me the crucial importance of situating music in its cultural context.

I remain especially grateful to Maribeth Payne, who first acquired *And the Beat Goes On* for the original Schirmer books, and to Richard Carlin, who shepherded the book through its first publication. Thanks also to many of my former colleagues, especially John Murphy, now professor of jazz studies at the University of North Texas, and Paul Paccione and James Caldwell of Western Illinois University, for their willingness to share their time and expertise. Their suggestions and insights have been most welcome. And I would like to acknowledge my debt to three senior American music scholars: Richard Crawford, Charles Hamm, and the late H. Wiley Hitchcock. Separately and collectively, they have provided scholars and students with an inclusive and integrated view of American music. For me, their work has been a source of information and inspiration.

The best for last! My heartfelt thanks to my family: my wife, Marie Jo De Maestri; her daughters, Eva and Helena Kranjc; and our son, Gabriel. They not only have made my work as easy as possible but also have given me the best possible motivation for doing it.

Michael Campbell

ABOUT THE AUTHOR

MICHAEL CAMPBELL is a writer and a pianist. A California native, he is a Phi Beta Kappa graduate of Amherst College and holds a doctorate from Peabody Conservatory, where he studied piano with Leon Fleisher. As a commercial musician, he has assisted such artists as Angela Lansbury, Gladys Knight and the Pips, Bob Hope, Redd Foxx, Ethel Merman, and Don McLean. As a concert pianist, he has performed a broad range of repertoire, including his own transcriptions of recordings by Art Tatum, Jelly Roll Morton, and other legendary jazz pianists.

He has presented papers on Cole Porter, the evolution of popular music, and the search for the first rock and roll record, and has contributed articles on Porter and Harold Arlen for a forthcoming book on popular song. Campbell is the author of two music texts, *Popular Music in America: The Beat Goes On* and *Rock and Roll: An Introduction,* coauthored by James Brody. For many years Campbell taught at Western Illinois University. He now lives in Rhode Island, where he devotes his time to research and writing.

INTRO

We begin with the most basic question of all: What is popular music? The most comfortable answer to this question might take its cue from Supreme Court Justice Potter Stewart's opinion on hard-core pornography: We might not be able to "define the kinds of material [we] understand to be embraced within that shorthand description . . . but [we] know it when we hear it."

What Is Popular Music?

The most direct answer to this question is music that appeals to a large percentage of a population. But if we use popularity as the sole defining characteristic of popular music, we immediately run into problems. Is a CD by a classical performer popular music if it goes platinum, as some have? Is punk a popular style even though such significant punk bands as the Sex Pistols and the Ramones never hit the Top 40 in the United States? Clearly, popular music embraces more than music that sells in large numbers. Popular music embraces an array of attitudes, a family of sounds, and an industry that supports it, all of which distinguish it from classical and folk music. We will consider all of these connotations from a historical perspective.

Popular Music Is Familiar and Widely Heard

People make choices about everything—foods, friends, homes—and it would be very surprising if they did not make choices about the music they preferred. We know that certain songs were widely known to the Greeks and the Romans. Popular songs found their way into classical compositions; Mozart, for example, wrote variations on "Twinkle, Twinkle, Little Star." Some songs became well-known because they served a larger purpose. Faithful Lutherans knew Martin Luther's hymns because he set out to compose simple words and melodies that everyone could remember and sing.

This is just to say, however, that a component of popular music is familiarity. We are still a long way from an understanding of pop music as we know it.

Is punk a popular style?

© iofoto/iStockphoto

Popular Music Is Profitable

Popular music began to take on the trappings of business—and the component of profitability as a measuring stick—with two important developments in the eighteenth century: the growth of the middle class in Europe and America, and improvements in music publishing. The emergence of a middle class, especially in England, expanded the audience that would pay for entertainment at music halls. Publishers began to offer songs, dance music, and instrumental pieces for the amateur home performer, most often a pianist—pieces that were relatively easy to play and attractive to middle-class tastes. Profitable music tended to be appealing, simple, current, and unpretentious. Then, as now, the audience for more sophisticated and difficult music was significantly smaller.

Almost all of the music of the eighteenth century was current, compositions written and performed for their time. The notion of "classical music"—that is, the continuing performance of music of the past—was an almost negligible part of the musical landscape for most of the century.

John Gay's *The Beggar's Opera*—a play with musical numbers woven into the plot—introduced the ballad opera, one of the most popular kinds of public entertainments. At the time, the most

Ultimately, the marketplace rules, for better or worse

esteemed musical **genre,** or stylistic category, was opera, and the most prestigious opera drew its plots from classical literature and mythology. The music of *The Beggar's Opera* came from several levels of society, from popular dances and songs, to classical works and parodies of them. An "opera" about the seamy side of everyday life in London—an opera that lacked the grand themes explored in mythology—was a drastic change in 1729 and proved very popular.

These qualities—appeal, simplicity, currency, and lack of pretense—are still part of the pop music world. In the eighteenth century, however, the musical difference between aristocratic music and more common music was one of degree, not kind. All of the music used the same musical language at varying levels of complexity; publishers simplified aristocratic music to make it accessible to a broader, less sophisticated, middle-class audience. This held true until the vogue for blackface minstrelsy in the 1840s.

Popular Music Is a Different Sound from Classical or Folk Music

With minstrelsy in the nineteenth century, the idea of popular music as we know it begins to take shape. It is different from classical or folk music in sound, style, attitude, purpose, and audience. In the twentieth century, through the infusion of African-derived musical values and with the continued growth of the classical music industry, the differences increased. Today, although each crosses over to the other's market, classical and popular music represent two different sound worlds and two different esthetics.

Thus **popular music** can simply be music that appeals to a mass audience, is intended to have wide appeal, and has a sound and a style distinct from classical or folk. When a particular song or piece of music has all three of these qualities, it is easy to classify as popular music. "Maybellene," the song discussed in Chapter 1, is a good example. It was measurably popular (it had wide sales); both Berry and the Chess brothers intended that it be popular (they were looking for a hit); and its sound was new, distinctly different from folk music or stylized classical music.

Popular music embraces an array of attitudes, a family of sounds, and an industry that supports it, all of which distinguish it from classical and folk music.

Popular Music Is Positioned in the Center

Popular music is usually positioned between classical music on the one hand and folk or ethnic music on the other. A three-tiered musical world has developed that corresponds roughly to the social standing of the respective audiences. Classical music is associated with the upper class; it helps sell Swiss watches and luxury cars. Popular music is for the middle class—the largest portion of the population—and helps sell fast food and trucks. Folk music has been associated with isolated, largely rural, working-class people—those cut off geographically and economically from mainstream culture—and doesn't help sell anything. Ethnic music is similar in this respect, although the isolation may have more to do with cultural identity and language than geography or economics.

Popular Music Arises from Synthesis

Some of the most interesting music in the popular tradition has arisen from musicians' exploring the boundaries between popular and classical music on the one hand, and popular and folk/ethnic music on the other. Among its many virtues, classical music nurtures craft; its greatest artists are extraordinarily skillful in manipulating musical materials. Craft, whether in composition or performance, can become an end in itself. Musicians develop skill because it interests them to do so and has become necessary to the full expression of what they have to say musically. How else does one account for the extraordinary and expressive virtuosity of musicians such as guitarist Eddie Van Halen (heavy metal) and trumpeter Wynton Marsalis (jazz)? When musicians working in popular styles like heavy metal and jazz assimilate some of the values of classical music, they may deliberately forsake a larger audience to preserve their artistic vision.

The goal of folk/ethnic–popular fusions is to broaden the audience, not leave it behind. The creative concern for the folk or ethnic performer is whether to add outside elements to one's own style. Because the connection between folk musicians and their audience is more immediate and less influenced by market values, the bond between the music and its culture is typically stronger. Numerous folklike styles have come from disenfranchised, largely poor populations, some in rural, isolated areas and more recently in cities. Both punk and rap are folklike because they emerged in urban areas within underprivileged populations that were outside the mainstream and because the music expressed the attitudes and emotions of their respective subcultures.

Popular music owes its identity and its evolution to a process of creative and open-minded synthesis.

The assimilation of less popular styles into the popular music **mainstream**—that is, the prevailing popular style(s)—may have either a homogenizing or an energizing effect on the creative process. The homogenization that occurs when established acts reinterpret a fresh sound in the prevailing style may suppress or erase altogether the defining qualities of the new style. For example, in the early years of rock and roll, some white artists—including Pat Boone, who sang a notoriously bland version of Little Richard's raucous "Tutti Frutti"—made cover versions of rhythm-and-blues songs. Although these homogenized covers often sold better than the originals, they so diluted the music with mainstream pop elements that they sacrificed the integrity of the new sound.

Alternatively, the mainstreaming process may create an exciting new synthesis—a new sound—as when British rockers absorbed the "deep blues" of Muddy Waters and others into their music, or when both British and American musicians integrated reggae rhythms and textures into pop music during the late 1970s and early 1980s.

The Central Fact of Popular Music

Such borrowings highlight a central fact: Popular music owes its identity and its evolution to a process of creative and open-minded synthesis. From its beginnings to the present, the new sounds in popular music have emerged from the blending of different kinds of music—often so different as to be musically and culturally opposite. Popular music blurs racial, economic, geographical, cultural, and class boundaries. Ultimately, the marketplace rules, for better or worse. We encounter this synthetic process from the outset of our survey, in the music for the minstrel show. And we will encounter it again and again as we observe popular music grow into a global musical language with countless dialects. We begin in the middle.

Talking about Popular Music

UNIT 1

Sometime early in 1955, Chuck Berry (b. 1926) "motorvated" from St. Louis to Chicago to hear Muddy Waters perform at the Palladium Theater. For years Berry had idolized Waters, the leading electric bluesman of the postwar era. After the concert, Berry went backstage to meet him. When he asked Waters how he might find a record deal, Waters suggested that he get in touch with Leonard Chess, the owner of Chess Records, the small independent label for whom Waters recorded. Two weeks later, Berry was back in Chicago, giving Leonard Chess a demo tape that contained four songs. Among them was Berry's remake of a country song called "Ida Red," which he titled "Maybellene." Chess liked the song, so Berry recorded it soon after; it was released on August 20, 1955.

"Maybellene" caught the ear of disk jockey Alan Freed, a strong and influential supporter of rhythm and blues, and the man who gave rock and roll its name. While he was a disk jockey in Cleveland, Freed had begun using "rock and roll" in 1951 as code for "rhythm and blues." The term caught on after Freed moved to New York in 1954. By the time "Maybellene" was released, rock and roll was in the air and on the charts. With Freed promoting "Maybellene" by playing it frequently on his radio show, the song quickly jumped to No. 5 on the *Billboard* "Best" chart.

The story of "Maybellene"—a black artist with a new sound crossing over to the mainstream, an independent label looking to break through to the big time, a disc jockey trading influence for favors (Freed received partial songwriting credit on "Maybellene," and the royalties that went with it, in return for extensive on-air promotion of the song)—is but a short chapter in a saga dating back to the emergence of popular music: the complex, often contentious, interaction among those who create the music and those who try to profit from it. From the start, this interaction has involved power, money, class, race, and gender. It will be a recurrent theme in our survey.

The early history of "Maybellene" is a compelling story, and no music-specific knowledge is necessary for understanding it. But what about the song itself? Supposing that you had been present at the recording session and wanted to tell your friends about it? It wouldn't be hard to convey your enthusiasm, but could you describe its musical features accurately and specifically enough that your friends could recognize the song if they heard it on the radio?

CHAPTER 1
Talking about Popular Music

A hypothetical phone call, late at night on May 21, 1955.

You: Hey, I was just down at Chess Records . . . you know, that label down on the south side that records all those black blues singers? Anyway, they had this guy named Chuck Berry, up from St. Louis. He brought a couple of songs, this slow blues song that he called "Wee Wee Hours" and this remake of a country song that Bob Wills did, called "Ida Red." The Chess brothers didn't like the name "Ida Red," so Berry saw this mascara container on the floor and called the song "Maybellene." Maybelline makes cosmetics, but Maybellene's the girl in the lyric. Crazy, huh?

Your Friend: Why is Berry recording a country song on a blues label?

You: Well, it didn't sound too much like country when he got through with it.

Your Friend: How so?

You: First he starts the song with this nasty guitar *riff*—just him. The sound is funny—edgier than a country or jazz guitar player—or even a blues guy. Sounds like he had his amp set too high, 'cause the sound was a little distorted. Then the rest of the band joins in—just a *rhythm section* plus some guy playing maracas, of all things. They lay down this fast honky-tonk *two beat*—that's where you hear the country—but the *backbeat*'s a lot stronger—almost overpowers the bass player. For the vocal, Berry dumps the *chorus* that Wills used and plugs in his own. It's just a basic *twelve-bar blues* about a girl who can't stop cheating on him. But the *verse*—he takes that from Wills, almost talking over one chord—is all about a car chase.

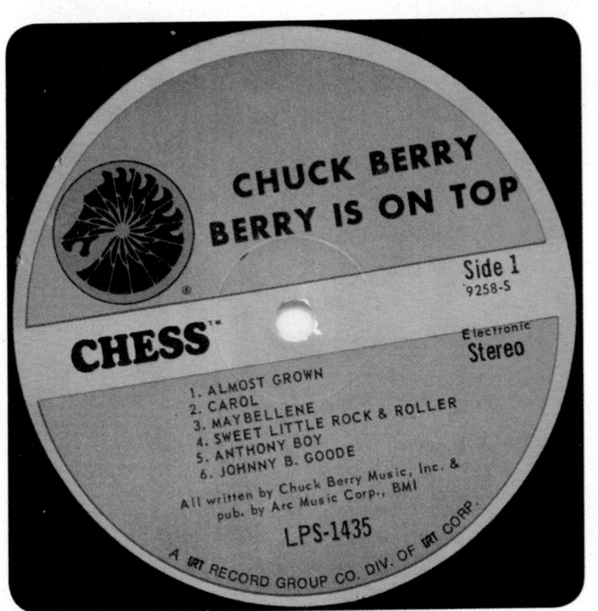

© GAB Archive/Redferns//Getty Images

Your Friend: Does Berry play a solo?

You: Yeah, in the middle of the song. And you know what? The band shifts into a swing rhythm, which is cool, 'cause Berry's solo is mostly a bunch of syncopated riffs.

Your Friend: What happens then?

You: Berry sings another chorus and he finally catches up with Maybellene's Cadillac in the last verse. After the last chorus, it just kind of fades out. . . .

Your Friend: So you like it?

You: Yeah, it's different—good story, good beat, Berry sounds like he's having a good time. I think it's gonna be a hit.

This hypothetical exchange illustrates the power of terms that can describe musical events and features with some precision. If the two friends were familiar with the broader popular music scene ca. 1955 and understood the terms highlighted in italics, the friend who received the call would have such a clear idea of what to expect that he would be able to recognize the song even before Berry sings, and anticipate many of its major features.

Meaningful discussion of any subject—geometry, automobiles, garden plants, early rock and roll—requires a vocabulary of terms that describe elements and features of the subject clearly and specifically. When users have learned a sufficient number of related terms, they can use the terms to identify, compare, and contrast not only the instances they have already encountered but also similar instances: for example, sedans, coupes, and convertibles are cars; pickups are trucks, which are not cars.

Terms do not have to be technical to be useful. *Black-eyed Susan* is far more useful for just about everyone except botanists than *Rudbeckia hirta;* the same is true for *daisy* and *Bellis perennis*. Similarly, the terms used throughout this text are useful, but not technical. Understanding them requires no advanced skills or training, only focus and concentrated listening. In this unit, we define several frequently used terms and connect them to the elements of music.

The Elements of Music

The terms used by the enthusiastic caller are specific realizations of the elements of music. *Rhythm section* implies a particular **instrumentation;** *two beat, backbeat, swing,* and *syncopation* are features of **rhythm;** *riffs* are building blocks of **melody;** *blues progression* pertains to **harmony;** *verse, chorus,* and *twelve-bar blues* refer to **form.** These and two other elements, **dynamics** and **texture,** grow out of the properties of musical sound.

The Properties of Musical Sound

Almost every musical sound has four properties: timbre, pitch, intensity, and duration. **Timbre** (pronounced "*tamber*") refers to the tone color of a musical sound. It is the term we use to describe the characteristic sound of a voice or an instrument. When we want to describe the different sounds of the same melody played on a piano and an electric guitar, we say that they have different timbres.

Pitch describes how high or low a musical tone sounds. Our sense of low and high is a function of how fast the object creating the tone is vibrating: The faster the vibration, the higher the tone. We also distinguish between sounds with definite pitch, because they vibrate at a consistent frequency, and sounds with indefinite pitch, which do not. Many percussion sounds, including those made on a drum set, convey only a general sense of high and low.

Intensity describes how loud a musical sound is. In popular music, simple descriptive terms like *loud* and *soft* usually suffice. **Duration** refers to the length of a musical sound. We typically relate the length of a sound to the beat: for example, "This note lasts (has a duration of) two beats."

The Elements of Popular Music

The elements of a musical performance grow out of these four qualities of sound. **Instrumentation,** which grows out of timbre, identifies the voices and instruments heard in performance. **Performance style** describes the way the musicians sing and play the instruments; it offers a more finely tuned understanding of sound choices. Pitches combine into *melody* and *harmony*. Intensity becomes *dynamics* on a large scale (the dynamic level of a typical heavy metal band is loud) and **inflection** on a smaller scale, such as the gradations of loudness from syllable to syllable in a vocal line. Duration grows into *rhythm* as soon as more than one note is sounded.

Two other elements emerge from instrumentation, pitch, and rhythm as the music unfolds in time. *Texture* describes the relationship among the various parts—in "Maybellene," the roles played by Berry's voice and the five instruments behind it. *Form* describes the organization of music in time. We reverse engineer definitions for the terms used in the phone call by presenting them within a discussion of the element(s) they exemplify.

© CWLawrence/iStockphoto

A tuning fork vibrates at 440 cycles per second and produces a definite pitch in the mid-range of a woman's voice; string and wind players typically use this pitch to tune their instruments.

Listen to what happens in the first 15 seconds of "Maybellene."

- Berry begins the song alone. He plays loudly, and his guitar sound has a little distortion; the loudness and the distortion give the sound an edge.
- The rest of the musicians quickly join in; they establish a clear two-beat rhythm at a brisk tempo.
- Berry sings the chorus of the song; it begins with two complementary riffs.

In this briefest of time spans, Berry provides the three most familiar elements of popular music: its distinctive sounds, its propulsive rhythms, and its accessible melodies. We discuss each in turn in the chapters that follow.

LISTENING CUE · **"Maybellene" (1955),** Chuck Berry. Berry, electric guitar and vocal; Willie Dixon, string bass; Jasper Thomas, drums; Johnnie Johnson, piano; Jerome Green, maracas.

Listen to this selection in CourseMate.

CHAPTER 2

The Sounds of Popular Music

"Maybellene" begins with Berry playing alone. Within a few seconds, the other band members join in. In just this short excerpt, we hear three key features of the sound world of popular music: the diverse and heterogeneous sounds that are incorporated into the music; the rhythm section, its core instrumental sound; and the cultivation of a distinctive performing style.

Berry and his cohorts exemplify the singular open-mindedness of innovative popular musicians. Certainly since the middle of the nineteenth century, more progressive performers have sought out new instruments and new ways of playing them. The instruments can, and have, come from almost anywhere.

Sources of Instrumental Sounds in Popular Music

The unparalleled variety of instrumental sounds in popular music comes from five sources:

1. Instruments inherited from popular music's antecedents and contributing styles
2. New ways of playing these inherited instruments
3. Creation of new instruments specifically for use in popular music
4. Use of electronic technology for sound modification
5. Use of "found" instruments

Popular music has developed from several different musical genres; all have added their instruments to the mix. Most nineteenth-century popular music used the same instruments as classical music, including the piano and guitar, plus many of the instruments of the orchestra and band—especially trumpet, trombone, clarinet, tuba, violin, and drums and cymbals. African-American musicians created new sounds on these instruments; many of these sounds were influenced by blues style (the moan of a saxophone; the use of a toilet plunger as a mute for brass instruments) or emphasized the percussive component of the sound (the sharp strum of a banjo or the plucking of a string bass). As new styles have been incorporated into popular music, their instruments have enriched its sound world. Anglo-American folk music and country music added banjo (actually a white adaptation of an African instrument recreated by slaves in America), fiddle, and steel guitar. Latin music added an array of percussion instruments: conga drum, bongos, timbales, claves, and more. Newly created instruments like the Hammond organ and the vibraphone also found a home in popular music.

Instruments designed expressly for use in popular music have also helped shape its sound. Most of the instruments used in contemporary popular music were invented principally, even exclusively, for that purpose. These include not only the drum set but also an almost unlimited array of electronic instruments: electric bass, various electronic keyboards—even synthesized drums and wind instruments.

Electronics can also drastically modify the sound of existing instruments. Sometimes amplification results in such a dramatic change in timbre and leads to such significant changes in the design and setup of the instrument that, in effect, it becomes a new instrument. The solid-body guitar is a familiar example. Signal processing can also reshape the basic timbre of an instrument, as guitarist Jimi Hendrix proved so convincingly.

At the opposite end of the technology spectrum are "found" instruments—instruments created from materials close at hand but intended for other uses or for no use at all. Most of these are percussion instruments that now exist in a more refined, commercial form after becoming well established. These include a handclap; a tap dancer's feet; the bones of the early minstrel show; a host of Afro-Cuban percussion instruments—claves, cowbell, gourd, and the like; the pans of calypso, originally steel drums used to store oil; and the turntable, used by rap DJs for scratching.

We hear examples of all of these sources in "Maybellene":

- The piano and string bass come from European music; so does the original version of Berry's guitar.
- Bassist Willie Dixon plucks the strings of the string bass rather than bowing them. This technique, called *pizzicato,* is relatively rare in classical music but the norm in popular music.
- Jasper Thomas's drum set evolved from the primitive drum sets that appeared just after the turn of the twentieth century in early jazz bands and dance orchestras.
- Amplification made the guitar far more powerful, and it enabled Berry to develop an aggressive sound.
- Jerome Green's maracas evolved from a percussion instrument created by filling a hollow gourd with seeds.

The Rhythm Section

"Maybellene" offers an easily recognizable instance of the core instrumental sound of popular music, the rhythm section. The **rhythm section** is a heterogeneous group of instruments that includes at least one chord instrument, one bass instrument, and one percussion instrument.

© Branex/Dreamstime.com

The most common chord instruments are of two types: strummed and keyboard. Strummed instruments include banjo and guitar, both acoustic and electric. Keyboard instruments include piano, organ, electric piano, and synthesizer. Bass instruments include tuba (brass bass), string bass, electric bass, and synthesizer bass. The main percussion instrument is the drum set. Occasionally, other percussion instruments, especially the conga drum, have augmented the rhythm section or substituted for the drum set. More recently, synthesized drum sounds have replaced human drummers.

The rhythm section has been a fixture in popular music for almost a century. The first rhythm sections, heard in the dance orchestras and jazz bands of the twenties, consisted of an instrument from the marching band (brass bass), an instrument assembled from the drum line of a marching band (the drum kit), an instrument from the minstrel show (banjo), and the all-purpose instrument of the time (piano). By the thirties, the string bass had largely replaced the brass bass, and the acoustic guitar had replaced the banjo. Throughout the first half of the century, the rhythm section was in the background. Its primary role was to provide support for vocalists or melody instruments like the trumpet and saxophone. That would change around mid-century.

There were two significant changes in the rhythm section after 1950. The first was the increased use of amplification. The electric guitar caught on after World War II, especially in blues and blues-derived music. By the 1960s, the electric bass had replaced the string bass in rock and rhythm and blues, and electronic keyboards had become an increasingly popular alternative to the acoustic piano. The other change was the increased prominence of the rhythm instruments. In electric blues and then in rock, the rhythm section became the nucleus of the band; other instruments, such as saxophones, were optional. "Maybellene" evidences an early stage in this process: Berry's guitar is the only amplified instrument, and the rhythm section is the entire band.

The major development in the last quarter of the twentieth century was the electronification of the rhythm section. With the rapid development of synthesizers in the 1970s and digital instruments in the 1980s, synthesized bass, chord, and percussion sounds augmented or replaced acoustic and electronic rhythm instruments.

Although the instruments of the rhythm section have changed drastically over the past century, their role remains much the same. Rhythm instruments of all kinds—from banjos and brass basses to digital keyboards and drum machines—provide harmony, a bass voice, and percussive sounds.

Performance Style

Instrument choice is one dimension of the sound variety in popular music; another is the varied ways in which musicians sing and play. Consider this list of singers who had or participated in No. 1 hit singles or albums in 1960:

- Elvis Presley, the king of rock and roll, the white man with the "negro feel"
- Ray Charles, who brought a unique merging of blues and gospel to pop and country music
- Marty Robbins, a popular country singer who was part of the mainstreaming of Nashville in the late fifties
- Chubby Checker, a Fats Domino fan who made a career out of one dance, the Twist
- The Drifters, one of the classic black vocal groups of the fifties and early sixties
- The Kingston Trio, pleasant-voiced young men who were part of the folk revival in the late fifties/early sixties

Most of these performers have a distinctive performance style. The cultivation of a personal sound is the ultimate extension of the timbral variety of popular music; in effect, it is variety at the most local level.

Moreover, one measure of excellence in popular music is *innovation,* the ability to develop a fresh, distinctive, and personal sound. Berry's guitar style, with its frequent double notes and slight distortion, had a sharper edge than the electric guitar sounds used in jazz and country music, and a brighter sound than usually heard in electric blues.

Among the reasons that "Maybellene" brought a fresh sound to the pop charts were Berry's edgy guitar playing and singing. Another was forming the entire band from rhythm-section instruments. In pre-rock pop, rhythm sections supported voices and melody instruments. In rock, the rhythm section became the nucleus of the band; other instruments, such as saxophones, were optional.

In "Maybellene" and most of the music that we hear, we react first to the sounds that we hear. Often, our next response is to the beat. We explore what we mean by *beat* and other aspects of rhythm in the next chapter.

CHAPTER 3
Rhythm in Popular Music

In the excellent documentary *Rock and Roll: The Early Years*, there is a clip of a white preacher denouncing the evils of rock and roll. He asks rhetorically what it is about rock and roll that makes it so seductive to young people, then immediately answers his own question by shouting, "The BEAT! The BEAT! The BEAT!" pounding the pulpit in time to his words. The preacher might have been thinking of "Maybellene," which has a strong, fast beat—to keep up with the Coupe de Ville that Berry is chasing in his V8 Ford. It *was* the beat that drew teens to rock and roll during the 1950s.

This meaning of **beat**—that quality of music that makes you want to want to tap your foot—is the most basic and familiar one. However, two other meanings of *beat* are in common use in popular music. The differences among them are exemplified in these three sentences:

- The tempo of "Maybellene" is about 140 beats per minute.
- "Maybellene" shifts between a two-beat and a four-beat rhythm.
- "Maybellene" has a great beat; it makes you want to dance to the music or drive faster.

In the first sentence, *beat* refers to the regular measure of time; in the second, it refers to the fundamental rhythmic organization, to which all other rhythmic features relate; and in the third it refers to the full range of rhythmic events that interact to make the rhythm compelling. Let's consider each in turn. Our goal here is to describe these three distinct meanings of beat, using its realizations in "Maybellene" as a springboard for a more general understanding of rhythm in popular music.

"Timekeeping" Beat

If you tap your foot as you listen to "Maybellene," you will almost certainly align your foot taps with the bass notes. Except for a brief stretch during Berry's guitar solo, the bass notes mark off equal increments of time at a rate a little bit faster than two times per second. We identify this particular regular rhythm as the beat because it lies in our physical comfort zone.

We use the word **tempo** to refer to the *speed* of the beat. We generally measure tempo in beats per minute: The tempo of "Maybellene" is on the fast side at 140 beats per minute. Tempos in danceable popular music generally range between 110 and 140 beats per minute (bpm); marches and disco songs are in the mid-range,

© Roberto A Sanchez/iStockphoto

around 120 beats per minute. Tempos outside this range may connect powerfully to the musical message: The frenetic tempos of punk (often around 160 to 170 bpm) reinforce the confrontational nature of the style; by contrast, the languid tempos (often between 60 and 70 bpm) of so many doo-wop songs encourage the slow dancing that enhances the romance expressed in the lyrics.

Beat and Measure

In popular music, beats may coalesce into groups of two, three, four, or even five—Dave Brubeck's "Take Five" is a famous, if rare, example of five-beat groupings. Two and four are the most common. We call a consistent grouping of beats a **measure,** or **bar.** The measure represents a slower regular rhythm. And because it is slower, it is a more convenient form of rhythmic reference for longer time spans: For instance, we refer to the form of the chorus in "Maybellene" as a twelve-bar blues rather than a twenty-four- or forty-eight-beat blues.

In "Maybellene," you can hear the relationship between beat and measure as soon as the other instruments enter. Berry's accompaniment sets up an oscillating pattern that repeats every two beats; as a result, we hear each measure as encompassing two beats during much of the song.

This meaning of *beat* is the most generic: it and the terms associated with it—*tempo, measure,* and *bar*—could be applied to a wide range of music: pop, jazz, classical, rock, R&B, and almost any other music with a steady pulse. By contrast, the second meaning of *beat* is specific to twentieth-century popular music.

"Style" Beats

Musicians often use the term *two-beat* to identify the rhythmic foundation used in the vocal sections of "Maybellene." A **two-beat rhythm** features two bass notes per measure alternating with chords played on the backbeat. In "Maybellene," Berry alternates between bass and chord underneath his vocal; the bassist reinforces the bass note, while the drummer emphasizes the backbeat with sharp raps on the snare drum.

The **backbeat** is a percussive sound on the second of a pair of beats, or—in this case—on the second half of a beat. The percussive sound can be as simple as a handclap or finger snap, or it can be a rap on the snare drum, the closing of the cymbal, or an energetic strummed chord. As heard in a two-beat rhythm, it is an African-American reinterpretation of the afterbeat of a march or polka (both popular dance forms in the latter part of the nineteenth century): OOM-pah becomes OOM-chuck.

During Berry's solo in the middle of the song, the bassist shifts from two notes per measure to a "walking" bass line with four notes per measure. The backbeat remains constant: The drummer continues to rap it out on the snare drum. As a result, the tempo doubles, as if Berry and his group shifted into a higher gear right along with the narrator's V8 Ford. Typically, when the rhythmic foundation of a song features a walking bass or other steady timekeeping four times a measure, we think of it as a **four-beat rhythm.** In this context, with the breakneck tempo and two-beat frame, the matching of bass line to the beat is not as immediately apparent as it will be in subsequent examples.

© Marcin Pawlik/iStockphoto

We identify both the two-beat and four-beat rhythms as **style beats** because they are the most pervasive feature of the dominant (or co-dominant) style of the music of a particular era. Almost all of the songs published during the 1920s and 1930s were subtitled "a foxtrot"; the foxtrot remains the most familiar version of a two-beat rhythm. Beginning in the late 1930s, the newly popular four-beat rhythm became the rhythmic foundation of swing. It most clearly differentiated swing from the more sedate "sweet" foxtrot songs. Similarly, the vast majority of rock songs from the 1960s and 1970s have a rock beat, although they differ widely in instrumentation, vocal style, and melodic approach. Although it connects to rock and roll, "Maybellene" does not have a rock beat. The lack of a rock rhythm identifies "Maybellene" as a song from the very beginning of the rock era, before Berry and others defined the essential features of rock rhythm.

So, the word *beat* in the phrase "two-beat" has a meaning distinctly different from the first meaning of "beat," which refers to the regular rhythm to which we most easily respond. Both are relatively specific: We can say the "Maybellene" has a tempo of about 140 beats per minute and that it also has a two-beat rhythm because of the alternation of bass note and backbeat. The third meaning of beat is more subjective: What constitutes a "good beat" is a matter of taste. Still, there is close correspondence between what makes big-band swing, and rock bands rock.

"Good" Beat

For most people, what gives a song a "good" beat is the interplay among all the rhythms present in a performance or recording, especially when the rhythms are syncopated. A **syncopation** is an accent that does not line up with the beat. An **accent** is a note, chord, or non-pitched sound that is emphasized in some way, so that it stands out. Often, accents stand out because they are louder or longer than the notes around them. Many of the accented syllables in the chorus of "Maybellene" are syncopated: for example, "can't" and "oh." Similarly, the last syllable in each line of the lyric—"hill," "Ville," and so on—in the storytelling part of the song is syncopated. It is the interplay between the steady style beat and the syncopated accents that gives the song so much rhythmic vitality.

In popular music, as in all other kinds of music, rhythm includes more than the beat. In its fullest meaning, rhythm is the time dimension of musical sound: It encompasses any musical event heard as a function of time. Still, "beat" in all three of its meanings is central to an understanding of rhythm. Most often, it is the rhythmic point of entry into a performance and its main point of reference. Whether it's the relentless throb of a disco hit, the elegant sway of a Cole Porter foxtrot, the supercharged tempos of punk, or the sequenced syncopations of rap and hip-hop, rhythm is at the heart of our experience of popular music.

CHAPTER 4
Melody and Harmony, Texture and Form

The chorus of "Maybellene" begins with two short phrases: One ("Maybellene") is three syllables, the other ("why can't you be true?") is five. Both have a lot of empty space around them. Then they are repeated immediately, with only slight variation. These four phrases are riffs. They stand out sharply, both in the chorus and in the song overall, because the verse is sung mostly to a single note. By keeping the main melodic idea short and set off from the music around it, Berry makes it easy to latch onto the riff. It's one of the hooks that pulled listeners in back in 1955.

Riffs: Melodic Building Blocks

In popular music, melodies typically grow out of riffs. **Riffs** are short, easily remembered, and often syncopated melodic ideas. When sung, riffs are typically set two to seven syllables; instrumental riffs tend to be of comparable length. Their brevity makes them easier to remember. In songs like "Maybellene," riffs are both the main melodic point of entry and the building blocks of **melody.** They can give melody a distinctive rhythm and contour (the pattern of rise and fall), which in turn makes it stand out from more generic patterns, such as repeated chords or repetitive bass lines.

© Jeff deVries/iStockphoto

In popular music, building melodies from short melodic ideas dates back to the minstrel show, but most nineteenth-century popular song employed longer, more spun-out phrases. Riffs began to appear in popular song around 1910; within a decade, the riff had become the customary starting point for melody in popular music.

In "Maybellene," Berry develops the title-phrase riff into a complete melody via a statement/response approach: "Maybellene" is answered by "why can't you be true," and the entire unit is repeated with subtle variation. On the next larger level, this statement/response phrase becomes a statement, which receives a more extended response after its repetition.

Because of their brevity and because they could be syncopated, riffs enabled songwriters to impart a conversational rhythm to the lyrics; for example, the rhythm of "Maybellene" and the rest of the chorus as Berry sings it closely approximates speech rhythm. Indeed, one of the most interesting features of "Maybellene" is the smooth continuum between speech and song: The chorus has a melody, while the verses, which focus around a single note, are more than speech but less than conventional song.

The innovative sounds, compelling rhythms, and memorable riffs heard in songs like "Maybellene" draw listeners in. Supporting these points of entry are two key background elements: harmony and texture. Harmony refers to chords; texture refers to the relationship among the parts—melody, bass line, and others. Each has a complementary relationship to melody: A melody note, and especially a prominent melody note, is often part of the chord supporting it; the melodic line is usually the most prominent part of the texture.

Harmony

In music, **harmony** is the study of **chords:** what they are, how they are formed, how long they last, and how they succeed each other. If you have ever sung or heard a four-part hymn, you are already acquainted with all four of these concepts. When all four parts sing at the same time, they produce simultaneous complementary groups of pitches, or chords. The top, or soprano, part is the melody. The series of chords formed by the four parts is the harmony.

The other qualities of harmony are just as clearly evident in a hymn. Typically, chords change in a steady rhythm, once every syllable. Because chord change is usually clear and regular, the sequence of chords is easily heard. Chord sequences often become predictable, especially at the ends of phrases.

Chords are most easily recognized when all pitches sound at the same time. But there are other ways of presenting harmony; most of them are subtler. For example, accompaniments in a two-beat rhythm typically present the lowest note of the chord (the bass), followed by the rest of the chord notes. Or chord pitches may occur one after the next. We use the term **arpeggio** to describe a chord in which the pitches are presented in succession: The opening notes of "The Star Spangled Banner" form an arpeggio.

The most basic harmonies in popular music are a group of three chords, commonly identified as I, IV, and V. These have served as the main chords in popular song since its beginnings as a commercial music in America: many nineteenth-century songs are harmonized only with these basic chords. In the twentieth century, I, IV, and V were the most widely used chords in pre-rock popular song, formed virtually the entire harmonic vocabulary of blues and early country music, and became focal chords in rock.

Chords often appear in a consistently used sequence called a **chord progression.** In a chord progression, there is a sense of connection between the chords. The chords are not simply following each other but forming a larger unit that leads toward a goal chord. Certain chord progressions appear so regularly that they create a sense of expectation. When we have heard part of the progression, we have a sense of what will come next.

In "Maybellene," the supporting harmony alternates between the twelve-bar blues progression in the chorus and solos, and resting on the I chord in the verses. The blues progression is outlined below in the discussion of form.

Texture

We use the term *texture* to identify the rest of the story for sound, melody, and rhythm. For each element, it completes the picture, going beyond the point of entry to encompass the full range of activity. When evaluating texture in relation to sound, we consider the number of voices and instruments, the range between the highest and lowest sounds, and the areas in which sounds are concentrated. This provides an overall impression of textural density—thick or thin, dark or light. Density often has a subtle but profound impact on mood. The sound of jazz in the 1920s is often upbeat, in part because of the concentration of instruments in a higher register. By contrast, the dark, even threatening sound of electric blues, hard rock, and rap owes much to the concentration of parts in a lower register: prominent bass and low-pitched percussion sounds. In "Maybellene," the most prominent sounds come from Berry himself: His singing is in a middle range, and his guitar accompaniment is in a low-middle range.

The melodic dimension of texture is concerned mainly with the distribution of melodic interest. The melody is, by default, among the most interesting lines because it has a distinctive rhythm and melodic contour (the rise and fall in pitch of a melodic line). Using the melody as a yardstick, we observe whether other parts, if any, are of comparable melodic interest, and which parts are of lesser interest. In the vocal sections of "Maybellene," the melody—Berry's vocal line—is not sufficiently self-contained to stand alone, but it is far more distinctive than the bass line or the minimal melodic pattern formed by the chordal accompaniment. The walking bass line during the guitar solo is more interesting melodically, but not comparable in interest to Berry's riff-laden line. The intermittent piano fills have a distinctive profile but do not coalesce into a continuous line.

The rhythmic texture of popular music is likely to be fuller than the melodic texture because there are usually drums and/or other nonmelodic percussion instruments in a popular music performance. All instruments, pitched and unpitched, enrich the rhythmic texture in popular music. One aspect of rhythmic texture is its density, how many voices and instruments are contributing to the rhythmic flow.

Another aspect of rhythmic texture is the role of the various parts—whether they reinforce the beat or another regular rhythm that moves faster or slower than the beat, push against it, or float above it. The beat offers a familiar point of reference for rhythmic texture. However, those parts that confirm the beat are likely to be the least interesting parts of the texture. Strict timekeeping may produce a clear beat but little interest. A good beat, in the qualitative sense, depends on the interplay between those rhythmic layers marking or implying a regular rhythm and those that conflict with it or soar over it. In "Maybellene," bass, drums, maracas, and guitar mark the beat and backbeat during the vocal sections; the rhythmic interest comes almost exclusively from Berry's vocal line.

In observing texture, we will concentrate on general observations: impressions of density (thick/thin), register (high/low, concentrated/separated), melodic interest (concentrated in one part/diffused among several parts), rhythmic activity (active/quiet), beat keeping (clear/implied), and rhythmic play (syncopated/unsyncopated).

The familiar points of entry in sound, melody, and rhythm may draw us into a song, but it is often the harmony and texture that sustain our interest, even through several listenings. We can easily assess the validity of this statement by this simple test: Sing the melody and tap the beat and backbeat of "Maybellene" (or any other song that you like), then compare the result to the recording. The melodic and rhythmic points of entry are just a small fraction of the sound world of the song, even if they are the most prominent. That is why even "first-take" observations of harmony and texture help round out our impression of a song.

Form

When you look at a photograph of Chuck Berry, you can take in the whole image in a glance. You can't do that with his music because it unfolds in time. Your sense of the organization of a musical performance—its *form*—comes gradually, as you hear clues that one section has ended and a new one has begun. Eventually, the clues coalesce into a pattern, and you grasp the organization of the performance as a whole.

In most of the music that you will encounter in this text, you will observe form at two levels: the form of a section and the form of the performance as a whole. "Maybellene" uses two common formal templates. The overall form of the song is usually identified as verse/chorus form, whereas the chorus uses blues form.

Verse/Chorus Form

Verse/chorus form is a vocal-based form that contains two main elements, both of which are repeated. They differ in their relationship to the lyrics of the song. In the verse, the same melody sets different lyrics; in the **chorus** (also called the **refrain**), both words and music remain much the same every time. Within this general guideline is almost limitless possibility for variation. "Maybellene" begins with the chorus. This is a departure from the more typical pattern of beginning vocal sections with the verse and following it with the chorus.

The graphic of the overall form of "Maybellene" shows the alternation of chorus and verse. ("I" refers to the short guitar intro; "T" refers to the short tag at the end of the song.)

Verse/chorus form in American popular music is as old as the first minstrel-show songs of the 1840s, and it soon became a standard feature of all popular song. During the first half of the twentieth century, the verse all but disappeared in performance, although most popular songs, and especially those written for musicals, had verses. During the rock era, the verse returned; Berry's song was among the first crossover hits to feature verse and chorus.

Each of the verses contains six lines of lyrics; they are half sung/half spoken over the I chord. Both the chorus and the guitar solo use the twelve-bar blues template as the sectional form.

Blues Form

The chorus of "Maybellene" uses the most characteristic version of **twelve-bar blues form.** This version of blues form contains three melodic phrases in each statement of the form. Each phrase and the pause that follows lasts four measures, so one statement of the complete form takes twelve measures: hence, twelve-bar blues. When sung, the phrases are a rhymed couplet, with the first line repeated. A harmonic progression using only I, IV, and V supports the melody according to a well-established pattern: Each phrase begins with a different chord—I, then IV, and finally V—and remains on or returns to the I chord halfway through. The graphic below shows how lyrics, melody, and harmony combine to outline the traditional twelve-bar blues form.

First phrase	"Maybellene . . .		true?"	
Measures 1–4	**I**		**I**	
Second phrase	"Oh, Maybellene . . .		true?"	
Measures 5–8	**IV**		**I**	
Third phrase	"You done started . . .		do."	
Measures 9–12	**V**		**I**	

The foundation of twelve-bar blues form is its chord progression. Songs in blues form can have a different phrase structure or they may not have a predetermined melodic form at all; that is the case during Berry's guitar solo. In all cases, it is the chord progression that provides common ground. In its familiarity and adaptability, a blues progression is like a pair of old jeans: Both are durable and well broken in yet extremely flexible and adaptable, and neither goes out of style. For generations, the chord progression has been familiar to musicians—who have borrowed it from the blues for use in popular song, jazz, Latin music, rock and roll, and rock—and their audiences.

In "Maybellene," the twelve-bar blues form serves as the formal template for the chorus of the song. The overall form alternates between chorus and verse, with a guitar solo serving as an interlude (and an opportunity for Berry to showcase his guitar playing) between vocal sections. Both blues form and the use of a chorus help listeners find and maintain their bearings as the song unfolds. Their ease of use is one reason for their frequent use in popular music.

CHAPTER 5
A Matter of Style

For the historically inclined listener, "Maybellene" presents a fascinating paradox. It is arguably one of the most important recordings in the history of rock, but if Berry had stopped recording at that point in his career, it's possible, even likely, that rock would have evolved in a quite different direction. An understanding of musical style sheds light on this intriguing circumstance.

CHUCK BERRY, the architect of rock 'n' roll

Musical Style

Musical **style** is a set of characteristic musical features that typifies a body of music. These features are, in essence, a statistical summary of what one expects to hear in the style; for example, most rock songs of the 1960s and 1970s have a rock beat. Musical style is comprehensive. It includes musicians' choices regarding all the elements of music, although some may play a more prominent role than others in defining the style. For example, distortion is the sound signature of heavy metal.

Style is a three-dimensional phenomenon in that some characteristics of a style may occur in several styles, whereas others occur in a smaller range of music. For example, the backbeat has been a common feature in popular music from the 1920s to the present. By contrast, the two-beat rhythm through which it was introduced was wildly popular in popular song and dance music during the 1920s and 1930s. After World War II, it was widely used in country music and more conservative pop. By the time "Maybellene" hit the charts, the two-beat rhythm was an anachronism.

Because style is three-dimensional, it is possible to hear connections and patterns of influence from style to style. In "Maybellene," the instrumentation (electric guitar plus full rhythm section) comes from postwar electric blues; Berry's riff-based solo over a four-beat rhythm comes from swing via up-tempo rhythm and blues. Berry almost certainly adapted the two-beat rhythm from honky-tonk, a popular country music style in the post-WWII era. It is also possible to hear the innovative features present in a song or in the work of a particular act. In "Maybellene," we hear Berry's fresh mix of blues and verse/chorus forms (framing verses with a blues-based chorus) and his more aggressive approach to blues guitar style (the occasional bent notes and the edge to his sound).

Musical Style and Style Labels

We often use one- or two-word terms to identify a style. Our caller in the previous chapter referred to *swing, blues, jazz, country,* and *honky-tonk.* Style labels are useful to the extent that they call to mind a specific set of musical characteristics. For this reason, "Maybellene" produces a stylistic paradox. We can label it "early rock and roll" and justify this label because of its creator and its historical position. It is certainly innovative in its fusion of honky-tonk and several blues substyles. But it gives no hint of the new rhythms that would soon differentiate rock and roll from every other popular style: the more active rock beat that would be the rhythmic signature of rock-era music and rock's most pervasive style feature. Berry was the musician most responsible for this evolutionary leap, but his rock-defining songs would come later.

So, "Maybellene" is an exception that proves the rule. Most of our musical examples are more representative of the styles they exemplify. In our survey, we are interested both in the ways in which an example typifies a style and

the ways in which it departs from it. To this end, consider revisiting "Maybellene" at the beginning of Unit 10, after you have heard several different blues styles, verse/chorus songs, and western swing and honky-tonk, to hear how Berry blended and reshaped these diverse influences into a new sound and to hear how it differs from the examples that follow.

Style and Meaning

Try putting the sound of "Maybellene" out of your mind, then read the lyrics of the song. The chorus seems to be about a failed relationship; the verses are about cars. Read as text, out of the context of the song, the verses vividly evoke the drag races that were so much a part of 1950s mythology—with the added twist that one of the drivers is a woman. The effect is almost cinematic. However, it is the music that conveys the energy and excitement of the chase. The brisk tempo, driving rhythm, shift in gears during the guitar solo, and the rapid, almost breathless, delivery of the verse all help bring the words to life.

When words and music work together in popular music to convey the meaning of a song, the words express the meaning, but the music helps listeners *feel* the message expressed in the words. However, with few exceptions, musical sounds are inherently abstract. Unfamiliar sounds seem meaningless to observers. The numerous comments by explorers and missionaries regarding African and Native American music are evidence of that; so are the reactions of cultural snobs to ragtime, blues and jazz in the early years of the twentieth century. The conventions of a style bridge this gap, serving as an interface between musician and listener. As they become familiar, listeners can connect them to nonmusical experiences: the rise and fall of a melody as highly inflected speech, the energy of a fast tempo, the dark or subdued mood often implied by sounds clustered in a low register, the satisfying resolution of musical tension at the end of a chord progression. Cumulatively, imaginative handling of the musical elements can express mood and feeling with enormous power, as we will discover again and again.

UNIT 1

LOOKING BACK, LOOKING AHEAD

OUR TWO MAIN OBJECTIVES in these opening chapters were to define the terms that our caller used to describe features of "Maybellene" and to describe the elements that the terms exemplify in more general terms. "Maybellene" has been useful in this regard because so many musical features—for example, its rhythm section–based instrumentation, rhythmic features like the backbeat and style beats, its use of riffs to build a melody, the blues progression, and verse/chorus form—occur not only in this song but also in a wide range of popular music. These musical features may be realized in quite different, even individual, ways, but they are commonplace throughout popular song. We often use style labels, like *rock and roll,* to succinctly identify the particular ways of realizing the elements of music in a given style.

This is the foundation for the style-based discussions of virtually all of the musical examples presented in this book. For almost all of the examples discussed in the text, you will find the following:

1. Things to "Listen For," key observations that highlight prominent style features, to help you identify the song and its style quickly and accurately.
2. Concise summaries of key points to "Remember" that highlight noteworthy aspects of the song, connect it to other music, and offer interpretations of the expressive meaning of musical features. For example, in "Maybellene," we might observe the following:
   - A song about cars and driving, a popular teen theme in the 1950s and early 1960s
   - Strong influence of blues: conventional blues form in the chorus, electric blues band instrumentation, blues-inspired bent notes, and aggressive guitar sound
   - Country influence evident in the honky-tonk–style, hard-driving, two-beat rhythm
   - Mix of blues, rhythm and blues, and country influences, anticipating important direction in rock and roll

Our survey of popular music ends close to the present time. It begins in the next unit with a brief overview of the sources of the first distinctively American popular music.

The Beginnings of American Popular Music

UNIT 2

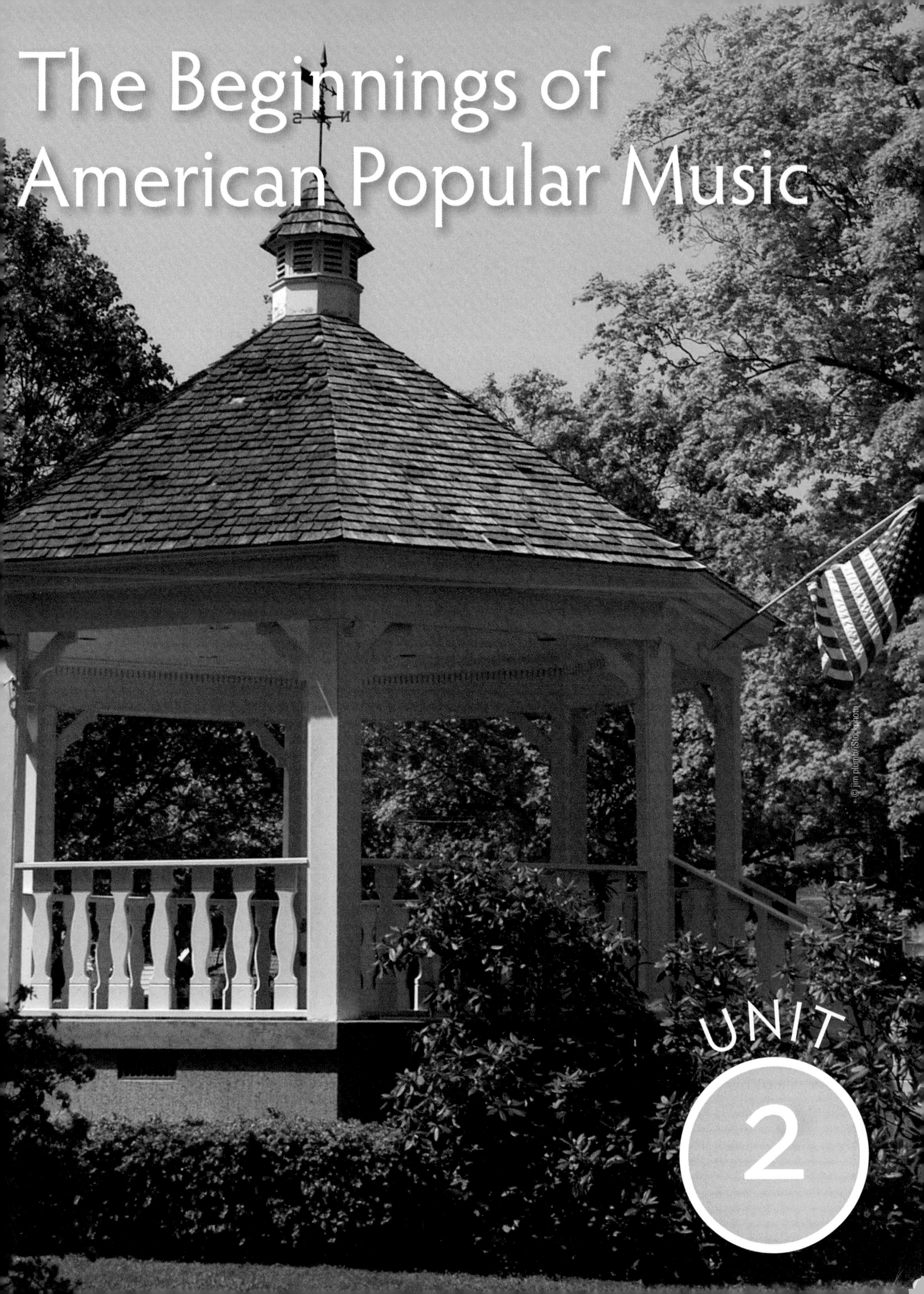

© jim plumb/iStockphoto

UNIT 2

We begin close to the end. The top 20 albums on the *Billboard* 200 year-end chart for 2010 are a grab bag of styles: country (Lady Antebellum), country rock (Zac Brown Band), and country pop (Taylor Swift, Carrie Underwood); hip hop (Eminem, Drake); contemporary pop, often with a substantial techno influence (Lady Gaga, The Black Eyed Peas, Justin Bieber); sophisticated R&B (Sade, Alicia Keys, Usher); throwbacks to classic pop singers (Michael Buble) and early 1970s singer-songwriters (John Mayer); and a couple of great voices singing Christmas music (Andrea Bocelli) and anything she wants (Susan Boyle).

The *Billboard* 200 measures album sales without regard to genre; if an album is selling well, it's on the charts. The year-end charts list the best-charting albums of the previous year. In 1991, *Billboard* began using data from Nielsen SoundScan, which tracks sales from 14,000 retailers and, more recently, online services. It was a far more accurate measure of record sales than the previous system. Because it's strictly quantitative, there is no bias in the reporting of information.

Both the diversity of the *Billboard* 200 and the profusion of charts—from classical crossover, country, Christian, and contemporary jazz, to rock, rap, reggae, and rhythm and blues—highlight the extraordinary range of popular music at the beginning of the twenty-first century. It's truly a global industry, with music coming from and going to every part of the world. Those who create the music face no apparent social or cultural boundaries. The artists include women and men; old and young; white, black, and every shade in between; American and foreign; urban and rural; gay and straight. They draw on sounds and styles whose roots stretch across four continents—Europe, Africa, and both Americas. They blend them together according to their artistic vision, perhaps their sense of what will succeed commercially, or maybe something of both. There is no dominant style and no cultural pecking order. The top of the charts is, in principle, open to any artist.

It wasn't always that way. A century ago, the business of popular music was still a new industry. A dazzling variety of stage entertainment captivated audiences around the country; a flood of songs streamed out of publishing companies along Tin Pan Alley; and the first commercial sound recordings found their way into the homes of the well-to-do. However, whites dominated every aspect of the business; black songwriters and entertainers had very little exposure and even less leverage. For many Americans, the most persistent images of African Americans came from the minstrel show, where blacks made themselves up with burnt cork in order to look as whites thought they should, and from the grotesque caricatures on sheet music covers. Ragtime, the first authentic black music to cross over into the pop world, was forbidden fruit for the young, provocative music for open-minded musicians, and sinful music for the "respectable."

Two centuries ago, the idea of popular music as we understand it today did not exist in America. There was music that was popular, but most of it came from Europe or imitated European music. There was commercial publishing and public performance, but there was no industry to provide and profit from mass musical entertainment.

Our account, then, begins in the early nineteenth century. In this unit, we briefly describe the three main sources of American popular music, then highlight important nineteenth- and early twentieth-century developments, from the parlor song and minstrel show music at mid-century to the rise of Tin Pan Alley, the growth of stage entertainment, and the popularity of the concert band, all around the turn of the century.

CHAPTER 6
Sources of Popular Music

The music of our time is fully integrated. It has deep musical and social connections to the cultures of Europe and West Africa, whose musical traditions are so contrasting as to seem almost mutually exclusive. Yet, as popular music evolved from the minstrel show to the present, it seamlessly blended musical elements from these quite different and often antagonistic cultures into new kinds of music.

The African musical tradition was the sand in the oyster.

Popular music in America has been the product of a long evolution that began with the arrival of African slaves in the New World. The African musical tradition was the sand in the oyster—the agent of change that ultimately produced the popular music of the twentieth century, from rags to rap. The oyster was the music that European settlers had brought with them to the New World: the upper- and middle-class music of the cities and the folk traditions of the countryside and the mountains. To highlight the differences among these three traditions, we present three sets of excerpts. The first set demonstrates the close connection between African culture and the music of the African diaspora in the Americas. The second set includes excerpts of folk song and dance music. The folk song comes from the British Isles and is sung by an American; the dance tune is American but descended directly from the dance music of the British tradition. The third set demonstrates the smooth musical continuum between art music and commercial music in the early years of the nineteenth century.

African Influences

We don't know much about the music of the slaves in the United States during the early nineteenth century. We have some anecdotal evidence, written mostly by white observers who found their music baffling. But we do know that drums were largely outlawed on the southern plantations because slave owners feared that blacks were using them as a means of communication. As a result, extensive use of percussive instruments, perhaps the most crucial element of African music making, was all but eliminated. In Cuba, Brazil, and elsewhere in Latin America, African traditions were stronger because slaves were allowed to re-create their drums, rattles, and other instruments.

Because we have virtually no hard evidence of the music made by people of African descent during the years of slavery, we must infer the nature and extent of the musical connection. The most informative path has been to compare field recordings of African folk musicians with those of musicians of African descent living in the New World. Often there are striking correspondences or retentions, such as a Mississippi bluesman sounding uncannily like a man from Senegal. We hear next Cubans singing in an old Yoruba dialect as they drum and dance during a *santería* ceremony.

From Nigeria to Cuba: *Santería*

Santería is the adaptation of Yoruba religious practices by Cuban descendants of African slaves, mainly from what is now Nigeria. In the traditional religions of the Yoruba people, initiates seek to establish a personal relationship with a patron spirit, called an *orisha,* who serves as an intermediary between the person on earth and God—much the same as a saint in the Catholic Church. Because of the parallel roles of *orishas* and saints, this adaptation of Yoruba religious practice in Cuba has become known as *santería,* or "the way of the saints." Music and dance are integral components of *santería* ceremony; it is through music and dance that initiates communicate with their personal *orisha.*

LISTENING CUE • **"Song for Odudua,"** Santería Musicians

Listen to this selection in CourseMate.

In the example presented here, the leader is singing in an old-fashioned Yoruba dialect: he is inviting Odudua, an *orisha,* to aid them. Soon drums, then voices, enter. The music settles into a steady rhythm, with the leader singing in alternation with the group. In this recording we hear several musical features that would be assimilated into the popular tradition:

- Prominent percussion: more specifically, drums similar to conga drums
- Complex rhythms, with constant syncopations in the percussion parts
- **Call and response,** an exchange between leader and group
- Melody built on an African pentatonic (five-note) scale.

The debt of popular music—of virtually all kinds—to African music is extensive and unmistakable. It includes these key features:

- An unvarying beat or other regular rhythm
- Several layers of rhythmic activity, which often create syncopations and other forms of rhythmic conflict
- Percussion instruments and percussive playing techniques
- Riff -like melodic ideas
- Layered textures

Few whites in the United States, Cuba, or elsewhere in the Americas would have heard sounds like these during the nineteenth century. Before the Civil War, the only place in the South where African Americans could revive their musical heritage was Congo Square in New Orleans. Nevertheless, despite numerous obstacles, all of these African musical features—rhythms, instruments, riff-based melodies, and the like—would gradually reshape popular music.

Folk Music from the British Isles

The members of the lower classes who emigrated from the British Isles to North America brought their music with them: songs and dances dating back centuries are still sung and played. For those people living in more isolated areas, such as the Appalachians, the traditions remained largely untouched by outside influences until well into the twentieth century.

Anglo-American Folk Dance

The most popular dances brought from the British Isles were up-tempo jigs and reels, typically played by a fiddler. We have no way of knowing exactly how this music sounded in the early nineteenth century, but we do know some of the songs and can infer some of the key features of the style from the earliest country recordings and contemporary accounts. This early recording of "Old Joe Clark"—one of the first country music recordings—reveals musical features that were almost certainly present in Americanized versions of British folk music, as heard in the nineteenth century.

Fiddlin' John Carson, who sings and plays the fiddle on this recording, grew up in northwest Georgia, at the southern end of the Appalachian Trail. Carson was among the very first country musicians to record; his playing and singing are representative of a tradition that had changed little over several generations.

Library of Congress, Prints and Photographs Division, Washington, DC

Despite cultural barriers, musical exchanges between blacks and whites went in both directions.

This song is somewhat unusual in that it combines song and dance. Many fiddle tunes were strictly instrumental, but here, vocal and instrumental statements of the melody alternate. Each statement of the melody

LISTENING CUE • **"Fare You Well Old Joe Clark,"** excerpt, traditional (1924), Fiddlin' John Carson. Carson, vocal and fiddle.

Listen to this selection in CourseMate.

includes a verse and a chorus. Their relationship is apparent from the lyric: the chorus retains the same words and melody, whereas the verses keep the melody but change the words. When he's singing, Carson performs two slightly different versions of the melody; the instrumental versions are more elaborate. There is only a drone—a sustained low note—as accompaniment. The song has a moderately fast tempo and a clear, danceable beat; for centuries, fiddlers were often one-man dance bands among rural whites in the South. Among the qualities that would find their way into popular music are these:

- Down-home, good-humored attitude
- Story told in everyday language
- Melody set to a danceable beat
- Rough, untrained singing voice
- Verse/chorus form

All of these qualities would surface in the music for the minstrel show. It's possible that the form of "Old Joe Clark" could have been influenced by minstrel show songs, because most of the stories of its origin point to events taking place after the Civil War. In other respects, however, the style seems a direct ancestor of music for the minstrel show.

Upper- and Middle-Class European Music

Throughout the eighteenth and nineteenth centuries, the upper and middle classes in Europe and America shared a common musical language. We know its most sophisticated statements as classical music: the music of Bach, Handel, Haydn, Mozart, Beethoven, and Schubert, among others. However, there was also a vast body of popular song and music for social dancing that used a simpler form of the same musical language; so did patriotic music (e.g., national anthems such as "God Save the King") and hymns and other church music. Through the middle of the nineteenth century, there was a smooth stylistic continuum among these different types of music.

"Woodman, Spare That Tree" is a song by Henry Russell (1812–1900), the Elton John of the 1830s, an English songwriter, singer, and pianist who enjoyed extraordinary success in America. Russell claimed to have studied composition with the Italian opera composer Vincenzo Bellini before immigrating briefly to the United States; "Woodman, Spare That Tree" clearly shows the influence of Italian operatic style.

"Woodman, Spare That Tree" is set for voice and piano. Musical interest centers on a flowing melody; the simple arpeggiated accompaniment is clearly subordinate. It has a moderately slow tempo with a clear, if lightly marked, beat, and it uses the harmonic language heard in almost all of the urban music of the eighteenth and early nineteenth centuries.

"Woodman, Spare That Tree" may seem miles away in style and spirit from not only "Old Joe Clark" but also "Maybellene." But several of the musical features that it exemplifies became part of the sound of popular music. Among them are these:

- Chords and chord progressions
- Melody-and-accompaniment texture, with the flowing melody on top, bass on the bottom, and chords in between
- Hierarchical form, in which phrases coalesce into larger formal units
- The piano

Neither African music nor most of the folk music brought from the British Isles uses harmony; it is specific to urban upper- and middle-class music of Europe. So are many of the instruments of popular music, although popular musicians created new sounds from them. Classical music, and the music modeled after it, also served as the de facto standard of excellence. Aspiring to art would remain a persistent countercurrent in popular music throughout the twentieth century, from Scott Joplin's "classic" rags to the beautifully crafted albums of Radiohead.

American Popular Music, from Sources to Syntheses

If you compare the musical examples in the chapter, you can gain a clear picture of the deep contrast between musical traditions, especially between the urban European

LISTENING CUE · **"Woodman, Spare That Tree,"** excerpt, (1837), Henry Russell Douglas. Jimerson, vocal.

Listen to this selection in CourseMate.

music popular during the first part of the nineteenth century and West African music. Here are some of the key differences between the two traditions:

	Urban European	**West African**
Instrumentation	Chord instrument (piano) is the only instrument	Several percussion instruments (including handclaps); also a plucked instrument
Harmony	Chords	No chords
Melody	Long, flowing melody	Short phrases ending in long notes
Rhythm	Gentle beat keeping	Strong beat keeping
	No syncopation	Lots of syncopation in drum parts

In short, there is virtually no common ground between the urban European and West African traditions. The extreme contrast between them makes the emergence and evolution of a distinctively American popular music from their ongoing interaction even more remarkable. Popular music acquired a distinct identity only when it began to synthesize these disparate traditions into a new sound. We encounter the first such synthesis in the music of the minstrel show.

CHAPTER 7

The Parlor Song

In a famous letter to his publisher E. P. Christy, Stephen Foster (1828–1864) reveals his ambivalent attitude about his "Ethiopian songs"—songs he wrote for the minstrel show. He wrote, "As I once intimated to you, I had the intention of omitting my name from my Ethiopian songs, owing to the prejudice against them by some, which might injure my reputation as a writer of another style of music, but I find that by my efforts I have done a great deal to build up a taste for the Ethiopian songs among refined people by making the words suitable to their taste."

Foster wrote the letter in May of 1852, almost a year after the publication of "Old Folks at Home," perhaps his most famous song. The published version of the song shows Christy as the composer of the song, which was already well on its way to becoming one of the most popular American songs of all time. In the wake of its success, Foster was obviously having a serious case of the druthers, as well he should. Nevertheless, the fact that Foster would have previously agreed to withhold his name from the covers of his minstrel show songs implies a deep division between "highbrow" and "lowbrow" in American cultural life during the middle of the nineteenth century.

America declared political independence from Great Britain in 1776. Cultural independence in art, theater, literature, and especially music took quite a bit longer.

Library of Congress, Prints and Photographs Division, Washington, DC

THE AMERICAN PARLOR, CA. 1860

Virtually all of the commercially produced music one might hear in the United States during the first decades of the nineteenth century came directly or indirectly from the British Isles: orchestral and choral music in public performance; opera; music published for home performance; and hymnals for church use.

Cultural Life in Early Nineteenth-Century America

America was mostly wilderness at the beginning of the 1800s. In 1790, New York, then as now the largest city in the country, had a population of about 33,000 people. By 1840, its population had grown almost ten times, to about 312,000. The next-largest cities, Baltimore and New Orleans, had populations of just over 100,000. America remained mostly rural until well into the twentieth century, but its cities grew, and a cultural divide developed between the largely urban, literate middle and upper classes and the poorly educated, less mannered lower classes of city slums and rural counties. All forms of entertainment, including music, reflected this gulf. During the nineteenth century, the distinction was commonly expressed as *highbrow* (urban and cultivated) versus *lowbrow* (rural and vernacular).

Stephen Foster and the Parlor Song

The more respectable members of a growing middle class aligned themselves with highbrow taste in all aspects of culture. Musically, it was most evident in the songs they preferred. As they did with other aspects of culture, they looked to England for inspiration.

In the early nineteenth century, the most popular songs in England were the folk-song settings of Thomas Moore (1779–1852). Moore, an Irish poet and musician who lived in England most of his career, set his own poems to traditional Irish folk melodies. A skilled singer and pianist, he made these adaptations himself and published them in ten volumes between 1808 and 1834. According to Charles Hamm, they were, along with the songs of Stephen Foster, "the most popular, widely sung, best-loved, and durable songs in the English language of the entire nineteenth century." Not far behind were the Scottish song settings by Robert Burns, including the still familiar "Auld Lang Syne."

These folk-song settings, circulated in sheet music versions, were genteel and "correct" according to the musical standards of the day. In this form, they appealed to and circulated among musically literate members of the middle and upper classes. They helped spawn new kinds of popular music, including the most popular genre in nineteenth-century America: the **parlor song.**

Parlor songs resemble the art songs of classical music in their setting for voice and piano, but were more modest in their expressive range and musical requirements. They told sentimental stories, which were set to simple melodies with generally modest accompaniment.

Parlor songs derive their name from their typical setting. In the era before mass media, those who wanted music generally made it themselves. Young ladies from middle- and upper-class families often received musical instruction. After dinner, families would gather in the parlor, where they would sing and play songs like "Jeanie with the Light Brown Hair."

Stephen Foster (1826–1864) was the most important songwriter in nineteenth-century American popular music. He was versatile and skillful, and his songs were well written and often inspiring and innovative. Success came early with minstrel tunes like "Oh, Susanna!" and "Camptown Ladies." Particularly in the 1850s, at the apex of his career, Foster was a composer of real skill. His best songs far outshine the work of his contemporaries and successors. The relative simplicity of his style came about by choice, not default, as he sought to create a specifically popular style.

STEPHEN FOSTER in 1859, at the height of his career.

The parlor song was an integral part of Foster's musical world from the beginning of his career. His first published song, "Open Thy Lattice, Love" (1844), is a fine example of the genre. Among the most memorable of his parlor songs was one he composed about a decade later, after his career as a songwriter was well under way. "Jeanie with the Light Brown Hair" is a typical, and especially pretty, example of the parlor song genre. Its roots in the folk music of the British Isles are most apparent in Foster's use of an Anglo-American pentatonic scale. The major musical difference is, of course, the addition of a rich, if understated, piano accompaniment.

Foster was the most popular and most admired of the first generation of American songwriters. The sentimental songs that he and his contemporaries composed marked the beginning of the American popular mainstream. Quickly overshadowing them was a humbler but ultimately far more influential kind of song: a song composed (or borrowed) for the minstrel show.

LISTENING CUE • **"Jeanie with the Light Brown Hair" (1854),** Stephen Foster. Richard Lalli, vocal; Michael Campbell, piano.

STYLE Parlor song • **FORM** The melody contains four phrases in the form AA^1BA^2, where A is the first melodic idea, A^1 and A^2 are different versions of the idea, and B is a contrasting melodic idea.

Listen For . . .

INSTRUMENTATION
Voice and piano

RHYTHM
Subtle pulse at moderately slow tempo, with occasional suspension of timekeeping

MELODY
Long, flowing lines, ending in clearly punctuated phrases

TEXTURE
Melody plus simple accompaniment

Remember . . .

SENTIMENTAL TEXT
Saccharine portrait of Jeanie in the lyrics resonated well with respectable families in nineteenth-century America.

SONG FOR HOME USE
Singers and pianists of modest skills could comfortably perform parlor songs at home.

IRISH CONNECTION
Like many folk and folk-inspired songs from the British Isles, "Jeanie" uses a pentatonic (five-note) scale.

BEAUTIFUL MELODY
Melody is the main focus and the feature that gives the song its character; accompaniment is generic; no underlying dance rhythm.

Listen to this selection in CourseMate.

CHAPTER 8
Minstrelsy

The first minstrel show—billed as an "Ethiopian Concert"—took place in Boston in February 1843. It featured the Virginia Minstrels, four veteran blackface performers, none of whom were from the South. These all-around entertainers sang, danced, and played fiddle, banjo, tambourine, and bones, and their first evening of entertainment was an immediate success. Following their lead—and hoping to match their success—other minstrel troupes formed almost overnight. Within a few years, troupes were crisscrossing the country, and many cities had their own resident troupe. The size of the minstrel troupe also grew (and would continue to grow after the Civil War). Christy's Minstrels, formed in 1844, soon added other performers and then an orchestra.

It is difficult to give a precise description of the minstrel show because it lacked a consistent form and evolved so quickly. In the twenty years prior to the Civil War, minstrelsy developed from small-group acts to a full evening's entertainment, with a large troupe and orchestral accompaniment. Audiences at the early minstrel shows were the forerunners of today's raucous rock-concert or soccer-match crowds. Rowdy patrons provoked "minstrel programs [to list] 'Rules of Hall,' which pleaded with the audience not to whistle during the performances and not to beat time with their feet."

The Minstrel Show

The **minstrel show** was a high-spirited, often improvisatory stage entertainment performed in **blackface:** both white and (later) black performers applied burnt cork to darken their complexion. By its very nature, the minstrel show was loosely structured (and remained loose even as the size of the troupe grew). There were at least three minstrels: the interlocutor and the two endmen, **Tambo and Bones,** so named for the tambourine and the bones that they played. The troupe sat in a semicircle, with the **interlocutor** in the center and the **endmen** at either side. The rest of the troupe filled the gaps between the interlocutor and the endmen. There was no plot or storyline, although there were stock routines and consistent characters. The subject matter provided the continuity in a string of comic exchanges between the interlocutor, who spoke with a resonant voice, proper diction, and a rich vocabulary, and the endmen, who spoke in a caricature of African-American speech. These exchanges bonded together a varied assortment of songs and dances. The interlocutor controlled the pacing of the show. According to the mood and the response of the audience, he would allow routines to continue or cut them off.

The minstrel show grew out of the blackface entertainment of the late 1820s and 1830s. The first important blackface entertainer was George Washington Dixon, who created a sensation in New York with his performance of "Coal Black Rose." During the 1830s, the most popular performers of the era built their routines around two stock characters: the city slicker, Zip Coon, and the country bumpkin, Jim Crow.

Jim Crow was first: In 1832, Thomas Dartmouth Rice observed (or claimed to have observed) an African-American street entertainer in Cincinnati doing a song and dance with a peculiar hop step, which he called "Jumping Jim Crow." He copied the man's routine and introduced it on-stage shortly thereafter with great success. Jim Crow's city counterpart acquired a name two years later, when in 1834 Dixon and Bob Farrell, another blackface entertainer, introduced the song "Zip Coon" on-stage.

The first minstrel shows simply constructed a full-length show from various routines about the two most popular blackface characters. The opening section portrayed the city slicker, and the closing section portrayed the country bumpkin. Within a few years, the show had grown into three distinct parts. The opening section alternated highly ritualized minstrel material with a balladeer singing popular parlor songs. The second section, called the **olio** (an Anglicization of the Spanish word *olla* for "stew"), was the variety portion of the show and featured a wide range of acts. Many of these were novelty routines; others were **burlesques** (humorous parodies) of cultivated material—Shakespeare's plays or Italian operas, for example. The final section was an extended skit. Originally based on idealized plantation life, the skits later became topical comedy sketches. The show concluded with a **walkaround,** which featured the entire minstrel troupe in a grand finale of song and dance.

By the end of the nineteenth century, the walkaround had evolved into the cakewalk. By most accounts the **cakewalk** originated as a contest among slaves: couples danced for a prize, generally a cake. The winners were the "pair that pranced around with the proudest, high-kicking steps." By the 1890s it had become a dance fad, moving from the stage to the dance floor, where couples competed in contests for prizes larger than a cake. Its signature short-LONG-short rhythm was the first persistent use of syncopation in popular music; it would find its way into much turn-of-the century American song and dance music.

Dan Emmett and Music for the Minstrel Show

Dan Emmett's "De Boatmen's Dance," heard here in a 1978 performance by Robert Winans, illustrates the sound of early minstrel show music. Emmett (1815–1904) was a

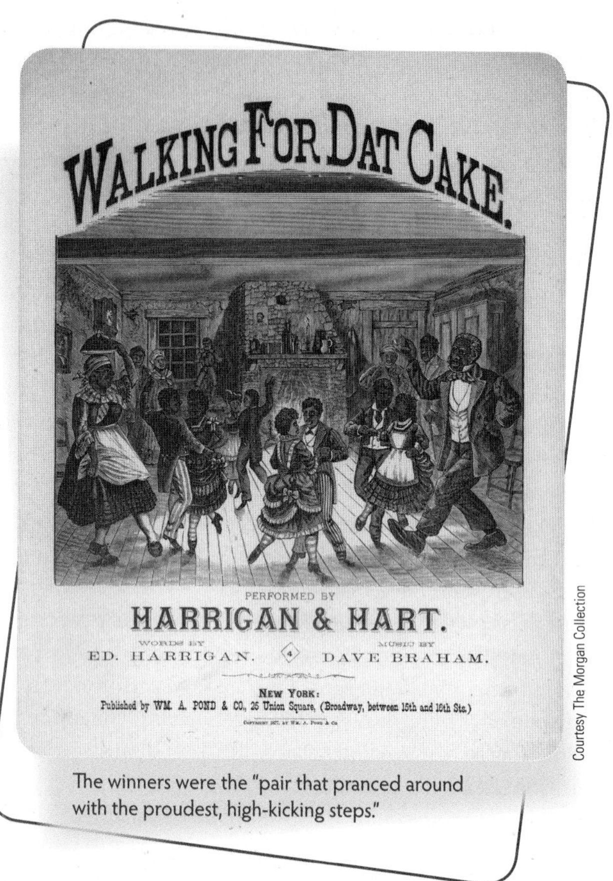

The winners were the "pair that pranced around with the proudest, high-kicking steps."

blackface entertainer in the 1830s and one of the founding members of the Virginia Minstrels. He also composed (or adapted from folk repertory) a number of songs for the minstrel show, including "Dixie." Among his contemporaries, only Stephen Foster surpassed him as a minstrel show songwriter. "De Boatmen's Dance" was one of the songs in the first Virginia Minstrels show in 1843.

Even a casual comparison makes clear the affinity between "De Boatmen's Dance" and Fiddlin John Carson's "Old Joe Clark." Both have lyrics that describe a series of "scenes" in down-home language. Both feature voice and fiddle, an upbeat tempo with a clear beat, alternation of singing and playing the melody, and a form that alternates verse and chorus. In this song there are two choruses: one is sung in harmony, the other in **unison**—that is, with more than one voice and/or instrument performing the same melody. The use of a chorus, in which both words and music are repeated again and again, would become more common in popular music after the Civil War, when songwriters and publishers cultivated a distinctively popular song style. It is easy to imagine the song supporting action on stage as the troupe acts out the scenes described in the song or simply dances.

Perhaps the most crucial difference between "Old Joe Clark" and "De Boatmen's Dance" is the latter's use of harmony. Clearest in the chorus and implicit throughout the rest of the song, the use of harmony connects "De Boatmen's Dance" to the cultivated parlor songs of the period. This addition of urban harmony to folk content and rhythm created a mix with a different sound and attitude. So did the use of African-American images and sounds.

LISTENING CUE · "De Boatmen's Dance" (1843), Dan Emmett. Ensemble directed by Robert Winans.

STYLE Minstrel show song • **FORM** Verse/chorus: In each statement of the form, two choruses frame the verses. Both choruses are short; the verse has four short phrases.

Listen For . . .

INSTRUMENTATION
Voices, fiddle, banjo, tambourine, and bones

RHYTHM
Bright, steady tempo, with a clear beat
Fast rhythms in banjo and syncopated patterns in fiddle and bones

MELODY
Simple, three-phrase melody based on pentatonic (five-note) scale

TEXTURE
Some harmony in the first segment of the chorus; otherwise, voices and pitched instruments sing and play different versions of the melody.

Remember . . .

FOR STAGE ENTERTAINMENT
Song is part of an all-around show with singing, dancing, and joke telling

CHORUS-BASED FORM
Two choruses frame each statement of the verse.

DANCE RHYTHMS
Song uses a bright dance rhythm.

MINSTREL SHOW LYRICS
A pale imitation of black speech brings earthier element into popular song.

Listen to this selection in CourseMate.

Black Faces and Black Sounds

Without question, African-American music influenced the sound of early minstrel performers. Bones and tambourine formed the first "rhythm section," and the banjo developed from African instruments. But the music of the early minstrel show had little relation to authentic African-American music; in fact, it had much more in common with the folk music of rural settlers, and many minstrel songs passed into the oral tradition of country music. "Zip Coon," for example, became the fiddle tune "Turkey in the Straw." The song lyrics were not authentic either, but were written in pseudo-dialect. A line from "Zip Coon" shows the inconsistency in language: "I went the udder arter noon to take a dish ob tea." Some words are in alleged dialect; others remain unchanged.

Although it is clear from drawings and accounts of the period that at least some white minstrels keenly observed the appearance, speech, and dancing of black Americans, "Jim Crow," "Zip Coon," and other minstrel songs were in fact crude parodies of the African-American life that minstrels attempted to capture in song and dance. In the years before the Civil War, the majority of minstrel performers had only incidental contact with the African Americans whom they supposedly portrayed. Most minstrel troupes resided permanently in northeastern cities—New York especially—that were far from soutern plantations.

There is compelling, if indirect, evidence to suggest that white minstrels did not capture the *quality* of African-American music making. After the Civil War, performances by black minstrels were so much more successful than the white minstrels that the white minstrel show evolved away from traditional minstrelsy.

Routes to Popularity: Written and Oral Traditions

In the middle of the nineteenth century, the two outlets for minstrel show songs were sheet music and the stage. Publication via sheet music was the established practice. However, many minstrel show songs were simple enough, repetitious enough, and coherent enough melodically that the audience could remember the tune after only a few hearings. To take advantage of this accessibility, publishers put out **songsters**—books with just the lyrics to popular songs of the day—on the assumption that those who bought them already knew the melody and simply needed to be reminded of the words.

The still-familiar minstrel-show songs of Stephen Foster have come down to us both ways. We can easily learn songs like "Camptown Ladies," "Oh! Susanna," and "Old Folks at Home" by hearing them or by reading them from the music. Although created as popular songs, they have attained a folklike status; the song is simply out there. What is novel about this state of affairs is the fact that the song existed simultaneously in a more or less official version (the sheet music) and in the multiple versions created by those who learned it by ear. However, unlike the published scores of Foster's parlor songs, the sheet music of the minstrel show songs was not an authoritative guide to performance. It was simply the best way to get the song out to the public and make some money from it.

The sheet music versions of Foster's minstrel show songs would have sounded very different in the minstrel show, their real home—there would have been fiddle, banjo, tambourine, and bones supporting the vocals instead of piano, and the minstrels probably danced as they played. In terms of musical identity, this kind of popular song would occupy a middle ground between classical music, where the printed score preserved the composer's musical vision, and folk music, where there is no single authoritative source.

The two decades before the Civil War saw the birth of popular music; the three decades after the Civil War saw the birth of the popular music industry.

Social Acceptance and Synthesis

With our multicultural mindset, it is hard to imagine the kind of contempt "respectable" people felt toward the minstrel show. However, in mid-nineteenth century America, the more respectable members of American society looked down their noses at "the Ethiopian business." Many considered the early minstrel show and anything associated with it to be low-class entertainment, although some patronized the shows. Nevertheless, minstrelsy and the music for it had gained a firm toehold in American life by the Civil War. Foster played a significant role in making it more palatable by creating a new genre, the "plantation song." Foster's innovative synthesis brought the sentimentality of middle-class song into the rough-and-tumble world of the minstrel show, and with it, a more human portrayal of blacks.

Acceptance was not universal. John Sullivan Dwight, whose *Journal of Music* served as the semiofficial arbiter of good taste among the cultivated, admitted that "Old Folks at Home," Foster's most famous plantation song, was indeed popular but likened the song to a "morbid irritation of the skin." "Old Folks at Home" would become the best-known song in nineteenth-century America: estimates of sheet music sales of the song during the latter half of the century reach as high as 20 million, and the song remains familiar to this day.

The popularity of Foster's minstrel show songs was the clearest signal that a distinctive new musical style, one that was both popular and American, had emerged. His songs have remained part of our collective memory for more than a century and a half, whereas much of the more-genteel music that Dwight championed is long forgotten.

Minstrelsy and American Popular Music

American popular music—music that is distinctively and recognizably American, a commercial enterprise, and widely popular—began with minstrelsy. There had, of course, been music that was popular in America before minstrelsy—we still sing the revolutionary-era tune "Yankee Doodle"—but there was no popular music that sounded distinctively American until the appearance of minstrel show songs like "Camptown Ladies" and "De Boatmen's Dance."

Even in its published form, the minstrel show song introduced two innovations that would become a permanent part of popular song: use of a recurrent chorus and dance rhythms. And as performed onstage, it introduced the mixed-timbre accompaniment, complete with percussion—tambourine and bones.

Minstrelsy would give blacks their first substantial opportunity to enter the entertainment business. Black minstrel troupes took the stage right after the end of the Civil War, and they were popular from the start, drawing crowds as big as, or bigger than, the white troupes did. Promoters billed black minstrels as authentic portrayers of plantation life, although they were forced to perpetuate the stereotypes of the early minstrel show. Bert Williams, the great African-American vaudeville performer of the early twentieth century, complained that he and other black performers had to appear in blackface so that they looked the way white people thought they should.

American popular music—music that is distinctively and recognizably American, a commercial enterprise, and widely popular—began with minstrelsy.

Nevertheless, in the late nineteenth century, minstrelsy was the main route to a career for black popular performers. W. C. Handy, the "father of the blues" and himself a minstrel in the 1890s, noted that "All the best [African-American] talent of that generation came down the same drain. The composers, the singers, the musicians, the speakers, the stage performers—the minstrel show got them all."

The minstrel show was America's first indigenous popular music and its first musical export. It brought freshness to America's cultural life. Because of this, it is doubly unfortunate that its most indelible image is its demeaning stereotypes of African Americans. Minstrelsy cultivated prejudice and ignorance in some and reinforced it in others. Still, the positive contributions of the minstrel show include four important firsts, all of which figure prominently in subsequent generations of popular music:

- It was entertainment for the masses.
- It used vernacular speech and music.
- It created a new genre by synthesizing middle-class urban song and folk music.
- It was the first instance of a phenomenon in American popular music that has continued to the present day: that of invigorating and transforming the dominant popular style through the infusion of energetic, often danceable music.

The Popular Music Industry

The two decades before the Civil War saw the birth of popular music; the three decades after the Civil War saw the birth of the popular music industry. The minstrel show had demonstrated that stage entertainment offered an excellent way to promote songs. Brisk sales of Stephen Foster's songs had revealed a large and lucrative market for sheet music. Those who ran the music business soon capitalized on both revenue streams.

CHAPTER 9
Popular Song at the Turn of the Twentieth Century

After the Civil War, both stage entertainment and music publishing became more commercially oriented. Stage entertainment expanded and diversified, while an increasing number of music publishers began to publish only popular songs in order to maximize profits.

By the 1890s, the popular music industry was up and running. Musical comedy and vaudeville competed with the minstrel show for the stage entertainment dollar. Charles Harris's 1892 hit "After the Ball" confirmed what music publishers already suspected: the existence of a large market for popular song. And after three decades of being confined to minstrelsy, blacks branched out into other facets of the entertainment business.

Tin Pan Alley

In the 1880s, a different breed of music publisher opened for business in New York City. Whereas traditional publishers issued music of all kinds, the new publishers sold only popular songs and marketed them aggressively. They hired **song pluggers,** house pianists who could play a new song for a professional singer or a prospective customer. At first, the publishers congregated in the theater district around Union Square (14th Street), but most soon moved uptown to 28th Street, still near enough to the theaters to have access to performers. Writer Monroe Rosenfeld dubbed 28th Street **"Tin Pan Alley"** because the sound of several song pluggers auditioning songs at once reminded him of crashing tin pans.

New York City became home to both popular stage entertainment and popular-music publishing. The new flood of immigrants, among them Irish, Germans, and then Jews, plus the migration of African Americans into the city, swelled New York's population. Many immigrants found work in show business as performers, songwriters, theater owners, agents, or publishers. New York was the center of popular music for decades, challenged only by Hollywood and talking movies.

African-American songwriters found wider acceptance for their work. In the 1890s, Gussie Davis became the first black songwriter to achieve success on Tin Pan Alley. The songwriting team of Bob Cole and the brothers J. Rosamund Johnson and James Weldon Johnson supplied music for their own shows and for interpolation into other productions. African-American musicians of the time usually wore many hats. For example, the most lasting contribution of the Johnson brothers was not their popular songs but their arrangements of Negro spirituals. They would publish two sets of them, in 1925 and 1926. Will Marion Cook, musical director for the Walker-Williams Company in the 1900s, also composed songs in a style influenced by African-American folksong. Later, he directed one of the leading syncopated dance orchestras of the time.

"After the Ball" and the Music Business

Charles Harris's 1892 popular song "After the Ball" was the first big Tin Pan Alley hit, eventually selling more than 5 million sheet-music copies. An early recording of "After the Ball," sung by George Gaskin, one of the Irish tenors who were so popular around the turn of the century, was a bestseller in 1893. (*Bestseller* is a relative term, however, as commercial recording was only three years old at the time, distribution was difficult, and both records and record players were expensive.) The story of its road to success tells us a lot about the growth of stage entertainment and music publishing, the way they operated, and the extent to which they intertwined.

Harris was a self-taught songwriter and performer (on the banjo). He never learned to read or write music and had to hire a trained musician to notate his songs. But he made up for his lack of training in determination, nerve, and business savvy. While living in Milwaukee, he wrote "After the Ball" for a friend. Harris then approached several popular singers whose tours with vaudeville took them through Milwaukee and asked them to perform the song in their shows. The first three, two vaudeville stars and a ballad singer in a minstrel show, unceremoniously turned him down. He finally persuaded the fourth—who was starring in a touring production of *A Trip to Chinatown,* one of the most popular musical comedies of the 1890s—to interpolate the song into the show. Reportedly, Harris convinced the star by representing himself as a correspondent for the New York *Dramatic News,* promising a glowing review and paying the star $500.

"After the Ball" was such a great success in the show that Julius Witmark, one of the new breed of Tin Pan Alley publishers, offered Harris $10,000 for the rights to the song. Instead, figuring that he could make more money publishing it himself, Harris set up his own publishing house. As it turned out, he was correct. He understood public taste and had a knack for spotting potential hits. Although he never wrote another song as successful as "After the Ball," Harris made a fortune publishing his own songs and those of other songwriters.

In the wake of its success, even more publishers restricted their catalogs to popular song, and by 1900 very few hit songs were published away from Tin Pan Alley. Harris's decision to go into business for himself suggests that songwriters seldom realized either fame or fortune: it was the publisher who saw most of the profits, and the singers who enjoyed the celebrity.

Part of a publisher's profits went toward recruiting singers to perform the publisher's songs. Then, as now, the surest route to popularity was performance by a star of the day, even when the song was intended primarily for the home market. It was standard practice to secure performances with gifts and bribes, just as record companies bribed disc jockeys sixty years later. The principle—or lack of principle—was the same; only the players and the terms of the deals differed.

Waltz Songs

By the 1890s, dance rhythms, an integral feature of songs for the minstrel show, began to be used even in songs with sentimental texts. The waltz was the first dance rhythm to enjoy widespread use: many of the most memorable songs of the 1890s and 1900s had a waltz beat. In *Yesterdays,* his chronicle of popular song, Charles Hamm lists sixteen commercially successful songs (most had sales of at least 1 million copies of sheet music) from these two decades—thirteen of which have an accompaniment in waltz rhythm. Among the still familiar **waltz songs** from the turn of the century is the 1908 hit "Take Me Out to the Ball Game."

"Take Me Out to the Ball Game" is a true product of Tin Pan Alley. Its composer, Albert von Tilzer, was the younger brother of Harry von Tilzer, the most successful songwriter of the period and a partner in a very profitable music-publishing firm. The younger von Tilzer worked for his older brother's publishing house.

The lyric is fun and very much in the present, neither sentimental nor nostalgic. The language is simple, direct, and slightly slangy, and it tells of the imaginary Katie Casey's love affair with baseball. The music is as jaunty as the lyrics. The band's *OOM-pah-pah* waltz rhythm gives the song a bounce, and the rhythm of the melody swings from one strong beat to the next. Like the parlor song, "Take Me Out to the Ball Game" is all about melody; once the voice enters, everything else stays in the background. The rhythm of the melody governs the rhythm of the lyrics, which is quite different from speech rhythm.

The song uses a verse/chorus form: the verse tells us about Katie; the chorus states, then restates, the song's main theme. This form was more widely used than any other from the 1860s through the 1910s. Gradually, however, perhaps because the chorus was more memorable and central to the song, performers began to ignore the verse. The verses of "Take Me Out to the Ball Game" all but disappeared from our collective memory decades ago.

The verses of "Take Me Out to the Ball Game" all but disappeared from our collective memory decades ago.

LISTENING CUE • **"Take Me Out to the Ball Game" (1908),** Albert von Tilzer, music; Jack Norworth, lyrics. Harvey Hindermyer, vocal.

STYLE Waltz song • **FORM** Verse/chorus: Both verse and chorus are long; the chorus stands alone. The form of the chorus is A A[1].

Listen For . . .

INSTRUMENTATION
Solo voice with band instrument accompaniment

PERFORMANCE STYLE
Over-enunciated singing typical of early recordings; quasi-operatic voice

RHYTHM
Waltz rhythm *(OOM-pah-pah)* at a fast tempo; rhythm of the words not speech-like

MELODY
Flowing phrases, each four measures long, with a rest at the end

Remember . . .

ACOUSTIC RECORDING
Very early commercial acoustic recording; poor fidelity

EXPANDED VERSE/CHORUS FORM
Bigger verse/chorus form; chorus can stand alone.

WALTZ SONGS
Not for dancing, but with a clear dance rhythm in accompaniment

LIGHT-HEARTED SONG
Lyrics show shift away from nineteenth-century sentimentality.

Listen to this selection in CourseMate.

In time and in topic, "Take Me Out to the Ball Game" is a long way from the minstrel songs "De Boatmen's Dance" and "Camptown Ladies." Still, we find in this song the legacy of the minstrel show and the revolution it sparked. It is apparent in the everyday language of the lyric, the dance rhythm that supports the melody, and the verse/chorus form—the most widespread influences of minstrel show songs. Songs like "Take Me Out to the Ball Game" show the shift in popular music during the latter part of the nineteenth century. Although sentimental songs were still popular—"After the Ball" is a real tearjerker—high-spirited songs about everyday life became common. Its musical complement was the use of a dance rhythm—waltz rhythm was the most popular, but march and polka rhythms were also used.

Hindermyer's recording of the song reminds us that recordings were at best an imperfect way to get the song to its audience. If one wanted to hear a professional performance of a popular song, the best strategy was to hear it performed live. In 1900, audiences had many options.

Stage Entertainment

Stage entertainment with music exploded after the Civil War. The spark came from the minstrel show, whose appeal made it clear that there was a market for popular entertainment. Improvements in everyday life, from elevated trains in cities to electric lights in theaters and streets, made it easier to draw audiences and made the theaters safer venues. And the potential audience grew dramatically as immigrants from all over Europe poured into the United States. In just a few decades, stage entertainment with popular music went from a happy accident to a significant industry.

By 1870, three entertainment genres incorporated popular music: the minstrel show, vaudeville, and musical comedy. **Vaudeville** was a variety show, pure and simple. It featured a series of acts—singers, dancers, comics, acrobats, magicians, jugglers, and the like—without any pretense of dramatic unity. Acts came on stage, did their routines, and left, not to return for the rest of the show. By contrast, musical comedies had plots, but they served more as scaffolding for a string of songs than dramatically credible stories enhanced by the music.

A fourth genre, **operetta,** was imported from England during the 1870s. The operettas of Gilbert and Sullivan enjoyed great success in the United States, and by the early twentieth century, European operetta composers had begun to emigrate to the United States: the Irish composer Victor Herbert was the most prominent. Operetta would remain part of mainstream musical life through the 1930s.

The slow demise of the minstrel show at the end of the nineteenth century created a void for a breezy, loosely jointed show with lots of song and dance and a skimpy plot to hold it all together. The public craved shows that were topical, upbeat, aimed at the masses, and full of comedy, song, and dance. The **revue,** a series of song and dance numbers held loosely together by a topical story line, filled that void for more than twenty-five years.

Two things stand out about song on the American stage around the turn of the century: most songs had little dramatic connection to their context, and most songs did not sound particularly American. Recall that vaudeville had no plot, just a sequence. The minstrel show had songs, but not much of a story. Revues used some kind of story line to hook a string of songs together with comedy and dance routines. Although it generally began with a real plot, musical comedy wasn't much better. **Interpolation,** in which the plot of a musical comedy was adapted to include a currently popular song, was the rule of the day; plots accommodated songs, as the history of "After the Ball" exemplifies. Only in operetta do we find a consistent connection between song and story.

Today we expect songs in musicals to serve a dramatic purpose, even though the song may become popular outside of the show. The idea of introducing a song into a show just because it is popular, or in the hope that it will become popular, seems a crude practice dramatically. However, viewed as a transitional step on the way to dramatically credible musical theater or as a way to connect popular song and popular stage entertainment after the Civil War, interpolation is more understandable. Compared with the minstrel show, which had a deliberately loose story line (when it had one at all), and vaudeville, which was a plotless variety show, the surprise is not that the plot of a musical comedy was fair game for interpolation, but that it had a plot at all.

Moreover, most songs lacked a recognizably American musical character: before 1900, very few songs evidenced musical features with a distinctively American sound. That began to change with the increasing popularity of songs by black songwriters and the production of musical comedies by George M. Cohan.

George M. Cohan: Toward an American Musical Comedy

Born into a family of vaudeville performers, George M. Cohan (1878–1942) came into prominence around 1900 with a string of successful musicals that included many still familiar songs and that were more tightly knit dramatically than their predecessors. Cohan was a one-man entertainment industry, adept at all phases of the theatrical business: songwriting, performing, directing, and

The Kobal Collection/Art Resource, NY

Film still from the 1942 film of George M. Cohan's *Yankee Doodle Dandy* with James Cagney (center) in the title role. When Cohan saw Cagney's portrayal of him in the film he said, "My God, what an act to follow!"

producing. He was among the most important and versatile entertainers of his age.

But it is as a patriotic songwriter that Cohan's legacy endures. His **patriotic songs** have the energy of a great march, a vigorous melody, a hint of syncopation, and clever lyrics without a trace of nineteenth-century sentimentality. With the exception of Irving Berlin, no American songwriter before or since has embodied patriotic sentiment so successfully in words and music.

In addition to their memorable songs, Cohan's musicals were also noteworthy because their books (scripts for nonmusical sections) and song lyrics used everyday speech, a practice that Cohan readily defended. As musical theater historian Gerald Bordman notes:

> A number of traditional reviewers assailed excessive dependence on slang. Cohan retorted that that was the way his characters would talk could they have come to life on stage. He was not writing "literature," he was creating an entertainment about people with whom his audience could identify.

Cohan's musicals were a people's music, written for "the plumber and his lady friend in the last balcony." We see this in the lyric of "The Yankee Doodle Boy" from Cohan's musical *Little Johnny Jones* (1904). The verse contains several slang expressions that give the song an easy familiarity: "all the candy"; "ain't that a josh"; and "phony"—early twentieth-century street talk.

"Yankee Doodle Boy" is one of the most memorable of Cohan's patriotic songs. In the musical, it helps establish the character of Johnny Jones, a jockey who has come to England to ride in the Derby. Jones, played by Cohan in the original production, is, in Bordman's words, "the cocky, slangy, identical twin of his creator." These qualities certainly come across in the song. It is an early example of the best kind of theater song—one that enhances the action on-stage but has a life apart from the show.

Cohan's musicals are seldom produced today—indeed, they might be hard to reconstruct. Still, his music has survived. Other than Stephen Foster's songs, Cohan's are the oldest still around in our time. Songs such as "The Yankee Doodle Boy," "Give My Regards to Broadway," and "You're a Grand Old Flag" are still very much in the air. James Cagney's portrayal of Cohan in *Yankee Doodle Dandy* (1942) and the musical *George M.* (1968) have helped keep Cohan and his music alive and in the public eye.

LISTENING CUE · "The Yankee Doodle Boy" (1904), George M. Cohan, Richard Perry, vocal.

STYLE "March" song · **FORM** Verse/chorus: Both verse and chorus are long; the chorus can (and does) stand alone. Form of the chorus is A, A^1.

Listen For . . .

INSTRUMENTATION
Voice, plus piano and drums (added to give march-like feel)

RHYTHM
March-like rhythm (*OOM-pah*) at a fast tempo.
Fast-moving rhythms in melody with occasional single syncopation

MELODY
Fairly long phrases in verse and chorus, with regular pauses.
Extensive quotation of existing songs interpolated into melody

Remember . . .

"SAMPLING" CA. 1904
Cohan quotes several patriotic tunes and a popular song of the day.

THE COMMON TOUCH
Colloquial lyrics and a bright catchy tune

PATRIOTIC CHARACTER
Patriotic tunes, plus a crisp march rhythm

CAKEWALK RHYTHM
The simple syncopation of the cakewalk is used throughout: "ain't that a josh."

Listen to this selection in CourseMate.

CHAPTER 10
The Concert Band

The World's Columbian Exposition of 1893 was the last of the great nineteenth-century World's Fairs. It was held in Chicago, mainly in Jackson Park, located on the South Side along Lake Michigan, and on the Midway, a green median that connects Jackson Park with Washington Park, several blocks to the west.

Music was a major attraction at the fair. The most prestigious musical ensemble presented at the fair was the Exposition Orchestra, an augmented version of the newly formed Chicago Symphony, which was conducted by Theodore Thomas. However, concert bands proved to be far more popular attractions—to the point that exposition organizers canceled the last several concerts of the Exposition Orchestra because of consistently poor attendance.

The marquee musical attraction was the band led by John Philip Sousa. The previous year, Sousa had stepped down as conductor of the Marine Band to form his own ensemble, which he called the New Marine Band. Their appearance at the fair was one of their first important engagements; thousands attended each of the concerts.

The Concert Band

The most popular instrumental ensemble in late nineteenth-century America was the **concert band.** In an era without radio, TV, and other forms of mass communication, touring concert bands, as well as the municipal bands found in almost every town, were a primary source of musical entertainment. They supplied their audiences with a broad range of music: classical selections arranged for band; current hit songs; and, of course, marches, which (ironically) they usually played sitting down.

Bands had been a part of American life since the Revolution. Almost every city and town, large or small, had a municipal band. They performed on most public occasions and gave concerts in season. After the Civil War, some of the bands that had formed in major cities became professional ensembles, playing at concerts, dances, and other public occasions. By the latter part of the nineteenth century, the instrumentation of the concert band had stabilized. Bands were composed of woodwinds, brass, and percussion instruments. Trumpets, trombones, clarinets, and percussion were typically the most prominent.

Sousa and the Concert Band

From the 1890s through the 1920s, the most popular concert band in the United States was John Philip Sousa's New Marine Band. Sousa (1854–1932) was the most prominent bandleader and band composer of his era. He had established his reputation as a composer and conductor with the Marine Band, which he directed for twelve years, then formed his own band in 1892. For the remainder of his career, he led his band on annual tours throughout the United States, as well as several tours to Europe and one world tour, giving over 10,000 concerts. Sousa's band was known for its precision and musicianship and for the excellence of its soloists, several of whom subsequently led bands of their own.

A typical Sousa band concert included **marches** (music composed in regularly accented, usually duple meter, appropriate to accompany marching), original works for band, solos featuring the band's virtuoso instrumentalists, arrangements of well-known opera overtures, symphonic poems, program music, and the popular music of the day. The latter included the latest in syncopated music, such as the cakewalk "At a Georgia Camp Meeting," originally published as a solo piano piece. In fact, many European listeners first gained exposure to ragtime's syncopated rhythms through Sousa's performances abroad.

The role of professional bands in American musical life around 1900 was much like that of the contemporary pops orchestra. Both feature varied programming: a mixture of popular classical music and popular music, with star soloists. And both direct their programs at a

JOHN PHILIP SOUSA in 1900

Library of Congress, Prints and Photographs Division, Washington, DC mass audience. Sousa was keenly aware of the difference in the roles of the concert band and the symphony orchestra. Comparing himself to Theodore Thomas, the founder and conductor of the Chicago Symphony, Sousa remarked that Thomas "gave Wagner, Liszt, and Tchaikovsky, in the belief that he was educating his public; I gave Wagner, Liszt, and Tchaikovsky with the hope that I was entertaining my public."

Stars and Stripes Forever, a Famous March

Although he composed other kinds of works—songs, operettas, and band suites—Sousa made his reputation as a composer of **marches.** Their popularity earned him the title "The March King" and made him America's best-known composer during his lifetime. He wrote 136 marches between 1876 and 1931, but most of the best known were written between 1888 and 1900: *Semper Fidelis* (1888), *The Washington Post* (1889), and *Hands Across the Sea* (1899) are a few.

Sousa's most famous march, and probably the most famous American march of all time, is *Stars and Stripes Forever.* Conceived of in 1896 and published the following year, during Sousa's peak decade as a composer, it is the quintessential Sousa march. It has stirring and lyric melodies, subtle variation in accompaniment and rhythm, and a rich texture, with several layers of activity. A typical Sousa march has a modular form, assembled from a series of melodies or "strains" that are sixteen or thirty-two measures in length. There are two main sections, the march and the **trio;** the trio is in a different key. Each strain is repeated at least once.

Sousa's marches are the instrumental counterpart to the songs of Foster and Cohan. They share three important qualities. First, the most famous works by all three composers were immediately popular and have remained among the best-known music from their eras. Second, they are musically significant, the best examples of their genres. Third, they are (almost indefinably) American, without extensive or obvious black influence. With ragtime, they comprise the most important legacy from American popular music before World War I.

Simply because they—and the bands that played them—were so popular, marches by Sousa and others had an impact well beyond the parade and concert venues. The two-step was a popular social dance inspired by Sousa's *The Washington Post*. The rhythm and spirit of the march animated popular song, as we discovered earlier. Most important perhaps, the march and the concert band also played a seminal role in the development of ragtime, syncopated music, and jazz.

LISTENING CUE · ***Stars and Stripes Forever* (1897),** John Philip Sousa. The Sousa Band, 1903.

STYLE March **FORM** · Multisectional form of march; four strains in the form AABB/Trio (CDCDC)

Listen For . . .

INSTRUMENTATION
Full concert band, with woodwinds, brass, and percussion

RHYTHM
Duple meter, at a brisk tempo, with clear marking of the beat in accompaniment throughout, except for breaks

MELODY
Instrumental-style melodies for the most part: fast-moving notes, wide skips.
Trio has lyrical melody.

TEXTURE
Melody plus simple accompaniment, with countermelodies a striking feature of the trio when repeated; accompaniment stops during breaks.

Remember . . .

MARCH RHYTHM
OOM-pah: bass note on the beat, chord on the afterbeat, with variants or breaks for rhythmic interest

MARCH FORM
Four strains, with a pronounced contrast in the third strain. The break is an exceptional feature.

THE CONCERT BAND
Large ensemble, with clarinets the most numerous instrument. Trumpets, trombones, clarinets, piccolo, and percussion are featured.

AMERICAN MUSIC
Sousa's marches sound musically American because of their vitality and rhythmic energy.

Listen to this selection in CourseMate.

UNIT 2

LOOKING BACK, LOOKING AHEAD

THE AMERICAN MUSIC LANDSCAPE during the first few decades of the nineteenth century provides virtually no clues as to the direction popular music would soon take. Virtually all of the commercially disseminated popular music came from Europe. Only the emergence of blackface entertainment in America gave a glimpse of future developments. However, by the turn of the twentieth century, America had its own popular music, recognized as such at home and abroad, and a rapidly growing industry to promote it.

The birth of a recognizably American popular music and the growth of the popular music industry are the two most significant developments in nineteenth-century popular music. They encompass several important trends that continue through the twentieth century, including these:

- **The infusion of rhythm into popular music.** Dance rhythms in support of popular song are an innovation of minstrel show music; by the end of the century, they are customary in almost all kinds of popular song.
- **Impact of "low-brow" styles.** In popular music, the impetus for change comes from the more marginalized segments of American society: rural folk traditions, white and black, at mid-century, then African-American elements around the turn of the twentieth century.
- **Innovation through synthesis.** Innovation in popular music is mainly a matter of integrating diverse, even contradictory, musical elements into a new sound. The minstrel show song and Foster's plantation songs evidence this trend.
- **Increased role of blacks.** The presence of African Americans in the popular music industry, begun in earnest after the end of the Civil War, continues during the latter part of the nineteenth century. Blacks begin to break through into genres other than minstrelsy around 1900.

The new century would bring vibrant new music, mainly through a comprehensive infusion of African-American music: ragtime, syncopated dance music, blues, and jazz. We encounter these styles in the next unit.

The Emergence of Black Music

LIVE JAZZ

UNIT 3

UNIT 3

Sometime in 1914, Jim Europe sat at the piano during a break between dance numbers. He was playing a song that he'd played many times before, W. C. Handy's "Memphis Blues." Irene and Vernon Castle, who had heard him play it over and over, approached him and asked him to turn it into a dance number. Europe did, and the Castles created a new dance, the foxtrot. The Castles' casual request marked the beginning of the modern era in popular music.

This new music sounded modern mainly because it incorporated unmistakable elements of black music. In the first twenty-five years of the twentieth century, black music exploded into American life. Ragtime, syncopated dance music, blues, and jazz—all found an audience among blacks and whites and eventually blended with the mainstream styles to produce a new kind of popular music.

CHAPTER 11
Ragtime

Among the bigger hits of 1896 was a song entitled "All Coons Look Alike to Me." In our own time, a title like that would be considered indisputably offensive. However, the end of the nineteenth century was a low point in post–Civil War race relations; in the same year that the song appeared, the Supreme Court's decision in *Plessy v. Ferguson* ratified the "separate but equal" policy that became the law of the land until the 1950s. In this environment, most mainstream Americans seemed not to find derogatory racial terms particularly offensive.

As it happened, the composer of "All Coons Look Alike to Me" was Ernest Hogan, one of the leading black entertainers of the time. His song is romantic: It describes a young man who has eyes for only one girl; other girls "look alike" to him. However, in a climate where the majority of Americans assumed that blacks were inferior, a love song between blacks was not socially acceptable outside the black community. So Hogan found himself with a bitter choice: buy into the stereotypes of the time—even as he tried to undermine them somewhat in the lyric—or fail to get the song published.

Hogan's music is the good news that balances the bad news of the title. In the published version of "All Coons Look Alike to Me," the repetition of the chorus features a "Negro 'rag' accompaniment." This was the first published example of raglike piano style. The first published piano rags, including Scott Joplin's "Original Rags," appeared a year later.

Ragtime Emerges

The history of **ragtime** begins in the years after the Civil War. Black musicians in the Midwest had been playing ragtime—or at least syncopated music—well before the first rags were published in the 1890s. During this same period, black pianists in bars and bordellos up and down the East Coast played what would soon be called "ragtime," according to several contemporary accounts.

During the 1893 World Columbian Exposition, ragtime pianists from all over the country migrated to Chicago. Among them were most of the St. Louis ragtime pianists, including Scott Joplin. They found employment and valuable exposure in the restaurants, saloons, and brothels in the vicinity of the exposition.

Toward the end of the century, composers and songwriters began to use the terms *rag* and *ragtime* to identify a new style. With the publication of Joplin's "Maple Leaf Rag" in 1899, *ragtime* became a household word.

Joplin's "Maple Leaf Rag" was the first commercially successful **piano rag.** It did not so much start a craze for syncopated music as give it a major push along two lines: It introduced more complex African-inspired rhythms to popular music, and it made them available in sheet-music form. The rhythms of Joplin's early rags were more intricate than the syncopated songs and dances of the 1890s. Rhythmically, they found a midpoint between the improvised style of black ragtime pianists and the cakewalks and ragtime songs of the period.

And because ragtime was the first black music that looked on paper the way it sounded in performance, any competent pianist, black or white, who was able to read music could buy the sheet music to Joplin's "Maple Leaf Rag" and perform it in a reasonably authentic manner. At a time when recordings were limited; films were silent; radio and television, nonexistent; and live entertainment, especially by black performers, relatively rare outside of the big cities, sheet music was the best way to absorb new music.

Scott Joplin

The classic piano rags of Scott Joplin (1868–1917) are the most enduring music of the ragtime era. Several have remained familiar, especially since the ragtime revival of the 1970s; Joplin's piano rags remain the core of the ragtime repertoire. A professional musician from his teenage years, Joplin played in saloons and clubs along the Mississippi River Valley and eventually in Missouri. (The "Maple Leaf Rag" is named after the Maple Leaf Club in Sedalia, Missouri, where he worked from 1894 until the turn of the century.) He also received formal musical training in the European tradition, principally through study at George R. Smith College in Sedalia, and was a fluent composer and arranger in the popular white styles

SCOTT JOPLIN

© Pictorial Press Ltd/Alamy

of the day. After the turn of the century, Joplin devoted most of his professional efforts to legitimizing ragtime. In addition to a steady stream of piano compositions, mostly rags, he composed a ballet, *The Ragtime Dance,* and two operas, *Treemonisha* and the now lost *A Guest of Honor.* (Joplin received a posthumous Pulitzer Prize for *Treemonisha* in 1976 on the occasion of its revival.)

The Sound of the Piano Rag

In Joplin's own performance of "Maple Leaf Rag," we can hear virtually all the significant features of traditional piano ragtime. The piano rag is based on the march. (At this time, marches were almost as popular on the dance floor as during a parade.) Joplin and his peers simply transformed the march into ragtime by adding idiomatic, African-inspired syncopation and adapting the style to a single instrument, the piano.

Ragtime Enters Popular Culture

Although initially referring to piano music, the word *ragtime* quickly came to identify almost any syncopated music and even some that was not. For example, Irving Berlin's 1911 hit "Alexander's Ragtime Band" is a thoroughly modern song for the time, but it does not have even the modest syncopation of earlier ragtime songs. Ragtime songs, written and performed by both blacks and whites, were often interpolated into Broadway shows. "Under the Bamboo Tree," a hit song by black musicians James Weldon Johnson, J. Rosamond Johnson, and Bob Cole, first appeared in the show *Sally in Our Alley,* sung by Marie Cahill, an Irish-American singer. (It is difficult to imagine how they worked the lyrics—about a jungle maid—into the plot and how Cahill passed herself off as an African queen.)

". . . the 'Ragtime Evil' should not be found in Christian homes."

LISTENING CUE • **"Maple Leaf Rag" (1899),** Scott Joplin. Joplin, piano (piano roll, 1916).

STYLE Piano rag • **FORM** Multisectional form of march, four strains in the form AABBA/CCDD

Listen For . . .

INSTRUMENTATION
Solo piano

RHYTHM
March rhythm *(OOM-pah)* in accompaniment much of the time; syncopated ragtime patterns in melody

MELODY
Instrumental-style melody: rapid arpeggiated figuration

TEXTURE
Thick texture: harmonized melody plus bass/chord accompaniment

Remember . . .

SOUND OF THE PIANO RAG
Its most characteristic feature is syncopated figuration.

MARCH CONNECTION
A piano rag is like a march with syncopation played on the piano.

RAGTIME, PUBLISHING, AND THE SPREAD OF BLACK MUSIC
Published rags gave mainstream America its first encounter with authentic black musical style.

Listen to this selection in CourseMate.

As it spread across the country, ragtime met with resistance from virtually every corner of the establishment. It was considered immoral, fit only for the saloons and brothels where it was played, and deemed musically déclassé—the product of an inferior race incapable of the musical sophistication that Europeans had achieved. And it was considered a cause of moral decay. According to one writer, "the 'Ragtime Evil' should not be found in Christian homes."

There were, of course, overtones of racial prejudice in virtually all of these arguments. During this low point in race relations, few whites accepted blacks as equals, so it is not surprising that many found ragtime's mix of black and white influences unacceptable.

Serious musicians stood divided on the question of ragtime's worth. Daniel Gregory Mason, one of the guardians of the cultivated tradition, sought to demean ragtime by drawing an unfavorable comparison between its syncopated rhythms and those found in Beethoven's and Schumann's music. Charles Ives, the most important American classical composer of that generation and an after-hours ragtime pianist, responded that the comparison showed "how much alike they [ragtime and Schumann] are."

In retrospect, the reaction against ragtime (and the blacks who created it) was even stronger than the reaction would be against rock and roll a half century later. However, the end result was the same: Ragtime, like rock and roll, won out.

Courtesy Duke University Rare Book, Manuscript, and Special Collections Library

JOPLIN and his peers simply transformed the march into ragtime by adding idiomatic, African-inspired syncopation and adapting the style to a single instrument, the piano.

The Legacy of Ragtime

Ragtime's legacy to American music includes these three contributions:

- A body of music of enduring value and appeal
- A number of firsts in the history of African-American music
- The catalyst for the revolution that produced the modern era in popular music

The Classic Piano Rag

The classic piano rags of Scott Joplin and other distinguished composers represent a repertoire of real artistic worth and individuality; there is no other music like it. From musical evidence in Joplin's works, we can also infer his dedication to bringing ragtime under the European classical music umbrella. The later rags are more melodious and less syncopated, and in both his tempo indications for rags and his written commentary on the correct performance of ragtime, Joplin constantly admonishes pianists against playing ragtime too fast; ragtime played at a slower tempo gains dignity.

As his later compositions showed, Joplin saw ragtime as a vehicle for serious artistic expression as well as entertainment. Accordingly, he thought of himself as a composer of art music in the tradition of the nineteenth-century nationalist composers. He believed that he had elevated a folk-dance music to concert status, in much the same way that Polish composer Frédéric Chopin had elevated the *mazurka* (Polish folk dance) and Viennese composer Franz Schubert the *ländler* (Austrian folk dance) in classical music.

Joplin's disciples approached ragtime composition with a similar seriousness of purpose, and his publisher, John Stark, identified him as a composer of "classic" rags. In keeping with his purpose, the classic ragtime style of Joplin and his disciples was the most conservative, or European, of the ragtime piano styles current around 1900. The East Coast ragtime of Eubie Blake and the New Orleans style of Jelly Roll Morton are considerably more syncopated than Joplin's music.

Ragtime and the Preservation of African-American Culture

Ragtime, or at least the classic ragtime of Joplin and his peers, enabled African Americans to become more aware of their own culture. Prior to ragtime, black folk music had been passed on through oral tradition. Each new generation of blacks would learn the songs, dances, and religious music of their culture by hearing them and singing or playing along. It is frustrating to read pre-twentieth-century descriptions of black music; attempts by interested white musicians to capture black folk music in notation fall far short of the mark, no matter how sincere they may have been.

Joplin's work marked the beginning of a movement among historically conscious black musicians to preserve their musical heritage. W. C. Handy, the "father of the blues," began collecting blues melodies and assembling them into songs, just as Joplin had done with rags. James Weldon Johnson and J. Rosamond Johnson, brothers who were also active Broadway composers, assembled and arranged spirituals, fitting them with piano accompaniments for performance at home, at church, and even in the concert hall.

Ragtime also represented the first documented instance of African Americans filtering through their own musical heritage the European music to which they had been exposed. By comparing pieces in rag style with their original versions and models, it is possible to identify the specifically African-American elements in the rag.

Ragtime as a Catalyst for Change

Ragtime had a widespread impact on other musical styles. It loosened up popular music (both song and dance), helped shape jazz in its early years, and aroused the interest of several of the most important classical composers in the early twentieth century. Ragtime also made popular music livelier. Its beat had more of a bounce, and its syncopated rhythms permitted a rapid yet relatively natural delivery of the words.

Even at the peak of its popularity, and despite its notoriety, however, ragtime was never the dominant popular style. Mainstream popular music remained largely unsyncopated, as we discovered in "Take Me Out to the Ball Game." But no music from its era was more influential, and no music of the period remains more popular. Even more important, it opened the doors of popular music to other, more African styles. Syncopated dance music, blues, and jazz would soon follow ragtime's path toward the popular mainstream.

CHAPTER 12
Syncopated Dance Music

In the two decades between 1905 and 1925, Americans went dance crazy. Early on, much of the music that they danced to was ragtime, but over time the music for these new dances diversified to include popular songs set to a danceable beat. The most popular and enduring of the new dances was the foxtrot.

Ragtime Dance

Almost as soon as it appeared, ragtime became music for social dancing. Piano rags were scored for the dance orchestras of the period. Joplin's famous "Red Book" (so called because it had a red cover), a collection of dance-orchestra arrangements of his popular rags, is the best-known example. Original dance music in a syncopated style also appeared throughout the late 1890s and into the 1910s.

As the cakewalk fad faded away, other dances took its place, most of them adapted or borrowed from black folk dances. The most notorious of these new dances was a group of **animal dances.** The grizzly bear, the chicken glide, and the turkey trot all became popular in certain circles around 1910. "Respectable" citizens reacted violently to these dances, which were associated with sleazy establishments and disreputable people. As recounted in Sylvia Dannett and Frank Rachel's book, *Down Memory Lane: The Arthur Murray Picture Book of Social Dancing:*

> A Paterson, New Jersey, court imposed a fifty-day prison sentence on a young woman for dancing the turkey trot. Fifteen young women were dismissed from a well-known magazine after the editor caught them enjoying the abandoned dance at lunchtime. Turkey trotters incurred the condemnation of churches and respectable people, and in 1914 an official disapproval was issued by the Vatican.

The turkey trot was one of the most popular dances. By all accounts it was simple and awkward, but it permitted "lingering close contact," a novelty at the time. Body contact between couples (presumably) delighted the dancers but scandalized the more conservative segments of American society and provoked a hostile backlash. A more refined dance, the **foxtrot,** soon replaced it.

James Reese Europe and the Foxtrot

James Reese Europe (1881–1919) had come to New York in 1905 from Washington, D.C., and quickly immersed himself in the popular music world. By 1910 he had organized the Clef Club, an organization for black musicians that was part union and part booking agency. In 1912, he directed the 150-piece Clef Club Orchestra in a concert at Carnegie Hall, then as now America's musical mecca. Designed to showcase the achievements of African-American musicians, the concert impressed members of New York's high society, and soon Europe and his Society Orchestra were in demand for parties given by the Rockefellers and other wealthy families.

Published in 1915, this early foxtrot sheet music is evidence that the dance caught on quickly.

> *"A Paterson, New Jersey, court imposed a fifty-day prison sentence on a young woman for dancing the turkey trot."*
> —The Arthur Murray Picture Book of Social Dancing

Europe's star rose even higher when Irene and Vernon Castle chose him and his orchestra to accompany them. Fresh from Europe, where they had wowed Parisian audiences with their rendition of the tango, the Castles took New York by storm, appearing in a series of Broadway productions between 1912 and 1914 and in vaudeville, starring in silent films, and opening a dance studio and a supper club.

Among the dance pieces that Europe composed for the Castles was "Castle House Rag." Europe's orchestral rag

LISTENING CUE · **"Castle House Rag" (1914),** James Reese. Europe Europe's Society Orchestra.

STYLE Syncopated dance music · **FORM** March-inspired multisectional form, with five strains plus drum solo

Listen For . . .

INSTRUMENTATION
Unusual instrumentation includes violins and cello, flute and clarinet, cornet and baritone horn, piano, bells, and drums.

RHYTHM
March-like rhythm at a brisk tempo;
simple syncopation in melodies; syncopated accents in drum solo

MELODY
Contrasting activity in instrumental-style melodies

TEXTURE
Melody plus simple accompaniment (accompanying parts not always easily heard because of primitive recording equipment)

Remember . . .

SYNCOPATED RHYTHMS
Most strains have simple, rag-influenced syncopations.

DANCE ORCHESTRA IN TRANSITION
Violins connect to Europe; winds, brass and especially percussion connect to 1920s dance orchestras.

CUTTING LOOSE
Musicians break free of tight arrangement only at the end.

SPRAWLING RAG
Short strains and fast tempo = four additional strains plus drum solo

Listen to this selection in CourseMate.

evidences the spread of ragtime and shows the evolution of the genre away from the classic piano style. In addition to Europe's multi-instrumental setting, other differences between it and a classic Joplin rag include these:

- *A faster tempo.* The tempo of ragtime music gradually accelerated during this period (despite Joplin's admonition to the contrary), so the beat of this song moves considerably more quickly than "Maple Leaf Rag." It is about the same speed as up-tempo music from the early 1920s (we hear two examples in the next chapter: "Charleston" and "Fascinating Rhythm."
- *Less syncopation and less "ragged" melodies.* Overall, there is less rhythmic conflict in this piece than in a classic rag, and the figuration is less complex—probably because it would have been challenging to perform on melody instruments at such a fast tempo. There are exceptions, most notably the transition into the trio-like third section and the drum solo at the end.
- *A chance to improvise.* The last two sections allow the musicians, particularly drummer Buddy Gilmore, the chance to depart from the carefully scripted arrangement used throughout most of the performance.

Jim Europe's life ended abruptly when one of his musicians, angry about Europe's discipline attacked him and severed his jugular vein. At the time, Europe was probably the most popular and respected black musician in the United States. He worked tirelessly to raise the stature of African-American musicians. Justified or not, newspapers eulogized him as the "jazz king."

Some writers have speculated that if Europe hadn't died, popular music would have been quite different. The few recordings by his dance orchestra do not lend much support to this notion, and two circumstances argue against it. One was the proliferation of dance orchestras, both black and white, beginning the year of Europe's death and continuing into the 1920s. The other was the emergence of two other black styles: jazz and blues.

Europe's most far-reaching contribution to popular music was his integral role in developing and popularizing the foxtrot, which would become the dominant social dance of the 1920s and 1930s. For the first time, social dancing to a clearly black beat became acceptable to a significant portion of the population. Foxtrotting caught on with all levels of society, from the Rockefellers on down. Although it may not have been condoned in all quarters, dancing to syncopated music was no longer a criminal offense. By the mid-1930s, dancing "cheek to cheek," as Fred Astaire and Ginger Rogers did on-screen, was not only socially acceptable, but the epitome of elegance.

Syncopating the Mainstream

The success of syncopated dance music was a milestone in the mainstreaming of black popular music. Still, it was only a step toward equal opportunity, equal treatment, and dignity. During the early 1910s, James Europe got dance engagements in part because white bands refused to play the new syncopated music—they considered it beneath them. Only when the foxtrot caught on did white bands hop on the syncopated-music bandwagon.

CHAPTER 13

Early Commercial Blues

In his autobiography, W. C. Handy tells of an encounter late one night in 1903. While waiting for a train, Handy heard a young black man singing and playing a guitar, using a knife on the strings—similar to the bottleneck style of other blues guitarists. He described the sound as "the weirdest I'd ever heard." That "weird sound" was almost certainly the blues; Handy's account suggests that the style was already well established by that time. The story and its aftermath encapsulate the history of the blues in the first part of the twentieth century. There is not one history, but two. One is familiar, the other largely unknown. Partly as a result of this experience, Handy would go on to play a leading role in the emergence of blues as a commercial music during the first quarter of the twentieth century. It was the commercial versions of the blues that would shape the sound of popular music so profoundly in the early modern era.

That "weird sound" was almost certainly the blues.

By contrast, like the young man at the station, a whole generation of bluesmen would remain anonymous. We have almost no anecdotal information about the early history of blues as a folk music, and no musical evidence until the mid-1920s, when a few record companies began to record folk bluesmen like Blind Lemon Jefferson. The influence of this branch of the blues on mainstream music occurred in the rock era, and only after many of its leading performers left the South for northern cities like Chicago. We consider such "folk blues" in Unit 6. In this chapter, we focus on the commercial blues styles that emerged in the first three decades of the twentieth century.

The First Commercial Blues Styles

Commercial blues entered the larger world of popular music in four stages. The first began around the turn of the century, when the first professional blues performers launched their careers. The second occurred in the early teens with the publication of blues songs. In the third stage, which began in the late teens, blues style helped shape the sound of jazz. Finally, a group of "classic" blues singers, many of whom had started their careers years before, began to record.

© George Bailey/iStockphoto

The First Professional Blues Musicians

By the time of Handy's encounter, blacks had begun to sing and play the blues professionally. The great blues singer Ma Rainey, who would record extensively in the 1920s, recalls that she was inspired to sing the blues after hearing a girl sing the blues at a theater in St. Louis in 1902, and several of New Orleans's first generation of jazzmen recall playing the blues before the turn of the century. Early in the century, the audience for blues—folk, semiprofessional, and professional—were blacks, mainly in the South, and those whites who had extensive contact with blacks and/or who frequented the bars and bordellos where black musicians performed. However, as blacks migrated to urban areas in both the North and the South, they took the blues with them. After the move to the cities, what had been private or small-group entertainment in the rural South became music for public performance. Blues singers, most of them women, toured on the black vaudeville circuits and performed wherever they got paid. Ma Rainey was among the first; Bessie Smith joined her in the teens. They and other blues singers remained unknown to most Americans (both white and black) until the 1920s. The blues that reached these larger audiences were filtered through other styles. In the meantime, however, white America got its first taste of the blues.

Blues in Print: The First Published Blues Songs

W. C. Handy's "Memphis Blues" was part of a wave of blues songs that appeared during the 1910s. Handy composed several more, most notably "St. Louis Blues" (1914), the most frequently recorded song in the first half of the twentieth century. These published songs are a pale imitation of the blues that Ma Rainey and Bessie Smith were singing in tent shows and on the black vaudeville circuit. Still, they mark the entry of the blues into the mainstream; it was this distinction that enabled Handy to claim with some justification that he was the "father of the blues." Although he certainly didn't invent the blues, he published sheet music editions of his compositions, thereby disseminating many of its conventions, such as the twelve-bar form, and bringing them into the world of popular music.

Blues, Jazz, and Dance Music

During the teens, a few instrumental groups recorded the published blues songs of Handy and others, but the performances had little to do with blues style as heard only a few years later in the singing of Bessie Smith. In 1917, the first jazz recording was released; it featured the all-white Original Dixieland Jass [*sic*] Band. One side of the record was "Livery Stable Blues," a song in blues form replete with barnyard sounds. A host of bands, black and white, followed in their footsteps; Europe's 369th U.S. Infantry "Hellfighters Band," a military band he brought to Europe at the end of World War I, recorded several of Handy's blues songs. These recordings brought the instrumental performance of blues closer to the style of the black blues singers. However, authentic blues style in instrumental music would only appear on record when the top black jazz bands, which had been playing blues-based jazz since the turn of the century in New Orleans, began recording in the early 1920s; we hear King Oliver's Creole Jazz Band in the next chapter.

What ragtime and syncopated music did for the hips and the feet, blues did for the heart and soul.

Classic Blues

The blues recorded during the 1910s were strictly instrumental. That changed almost overnight with the release of Mamie Smith's "Crazy Blues" in 1920. "Crazy Blues" is not a blues song in the full sense of the term. Rather, it is a blues-influenced popular song sung in a bluesy, distinctively black singing style. The recording caused a sensation and encouraged record companies to seek out other, similar singers.

The growth of commercial radio gave the record companies added motivation to recruit black blues singers. Because people didn't want to pay for what they could get for free, record companies were forced to seek out smaller markets—blacks, southern whites, and various ethnic groups—where they would not face competition from mainstream radio.

Chief among them was the so-called race-record market. **Race records** were recordings of black performers, targeted at a black audience. The featured styles were blues and jazz. Both major labels and the 1920s equivalent of indie labels recorded black jazz and blues musicians. Columbia Records, the company that recorded Bessie Smith, was one of the top labels of the era; Paramount, which recorded the folk bluesman Blind Lemon Jefferson, was a sideline for a Wisconsin furniture manufacturer. It is on race records that we hear the sounds of classic blues.

Courtesy The Morgan Collection

This photo, shot when Bessie Smith was about thirty, shows her looking both elegant and vulnerable. Smith was a big woman with a big voice; other publicity shots show a more rambunctious side of her personality.

Bessie Smith

The recordings of Bessie Smith (1894–1937) epitomize **classic blues**. They are "classic" blues because they embody the three defining aspects of the blues: its form, style, and feeling. Most of her recordings are conventional twelve-bar blues with call and response between singer and an instrumentalist. Typically, the songs are personal, and she sings them with a rough, full voice, with support from jazz musicians. The accompaniment varies from recording to recording, from just a pianist to a full jazz band. We hear a famous example next, recorded in 1928 at the peak of her career.

In "Empty Bed Blues," Smith begins by singing about her man troubles. For most of the song, she describes their lovemaking, sometimes in metaphor ("coffee grinder," "deep sea diver") and sometimes directly. All of this makes his infidelity even more painful.

Particularly since the emergence of punk and rap, we are used to music being "real"—a no-nonsense, no-holds-barred representation of our lives. In popular music, classic blues is where *real* begins. Not only the subject of the lyrics but also the range of emotions they describe and the frankness with which Smith sings them were without precedent. She tells us how good it is with her man and how devastated she is when he's with someone else.

Smith sings with a rough, rich, powerful voice. Most phrases start high and end low, and cover a narrow range. She inflects key words to intensify their emotional power; her delivery is speech intensified into song. Smith is backed by two good jazz musicians of the time, trombonist Charlie Green and pianist Porter Grainger. Green, in particular, tries to emulate and extend the blues vocal style: his playing is full of swoops, smears, and bent notes—all of which mimic the expressive inflection heard in great blues singing.

The earthy, direct lyrics; Smith's singing; and the use of several blues conventions—the twelve-bar form, call and response between voice and instrument, and phrases that start high and end low—all of these features exemplify blues as a form, elements of blues style, and the way blues style can convey deep feeling. Through songs like this, listeners could tap into the expressive power of the blues.

Smith's audience included not only black Americans but also a small, devoted group of white fans. She was admired enough to appear in a short film, an extremely unusual circumstance for a black blues singer in the late 1920s. The blues that she epitomized penetrated almost every aspect of popular music, as we will hear in the next chapter.

The Great Depression hit Americans hard—and blacks especially hard. Too few could afford to buy records or attend the theaters and clubs where these blues singers performed. As a result, the market for this kind of commercial blues singing had all but dried up by the early 1930s.

The Legacy of Blues Style

Through this multistage infusion of blues styles, both the idea and the sound of the blues entered the popular mainstream, touching social dancing (there was a

LISTENING CUE • **"Empty Bed Blues" (1928),** Bessie Smith. Smith, vocal; Charlie Green, trombone; Porter Grainger, piano.

STYLE Classic blues • **FORM** Blues form (strophic form with five choruses that use twelve-bar blues form)

Listen For . . .

INSTRUMENTATION
Voice, trombone, and piano

PERFORMANCE STYLE
Smith sings with a strong, gravelly voice. Her singing is highly inflected.

RHYTHM
Four-beat feel, but with two-beat accompaniment in piano; subtle rhythmic play, moving ahead or behind beat

MELODY
In voice; medium-length phrases in a narrow range start high and finish low.

Remember . . .

BLUES FEELING
A characteristic "my man's gone now" blue mood, in the lyric and in Smith's singing

RACY LYRICS
Talking about sex through metaphors like "deep sea diver"

ESSENCE OF BLUES STYLE
Big, rough voice; high-to-low phrases; subtle timing and inflection

STANDARD BLUES FORM
Five choruses of a conventional twelve-bar blues

Listen to this selection in CourseMate.

popular dance in the early 1920s called “the blues”), popular song, jazz, and pop-based concert music. We even find evidence of blues in musical theater. When composer Jerome Kern wanted to tell the audience of his landmark musical *Show Boat* that the character who sings “Can’t Help Lovin’ Dat Man” is a light-skinned mulatto passing for white, he added blues touches to the song.

What ragtime and syncopated music did for the hips and the feet, blues did for the heart and soul. All of this filtered into popular music. The music of the 1910s and 1920s was the first generation of popular music to be shaped by the blues. It would not be the last.

CHAPTER 14
Early Jazz

Legend has it that Buddy Bolden was already blowing everyone away in New Orleans before 1900. Bolden was the first of the great New Orleans cornetists. (A cornet is a close cousin of the trumpet.) But we don't know what his music sounded like, or what jazz might have sounded like then, because we have no recordings of him or any other jazz musician from that time.

The Roots of Jazz

We do know that New Orleans was regarded as the birthplace of **jazz** and that contemporary accounts date its beginnings sometime around the turn of the twentieth century. It flourished in the rich cultural mix that was New Orleans: whites of English and French descent, blacks, immigrants from the Caribbean and Europe, plus many citizens of mixed race. Music was part of this mix: brass bands for parades, and pianists and small groups for the bars, honky-tonks, and houses of prostitution, which was then legal in New Orleans. New Orleans and its visitors simply let the good times roll.

Throughout much of the nineteenth century, New Orleans had been a relatively hospitable environment for blacks. During slavery, Congo Square (now Louis Armstrong Park) was the only part of the South where people of African descent could legally gather and play drums and other percussion instruments. Before the Emancipation Proclamation, there were more free blacks in New Orleans than anywhere else in the United States, and New Orleans developed a complex social structure. It assigned social status by race and ethnic heritage—not just whites and blacks but also those of mixed race. "Creoles of color," those with ancestors from both France and Africa, enjoyed a higher social standing than ex-slaves. They lived in better neighborhoods, were better educated, and had more freedom. An aspiring Creole musician received traditional classical training, whereas black musicians typically learned to play by ear. Creoles of color tended to look down on the ex-slaves. Many emulated white culture rather than black.

What blues did for the heart and soul, jazz did for the spirit.

The Jim Crow laws enacted in the wake of *Plessy v. Ferguson* changed this. Race in New Orleans became simply "white" and "colored." Grouped together with no legal difference between them, black and Creole musicians began to work with one another. Jazz gained the spontaneity of improvisation and the feeling of the blues from the blacks, and the discipline and the traditional virtuosity of classical training from the Creoles.

In 1898, a New Orleans alderman named Sidney Story proposed that legal prostitution be restricted to a relatively small section near the French Quarter. Story's proposal became law, and the section of the city where prostitution was legal became known, ironically, as Storyville. Most jazz musicians worked in Storyville. However, in 1917 a series of unsavory incidents involving sailors of the U.S. Navy brought Storyville to the attention of the Secretary of the Navy, who threatened to shut down the New Orleans naval base if the city fathers didn't close Storyville. They did. The closing of Storyville put many jazz musicians out of work and forced them to look elsewhere. Many moved out of town, and Chicago became a prime destination.

The New Orleans Jazz Band

The early history of jazz that we can document in sound begins in the early twenties, when black jazz bands began to record with some frequency. The standard **New Orleans jazz** band blended the instrumentation of three key popular music genres. From the marching band came the clarinet, cornet or trumpet, trombone, tuba, and drum line, now consolidated into the drum set; from the minstrel show came the banjo; and from the saloons and bordellos (and other places where one could hear professional ragtime pianists) came the piano.

The band has two parts: the front line and the rhythm section. The **front line** (so called because the musicians stand at the front of the bandstand) is typically three instruments: clarinet, trumpet or cornet, and trombone. The front-line instruments play melody, usually within a well-defined range and within well-defined limits, particularly when playing together.

- The cornet (trumpet) is the mid-range instrument that usually carries the melody.
- The clarinet takes the highest part, playing a fast-moving countermelody to the main part.
- The trombone carries the lowest melodic part, usually in the form of "commentary" on the melody and the clarinet part.

The standard rhythm section of the time consisted of banjo, piano, brass bass (or tuba, the lowest-pitched of the brass instruments), and drums. The rhythm section marked the beat and supplied the harmony.

All three (or four, when there's an extra cornet or saxophone) melody instruments typically play at the same time, a practice called **collective improvisation,** which means that the performers simultaneously make up the music together as they play, rather than playing music that they or someone else has already written.

Collective improvisation requires teamwork: Everyone has to know not only his or her own role but the others' roles as well. In this respect, collective improvisation in jazz is like a fast break in basketball; the cornet or trumpet player is like the ball handler. Both are located in the center of the action—mid-range melody for the musician, center court for the basketball player. Other players flank the center and react to what the player controlling the action does. In both cases, the process is spontaneous, but it occurs within prescribed and well-understood boundaries.

© Frank Driggs Collection/Getty Images

KING OLIVER'S CREOLE JAZZ BAND IN 1923. From left to right: Honore Dutrey, trombone; Baby Dodds, drums; King Oliver, lead cornet; Louis Armstrong, slide trumpet; Lil Hardin (Armstrong's future wife), piano; Bill Johnson, banjo; and Johnny Dodds, clarinet.

King Oliver's Creole Jazz Band

Joe "King" Oliver (1885–1938) was one of the major figures of early jazz. His reputation rests on his achievements as a bandleader and a cornet player. Like many New Orleans musicians, he emigrated to Chicago in search of a better-paying job following the closing of Storyville. By 1920, he had assembled several of his New Orleans expatriates into King Oliver's Creole Jazz Band, the finest traditional New Orleans-style jazz band preserved on record.

Although in "Dippermouth Blues" Oliver and clarinetist Johnny Dodds play solos, most of the performance proceeds with all instruments playing simultaneously, with no one instrument completely dominant. This is the quintessential New Orleans jazz sound.

"Dippermouth Blues" is a blues song in form and style. Each section is twelve measures long, with the

LISTENING CUE • **"Dippermouth Blues" (1923),** Joe Oliver. King Oliver's Creole Jazz Band featuring Oliver, cornet; and Johnny Dodds, clarinet.

STYLE New Orleans jazz • **FORM** Blues form (strophic form with nine choruses that use twelve-bar blues form)

Listen For . . .

INSTRUMENTATION
Front line: two cornets, clarinet, and trombone; rhythm section: piano (barely heard), banjo, and drums/percussion

PERFORMANCE STYLE
Instrumental counterpart to blues vocal style: lots of bent notes and slides into notes, imitating the voice

RHYTHM
Four-beat rhythm (kept by banjo and felt by entire band) at fast tempo; lots of syncopation and other forms of rhythmic play, especially anticipating or lagging behind the beat in solos

TEXTURE
In most choruses, collective improvisation in the front line (three independent lines, all improvised); the rhythm section keeps time.

Remember . . .

JAZZ RHYTHM
Rhythm section chunks out steady four-beat rhythm; horns syncopate over rhythm section timekeeping.

BLUES INFLUENCE
Twelve-bar blues harmonic progression; blues style, especially in Oliver's solo

NEW ORLEANS JAZZ INSTRUMENTATION
Standard New Orleans jazz band: front line (clarinet, cornet[s], trombone) plus rhythm section (here, banjo, piano, and drums)

COLLECTIVE IMPROVISATION
Front-line players improvise at the same time.

Listen to this selection in CourseMate.

characteristic harmonic pattern of the blues. It is also a blues song in style, which is most apparent in Oliver's famous cornet solo. As a cornet player, Oliver developed an influential style deeply rooted in the blues. His solo in "Dippermouth Blues" was one of the most frequently imitated jazz solos of his generation. His playing parallels the heightened inflection, narrow range, and unconstrained rhythmic delivery of a blues singer. The manner in which he slides in and out of important notes is an instrumental counterpart to blues vocal style.

"Dippermouth Blues" shows the "deep blues" roots of early jazz. Most early jazz recordings show at least some influence of blues style, and many of them—almost half, it would seem—are based on blues form. From the beginning, jazz musicians have liked to improvise on the blues chord progression because the chords are simple and change relatively slowly. This gives the musicians plenty of time to invent ideas—such as blues-like riffs (as in Oliver's solo) or faster running lines.

Playing second cornet on "Dippermouth Blues" was Louis Armstrong, who had come to Chicago in 1922 at Oliver's invitation. Armstrong would leave Oliver and move to New York , where he became the most influential jazz musician of his era. His work in the late 1920s would set the standard for the two most distinctive qualities of jazz: swing and improvisation.

The Essence of Jazz: Swing and Improvisation

The two qualities that most readily distinguish jazz from other popular genres are swing, its distinctive rhythmic conception, and improvisation, its spontaneous dimension. The ability to play with time and create in the moment have been measures of artistry in jazz performance certainly since the late 1920s; both are abundantly evident in the playing of the most admired and influential jazz musicians, from Armstrong to the present.

Swing

The most essential element in jazz is swing, as Duke Ellington asserted in his 1932 song "It Don't Mean A Thing (If It Ain't Got That Swing)." Here is a succinct definition of **swing:** rhythmic play over a four-beat rhythm. Both the four-beat rhythm and the rhythmic play over it were paradigm-shifting innovations. They were the clearest indications that jazz—and the popular music that it influenced—had embraced an entirely new rhythmic conception. The black musicians who created jazz kept the metrical structure of European music but interpreted it through an African sensibility. Instead of accenting the first beat of each measure, jazz musicians typically stressed all beats equally—or played rhythms that used that feel as a point of departure. In the Armstrong recording we hear next, the pianist and guitarist typically play chords on each beat; each receives the same amount of emphasis.

But in isolation the undifferentiated beats of the rhythm instruments do not produce swing. Swing results from the interplay between the beat and the syncopated accents and irregular patterns that conflict with the steady timekeeping of the rhythm instruments. It is this interplay that makes the rhythm so irresistible.

Improvisation

Improvisation in music is the act of creating new music in the moment—as one is singing or playing—rather than re-creating someone else's composition. The first generation of jazz musicians improvised by inventing new melodies for an existing song: a blues, a popular song, or a melody (and the accompanying harmony) created specifically as a point of departure for improvisation. In the Oliver example, the new melodies—for example, Oliver's solo—are created over a conventional blues progression; in Armstrong's "Hotter Than That," the melody and the chord progression were composed expressly for the recording session.

Improvisation is not unique to jazz. Through the early nineteenth century, classical composers were typically also adept improvisers: Bach, Mozart, and Beethoven were renowned for their improvisational ability. However, the practice largely died out in European classical music during the nineteenth century. Only with jazz did a sophisticated form of improvisation once again become an integral component of a new genre.

Louis Armstrong: Jazz as a Soloist's Art

Early in 1924, Armstrong married Lil Hardin, the pianist with Oliver's band. Soon after, they moved to New York, where Louis joined Fletcher Henderson's hot dance orchestra. In New York, Armstrong was a regular in the studio as well as the bandstand, recording with Henderson, a host of blues singers (including Bessie Smith), and the pianist Clarence Williams. Williams, who doubled as Okeh Records' A&R (artists and repertoire) man, noticed that the recordings on which he used Armstrong sold better than others. So in 1925 he offered Armstrong the chance to record as a leader rather than as a sideman. Armstrong, who had returned to Chicago, proceeded to record with what amounted to a studio band of his New Orleans friends plus Lil (and, somewhat later, pianist Earl Hines). Okeh billed them as Louis Armstrong's Hot Five or Hot Seven (depending on the number of players). Armstrong's groups made dozens of recordings, and made jazz—and music—history in the process.

LISTENING CUE • **"Hotter Than That," (1927),** Lil Hardin. Featuring Armstrong, vocal and trumpet; Kid Ory, trombone; Johnny Dodds, clarinet; Lil Hardin Armstrong, piano; Johnny St. Cyr, banjo; Lonnie Johnson, guitar.

STYLE 1920s Jazz • **FORM** Several improvised choruses on a melody based on popular song form: AA[1]

Listen For . . .

INSTRUMENTATION
Front line: clarinet, trumpet/voice, and trombone; rhythm section: just piano and banjo, giving way to guitar

PERFORMANCE STYLE
Armstrong's instrumental and vocal conception much the same: musical feel is almost identical; main differences are timbre and range.

RHYTHM
Four-beat rhythm at fast tempo; abundant syncopation in fast-moving melody lines

TEXTURE
Melody with steady timekeeping and harmonic accompaniment; collective improvisation at end

Remember . . .

SWING
Swing-producing rhythmic play especially evident in Armstrong's singing and playing

IMPROVISATION
Performance almost completely improvised, including opening chorus; underlying harmony the basis of improvisation

SOLO-ORIENTED JAZZ
Solo orientation—with collective improvisation only at end—signals shift away from collective improvisation.

EXPRESSIVENESS
Armstrong's arsenal of expressive devices includes vibrato (rapid oscillation in pitch) on long notes, slides into high notes, and rhythmic play over the four-beat rhythm.

Listen to this selection in CourseMate.

Louis Armstrong was the first great soloist in jazz. Every aspect of his playing—his beautiful sound; the bent notes, slides, shakes, and other expressive gestures; his melodic inventiveness; and above all, his incomparable sense of swing—inspired jazz and popular musicians of the era: Bing Crosby was a regular at the clubs where he worked; so were numerous jazz musicians. His playing became the standard by which other jazz musicians measured themselves. Recordings like "Hotter Than That" (written by Lil Hardin) captured an exuberance that is unique to early jazz, and especially the playing of Louis Armstrong. It invites a different kind of movement—foot tapping, head bobbing, lindy hopping. It comes from the particular interaction of the relentlessly pulsing beat, the ebb and flow of harmonic tension, and Armstrong's extraordinarily varied and subtle rhythmic play, with its note-to-note variation in accent, timing, and expressive gesture.

There is no known precedent for the swing heard in early jazz. No earlier music that has come down to us, not even ragtime, creates a comparably infectious rhythm. Its defining features are far too subtle to commit to notation and seem to elude precise definition. Indeed, Armstrong, when asked to explain swing, responded with something like "If you have to ask, you'll never know."

Armstrong's influence was pervasive: swing became common currency when the musicians who followed him absorbed his lessons on how to swing and audiences responded to this vital new rhythm.

Jazz in America during the 1920s

With the influx of New Orleans jazz musicians into northern cities and the recording of both white and black musicians, jazz became a truly national music in the early 1920s. Chicago and New York were the hot spots. Chicago was wide open—Al Capone and other gang leaders all but ran it—and musicians found ample employment opportunities in speakeasies and ballrooms. A generation of white musicians, among them Bix Beiderbecke and Benny Goodman, absorbed the sound of the New Orleans musicians firsthand, much as white rockers absorbed Chicago blues style in the 1960s. New York had top dance orchestras, including those led by Fletcher Henderson and Duke Ellington. Armstrong and other top jazzmen relocated there in the latter part of the 1920s.

What blues did for the heart and soul, jazz did for the spirit. The jazz of the early 1920s was exuberant, optimistic, spontaneous, and fast paced. It suggested illicit pleasures, if only because it so often accompanied them. In these respects it captured—and often inspired—the mood of the country, which accelerated through the decade until everything came crashing down in 1929. More than any other music, jazz would become the soundtrack of the decade. Small wonder that novelist F. Scott Fitzgerald and others called the 1920s the Jazz Age.

UNIT 3

LOOKING BACK, LOOKING AHEAD

THE PUBLICATION OF JOPLIN'S "Maple Leaf Rag" in 1899, only three decades earlier, gave piano-playing Americans of all races firsthand contact with an authentic African-American music. *Rag* was just beginning to be a dirty word. *Jazz* and *blues* were obscure, nameless musical styles.

By 1929, everyone was dancing the foxtrot, and *blues* and *jazz* were household words. Black music was on record, on the radio, in the theaters, and even occasionally on film.

In the first three decades of the twentieth century, black music gained a secure place in American musical life. Joplin, Europe, Smith, Oliver, Armstrong, and many others left a legacy that we still value, and they helped bring a wave of black musical styles into popular music. Ragtime was first. Syncopated dance music grew out of the ragtime dances of the 1900s and became popular in the early teens. Blues (as published songs) and jazz (as performed by white musicians) caught on shortly thereafter, and both flourished in the 1920s.

Moreover, these emergent styles were the catalyst for the wholesale transformation of popular music. In large part because of their contributions, popular music entered the modern era. We encounter this revolutionary development in popular song in the next chapter.

Popular Song in the Modern Era

UNIT 4

Courtesy of the author

UNIT 4

Among the new talking films cranked out in 1928 were a series of shorts featuring Eddie Peabody. Peabody was "The King of the Banjo," a gifted instrumentalist who was a vaudeville star and recording artist. In one of the films, he teamed up with Hal Kemp's Collegians, a popular dance orchestra of the era. The name of the band was pretty much on the mark: Kemp had formed the Carolina Club Orchestra while attending the University of North Carolina, and brought several band members with him to New York when he went professional.

The short, titled "Eddie Peabody, the Banjoy Boy and 'His College Chums,'" begins with Kemp's band, portrayed sitting around in the commons room of a fraternity, playing a good-humored version of their hit "I Don't Care": they clown their way through the group vocal chorus. Toward the end of the song, Peabody, wearing a raccoon coat, bounces into the room, tosses the coat away, then conducts the end of the song while spinning around. He tells Kemp's band that they'll sound fine at the varsity show. One of the band members asks Eddie what he's going to play; he replies, "I was thinking about . . . that new popular song, called 'High Up On a Hilltop.'" Peabody sings a chorus, then plays most of the next chorus in his trademark harmonized melody style. The centerpiece of the film is Peabody's classically inspired version of Irving Berlin's "Blue Skies," but he also shows off his mastery of the lap guitar and a pint-sized violin. There's no story to speak of; more than anything else, it's a 1920s-style music video.

Everything about the scene is modern—up to date ca. 1928. It's most obvious in the fact that the film has sound; the technology had become commercially viable only in the previous year. Kemp and his sidemen, most only a year out of school, try to act out the good times of college life, which was a popular theme in the media. Kemp's dance orchestra features saxophones and a big rhythm section. The music is relentlessly upbeat; the songs involving Peabody and the band bounce along over a foxtrot rhythm. This was the Jazz Age, after all—at least for another year.

"High Up On a Hilltop" is a "lilting fox trot," according to the sheet music. The chorus, which Peabody and Kemp's Collegians perform twice, begins with the title phrase set to a six-syllable riff. The flow of the lyric is almost conversational. The song was written by Abel Baer, Ian Campbell, father of the author of this text, and George Whiting.

All of this—the music, the high spirits, and the technology—represents radical change from the popular music at the turn of the century. In this unit, we explore what makes the popular songs of the 1920s modern, discuss how technology not only transformed the dissemination of popular music but also reshaped its sound, and consider its impact on American society.

CHAPTER 15

The Early Modern Era: Music, Society, and Technology

The fifteen years between 1914 (the start of World War I) and 1929 (the start of the Great Depression) marked the beginning of the modern era, not only in popular music but also in art, literature, and American life. To be modern in America during the 1920s meant moving and living at a faster pace. It meant believing in progress, especially material progress. It meant moving out of the country and into the city. It meant taking advantage of new technologies, from automobiles and air conditioning to the zippers that were now featured on clothing, luggage, and a host of other products. It meant buying into fashionable intellectual ideas and artistic trends. And it meant listening—and dancing—to a new kind of music.

The emergence of a distinctively American popular music expressed both the fact and the nature of America's coming of age. With its intercession in World War I, the United States had become a world power, a player on the world stage. Business, applying the assembly-line procedures used so successfully by Henry Ford and the management techniques of Frederick Winslow Taylor, grew in size and efficiency. New products, particularly electrically operated home appliances, made domestic chores significantly easier. Skilled workers had more money to spend and more time to spend it.

As a result, the entertainment industry flourished. Much of this entertainment, particularly popular music and films, projected a uniquely American cultural identity and a distinctly modern attitude. Politically, economically, and culturally, the United States relied much less on Europe for inspiration and guidance.

"Does Jazz Put the Sin in Syncopation?"

—Ladies Home Journal, *1921*

Sex, Booze, and All That Jazz

The teens and twenties saw enormous social change in America. Immigration and migration, Prohibition and its consequences, and a sexual revolution that dramatically redefined the place of the woman in American society all reshaped life in the modern era.

People on the Move

Immigration from abroad, especially during the teens, and internal migration within the United States, especially by African Americans, swelled cities like New York and Chicago. The biggest influx of people from abroad came in the teens. A backlash against this new wave of immigrants resulted in laws severely restricting immigration. By 1931, more people were leaving the United States than entering it, a trend that has since been reversed.

Large ethnic and minority populations in such cities as New York and Chicago helped support their resident musicians and entertainers. Most of the great songwriters of the period between the wars were Jewish or black: Irving Berlin, Jerome Kern, Richard Rodgers, Harold Arlen, George Gershwin, Duke Ellington, and Thomas "Fats" Waller. So were many vaudeville stars: Eddie Cantor, Al Jolson, Bert Williams, and Fanny Brice. Black musicians supplied dance music and entertainment for all levels of society in the 1910s and 1920s, although bands remained segregated until the late 1930s.

Prohibition

In an effort to eliminate workers' "blue Mondays" (worker absenteeism or poor performance caused by excessive weekend drinking), among other alcohol-related social problems, the Temperance movement succeeded in getting the Eighteenth Amendment passed. Although it didn't stop Americans from drinking, Prohibition did make producing or purchasing alcohol illegal. The 1920s became the era of bathtub gin (and other kinds of homemade liquor) and **speakeasies**—clubs that required a softly spoken password for admission.

Prohibition meant work for many popular musicians. Jazz spread from New Orleans throughout the country by way of Chicago's speakeasies, as Joe "King" Oliver, Louis Armstrong, and other early jazz greats moved north in search of more and better-paying work. Benny Goodman, the "king of swing," also got his professional start in a Chicago speakeasy.

The New Woman

The passage of the Nineteenth Amendment, which gave women the right to vote, ended a long and difficult chapter in the history of women's rights. It also signaled a major shift in American attitudes toward women and their place in society. One product of this change was a new kind of young woman.

This "new woman" appeared in the 1920s. Freed from some of the drudgery of housework by a wave of new appliances and with more cash in hand, she consumed—and became a target of advertisers. Liberated from Victorian morality by trendy interpretations of Freudian ideas, she indulged in "petting" with all-too-eager young men. Inspired by Irene Castle, the queen of the foxtrot, she cut her hair and dressed in short, loose-fitting dresses. Tempted by illicit liquor, cigarettes, and other accoutrements of fast living, she partied hard. She was called a "flapper," and she danced, and danced, and danced to the new syncopated music. Her parents were, not surprisingly, horrified by this behavior. And, then as now, popular music was judged one of the causes of her moral degradation. To cite just one example, an article appeared in a 1921 issue of the *Ladies Home Journal* entitled "Does Jazz Put the Sin in Syncopation?"

Library of Congress, Prints and Photographs Division, Washington, DC

Compared with the suffragists who had fought so hard for the right to vote and the members of the Women's Christian Temperance Union who decried the evils of alcohol, the flappers seemed frivolous and hedonistic. But what they represented—women who had the power to make choices, however misguided or silly they might seem in retrospect—was not frivolous. The battle for equal rights had a long way to go, but the flappers reaped the benefits of a significant victory and the change in attitude it symbolized.

Flappers were too-easy targets. Young men in the 1920s were certainly just as frivolous as their female counterparts. And how to label the fiscal foolishness of so many of their parents who hopped on the stock market bubble until it burst in 1929? Jazzy, bluesy, get-up-and-dance-to-it popular music was the soundtrack to all these changes. How people heard it is the next part of our story.

The First Technological Revolution: From Radio to Talking Pictures

In 1919, if you were living in Omaha or Oklahoma City and wanted to hear a hit song, you had few choices. You could buy the sheet music and play it yourself—or get a friend to play it for you. That was a popular choice; sheet music sales peaked in the teens. Or you could buy an **acoustic recording,** like those we've heard by Jim Europe and Harvey Hindermyer. Or you could pay to see a vaudeville show passing through town, where you might hear one of the acts sing the song. Otherwise, you'd probably have to go out of town—to places like New York or Chicago. In 1929, you had many more choices. You could still buy the sheet music and go to the theater to hear a vaudeville act. But you could also turn on the radio and find a local musician playing the song or tune in to a network broadcast of one of the top hotel bands from New York City. You could go into Woolworth's and buy a record of the song; it would sound a lot better than the recording from ten years earlier. And if a film musical featuring the song was in a local theater, you could go to the movies to hear and see the song performed onscreen.

At no time—not even our own—has the way in which popular music reached its audience changed so fundamentally. In 1919, the majority of the audience learned pop songs by looking at them—that is, by playing through the sheet-music versions. In 1929, more people learned songs by ear: on the radio, on record, at the movies, and in live performances. The advances in our own time—MP3s, streaming audio, worldwide access, and the like—don't change the way we learn the music. We listen to it through the media, just like our parents and grandparents did. The shift from eye to ear happened in the 1920s.

The new media appeared in stages: first radio, then electric recordings, followed by amplified live performances, and finally talking films. Each new medium represented another application of an innovative technology.

Radio Broadcasting

In 1920, the first commercial radio station, KDKA in Pittsburgh, began broadcasting. Within two years, the number of commercial stations had grown from one to more than 200. With few exceptions, each radio station, hiring local musicians and personalities to provide entertainment, generated its own programming.

Important technological advances accompanied the rapid growth of commercial radio. None was more important than the conversion from acoustic to electric broadcasting. Many of the earliest radio studios were equipped with long, conical horns similar to those used in acoustic recordings, into which performers spoke, sang, or played. These horns soon gave way to **microphones** that converted sound into electric impulses, which were then converted into the broadcast signal or transmitted to network affiliates for local broadcast. **Amplifiers** and loudspeakers were used to reconvert the electric impulses into sound. This new technology improved quickly.

In 1925, the National Broadcasting Company (NBC) began broadcasting simultaneously on twenty-five affiliates throughout the Northeast and the Midwest with a gala concert. Although American Telephone and Telegraph (AT&T) had already experimented with broadcasts over several stations from one source, it was NBC's debut that celebrated the birth of a new industry: network radio. Soon performances emanating from one location could be broadcast throughout the country and provide the nation with an unprecedented sense of unity.

© ginosphotos/iStockphoto

Electric Recording and Amplified Live Performance

Microphones, amplifiers, and speakers found immediate application elsewhere, in recording, live performance, and instrument manufacture. In 1925 the recording industry converted from acoustic to **electric recording** almost overnight. As in broadcasting, microphones replaced the cumbersome and inefficient horns used for acoustic recording. The result was a dramatic improvement in recorded sound.

The most obvious benefit of amplification was greater volume in performances both live and recorded. Amplification had an even more far-reaching effect, however, on the *sound* of popular music, first by enabling small-voiced singers to record and perform and then by boosting and transforming the sound of existing instruments and making possible an increasingly broad array of electronic instruments.

Before commercial radio, popular singers performed in theaters and auditoriums without any amplification. Many had classically trained, quasi-operatic voices suitable for the operettas fashionable in the early part of the century and for the more serious and conservative popular songs. Others, like Sophie Tucker, Bessie Smith, and Al Jolson, belted out their songs in a full voice that filled the theater.

Aided by this new technology, a new generation of singers broadened the spectrum of vocal styles heard in popular music. By 1929 listeners could choose from the intimate crooning of Bing Crosby; the jazz-inflected, conversational style of Louis Armstrong; the patter of Fats Waller; the faint sounds of "Whispering" Jack Smith; and many others who would not have succeeded in live performance or recording before the electric revolution of 1925.

Talking Films

On October 6, 1927, *The Jazz Singer,* starring Al Jolson, premiered. Although there had previously been other films with sound, this was the first talking picture. Jolson sang, talked, and acted over the soundtrack. The public loved it, and soon Hollywood was churning out talking pictures, even as theater owners were scrambling to add sound systems to the theaters.

Soon popular music was firmly entrenched on the screen. Vaudeville performers filmed their acts. Broadway stars trekked off to Hollywood, and in the 1930s songwriters would follow. By 1929 moviegoers could have seen the first film versions of *Show Boat, Rio Rita* (a spectacular adaptation of another Broadway musical), and *Broadway Melody of 1929,* the first musical and the first sound film to win an Academy Award for best picture.

The sound technology, called Vitaphone by Warner Brothers, the film studio that developed it, was good enough to make the sound realistic. Earlier attempts to merge sound and film had failed because the sound quality was so poor. The talking film was yet another adaptation of the technology that had transformed radio, recording, and live performance.

The changes in the entertainment industry during the 1920s were staggering: radio, network radio, amplification in live performance, decent recording quality, and talking pictures. All of these dreams of 1919 were reality in 1929. The closest parallel might be the Internet explosion in the 1990s; at no other time has so much world-transforming technology appeared in such a short period.

The Modern Era in Popular Music

The soundtrack for these momentous changes in American life was the new popular music created between the two World Wars. It was strikingly different from the mainstream popular music from the turn of the century, for three main reasons: (1) the application of the new technology; (2) the infusion of black musical features—riffs, rhythms, instruments, performing styles; and (3) the more open and vibrant sensibility expressed in the songs and their performance.

Despite this revolutionary transformation of the popular music mainstream, there is no umbrella term in general use that distinguishes this music from the music that came before or after. The popular song of the long period from the late nineteenth century through the early 1960s (just before the ascendancy of rock) is typically identified as "Tin Pan Alley" song, or simply "pop," but the term *Tin Pan Alley* covers a broad range of styles and eras.

In our view, the revolutionary developments of the 1910s and 1920s in popular music marked the beginning of a new era. For ease and clarity of reference, then, we're labeling the period from the early 1910s to the early 1960s the **modern era** in popular music. This new popular music was modern because it became increasingly dependent on new technology for performance and dissemination; it took a leading role in improving race relations; and it introduced into popular music so many features that are still part of the sound of popular music, such as the rhythm section, the backbeat, riff-based melodies, and conversational lyrics.

CHAPTER 16
The New Rhythms of Popular Song

In describing the composition of his enduringly popular *Rhapsody in Blue*, George Gershwin said, "It was on the train, with its steely rhythms, its rattle-ty bang, that is so often so stimulating to a composer. . . . I frequently hear music in the very heart of noise." Gershwin was among the musicians most in tune with the new rhythms that increasingly dominated popular song during the late 1910s and 1920s. Like the world around him, his music vibrates with energetic, often fascinating rhythms, as we hear shortly. We discuss the new rhythms of popular song, exemplifying them with two songs from the early 1920s.

The New Rhythms of Popular Song

Rhythm provided the first evidence of a new kind of popular song. Around the time that Jim Europe formed his Clef Club Orchestra, songwriters like Irving Berlin were adapting the more flexible rhythms of ragtime to popular song. This became manifest mainly in two features: (1) the isolation of a short melodic idea and (2) a melodic rhythm that flows close to the cadence of everyday speech. Still-familiar songs like Berlin's "Alexander's Ragtime Band" (1911) and "You Made Me Love You," a big hit for Al Jolson in 1913, begin with one or more short phrases set off with silence and whose rhythm approximates that of speech: "Come on and hear"; "You made me love you." The rest of the melody mixes long and short phrases, but their rhythm also comes close to speech-like delivery of the words.

This practice contrasts sharply with the practice in turn-of-the-century songs: a simple recitation of the lyrics of "Take Me Out to the Ball Game" or "Yankee Doodle Boy" will point up the discrepancy between the lyrics as spoken and the lyrics as sung. What made the conversational rhythm possible was the division of the beat into long and short durations. This enabled songwriting teams to match the natural accentuations in the words to the flow of the melody. The difference between the two approaches to rhythm can be summarized this way: Before the modern era, the rhythm of the words was adapted to the rhythm of the melody; with the modern era, the rhythm of the melody was adapted to the rhythm of the words.

Popular song and dance music were still distinct at this point: "Castle House Rag" does not have a singable melody, and popular song was typically not used for social dancing. However, there was mutual awareness, as the occasional "dance instruction" song evidences. The opening lines of the 1913 song "Ballin' the Jack," written by the black songwriting team of James Henry Burris and Chris Smith, explains how to do the dance of the same name:

> First you put your two knees / Close up tight.
>
> Then you sway it to the left / Then you sway it to the right.
>
> Step around the floor / Kind of nice and light.
>
> Then you twist around and twist around / With all of your might.

Songs like this were the modern-era counterparts to Chubby Checker's early 1960s dance-instruction song, "The Twist." Still, popular song did not become dance music until after 1920. With the rise of the dance orchestra and a new generation of songwriters, popular song acquired its trademark style beat and a large dose of syncopation. New dances ushered them into the mainstream.

Dance Fads of the 1920s

The 1920s began with a second wave of dance crazes: the black bottom, the shimmy, the blues (yes, there was a social dance called "the blues"), and, above all, the Charleston. Like the ragtime dances of earlier decades, these began as African-American social dances and found a new home among younger whites. Dancing to syncopated music had become commonplace and socially acceptable, but these new dances were the cutting edge, a more energetic alternative to the foxtrot.

The Charleston

The most popular and enduring of these new dances was the **Charleston.** The dance goes back to at least the early twentieth century, and there is apparently a connection to Charleston, South Carolina. It was danced in Harlem as early as 1913, but it didn't become well-known until 1923, when it was introduced on-stage, most notably in an all-black musical production, *Running Wild.*

The dance was done to the song of the same name, "Charleston," written by James P. Johnson (1894–1955), who is much better known as a superb stride pianist. (**Stride piano** is a jazz piano style with deep roots in ragtime.) "Charleston" was Johnson's most memorable hit. It had lyrics by Cecil Mack, but they are seldom sung. Then and now, we almost always hear it as an instrumental strictly for dancing.

Johnson's song is the textbook for the new syncopated foxtrot. The chorus presents not only the two-beat rhythm that is the rhythmic foundation of the dance but also its signature syncopation. It consists of a two-note riff over two beats, with the accent on the second note.

LISTENING CUE • **"Charleston" (1923),** James P. Johnson. Paul Whiteman and His Orchestra.

STYLE Foxtrot dance • **FORM** Three statements of the chorus—ABAC—with introduction, verse, and interlude

Listen For . . .

INSTRUMENTATION
1920s rhythm section: tuba, banjo, piano, drums
Melody instruments include saxes doubling (switching from one instrument to another) on clarinets, trumpets, and trombones; violin reinforcing melody; occasional hot vocal.

RHYTHM
Basic foxtrot rhythm (bass note and backbeat in alternation) at a fast tempo
Most popular 1920s syncopation: "Charle-" on the first beat; "ston" just before the second beat

TEXTURE
Rich texture: voice/lead instrument plus secondary horn parts (riffs, sustained chords) and rhythm section

Remember . . .

FOXTROT RHYTHM AND SIGNATURE SYNCOPATION
Foxtrot = bass alternating with chord on backbeat
Signature syncopation = "Charleston"

FORMING THE RHYTHM SECTION
Sound and beat-keeping role of rhythm section, a new sound in 1920s music

SAXOPHONE
Warmer and fuller sounding than clarinet; most enduring new instrumental sound of 1920s

DANCE MUSIC/DANCE ORCHESTRA
Dance orchestra, with occasional grouping by sections, plays song intended for dancing

Listen to this selection in CourseMate.

We hear the riff all by itself at the beginning of the chorus; the words are "Charle*ston*, Charle*ston*." The first note comes with the first beat, and the second note comes just *before* the second beat; the anticipation of the second beat produces the syncopation. This riff, either in the most basic form heard here or in various elaborations, was the rhythmic key to countless songs of the late teens and twenties.

The Dance Orchestras of the 1920s

The recording heard here, by Paul Whiteman and His Orchestra, documents the emergence of the modern dance orchestra. During the teens, black groups like Jim Europe's Society Orchestra provided most of the syncopated dance music. By the end of the decade, white bands were also offering this jazzy new music. Among the first was the orchestra of Paul Whiteman.

By the early 1920s, Whiteman had plenty of company. Dance orchestras led by Guy Lombardo, Fred Waring, and Isham Jones (who was also a fine songwriter; among his hits was "It Had to Be You") found work in hotels in resorts and major cities. Black bands also modernized: among the best was the Fletcher Henderson Orchestra, which performed at the Roseland Ballroom, one of New York's hot spots.

These new dance orchestras brought a fresh sound to popular music. Two important reasons were the use of a complete rhythm section and the prominent role of the saxophone.

Duke University Rare Book, Manuscript, and Special Collections Library

A sheet music cover from 1920 with a couple dancing in close embrace. Among the instruments in the silhouetted orchestra are a trombone, clarinet, saxophone, strummed instrument, piano, violin, and drum set.

The Rhythm Section in the Dance Orchestra

It is in the early 1920s that the rhythm section takes shape. We heard it in the recording by King Oliver, and we can hear it even more clearly in the "Charleston." It is an essential part of the sound of the dance orchestras of the 1920s, and it is a key element in the new, more modern sound of popular music. Since that time, the instrumentation of the rhythm section has changed, but its basic components have not. A complete rhythm section always has at least one chord instrument, a bass instrument, and a percussion instrument.

The rhythm section's most fundamental role—to supply the beat and the harmony—also remains essentially the same. In the "Charleston," tuba and banjo lay down the *OOM-chuck* rhythm of the two-beat throughout most of the song and outline the harmony.

The Saxophone: A New Sound of the 1920s

The saxophones that are so prominent in the recording of "Charleston" represent the most enduring new sound of the 1920s. There were other new sounds during the same time; the ukulele was an even bigger novelty when Hawaiian music was intermittently in vogue during the decade. But it was the sax that would ultimately become an integral part of the sound of popular music. James Reese Europe was the innovator; his was one of the first dance orchestras to feature the saxophone. But it did not become a staple in the dance orchestra until arrangers began to group instruments into sections. The more massive sound and the broader range of the saxophone family (most bands used three different saxes—alto, tenor, and baritone) made them a more effective counterpart to the brass instruments than the clarinets that were popular in jazz bands and early dance orchestras.

With the consolidation of the rhythm section and the addition of saxophones, orchestras got larger, and the melody instruments were grouped into sections: brass (trumpets and trombones), winds (clarinets and saxophones), and strings (mostly violins). Typically, the musical spotlight would shift from one section to the next, often quickly, as if the two were talking back and forth. These changes are evident in Whiteman's recording. What's missing is the singer. Singers certainly did record, as we hear, but almost never with dance orchestras before 1925.

Rhythm Songs

The energy and high spirits of the modern era are evident not only in dance numbers like "Charleston" but also the aptly named rhythm songs that began to appear in the mid-1920s. As its name implies, a rhythm song is a song in which the primary interest comes from its rhythm rather than the flow and contour of its melody. Rhythm songs can be simple; the 1925 hit "Yes Sir, That's My Baby" and George Gershwin's "I Got Rhythm" (the title applies to the song as well as to the person singing) simply repeat a syncopated pattern with little variation. Or they can be more complex manipulations of a series of notes. Irving Berlin's 1929 hit "Puttin' on the Ritz" applies varying rhythms to a four-note chord; Cole Porter's "Anything Goes," the title song of his 1934 musical, does the same to a three-note pattern. In either case, there is little or no melodic variation or development, just the tricky, syncopated rhythm.

George and Ira Gershwin's "Fascinating Rhythm" is a spectacular early example of the rhythm song. The riff that opens the song contains six syllables: "Fas-cin-a-ting rhy-thm"; together with the pause that follows, they

LISTENING CUE • **"Fascinating Rhythm" (1924),** George and Ira Gershwin. Fred and Adele Astaire, vocals; George Gershwin, piano.

STYLE Rhythm song • **FORM** Verse/chorus song, verse heard only once and chorus repeated, chorus ABAB[1]

Listen For . . .

INSTRUMENTATION
Voices and piano

PERFORMANCE STYLE
Gershwin's aggressive piano style: heavy bass/chord or rapid chords in accompaniment; harmonized melody or figuration

RHYTHM
Foxtrot rhythm in accompanying pattern; abundant syncopation in melody in both verse and chorus

MELODY
Phrase built from repeated, rhythmically displaced riff

Remember . . .

FASCINATING RHYTHM
Displacement of repeated riff puts emphasis on rhythm.

SONG FORM IN TRANSITION
ABAB[1] form connects back to ca. 1900 songs; reduced role of verse anticipates common practice in modern era.

GERSHWIN'S SKILLED PIANO PLAYING
Gershwin was an excellent pianist, here supplying melody, melodic responses, and varied accompaniment.

Listen to this selection in CourseMate.

last 3½ beats. Gershwin repeats the riff three and a half times; each restatement of the riff starts a half a beat earlier than the previous one. As a result, the "fascinating" rhythm goes out of phase with the beat:

1		2		3		4	
Fas	ci	na	ting	Rhy	thm		You've
1		2		3		4	
got	me	on	the	go		Fas	ci
1		2		3		4	
na	ting	rhy	thm		I'm	all	a
1		2		3		4	
qui	ver						

We hear this fascinating rhythmic trick in the song, as performed by Gershwin himself. In retrospect, it's not surprising that George Gershwin composed "Fascinating Rhythm" and several other rhythm songs, because, more than any other songwriter, Gershwin incorporated the rhythmic language of ragtime and syncopated dance music into his songs. Typically, his songs, even his ballads, grow from a riff-like figure that's short and rhythmically interesting. "I Got Rhythm" applies to the song as well as to the person singing.

Song and Dance

"Charleston" is a syncopated song by a black musician performed by a white band; although it has lyrics, it is music for dancing. "Fascinating Rhythm" is a song for a Broadway musical by a white songwriter whose composing and playing betray the obvious influence of the new black music. As performed by the Astaires and Gershwin, it is not for dancing. In the early 1920s, popular songs were either music for dancing (when performed by dance orchestras) or music for listening (when sung), but not both. The electrical revolution that occurred around 1925 helped make it possible to merge song and dance.

CHAPTER 17
The Integration of Popular Song

A new kind of popular song flooded the market in the late 1920s. It was upbeat and up-tempo. You could sing it *and* you could dance to it. It captured the high spirits of the age. And it leveraged the new electric technology to embed its catchy riffs in listeners' ears.

The Record and Recording

In referring to recordings, we commonly distinguish between "albums" and "singles." The term *album* is an anachronism; it hasn't been an accurate description of the delivery format of recordings for over half a century. The term came into use in the modern era to describe recordings bundled together. Early on, they were most often used for classical music. A 12-inch, 78-rpm (revolutions per minute) recording lasted about 4 minutes. Because most major classical compositions last longer than 4 minutes, a recording of a major classical work, such as a symphony by Beethoven or Brahms, would be spread over several discs. These discs were packaged in an *album,* with a cover, binding, and sleeves for each disc. The invention of the LP (long-playing record) made it possible to record entire pieces on one disc instead of several. Despite this, LPs were still called albums; a recording with two discs, like the Beatles' *White Album,* was a double album.

During the modern era, albums were relatively rare. Far more common were single recordings, which contained two songs, one on each side of a 10-inch disc. These records could hold about 3 minutes of music per side. Consequently, musicians had to structure their performances so that they would finish around the 3-minute mark.

The use of popular song as dance music and the constraints of the 3-minute recording drastically reshaped the form and presentation of popular song. Instead of the alternation of verse and chorus common in the early years of the century, performances typically featured several statements of the chorus, both instrumental and vocal; the verse was often simply used as an interlude or eliminated altogether. In addition, songwriters revived and adapted a venerable form that put the memorable melodic material in listeners' ears three times a chorus, instead of two. The recording we discuss next demonstrates how bands molded the performance of the song to optimize its impact on a 3-minute recording.

A New Kind of Popular Song

In the wake of the 1925 electrical revolution, the modern-era popular song assumed its mature form. Technology made possible the merger of song and dance on record and in performance, and made it all easier to hear. It sent over the air and captured on disc and film the

LISTENING CUE • **"Sunday" (1927),** Clifford Gray and J. Fred Coots. Jean Goldkette Orchestra, with the Keller Sisters, vocals.

STYLE Foxtrot song • **FORM** Four statements of the chorus (AABA), with verse as interlude

Listen For . . .

INSTRUMENTATION
1920s dance orchestra: brass, saxes, vocal, violin, over rhythm section, with banjo alternating with guitar

RHYTHM
Two-beat rhythm with a jazz feel: four-beat rhythm in vocal chorus
Substantial syncopation, especially at end of vocal chorus

MELODY
Riff pairs the building blocks for A section and bridge

TEXTURE
Contrasts: full band; sections (e.g., trumpets); group vocal; solos and duets: all over steady rhythm

Remember . . .

AABA POPULAR SONG
Newly revived AABA form the most popular song form after 1925

MAXIMIZING MEMORABLE MELODY
Form and chorus-oriented performance designed to maximize listeners' contact with opening phrase: heard twelve times in 3 minutes

JAZZY FOXTROT
Mostly two-beat rhythm throughout but with a jazz-like swing in melody; swing rhythm by guitar underneath vocal

INTEGRATION OF SONG AND DANCE
Instrumental choruses sandwich a vocal chorus = music for dancing and singing

Listen to this selection in CourseMate.

giddy energy and exuberance of the jazz. The recording discussed next typifies this vibrant new sound.

"Sunday" was a hit in 1927 for the songwriting team of Clifford Gray and J. Fred Coots. (Coots is best remembered for the Christmas evergreen "Santa Claus Is Coming to Town.") The song first appeared in the revue *The Merry World*, and when it caught on, several bands recorded it, among them the one led by Jean Goldkette.

The song is up to date in both words and music. The lyrics are simple and tell us about the life of a young person working long hours. (Among other things, we learn that workers in the 1920s had a six-day workweek.) From the words, the mood could be either up or down, depending on whether the focus is on Sunday or the rest of the week. In either event, the lyrics are full of the exaggerated feelings that so often accompany infatuation.

One of the novel features of this recording of the song is the absence of a sung verse. We hear a fragment of the verse played by the band just before the voices come in, but we never hear it sung.

JEAN GOLDKETTE and his orchestra, ca.1923. From right to left: Jean Goldkette (glasses, slide trombone), Jimmy Dorsey (trumpet), Bix Beiderbecke (clarinet), Paul Mertz (piano), Chauncey Morehouse (drums), and Howdy Quicksell (banjo).

AABA Form

The chorus of "Sunday" resonates with the faster pace of life in the 1920s. It consists of four short sections. The first, second, and last sections are just about the same (there are minor differences between the first and the second sections); the third is different. We usually refer to this form as AABA form: A is the first section of the chorus and any repetition of it, and B is a new section. AABA form was not new to popular music, but it was not widely used before 1925. After that year, however, a decided majority of popular songs used AABA form or some variant of it until well into the rock era.

The A section consists of three phrases, two that are rather short and a third that's about twice as long. The first phrase is built from two riffs: "I'm blue" and "every Monday." The other two alter the scheme a little. The B section starts with the same rhythm as the A section but with a different melody. The music moves fast, both within and among the sections. The phrases within each section are short and snappy. Performed at the brisk, Charleston-like tempo heard here, the song flies by.

Even at first hearing, we notice a big difference between this recording of "Sunday" and all the others that predate it. The song begins like a dance number, with the band playing the melody over a strong, jazz-inflected, two-beat rhythm. Midway through, however, we hear the song sung by a female trio. The band returns for a final chorus. From the late teens on, almost all new pop songs were foxtrots. (Sheet music covers and record labels make this clear.) In this sense they were for both singing and dancing. However, it wasn't until the electrical revolution that it became routine to include both instrumental statements by a full dance orchestra and a vocal on the same recording. The practice of sandwiching a vocal between dance-oriented instrumental statements of the melody remained popular through the early 1940s.

Jean Goldkette's Orchestra

Born in France and trained as a concert pianist, Jean Goldkette (1899–1962) came to the United States in 1911 and found work in Chicago as a musician during his teens. In 1915, he heard a Dixieland jazz band and started playing in, and then leading, dance orchestras. By the mid-1920s, he had put together what many considered the best jazz orchestra of the time. Among the band members were several of the top white jazz musicians in Chicago, including Bix Beiderbecke. They did well on record ("Sunday" sold very well), but not well enough in the ballrooms. (It was probably an early example of an age-old problem among jazz musicians: playing music that's too hip for the room.) Goldkette disbanded his orchestra in 1927, and most of the top players soon joined Paul Whiteman's band.

Goldkette's band offers a jazzier version of the dance orchestra sound of Paul Whiteman. Again we hear the band grouped into sections. The first half of the last chorus has a particularly nice stretch for the trumpet section. There are also improvised solos for trombone and clarinet. The vocal trio that sings the third chorus sounds like flappers look: The nonsense syllables "vo-de-o-do" are a sound of the times, much like interjections such as "go, man, go" in early rock and roll.

A special feature of Goldkette's band was the use of both banjo and guitar in the rhythm section. The tuba and the banjo lay down a straightforward two-beat rhythm, while guitarist Eddie Lang strums chords on every beat, which gives the song a jazzy feel. (Lang's strumming is easy to hear in the vocal chorus.) This combination of rhythms is a main source of the song's bounce.

In recordings like "Sunday," the jazz feel is evident throughout. Many of the top dance orchestras employed good jazz musicians, and the black dance orchestras, led by Henderson, Ellington, and others, attracted a substantial mainstream following. The sounds of jazz (and jazz-like music) pervaded the music of the 1920s: the decade was, after all, the Jazz Age.

The New Sounds of Modern-Era Popular Song

With recordings like "Sunday" the revolution that produced the modern era in popular music is just about complete. The interaction of black music with white popular song and the integration of new technology comprehensively reshaped the mainstream popular style. Among the most significant and evident changes were these:

- *The merger of song and dance.* Popular songs before 1910 had used dance rhythms but were not sung as music for social dancing. By 1920, popular song had become dance music. By the late twenties, performances of popular songs were singable and danceable.
- *The formation of the syncopated dance orchestra.* Although dance orchestras had existed in America since colonial times, none sounded like those of Jim Europe in the teens and those of Whiteman, Goldkette, and so many others in the twenties. Two key differences in the instrumentation distinguished these new dance orchestras: the full rhythm section and the use of the saxophone. Violins, long the main melody voice of the dance orchestra, lost status during the twenties. In orchestras like Paul Whiteman's, they played a less prominent role. In the jazz-influenced dance bands like those of Henderson and Ellington, they disappeared altogether.
- *A foxtrot beat.* Most songs in the twenties were foxtrot songs. In performance a two-beat rhythm, played by tuba and banjo (or other bass and chord instruments) in alternation, supported the melody. The two-beat rhythm, with its crisp backbeat, was the first of the African-American rhythms to reshape popular music.
- *New instrumental styles.* Popular instrumentalists, especially wind and brass players, cultivated ways of playing their instruments that distinguished them from band and orchestra performers. Brass players used mutes, plungers, and other timbre-altering devices. All wind (brass, sax, and clarinet) players used **vibrato,** a subtle alteration of the pitch of a note. Much of this came from jazz and blues.
- *Snappy, riff -based melodies.* Blues and ragtime influenced the melodies of popular song even more directly. The influence is evident in three characteristics: the use of riffs, rhythms that flow like speech, and syncopation. All three in combination created melodic rhythms that closely corresponded to the natural inflection and rhythm of American vernacular speech.
- *Conversational lyrics.* Lyrics matched the spirit and the feel of the melodies. More often than not, words were one syllable; phrases and sentences were short. Colloquial expressions replaced the more formal language of nineteenth-century song.
- *A chorus-oriented form.* Except in musical theater, verses were all but scrapped. A performance of a song consisted primarily of several statements of the chorus. A fragment of the verse might be used as an interlude, particularly in dance-band arrangements. Further, the form of the chorus was itself fast paced: four short sections, almost always in AABA form.

Any one of these changes would have been significant. Taken together, they represent a comprehensive transformation of popular music. Certainly, they are on a par with the changes that took place during the first fifteen years of the rock era. Add to that the advent of electric technology and its impact on how the music reached its audience: the result was a revolution in popular music. There was one more step: modernizing popular singing.

CHAPTER 18
Mainstreaming the Blues

Ethel Waters's first big hit was "Dinah," a popular song that she recorded in 1925 shortly after switching from Black Swan records to Columbia. After Waters (1896–1977) survived a horrific and abbreviated childhood—her mother was only 13 when she gave birth to her; Waters herself married at 13 and quickly divorced—she began her musical career at age 14, touring on the black vaudeville circuit and performing in black nightclubs. Around the time she changed record labels, she crossed over to what blacks of the era called "white time," performing for white audiences on Broadway, then touring on a big-time white vaudeville circuit.

Waters was the first black performer to succeed as a mainstream popular singer. Columbia recorded Bessie Smith as a blues singer for the race record market, but recorded Waters as a bluesy pop singer for whites and blacks. She was in the vanguard of a wave of black entertainers who gained a presence in popular music.

The 1920s, a Breakthrough for Black Musicians

The 1920s saw a resurgence of musical productions by black Americans in New York, both uptown and downtown. *Shuffle Along,* a 1921 musical that featured Noble Sissle and Eubie Blake as songwriters and performers, made the first big splash. The show was notable in that it included a romantic scene; in the minstrel show, blacks were not permitted to express their emotions honestly or realistically. Still, the conventions of minstrelsy permeated such shows; many of the performers blacked up, and the plots (and scenery) often perpetuated minstrel-show stereotypes. Other shows soon followed, both book shows and revues: Lew Leslie's *Blackbirds* series was popular into the 1930s. Leslie also booked black acts at the Cotton Club, a famous Harlem nightclub, where Duke Ellington performed for many years. Downtown, intrepid and light-footed New Yorkers could dance to Fletcher Henderson's band at the Roseland Ballroom, or they might join Bing Crosby at a speakeasy to hear the music of Louis Armstrong. In Chicago, if you were an associate of Al Capone, you might have heard pianist/songwriter Fats Waller at his birthday party in 1926—Waller was kidnapped at gunpoint after a gig and brought to the party as the surprise guest entertainer. By the end of the decade, Waters, Smith, and others had appeared in talking films. Those who knew the right record stores could find race records by Bessie Smith and Louis Armstrong; the less adventurous could still find records by Waters in their local department store.

© Moviestore Collection Ltd/Alamy

AL JOLSON, in a scene from *The Jazz Singer* (1927), performs in blackface.

Still, the increased opportunities for African-American entertainers were only a modest advance toward a truly integrated music business. Stereotypes from minstrelsy still pervaded popular culture. The white singer Al Jolson blacked up in *The Jazz Singer,* the first talking film, and Busby Berkeley's visually spectacular films from the early 1930s occasionally featured performers in blackface. Bandstands were not integrated, and black performers had to conform to the expectations of the whites who ran the business. An outrageous remark by producer Lew Leslie shows the obstacles that they faced:

> They (white men) understand the colored man better than he does himself. Colored composers excel at spirituals, but their other songs are just "what" (dialect for "white") songs with Negro words.

Still, opportunities for black musicians in 1929 were far better that they had been in 1919. And as black performers entered the mainstream, popular music gained a tinge of the blues.

Mainstreaming the Blues

Blues helped shape modern popular song via two paths. One was indirect and relatively unobtrusive: Blues helped shape jazz, which in turn shaped popular song and its performance. The other was more direct and more obvious: Blues songs and blues singing served as model and inspiration for songwriters and singers. Popular musicians drew on all three dimensions of the blues revealed in the performances of classic blues singers: feeling, style, and form.

It is as song that the power of the blues is fully manifest. This power is—or can be—apparent in the use of key elements of blues style and the expression of blues feeling. As a result, the blues tinge in popular music evident in the 1910s, when instrumental blues were introduced, becomes a darker hue in the latter part of the 1920s.

In the 1920s, vocal blues influenced both the songs and the singing of them. Songwriters evoked the mood of blues songs, although pop song lyrics were never as direct or powerful as a blues, and they occasionally incorporated blue notes—produced by interpolating notes from a pentatonic scale into a conventional scale—usually at expressive moments.

Singers, black and white, brought blues style and feeling into their music, in varying degrees. Indeed, the blues helped spawn a new genre: the torch song. A **torch song** was a song about unrequited or lost love. Torch singers, like the classic blues singers, were women; most were white. They typically delivered a torch song that evoked, at least to some degree, the mood of the blues; it was a strong contrast to the generally peppy music of the time.

Blues in Popular Song

Ethel Waters's recording of "Am I Blue?" shows the decided influence of the blues on popular song and its performance. The song is not a blues, although in this performance one chorus of a blues is interpolated between statements of the chorus. But it tells a blues-like story of a woman who's lost her man and has a tinge of blues in the melody: the blue note at the end of the A section, on the syllable "tell." Waters's singing is not as gritty as Bessie Smith's, but she inflects the melody with the kind of nuance associated with blues singing, especially toward the end, when she sings responses to the instrumental statement of the melody.

"Am I Blue?" was a huge hit in 1929. Both the evocation of blues feeling in words and melody and Waters's blues-tinged singing were exceptional in the popular music of the 1920s. Nevertheless, the fact of its popularity demonstrates the emerging influence of the blues on popular song and its performance. Its impact would deepen in the decades to follow.

LISTENING CUE • **"Am I Blue?" (1929),** Grant Clarke and Harry Akst. Ethel Waters, vocal.

STYLE Blues-influenced modern-era song • **FORM** Verse/chorus song: chorus (AABA) heard twice; vocal interlude in blues form

Listen For . . .

INSTRUMENTATION
Voice and dance orchestra, including bowed string bass in rhythm section

PERFORMANCE STYLE
Waters sings with rich, pleasant pop voice; abundant blues and jazz influence evident in rhythmic freedom and expressive nuance.

RHYTHM
Foxtrot rhythm at moderate tempo; sudden shift to slower tempo and four-beat feel in blues interlude

MELODY
A section built from short riff; B section has longer phrases.

TEXTURE
Mainly melody plus accompaniment in choruses; vocal obbligato in last chorus an appealing novelty

Remember . . .

BLUES INFLUENCE: SONGWRITING
Title and mood of lyric; nice blue note at end of A section; blues interlude specific to this recording

BLUES INFLUENCE: PERFORMANCE
Influence of blues style evident in vocal responses in second chorus, bending notes, rhythmic freedom, and intense inflection

MODERN POPULAR SONG
Typical late-1920s song in form (AABA), basic rhythm (foxtrot), and construction (built from a simple riff)

Listen to this selection in CourseMate.

CHAPTER 19
Popular Singing after 1930

Modern popular song emerged during the 1920s; modern popular singing emerged in the 1930s. The main reason for the gap between songwriting and performance was the limitations of technology in the early 1920s. The new technology that emerged at mid-decade opened the door for a host of new singers who would not have had professional careers previously. Among them were light-voiced singers like Gene Austin, Cliff "Ukulele Ike" Edwards, and even "Whispering" Jack Smith. However, the two most influential new singing styles were crooning and jazz singing. Among the early crooners were Rudy Vallee—who was famous for singing into a megaphone—Russ Columbo, and Bing Crosby. The more jazz-oriented singers included Louis Armstrong, whose singing would prove as influential to pop vocalists as his playing was to jazz musicians, and Fats Waller.

Bing Crosby: Quintessential Crooner

The dominant popular singer of the 1930s and 1940s was Bing Crosby (1903–1977). No singer sold more recordings, appeared in more films, or starred on more radio programs. During this period, Crosby had an impeccable public persona—affable, good-humored, easygoing; it was a perfect complement to his **crooning,** an intimate, pleasant singing style.

Crosby joined Paul Whiteman's band in 1926 as part of a vocal trio, the Rhythm Boys. During his three years with Whiteman, Crosby sang as part of the group and occasionally as a solo singer. When he wasn't singing for Whiteman, he frequented the clubs where Louis Armstrong performed. It was from Armstrong that he learned how to swing; by the late 1920s he was an excellent jazz singer, as his recordings with Whiteman as a solo singer evidence. (In the thirties, after he had become a big star, he repaid this musical debt by insisting that Armstrong be included in the 1936 film *Pennies from Heaven.*) Crosby was cool before it was cool to be cool and hip before it was hip to be hip.

Many writers have observed that Crosby was the first singer to really use the microphone well. He developed a low-key style that was as conversational as the lyrics he sang. Coming through the radio or phonograph, he sounded as though he were in the same room as his listeners. The new technology made this kind of intimacy possible; Crosby was the first to capitalize on it in a big way. He soon had many imitators.

© Metronome/Getty Images

BING CROSBY was the first singer to really use the microphone well.

After he left Whiteman in 1929, he diversified his repertoire and became known mainly for his comfortable crooning of ballads. "White Christmas" was the most famous of his more than 300 hits and his 4,000-plus recordings. However, in many of his recordings, his singing shows his affinity with jazz and a tinge of the blues (which came to him mainly through Armstrong). When blended with the easy delivery that the microphone made possible, it became the most influential and popular style of the era. We hear a fine example of Crosby's singing in his 1933 recording of Harold Arlen's "I've Got the World on a String."

Crosby's singing was modern because it was personal and personable. During the time that Crosby recorded "I've Got the World on a String," radios and record players were pieces of furniture, not portable devices, and there was no other commercial home medium—television would still be a novelty two decades later. Over the air or on record, Crosby sounded as if he were in listeners' living rooms, singing just for them. This contrasted sharply with the singing of song belters like Al Jolson, who were used to singing in theaters with no amplification.

Crosby's sound and style complemented the words and music of the new modern-era songs. The lyrics captured the tone and cadence of everyday speech; most words were a single syllable: "I've got the world on a string . . . "; "Why not take all of me?" The best melodies magically matched the flow of the words while still retaining sufficient interest to stand alone.

Crosby's relaxed delivery also complemented one of the important depression-era trends in popular song performance: a greater emphasis on melody. During the early 1930s, one direction in popular music was characterized by slower tempos; less syncopation and rhythmic activity; and smoother, more subdued sonorities—the

LISTENING CUE • **"I've Got the World on a String" (1932),** Ted Koehler and Harold Arlen. Bing Crosby, vocal, with the Dorsey Brothers Orchestra.

STYLE Blues-influenced modern-era song • **FORM** Chorus-oriented song in AABA form; verse used as introduction

Listen For . . .

INSTRUMENTATION
Voice and dance orchestra, with violin, and with Dorsey brothers featured (clarinet, trombone)

PERFORMANCE STYLE
Crosby's conversational crooning; use of mutes by trumpet and trombone

RHYTHM
Alternation between out-of-tempo beginning and swing rhythm in second chorus

MELODY
A section = long descending phrase from opening riff; B section = variations on repeated note

TEXTURE
Melody with rich, unobtrusive accompaniment in out-of-tempo sections. In-tempo sections feature melody plus steady timekeeping in rhythm, statement/response exchanges.

Remember . . .

BLUES-INFLUENCED POPULAR SONG: SONGWRITING
Arlen wrote several songs for the Cotton Club in the early 1930s; most show a blues influence, particularly in the descending curve of the melody. This song shows the happy side of the blues.

CROSBY'S CROONING
Crosby's mastery of the microphone and easy delivery were the model for a subsequent generation of singers. No singer of the era was more popular and more influential.

DOMINANCE OF MELODY
Crosby sings all the way through, and timekeeping only occurs in the latter part of the song. Although the in-tempo sections have a swing rhythm, this is not a performance intended for dancing.

Listen to this selection in CourseMate.

use of mutes in Crosby's song is an instance of that. By the late 1930s, this direction would be called "sweet," the opposite of swing. During the course of his career, Crosby's singing moved away from the jazz-inflected style of his Whiteman days toward the reassuring, if sentimental, crooning that was his trademark. Still, he remained comfortable in a jazz context, as his onscreen duets with Armstrong evidenced.

Crooning helped listeners connect to the singer as a person. Another kind of singing, which we will call **song interpretation,** made listeners aware of how the singer felt. We encounter a seminal example of this approach to popular song performance in the music of Billie Holiday.

Billie Holiday and Song Interpretation

Blues and modern popular song are both first-person music. However, blues is inherently a more first-person music because the singer often wrote the song—or could have written it—and because both song and singer can communicate deep feeling directly. As you listened to Bessie Smith describe her empty bed, you could feel that she was sharing a chapter in *her* life. Popular song is more generic, if only because those who write popular songs cannot make their songs as autobiographical as a blues. They compose knowing that someone else will sing them—of the important white songwriters, only Harold Arlen sang professionally. Indeed, their hope was that many singers would perform and record the song because it was a hit.

Crooning, like Waters's blues-tinged singing, made the singing of popular song a more personal statement. In the 1930s, however, there emerged another way of singing popular songs that seemed to come from even deeper inside the singer. Its two most important and influential models were Louis Armstrong and Billie Holiday, whom we hear next.

Billie Holiday claimed that her two biggest influences were Bessie Smith and Louis Armstrong. She admired Smith's power and Armstrong's style. Smith and Armstrong, along with Bing Crosby and Ethel Waters, helped chart a new path in popular singing. It was Billie Holiday, however, who took the next major step.

Born Eleanora Harris, Billie Holiday (1915–1959) led an unimaginably difficult life. Both she and her mother were born out of wedlock, and both were arrested for prostitution in 1929, when Holiday was only fourteen. Shortly after, she started her musical career singing at tables in Harlem nightclubs. These were not glamorous places like the Cotton Club, but rough bars where the girls were expected to do more than just sing. She became

LISTENING CUE • **"All of Me" (1931),** Seymour Simons and Gerald Marks. Eddie Heywood and His Orchestra, with Billie Holiday, vocal, and featuring Lester Young, tenor saxophone.

STYLE Pop song interpretation • **FORM** Two choruses plus interlude of a song in ABAC form

Listen For . . .

INSTRUMENTATION
Holiday's vocal, backed by a band featuring trumpet, three saxophones, and full rhythm section (guitar, piano, bass, drums)

PERFORMANCE STYLE
Holiday's unique vocal timbre and expressive blues-tinged inflections give her singing a distinct personality.

RHYTHM
Moderate tempo; swing (four-beat) rhythm marked by guitar and bass; lots of rhythmic play in Holiday's singing

MELODY
Develops from a three-note riff; succeeding versions of riff keep the rhythm but assume a different melodic shape.

Holiday reshapes the melody in second chorus, flattening it out to make it more blues-like.

Remember . . .

HOLIDAY, BLUES, JAZZ, AND POP
Holiday sings pop songs with the feeling and style of blues and the swing and freedom of jazz.

HOLIDAY'S VOICE
A unique, unconventional vocal sound that set her apart

POP SINGERS VS. SONG INTERPRETERS
Holiday was among the first important song interpreters, using songs to project her experience—and reshaping them in the process.

Listen to this selection in CourseMate.

an alcoholic and a drug addict, and she died at age forty-four after a steady decline in her ability to perform.

We hear her ability to transmute popular song into personal statement in her 1940 recording of "All of Me." A small band led by Eddie Heywood and featuring saxophonist Lester Young provides accompaniment.

"All of Me," written in 1931 by Seymour Simons and Gerald Marks, is a standard; it remains one of the most popular songs from the 1930s, and over the years hundreds of artists have recorded it. Billie Holiday's version shows how she brought the deep feeling of blues and the swing of jazz into popular singing.

In essence, Holiday projects *herself* through the song. As we listen to her recording, we are less concerned with the words than with how she delivers them. Her performance transcends the sentimental lyrics to express the real and almost universal pain of lost love, with an immediacy that the song by itself can't begin to attain. As written, words and music send one message; her voice sends a second, much deeper one. Hers is not a pretty sound, but it remains one of the most individual timbres ever to emerge in the popular tradition.

We notice this most clearly in the second chorus, as Holiday transforms this straightforward popular song into a blues song. The range of the melody narrows considerably, and most phrases begin high and end low. She sings this chorus in the top part of her range, giving her voice a particular urgency. The inflection of the melodic line becomes more intense, especially on the words "lips," "eyes," and "cry." The note values lengthen

The Kobal Collection/Art Resource, NY

BILLIE HOLIDAY in a scene from *New Orleans* (1946). It was her only film appearance. In the film, she plays a maid and is the girlfriend of Louis Armstrong, seen here playing a cornet (not a trumpet).

and the rhythm becomes freer, suggesting even more strongly than before that Holiday sings because simple speech cannot convey the emotion she wishes to express. She saves the very top note in the song for the climactic phrase, "Why not take the rest?"; as her voice descends, we can feel her despair. Her performance transcends the lyrics to express the real anguish of lost love.

Billie Holiday's art is not one of technical virtuosity. Nor is it a style of conventional beauty. Instead, she communicates her feelings directly, unfiltered by stylistic conventions, a conventionally pretty vocal sound, or a literal adherence to the original melodic shape of the song. Like other great performers, she is a style unto herself: instantly recognizable; broadly influential; and widely, if unsuccessfully, imitated.

Like Waters, Holiday brought blues style and blues feeling into the singing of popular songs. Her work showed how one could use a popular song as a window to a singer's heart and soul. In essence, she made popular singing a more autobiographical art, through her reshaping of a melody and the timing of her delivery. Her influence was evident on the next generation of pop singers, both women and men, and black and white, as we discover in Chapter 32.

CHAPTER 20

Popular Song on Stage and Screen

Sometime after eight o'clock on the evening of December 27, 1927, Paul Robeson, a young African-American actor-singer, stepped into the spotlight of the Ziegfeld Theater in New York to sing a song about a river. Robeson, the valedictorian of his class at Rutgers, a two-time All-America football player, and a graduate of Columbia Law School, had decided to pursue a career in entertainment. His opening number, "Ol' Man River," about as far removed as possible from the parade of chorus girls that usually opened Broadway productions, was a remarkable beginning to *Show Boat*, a remarkably innovative musical.

The Kobal Collection/Art Resource, NY

PAUL ROBESON in his role as the stevedore in *Show Boat*, 1936

Musical Stage Entertainment in the 1920s

The 1920s were the heyday of stage entertainment in the United States. Vaudeville was still going strong. Revues were doing well. The most famous were the *Ziegfeld Follies*, presented annually from 1907 to 1927. Musical comedies, with music by American composers such as George Gershwin, Irving Berlin, and Jerome Kern, competed with operettas, composed mainly by Europeans (Herbert, Romberg, Friml) who had emigrated from Europe to the United States.

Virtually all of this was fluff. The plots for musical comedies were lighthearted, comparable in dramatic depth to an average sitcom. Operettas had fantasy plots: the long-ago-and-far-away storylines still prevailed. There was a lot of singing and a lot of dancing; shows usually opened with a string of chorus girls kicking away. And there was also a lot of comedy. These productions were fun, designed to entertain and occasionally to titillate. But they didn't go much deeper than that.

All of this contrasted sharply with grand opera, which flourished in the United States during the early years of the twentieth century. New York's Metropolitan Opera company, which debuted in 1883, toured extensively throughout the United States. It featured the top singers and conductors of the day, including the tenor Enrico Caruso, arguably the most celebrated singer of the early twentieth century.

Show Boat would bridge the gap between grand opera and these lighter musical entertainments by weaving elements of both into a new genre.

The Innovations of *Show Boat*

Show Boat was a collaboration between songwriter Jerome Kern (1885–1945) and lyricist and librettist Oscar Hammerstein II (1895–1960). The musical was based on Edna Ferber's 1926 novel *Show Boat*. Kern first persuaded Ferber to let Hammerstein and him adapt the novel to the stage, then presented the story and some of the songs to Florenz Ziegfeld, who committed his considerable energy and financial resources to the project. It was a lavish production in every respect.

Ferber's novel dealt with serious issues seriously, even as it portrayed a chapter in American life that had all but disappeared. *Show Boat* chronicles the life of the Hawkes family over a period of about forty years and three generations. The patriarch, Captain Andy, runs a showboat, a riverboat that cruises up and down the Mississippi, stopping at river cities to provide theatrical productions to the townsfolk. The plot centers on the marriage between Magnolia, the Hawkes's daughter, and Gaylord Ravenal, a good-looking, good-for-nothing gambler. They go through many hard times, including a separation that lasts years, before they are reunited at the end. Any happiness is certainly tempered by the heartache they have known. A key subplot involves Julie, a light-skinned mulatto, and her white husband, Steve. They are the principal actors in the production put on by Captain Andy. She is exposed as nonwhite by a jealous suitor, and because of a law against miscegenation (interracial marriage), the couple must leave the showboat. Julie returns some years later, working as a cabaret singer, and obviously the worse for having become an alcoholic. Another recurrent theme is the life of the stevedores along the Mississippi. Their presence is a commentary on the hard lot of African Americans after the Civil War.

Show Boat was entertainment, not exposé, although it was entertainment with a message. And seen from our current perspective, it may seem politically incorrect. There are reverberations of the minstrel show in the lyrics to "Can't Help Lovin' Dat Man" and other songs sung by blacks. Julie was portrayed by the white torch singer Helen Morgan rather than a light-skinned black singer. But this was the 1920s. Jim Crow laws were still on the books in the South; the Ku Klux Klan was on the rise; professional baseball was still segregated; and Al Jolson had blacked up for *The Jazz Singer,* which had come out less than three months earlier. Seen against this backdrop, *Show Boat* was a major statement, simply by raising such difficult issues.

Jerome Kern and the Modern Popular Song

Jerome Kern was the elder statesman among the great songwriters active in the 1920s and 1930s; he had his first hit song in 1905. Moreover, Kern received traditional musical training in New York and Germany, and spent much of the 1900s and 1910s traveling between New York and London, where he supplied dozens of songs that were interpolated into shows.

By training, experience, and inclination, Kern, of the major songwriters, was least in touch with the sounds and rhythms of the new black-influenced popular music. Even the songs from late in his career ("The Way You Look Tonight," "All The Things You Are") favor European values: flowing melodies, surprising harmonies, and rhythms with little or no syncopation. As a songwriter, he was the anti-Gershwin.

Kern was the first important American songwriter to concern himself seriously with the integration of music and drama. Between 1915 and 1918, he collaborated with Guy Bolton on a series of musicals for the Princess Theater, a small venue in New York. These shows owed more to the operetta tradition that had begun in the United States with Gilbert and Sullivan and continued with other European-born composers, such as Victor Herbert, Sigmund Romberg, and Rudolf Friml.

In *Show Boat,* Kern and Hammerstein set out to integrate—or at least Americanize—operetta. The "musical play" featured an American take on the typical operetta plot: Long ago was the turn of the century, and the Mississippi River was, for 1920s New Yorkers, far enough away. To help convey this, Kern incorporated still-popular hits from the turn of the century, including "After the Ball."

Most of Kern's original songs for *Show Boat* show a closer affinity with European-inspired operetta than they do with the new music of the 1920s. The significant exceptions were the songs for black characters. To support the plot musically, Kern drew on black-influenced music familiar to him and much of his audience. In the case of "Ol' Man River," Kern evoked the spiritual to convey the dignity of the hardworking, mistreated, and underpaid black laborers. The dramatic function of "Can't Help Lovin' Dat Man" is to suggest Julie's mixed racial heritage, well before the scene where Julie and Steve, her husband, are forced to leave the showboat.

LISTENING CUE • **"Can't Help Lovin' Dat Man" (1927),** Jerome Kern and Oscar Hammerstein II. Helen Morgan, vocal.

STYLE Blues-influenced modern-era song • **FORM** Verse/chorus song: chorus (AABA) heard 1½ times; interpolation from another song

Listen For . . .

INSTRUMENTATION
Voice plus mix of pop and orchestral instruments, including strings, bassoon, strummed guitar.

PERFORMANCE STYLE
Morgan sings with quavery, quasi-operatic voice.

RHYTHM
Foxtrot rhythm at moderate tempo in chorus; shift to heavy four-beat rhythm in verse

MELODY
A section built from four-note riff; B section has longer phrases. Descending contour and blue note show blues influence.

Remember . . .

POSITIONING *SHOW BOAT* MUSICALLY
Mix of classical (Morgan's singing, orchestral accompaniment) and contemporary pop (blue notes, melodies growing from riffs) features imply middle ground between conventional stage entertainment and opera.

MAINSTREAMING BLUES INFLUENCE
The influence of contemporary black music—blues, jazz, dance music—is evident in the rhythm and melody, although filtered through a mainly European sensibility.

MODERN POPULAR SONG
In the form of the chorus (AABA), construction of melody from riffs, conversational rhythm of lyric, and use of two- and four-beat rhythms, "Can't Help Lovin' Dat Man" is a modern-era foxtrot song.

Listen to this selection in CourseMate.

When Queenie, the black cook, hears Julie singing "Can't Help Lovin' Dat Man," she asks Julie how she knows the song, because "Ah didn't ever hear anybody but colored folks sing dat song." In 1927, the most familiar "colored-only" songs were the classic blues of Bessie Smith and others. For numerous reasons—among them the racial climate at the time, the jarring musical contrast it would have created, and Kern's own musical predilections—Kern chose instead to compose a blues-influenced popular song rather than an authentic blues.

"Can't Help Lovin' Dat Man" is an up-to-date song for 1927, in the style of its lyrics, its melodic construction, its use of dance rhythms, and its form. Although the awkward imitation of black speech (downplayed in Morgan's performance) reeks of the minstrel show, the lyrics are typical of the modern era in popular song. The diction, with a preponderance of one-syllable words, is close to everyday speech, and the song is a gentrified blues lament.

A New Kind of Musical Theater

Show Boat was the first of the great modern musicals. It elevated the level of discourse in musical theater, dramatically and musically. Through the example of *Show Boat,* musical theater became a more elite entertainment, even as vaudeville and the revue disappeared from the stage, a casualty of the onset of the Depression and the rise of talking film. Many of the top songwriters on Broadway, including Kern and Gershwin, moved to Hollywood, where they composed memorable songs for film musicals. Those who stayed behind, most notably the team of Richard Rodgers and Lorenz Hart, created musicals that followed the lead of *Show Boat* in musical sophistication and dramatic substance. However, their musicals enjoyed relatively modest success, and they are seldom revived. Only with the Rodgers and Hammerstein musicals, beginning with *Oklahoma!* (1943), did the musical enjoy critical acclaim and commercial success comparable to *Show Boat.*

© Michael Ochs Archive/Getty Images

FRED ASTAIRE and **GINGER ROGERS** in a scene from the RKO musical *Swing Time,* 1936

During the 1930s, mass entertainment shifted from stage to screen: The film musical flourished as vaudeville and the revue all but died out, and light-hearted musical comedy struggled. Among the most popular film musicals of the 1930s were those that featured the unlikely pairing of Ginger Rogers and Fred Astaire.

The Acceptance of the Modern Popular Song

The setting for the big scene in *Top Hat,* a 1935 film that starred Ginger Rogers and Fred Astaire, is a posh supper club, with tables adjacent to a large dance floor, where an orchestra plays in the background. Fred walks into the club and spies Ginger, who is sitting with a woman whom she thinks is Fred's wife. Dressed formally in white tie and tails, Fred asks Ginger, in her long evening gown, to dance. Ginger reluctantly agrees. At the beginning of the number, Fred sings "Cheek to Cheek" while they're dancing. Initially, Ginger keeps her distance, but by the time Fred has finished singing and the orchestra has taken over, they've drifted off to their own private ballroom to perform a dance that's far more elaborate than the foxtrot they danced earlier in the scene. By the end of the number, Ginger is completely smitten with Fred. Shortly after, she comes to her senses, slaps him, and flounces away.

For millions of Americans, the Fred and Ginger movies were a chance to escape the misery of the depression and to dream of rubbing shoulders with the rich. They were enormously popular, mainly because of the great songs and Fred and Ginger's skillful dancing; the music and their dancing made their otherwise unlikely romantic pairing credible, if only for a few moments. "Cheek to Cheek," the most popular song from the film, was arguably the most popular song of the 1930s.

The Sophisticated Foxtrot Song

Irving Berlin's "Cheek to Cheek" is an elegant, expansive foxtrot. Compared with the songs earlier in this unit, "Cheek to Cheek" is longer, more melodious, and less syncopated. It has a more moderate tempo, and the basic foxtrot that Fred and Ginger dance at the beginning is far less vigorous than the Charleston—Fred can easily sing to Ginger as they dance. That he can do both at the same time emphatically confirms the integration of song and dance, and their artful dancing makes clear how far up the social ladder the foxtrot song has moved.

LISTENING CUE • **"Cheek to Cheek" (1935),** Irving Berlin. Fred Astaire, vocal.

STYLE Modern-era foxtrot • **FORM** Expansive form: AABBCA, with each A section twice the typical length

Listen For . . .

INSTRUMENTATION
Vocal, with dance orchestra featuring violins plus rhythm section (string bass and guitar stand out; piano plays fills), muted trumpet, saxophones

PERFORMANCE STYLE
Astaire has soft, reedy voice; he sings with subtle phrasing.

RHYTHM
Two-beat rhythm with discreet backbeat at moderate tempo through most of the song; B sections have four-beat rhythm.

MELODY
A section melody grows cleverly from simple two-note riff ("Heaven") into long arch.

Contrast from section to section: A = long arch; B = quick rise and fall (mountains); C = dramatic skips, jagged rhythm

Remember . . .

CLASSY CHEEK-TO-CHEEK DANCING
Classy song and classy dancing mean that modern popular music is acceptable at almost every level of society.

LONG SONG
"Cheek to Cheek" is more than double the length of the typical popular song.

MELODIC ECONOMY
Berlin builds expansive phrase out of simple two-note riff.

WORDS AND MUSIC
Melody of all three sections reinforces meaning of lyric.

Listen to this selection in CourseMate.

Song, Dance, and the Shift to Modern Social Values

Everything about the scene is more mature and upscale than the images of the frantic flappers of the twenties. Ginger is twenty-four and clearly a woman. Fred is thirty-six and looks as if he were never an adolescent. Their clothes must have cost a fortune, especially by thirties' standards. Elegance replaces energy; Ginger is wearing an evening gown instead of a flapper dress. The rough edges and vigorous movements of the Charleston are gone; the gliding movements of the foxtrot and the artistic dancing at the end of the scene take their place. The song offers a gentle "Heaven" instead of the syncopated "Charleston."

If you had to select one song to signal the end of the revolution that ushered in popular music's modern era, "Cheek to Cheek" would be a top candidate. The title, the lyrics, the lush setting, the elaborate dancing, and Berlin's wonderful song—all send the same message: It's okay to dance cheek to cheek, and when it's done by Fred and Ginger, it's about as classy as popular culture gets. The deep penetration of this suave and sophisticated sound into all levels of society essentially marginalized those who found popular music and its social setting objectionable.

Dancing elegantly and cheek to cheek required "lingering close contact." In 1935, this was the norm; the other couples are also close together. It was no longer scandalous—indeed, Ginger's dinner companion vigorously gestures for her to draw Fred closer. All of these changes confirm a new, more modern era—in popular music and in American life.

"Cheek to Cheek" and so many songs like it helped people dream, to escape the harsh reality of Depression-era America and experience vicariously the lifestyle depicted in *Top Hat*. For many people of this era, melodious popular song was the music of romance. Just like Fred and Ginger, couples often had "their" song—the song they fell in love to. Granted, it didn't pay the rent or feed the children, but it allowed people to forget about their day-to-day cares, at least for a few minutes.

UNIT 4

LOOKING BACK, LOOKING AHEAD

THE EIGHT EXAMPLES INCLUDED in this unit help document one of the two most eventful periods in the history of popular music; only the rock revolution of the 1950s and 1960s is comparable in significance. Compared with the music from the first part of the century, almost every aspect of this music—and the business surrounding it—had been significantly altered.

A media revolution transformed the way audiences encountered popular music: Through radio, electric recording, and film, Americans learned popular music by listening to it more than they did by reading the sheet music. Moreover, it opened the door to a host of new sounds—sounds that could be preserved on recordings or broadcast over the air, but not transmitted very faithfully via sheet music. These include not only jazz and the new popular singing styles but also a variety of blues and blues-based styles and country music (which we hear in Unit 7).

Many of the new sounds emerged through the wholesale infusion of African-American elements into popular styles. Most fundamental were the rhythmic changes. First came the transformation of the march into the foxtrot, mainly by converting the after beat into a crisp backbeat and adding syncopation. The more active and swinging rhythms of jazz and the relaxed, free delivery of the blues penetrated popular song and its performance soon after the emergence of the foxtrot.

Song and dance, separate at the turn of the century (although songs often had a dance rhythm), came together in the 1920s, first with the performance of popular songs by dance orchestras and then by interpolating vocals between instrumental sections. Popular songs also changed, not only in rhythm and melodic style but also in form. Performances typically consisted of several statements of the chorus; the verse was ignored or used as an interlude between choruses. AABA form, which repeated the catchiest part of the melody many times, largely displaced earlier forms. The newly formed rhythm section provided the beat underneath the melody; the newly popular saxophone often played it.

The infusion of blues and jazz into mainstream music also produced a small but measurable improvement in race relations. The numerous black musicals and revues, black dance orchestras like those of Henderson and Ellington, the jazz of Armstrong and Oliver, Kern and Hammerstein's sympathetic portrait of Joe in *Show Boat*, the emergence of entertainers such as Ethel Waters and Fats Waller—all of these developments moved public perception of African Americans away from the minstrel show stereotypes and toward real people. Moreover, many acknowledged not only their person but also their genius: Crosby found in Armstrong and his music something that he could find nowhere else.

Perhaps because it is an art of the ear, music has been the most colorblind facet of the entertainment world. The majority of good musicians have been most concerned with only one thing: how well one sings or plays the music that they like. Partly because of this, racial barriers came down faster in popular music than in any other segment of American society.

The best music, black and white, helped speed this process along. There was still a long way to go in 1940, but the popular-music business had at least started down the road, with American society following along. Giving it a strong push toward a barrier-free world was a new kind of dance music: swing.

The Swing Era

UNIT

5

UNIT 5

During the 1920s, Fletcher Henderson led one of the top hot dance orchestras in New York. Among the musicians who worked for him were Louis Armstrong and Coleman Hawkins, who would become the most influential saxophonist of the swing era. However, Henderson was a better musician than businessman. In 1934, desperate for cash, Henderson sold arrangements to Benny Goodman, whose band had just been engaged to present *Let's Dance*, a late-night radio show that was broadcast across the country.

After the contract for the radio show expired, Goodman and his band embarked on a cross-country tour, just to keep working. By the time they reached Los Angeles, they were disheartened; at almost all of their previous stops, the managers of the ballrooms had wanted sedate waltzes and foxtrots. Gun-shy from the cross-county trip, Goodman began the evening playing the syrupy music they'd been forced to play on the tour. But the capacity crowd that greeted Goodman's band at the Palomar Ballroom was part of their radio audience (midnight in New York meant nine o'clock in Los Angeles) and loved their new, swinging sound. The crowd was perplexed and gave the band a lukewarm response. Sensing their indifference, Goodman and the band decided to go down in flames—they pulled out a swing tune, and the crowd went wild. This was the music that they'd come to hear, and they let the band know it. The concert at the Palomar Ballroom, which was broadcast nationwide, was a huge success. Many cite it as the event that kick-started the swing era.

Goodman and the band decided to go down in flames—they pulled out a swing tune, and the crowd went wild.

CHAPTER 21
Big-Band Swing

We call the years between 1935 and 1945 the swing era. Swing had bubbled outside the mainstream since the early 1930s, mainly in the music of urban black dance orchestras, most notably those of Duke Ellington and Fletcher Henderson, and Midwest bands, like Bennie Moten's, which used Kansas City as their base. (Count Basie took over Moten's band after Moten's death in 1935.) However, in the wake of Goodman's triumphant appearance in Los Angeles, swing became a truly popular music. Following in Goodman's footsteps, a parade of big bands, white and black, competed for air play, ballroom engagements, and record dates. In addition to Goodman, the most notable bands were those led by both Dorsey brothers, Glenn Miller, Artie Shaw, Count Basie, and Duke Ellington.

The Sound of Big-Band Swing

The sound of big-band swing evolved directly from the jazz-influenced dance orchestras of the 1920s. The two most important developments were the expansion and transformation of the dance orchestra and a fundamental change in the rhythmic foundation of the music.

In 1940, the year in which he recorded "Ko-ko," Duke Ellington's orchestra included fifteen musicians, with the following instrumentation:

- Two trumpets and a cornet, a close relative of the trumpet
- Three trombones (two slide trombones and one valve trombone)
- Five saxophones (two alto saxophones, two tenor saxophones, and one baritone saxophone; Barney Bigard, one of the tenor saxophonists, doubled [alternated] on clarinet)
- Four rhythm instruments: guitar, piano (Ellington), bass, and drums

This was the minimum size for a big band during the height of the swing era. It represented an expansion in the size of the horn sections of many of the hot dance orchestras of the 1920s. These bands typically contained three saxophonists (who also played clarinets at times) and three or four brass instruments.

The expansion of the dance orchestra coincided with an increase in the use of riffs. From the early 1910s, riffs had been the seeds from which so many popular songs grew. In big-band swing, riffs became more repetitive (reflecting the influence of blues) and more pervasive. "Melodies" often

© Frank Driggs Collection/Getty Images

FLETCHER HENDERSON'S Orchestra in New York ca. 1924. The band features Henderson (seated at piano) and Louis Armstrong on trumpet (center, back). The saxophonists are (left to right) Coleman Hawkins, Buster Bailey, and Don Redman (alto).

consisted of a conversation among the sections, which traded riffs back and forth, rather than a single dominant line. This was an adaptation of the long-standing African practice of call and response, heard in a wide range of black vernacular music. In addition, one or more sections typically supported solos with riffs. Often, a horn player in Count Basie's orchestra, which featured several strong soloists, would invent a riff during another musician's solo; the other members of the section would harmonize it.

Swing Rhythm and the Rhythm Sections

The foundation for the stacks of riffs generated by the horn section was the steady pulse laid down by the rhythm section. Between 1930 and 1940, the rhythm section went through a wholesale transformation. Acoustic guitar replaced banjo; string bass replaced tuba; and the drum set gained an important new component, the hi-hat cymbal. The changes reflected the shift in underlying rhythm from the two-beat of the foxtrot to the four-beat rhythm of swing. Instead of tuba and banjo alternating on the beat and backbeat, both string bass and guitar marked each beat: the bassist, with a walking line—one note on each beat—and the guitarist, by strumming chords. Often the drummer also thumped out the beat on the bass drum. The backbeat was present, but more subtly; the drummer closed the hi-hat on the backbeat, and the guitarist strummed more vigorously on the second and fourth beats. (Films of swing-era guitarists often show them strumming up on the first and third beats and strumming down on the second and fourth beats.)

The novel element in swing rhythm was not the four-beat feel; that is present in classic jazz and blues recordings of the 1920s, such as "Hotter Than That" and "Empty Bed Blues," and became a common alternative to the two-beat rhythm by the end of the decade. Rather, it is the persistent timekeeping by a full rhythm section—guitar, bass, and drums—supporting the extensive syncopation in the riffs and call-and-response exchanges between sections. Swing *swings* because of the interplay between the timekeeping of the rhythm section and the syncopations everywhere else.

Fletcher Henderson and the Roots of Big-Band Swing

The early 1930s were the worst years of the Great Depression. Times were very tough: One person in four was out of work. The devastation of the Dust Bowl—severe droughts that paralyzed agriculture and uprooted families—reached its peak. The adversity affected African Americans disproportionately because so many doors were already closed to them. In spite of this, a few black bands managed to find enough work to live on. Their music was the main source of big-band swing.

The man most responsible for shaping the sound of big-band swing was Fletcher Henderson (1897–1952). Henderson is one of the shadow figures of popular music. We know that he came from a black middle-class family in Georgia and got his musical training from his mother, a piano teacher. He came north in 1920 to study chemistry but soon found work with the Pace-Handy music company, first as a song plugger in its publishing business, then as a jack-of-all-trades for Harry Pace's Black Swan Records. We know that during the 1920s he led one of the top bands in New York; they performed at the Roseland Ballroom and made it *the* place to go for great dancing. But hard times and Henderson's lack of business and leadership skills made it difficult to keep his band together. Still, he continued to find work for the band through the early years of the Depression.

We have conflicting accounts of Henderson the person and Henderson the musician. Most agree that he was far from a dynamic leader. Some accuse him of laziness; more claim that he was a terrible businessman. He owes his fame to his skill as an arranger, but even his musical contributions have been subject to doubt. Some scholars deflect credit to other musicians, notably Don Redman, who arranged for Henderson's band in the late 1920s, and Benny Carter, who did the same in the early thirties. We will probably never know the truth.

Nevertheless, Henderson was a major player behind the scenes for more than twenty years. He attracted to his band some of the best black jazzmen of the time, from Louis Armstrong to Coleman Hawkins, to Lester Young. And, most important, it was his arrangements that Goodman used to popularize swing. We hear a example of his approach in his 1934 recording "Wrappin' It Up," which conveys the essence of how to compose and play big-band swing. The first few seconds describe swing: syncopation over a steady four-beat rhythm. The rhythm section lays down the beat. The horns (brass and saxophones) play a simple riff that is out of phase with the beat. The swing results from the conflict between the beat and the syncopated riff.

LISTENING CUE · **"Wrappin' It Up" (1934),** Fletcher Henderson. Fletcher Henderson and His Orchestra.

STYLE Big-band swing · **FORM** Several choruses, some arranged and some improvised; chorus form = ABAC

Listen For . . .

INSTRUMENTATION
Small-scale swing band: three trumpets, two trombones, four saxophones (doubling on clarinet), plus full rhythm section (acoustic guitar, piano, string bass, and drums)

RHYTHM
Clear four-beat rhythm at a bright tempo laid down by the rhythm section; lots of syncopation in the horn parts, especially introduction and first chorus

MELODY
Melody constructed from a series of short, repeated riffs, especially A and B phrases

TEXTURE
Strong contrasts: extensive use of call and response; in ensemble sections, harmonized riffs over rhythm; in solo sections, background chords or riffs

Remember . . .

SWING RHYTHM
Syncopation over four-beat rhythm

SWING BAND
Four sections: rhythm (guitar, piano, bass, and drums), trumpets, trombones, and saxes

SWING TUNE
Riffs and responses: frequent call and response between horn sections

Listen to this selection in CourseMate.

The melody of the song grows out of another simple riff. In this respect, it's like so many of the songs from the twenties. What's different is the way it proceeds. Instead of developing the melody by varying the riff, Henderson simply repeats it one or more times, then shifts to another riff. Creating a melody by repeating a riff, rather than developing it, is one of the trademarks of big-band swing.

Another common feature is the call and response among the sections. Henderson's band features a four-man saxophone section, plus three trumpets and two trombones. Often saxes and brass exchange riffs; in the opening, the brass "comment on" or "respond to" the sax riff , as if they were saying, "Yeah!"

Henderson and his orchestra never hit it big, as Goodman and Glenn Miller did, or even like other top black bandleaders, such as Count Basie, Jimmie Lunceford, or Duke Ellington. Still, with arrangements like this one, Henderson laid the groundwork for **big-band swing:** saxes and brass exchanging riffs over a propulsive four-beat rhythm. In the wake of Goodman's success, this arranging style became the default sound of big-band swing.

The swing era was the one time that jazz was a truly popular music.

Swing as Popular Music

In the now obscure and otherwise forgettable 1941 film *Sun Valley Serenade,* there is a scene where Glenn Miller's band performs a number entitled "Chattanooga Choo Choo." The movie tanked, but the song became one of Miller's biggest hits, selling more than a million copies in less than three months. As a publicity stunt, RCA (Glenn Miller's record label) coated one of its records with gold lacquer and presented it to him on a radio broadcast in February 1942. Because of this, "Chattanooga Choo Choo" was the first certified "gold" record. (Later, the Recording Industry Association of America [RIAA], the trade group that represents U.S. recording interests, would set the benchmark for a gold record at 500,000 units.)

Glenn Miller: Singing, Swing, and Popular Success

Swing as jazz was usually an instrumental music. Swing as popular music was usually a vocal music. There were a few big hits that were strictly instrumental: Glenn Miller's "In the Mood" and Count Basie's "One O'Clock Jump" stand out. However, most of the hit songs recorded by swing bands were popular songs sung and played in a swing style. Also popular were swing-based novelty numbers—vocals where the melody resembles a riff -type swing melody. We hear a famous example of this style next.

GLENN MILLER and His Orchestra performing "Chattanooga Choo Choo." Tex Beneke (center) and the four Modernaires can be seen in a semicircle behind Miller (front on the trombone).

Glenn Miller (1904–1944) led the most popular band of the era. Goodman was the "King of Swing," and Count Basie and Duke Ellington were among its royalty, but no band was more popular than Miller's. One reason was his ability to move effortlessly between swing and sweet. For every "In the Mood" hit (swing), he had a "Moonlight Serenade" (sweet). Among the band's biggest hits was "Chattanooga Choo Choo." The recording is a real period piece; it can belong only to the swing era. The song sounds like an instrumental riff-based song ("Pardon me, boy") that acquired words along the way. In particular, the melody of the B sections moves quickly and skips around (it's easier to play than it is to sing). Although there's the obligatory sweetheart at the end, the song is about a train ride, much like Berry's "Maybellene" is about a car chase.

Tex Beneke, one of the saxophone players in Miller's band, sings the lead vocal. The Modernaires, a close-harmony vocal group that had joined Miller in 1939, back up Beneke and occasionally step into the spotlight. Close-harmony groups like the Modernaires and the Andrews Sisters were also part of the sound of swing-based popular music.

With its vocal, special effects, riffs, syncopation, and growled/smeared/bent notes in the horns—all sounding over a firm four-beat rhythm at a brisk tempo—"Chattanooga Choo Choo" epitomizes swing as a popular style. The music is exuberant. It's fun in both words and sounds—the kind of sound that put smiles on peoples' faces and got them out on the dance floor.

LISTENING CUE • **"Chattanooga Choo Choo" (1941),** Glenn Miller. Glenn Miller and His Band, with Tex Beneke and the Modernaires, vocals.

STYLE Big-band swing • **FORM** Expanded popular song form (AABBAA[1]) vocal chorus surrounded by verse, introduction, plus fragmentary statements of form

Listen For . . .

INSTRUMENTATION
Lead singer and close-harmony vocal group plus full big band: saxes/clarinets, trumpets, trombones, and rhythm; plus train noises at beginning

PERFORMANCE STYLE
Beneke's vocal style is neither personal nor suave; his "stepped-out-of-the-band" sound works well here.

RHYTHM
Strong swing rhythm except for bridge; lots of syncopation—in melody, where phrases end on an offbeat, and in many of the answering riffs

MELODY
A section: from simple riff to instrumental-type melody;
B section: instrumental-type melody, but sung

TEXTURE
Layers of riffs, generally in call-and-response arrangement, with rhythm section underneath

Remember . . .

NOVELTY SONG
A swing tune about a train ride, not love

INSTRUMENTAL SONG
Instrumental-style swing tune with lyrics added

IMAGINATIVE DESIGN
Bigger than usual form (two statements of bridge, B), train sounds, pause before end—all distinctive touches

Listen to this selection in CourseMate.

In the fall of 1942, Glenn Miller joined the army, to lift the spirits of the soldiers at war. Two years later, his plane disappeared en route to France, and his body was never recovered. Miller's death seemed to signal the end of the swing era. After the end of World War II, a few bands kept going, but most disbanded. Goodman's appearance at the Palomar Ballroom and Miller's death frame the swing era. These events, and the memorable events in between, sharply define a time, place, and mood. Only the rock and roll of the 1950s evokes such strong associations in image and sound.

Miller's death in 1944 seemed to signal the end of the swing era.

Swing and Sweet

Swing was not the dominant music of the decade. While Goodman and his band were appearing on late-night radio, Bing Crosby was crooning in prime time. Two camps quickly formed: those who liked swing, the energetic new dance music, and those who preferred **sweet,** the foxtrot song, now grown more melodious, less syncopated, and (usually) slower. Bands usually specialized in one or the other, although most of the top bands were capable of performing both styles. Swing and sweet were comparably popular through the end of World War II. Still, it is swing that put the musical stamp on the decade. The music seemed to capture—even create—the increasingly optimistic mood of the country as it fought off the Depression. The swing era was the one time that jazz was a truly popular music.

CHAPTER 22
Jazz in the Swing Era

Big-band swing got the dancers into the ballroom and onto the dance floor, but when jazz musicians played for fun or bragging rights, they usually did so in small groups. Often, they congregated in after-hours clubs for late-night jam sessions. These would start after an evening of playing for dancing and often continue until the next morning. These jam sessions were often called "cutting contests": They were competitive events where musicians would try to "cut"—that is, outdo—each other.

Jazz pianist Mary Lou Williams recalled one such session in Kansas City, a jazz hotbed in the 1930s. Coleman Hawkins, one of the great tenor saxophonists of the era, was traveling through town with Fletcher Henderson's band, and after his gig he went to an all-night club, where he took on three terrific Kansas City musicians, including Ben Webster, who went on to play with Ellington, and Lester Young, who was Count Basie's most inspired soloist. They started playing, and Hawkins, who was the reigning king of his instrument, wouldn't leave the bandstand until he had outdueled the others. The session went on into the night, and finally Webster went to Mary Lou Williams's house at four in the morning to wake her up, because they were still playing hard and the piano player in the rhythm section was worn out.

The music that jazz musicians played for themselves and for listeners was different from the swing they played for dancers. Swing was present in both styles, but jazz generally featured more extensive and elaborate improvisation, as we hear in recorded performances by Benny Goodman, Count Basie, and Duke Ellington.

Small-Group Jazz in the Swing Era

Although big-band swing was more commercially successful and better known, small-group jazz remained a vital part of the jazz scene through the thirties and early forties. Many of the important bandleaders of the swing era—not only Goodman but also Duke Ellington, Count Basie, Artie Shaw, and Lionel Hampton—also performed or recorded with small groups, either from their own band or assembled specifically for a recording session. "I Found a New Baby," the recording discussed next, brings together two of these bandleaders, Goodman and Basie.

Benny Goodman

Benny Goodman (1909–1986) earned his reputation as the King of Swing mainly from his work as leader of the first popular swing-era big band. But his small-group

LISTENING CUE • "I've Found a New Baby" (1941), Jack Palmer and Spencer Williams. The Benny Goodman Sextet (Benny Goodman, clarinet; Charlie Christian, guitar; Artie Bernstein, bass; Cootie Williams, trumpet; Count Basie, piano; Jo Jones, drums).

STYLE Small-group swing • **FORM** Several improvised choruses on pop song; chorus form = AABA

Listen For . . .

INSTRUMENTATION
Clarinet, trumpet, tenor saxophone; rhythm section of guitar (alternating between electric and acoustic), string bass, piano, and drums

PERFORMANCE STYLE
All soloists play with considerable blues-tinged inflection; trumpeter Cootie Williams uses a mute.

RHYTHM
Swing comes from frequent syncopations against rhythm. Varied rhythmic activity—riffs, running lines, melodic phrases with rhythmic contrast

MELODY
The song is based on a short riff. The solos are instrumentally conceived: fast-moving and wide-ranging lines or riffs.

Remember . . .

JAZZ REPERTOIRE
Jazz musicians began improvising on popular songs in the late 1920s; by the late 1930s, many jazz recordings used a familiar song or a blues as a point of departure.

IMPROVISATIONAL STYLES
Several different improvisational styles, from simple riff exchanges to complex streams of notes

CONVENTIONS OF JAZZ IMPROVISATION
Jazz musicians rely on harmony, rather than melody, as framework for improvisation; they typically create new or substantially modified melodies over the chord progressions of the song.

Listen to this selection in CourseMate.

BENNY GOODMAN CA. 1935

© Pictorial Press Ltd/Alamy

recordings during the swing era, live and in the studio, are an even more valuable part of his legacy.

Goodman's recording of "I've Found a New Baby" is particularly instructive in three ways. It gives us our first example of a jazz performance of a popular song; it presents, even more clearly than the big-band recordings, the timekeeping in the rhythm section that was the foundation of swing style; and it illustrates several improvisational strategies, including melodic paraphrase (in Goodman's statement of the melody), harmonically based running notes (in guitarist Charlie Christian's solo), and repeated riffs (in Basie's solo).

In this performance, both connotations of "swing" are apparent: swing as a rhythmic feel and swing as a style. The performance swings because of the rhythmic interplay of the soloists with the rhythm section. This interplay takes several forms: the marked syncopations of the opening riff, Goodman's bent notes that glide over the beat, and, in Christian's solo, phrases that end abruptly off the beat and the on again/off again accents at the end. The most recognizable elements of swing style are the explicit beat keeping of the rhythm section and the call-and-response exchange of riffs in the second chorus.

The Goodman group's "I've Found a New Baby" is swing as jazz, closely related to a popular style. It is music for listening, not dancing, and it demonstrates the central place of improvisation in typical jazz performance.

Goodman, Music, and Race

Goodman lived for music, so he picked his partners with his ears, not his eyes. He was passionate about playing with the best, and this passion trumped every other consideration, including race. In a potentially career-damaging move, he hired black pianist Teddy Wilson in 1935, not long after the band's big success in Los Angeles; he, Wilson, and drummer Gene Krupa would perform as a trio, separate from the rest of the band. The following year, he expanded the trio to a quartet by hiring black vibraphonist Lionel Hampton. At his landmark Carnegie Hall concert in January 1938, he featured not only the quartet with Wilson and Hampton but also members of the Count Basie and Duke Ellington orchestras, who joined him for a jam session. His recording of "I Found a New Baby" features four black musicians: trumpeter Cootie Williams; Charlie Christian; Count Basie; and Basie's drummer, Jo Jones. Goodman integrated the bandstand and did more than any other white musician to break down the color barrier in music and American life.

Count Basie: Improvisation in Big-Band Swing

Count Basie (1904–1984) was moonlighting when he recorded with Goodman. Most of the time, however, he was busy leading his own big band, which was renowned for its propulsive rhythm section and gifted soloists. Whether by design or economic necessity—arrangements cost money—many of the Basie band's hits grew out of "head" arrangements, those created mainly in performance, with relatively little preplanning beyond the melody and supporting chord progression and a rough outline of the sequence of events. Here's how the band's 1938 recording of Basie's "Jumpin' at the Woodside" might have come about:

Basie and the other band members are gathered for a rehearsal at Kansas City's Woodside Hotel (hence the title), where many of the band members stayed. Basie tells them that they need another arrangement. He plays a simple riff; the saxophones pick it up immediately. That's the A section of the melody. He plays a familiar four-chord progression for the bridge and asks the alto saxophonist Caughey Roberts to improvise on the progression. That's the tune. They try it out, then Basie asks the brass players to come up with a riff that responds to the saxes. They decide to play the melody through twice; the second time trombones add their own riff and Basie takes the solo during the bridge.

Basie then tells the band, "Buck (trumpeter Buck Clayton), you take the first solo, and Pres (tenor saxophonist Lester Young), you take the second one. The rest of you, find riffs to play behind the solos." Basie then plays a simple two-bar bass line and tells the rhythm players to come in one by one. They do, and the band plays the arrangement through Young's solo. During the horn solos, members of other sections (e.g., trombones and saxes during the trumpet solo) work out back up riffs and occasionally sustained chords. Basie then asks "How are we going to end it?" The band decides to finish by repeating the A section over and over, beginning with an exchange between clarinet and trombone, and gradually accumulating riffs from the saxes and trumpets. The sax riff replaces the original version of the riff, while the clarinet player continues to solo as an obbligato.

LISTENING CUE · **"Jumpin' at the Woodside" (1938),** Coumt Basie. Count Basie & His Orchestra.

STYLE Big-band swing · **FORM** Several choruses on an AABA form song

Listen For . . .

RHYTHM
Classic swing rhythmic foundation: bass and guitar marking the beat, drums keeping time and marking backbeat; frequent and complex rhythmic play created by frequent syncopations over swing rhythmic foundation

MELODY
Bare-bones melody: simple riff repeated multiple times

TEXTURE
Dense texture, especially in second chorus and ending, because of several layers of riffs, or riffs behind solos, all over steady timekeeping

Remember . . .

TERRIFIC RHYTHMIC ENERGY
Fast tempo, strong swing rhythm, and layers of syncopated riffs create great energy.

HEAD ARRANGEMENT
"Jumpin' at the Woodside," with its simple A section melody, improvised bridge, heavy reliance on solos, and layers of riffs, sounds like a head arrangement that was worked out by the band in rehearsal rather than written out beforehand.

SPOTLIGHT ON SOLOISTS
This performance showcases tenor saxophonist Lester Young, one of the top jazz musicians of this era.

Listen to this selection in CourseMate.

The Count Basie Orchestra was the swingingest of the swing bands: No band generated greater rhythmic excitement and energy. They were not as versatile or as polished as other bands; their arrangements tended to be simpler; and they didn't do sweet. But they offered strong solo players—some of the best of the time—and a spontaneity and synergy among sections that's hard to achieve when everything is so well scripted beforehand. They remain one of the great bands of the swing era.

The contrast between Count Basie and Duke Ellington, another swing-era royal, is striking: Basie and his band relied heavily on improvisation and spontaneous interaction; Ellington was the greatest composer of the swing era and arguably the greatest jazz composer.

Duke Ellington, Painter in Sound

The most distinctive big band of the swing era was the one led by Edward "Duke" Ellington (1899–1974). The quality that most distinguishes Ellington's music from that of all other bands was sound color. His masterpieces, like "Ko-ko," offer a dazzling variety of timbres unmatched by any other band of the era. The difference might be described in this way. Imagine the three basic timbres—trumpets, trombones, and saxophones—as primary colors. Arrangers of the era typically used these timbres as one might use crayons. By contrast, Ellington used timbres as an artist might use oils on a palette, blending them to produce a far greater range of shades and hues.

Ellington's unique sound has three principal sources: his own musical imagination; a long apprenticeship in New York nightclubs; and a core of musicians, some of whom remained in his band for their entire career. Ellington's creativity was evident almost from the start of his professional career, when he led a band called the Washingtonians—Ellington had been born and raised in Washington, D.C. The high point of his tenure in New York was his extended run at the Cotton Club, a Harlem nightclub. He and his orchestra performed there from 1927 to 1931; radio broadcasts from the club and recordings made him a national celebrity by the early 1930s. At the Cotton Club, Ellington had to provide what his manager Irving Mills called "jungle music." Although Ellington's music bore virtually no resemblance to sub-Saharan African music, it did encourage his musicians to develop novel effects.

From the late 1920s to 1943, when he and his orchestra made their Carnegie Hall debut, the membership of the band remained remarkably stable. He gradually added musicians over the years, from ten musicians around the time he started at the Cotton Club to the fifteen heard on "Ko-ko." Few musicians left Ellington's band during this period; some had been with him since the Washingtonian days.

What made Ellington's musicians special was their individuality. Most of the horn players had a special sound. Some derived their sound from the choice of instrument, for instance, the valve trombone instead of the more conventional slide trombone. Others, like baritone saxophonist Harry Carney, had a distinctive tone. Still others cultivated unusual effects; Ellington always had brass players who could produce growls and other effects through

© Michael Ochs Archives/Getty Images

DUKE ELLINGTON (on piano), Sonny Grier (on drums), and Ellington's orchestra, performing "Take the A Train" in the film *Reveille with Beverly*

the use of mutes. For Ellington, the band was a laboratory for constant experimentation. We hear the fruits of this association in "Ko-ko," a masterpiece recorded in 1940.

At first glance, the phrase "jazz composer" sounds like an oxymoron because, throughout its early history, jazz was largely an improviser's music—to the extent that it was hard to conceive of jazz without improvisation. Although he was certainly an able improviser at the piano, Ellington is remembered as the greatest composer in the history of jazz, in part because of the special sound worlds he creates: vibrant and varied timbres, exotic harmonies, and careful use of register and dynamics.

His compositions also shed light on Ellington's solutions to a major issue in jazz composition: imparting a sense of structure. "Ko-ko" is a composition—there is no extended improvisation—built on a blues progression. But Ellington controls the pacing, starting in a low register and ascending, and quickening the rhythms of exchanges between sections, so that the composition reaches two peaks, one just before the bass solo and the other at the very end. This sense of compositional architecture was rare in the jazz of the 1930s and 1940s. Inventive use of timbre, colorful harmonies, and handling of rhythm put Ellington's music "beyond category." No other jazz composer of his era brought his combination of craft and imagination to the work.

"Ko-ko" provides a useful perspective on the connection between swing, improvisation, and the essence of jazz. "Ko-ko" is jazz most fundamentally because it swings. A skilled improviser can play with time in a way that is virtually impossible to notate comprehensibly. In "Ko-ko," this subtlety is not present; in its place is a collective understanding of how to push against the beat. The sax riffs in the first chorus amply demonstrate this.

LISTENING CUE • "Ko-ko" (1940), Edward "Duke" Ellington. Duke Ellington and His Orchestra.

STYLE Big-band swing • **FORM** Several arranged choruses over twelve-bar blues, with introduction that returns at the end

Listen For . . .

INSTRUMENTATION
Full big band: two trumpets and cornet, two slide trombones and valve trombone, five saxophones, and rhythm section (guitar, bass, drums, and piano)

PERFORMANCE STYLE
Several band members cultivated distinctive sounds (trombonist Sam Nanton's use of a plunger mute).

RHYTHM
Four-beat swing rhythm in rhythm section, with syncopated riffs pushing against the beat.
"Exchange" rhythm, that is, the rhythm created by the call and response between sections; initially eight beats per call/response pair, but compressed at middle and end

TEXTURE
Multilayered texture over steady rhythm section; considerable variation in density—the number and spacing of parts—and register: effective use of extremes in both variables

Remember . . .

ELLINGTON = SOUND PAINTER
For Ellington, timbral variety is like paints on a palette: "Ko-ko" spotlights trombones, first as a section, then individually. Timbre and register change from chorus to chorus.

USE OF REGISTER
Registral placement contributes to pacing of piece. On largest scale, it goes from low to high: the very low repeated note by baritone sax to final flourishes at end.

BEYOND BIG-BAND SWING
Ellington starts from big-band swing conventions, but his treatment of them is more imaginative, more sophisticated, and more individual—and because of this, closer to art.

Listen to this selection in CourseMate.

UNIT 5

LOOKING BACK, LOOKING AHEAD

SWING brought a new and welcome energy to popular music, lifting people's spirits as America lifted itself out of the Depression. Among the enduring images of the swing era are dancers frenetically jitterbugging and Lindy-hopping around ballroom dance floors. The strong, syncopated four-beat rhythms of swing were the counterpoint to the more sedate foxtrots of the sweet bands.

By the end of World War II, the swing era was over, but the sound of swing did not disappear. Many swing-era musicians found steady employment in recording studios, where they played behind many of the top pop singers of the postwar era. This kind of singing was the most popular continuation of swing—but it was not the only one. Swing also helped spawn bebop, a daring new, listening-oriented jazz style, and an upbeat brand of rhythm and blues.

Blues and Black Gospel Come in from the Outskirts, 1925–1950

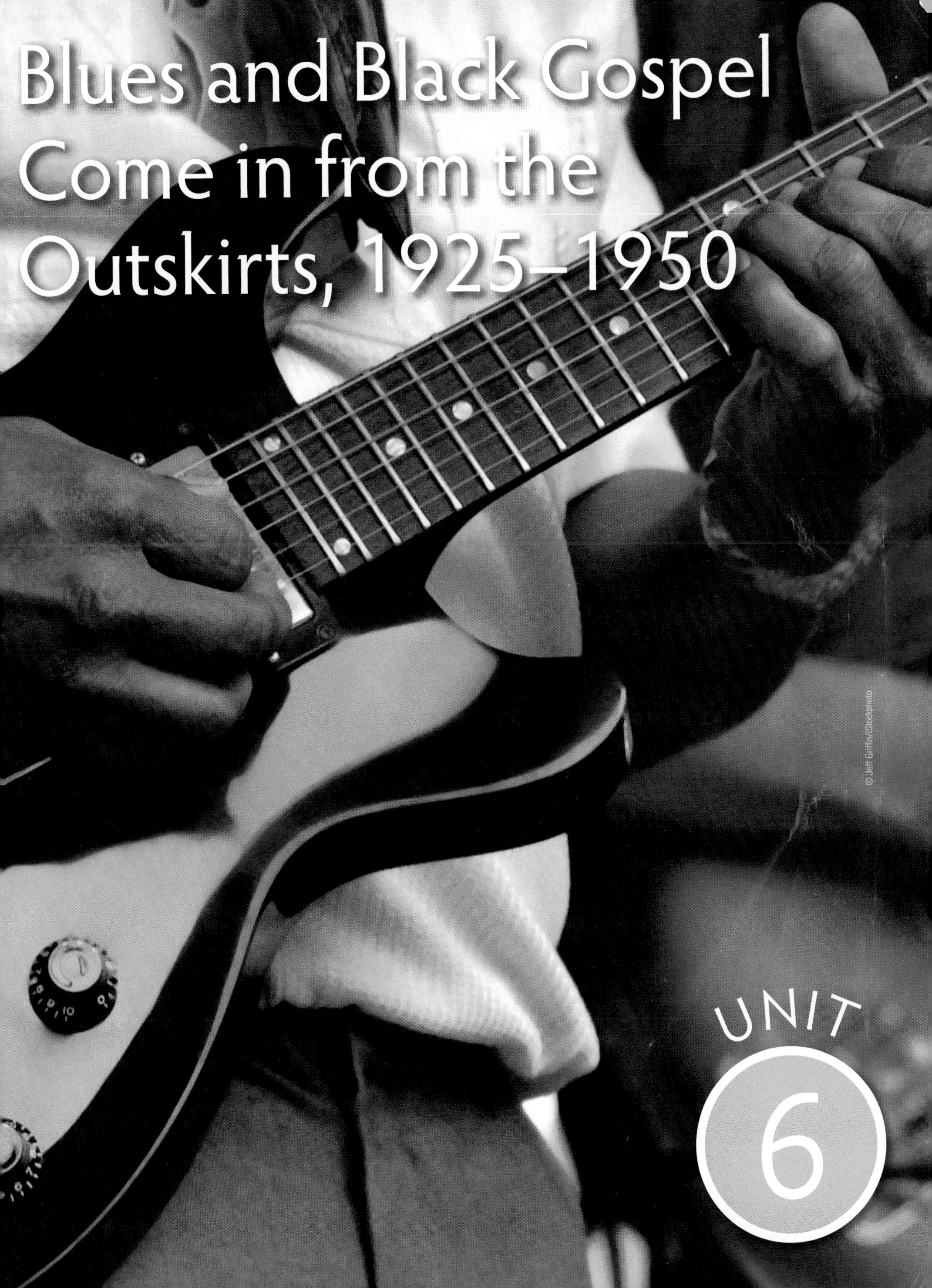

UNIT 6

UNIT 6

In 1961, Columbia Records (now Sony) issued *King of the Delta Blues Singers*, a compilation of several 78s recorded by bluesman Robert Johnson in 1936 and 1937. Most of Johnson's records, intended from the start for a small slice of the market, sold only in the hundreds. At the time that *King of the Delta Blues* was released, Johnson's music was known mainly to blues enthusiasts. Among them was talent scout extraordinaire John Hammond.

John Hammond helped shape both the swing and rock eras. As Benny Goodman's friend and future brother-in-law, he urged Goodman to hire black musicians such as Charlie Christian, whom he'd discovered. Hammond also gained national exposure for Count Basie's orchestra and organized the "From Spirituals to Swing" concerts at Carnegie Hall, which showcased a wide range of African-American vernacular music. During the early rock era, he signed Bob Dylan and Aretha Franklin to Columbia, although not as rock or rhythm-and-blues stars. Dylan began his career as a folk singer, and Aretha found her groove only after she signed with Atlantic Records. Hammond later signed Bruce Springsteen.

However, Hammond's most far-reaching impact on rock was his orchestration of the reissue of several of Johnson's recordings. Hammond had known about Johnson since the 1930s; he tried to locate him for the first of the "From Spirituals to Swing" concerts, but Johnson was already dead. At the height of the folk revival, Hammond persuaded Columbia to release several of Johnson's recordings on LP.

Copies of the LPs found their way to Great Britain, and British as well as American rock musicians went to school on Johnson's music. In particular, Eric Clapton has covered Johnson's music throughout his career.

The posthumous reissues of Johnson's recordings have enjoyed commercial success and critical acclaim. The various compilations have sold over 1,000,000 units, a number that Johnson might have found unbelievable. They have appeared on several lists of important recordings: *Rolling Stone* ranked one such compilation, *King of the Delta Blues Singers,* 27th on the 2003 list of the 500 greatest albums of all time.

In this unit, we survey three developments in black music between 1925 and 1950: the recording of what is usually called country blues; the emergence of up-tempo, piano-based blues styles; and the beginnings of black gospel music. None of this music found its way to the mainstream during the era in which it was created, although white takes on boogie-woogie were a novelty around 1940. We consider them in this text because of their profound and pervasive influence on the music of the rock era.

CHAPTER 23
Country Blues

In the latter part of the twenties, Paramount Records advertised the music of Blind Lemon Jefferson as "real old-fashioned blues by a real old-fashioned blues singer." As Paramount's ad intimates, Jefferson's blues was an old style that was new to records. Jefferson was the first major country blues singer to record. From 1926, the year of Jefferson's first recording, until about 1940, **country blues**—so called because the bluesmen came mainly from rural locales throughout the South—carved out a small but viable niche in the record industry.

The Roots of the Blues

Compared to Handy's published blues, the blues of jazz musicians, and the classic blues of Bessie Smith and Ma Rainey, country blues was late to market. Indeed, much of this music might never have been recorded if record companies were not compelled to search for minority audiences after the explosion of radio during the 1920s caused mainstream record sales to plummet.

Anecdotal evidence, such as Handy's story about the chance late-night encounter with the young man at the railroad station, suggests that country blues were already part of life in the South by 1900. Bluesmen would remain fixtures in both cities and towns across the South, from Texas and Oklahoma to Georgia and the Carolinas, through the 1930s.

The environment in which they created their music helped produce a style with strong connections to African culture. In the first half of the twentieth century, Jim Crow laws enforcing rigid segregation throughout the South had particular power because so few African Americans had any economic, legal, or political leverage. Sharecropping, with its poor wages, few rights, and high prices at the company store, kept many blacks almost as dependent as they had been during slavery. Some men—roustabouts and stevedores—worked along the Mississippi River, building up the levees or moving cargo on and off the riverboats. Pay for this work was marginally better than for share cropping—although it would make today's minimum wage seem like a fortune—but working conditions were harsher. White overseers carried guns to enforce discipline, and men labored long hours and lived in squalid work camps.

Most rural black Americans had little direct contact with white society, and none of it was on an equal footing. Moreover, in these days before television, few had much awareness of the outside world. Perhaps because they were isolated in so many ways, rural blacks rediscovered, or perhaps reinvented, many aspects of the cultures their ancestors had left behind in Africa. We sense this when Muddy Waters, who grew up in the Mississippi Delta, sings about "mojo" or when we discover that Bo Diddley's stage name mirrors that of the diddley bow (which he claims never to have heard of), an instrument similar to those found in West Africa, or when we hear a group of laborers singing a work song.

In the rural South, near Natchitoches, Louisiana, a store with live fish for sale.

Marion Post Wolcott/Farm Security Administration/Library of Congress, Prints and Photographs Division, Washington, DC

The Blues and African Culture

The blues is the most African of the African-American musical traditions that emerged during the early years of the twentieth century. West African cultures most often create music communally. However, within these cultures there is a direct precedent for the blues-man, the *griot*.

In West African culture, the ***griot*** fulfills many roles. He is the healer (the witch doctor); the tribe historian (he preserves its history in his songs); and, along with the master drummer, its most important musician. Although the *griot* is respected for his abilities, he is sometimes feared, or at least distrusted. As a result, he often stands outside of tribal life.

The *griot*'s incarnation in African-American culture has been the bluesman. Like the *griot*, he told stories through songs and earned admiration and respect for this ability, but he also lived on the fringes of society. Many bluesmen traveled around in search of work and company. The bluesman led a life much different from that of the sharecropper or the roustabout—working when others played, and playing around when others

John A. and Alan Lomax Collection, Library of Congress, Prints and Photographs Division, Washington, DC

BLIND WILLIE McTELL plays a twelve-string guitar in a hotel room in Atlanta, Georgia, for a John Lomax field recording.

worked. And like the *griot,* the bluesman was a part of life in the South, yet apart from it. The solitary aspect of country blues links it to the *griot* and differentiates it from most other African-American folk styles, including work songs and spirituals, which are based on collective music making.

The Life of a Bluesman: Blind Willie McTell

Today if you drive past 295 Ponce de Leon Avenue NE in Atlanta, you may be tempted to stop for a couple of Krispy Kreme doughnuts. However, back in the 1930s, you'd find barbeque at this location, which was home to the Pig 'n' Whistle. Customers would drive up to the restaurant, which occupied a big lot on one of Atlanta's main east–west routes. Most evenings, they could hear Blind Willie McTell (1898–1959) playing outside for tips. It was the closest McTell got to a steady gig.

McTell was one of several blind bluesmen. We encounter Blind Lemon Jefferson next, and there were also Blind Boy Fuller, Blind Blake, and several others. Being black and poor in the South during the early years of the twentieth century was hard enough; being born without sight or losing it early in life made subsistence an almost insurmountable challenge. For the blind with talent and the determination to nurture it, a musical career, however precarious, offered an opportunity for some independence and income, and a life beyond the menial tasks for which they had been trained.

Still, blind or sighted, most bluesmen led a precarious life. They entertained on street corners and at almost any social occasion—fish fries, parties, picnics, and the like—to make money, if only enough for their next drink. Some, like Robert Johnson, played (or at least recorded) only the blues; others, like McTell and Leadbelly, were *songsters* who had a large and varied repertoire of folk songs, hymns, ragtime, and popular songs: McTell once toured with blackface minstrels.

Bluesmen often traveled from town to town. McTell, who was born about 40 miles from Augusta, Georgia, moved around the state, sometimes using Atlanta as a home base, and traveled through the Carolinas. Many would stay long enough to earn some money and entertain the ladies, especially when their men were off working. McTell relied on friends (including a woman for whom he bought a car) or public transportation to get from place to place. For the husbands of his female companions, the bluesman was often the notorious "back-door man," sneaking out the rear of the house as the man came home. Many viewed the bluesman's arrival in town as a mixed blessing.

Although they gained a local reputation, early bluesmen largely lived and died in obscurity. They left few recordings and even fewer details of their lives, as biographers of Robert Johnson and McTell have discovered to their frustration.

Still, it is the recordings that constitute such a valuable legacy, far more important than their popularity might indicate. McTell recorded periodically during the late 1920s and 1930s, and in 1940 for folklorist John Lomax. Among his earliest recordings was "Travelin' Blues."

"Travelin' Blues," recorded in 1929, shows both his obvious skill as a performer and the connection between the bluesman and the *griot*. Much of the vocal line is spoken; McTell moves smoothly from speech to song, when he asks the engineer for a ride. He provides another perspective on the understanding of blues as intensified speech.

McTell's guitar playing is extraordinary. He preferred a twelve-string guitar, because it produced more sound. In this recording, he does the work of two guitarists: He maintains a fast, ragtime-like accompaniment throughout, and occasionally overlays the accompaniment with bottleneck-style riffs to evoke the sound of a train bell or to respond to vocal lines.

In songs like "Travelin' Blues," the connection between the bluesman and the *griot* is evident: like his West African counterpart, McTell tells a story by speaking and occasionally singing over his own instrumental accompaniment.

McTell was one of the major exponents of the blues characteristic of the Southeast. We hear a markedly different approach in the music of Blind Lemon Jefferson.

LISTENING CUE • **"Travelin' Blues" (1929),** Blind Willie McTell. McTell, vocal and twelve-string guitar.

STYLE Early country blues • **FORM** Spoken narrative over accompaniment alternating with slightly modified blues form

Listen For . . .

INSTRUMENTATION
Voice and twelve-string acoustic guitar

PERFORMANCE STYLE
McTell uses a bottleneck on one string while maintaining the accompaniment on other strings.

RHYTHM
Active rhythms at a fast tempo

MELODY
All three phrases of the blues melody start high and finish low

TEXTURE
Occasional call and response between vocal phrases and their imitation using the bottleneck style

Remember . . .

STORYTELLING BLUES
"Travelin' Blues" is a slice of McTell's life. It is, for the most part, emotionally neutral: The sung blues is the most expressive part of the track.

ONE GUITARIST OR TWO?
Remarkable guitar playing, often with melodic figures played at the same time as the intricate accompaniment

SOUND IMAGINATION
McTell creates an array of evocative sounds: the train chugging, the bell ringing, and the mimicking of the voice. It is another instance of the search for new sounds by African-American musicians.

Listen to this selection in CourseMate.

Blind Lemon Jefferson: "Old-Fashioned Blues"

"Country blues star" sounds like a contradiction in terms. Compared to the pop market, or even the market for classic blues singers, the market for "old-fashioned blues" was exceedingly modest. But there was a market, and Blind Lemon Jefferson (1894–1929) was the first to capture it.

Jefferson was born near Wortham, Texas, a small town about 80 miles south of Dallas. Early in his career, he was an itinerant street musician; by 1917, he had settled in Dallas, where he developed a following in the black community. His reputation grew sufficiently that "Ink" Williams, a talent scout for Paramount records, brought him to Chicago at the end of 1925 to record for the label. Jefferson recorded frequently until his death in 1929, and his records sold well enough that he was reportedly given a car and a chauffeur by Paramount in lieu of cash payment of his record royalties.

BLIND LEMON JEFFERSON

For many serious students of the blues, the purest blues has been the country blues of artists like Jefferson. Its "purity" lies in its freedom from commercial influences. We hear no pop, no jazz, no horns in country blues—just a man and his guitar. In "Black Snake Moan" (1927), one of Blind Lemon Jefferson's first recordings, the distance from European practice is striking. There is no chord progression; only the I chord that Jefferson occasionally strums as a tag to the intricate running figure that serves as the instrumental response. Although lyrics are a series of rhymed couplets with the first line repeated, there is no steady pulse underneath his vocal line. As a result, the predictable regularity of conventional blues form is not present.

His lyrics are rich in metaphor and graphic in subject—it's not difficult to imagine what his "black snake" is, even out of context. His singing is more moan than anything else; phrases start high and end low. The most striking feature of his guitar playing is the elaborate response figure, which briefly establishes a steady beat.

LISTENING CUE • **"Black Snake Moan" (1927),** Blind Lemon Jefferson. Jefferson, vocal and guitar.

STYLE Early country blues • **FORM** Blues form (strophic form with six choruses that use rhymed couplet lyrics, but not conventional twelve-bar blues progression)

Listen For . . .

INSTRUMENTATION
Voice and acoustic guitar

PERFORMANCE STYLE
Jefferson's moaning, rough-edged voice, half-talking, half-singing style typifies country blues.

RHYTHM
No steady tempo; alternates between out-of-tempo vocal and occasional steady tempo in response figures

MELODY
First line phrases start high, finish low; answering phrase has flatter contour.

HARMONY
Mostly one chord; chord under answering phrase indistinct—not V

Remember . . .

SEXUAL METAPHOR
Like many blues lyrics, song uses metaphor to describe sexual matters.

BLUES VOCAL STYLE
Moaning; starting high, ending low; half-singing, half-talking, rough voice all characteristic of blues style

BLUES FORM
Lyric is regular; music has irregular phrase lengths, static harmony, varying tempo.

Listen to this selection in CourseMate.

The market for country blues would remain small but stable, despite the onset of the Depression; most of the recordings of country bluesmen before the blues revival of the early rock era date from the 1930s. Among the most outstanding are those of Robert Johnson.

The Sound of Country Blues in the Delta: Robert Johnson

Country blues was part of life across the South and Southwest. However, if blues had a home, it was the Delta region of Mississippi, which is in the northwest part of the state. It is there that we find what Robert Palmer called "deep blues"—the starkest, most powerful expression of blues feeling.

Many important bluesmen, including Charley Patton and Son House, called the Delta home. Others, like Muddy Waters and Howlin' Wolf, grew up there, then moved north. The most esteemed of the early Delta bluesmen was Robert Johnson (1911–1938).

Johnson is a strong contender for the title of most mysterious figure in the history of popular music. He lived and worked in obscurity, and was virtually unknown outside of the Delta region during his lifetime. Although he spent most of his life in the Mississippi Delta, he made his only recordings in Texas: San Antonio in 1936 and Dallas in 1937. There are at least three different versions of his death, the most likely being that he drank whiskey poisoned with strychnine (by the jealous husband of a woman he'd been visiting) and died soon after.

The reissue of Johnson's recordings helped a generation of rock musicians discover his music. Top 1960s rock acts recorded his songs: among them were the Rolling Stones, who covered "Love in Vain" and "Stop Breakin'

The crossroads of Highways 61 and 49 in Clarksdale, Mississippi, where according to legend, Robert Johnson sold his soul to the devil in exchange for extraordinary skill on the guitar.

Down," and Eric Clapton, who has covered several Johnson songs over the course of his career.

In Johnson's 1937 recording "Hellhound on My Trail," the lyrics are filled with vivid images—"blues fallin' down like hail, . . . hellhound on my trail"—and he delivers them straight. On this important recording, we listen to what the words have to say and how Johnson delivers them. His guitar playing is extraordinary. Johnson can make his guitar mimic his voice, provide strong accompaniment in a shuffle rhythm (a shuffle rhythm divides each beat into two unequal parts; long/short), or serve as another voice.

By the time Johnson made his last recordings in 1937, country blues had peaked as a commercial style, at least in the eyes of the record executives. It went into decline for about two decades, resurfacing only as part of the folk revival around 1960. Johnson's recordings were among those reissued on LP about this time.

Country blues, and especially Johnson's music, hit British blues-based rock bands like a heavyweight's right hand, partly because it leapfrogged a generation and partly because it defined the essence of the blues, which inspired so many British rock musicians to get real.

LISTENING CUE • "Hellhound on My Trail" (1937), Robert Johnson. Johnson, vocal and guitar.

STYLE Country blues • **FORM** Blues form, but with varying bar lengths, phrase lengths; more static harmony

Listen For . . .

INSTRUMENTATION
Voice and acoustic guitar

PERFORMANCE STYLE
Guitar part often contains both strummed chords and melodic answer to the vocal phrase.

RHYTHM
Lazy tempo; guitar keeps intermittent shuffle rhythm (a shuffle rhythm divides each beat into two unequal parts; long/short).

MELODY
First line phrases start high, finish low; answering phrase has flatter contour.

HARMONY
Not quite a blues progression (second phrase uses the same harmony; third phrase goes to V, then back to I)

Remember . . .

DARK IMAGES
("hellhound . . .") evoke the world of the Delta bluesman

BLUES VOCAL STYLE
Strong, unfiltered, raw, powerful, acrid quality; phrases starting high, ending low; half-singing, half-talking style

GUITAR ROLES
Accompanist, responder, reinforcer: sometimes two at a time

Listen to this selection in CourseMate.

CHAPTER 24

Good Time Blues

Blues is a bipolar music. The most characteristic forms of the blues are songs that convey a "blue" mood: sadness, heartache, and longing. The blues of Smith, Jefferson, and Johnson project these moods powerfully; Waters's "Am I Blue?" is a pop reflection of this sensibility.

But blues can also accompany good times. There are blues songs that are fun—even funny at times—and upbeat in mood and tempo. We heard this kind of exuberance in King Oliver's "Dippermouth Blues" and encounter it in songs that illustrate two important blues styles of the late 1920s and 1930s, hokum and boogie-woogie.

Hokum

New, more urban blues styles began to appear on record in the late twenties. They featured singers who sounded bluesier than pop or jazz singers, but not as emotionally charged as Bessie Smith or as raw as the country bluesmen. The accompaniment, typically piano and guitar, gave the music a stronger, more consistent beat than country blues, but it was not as elaborate as the jazz accompaniments of the classic blues singers.

Among these new blues styles was **hokum,** a novelty style that was popular between the two world wars. Hokum songs showed an entirely different side of the blues: upbeat, salacious, good-humored, and light-hearted. They were miles away from the elemental power of Johnson's.

Perhaps the most famous hokum blues is "It's Tight Like That," a 1928 recording featuring pianist Georgia Tom (1899–1993) and guitarist Tampa Red (1904–1981), who advertised themselves as the Hokum Brothers. The real name of Georgia Tom of the Hokum Brothers was Thomas A. Dorsey. Dorsey turned his back on the blues shortly after this recording to devote himself to black gospel, where he would play a seminal role in its development.

"It's Tight Like That" is also an early example of a verse/chorus blues form. The harmonic form of the song is a twelve-bar blues, but lyrics replace the conventional rhymed couplet with a verse/chorus scheme. The first four bars describe a scene; the last eight repeat the same words and melody.

The lyric is humorous, with sexual overtones, for example, "another mule kicking in my stall." It's another way of getting the message across without being explicit. Toward the end of the song, lyrics move away from the barnyard to other ways of describing sex (or the lack of it).

Many features of the style, most notably the bright tempo, humorous lyric, and verse/chorus blues forms, resurfaced in post–World War II blues-based styles, such as the jump-band rhythm and blues of Louis Jordan and others and most of Chuck Berry's breakthrough hits.

In "It's Tight Like That," Tampa Red's guitar playing dominates the accompanying; Georgia Tom's piano playing is very much in the background. In the next example, the piano is the only accompanying instrument; it was the only one needed.

LISTENING CUE • "It's Tight Like That" (1928), Tampa Red and Georgia Tom. The Hokum Brothers.

STYLE Hokum (salacious, up-tempo blues style) • **FORM** Early verse/chorus blues form. First four bars briefly describe a scene; the last eight repeat a chorus based on title phrase.

Listen For . . .

INSTRUMENTATION
Voices plus acoustic guitar and piano

PERFORMANCE STYLE
Bent notes in guitar solo

RHYTHM
Bright tempo, syncopation in melody

MELODY
Narrow range throughout; riffs in chorus

HARMONY
Conventional blues progression

Remember . . .

UPBEAT BLUES
This is a happy blues. It moves at a bright tempo with a strong beat.

GOOD-HUMORED LYRIC WITH SEXUAL INNUENDO
This is literally barnyard humor: sexual matters are described via animal metaphors.

INSTRUMENTATION AND REGULAR BLUES PROGRESSION
Two accompanying instruments require coordination of harmony; conventional blues progression used throughout.

VERSE/CHORUS BLUES FORM
In its approach to blues form, there is a direct line from songs like this to many of the Chuck Berry hits of the 1950s.

Listen to this selection in CourseMate.

Boogie-Woogie

Boogie-woogie is a blues piano style that chases the blues away. It is typically exuberant, even boisterous, loud, and strong. Originating in the rural South during the early years of the century, boogie-woogie was born of necessity. Its creators were pianists who performed in noisy working-class bars and clubs, variously called juke joints, barrelhouses, and honky-tonks. To be heard over the crowd, pianists created a powerful two-handed style in which they played an active left-hand pattern in the lower part of the instrument and repeated riffs on the upper part. By the late 1920s, pianists were playing boogie-woogie in such urban centers as Chicago, New York, and Kansas City. It flourished in the 1930s and 1940s, spreading beyond black neighborhoods into mainstream America. The Andrews Sisters scored a hit with "Boogie Woogie Bugle Boy"; Tommy Dorsey's "Boogie Woogie" (an arrangement of Pine Top Smith's 1929 recording "Pine Top's Boogie Woogie") was his biggest instrumental hit.

Among the most famous boogie-woogie performances is the 1936 recording of "Roll 'Em, Pete," featuring blues shouter Joe Turner (1911–1985) and pianist Pete Johnson (1904–1967), one of the kings of boogie-woogie piano. Turner grew up in Kansas City and started his career by singing while tending bar. After teaming up with Johnson through the early 1940s, Turner became a prominent figure in the postwar rhythm-and-blues scene.

"Roll 'Em, Pete" is a straightforward blues in form, the kind that Turner could have made up on the spot. (The title of the song apparently came from the patrons of the club where Turner and Johnson worked. They would shout, "Roll 'em, Pete," as Johnson played chorus after chorus.) In its power, Turner's singing is reminiscent of Bessie Smith's classic blues, but "Roll 'Em, Pete" is good-time music. There's a smile in Turner's voice that matches the exuberance of Johnson's playing. In this recording, Pete Johnson sets up a steady rhythm in the left hand that divides each beat into two parts and builds piles of riffs on top of the left-hand pattern. In a medium-tempo boogie-woogie song, the division of the beat is uneven: a long/short pattern. At really fast tempos, however, it is difficult if not impossible to sustain the long/short rhythm in the left hand. So, in "Roll 'Em, Pete," the rhythm tends to even out so that each beat is divided in two halves of equal length.

Boogie-woogie's flirtation with the mainstream was brief. After World War II, boogie-woogie piano playing was heard mainly in rhythm and blues. The driving left-hand rhythm heard in "Roll 'Em, Pete" would resurface in the music of Chuck Berry and become the rhythmic foundation of rock 'n' roll, then rock.

LISTENING CUE • "Roll 'Em, Pete" (1936), Joe Turner and Pete Johnson. Turner, vocal; Johnson, piano.

STYLE Boogie-woogie • **FORM** Conventional twelve-bar blues form

Listen For . . .

INSTRUMENTATION
Voice and piano

PERFORMANCE STYLE
Blues "shouting": big, rough-voiced singing

RHYTHM
Bright tempo with active, steady rhythms

MELODY
Narrow range throughout

HARMONY
Conventional blues progression

MELODIES CONSTRUCTED FROM REPEATED RIFFS
Both the vocal line and the melody lines in the instrumental choruses typically begin with a repeated riff, then break off into a more elaborate line toward the end of the chorus.

CONVENTIONAL BLUES FORM AND HARMONY
Like Bessie Smith's blues, this is a straightforward blues in lyrics, harmony, and form. This would remain the most widely used version of blues form in the early rock era.

STRONG PIANO PLAYING
Boogie-woogie is a piano style designed to be heard over a crowd; strong, active, steady left hand, lots of double notes in right hand.

Remember . . .

BOOGIE-WOOGIE = SOURCE OF ROCK RHYTHM
At a faster tempo, shuffle rhythm evens out. Berry would adapt patterns like this to his rhythm guitar playing; they would become foundation for rock rhythm.

Listen to this selection in CourseMate.

CHAPTER 25
Black Gospel

In 1921, Thomas A. Dorsey (1899–1993) attended the final session of the National Baptist Convention. He was initially reluctant to go because he was, as he put it, "in the blues business," and not connected with any particular faith. However, his uncle cajoled him into accompanying him, and ultimately, he was glad he did: hearing W. M. Nix sing "I Do, Don't You?" changed his life. In his words:

> My inner-being was thrilled. My soul was a deluge of divine rapture; my emotions were aroused; my heart was inspired to become a great singer and worker in the Kingdom of the Lord. . . .

Dorsey would maintain a career as a blues pianist through the 1920s, but he soon began to write what he called "gospel songs":

> In the early 1920s I coined the words "gospel songs" after listening to a group of five people one Sunday morning on the far south side of Chicago. This was the first I heard of a gospel choir. There were no gospel songs then, we called them evangelistic songs.

His first **gospel** hit, "If You See My Savior, Tell Him That You Saw Me," which he composed in 1926, was a sensation at the 1930 Baptist Jubilee convention. After it caught on, Dorsey devoted himself full time to black gospel. He would become the key figure in the development of the music that he named and shaped.

Black Gospel Music

For much of the past century and into our own time, gospel music has been the most important and influential form of African-American religious music. It emerged as a new form of sacred music around 1930. Soon it became the most popular religious music within the black community due to the excellence of its major performers, the inherent appeal of the music, and tireless promotion by its key figures.

Black **gospel** blends white Protestant hymnody, the black spiritual, and more fervent religious music with the blues. Not surprisingly, considering his professional background and prominent role in the development of the music, it was Dorsey who brought the blues into gospel. Despite strong prejudices against secular influence on sacred music among certain segments of the black community, Dorsey didn't turn his back on the blues when he devoted himself to gospel music. As he said: "You see, when a thing becomes a part of you, you don't know when it's gonna manifest itself. And it's not your business to know or my business to know." It was the tinge of the blues that distinguished gospel from the spiritual and other forms of African-American sacred music.

Congregation and singers at a Gospel revival.

© Gerri Hernández/iStockphoto

Still, despite the blues influence, gospel music stood apart from secular African-American music. Its message was different from that of the blues. Blues comments on everyday life—good times and bad. Gospel, by contrast, is strictly good news. Again in Dorsey's words:

> This music lifted people out of the muck and mire of poverty and loneliness, of being broke, and gave them some kind of hope anyway. Make it anything [other] than good news, it ceases to be gospel.

The Early Years of Gospel

In its first two decades, gospel was a world unto itself. Performers traveled from stop to stop along the "Gospel Highway," churches and conventions where black believers congregated. Through the first decade, the music remained virtually unknown outside the black community; it gained a wider audience after World War II.

Dorsey was the glue that held the movement together during its formative stage. Although he credited Charles Tindley, another dynamic preacher and songwriter, as a major influence, Dorsey not only gave gospel music its name but also wrote about 1,000 songs (they were so popular that gospel songs were often called "Dorseys"). He discovered such top singers as Mahalia Jackson and Clara Ward, and organized major tours and events (he started the National Convention of Gospel Choirs and Choruses in 1933). No one did more to shape the sound of gospel music and put it on the musical map.

Gospel represented both a repertoire and a way of performing. Gospel songs included traditional hymns such as "Amazing Grace" and newer compositions by Tindley,

The Golden Gate Quartet on NBC Radio in the 1940s

Dorsey (such as "Precious Lord"), and W. Herbert Brewster ("How I Got Over"). There were two distinct performing traditions in early gospel music: male quartets and female solo singers. Mixed-gender groups were relatively uncommon, even in the forties and fifties.

One reason why male gospel singers formed into groups while females generally sang solo in the early days of gospel is that a male quartet can present complete harmonies in low and middle registers, which eliminates the need for accompanying instruments—as we hear in the Golden Gate Jubilee Quartet's recording. By contrast, a female group would not have a voice in the lower ranges, so that a performance would virtually demand some kind of instrumental accompaniment.

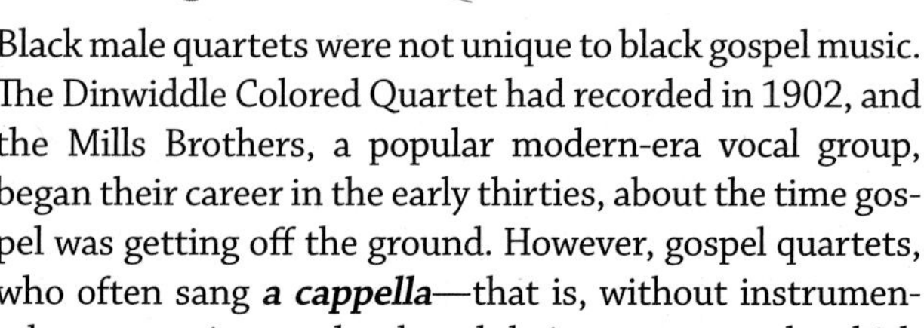

"This [gospel] music lifted people out of the muck and mire of poverty and loneliness."
—Thomas A. "Georgia Tom" Dorsey

Male Quartets

Black male quartets were not unique to black gospel music. The Dinwiddle Colored Quartet had recorded in 1902, and the Mills Brothers, a popular modern-era vocal group, began their career in the early thirties, about the time gospel was getting off the ground. However, gospel quartets, who often sang ***a cappella***—that is, without instrumental accompaniment, developed their own approach, which would often add rhythm section–like support to the lead vocal: not only harmony, but also a strong beat.

LISTENING CUE • **"Golden Gate Gospel Train," traditional (1937),** The Golden Gate Jubilee Quartet.

STYLE Black gospel • **FORM** Strophic, with last line of each verse serving as the chorus

Listen For . . .

INSTRUMENTATION
Four male voices

PERFORMANCE STYLE
Percussive vocal effects; train noises: sound imagination

RHYTHM
Syncopated accompaniment patterns under lead vocal

MELODY
Phrases start high, end low; built on pentatonic scale

HARMONY
Static: only one chord

Remember . . .

PERCUSSIVE VOCAL SOUNDS
Backup singers create percussive vocal sounds instead of using words.

PENTATONIC SCALE
Another example of black pentatonic scale, in a setting quite different from the blues

SYNCOPATED RHYTHMS IN ACCOMPANIMENT
Rhythms underneath lead vocal are much like the rhythms of a horn section in a big band behind a soloist.

RIFF-BASED MELODY
As in blues songs, melody grows out of repeated riffs, most of which start high and finish low.

STATIC HARMONY
Only one chord; anticipates more rhythmic forms of soul and—later—funk

Listen to this selection in CourseMate.

We hear this in "The Golden Gate Gospel Train," a song recorded by the Golden Gate Jubilee Quartet in 1937. The recording shows how resourceful such groups could be in depicting images in sound. The group replicates the sound of the train whistle and bell, as well as the chug of the engine. More important, the singers back up the lead vocalist with an accompaniment that supplies more rhythm than harmony. Both the static harmony and the percussive vocal sounds anticipate rock-era music, especially funk and rap. Other prominent African-derived elements include a melody of mostly descending phrases constructed from a pentatonic scale, blues-like inflection, and an active rhythmic texture.

Female Gospel Soloists

Women were the brightest stars on the gospel circuit. Vocalists such as Mahalia Jackson, Clara Ward, and Shirley Caesar sang alone, or at least in the forefront. Their accompaniment often included both piano and Hammond organ, both popular instruments in black churches; backup vocalists were optional.

The best gospel solo singers of the era sang with rich, resonant voices. They occasionally colored their singing with blues-like inflection and, more distinctively, expressive melismas (recall that a melisma is a group of pitches sung on a single syllable). During the thirties and forties, it was a sound distinct from every other kind of singing related to popular music: pop, jazz, country, blues, and others.

MAHALIA JACKSON

Mahalia Jackson's 1947 recording of "Move On Up a Little Higher" showcases her rich, blues-inflected voice. Dorsey may have brought the blues into gospel, but it was Mahalia Jackson (1911–1972) who adapted the feeling and style of her idol, Bessie Smith, to gospel singing.

Black gospel, especially when sung by women, gave the Hammond organ an early toehold in a style related to popular music. The Hammond organ was invented in the thirties and immediately found a home in churches, white and black, that could not afford a pipe organ. By contrast, it was a novelty instrument in popular music

LISTENING CUE • **"Move On Up a Little Higher" (1947),** W. Herbert Brewster and Virginia Davis. Mahalia Jackson, vocal.

STYLE Black gospel • **FORM** Strophic, with verses of varying length

Listen For . . .

INSTRUMENTATION
Vocal, piano, and organ

PERFORMANCE STYLE
Jackson's rich voice, with occasional melisma

RHYTHM
Slow tempo with "swinging" two-beat rhythm

MELODY
Mix between major scale and pentatonic scale (source of "blue notes")

HARMONY
Mostly static: only one chord, until the end of each verse; then progression away from and back to tonic

Remember . . .

VOCAL STYLE
Jackson's rich, blues-tinged voice and use of melisma would influence numerous black vocalists in the early years of the rock era.

USE OF HAMMOND ORGAN
Hammond organ, first sold in 1930s, would become a popular keyboard instrument in sixties rock. This is an early use of it in a non-pop setting.

RICH, BLUES-TINGED HARMONY
The static harmony and chord choices in the opening part of each verse show the influence of the blues. The quick progression at the end mixes blues notes into a conventional progression.

Listen to this selection in CourseMate.

and jazz; one heard it playing background music on radio soap operas and in cocktail lounges. It became a viable jazz instrument around 1960 and in rock and soul toward the end of the sixties.

From the 1950s until her death in 1972, Jackson was the Queen of Gospel: the face and voice of black gospel music not only within the black community but also to the wider public in America and abroad. She sang at John F. Kennedy's inauguration and supported the Civil Rights Movement during the 1960s. She exerted considerable influence on important rhythm-and-blues artists of the 1950s and 1960s, especially Aretha Franklin, the Queen of Soul, who heard her sing at her father's church.

Gospel Harmony

As it developed during the thirties and forties, gospel took its harmonic language from nineteenth-century European hymns and colored it with blues harmony. This produced a distinctive harmonic vocabulary, richer than blues, country, and rhythm and blues, yet distinct from the pop music of the same era.

Implicit in this distinctive harmonic approach is a message of hope. Even in "Move On Up a Little Higher," which has relatively static harmony throughout much of the song, there is a slight harmonic digression just before the end and a quick, straightforward return to the home key. This seems to suggest that no matter how stuck we are—harmonically or in life—we will find happiness when we go home—to the Lord, to heaven, and to the tonic. This kind of harmonic tension and release—drift away from the tonic chord, then return to it—is not present in conventional blues harmony in the same way; indeed, in one-chord songs like "Black Snake Moan," there is no possibility of harmonic tension.

The harmonic tension and release found in many gospel songs parallels the tension and release used in pre-rock pop. It has survived in rock-era music mainly in songs about love and happiness, most notably mainstream pop, by black and white acts.

UNIT 6

LOOKING BACK, LOOKING AHEAD

ALL OF THIS MUSIC—the numerous blues styles and black gospel—existed on the fringes of the popular music industry. The music was recorded commercially, but its target audience was narrowly circumscribed. As a result, it seldom achieved much traction in the marketplace before the end of World War II. Only boogie-woogie gained any notoriety. However, mainstream audiences encountered it mainly through white takes on the style, such as Tommy Dorsey's big-band "Boogie Woogie," rather the original versions. Mahalia Jackson's "Move On Up a Little Higher" actually made the charts, and she would soon gain international celebrity. But black gospel as a genre would, like the blues styles, largely remain under the radar through the 1950s. However, all three blues styles—country blues, hokum, and boogie—and black gospel would exert far more influence on rock-era music than their market share might suggest.

The Impact of Blues and Black Gospel Music

The blues styles helped shape two generations of rock. The rock and roll of Chuck Berry and Little Richard took its rhythm from fast boogie-woogie and its energy, exuberance, and multiple approaches to blues form from both boogie-woogie and hokum. In the 1960s, British rockers would dip deep into the blues, particularly the Delta blues of Robert Johnson and the amplified version that Muddy Waters created after he moved north. The rock of the Rolling Stones, the Who, Led Zeppelin, Cream, and numerous other acts evidences the profound influence in style and spirit of this most elemental blues style. Rock is inconceivable without these blues styles.

The most pervasive influence of gospel music—by far—was as a training ground for several generations of African-American singers. So many of the stars of the 1950s and 1960s, both solo artists and groups, began their performing careers as gospel singers, then traded the sanctuary for the stage—and the recording studio: Sam Cooke is the outstanding example. In effect, the church became a conservatory for so many rhythm and blues performers. They would graduate into doo-wop groups, Motown acts, girl groups, or solo careers. Few of the white teens listening to "Earth Angel" or so many other doo-wop hits were familiar with the sound of black gospel music, but they heard its echoes in much of the new sounds of rhythm and blues.

Gospel's legacy to rock-era popular music is substantial. Doo-wop, 1960s girl groups, Motown, and soul are inconceivable without gospel. Singing—the presence of both lead and backup singers, the vocal sounds and styles of the lead singers, call and response between lead and choir—is its most obvious contribution. In addition, its distinctive rhythms (especially the heavy backbeat), the Hammond organ, and rich harmony also filtered into rock-era music, both black and white.

In 1955, Ray Charles would scandalize the black church community by giving the gospel hymn "Jesus Is All the World to Me" new words and a new beat: the new song, "I Got a Woman," was his first big hit. Blues singer Big Bill Broonzy summed up what Charles had done and why it outraged so many when he said, "He's crying, sanctified. He's mixing the blues with the spirituals. He should be singing in a church."

If Broonzy had reflected a little on the history of black gospel, he might not have judged Charles so harshly. With Charles's late 1950s R&B hits, it was as if the connection between blues and black gospel had come full circle: Dorsey had brought the blues into African-American sacred music; Charles simply brought the sacred back into rhythm and blues.

It's not hard to understand Broonzy's objection, because here is a clear difference in intent and result between the blues and black gospel: one is for Saturday night and the other is for Sunday morning. Yet there is also common ground, as Charles demonstrated. By the 1960s, both the blues and black gospel were reshaping the sound of popular music, sometimes individually and occasionally in tandem. By the end of the decade, elements of both styles had become common currency.

Country and Folk Music Come in from the Outskirts

UNIT 7

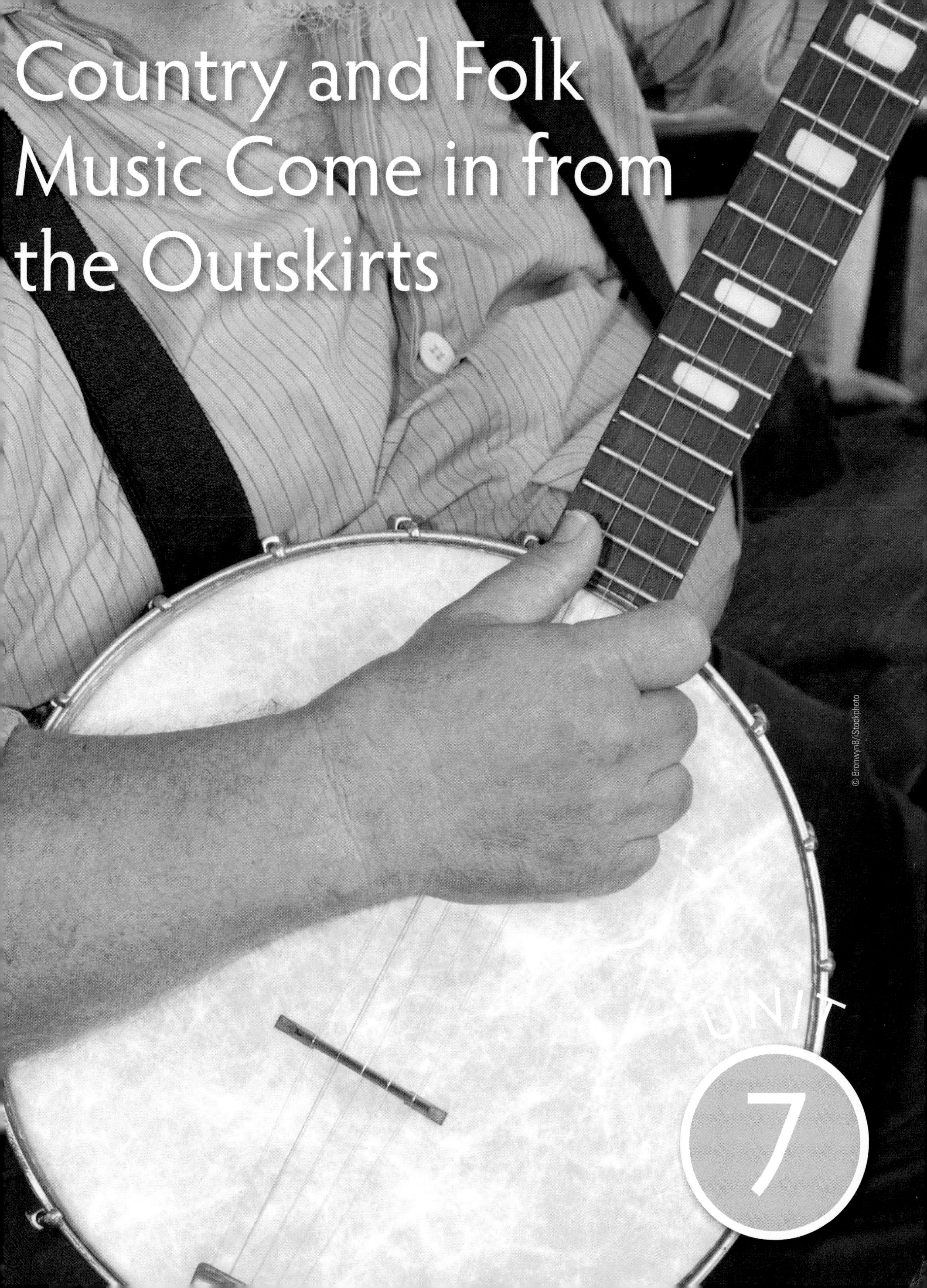

UNIT 7

What's the difference between country music and folk music? It depends on when you ask. If you asked in 1920, the answer would simply be "there is no difference": country music was a folk music. If you asked in 1960, the answer would be that the two styles shared little more than a common heritage and the fact that neither was a true folk music: Both had an industry behind them. One was down-home; the other was downtown. They had different sounds, different identities, and different agendas.

Before there was "country" music and "folk" music, there was folk music from the country—that is, the southern Appalachians. The music that spawned both country and folk came originally from the British Isles: England, Scotland, Wales, and Ireland. America's first European settlers brought their music with them. Some found their way into the mountains of Virginia, the Carolinas, and Georgia, where they preserved many of the songs and dances from their home countries and created new ones based on the music they had brought with them.

Recordings of the first country musicians and field recordings of folk musicians convey a sense of timelessness: Seemingly the music had not changed significantly in decades, even centuries. Early sources, including anecdotal evidence and dance tunes publications that date back to the seventeenth century, support this impression. So does the fieldwork of English folklorist Cecil Sharp. During trips through the southern Appalachians between 1916 and 1918, Sharp discovered songs that went back centuries and that were no longer sung in England.

When Sharp visited the United States, there was no such thing as "country music" or "folk music." The music that he heard and transcribed for posterity was a real folk music. That is, it was music made by members of a group for their own entertainment and passed down—and around—by ear. The musicians were not professional, and there was no industry or agency to support, promote, and preserve this music. It just was.

That would change within a decade. By the end of the 1920s, country music was on the map, its first stars were on record, and WSM in Nashville was broadcasting the Grand Ole Opry every Saturday night. And beginning in 1928, the Library of Congress began collecting and archiving folk music from the United States and its territories. In this unit, we sample music that illustrates the common heritage and divergent paths of folk music from the 1920s through the early 1950s.

CHAPTER 26

The Emergence of Country Music

Look at a current map of the southeastern United States and you'll find a web of interstate highways crisscrossing Virginia and West Virginia, the Carolinas, Tennessee, Alabama, Mississippi, Kentucky, and Louisiana. Were you to drive down one of these interstates and pull off, chances are you would find modern gas stations with minimarkets, chain motels, and a belt-stretching array of fast-food restaurants. There would be cable or satellite TV in the motel rooms and probably phone service to anywhere, as well as a modem hookup for your laptop. This is the twenty-first-century American South.

So it may be difficult to imagine a time when there were only dirt roads, few cars, no phones, no electricity, no running water, no indoor plumbing, no television or radio, no CD players, and no Internet. Whole regions lacked most if not all of the conveniences that we associate with modern life, and many of those who lived in the southern Appalachians had little knowledge of the outside world. A trip to the nearest large city often produced severe culture shock.

So it is a sweet irony that country music, which developed in the backwater that was the rural south and which reflects the traditional values of southern culture, is the product of a modern technology.

The Emergence of Country Music

The folk music of white southerners became **country music** when commercial radio came on the air and commercial records of this music arrived in stores. Before long, clear-channel AM radio—50,000-watt stations like WSM in Nashville, which began broadcasting in 1925—covered most of the country when the sun went down. WSM became the radio home to the *Grand Ole Opry* in 1928. Radio's impact on what would become known as country music was enormous, not only through broadcasting but also because of its impact on the recording industry: artists' live appearances on *Grand Ole Opry* or WLS's *Barn Dance* boosted their record sales.

The new technology helped create a class of professional, or at least semiprofessional, country musicians. Appearances on radio and records led to opportunities for live performances. Bands or solo acts with a weekly radio show would fill in the days between broadcasts with engagements in cities and towns within the listening area of their radio station.

Library of Congress, Prints and Photographs Division, Washington, DC

By 1930, a guitar player in Oklahoma could learn Virginian Maybelle Carter's distinctive accompanying style simply by buying a record and copying it.

Recordings helped spread the sound of "old-time music" beyond the South. By 1930, a guitar player in Oklahoma could learn Virginian Maybelle Carter's distinctive accompanying style simply by buying a record and copying it. Just as important, this new technology helped connect rural southerners to the outside world. They could share their own music and discover other kinds. This contact with like-minded musicians and the outside would become the main impetus for the evolution of country music.

In little more than a decade, what had been simply a folk music transplanted centuries ago from the British Isles had split into country and folk, two worlds that were almost mutually exclusive. And each world divided further into several streams, some creating paths to the mainstream, others running counter to the trend. At the heart of it all were the central tensions of this music: between commerce and culture, between innovation and preservation, between old and new, between inside and outside, and between staying home and roaming far and wide.

Ralph Peer and the Business of Country Music

The key figure in making country music a business was Ralph Peer (1892–1960). Peer was arguably the most influential man in country music during its first three decades. He played an instrumental role in finding it, disseminating it, and making money for those who created it.

Peer grew up in Missouri and as a young man helped his father sell sewing machines and phonographs. He went to work for Columbia Records, moved to Okeh Records in 1920, and moved again in 1925 to Victor. As a talent scout and producer, Peer would go from town to town, setting up temporary recording studios wherever he could. Word would spread that he was coming, and musicians would come down from the hills to record for him. Peer always seemed to be at the right place at the right time. He was responsible for the first on-location recording and the first country recording to be released, Fiddlin' John Carson's "The Little Log Cabin in the Lane" (1923). A few years later, he helped give old-time music a new name: hillbilly music. The term *hillbilly* had been in use since the turn of the century to identify rural white southerners, but its musical association dates from a 1925 recording session with Al Hopkins, leader of a four-man string band (a small group consisting mainly of string instruments of various types). Peer, who was running the session, asked Hopkins to give his band a name. Hopkins replied, "Call the band anything you want. We are nothing but a bunch of hillbillies from North Carolina and Virginia anyway"; they became Al Hopkins and His Hillbillies.

Peer was an astute businessman. He negotiated a split of the publishing rights to the songs he recorded for Victor and created his own publishing firm, Southern Music, in 1928. Southern Music grew into one of the leading publishers of country music and made Peer a rich and powerful man.

Peer also played a key role in establishing BMI (Broadcast Music Incorporated), a music licensing organization sponsored by the radio industry. Music licensing was the mechanism by which those who created the music received payment from those who made money from it. ASCAP, the American Society of Composers, Authors, and Publishers, the dominant licensing organization since its formation in 1914, required five hit songs for membership—a requirement that in effect excluded almost everyone who was not part of the pop-music inner circle. In particular, country music songwriters and black musicians were on the outside, looking in. So were most of those just starting their careers.

Library of Congress, Prints and Photographs Division, Washington, DC

In 1923, Ralph Peer produced the first country recording, Fiddlin' John Carson's "The Little Log Cabin in the Lane."

When ASCAP proposed a massive increase in royalties from the agreement they had signed in 1932, broadcasters formed their own organization. They chartered Broadcast Music Incorporated in 1939; BMI opened its doors early the next year. Unlike ASCAP, BMI accepted all aspiring songwriters. Overnight, all musicians had a potential stake in the music industry. That was good news for those who had been on the outside, looking in, especially jazz, country, and blues musicians. Many joined BMI, which gave the organization some much-needed leverage. Peer's support played a big role in getting BMI off the ground.

Peer's musical and business interests went well beyond country music. Almost as soon as he began working for Okeh Records, he set up the first race record recording session, which produced Mamie Smith's "Crazy Blues," and he negotiated the rights to Victor's race records along with the hillbilly music he had been recording. By the early 1930s, he had branched into popular music; and after a trip to Mexico, he secured the rights to several Latin hits. He continued to diversify his catalog after World War II by signing up rockabilly and rhythm-and-blues artists.

As his pragmatic, entrepreneurial, and open-minded stance toward music suggests, Peer represented the progressive direction in country music. He helped transform a folk music into a powerful segment of the music business. However, Peer had nothing to do with one of the most popular country music recordings of all time.

Vernon Dalhart and Country Music's First Big Hit

Dalhart is a town of about 8,000 people in the northwest corner of the Texas panhandle, which is as about as far north as you can get and still be in Texas. Vernon is another Texas small town; it lies about 250 miles southeast of Dalhart. No interstate connects the two towns, but they are linked in popular music history by an alias.

Marion Slaughter (1883–1948) grew up near Jefferson, Texas, a small town about 20 miles east of the Louisiana state line and 50 miles south of the Oklahoma border. Perhaps because his family lived up to its name—Slaughter's father killed his mother's brother during a saloon fight when Slaughter was ten years old—Slaughter decided to change his name, not once but many times. He did it for the first time in 1912, shortly after he moved to New York. His first stage name was Vernon Dalhart: Allegedly, he had punched cattle in the panhandle as a young man. He began his professional career that year as an opera singer, and made his first recordings four years later, in 1916. By the end of the teens, he was recording many different kinds of music, from opera to minstrel-ish popular songs (he billed himself as Bob White on these recordings). In the course of his career, he would record under about two dozen names. However, Vernon Dalhart remained his first choice as a stage name.

Vernon Dalhart

Dalhart could record under several names, because he never signed a contract with any one company. During the 1920s and 1930s, he probably made more recordings than any other singer, for virtually every record label in business at the time. His various aliases gave him the freedom to move easily from label to label. He recorded "The Prisoner's Song" for Victor, which had just established a Country Records Department.

"The Prisoner's Song"

"The Prisoner's Song" is the song that has secured his place in history Dalhart recorded it in 1924 as the "B" side of a popular "event" song, "The Wreck of the Old 97." ("Event" songs have a long history in folk and country music—and blues; this one is about a train wreck.) The two sides represented a return to his Texas roots; at the same time, they show how far he had moved away from them.

The song is simple—and confusing. What's simple is the music. The melody consists of a single phrase with alternate endings. A simple three-chord accompaniment supports it. These are the same three chords that we encountered in the blues, but in an even simpler sequence. We hear a violist play the melody when Dalhart doesn't sing, and play an obbligato (a second, and secondary, melody) toward the end.

The lyric is both simple and confusing. Its language and the images that it portrays are simple enough, but the narrative meanders from one scene to the next, and

LISTENING CUE • **"The Prisoner's Song" (1924),** Guy Massey. Vernon Dalhart, vocal.

STYLE Early commercial country • **FORM** Strophic

Listen For . . .

INSTRUMENTATION
Voice, guitar, and viola

PERFORMANCE STYLE
Dalhart has a trained voice with only a hint of twang; classical viola playing instead of country fiddling.

RHYTHM
Simple timekeeping in accompaniment with no strong syncopations in the melody

HARMONY
Simple four-chord progression using the three basic chords repeated over and over

MELODY
Four short phrases, in a question/answer relationship

Remember . . .

STORY-TELLING SONG IN A SIMPLE SETTING
The lyric that tells a story, the simple, repetitive melody, and the strophic form suggest its origins as a folk song, or at least a folk-style song

UNLIKELY HIT
"The Prisoner's Song" is strikingly different from 1920s pop: a simple chord instrument instead of a rhythm section; no dance beat or syncopation; no riffs.

"CROSSOVER" COUNTRY
For non-country audiences, Dalhart's pleasant voice and clear enunciation and the classical viola offer more familiar sounds; the rough edges of old-time fiddle music are absent. The form and style of the song and Dalhart's slight twang give the recording a country flavor.

Listen to this selection in CourseMate.

we never learn why the protagonist is in jail—at the end of the song, the story still hasn't been told.

Oh! I wish I had someone to love me,
Someone to call me their own.
Oh! I wish I had someone to live with
'cause I'm tired of living alone.

Oh! Please meet me tonight in the moonlight
Please meet me tonight all alone.
For I have a sad story to tell you,
It's a story that's never been told.

I'll be carried to the new jail tomorrow,
Leaving my poor darling alone.
With the cold prison bars all around me
And my head on a pillow of stone.

Now I have a grand ship on the ocean
All mounted with silver and gold.
And before my poor darling would suffer, Oh!
That ship would be anchored and sold.

Now if I had wings like an angel
Over these prison walls I would fly.
And I'd fly to the arms of my poor darlin'
And there I'd be willing to die.

The confusion lies in its history, its style, and its success. Dalhart claimed that he heard the song from his cousin, Guy Massey—he insisted that it was a folk song that had been around for years, and it almost certainly was. But others involved in the recording, the guitarist Carson Robison and the producer Nat Shilkret, each claimed a share of the song.

As he sings, we hear traces of Dalhart's east Texas accent, but we also hear a trained voice far different from the harsh twang of most early country singers. And instead of fiddle and banjo, we hear a viola, played in a classical rather than a country style, and a guitar. All of this sends a mixed message: This is a country song, but it has taken a Saturday night bath and put on its best clothes.

Success versus Identity in Country Music

The song was a huge success—perhaps the second-best-selling song from the first half of the century, behind Bing Crosby's version of "White Christmas." And it seemed to come out of nowhere. Dalhart was popular enough: He had already made 400 recordings by 1924, the year he recorded "The Prisoner's Song," and he would make well over 1,000 before the end of his career. But this song represented a new direction for him—away from opera and pop and back toward his southwest country roots.

Perhaps it was the combination of simplicity and novelty. We don't know why it was popular, but we do know that it was. And it showed country musicians the surest path to commercial success—blend country with other, more popular styles.

"The Prisoner's Song" effectively brought to light what would become one of the ongoing tensions in country music: identity versus popularity. The tension comes from determining the extent to which those features that give country music its distinctive sound—for example, the vocal style and the characteristic instruments and playing styles—have to be toned down in order to broaden its appeal. Staying true to one's roots brought the approval and support of country music's core audience. Mainstreaming the style promised greater commercial success, and the fame and fortune that went with it. Country performers continue to find it a difficult balancing act.

CHAPTER 27
Country Music's Seminal Acts

At the tail end of July 1927, Ralph Peer got off the train with his recording equipment and set up a temporary studio in a hotel on State Street in Bristol, Tennessee, for an open call for musicians. Over the next four days, he recorded two of country music's most important and influential acts: the Carter Family on August 1 and 2, and Jimmie Rodgers on August 4. Country music historian Bill Malone contrasted them in this way:

> Rodgers brought into clear focus the tradition of the rambling man. . . . This ex-railroad man conveyed the impression that he had been everywhere and had experienced life to the fullest. His music suggested a similar openness of spirit, a willingness to experiment, and a receptivity to alternative styles. The Carter Family, in contrast, represented the impulse toward home and stability, a theme as perennially attractive as that of the rambler. When the Carters sang, they evoked images of the country church, Mama and Daddy, [and] the family fireside. . . . Theirs was a music that might borrow from other forms, but would move away from its roots only reluctantly.

The Carter Family

The Carter Family, one of the most influential groups in the history of country music, consisted of Alvin Pleasant "A. P." Carter (1891–1960); his wife, Sara (1898–1979; after 1933, his ex-wife); and his sister-in-law, Maybelle (1909–1978). All three sang, Sara played guitar and autoharp, and Maybelle developed one of the most widely imitated guitar styles in the history of country music. A. P. had grown up playing the fiddle and learning ballads and other songs from his mother, and he never lost his love for this music. The Carter Family performed and recorded traditional songs that A. P. had collected and arranged, often in an unpaid partnership with his black chauffeur. Among the best known was their 1928 recording of a song they called "Wildwood Flower." It had started out as a commercially published parlor song entitled "I'll Twine 'Mid the Ringlets"; but like so many nineteenth-century commercial songs, "Wildwood Flower" found its way into the oral tradition.

The sound of the Carter Family was an intriguing mix of old and new. Certainly the song was old, although not nearly as old as those Cecil Sharp had heard in 1918. Maybelle's singing exemplifies one **traditional country vocal sound**—flat, nasal, and without much inflection.

It is the accompaniment that begins the break with the past. There is no fiddle, just guitar, and a clear division between melody and accompaniment. The most important and influential feature of the accompaniment is Maybelle's **thumb-brush style.** She plays the melody on the lower strings and, between melody notes, brushes the chords on the upper strings.

The Carters' professional career lasted from their discovery by Ralph Peer in 1927 until 1943. After World War II, Maybelle and her daughters continued to tour as the Carter Family, and subsequent incarnations of the group performed through the 1960s.

LISTENING CUE • **"Wildwood Flower," traditional (1928),** The Carter Family.

STYLE Country ballad • **FORM** Strophic: four-line stanzas for each verse

Listen For . . .

INSTRUMENTATION
Voice and guitar

PERFORMANCE STYLE
Pure, plain vocal sound; innovative "thumb-brush" guitar style

MELODY
Four short phrases form an arch: rise, then fall

HARMONY
Three chords (I, IV, V); mostly I

Remember . . .

SAD STORY
Ballads often tell sad stories; this is one. Absence of overt emotion in singing belies pain of love lost.

PURE COUNTRY VOCAL STYLE
Strong, nasal sound, with no vibrato

GUITAR STYLE
Thumb-brush guitar style (melody on bottom, chords on top) borrowed by Woody Guthrie, then folk revivalists of 1960s

Listen to this selection in CourseMate.

Jimmie Rodgers

Jimmie Rodgers (1897–1933) had a brief but extraordinarily influential career. His musical legacy, preserved primarily through recordings, inspired an entire generation. According to Bill Malone, "Ernest Tubb estimated that perhaps 75 percent of modern country music performers were directly or indirectly influenced to . . . either through hearing Rodgers in person or through his recordings."

Born in Mississippi, Rodgers spent much of his childhood and early adult life around the railroad, at first accompanying his father, a gang foreman, and then working off and on as a railroad man, before contracting the tuberculosis that was to end his life so prematurely at age thirty-six.

Rodgers's first recordings made him one of country music's first stars. Almost immediately, he was making $2,000 a month in record royalties alone. For the rest of his life, he enjoyed great popularity throughout the South in personal appearances, radio broadcasts, and frequent recordings.

Forced to move to Texas because of his illness, he gained an especially strong following in the Southwest. The greater receptiveness of southwestern country music to outside influences is surely due in part to Rodgers.

The image of the rambling man roaming far and wide that Rodgers carefully cultivated in his songs had great appeal for his fans. Musically, Rodgers borrowed liberally from all the styles with which he came into contact: Tin Pan Alley song, blues, and jazz.

"Blue Yodel No. 11," one of thirteen blue yodels that Rodgers recorded, is a blues in its lyrics, melodic style, harmony, form, and style. Rodgers sounds natural and at ease singing a blues. He has captured essential elements of the blues singing style: rhythmically free and unstilted delivery of text, highly inflected phrasing (listen to the extra emphasis on "presents" in the third phrase of the first section), and a vocal style more expressive than pretty.

Country Music: Tradition versus Innovation

There is something almost karmic about Peer's August recording sessions with the Carter Family and Jimmie Rodgers. It's not surprising that the Carters came to Bristol; it was not far from their home. But Bristol was some distance from Rodgers's home in Mississippi. As it happened, however, Rodgers moved to Asheville, North Carolina, in 1927 and was working with musicians who came from Bristol. So it was seemingly coincidental that the two acts made their recording debuts within a few days of each other.

What makes this coincidence so striking is that the Carter Family and Jimmie Rodgers represent opposing trends. The Carters represented the conservative impulse in country music. They recorded traditional songs in the traditional style and performed them with traditional instruments. By contrast, Rodgers staked out the evolutionary path of country music. He drew on the blues, pop, jazz, and country music of the time, and wrote his own songs. The Carters preserved the past; Rodgers showed the way to the future of country music.

LISTENING CUE • **"Blue Yodel No. 11" (1929),** Jimmie Rodgers. Rodgers, vocal and guitar.

STYLE Blues sung by country singer • **FORM** Blues form, but with irregular timing and extension for yodel at end of each phrase

Listen For . . .

INSTRUMENTATION
Voice and two guitars (Rodgers and Burke)

PERFORMANCE STYLE
Blues inflections–stressed syllables, sliding into notes, and conversational pacing. The yodeling at the ends of sections is a Rodgers trademark.

RHYTHM
Lazy four-beat rhythm. Rodgers's singing plays off the beat, as is common in blues singing. Occasional confusion about timing.

MELODY
Short phrases that start high and finish low; most are derived from pentatonic scale.

HARMONY
Basic blues progression, with occasional modification of the timing

Remember . . .

COMMON BLUES SUBJECT
"Blue Yodel No. 11" is about man/woman problems.

RODGERS'S INFLUENCE
Rodgers was the most influential of the early country musicians. His assimilation of non-country styles—and especially black styles like blues and jazz—became the major inspiration for change in country music.

FIRST "WHITE MAN WITH A NEGRO FEEL"
Rodgers sings the blues idiomatically 25 years before Elvis.

Listen to this selection in CourseMate.

CHAPTER 28

Putting the "Western" in Country Music

In August, 1928, the Federal Radio Commission (FRC) issued General Order 40, which reallocated the AM radio spectrum among local, regional, and clear-channel stations. Local stations could broadcast at only 100 watts of power. Regional stations had an upper limit of 1000 watts. Clear-channel stations broadcast from 10,000 to 50,000 watts of power. The range of a radio signal correlates to its wattage. The listening area for local stations was only a few miles, but on a good night the signals from clear-channel stations could be heard hundreds of miles away. One objective of the FRC's general order was to make radio available to those in rural areas who were not served by local or regional stations.

As part of the reallocation agreement, the FRC divided the country into five regions and assigned frequencies among the three types of stations so that there would be no overlap during the day. However, local stations that shared a frequency with a clear-channel station whose signal reached into their service areas ceased broadcasting at sundown, to avoid interference with the clear-channel stations.

The Boundaries of Country Music

In large part because of clear-channel radio, country music soon spread beyond the South. When the sun went down, 50,000-watt stations like WSM in Nashville covered much of the country, so later that year listeners hundreds of miles from Nashville could tune in to the Grand Ole Opry every Saturday night. Five years later, NBC began broadcasting its National Barn Dance. Later in the 1930s, Mexican radio stations exceeded the 50,000-watt limit imposed by the FCC; some also broadcast country music. Even as record sales dipped, radio more than picked up the slack.

Country music also spread because of Depression-driven migration. Hard times compelled people from the South and Southwest to look elsewhere for work. Especially during the Dust Bowl of the early 1930s, they went west and north and brought their music with them.

Even as it spread west and north, country music retained its home base, becoming a regional music with an international following. Nashville quickly became its commercial and cultural center, a status it has maintained into the twenty-first century. Country music did not shift its operational base to New York or Los Angeles when it entered the popular-music mainstream; the music industry came to Nashville.

Location was—and is—an integral part of the identity of country music. During the 1930s and 1940s, it went hand in hand with the preservation of musical tradition, as Bob Wills would find out during his one appearance on the Grand Ole Opry. By contrast, change or countertrends in country music have often originated some distance from Nashville. We explore this idea through the music of two musicians who helped put the "western" in "country and western music."

Horse Operas

It was inevitable that there would be musical westerns. America had long had a love affair with cowboys and the Wild West. Kids idolized not only the good guys like Wyatt Earp and William "Buffalo Bill" Cody (at least we thought he was a good guy), but also bad guys like outlaws Jesse James and William "Billy the Kid" Bonney. Cowboy songs like "Home on the Range" and "Git Along, Little Dogies" were as much a part of everyday life as Foster's minstrel songs, patriotic anthems, and current hits. It simply remained for Hollywood to put everything together. Beginning in 1935, it did.

The first singing cowboy on screen was Gene Autry (1907–1998). As a young man, he got a job as a telegraph

Poster for Republic's 1936 film *The Singing Cowboy* with Gene Autry.

operator. Autry was passing the time singing and playing the guitar one day in 1926, when a man walked in to send a telegram. The man was Will Rogers, the most popular humorist of the twenties and thirties. Rogers asked Autry to keep singing, then suggested that he get a job in radio. After an unsuccessful audition for Victor in 1927, Autry landed a radio show in 1929. This led to a recording contract later that year. After much success on radio and record—he was featured on the Grand Ole Opry and National Barn Dance, and Sears, Roebuck sponsored his radio show and promoted his records—Autry made his way to Hollywood in 1934.

The next year, he starred in the film *Tumbling Tumbleweeds*. The film is generally considered to be the first musical western (or horse opera) because the plot depends on the singing ability of Autry's character. The success of the film created a demand for singing cowboys. Autry became one of the most popular Hollywood stars, and other singing cowboys, like Roy Rogers and Tex Ritter, were not far behind. For many Americans in the 1930s and 1940s—especially those who went to the movies but didn't listen to the Grand Ole Opry—this was country music.

Among Autry's most popular musical westerns was the 1939 film *South of the Border*. In it, Autry and his sidekick (cowboy stars always have sidekicks) are federal agents investigating some funny business in Mexico. Along the way, Autry stops long enough to sing a few songs, including the title track, "South of the Border."

"South of the Border" is the work of Jimmy Kennedy, an Irish lyricist, and a British songwriter named Michael Carr. The song is a pop songwriter's take on an American cowboy song. The short, unsyncopated phrases of the melody recall songs like "Home on the Range," but there are slick touches in both melody and harmony that betray the songwriter's skill and pop orientation. The rich string background is all Hollywood; the piano- and percussionless rhythm section is Hollywood's evocation of the string-band sound. Two of the featured instruments have regional associations: The accordion evokes Mexico, while the steel guitar represents the most distinctive new sound in country music.

Autry's singing has a distinct southwestern flavor. It is pleasant, without much of the twang we associate with country music. As such, it represents a country—or western—crossover style—the first of many for country music.

Western songs lay out a formula for country crossover success:

- Begin with a vocal sound that is recognizably country, but not intensely so.
- Sing a simple melody with a simple accompaniment based mainly on three chords.
- Add in some country instrumental sounds, then mix in a little pop sophistication: more complex chords, melodic lines, and forms.
- Package it with an appealing personality.

LISTENING CUE · "South of the Border" (1939), Jimmy Kennedy and Michael Carr. Gene Autry, vocals.

STYLE Hollywood-style cowboy song • **FORM** expansive AABA with short tag ("Ay, ay, ay, ay")

Listen For . . .

INSTRUMENTATION
Vocal, plus prominent strings, accordion, and steel guitar, guitar, bass

PERFORMANCE STYLE
Autry's pleasant voice features light country influence.

RHYTHM
Light two-beat rhythm, with no strong syncopations, throughout most of the song; shift to a Latinish rhythm in the bridge (B section) of the song

MELODY
A section consists of a series of short phrases with quick rise and fall.

TEXTURE
Secondary melodic figures by accordion and steel guitar answer vocal phrases.

Remember . . .

DETAILED STORY
Unlike the majority of pop songs, "South of the Border" tells a story.

COUNTRY TINGE
Autry's pleasant "western" sound, steel guitar, and guitar/bass rhythm section give the track a country-pop flavor.

HOLLYWOOD TRIMMINGS
Rich string sound, Latin sounds (accordion) and rhythms make the setting responsive to the lyrics (and the film) even as it also imparts a more pop-oriented sound.

Listen to this selection in CourseMate.

The formula certainly worked for Autry, and it would work for many more country and western singers for generations to come.

Putting the Swing in Country Music

Bob Wills (1905–1975) was country music's first maverick. Wills grew up in a musical family, learned mandolin and fiddle, and played with his father at local dances. However, Wills was drawn not only to the fiddle music he heard and learned growing up, but also the other new sounds of the 1920s, and especially blues and jazz; he reportedly rode 50 miles on horseback to hear Bessie Smith sing. Not surprisingly, when he formed the Texas Playboys (the band that would create his legacy) during the mid-1930s, he blended the country string-band sound with pop, blues, and jazz and country music's newest "traditional" instrument, the steel guitar, into a new style called **western swing,** a country take on big band swing and jazz.

In Wills' version of western swing, the blues and jazz influence was most often evident in the heavier beat, the fuller instrumentation, and the styles of many of the soloists. Wills surrounded himself with good musicians, and gave them ample opportunity to showcase their skills, as we hear on his 1936 recording of "Steel Guitar Rag."

"Steel Guitar Rag" features Leon McAuliffe playing the then-novel electric steel guitar. The **electric steel guitar** stands alone among contemporary popular instruments as the signature instrument for two—and only two—kinds of music: Hawaiian and country. These are two different musical worlds, yet the instrument sounds equally at home in both.

During the 1920s, there was a tremendous vogue for Hawaiian music. Hawaiian guitarists, playing the lap steel guitar, were a vaudeville staple, and most of the bigger music publishers published learn-at-home methods for the instrument. In search of a more powerful sound, instrument makers created the dobro, a guitar with a built-in steel resonator that also was played on the lap. (The term *dobro* reportedly comes from Dopyera Brothers, a family of Czech immigrants who created the first dobros in 1928; dobro also means "good" in Czech). The electric steel guitar, invented in the early thirties, soon replaced the dobro as the instrument of choice for lap guitarists. As with the steel guitar, the origins of the electric steel guitar are cloudy, but it seems safe to say that the steel guitar was the first electric guitar.

LISTENING CUE • **"Steel Guitar Rag" (1936),** Leon McAuliffe. Bob Wills and His Texas Playboys, featuring Leon McAuliffe, electric steel guitar.

STYLE Western swing • **FORM** ABC for the melody; solos only on A (A and C share same chord progression)

Listen For . . .

INSTRUMENTATION
Steel guitar in the spotlight, plus small horn section (trumpets and saxophones stand out) and rhythm section (including piano, bass, and drums)

PERFORMANCE STYLE
Occasional blues-influenced bent notes in steel guitar line

RHYTHM
Fast tempo; two-beat rhythm with a strong backbeat

MELODY
Riffs in A and B; rag-like figuration in B and C

HARMONY
I, IV, V most of the time, with long stretches on I

Remember . . .

BLUES INFLUENCE
A few blue notes in the melody and a few bent notes in McAuliffe's playing

JAZZ INFLUENCE
Improvising style in piano and sax solos; expanded instrumentation—Wills augments the traditional country band with a full rhythm section and a small horn section, plus the steel guitar; use of drums—Wills was the first important country bandleader to use drums.

HONKY-TONK BEAT
Countrified two-beat: clear OOM-pah rhythm with a crisp backbeat

COUNTRIFYING
Rhythm (two-beat), melody (blues/rag inspiration), and sound (steel guitar) all demonstrate country adaptation of outside influences.

BOB WILLS = COUNTRY PROGRESSIVE
Western swing would influence honky-tonk, rockabilly, and country rock.

Listen to this selection in CourseMate.

© Pictorial Press Ltd/Alamy

BOB WILLS (at the microphone) and His Texas Playboys in 1937, before their signature Stetson hats.

Wills' spotlighting an almost brand-new instrument on a strictly instrumental song is only the most prominent of several innovations. Wills and the Texas Playboys were not responsible for all of them, but, as the most popular band in the Southwest during the late 1930s and 1940s, they did more than anyone else to popularize them, and most of them eventually wove their way into the fabric of country music.

In his receptiveness to black music, Wills certainly drew on Jimmie Rodgers' legacy, and like Rodgers, Wills also left an enduring legacy of stylistic innovation in country music. No one did more to promote the sound of western swing than Bob Wills, and few did more to update the sound of country music. The impact of his music would become even more apparent after World War II.

The Expansion of Country Music

It was inevitable that country music would evolve as soon as it became a commercial music. The pressures of the marketplace and the curiosity and creativity of the musicians all but guaranteed it. The two examples discussed in this chapter demonstrate country music expanded stylistically as well as geographically.

The tracks by Autry and Wills also illustrate two important musical features of country music: its two dominant evolutionary paths and its retention of identity through change. "South of the Border" exemplifies the pop-oriented evolutionary direction. The pop trimmings—from the song itself, which Autry heard in Europe, liked, and brought back with him, to the rich string accompaniment—almost smother the country elements. This was Hollywood's conception of "western" music. By contrast, "Steel Guitar Rag" illustrates the evolutionary direction influenced by African-American music, particularly blues and jazz: The "rag" in the title implies as much. The full rhythm, strong beat keeping, horn sections, extended solos, and McAuliffe's bent notes—all features of black and black-influenced music—clearly show a dramatic departure from the traditional vocal and fiddle sounds of the first country recordings.

Still, country music retained and reshaped its identity through a two-part strategy: preserving its core features and "countrifying" the influences that it assimilated. The two most enduring musical elements of country music during this time are a clear, honest vocal style, often nasal and without vibrato or fullness, and the fiddle style popular for generations throughout the South, and elsewhere, through the minstrel show. Both have been least susceptible to change, seem to predate any outside influence, and still help define the country sound. Autry has a pleasant singing voice with enough of a twang to differentiate him from the crooners that were popular during the 1930s and 1940s.

At the same time, as they absorbed these various elements—popular songs, new instruments, blues riffs, and so on—into their music, country musicians typically gave them a decidedly country stamp. In country music, reinterpretation has often followed assimilation. Wills' western swing exemplifies this: It's good dance music, but the rhythmic feel of the music is distinctly different from the big band swing heard earlier in this survey. Even more, the steel guitar, borrowed from Hawaiian music by way of vaudeville, becomes the contemporary sound signature of country music, a complement to the fiddle.

Country music began the 1930s as a mainly regional music. It ended the 1930s with a broader audience, more varied styles, and two clear evolutionary paths. Its evolution would take another significant step after World War II.

CHAPTER 29

Folk Music in the 1930s and 1940s

In 1928, the Library of Congress established an Archive of American Folk Song within its Music Division. Through the efforts of Robert W. Gordon, its first director, it soon amassed a substantial and varied body of music. Among its early acquisitions were recordings of Native Americans, ex-slaves, Hawaiians, and folk songs and fiddle music from the Appalachians, collected by Gordon himself.

The first curator of the archive was John Lomax (1867–1948), who was born in Mississippi and grew up in Texas. While a graduate student at Harvard, he met George Kittredge, an eminent folklorist who encouraged Lomax's longstanding interest in cowboy songs. Lomax returned to teaching but was fired in 1917, when he came out on the wrong end of a tug of war between the president of the University of Texas and the governor of Texas (who was later impeached). After moving to Chicago, Lomax worked in banking for the next fifteen years.

About the time most people think about retirement, Lomax returned to the music that had been his passion since childhood. In 1932, he secured a contract from a leading publisher for a wide-ranging anthology of folk ballads. He had previously prepared a collection of cowboy songs in 1910, which had been well received. After signing the contract, he went to the newly established Archive of American Folk Song to examine its holdings. In 1933, he made the first of his field trips through the South, where, using equipment mounted in the trunk of his car, he recorded folksingers. Soon the Library of Congress became the locus of the contemporary folk movement. Lomax and his son Alan not only recorded folk musicians of all kinds during their field trips but also brought several to Washington, D.C.

By the early 1940s, the contemporary folk movement—"**folk music**" as a commercial music—had begun to take shape. The movement had three branches: professional performance opportunities for folk performers, composition of topical songs written and performed in a folk style, and the revival of folk songs by musicians who were not part of the culture that was home to the music.

Woody Guthrie and Contemporary Folk Music

Whether it's riding a horse on the range, hopping a train, or driving an eighteen-wheeler down the interstate, one of the enduring images in country music is the traveling man. But you wouldn't find America's greatest musical wanderer on the stage of the Grand Ole Opry, even though he was born in a small town in Oklahoma and borrowed his guitar style directly from Maybelle Carter. Instead, he forged a new path—one that helped create the contemporary folk movement.

WOODY GUTHRIE, 1943

NY World Telegram/Al Aumuller//Library of Congress, Prints and Photographs Division, Washington, DC

For Woody Guthrie (1912–1967), growing up was hard. His parents were pioneers. His sister died when a stove exploded; his father rode the oil boom, then went bust; and his mother ended up in a mental institution with an undiagnosed case of Huntington's chorea, a congenital disease that would curtail Guthrie's career and claim his life. He left home at sixteen, just before the stock market crash and a few years before the Dust Bowl drove so many Oklahomans west in search of a better life.

His first stop was Pampas, Texas, where his uncle, Jack Guthrie, nurtured his interest in country music. Before long, he had assembled the Corncob Trio and was doing what so many other country bands were doing. But his music soon went in a different direction, and in the early thirties he started writing songs. Here is how he described them in *Bound for Glory,* his novel-like autobiography:

> Some people liked me, hated me, walked with me, walked over me, jeered me, cheered me, rooted me and hooted me, and before long I was invited in and booted out of every public place of entertainment. But I decided that songs was a music and a language of all tongues.
>
> I never did make up many songs about the cow trails or the moon skipping through the sky, but at first it was funny songs of what all's wrong, and how it turned out good or bad. Then I got a little braver and made up songs telling what I thought was wrong and how to make it right, songs that said what everybody in that country was thinking. And this has held me ever since.

Guthrie makes clear that he is the champion of the working class. In the course of his career, he wrote songs—more than a thousand of them—told stories, and authored articles (for a Communist Party newspaper) that commented on social injustice, the lives of the poor and the unknown, and anything else that caught his sharp eye. He spent most of the 1930s crisscrossing the United States, sometimes hopping trains to get from one place to the next.

In 1940, he made his way to New York, where Alan Lomax (also a Library of Congress folklorist) discovered him singing at a "Grapes of Wrath" rally for farm workers. Within a year, Lomax recorded him at the Library of Congress and featured him on his radio show. Pete Seeger was also part of the liberal/radical circle in which Lomax moved, and Guthrie joined Seeger and two others in 1941 to form the Almanac Singers.

"Do-Re-Mi"

In "Do-Re-Mi," a song Guthrie wrote in 1937, we can hear what drew Lomax, Seeger, and working-class folk to his music. We don't listen to Guthrie's songs for the beauty of his singing; what Robert Christgau calls his "vocal deadpan" was the opposite of the crooning of Bing Crosby, whom Guthrie openly despised. And we don't listen for the sophistication of the accompaniment; Guthrie was fond of saying that three chords were one too many. We listen for the words.

With no sugarcoating, Guthrie tells the tough-times story of the desperate people who migrated west in search of a decent life. He gets his point across with a wry humor that intensifies the grim circumstances that he describes. This is a funny song that isn't funny at all.

Guthrie's music is centuries old and brand new at the same time. In his music are echoes of British broadside ballads, a tradition that dates back to the sixteenth century. (A **broadside** is a topical text sung to a well-known tune. Broadsides were, in effect, an urban folk music with printed words.) In fact, Guthrie occasionally fashioned new words to familiar songs, in true broadside and folk tradition. But in the musical context of the 1930s—the world of silver-screen pop, swinging big-band jazz, singing cowboys, and crooners—Guthrie's songs stood apart. From the late 1930s through the end of World War II, there was no sharper musical commentator on the inequities of life in America, no more persistent musical voice for social justice, and no more prolific musical advocate for the cause of the working class than Woody Guthrie.

He wrote and delivered his songs in a folk style, sometimes fitting old melodies with new words, but the songs were new. In so doing, he helped made folk a commercial music—even if much of the time his songs had an anticommercial message. He also made folk a living music. Others, most notably the Weavers, would follow in his footsteps.

Relocating Folk Music

For jazz aficionados, the Village Vanguard, located in New York's Greenwich Village, is Mecca. Dozens of top jazz musicians have recorded live in this small, triangular-shaped room, which holds only 123 people. However, during the 1940s, it was home to a different kind of music.

LISTENING CUE • "Do-Re-Mi" (1937), Woody Guthrie. Guthrie, vocals and guitar.

STYLE Topical folk song • **FORM** Verse/chorus

Listen For . . .

INSTRUMENTATION
Voice and guitar

PERFORMANCE STYLE
Twangy singing style; easy delivery of words; the Carter thumb-brush guitar style

RHYTHM
Moderate tempo; light beat keeping in regular accompaniment rhythm (no syncopation or rhythmic play)

MELODY
Long phrases at quick pace; narrow melodic range

HARMONY
Simple three-chord song

Remember . . .

TOPICAL SONG
Guthrie brought topical songs into Depression-era American life. Social commentary rare in any kind of song before World War II.

FOLK STYLE ACCOMPANIMENT
Guthrie adapted Maybelle Carter's thumb-brush accompanying style; link between traditional country and folk revival.

ANTI-POP/INSPIRATION FOR ROCK
Guthrie embraces reality instead of escaping it (as pop songs did); important influence on rock's "realness."

Listen to this selection in CourseMate.

Max Gordon opened the Village Vanguard in 1935 as a venue for variety entertainment. However, beginning in 1941, it became home base for the folk scene that was taking shape in Greenwich Village. Among the musicians who were part of this first folk revival were Woody Guthrie, Pete Seeger, and John Lomax's daughter Bess, plus the black bluesmen Sonny Terry and Brownie McGhee. The first night of folk music featured two black songsters, Josh White and Lead Belly; the 1940s came to an end at the Vanguard with a six-month run by the Weavers, a four-person folk group that sang traditional material from around the globe.

During the 1920s and 1930s, Greenwich Village became the New York destination for artists, musicians, writers, and those who appreciated the arts. Rents were still relatively cheap and the company was good. It was also a hotbed for left-leaning politics: Woody Guthrie was among those who moved there in the early 1940s.

So as country music moved away from its folk roots, Greenwich Village—urban, not rural, and progressive, not conservative—became an unlikely home for traditional music from the South, by both blacks and whites. The first "star" of the folk scene was Lead Belly.

Lead Belly, an Authentic Songster

Huddie Ledbetter (1888–1949), better known as Lead Belly, grew up in Louisiana and spent time in Dallas working with Blind Lemon Jefferson. He was sent to prison for murder in 1918 and won a reprieve in 1925 on the strength of his good behavior, which included entertaining prisoners and staff. By 1930, he was back in Angola Prison in Louisiana, where John Lomax recorded him for the Library of Congress, got him paroled, and brought him to New York the following year. Lead Belly continued to record for the Library of Congress and also began recording commercially, initially for the American Recording Company.

William P. Gottlieb Collection//Library of Congress, Prints and Photographs Division, Washington, DC

LEAD BELLY, photographed by William Gottlieb at the National Press Club, Washington, D.C., between 1938 and 1948.

Lead Belly sang the blues often and with authority, but he was much more than a bluesman. Within the black community he was known as a songster; he performed many different kinds of music, including blues, ballads, work songs, children's songs, and familiar folk songs, both black and white. The first songsters we know about appeared in the latter part of the nineteenth century; the tradition was dying out around the time Lead Belly came to prominence. Among Lead Belly's best-known recordings are the old frontier/children's song "Skip to My Lou" and "Goodnight, Irene," a nineteenth-century parlor song written by a black songwriter from Cincinnati, which would become a hit song for the Weavers and then for pop singer Jo Stafford and country singer Ernest Tubb. Lead Belly performed both songs without any trace of blues style beyond the inherent huskiness of his voice, and his guitar accompaniment is simple and straightforward, with no bent notes or syncopation. It is as if Lead Belly assumed a different musical persona when singing white songs.

From Folk to Pop

Among the most unlikely pop successes of the postwar era were the Weavers. The Weavers grew out of the Almanac Singers, a folk-singing group that included Woody Guthrie, Pete Seeger, Millard Lampell, and Lee Hays. The Almanac Singers were the spiritual forebears of the protest singers of the early 1960s. Politically, they leaned well to the left and advocated isolationism, a path that was rendered moot after Pearl Harbor.

After Woody Guthrie left the Almanac Singers to join the merchant marine in 1943, Seeger and Hays continued to sing together. In 1949, joined by Veronica "Ronnie" Gilbert and Fred Hellerman, they formed the Weavers. They all sang, and the three men played the accompanying instruments, Seeger on the banjo, Kellerman on guitar, and Hays on bass.

The six-month stint at the Village Vanguard was the Weavers' springboard to a brief flirtation with the pop limelight. They had begun recording for a small independent company, but their success caught the attention of the major record labels. The Weavers eventually signed with Decca Records, where Gordon Jenkins, one of the top pop arrangers of the day, provided lush string backgrounds.

Their first and biggest recording coupled a folklike Israeli song, "Tzena, Tzena," with "Goodnight, Irene." A comparison of their pop version with an earlier recording by Lead Belly gives some sense of the stylistic range of the music considered "folk."

LISTENING CUE • **"Goodnight, Irene" (1936; 1950),** Gussie Davis(?). Lead Belly; The Weavers

STYLE Folk ballad/pop version of folk song • **FORM** Verse/chorus

Listen For . . .

INSTRUMENTATION
(LB) Solo voice and guitar / (W) voices plus guitar, bass, violin(s) and choir

RHYTHM
Simple waltz-like accompaniment rhythm, with no syncopation in melody

MELODY
Simple three-phrase melody (short, short, long) in both verse and chorus

HARMONY
Basic chords: I, IV, V

TEXTURE
(LB) Simple melody plus accompaniment / (W) rich harmonies in voices and/or strings, plus bass/chord instrumental accompaniment

Remember . . .

BALLAD
A grim story, told succinctly and in fragments

SIMPLE SONG
Both melody and harmony are easy to learn and remember.

FOLK VS. FOLK-POP
Lead Belly's simple, plain folk style vs. Weavers' hearty harmony and arranger Jenkins's pop sophistication

Listen to this selection in CourseMate.

"Goodnight, Irene"

"Good Night, Irene" may have been written in the late nineteenth century, but like many nineteenth-century songs, it went quickly into oral tradition: Lead Belly claimed to have learned it from his uncle.

"Goodnight, Irene" is in the style of a folk ballad. It is a depressing story of a failed marriage; in one of the verses in Lead Belly's version, Irene seems to be underage when she marries. The story is told in plain language and is sung by Lead Belly in a matter-of-fact manner, with a simple accompaniment on the guitar. The emotional neutrality is in stark contrast with the powerful events in the story. The guitar accompaniment is simple; the chorus and the verse use just I, IV, V, the three basic chords, in a well-trodden progression.

By contrast, the Weavers' version is like dressing a farmer in a tuxedo. Jenkins's syrupy setting, with strings and choir behind the Weavers, clashes with the lyric of the song. The Weavers are closer in spirit to the folk tradition. Their singing is warm and hearty. It exudes an optimistic, "everything's all right with the world" spirit, which is one source of their appeal. But the close harmony in the chorus and supporting vocals in the verses have more to do with mainstream practice than traditional folk music. (In close harmony singing, the other notes of the chords are near in pitch to the melody note; all parts typically move in the same rhythm.)

The two versions of "Goodnight, Irene" offer an inside/outside perspective on the folk music scene during the 1930s and 1940s. Lead Belly's 1936 recording is like a sound snapshot: an authentic folk version of the song as it might have been heard on Lead Belly's home turf. By contrast, the Weavers' version reproduces the song but relatively little of the style.

The Weavers were the first ambassadors of folk music, but their time at the top of the pop market was short-lived. Their advocacy of leftist politics and causes made them a target of the McCarthy-era witch hunts. Although they continued to work through the fifties—a 1955 Carnegie Hall concert was the highpoint—they never recaptured their early success.

The Weavers' importance lies more in their influence than in their music. The folk revival of the late 1950s and early 1960s was a revival in two senses. The more obvious was the recapturing and updating of traditional folk music. But it was also a reenergizing of the Weavers' attempt to use the accessibility of folklike music to advance their political and social agenda—to address the inequities of American life and the need for social justice—by taking it to a broader audience.

CHAPTER 30
Honky-Tonk

A *honky-tonk* is a working-class bar. After the repeal of Prohibition in 1933, bars and dance halls catering to a working-class clientele sprang up all over the South and the Southwest, but particularly in Texas and Oklahoma. Those honky-tonks that catered to a white clientele typically featured country music, often performed by a live band. These bars were usually rough, noisy establishments, and musicians who performed in them needed a musical style that could be heard above the din. At the same time, their songs needed to articulate the problems and pleasures of the audience. Most of the traditional country repertoire, particularly sentimental or religious songs, would have been wildly inappropriate for a honky-tonk. Out of this environment came a new kind of country music, called (appropriately enough) **honky-tonk.**

© Allison Murray/iStockphoto

Country Music after 1945

In its January 8, 1944, issue, *Billboard* began its coverage of "folk" music by publishing a chart of the "Most Played Juke Box Folk Records." By the end of the decade, they had expanded their coverage to include record sales ("Best Selling Retail Folk Records," first published in May, 1948) and radio airplay ("Country and Western Records Most Played By Folk Disc Jockeys," first published in December 1949). The three charts were eventually consolidated into the "Hot C&W Sides" for the October 20, 1958 issue.

The proliferation of *Billboard* "folk" charts during the late 1940s and early 1950s—one each for radio airplay, jukeboxes, and record sales—indicated the growing popularity and broadening audience for country music. Other clues include the offer of a movie contract to Hank Williams (who died before he could fulfill it) and **cover versions** (recordings of a song by acts other than the first to record it) of country hits by pop artists. Patti Page's 1950 version of Pee Wee King's "Tennessee Waltz" was a huge hit, with sales of more than 6 million records; it was the most popular of several pop makeovers of country songs.

Country music's spike in popularity, fueled in part by the continuing migration of people from the South and Southwest to other parts of the country after those in the military returned home from the war, was one sign that a new era in country music had begun.

However, the most compelling evidence was in the music itself. A host of new artists rose to country stardom in the decade after World War II: Hank Snow, Eddy Arnold, Lefty Frizzell, Webb Pierce, Kitty Wells, Ray Price, and above all Hank Williams, Sr. The new sounds they created borrowed from pop and black music, which produced music far removed from the old-time fiddle music of the 1920s yet remained identifiably country. The most popular new style of the late 1940s and early 1950s was called honky-tonk. We encounter it in the music of Hank Williams and Kitty Wells.

Hank Williams

Hank Williams (1923–1953) was the quintessential country singer. Williams was born into a poor family in rural Alabama. While still in his teens, he performed in rough honky-tonks near his home and later in southern Alabama. His career received a boost from Fred Rose, a Nashville-based pianist, songwriter, and music publisher

HANK WILLIAMS

© Michael Ochs Archives/Getty Images

and one of the most successful promoters in the history of country music. Williams gained widespread exposure throughout the South and the Southwest through appearances on the *Louisiana Hayride* and the *Grand Ole Opry*.

Williams suffered from spina bifida, a birth defect affecting his back. Throughout his life he was in constant pain, which may have contributed to his alcoholism and which cost him his life before his thirtieth birthday. At the time of his death, he was the dominant figure in country music and the standard-bearer for the new sound of country music. A song that provided a major stepping-stone in his rise to the top was "Lovesick Blues," his first big hit.

"Lovesick Blues"

Williams recorded "Lovesick Blues" late in 1948 over the strong objections of Fred Rose and the backup musicians. "Lovesick Blues" was a curious choice for Williams, who typically recorded his own songs. It was a pop song from the early 1920s that had been recorded by Emmett Miller, one of the last blackface minstrels. Miller's 1929 recording of the song, on which he was backed by some of the top white jazz musicians of the day, was familiar to country audiences. Williams essentially copied Miller's version, including his yodels and occasional dropped beats; his instrumental accompaniment was a modern country band, with full rhythm and steel guitar, instead of a jazz band.

Williams's remake of "Lovesick Blues" is a more modern version of an established country practice: redoing an old pop song in a country style. Recall that the Carter family's "Wildwood Flower" was a reworking of a nineteenth-century parlor song; Williams simply takes advantage of recording technology to revive "Lovesick Blues," giving it a country sound and feel that the original did not have.

In "Lovesick Blues" (1949), we hear many of the elements that define the new sound in country music. The band behind Williams includes a full rhythm section, including drums, plus the "newly traditional" country instrument, the steel guitar. They lay down a two-beat rhythm with a crisp backbeat; it is in essence a country take on the foxtrot. (We heard this rhythm previously in Bob Wills's "Steel Guitar Rag.")

Williams's singing also blends old and new. It has a uniquely country timbre. It is thin, nasal, and flat yet intensely expressive, as plaintive or high-spirited as the song demands. It is also tinged by the blues that Williams heard from street-corner blues singers when he was growing up. In particular, he credited Rufus Payne, a local bluesman whom he befriended, with giving him "all the music training I ever had." Indeed, Williams referred to his own singing as "moanin' the blues." This fusion of country and blues was Williams's personal synthesis, one that made him perhaps the most easily recognized singer in country music until his untimely death.

Even more important, Williams unlocked the expressive potential of country music. Like Billie Holiday and Frank Sinatra, he is one of the great song interpreters.

LISTENING CUE • **"Lovesick Blues" (1948),** Irving Mills and Cliff Friend. Hank Williams, vocal.

STYLE Honky-tonk • **FORM** Verse/chorus song, verse heard only once and chorus repeated, chorus ABAC

Listen For . . .

INSTRUMENTATION
Voice, plus electric guitar, steel guitar, mandolin, string bass, and drums

PERFORMANCE STYLE
Williams's patented "moanin' the blues": blues-tinged country vocal style, with occasional yodel via Jimmie Rodgers

RHYTHM
Honky-tonk beat = countrified two-beat rhythm

HARMONY
Harmony closer to early twentieth-century songs (like "Take Me Out to the Ball Game") than to typical three-chord country song

TEXTURE
Melody with simple accompaniment, plus responses from steel guitar

Remember . . .

MOANIN' THE BLUES
Williams sings with a characteristic country twang, but with a grittiness that shows blues influence.

HONKY-TONK SOUND
Full, discreet rhythm section laying down a two-beat rhythm, plus steel guitar and electric guitar lead

COUNTRIFYING POP AND BLUES
Williams's first big hit was a cover of a 1920s pop song, not an original composition.

Listen to this selection in CourseMate.

The intensity of Williams's rendition invests this rather humdrum song with real feeling. He conveys it with the inherent fragility of his vocal sound—it comes close to breaking several times—emphatic inflection of the lyric, and the plaintive quality with which he sings the longer notes in the melody.

"Lovesick Blues" was Williams's ticket to an appearance on *Grand Ole Opry*. As Bob Wills discovered, the Opry management resisted non-country elements like drums. However, Williams's electrifying performance of "Lovesick Blues" earned him six encores and effectively washed away any significant resistance to the modern sound of honky-tonk. Williams played a key role in popularizing honky-tonk. Among the brightest new stars in this new style was a reluctant feminist, Kitty Wells.

Kitty Wells and the Heart of Country Music

Kitty Wells (b. Muriel Deason, 1919) had been on the fringes of country music for almost two decades when she was persuaded to record an "answer" song to Hank Thompson's "The Wild Side of Life," a No. 1 country hit for him in 1952. In the song, Thompson proclaimed his true love to a "honky-tonk angel," a woman who rejected him so that she could return to the "glamor of the gay night life." The song all but demanded a rebuttal, which was written by J. D. Miller; Miller took the title "It Wasn't God Who Made Honky Tonk Angels" from a line in the lyric of Thompson's song.

KITTY WELLS

By 1952, Wells's career had been stuck in neutral for more than a decade. She was married to Johnnie Wright,

LISTENING CUE · **"It Wasn't God Who Made Honky Tonk Angels" (1952),** J. D. Miller.
Kitty Wells, vocal.

STYLE Honky-tonk · **FORM** Verse/chorus song: both verse and chorus use same melody; words remain same in chorus, differ in verse. Form of melody = A A^1

Listen For . . .

INSTRUMENTATION
Voice, plus fiddle, steel guitar, and guitar/bass/drums rhythm section

PERFORMANCE STYLE
Typical country sounds: flat, clear vocal; flat, clear fiddle playing—no vibrato or special sounds, but with double notes

RHYTHM
Steady two-beat rhythm with crisp backbeat on guitar and drums

MELODY
Four phrases of moderate length, in a question/answer pattern

HARMONY
Simple progression over and over: I-IV-V-I

Remember . . .

WORDS IN FOREFRONT
Wells sings with a plain, sincere sound: no vibrato, no inflection, no affectation or special effects; it helps make the words easy to understand.

HONKY-TONK SOUND
The now-traditional sound of honky-tonk: full rhythm playing a two-beat rhythm with a crisp backbeat; steel guitar and fiddle as dominant instrumental sounds

SONG RECYCLING
Wells's answer song fits new words to Thompson's song, which is in turn based on sacred song "Great Speckled Bird" sung by Acuff.

COMMONSENSE FEMINISM
Pointing out the obvious—a courageous stance for Wells in male-dominated country music

Listen to this selection in CourseMate.

a popular country singer, but had not made much of an impact as a solo act; a four-year tenure at RCA had produced nothing of note. She had just signed on with Decca records in 1952, when Paul Cohen, a Decca executive, approached her about recording the song. Perhaps enticed by the $125 she would receive for the recording, she overcame her initial reservations and made history in the process. The recording sold 800,000 copies, topped the *Billboard* country disc jockey chart and reached the top ten on the best sellers and jukebox charts, and crossed over to the pop charts. Wells's recording was the first crossover hit by a female country singer. Almost overnight, she became one of the top stars of country music.

Several features of the song stand out: the primacy of the lyric and the role of music in supporting it, the sincerity and lack of artifice in Wells's singing, and the newly traditional sound of the accompanying instruments.

The song is a modern (for 1952) version of a long-established practice in British and American music: fitting new words to old songs. Thomas Moore had gentrified the practice with his *Irish Melodies*. In 1831, Samuel Francis Smith had given "God Save the King," the British national anthem, new words; Americans know the song as "My Country 'Tis of Thee." Woody Guthrie had given several old songs new lyrics. Thompson continued this practice by using the melody of "Great Speckled Bird," a white gospel song recorded by Roy Acuff in 1936. Miller's reuse of Thompson's melody was an obvious way of highlighting the fact that "It Wasn't God Who Made Honky Tonk Angels" was an answer song.

The use of a familiar melody shifts the spotlight to the words, which asserts that men are far more likely to be unfaithful than women. Wells's sincere vocal timbre and straightforward delivery of the words underscores the message. It resonated with everyone: audiences, industry executives and producers, and musicians and songwriters. Wells had opened the door for a new generation of female country singing stars.

The frankness of the song and Wells's singing of it is in sharp contrast to the popular music of the era. There is no stardust in her eyes. Rather, it is as if she's sitting with you at the kitchen table, pouring her heart out. In this respect, it's like the blues. However, because there is comparatively little musical interest—the melody is short and repetitive, its harmony is similarly simple, and the accompaniment is unobtrustive—there is even more focus on lyric; the music supports the storytelling, but it doesn't deflect attention from it.

Honky-Tonk and the Evolution of Country Music

In 1950, honky-tonk was new and old at the same time. By incorporating such mainstream features as a full rhythm section and a two-beat rhythm, it updated the sound of country music. At the same time, it maintained a strong connection with its roots. Its chief musical features show this mix of old and new:

- Song texts that speak plainly and personally about everyday life: love, alcohol, hard times, loneliness, work, or life on the road
- A nasal, often twangy vocal style
- Straightforward melodies, delivered plainly and directly with simple accompaniments, usually built from the three basic chords: I, IV, and V
- The old and new country instruments: fiddle and steel guitar
- A full rhythm section playing a countrified version of a popular dance beat

The features that connect honky-tonk most firmly to its heritage are the storytelling lyric, straightforward melody, the vocal style, and the use of the fiddle. However, all of these features have been updated. Unlike the ballads from which they are descended, the lyrics of honky-tonk songs are usually personal and cast in the present. The melodies have simple accompaniments. The vocal style often infuses a touch of blues or pop into the distinctive country twang. And the fiddle playing has lost its rough edges.

The elements brought in from other styles were countrified. Country music soon owned the sound of the steel guitar, not only because the music was so much more popular than Hawaiian music but also because it acquired a tinge of the bluesman's bottleneck guitar style. The distinctive honky-tonk beat is a country take on the foxtrot.

With honky-tonk, country music redefined itself. It preserved a distinctively country sound, one with secure links to its heritage, by retaining and adapting key features of the folk music that spawned it; imbuing those outside elements that it assimilated with a country sound; and speaking directly to its audience, who preferred stories told in plain language that it could relate to. At the same time, all of these evolutionary advances produced a style that defined a new era in country music.

Honky-tonk quickly became country music's traditional, almost timeless style, and it has remained the reference point for country music into the twenty-first century. For country traditionalists, it has provided periodic course correction, counterbalancing Nashville's ongoing romance with pop, from the "Nashville Sound" of the 1950s to the country pop singers of the new century.

CHAPTER 31

Bluegrass, a Neo-Traditional Style

Country music prizes its roots more than any other major genre. It let the world come to Nashville rather than relocating to the main media centers. Its institutions honor and preserve its past. It holds on to its core values rather than rejecting them in the quest for the next new thing. So it was fitting that one of the most distinctive sounds in postwar country music was bluegrass, a new take on its oldest tradition.

Bill Monroe and the Birth of Bluegrass

Bill Monroe (1911–1996), a singer and mandolin player, is known as the "father of bluegrass." He was responsible not only for the sound but also the name: Kentucky, where he was born, is the Bluegrass State. Monroe grew up surrounded by skilled folk musicians, including his uncle Pendelton Vandiver (whom he would remember in the song "Uncle Pen"). He took up the mandolin because no one else in the family played it.

Monroe began to build his career in the 1930s and arrived on the stage of the Grand Ole Opry in 1939. By that time, he was well on his way to assembling the sound of bluegrass. It would come together in 1945, when virtuoso banjo player Earl Scruggs joined Monroe's group.

© Pictorial Press Ltd/Alamy

BILL MONROE (second from the left) and His Blue Grass Boys about 1940.

Monroe's **bluegrass** music descends directly from the early string bands. The acoustic instrumentation (no electric instruments or amplification) and the mountain vocal style (the "high lonesome" sound) preserve important country music traditions. But there are some important differences as well:

- *Expanded instrumentation.* Monroe and the Blue Grass Boys offered a complete array of acoustic string instruments: fiddle, guitar, banjo, mandolin, and string bass.
- *Chop-chord mandolin style.* Bill Malone calls Bill Monroe's mandolin style "chop-chord." The chop-chord style, a percussive sound occurring in alternation with the bass, is the bluegrass counterpart to the honky-tonk backbeat.
- *Earl Scruggs's virtuoso banjo playing.* Scruggs updated the Appalachian three-finger banjo style. It combined the continuous stream of notes found in earlier banjo styles with the syncopated groupings of ragtime and the occasional blues lick—all at breakneck tempos.
- *Collective improvisation.* The texture and the form of a bluegrass recording have close parallels with New Orleans jazz. In both there is a dense, active texture resulting from simultaneous improvisation on several melody instruments over a timekeeping rhythm section, with occasional interruptions for a featured soloist. This collective improvisation harks back to the thoroughly blended texture of the string band, but there are more parts and their roles are more varied.
- *Exceedingly fast tempos.* String-band music was often dance music, but the tempos in many bluegrass songs are much too fast for all but the most agile dancers. This is listening music, although it invites a physical response. Part of the excitement of bluegrass is the skill with which its best performers reel off streams of notes at very fast speeds.

We hear all of these features in "It's Mighty Dark to Travel," a 1947 recording by Bill Monroe and the Blue Grass Boys. The recording features Earl Scruggs on banjo, Lester Flatt on guitar, and Bill Monroe on mandolin. Flatt and Scruggs would leave the following year to form their own group. By the end of the 1940s, other musicians were copying features of Monroe's music, and it remains the standard by which bluegrass groups are measured.

In the postwar era, bluegrass was the country music style closest to the old-time music of country fiddlers like

LISTENING CUE • **"It's Mighty Dark to Travel" (1947),** Bill Monroe. Bill Monroe and His Blue Grass Boys: Monroe, mandolin and vocal; Earl Scruggs, banjo; Lester Flatt, guitar and vocal; Chubby Wise, fiddle; and Howard Watts, bass.

STYLE Bluegrass • **FORM** Verse/chorus

Listen For . . .

INSTRUMENTATION
Vocals, banjo, fiddle, guitar, bass, and mandolin

PERFORMANCE STYLE
"High lonesome" mountain vocal sound

RHYTHM
Very fast tempo; strong two-beat rhythm with crisp offbeat chords; very active banjo and mandolin rhythms

MELODY
Vocal line consists of short phrases. Instrumental solos generally move at faster pace and with more skips.

Remember . . .

BLUEGRASS INSTRUMENTATION
The core bluegrass instrumentation: all strings, no drums or horns

BLACK MUSIC INFLUENCE: RAGTIME, BLUES, JAZZ
Banjo lines have rag-like figuration and a few blue notes; interaction among instruments recalls New Orleans jazz.

TEMPO AND TEXT
Very fast tempo vs. mournful lyric

Listen to this selection in CourseMate.

Fiddlin' John Carson. As such, it represented a countercurrent in country music. It would remain on the periphery of country music, although its stars remained widely admired. The sound of bluegrass charted in 1962, when Flatt and Scruggs's "The Ballad of Jed Clampett" served as the theme music for the television show *The Beverly Hillbillies*.

UNIT 7

THREE DECADES OF COUNTRY AND FOLK MUSIC

AN ALMOST VERTICAL LINE CONNECTS Kosse, Texas; Tioga, Texas; and Okemah, Oklahoma. Tioga, a small town due north of Dallas, was the birthplace of Gene Autry, the first of the singing cowboy movie stars. Bob Wills, the man most responsible for western swing, the hottest country sound of the 1930s, came from Kosse, a small town almost directly south of Dallas. Woody Guthrie, the man who made folk a contemporary music, was born in Okemah, mostly north and a little east of Dallas (and Tioga).

Autry died in Los Angeles, home of the motion picture industry. His music and the music of the other singing cowboys was the most visible segment of country music; it was the interface between country music and pop. Wills died in Tulsa. Although his group traveled to California and even appeared in films, his music remained familiar mainly to that slice of country music's core audience that was open to outside influences. Guthrie died in New York. He had essentially left country music behind to forge a new direction and find a new audience.

These three key figures encapsulate the evolution of country and folk music during its first three decades. All started from much the same place, but their career paths produced both geographical and musical separation—even alienation, in the case of Guthrie and folk music.

What had been a folk music transplanted from the British Isles as late as 1920 split into country and folk, two worlds that were almost mutually exclusive. And each world divided further into several streams, some creating paths to the mainstream, others running counter to the trend. At the heart of it all were the central tensions of this music: between commerce and culture, innovation and preservation, and staying home and roaming far and wide.

The first three decades of country and folk music make clear that tradition in country music is relative, not absolute. Both honky-tonk and bluegrass, the most "traditional" post–World War II country styles, evidence the assimilation of non-country elements, although they acquire a distinctively country sound as they are adapted to country music. Guthrie's topical songs use a traditional style to deliver contemporary, timely messages; at the height of their popularity, the Weavers embed folk material in a rich pop setting.

Country and folk would follow separate paths through the 1950s and into the 1960s. It remained for Bob Dylan to bring them together.

Latin Music in the United States, 1900s–1950s

UNIT 8

UNIT 8

In the late 1850s, Louis Moreau Gottschalk (1829–1869), a composer and pianist who was America's first classical music star, toured South America and the Caribbean. On his return, Gottschalk, a native of New Orleans, composed several piano pieces—the first noteworthy American music to show Latin influence. Native Latin music was not widely known in the United States, and Gottschalk's pieces were exotic novelties. But no one of importance followed Gottschalk's lead; other American musicians stayed home or turned to Europe for inspiration.

About a century later, CBS began broadcasting *I Love Lucy.* The show featured the real-life husband-and-wife team Desi Arnaz and Lucille Ball, portraying husband and wife Ricky and Lucy Ricardo. Ricky led a Latin band at the Tropicana nightclub; Lucy was a show-business wannabe. The commercial viability of a white woman married to a Latin musician was a hard sell to CBS executives, so Lucy and Desi spent $5,000 of their own money to make a pilot showing that the couple would be believable. CBS finally bought the idea, the show went on the air in 1951, and the result was the popular, now classic, sitcom of the 1950s (still showing on cable stations).

I Love Lucy highlights the blending of Latin music and Latin musicians into American life. By 1955, Latin music had become a subtle seasoning in popular music, jazz, and rhythm and blues, as well as an acceptable alternative to more conventional American music. In fact, the biggest hit of 1955 was a Latin song, Perez Prado's "Cherry Pink and Apple Blossom White."

In about a century, the place of Latin music in the United States had changed dramatically from exceptional oddity to part of the mix. In this unit, we briefly survey Latin music in the United States from the turn of the twentieth century through the early years of the rock era, with a particular focus on Cuban music.

CHAPTER 32

Latin Music in the United States, 1900–1960

The slave trade that brought Africans to the United States also brought them to other parts of the New World, particularly the Caribbean Islands and Brazil. Unlike their counterparts in the American South, however, slaves in Latin America and the Caribbean kept much of their culture. They merged their tribal religions with the various forms of Christianity introduced by European colonialists. They created Creole dialects—hybrid languages that were part European, part African. And because drums (banned in the slave-holding American South) were permitted in most other parts of the Americas, folk music from these regions remained much closer to its African roots than almost all African-American music. Afro-centric folk music from Latin America typically features more percussion instruments and a denser, more complex rhythmic texture. Both are prominent differences between Latin and American popular styles, as we will discover.

Latin Music in the United States

For the better part of a century, *Latin music* has been the American umbrella term for music that originated in countries in the Americas where Spanish or Portuguese was the native language, music created in the United States by Latin musicians, and music by Americans without a Latin heritage who adapted Latin elements—particularly the rhythms and characteristic percussion instruments—into their popular songs, dance music, and jazz.

© Carlosphotos/Dreamstime.com

THE TANGO

The Assimilation of Latin Music

The assimilation of Latin elements into popular music during the first half of the twentieth century took place in three stages that followed a roughly chronological progression, with considerable overlap.

- In the first stage, lasting until the early 1940s, Latin styles emerged as exotic novelties, usually dance fads that departed from mainstream fare. As they became popular in America, they moved away from their native forms, especially when played by the most popular bands.
- The second stage, lasting from the 1930s through the 1950s, saw the emergence of hybrid or transformed styles. These grew out of the interpretations of Latin music by American musicians—and, more significantly—the incorporation of American music into Latin styles. Because of their different rhythms and instrumentations, these Latin-influenced or Latin-derived styles remained distinct from mainstream pop music until well into the rock era.
- The third stage coincided with the emergence of rhythm and blues and rock and roll, as elements of Latin music became part of the fabric of these newly dominant styles. Latin rhythms helped shape the rhythms of rock-era popular music, and Latin instruments now appeared routinely in a broad range of musical styles. Latin music still stood apart from American popular styles, but the line distinguishing Latin from mainstream was, and is, not nearly so clear as it had been before rock.

The Habanera and Tango

The story of Latin dance music in the United States begins more than a century ago with the emergence of the Cuban **habanera.** Its name is probably an abbreviated form of *contra-danza habanera*—that is, a *contredanse* (a European ballroom dance) from Havana. Its characteristic rhythm is one of the first recorded instances of African influence on European music. Developing during the early part of the nineteenth century, the habanera spread beyond Cuba after 1850, traveling to Europe, the United States, and South America. In Europe the habanera caught on not only in Spain but also in France. The French composer Georges Bizet composed a habanera, based on what he thought was a well-known folk song, for his immensely popular opera *Carmen* (1875).

The habanera entered the United States by way of Mexico, where it had become popular in the 1870s. A Mexican military band performed the dance at an international exposition held in New Orleans in 1884–1885. The band was the musical hit of the event, and its popularity led to the publication of several of the most popular pieces in its repertoire. By the end of the century, the influence of the habanera was evident in more mainstream American popular music. The rhythmic signature of cakewalks and many ragtime songs is virtually identical to that of the habanera. However, its influence was seldom acknowledged: Scott Joplin's "Solace," which he subtitled "A Mexican Serenade," is a rare exception.

Musical evidence suggests that the *habanera* also went south to Argentina, where it became the rhythmic basis of the tango. The tango arrived in America in 1913 from Argentina by way of Paris, where Irene and Vernon Castle had captivated audiences with their dancing of the tango. Upon their return to the United States, they introduced it in a Broadway show, *The Sunshine Girl,* where it was a sensation. Almost overnight, the tango became the first of the twentieth-century Latin dance fads in the United States, then became a fixture in popular culture, especially in musicals and films. However, the tangos most familiar to American audiences were musical caricatures; for most Americans, authentic Argentine tangos remained an exotic and unfamiliar sound throughout the first half of the twentieth century.

As the crow flies, Buenos Aires is over 5,000 miles from New York City; Havana is a little over 1,000. Geography played a role in the greater popularity of Cuban dance music, if only because it was relatively easy for the Havana Casino Orchestra to travel from Havana to New York.

Mainstreaming Latin Music

The Havana Casino Orchestra, led by Don Azpiazú and featuring vocalist Antonio Machin, came to New York in 1930. Their visit was orchestrated by a producer who had heard them in Havana the previous year. Azpiazú's orchestra, featuring a large complement of Afro-Cuban percussion instruments, introduced New York audiences to the authentic sounds and rhythms of Cuban music. They were a sensation during their appearances at the Palace Theater, and their recording of "El Manisero" ("The Peanut Vendor") reportedly sold over 1,000,000 units. The surprising success of "El Manisero" sparked widespread enthusiasm for Latin music, sending publishers back to their catalogs for Latin numbers, producing numerous versions of the song by American performers, including Louis Armstrong, and inspiring a stream of Latin songs by American songwriters. The song also triggered the second Latin dance craze in the United States—the **rumba.**

LISTENING CUE · **"El Manisero" ("The Peanut Vendor") (1930),** Sunshine Marion, Gilbert Wolfe, and Simons Moises. Don Azpiazú and His Havana Casino Orchestra.

STYLE Rumba · **FORM** Open form: alternation of two sets of phrases, with variation in pitches and phrase length

Listen For . . .

INSTRUMENTATION
Voice, piano, bass, guitar, clarinets, trumpet (muted), and a battery of percussion instruments; most prominent percussion: maracas, claves, and timbales (shallow, single-headed drums tuned to different pitches)

RHYTHM
Reverse clave rhythm; other rhythms line up with clave pattern; steady activity in accompaniment

MELODY
Two melodic phrases, with either long notes or active lines whose accents line up with clave rhythm

TEXTURE
Melody with rich, percussion-heavy accompaniment

Remember . . .

REVERSE CLAVE RHYTHM
Played on claves; amplified by "in clave" clarinet riff that runs through song

LATIN PERCUSSION INSTRUMENTS
Claves, maracas, and timbales introduced to American ears

OSCILLATING HARMONY
Simple alternation between two chords; not a progression, thus making open-ended form possible

OPEN FORM
Extensible form—both vocalist and trumpeter can expand phrases—plus layered opening and fadeout ending show African roots, anticipate rock-era music.

Listen to this selection in CourseMate.

The Rumba

The rumba (also spelled *rhumba*) grew out of the *son,* an Afro-Cuban dance. The *son* apparently originated in eastern Cuba. Brought to Havana around the turn of the century, it flourished in the 1920s among all classes, with the growth of Cuban commercial radio. Many Cuban radio shows featured live performers; and because they were heard but not seen, Cubans of African descent gained access to audiences who would not normally have heard them perform.

The Afro-Cuban influence in Don Azpiazú's recording of "El Manisero" is most evident in the vocal, the prominent Latin percussion, and the reverse clave rhythm. Clave rhythm (so called because it is played on **claves,** a pair of cylindrical wooden sticks that are tapped together) is to much Cuban popular music what the backbeat is to American popular styles: a consistent point of rhythmic reference. The clave pattern consists of five irregularly spaced taps, spread over two 4-beat measures. In **reverse clave rhythm,** the second half of the pattern comes first. In other respects, the recording is comparable to American pop styles of the period. The trumpet is muted, and the piano style is halfway between Cuban and cocktail piano.

Americanized Latin Music: Cugat, Porter, and the Latin Song

With the success of "El Manisero," Latin music gained a toehold in the American pop world. American songwriters showed a greater sensitivity to Latin style—Irving Berlin's "Heat Wave" (1933) is a well-known example—and songs by Latin composers, such as Cuban Nilo Melendez's "Green Eyes," were on their way to becoming pop standards. Both stage and film musicals featured Latin music more prominently.

In particular, bandleader Xavier Cugat popularized Latin music in a hybrid style—rhythmically simplified and commercially acceptable to white audiences. His orchestra was the most visible evidence of a growing Latin musical presence in the United States.

Cugat (1900–1990), a Spanish-born violinist raised in Cuba, came to the United States in 1921 and worked as a violinist before forming his own bands. Cugat helped establish a commercial Latin style, initially through engagements at the Waldorf Hotels in New York and Los Angeles and performances on the radio show *Let's Dance,* then as the most filmed bandleader in Hollywood.

Cugat was Latin music's Paul Whiteman. Both wore moustaches and were rotund. Both were string players who became bandleaders. Both hired the best musicians. Whiteman's band included top jazzmen of the 1920s; Cugat's bands included top Cuban musicians. Both were showmen, but Cugat put more emphasis on the show—and on showing off. The band wore ridiculous uniforms, played corny arrangements, and did campy routines. Still, each bandleader was responsible for bringing his music into the mainstream. Whiteman was instrumental in making jazz and the dance orchestra popular during the twenties, whereas Cugat was making Latin music for the masses in the thirties, forties, and fifties.

Among Cugat's biggest fans was Cole Porter (1891–1964), then living at New York's Waldorf Hotel. Of the great Tin Pan Alley songwriters, Porter was the most open to the sound of Latin music, or at least the commercial Latin music that Cugat played. Porter wrote several Latin songs, beginning in the 1930s, identifying the rhythm variously as "rhumba" or **beguine** ("beh-*geen*"). What is noteworthy about most of Porter's Latin songs is that their lyrics have nothing to do with Latin culture. Apparently, he simply liked the feel of the rhythm. A spectacular exception is his most famous Latin song, "Begin the Beguine" (1935).

Cugat's recording of "Begin the Beguine" was one of the first; it was a hit—one of three for him that year. Although the song has a lyric, Cugat's orchestra performs it as an instrumental. Only two short vocal sections frame an instrumental statement of the melody. It is elegantly done. Violins play the opening phrase of the melody, while the rest of the orchestra supports the melody with the Americanized Latin rhythm and Porter's original offbeat accents. The rich overlay of percussion instruments, including claves, gives the performance a more authentic Latin sound.

American versus Latin Rhythms

For songwriters like Porter, "Latin" meant mostly a change in the rhythm, from an uneven division of the beat to an even division. In a typical foxtrot, the beat is divided into a long/short rhythm, with accented syllables often falling on the beat and unaccented syllables coming on the shorter part of the beat.

The Americanized Latin rhythm in "Begin the Beguine" divides the beat into equal parts. In Porter's Latin songs, the bass line typically has notes on the first, third, and fourth beats, while the accompaniment chords all come on offbeats. This pattern became the generic Latin rhythm of American popular music from the 1930s through the 1950s.

In "Begin the Beguine," the melody flows over this subtle, sinuous rhythm. Unlike "El Manisero," the clave pattern does not govern the accentuation of the melody;

LISTENING CUE · **"Begin the Beguine" (1935),** Cole Porter. Xavier Cugat and His Orchestra.

STYLE Beguine (Americanized Latin song) · **FORM** AA^{1}BA^{2}CC, expanded song form, with each phrase double the normal length

Listen For . . .

INSTRUMENTATION
Full downtown Latin orchestra, with the most audible being vocal, strings, rhythm section with piano, bass, and many Latin percussion instruments (bongos, maracas, and claves), trumpets, accordion, and marimba

RHYTHM
Beguine rhythm: bass on beats 1, 3, and 4; chords on every after beat; two kinds of rhythmic play: slow triplets float over accompaniment; offbeat accents in accompaniment

MELODY
Unfolds slowly from riff-like ideas that float over the beat rather than bounce off it; builds gradually toward the final climactic phrases

TEXTURE
Melody with rich, percussion-heavy accompaniment

Remember . . .

PORTER'S LONG SONG
A very long, well-integrated song, three times the length of a typical pop song

LATINESQUE SONG
Porter's take on Latin rhythms, delivered in Cugat's commercial Latin style; music sounds Latin, but is not in clave.

LATIN ORCHESTRA
A sweet band (note the violins) with Latin percussion instruments, plus accordion and marimba

UPSCALE MUSIC
Porter's song = significant step up in sophistication from late 1920s songs; Cugat's rendition, with strings, rich percussion, floating rhythms = comparably high-class

Listen to this selection in CourseMate.

COLE PORTER

in fact, the melody actually soars over the underlying rhythm, with long notes and slow triplets that do not line up with the Latin accompaniment (recall that a triplet divides the beat or other rhythmic unit into three equal parts). In Cugat's recording, a percussionist plays the claves, but the clave rhythm and the melody move independently. Here the clave rhythm is simply a strand in the rich tapestry of percussion sounds; it does not serve as the rhythmic reference point, as it did in "El Manisero."

Cugat's recording shows one important way in which Latin elements filtered into American popular music. American composers borrowed from the Latin music that they heard and interpreted it through their own musical understanding. Latin bandleaders like Cugat accommodated the American composer and played to the American public. Most American musicians ignored the clave rhythm because it was so foreign to their musical experience, but they found the rippling beguine accompaniment, with patterns similar to more familiar music, easy to adapt.

While Cugat was performing downtown at the Waldorf, a group of Latin musicians were creating a new kind of Latin music in the Hispanic section of uptown of uptown New York. From their efforts would come the third Latin dance fad, the mambo.

CHAPTER 33

Latin Music in the United States, 1940–1960

The establishment of a Latin district, or *barrio,* in New York dates back to the turn of the twentieth century, when, as a consequence of the 1898 Spanish-American War, Spain ceded Puerto Rico to the United States. Puerto Ricans were allowed to immigrate to the United States without restriction. Latins from other parts of the Caribbean soon followed, and by the late 1920s a substantial community of Cuban musicians resided in the United States. Some appeared in vaudeville or worked in society dance orchestras, but many also played for clubs and recorded for companies catering to the growing Latin community. New York was the most popular destination. Most Latins settled in upper Manhattan's east Harlem; Cubans shared their music with other immigrant Latinos and Americans of Cuban and Puerto Rican descent.

Among the Cuban musicians and, later, the Puerto Rican musicians who worked with them, there were two distinct Latin styles, downtown and uptown. The **downtown Latin style** was intended for the white American market. The **uptown Latin style** served the musical needs of the ever-growing Latin community in New York. This music was more African, with much heavier percussion and denser, more complex rhythmic textures. Its most popular expression was the mambo.

The Mambo

The **mambo** was the third of the twentieth-century Latin dance fads, after the tango and the rumba, but the first to develop on American soil. It merged authentic Afro-Cuban *son* with big-band horns and riffs. The style was born in 1940, when Machito (Frank Grillo), New York's first important *sonero* (lead singer in a *son* band), formed his own band, Machito's Afro-Cubans, and hired fellow Cuban Mario Bauza as musical director. Bauza had worked in the African-American swing bands of Cab Calloway and Chick Webb and wanted to combine Cuban rhythms with the horn sound of swing. Their new style provided an uptown alternative to the commercial Cugat sound.

By the late 1940s, the mambo had begun to attract notice outside of the uptown *barrio*. Downtown ballrooms like New York's Palladium Dance Hall served as venues for this new dance fad. The mambo caught on

Photo by Neil Stevenson/Rex USA, Courtesy Everett Collection

TITO PUENTE performing at the Royal Festival Hall, London, Britain, 1993. Note the expanded timbales setup of several drums, all about the same size.

with the non-Latin audience, although Americanized mambos enjoyed greater mainstream success. The dilution of the mambo as it entered the mainstream paralleled the watering down of the rumba in the early 1930s. What differentiated the fate of the mambo from that of the rumba was the presence of a stable, enthusiastic U.S. audience for Afro-Cuban–inspired music. In the 1930s, the audience for authentic Cuban music had been too small to support expatriate Cuban musicians. Twenty years later that audience had grown large enough to support the undiluted Afro-Cuban sounds of the mambo.

The presence of two "mambo kings" in the 1950s brings to light the division between commercial and Afro-Cuban Latin music. For white audiences pianist/bandleader Perez Prado was king. His recordings, many of them called simply "Mambo No. 1," "No. 2," and so on, offered the commercial sound of the mambo for the masses. The extent of his entry into the mainstream market can be gauged by the success of his biggest hit, "Cherry Pink and Apple Blossom White." But his style often had little to do with authentic Afro-Cuban music. In many of his recordings, Afro-Cuban rhythms and instrumentation are severely diluted or completely absent.

For Latins the "king of the mambo" during the 1950s was Tito Puente (1923–2000). Born in New York of Puerto Rican parents, Puente was an alumnus of Machito's band, in which he played timbales. By the early 1950s, he had formed his own band, for which he also composed and arranged. His style, with its heavy brass and full Cuban rhythm section, appealed much more strongly to Latin audiences than Prado's music did.

"Complicacion," which Puente recorded in 1958, shows a successful blend of American and Afro-Cuban

LISTENING CUE • "Complicacion" (1958), Francisco Aguabella. Tito Puente and His Band.

STYLE Mambo • **FORM** Multisectional form with two similar chorus-like sections

Listen For . . .

INSTRUMENTATION
Big-band horn section (full trumpet and sax sections) plus piano, bass, and full Afro-Cuban percussion section: conga drums, claves, cowbell, and timbales, among others

RHYTHM
Fast-moving rhythms in percussion parts, with no instrument consistently marking the beat; lots of syncopation: in percussion, vocal lines, *tumbao* (offbeat bass rhythm) and *montuno* (completely syncopated piano figures) patterns, and horn riffs

MELODY
A series of short riffs, usually repeated, in the instrument and group vocal lines. Solo vocal part has longer phrases.

TEXTURE
Thick, with several layers: lots of rhythmic activity in percussion parts, plus chords in horns

Remember . . .

MAMBO
Afro-Cuban rhythm (full percussion section and complex rhythms) plus big-band swing (horn sections playing riffs)

CLAVE RHYTHM
Hear it clearly at 0:28—**Yo la que-ri-a (x)** (bold syllables = clave rhythm)

RHYTHMIC FLOATING
Piano and bass often play against time rather than marking the beat; other instruments play fast patterns.

INSPIRACION
Inspiracion = Latin jamming; in big band jazz, horns solo; in mambo, percussionists improvise together

Listen to this selection in CourseMate.

elements. The instrumental accompaniment mixes big-band–style horns (brass and saxes playing riffs and sustained chords) with a full Latin percussion section.

Particularly in the second section, it is possible to hear key elements of Afro-Cuban rhythm. The repeated riff conforms to the clave rhythm, and several layers of percussion produce a dense texture with considerable rhythmic conflict. The bass plays the offbeat ***tumbao*** pattern, while the piano plays an active pattern, called a ***montuno,*** that recalls ragtime figurations but is even more syncopated.

UNIT 8

LOOKING BACK, LOOKING AHEAD

AT THE TURN OF THE TWENTIETH CENTURY, Americans were largely unaware of Latin music, and few acknowledged its indirect influence on the new syncopated rhythms in the cakewalk, ragtime, and popular song. By mid-century, Latin music had a firm toehold in American culture. Couples danced the tango, rumba, mambo, and cha-cha-cha and listened to Latin-tinged songs and jazz. Both Latin and American musicians were creating Latin song and dance music, including some with authentic Afro-Cuban instruments and rhythms.

However, for pop, jazz, and even commercial Latin musicians, the rhythms of the rumba and mambo were an alternative to the prevailing styles. It was impossible to mesh Latin rhythms, however diluted, with foxtrot or swing rhythm. Only with New Orleans rhythm and blues and, later, rock and roll did Latin rhythms and instruments blend smoothly—even imperceptibly—into the musical fabric, because adding Afro-Cuban elements no longer required adjusting the rhythmic foundation. By the 1960s, these elements were often part of the mix, rather than apart from the mainstream.

Popular Music Matures: Musical Theater, Modern Jazz, and Song Interpretation

UNIT 9

UNIT 9

We tend to filter our understanding of an earlier time and place through more recent developments and the current state of affairs. For contemporary audiences, the rise of rhythm and blues and rock and roll has eclipsed every other development in popular music during the 1950s.

However, the popular music landscape looked dramatically different to audiences in postwar America. Market share and mindshare belonged mainly to musical theater, modern jazz, and popular song. Musical theater enjoyed both popularity and prestige: The top Broadway musicals were regarded as elite popular entertainment. For mid-century audiences, modern jazz was swing's eccentric son. Whereas the more mainstream jazz musicians supported pop singers on stage and in the studios, bop and cool musicians performed mainly in jazz clubs that attracted a more adventurous and avant-garde audience that included beats and other hipsters as well as skilled and sophisticated musicians like conductor/composer Leonard Bernstein. With country, Latin, folk, and rhythm and blues, popularity and prestige typically reflected the extent of pop influence. The stronger the pop orientation—most evident in cover versions of country, Latin, and rhythm-and-blues hits—the greater the acceptance.

The postwar media revolution that reshaped the music industry highlights the relative commercial and cultural importance of the diverse popular music genres active around mid-century. Beginning in the late 1940s, television emerged as the new dominant mass medium. Sales mushroomed from 6,000 in 1946 to 2 million in 1949; by the mid-fifties, television was a household staple, and the first color sets were on the market. Pop had by far the strongest presence on television: non-pop acts may have occasionally appeared on network shows, but pop stars like Frank Sinatra and Perry Como hosted them.

Because television quickly took over radio's role as the primary source of all-purpose entertainment, radio stations began programming recorded music far more frequently. Most stations broadcast pop, especially during peak listening hours. Alternative programming was relegated to odd times—late at night, early in the morning.

Two new recording formats appeared the in the late 1940s: Columbia Records introduced **long-playing (LP),** or **33 rpm, records** in 1948 and RCA brought out the 7-inch **45 rpm single,** which held about three minutes of music, a year later. It took a while for these new formats to catch on because they required new record players, but 78 shellac discs were all but obsolete by the middle of the 1950s.

The new formats underscore the stratification of popular music at mid-century. During the 1950s, long-playing albums catered mainly to adult tastes: musical theater and film soundtracks, "easy-listening" pop, jazz, and classical music. Singles (both 45s and 78s) included a wide range of pop plus country, Latin, rhythm and blues, and more.

In this unit, we survey developments in musical theater, jazz, and popular song and singing in the decade and a half after 1945, sampling classic performances in each genre.

CHAPTER 34
The Golden Age of Musical Theater

For more than twenty years, lyricist Lorenz (Larry) Hart (1895–1943) and songwriter Richard Rodgers (1902–1979) persevered with considerable success through an increasingly difficult working relationship: Rodgers was a workaholic and Hart was an alcoholic. When Hart, whose health was deteriorating, declined an offer from Rodgers to turn a play by Lynn Riggs, *Green Grow the Lilacs* (1931), into a musical, Rodgers then turned to Oscar Hammerstein II, who had enjoyed great success with *Show Boat,* but little since then. Out of their first collaboration came *Oklahoma!* (1943), a musical based on Riggs's play. Critics loved it and audiences flocked to see it. *Oklahoma!* ran on Broadway for more than five years; its 2,248 performances far exceeded any previous run.

Rodgers and Hammerstein and the Golden Age of Musical Theater

The success of *Oklahoma!* marked the beginning of the golden age of musical theater and Rodgers and Hammerstein's reign as the preeminent composers of musical theater. The team followed *Oklahoma!* with several more musicals, including *Carousel* (1945), *State Fair* (1947, their only musical written specifically for film), *South Pacific* (1949), *The King and I* (1951), and *The Sound of Music* (1959). Their partnership, the most successful in the history of musical theater, ended only with Hammerstein's death in 1960.

Rodgers and Hammerstein's musicals built on the significant musical-dramatic innovations first introduced in *Show Boat:* depth of character portrayal, seriousness of plot, integration of song into the story line, and a willingness to challenge conventional practice. The extraordinarily enthusiastic public support for a dramatically credible musical inspired a wholesale shift in values, by both creators and audience.

Because of their innovative approach to musical theater and their tremendous critical and popular success—almost all of their successful Broadway musicals also became extremely popular films—Rodgers and Hammerstein's musicals were a major influence on other Broadway productions and the standard by which all other musicals were measured. This is reflected in such key matters as the choice and the source of subjects, dramatic integrity, and the musical language.

Musically, however, the Rodgers and Hammerstein musicals turned back the clock. Melody reigned supreme. Most characters sang with classically trained voices in a quasi-operatic style. Theater orchestras sounded more like symphony orchestras than swing bands. The songs abandoned the rhythmic innovations of the modern era; syncopation all but disappeared, and swing was in another musical world.

In a genre in which so much of the music is tuneful melody, it is challenging to make the music dramatically evocative. Kern could allude to black characters in *Show Boat* because the spiritual and blues were familiar genres with strong associations, but that was a special circumstance. More often, Rodgers and his peers made little effort to adapt their style to the story. The music from *Oklahoma!* bears almost no resemblance to country or western music, nor does the music for *South Pacific* have much relation to Polynesian music or even popular music during World War II. Instead, Rodgers made his music more dramatically compelling mainly by bringing to his songs some of the breadth and sophistication of classical music. He uses popular song conventions as a point of departure but expands and modifies them; their orchestration and performance complement these changes. We hear these developments in a performance of "Some Enchanted Evening," a love song from *South Pacific.*

South Pacific

South Pacific is a musical based on two short stories from a book by James Michener entitled *Tales of the South Pacific.* The plot takes place far away but not long ago; the action occurs during World War II. The story centers around the war and on love. There are two relationships, both of them with an interracial component. One involves Emile de Becque, a French plantation owner on a Polynesian island, and Nellie Forbush, a Navy nurse

LISTENING CUE • **"Some Enchanted Evening" (1949),** Richard Rodgers and Oscar Hammerstein II. Ezio Pinza, vocal.

STYLE Musical theater song • **FORM** Individualized popular song form: three long phrases (A, A^1, A^2) with an interlude (comparable to the bridge, but shorter) that also serves as the closing section

Listen For . . .

INSTRUMENTATION
Voice plus full orchestra, with violins and orchestral winds most prominent

PERFORMANCE STYLE
Pinza sings in operatic vocal style.

RHYTHM
Moderately slow two-beat rhythm, but not for dancing

RHYTHM/MELODY
Main melodic idea = "riff-inspired" six-note pattern, but with no syncopation

MELODY
A sections comprised of two long-arching phrases

Remember . . .

LOVE SONG
Soaring, expansive melody supports "love-at-first-sight" lyric.

CLASSICAL INFLUENCE = UPSCALE POP
Song and performance invest popular song with classical trappings: melody with almost no syncopation, rich harmony, operatic singing, orchestral accompaniment; all suggest alignment with classical music, the most prestigious musical tradition at mid-century.

BIG SONG
Long phrases, individual form, and slow tempo = one statement of form in three or more minutes

TURNING BACK THE CLOCK
Musical theater looks back to the musical past (melody-oriented song; classical music) rather than connecting with present to look to future.

Listen to this selection in CourseMate.

from Arkansas. The other involves Joe Cable, a Marine lieutenant, who falls in love with Liat, a beautiful local girl. Both couples talk about marriage, but neither of the Americans is willing to commit to a permanent relationship because of race: Liat is Polynesian, and Emile, a widower, has two biracial children from his first marriage. When Nellie rejects Emile's proposal, Emile and Joe lead an expedition behind Japanese lines. In a bittersweet ending that is a reflection of the times, Joe is killed in combat and Emile returns home. Nellie overcomes her prejudice, and they marry.

In post–World War II America, the racial element was problematic. In particular, there was a hostile reaction, especially in the South, to the song "You've Got to Be Carefully Taught," in which the lyric, sung by Joe, asserts that racism is learned, not inherited. Indeed, if Broadway were in the South, the marriage of Liat and Joe would have been so controversial that the show would likely not have made it to the stage.

Emile sings "Some Enchanted Evening" when he first meets Nellie; the song expresses his immediate infatuation with her, although he does so in the second person. Its lush orchestration, expansive form, and above all its soaring melody, sung with great dignity by opera star Ezio Pinza, enable Emile to linger in the moment.

As this excerpt from *South Pacific* demonstrates, the musicals of Rodgers and Hammerstein helped establish musical theater as the most prestigious popular genre during the 1950s. *West Side Story* would bring the musical to an even higher level of dramatic and musical sophistication.

Beyond the Broadway Musical: *West Side Story*

The idea of bringing Shakespeare to Broadway came late: Rodgers and Hart's *The Boys from Syracuse,* an adaptation of the playwright's *The Comedy of Errors,* opened only in 1938. A decade later, Cole Porter modernized and musicalized *The Taming of the Shrew* in *Kiss Me, Kate.* In 1957, Leonard Bernstein's *West Side Story* offered an even more radical Shakespeare metamorphosis.

Leonard Bernstein

West Side Story grew out of the collaboration of composer Leonard Bernstein, lyricist Stephen Sondheim, choreographer Jerome Robbins, and librettist Arthur Laurents. The key player was Bernstein (1918–1990). By the time he composed *West Side Story,* Bernstein had established himself as one of America's most multitalented musicians. He had an active career as a conductor, would become music director of the New York Philharmonic in 1958, and had already composed three Broadway musicals, an opera, two ballets, two symphonies, film sound

tracks, and numerous other works. He was an excellent pianist, whether performing the classical repertoire or his own compositions. He would become best known to the general public as a commentator on music, through television programs such as the *Young People's Concerts,* which began in 1959. He also wrote several widely read books on music. The breadth of Bernstein's skills and interests—he had strong affinities for jazz and theater music—is evident throughout the musical.

West Side Story

West Side Story, first staged in 1957 and filmed in 1961, was creative and innovative in its plot, music, and use of dance. Its inventiveness begins with its libretto, which puts a new twist on an old practice: Instead of using a long-ago time or an exotic locale, the collaborators took a timeless story—Shakespeare's *Romeo and Juliet*—and set it in contemporary New York.

Bernstein and his collaborators turned the Capulets and Montagues into two street gangs: the white Jets and the Puerto Rican Sharks. Tony, a friend of Riff, the leader of the Jets, and a former member of the gang, is the modern counterpart to Romeo. Maria, the sister of Bernardo, the leader of the Sharks, is the modern Juliet. She has just come from Puerto Rico to marry Chino, Bernardo's friend. Tony spies Maria at a dance and immediately falls in love. While Tony and Maria begin their romance, the two gangs plan a rumble (a gang fight). Maria learns of the fight and asks Tony to break it up. Despite Tony's efforts, the fight quickly escalates: Bernardo kills Riff, and Tony, now enraged, grabs Riff's knife and kills Bernardo. Tony visits Maria after she learns that he has killed her brother. In spite of this, they long to escape. They have a brief moment together before Chino shoots Tony, who is carried off by members of both gangs.

Although there are light moments, *West Side Story* is a tragedy: Laurents did nothing to soften the story of Shakespeare's famous star-crossed lovers. That he brought it into the present only made its impact more immediate. No earlier musical had ever approached the realism of *West Side Story.*

"Cool" and the Innovations of *West Side Story*

Among the most innovative features of the musical are Bernstein's music—both the songs and the dance music—and the total integration of dance into the show. In *West Side Story,* Bernstein brought his compositional range to bear in ways that songwriters, even those as skilled as Jerome Kern and Richard Rodgers, couldn't. His musical language is generally up to date. He wrote contemporary jazz for the Jets dance numbers. For the Sharks, he wrote Latin, or at least Latinate, numbers. (There is a mambo, for the dance in the gym, but other music for Puerto Rican characters, like "America," seems derived more from classical music by Latin composers than from Puerto Rican popular music.)

The love songs ("Maria," "Tonight," "One Hand, One Heart," "Somewhere") find a middle ground between Tin Pan Alley conventions and the more extensive development customarily heard in an opera aria. However, it is in the instrumental writing that Bernstein truly flexes his compositional muscle. In *West Side Story,* dance is functional, not decorative; choreographer Jerome Robbins was a full partner in the collaboration. For dance numbers, Bernstein often shook free of the constraints of popular song and composed extended, complex music that enhanced the expressive impact of the dance.

Among the most dramatically compelling dance scenes is that for "Cool." In the film version, it occurs after the rumble, when the gangs have fled the scene of the stabbings and the Jets have reassembled in a garage after scattering to avoid the police. Some of the Jets are almost boiling over in their urgency to gain revenge on the Sharks, but Ice, the de facto new leader, cautions them to be "cool." In this scene, dance speaks louder than words or song. It captures the repressed emotion of the gang, ready to explode at the slightest provocation and kept under control only by the force of Ice's will. Bernstein supports their nervous energy with a jazz ballet that features an extremely hip fugal section.

To characterize the Jets, Bernstein offers his take on modern jazz. Five years later, he might have used rock and roll, but when he began working on the musical, modern jazz was the "coolest" current music, and it had a distinctly "outsider" association during the 1950s. Bernstein's skillful evocation of modern jazz and Latin music was a distinct departure from the practice of Rodgers and Hammerstein and other golden-era theater composers, who seldom attempted to use musical style to evoke character or place. It would be one of Bernstein's most far-reaching innovations.

LISTENING CUE • **"Cool," (1957)** Leonard Bernstein and Stephen Sondheim. Original Broadway cast.

STYLE Jazz-influenced Broadway song and dance • **FORM** Two-phrase pop song, with expansion and interpolations • **GENRE** Musical theater

Listen For . . .

RHYTHM
Swing rhythm (but usually without walking bass), crisp backbeat, evident especially in finger snap/drum sections; lots of syncopation, from the opening riff on

MELODY
Melody grows out of a three-note riff. Both the melody of the vocal section and the new melodies in the central instrumental section tend to be angular with frequent melodic skips.

INSTRUMENTATION
"Everyday" voice (speaking and singing), full orchestra plus rhythm section and big-band instruments. Woodwinds (flutes, clarinets, etc.) featured throughout much of the instrumental sections.

HARMONY
Complex chords far removed from I-IV-V

TEXTURE
Considerable variation, from just percussion to full big band. Central section often has two or more melodic lines sounding simultaneously.

Remember . . .

HIP TALK, CA. 1957
Sondheim's lyrics, from the song's title on, make liberal use of 1950s slang: "cool," "daddy-o," "rocket in your pocket." But he combines words in clever ways, for example, "Breeze it, buzz it, easy does it."

COOL MUSIC
As Bernstein was writing the music for this show, rock and roll was just getting started. For adults, the coolest music was "cool" jazz. Bernstein's musical is in an authentic-sounding modern jazz style.

JAZZ/CLASSICAL FUSION
Bernstein seamlessly blends jazz and classical music here. The musical materials evoke the angular lines and rich and distinctive harmonies of jazz, the relentless ride pattern of the drummer was the jazz standard at the time, and the musicians play with a jazz feel. At the same time, there are no improvised solos, and the form and texture show the strong influence of classical techniques, most notably rich counterpoint, especially in the middle section.

Listen to this selection in CourseMate.

Before Oklahoma! *we remember mainly the songs; beginning with* Oklahoma! *we remember mainly the shows.*

Golden Age Musicals

The most succinct way to describe the difference between musicals produced before and after *Oklahoma!* is this: Before *Oklahoma!* we remember mainly the songs; beginning with *Oklahoma!* we remember mainly the shows. Few pre-1943 musicals are revived with any frequency; *Show Boat* and Cole Porter's lighthearted *Anything Goes* are the almost singular exceptions. By contrast, the musicals of Rodgers and Hammerstein, Lerner and Loewe (*My Fair Lady*), Frank Loesser (*Guys and Dolls*), and Leonard Bernstein (*West Side Story*) are performed regularly at all levels, from high school, college, and community theater productions to revivals on Broadway and London's West End.

A primary reason for the frequent production of the golden-age musicals is their success as dramas. They tell good stories well. Recall that the majority of the plots are based on existing literature, from Shakespeare to top contemporary writers. Moreover, song and dance are in the service of the story. As "Some Enchanted Evening" suggests, Rodgers tweaked popular song conventions to create songs that were distinctive and dramatically appropriate. The combination of compelling stories and appealing, artful music helps account for the frequent production of these musicals.

In the musicals of Rodgers and Hammerstein and those influenced by them, musical theater turned back the clock stylistically, even as most other styles continued along the evolutionary path of the 1920s and 1930s. As a result, musical theater grew apart from other musical developments of the era, such as jazz-influenced pop singing, rhythm and blues, country music, and Afro-Cuban music. Hammerstein's death in 1960 brought this era to a close.

Bernstein's landmark musical anticipated one of the most important new directions in late twentieth century musical theater. In the richness of its musical setting, breadth of musical numbers, and the evocative use of musical style to convey time and place, *West Side Story* anticipates the critically acclaimed musicals of Bernstein's lyricist Stephen Sondheim and other like-minded composers.

CHAPTER 35

Modern Jazz

In the first verse of his 1957 hit "Rock and Roll Music," Chuck Berry sings, "I've got no kick against modern jazz/ Unless they try to play it too darn fast/And change the beauty of the melody." In these three lines, Berry highlights the salient features of the new jazz style of the late 1940s and 1950s—and its reception. Bop, the trend-setting style of the 1940s, often featured performances at breakneck speed ("too darn fast"), with new melodies set to familiar chord progressions. "Salt Peanuts," the performance discussed in this chapter, moves at a tempo of about 300 beats per minute and features an acrobatic, angular melody that replaces the much simpler Gershwin song "I Got Rhythm" ("change the beauty of the melody"). And, like Berry, many listeners found the modern jazz that emerged after bop to be more accessible when the tempos dropped and the melodies became more tuneful.

"I've got no kick against modern jazz/ Unless they try to play it too darn fast/And change the beauty of the melody."
—Chuck Berry

Bop: A Music of Liberation

Bop (or **bebop**) was a radically new jazz style that seemed to appear out of nowhere. It took shape during the early 1940s at Minton's Playhouse, a Harlem jazz club, while a ban on instrumental recording was in effect. When bop musicians finally began recording in 1945, their music touched off a revolution in jazz.

Bop conveyed a new message: liberation. The message permeated every aspect of the music and the milieu in which it thrived. The freeing of jazz began with the music itself: The innovations of bebop gave the music and those who played it unprecedented freedom. Its emergence as a commercial music—music played not only for fun but also for enough funds to live on—would play a major role in freeing American culture from the idea that art in music was more or less the exclusive province of European white males. Bebop musicians would comprise the first counterculture, planting the seed for the revolution in mass culture for which rock was the soundtrack.

© Frank Driggs Collection/Getty Images

On stage in 1951 at Charlie Parker's nightclub, Birdland, in Manhattan, are (left to right) Tommy Potter on bass, Charlie Parker on alto saxophone, and Dizzy Gillespie on trumpet. On the right, briefly joining them, is tenor saxophonist John Coltrane.

These innovations were the product of a small circle of musicians, including drummers Kenny Clarke and Max Roach, pianists Bud Powell and Thelonious Monk, and trumpeter Dizzy Gillespie. However, the dominant figure in the formation of bop style was a saxophonist named Charlie Parker.

Charlie Parker and "Salt Peanuts"

Charlie Parker (1920–1955), known familiarly as "Bird" (a shortened form of "Yardbird," a nickname he acquired early on) came of age in Kansas City, Missouri, a jazz hotbed in the 1930s. By 1940, he was in New York and had joined with the handful of musicians who would create bebop. By 1945, the small circle of bop musicians had been recorded, and Parker would be bop's guiding force for most of his too-short life; he died at an early age from severe substance abuse problems. Heroin was the drug of choice for too many jazz musicians; Parker was the most conspicuous casualty.

We hear all of the key features of bop style in a 1945 recording of "Salt Peanuts," a tune written by trumpeter Dizzy Gillespie. It features Gillespie on trumpet and singing the signature riff, plus Parker on alto saxophone, and a rhythm section of piano, bass, and drums. In this recording, the salient features of bop style, which affected almost every musical parameter—rhythm, melody, harmony, sound, and texture—are clearly evident. Among the most significant innovations were these five:

- *The emancipation of the rhythm section*. In pre-bop jazz, the almost exclusive rhythmic role of the rhythm section was beat keeping. In bop, only the bassist consistently marked the beat, with a walking bass line.

LISTENING CUE · **"Salt Peanuts" (1945),** Dizzy Gillespie. Gillespie, trumpet and vocal; Charlie Parker, alto saxophone; Al Haig, piano; Curly Russell, bass; and Sidney Catlett, drums.

STYLE Bebop · **FORM** Several improvised choruses on a melody based on AABA popular song, with periodic interludes

Listen For . . .

INSTRUMENTATION
Alto saxophone, trumpet, piano, string bass, drums

RHYTHM
Walking bass keeps four-beat rhythm at very fast tempo. Fast streams of notes have offbeat accents (be-BOP) in improvised solos.

MELODY
Bop-style lines in solos and interludes: fast-moving, angular lines

HARMONY
Complex, clashing harmonies in introduction, interludes

Remember . . .

EMANCIPATED RHYTHM SECTION
Liberation of drummer and pianist (chord I instrument) from steady timekeeping

AGGRESSIVE SOUND
Both horns have edgy sound; not warm, like swing-era saxophone.

VIRTUOSITY
Improvisation at extremely fast tempos is a supreme technical challenge.

MUSIC FOR LISTENING
Bebop divorces modern jazz from any connection with dance because of fast tempos and prominent syncopation.

Listen to this selection in CourseMate.

Pianists "**comped.**" That is, they played chords intermittently to provide accents; these often fell on the offbeats. Drummers transferred the ride pattern from the hi-hat to the ride cymbal, which gave a more continuous sound, and played intermittent, syncopated accents. As a result, both drums and piano (or guitar) were almost completely liberated from the steady timekeeping of swing-era jazz.

- *Rapid tempos.* Tempo took a quantum leap in bop. One reason for this dramatic jump was simply the exhilaration the musicians felt improvising fluently at such daredevil speeds—bop was the downhill skiing of music. In addition, the brisk tempos were one way of separating musical wheat from the chaff during the after-hours jam sessions: it was bop musicians' most obvious method of excluding those who had not spent enough time in the woodshed to develop their skill.
- *Asymmetrical, irregular melodic lines.* Much of the repertory of bop musicians consisted of newly composed melodies set to the chord progressions of familiar popular songs and blues. In bop, the melodies matched the improvisational style of the musicians: Bop-style melodic lines typically consist of a stream of fast-moving notes ending on an offbeat accent (be-BOP).
- *Complex harmony.* Bop musicians enriched the harmonic vocabulary of jazz, interpolating new, more complex chords to the relatively simple harmony of blues and popular song.
- *An aggressive sonority.* Bop horn players, especially Charlie Parker and Dizzy Gillespie, turned their back on the warm, mellow timbres of swing-era horn players. Parker, in particular, opted for a full but penetrating sound, usually produced with little or no vibrato.

Bop was a hot music: aggressive sounds and high energy. It spawned a broad range of progressive jazz styles, some quite different from bop. The first post-bop style to emerge was "cool," which kept the intricacy of bop but took the edge off. One offshoot of cool was "West Coast" jazz, so called because so many of its players were based in Los Angeles or San Francisco. The keepers of the flame were the hard bop musicians of the 1950s, most of them black and based on the East Coast. More than any other, they built on the legacy of Charlie Parker, even as he was wasting away. These and other styles were collectively identified as "modern jazz." Most retreated from the high intensity of bop or veered off in another direction. Still, the imprint of bop was evident on virtually all of the new jazz of the early 1950s.

Jazz as Art

The currently fashionable—and largely accurate—description for jazz is "America's art music," but the identification of jazz as an American art came well after the fact. Armstrong's playing in recordings like "Hotter Than That" evidences the classic measures of artistry: mastery, expressiveness, inspiration, individuality. But it was not regarded as art because it was not like classical music, the one widely accepted art music, and it was heard in speakeasies, not concert halls. Benny Goodman's appearances at Carnegie Hall, with his own bands and as part of the "Spirituals to Swing" series, showcased the artistry of top swing musicians. However, swing as a style was still mainly dance music, despite the work of Goodman, Ellington, and others.

By contrast, bop was an art music from the start. Its originators created a style so novel, so complex, and so technically demanding that when it first became known, only a very few musicians—jazz, popular, or classical—were proficient enough to perform it capably. Its original venues were dingy nightclubs in Harlem and along 52nd Street in New York, a short distance from Carnegie Hall geographically but far away socially and culturally. However, around the time that bop emerged, promoters such as Norman Granz began booking jazz concerts. His "Jazz at the Philharmonic" tours began in 1944 and remained a part of the jazz scene through 1957. In the summers, with the creation of jazz festivals, jazz became outdoor concert music. The festival provided a concert-like setting with the focus squarely on the musicians, usually with a large audience in attendance; the outdoor location made it less formal and more relaxed than a traditional concert hall. There were festivals as early as the mid-1940s, but the first annually recurring festival was the Newport (Rhode Island) Jazz Festival, which began in 1954.

The most consciously art-oriented developments in modern jazz were jazz/classical syntheses. These took many forms. Among the most noteworthy were collaborations between Dave Brubeck, Leonard Bernstein, and the New York Philharmonic; a series of albums by Miles Davis and Gil Evans, who had first worked together to create cool jazz; and third-stream music, a concerted effort by the Modern Jazz Quartet, Gunther Schuller, and the Beaux Arts String Quartet to fuse jazz and classical music.

© Michael Ochs Archives/Getty Images

From the start, the Modern Jazz Quartet (left to right, vibraphonist Milt Jackson, drummer Connie Kay, bassist Percy Heath, and pianist John Lewis, seated), presented themselves formally, as befit the elegance of their music.

The third-stream experiment was the most extreme expression of the classicizing-jazz approach of the Modern Jazz Quartet. We encounter a more enduring example of their approach next.

The Modern Jazz Quartet: Jazz as Concert Music

A performance by the Modern Jazz Quartet was a formal affair. Often it took place in a concert hall. The Quartet—Milt Jackson, vibraphone; John Lewis, piano; Percy Heath, bass; Connie Kay, drums—would come onstage dressed in tuxedos and carrying themselves with elegance and dignity. As they began to play, the music would send much the same message. It was restrained, not extroverted, and more controlled than spontaneous. The intricacy and subtlety of their musical interaction elicited comparisons with classical chamber music—it was a comparison that the group, and especially John Lewis, enjoyed.

In a very real way, the Modern Jazz Quartet was swimming upstream. All except Kay, who joined the group in 1955, were veterans of the bop revolution; Jackson, Lewis, and Heath played with Dizzy Gillespie's big band at various times between 1945 and 1950. They continued to work together in the early 1950s, finally consolidating as the Modern Jazz Quartet in 1952. Partly because of their instrumentation—the vibraphone is not a loud instrument—and partly because of their temperament, they turned their back on many of the features of bop style. Unlike hard bop combos, which played at full throttle so much of the time, the Modern Jazz Quartet seldom stretched to bop's extremes in tempo, loudness, and aggressiveness.

Before long, however, audiences recognized their virtues; by the end of the 1950s, they were a jazz institution. They stayed together full time until 1974—an astonishingly long tenure for any musical group—and reunited for several months each year, beginning in 1981. They remained together until 1997.

Almost from the beginning of his career, John Lewis sought to bring elements of classical music into jazz: it would inform virtually all of his writing for the Modern Jazz Quartet. We hear a fine example of it in "Django," one of his works for the Modern Jazz Quartet. ("Django" is a tribute to Belgian jazz guitarist Django Reinhardt.) The version presented here is a 1960 recording of a European concert performance of Lewis's 1954 composition.

The one musical area in which bop and post-bop jazz styles were not revolutionary was form: performances

LISTENING CUE • **"Django" (1954, recorded 1960),** John Lewis. The Modern Jazz Quartet.

STYLE Modern jazz • **FORM** Large-scale arch form, with high point in middle; improvisation on an unusually structured four-section chord progression. There is no head, just solos over the progression.

Listen For . . .

INSTRUMENTATION
Vibraphone, piano, string bass, drums

RHYTHM
Varied timekeeping: from no steady pulse to steady walking bass. Delicate swing: solos, comping, and drum accents create rhythmic play over bass timekeeping.

HARMONY
Long, irregularly patterned progression in multiple keys

TEXTURE
Airy variant of postwar rhythm section interplay: timekeeping in bass and ride pattern; rhythmic play from chord instrument and drums

Remember . . .

MODERNIZING SWING
Rhythm section = less emphasis on timekeeping, more on rhythmic play (comping, offbeat drum accents)

IMPROVISATION WITHIN COMPOSITION
Arch form, control of activity behind soloists gives performance structure

CONCERT JAZZ
Modern Jazz Quartet members present themselves as concert performers in appearance, manner, and sound.

TIMELESS JAZZ STYLE
The core features of "Django"—approach to swing rhythm, interplay within rhythm, improvisational approach—become the standard for "straight-ahead" jazz after 1955.

Listen to this selection in CourseMate.

typically retained the head/solos/head formal plan. ("Salt Peanuts" is exceptional in this regard). By contrast, "Django" is a composition with a carefully planned architecture. In "Django," Lewis uses this variation form as a point of departure but goes well beyond it. To begin with, there is no head per se. The opening musical idea returns at the end; together they frame the improvised sections. Unlike other jazz performances we have heard, the opening material does not provide a harmonic template for improvisation. Lewis instead uses a quite different five-section plan.

A fragment of this material also serves as a keystone for the musical arch that Lewis creates by regulating the activity of the three rhythm instruments. Heath, the bassist, begins by playing one note every four beats, then every other beat, then finally walking, then playing an active riff. Lewis escalates his comping as Jackson's solo builds. Kay, the drummer, begins with silence, then with brushes, before changing over to sticks. (I had the opportunity to ask Connie Kay how much of this was predetermined; he told me that Lewis decided all but the subtlest details.) To ratchet down the performance back to its original tempo, Lewis directed the bass to slow down his riff.

We sense the arch through the carefully controlled escalation of activity by the rhythm section, from the outset through the end of Jackson's solo, and de-escalation through Lewis's piano solo and the slowing down of the riff by Heath. This gives the performance an entirely different feel. In most live jazz performances, especially small group performances, we are in the moment; solos could go on for a long time, and they often did. There is little sense of overall structure other than the opening and closing statements of the head and the harmonic plan used for improvisation. But Lewis's pre-performance decisions act like a guiding hand. "Django" unfolds like a six-minute breath: Inhale during Jackson's solo; exhale during Lewis's.

"Django" also makes clear that modern jazz does not need to be fast, loud, or assertive. There is certainly passion in the group's playing, especially during Jackson's solo, and the music swings. But there is also elegance, an elegance without real precedent in jazz or elsewhere. With the Modern Jazz Quartet, jazz truly became a concert music.

Modern Jazz = Jazz

With the ascent of rock, "modern jazz" was no longer modern. But so many of the innovations of bop—the interplay within the rhythm section, the increased harmonic complexity, an improvisational approach based on flowing streams of notes, performances based on newly composed jazz-oriented melodies or significant adaptation of existing songs—became standard practice and have remained the default jazz style to the present.

Bop and the array of post-bop styles also confirmed jazz as a listening-only music. It was music completely divorced from social dancing, at times because of its tempos, and almost always because of the emancipation of the rhythm section from routine timekeeping and the emphasis on improvisational brilliance rather than tuneful melody.

CHAPTER 36
Popular Song Interpretation

In 1984, the Smithsonian Institution released a five-CD box set entitled *American Popular Song: Six Decades of Songwriters and Singers.* Like similar sets for jazz, blues, musical theater, and country music, this set offered a balanced retrospective of the history of a particular genre over an extended period.

One of the most intriguing differences between the popular song anthology and the other sets is the gap between composition and performance. For the other genres, the majority of the performances were recorded around the time the song was created. In the popular song anthology, the majority of the songs were composed before 1945, whereas the majority of the performances were recorded after 1945 by artists whose careers began or peaked during the 1950s.

This unusual circumstance was the product of two parallel developments. One was a growing body of **standards,** popular songs that retained their appeal well after their initial popularity. The other was the shift in focus from song to singer: the most admired singers sought to individualize their performances—to transform a song into a personal statement.

Song Interpretation

The practice of personalizing a song performance, begun in the 1930s by singers such as Armstrong, Waters, Holiday, and Crosby, became the most highly regarded approach to popular singing after 1945. Singers like Ella Fitzgerald, Frank Sinatra, and Sarah Vaughan, all of whom had begun their careers as band singers, and Nat Cole, who began his career as a jazz-oriented lounge pianist in the early 1940s, became popular solo artists during the late 1940s and 1950s. A new generation of singing stars, including Tony Bennett and Dinah Washington, joined them. Their recordings remain some of the most treasured pop recordings of the era.

One distinguishing feature of all of these singers is the way in which they put their personal stamp on a song performance: Within seconds, we recognize their sound and style. Moreover, they and the arrangers with whom they worked often reconceived the song by changing its underlying rhythm, performing it at a different tempo, or introducing new instrumental colors. As a result, new versions of standards were distinctively different from earlier recordings, and songs introduced by singers like Cole and Sinatra became identified more with the singer than with the songwriter.

Song interpretation begins with a distinctive vocal style. None of the song interpreters has a conventionally pretty voice. For example, Sinatra's voice at the beginning of his career, when he sang with Tommy Dorsey's orchestra, was silkier; he was a real crooner. Years of fast living, cigarettes, and alcohol took away the sweetness and added a heavy dose of grit. Cole's voice was warm and husky from the start.

All are masters of pacing; they are not bound by the beat. Typically, they will, at the very least, mold the song to their style. This often involves reshaping the melody, perhaps with subtle changes in timing to make the delivery of the lyric more speech-like, or even with significant alteration of the contour. Especially with standards, they may reconceive the song completely: An uptempo song becomes a ballad; a Latin song swings.

All of this transforms the relationship between song and singer. When we listened to Astaire sing "Cheek to Cheek," the focus was on the song. He delivered it impeccably, in a way perfectly suited to his film character, but he did not open a window to his soul. The new generation of popular singers reversed this dynamic. When they sing a song, we sense that they are using the song to share their feelings and life experiences. In so doing, they make what is essentially an impersonal song—a song anyone can choose to perform—more personal. Their version of a song stands out; it may come to be regarded as the definitive interpretation of the song.

Nat Cole

Nat "King" Cole (Nathaniel Coles, 1917– 1965) parlayed his superb piano-based jazz conception, smoke-filtered voice, and winning personality into a major career. He was the most popular and important black pop artist of the postwar era. Cole formed a piano–guitar–bass jazz trio in 1937, which he continued to lead through 1951. He gradually incorporated vocals into the group's performances. Backed by the trio, he scored his first big hit in 1943 with "Straighten Up and Fly Right," a bouncy song with a cautionary lyric. After the war, he gravitated to the pop marketplace. Recording mainly with a large studio orchestra and supported by lush arrangements, he produced an almost unbroken string of pop hits, beginning with "(I Love You) for Sentimental Reasons" and "The Christmas Song" (both 1946). The majority of the hits that followed were smooth ballads with little obvious jazz influence. However, Cole's singing always evidenced two qualities that betrayed his jazz background: a distinctive sound—one of the most distinctive of the era—and exquisitely subtle timing. We hear both in his 1951 recording of "Unforgettable."

LISTENING CUE • **"Unforgettable" (1951),** Irving Gordon. Nat Cole, vocal.

STYLE Late modern-era pop ballad • **FORM** A A^1

Listen For . . .

INSTRUMENTATION
Voice, plus rhythm section, vibraphone, violins and other strings

PERFORMANCE STYLE
Cole's husky singing; violin pizzicato in instrumental section

RHYTHM
Two-beat rhythm, but with jazz feel

HARMONY
Unusually, song starts and ends in different keys.

TEXTURE
Voice, sustained strings, string countermelodies, rhythm section, including piano tinkling

Remember . . .

BALLAD TEMPO
Slow tempo, two-beat rhythm = ideal for romantic dancing

COMPLEX, EXPANSIVE SONG
Melody consists of two long arches (AB, AB^1)

LUSH SETTING
Rich texture, with warm sounds: Cole's singing, violins, plus rhythm and vibraphone occasionally

COLE'S SINGING
Cole's warm, husky voice one of the distinctive vocal styles of the era

Listen to this selection in CourseMate.

"Unforgettable" was a new song when Cole recorded it. It is more complex and expansive than most pre–World War II songs, and Cole's lush and languid version complements the long lines of the melody. The most distinctive features of the recording—Cole's singing and the timing of his delivery, the subtle sway of the jazz-tinged rhythm, the slow tempo, the warm string background, and the muted sound of the vibraphone—place it in the postwar era. This is music for slow dancing; the bouncy foxtrot is now out of date. Noticeably absent are the brass and saxophones of the big-band era; vibraphone and strings replace them with a softer musical cushion.

"Unforgettable" also illustrates the shift in emphasis from the song to the singer. Cole turned a new song by Irving Gordon, a little-known songwriter, into a hit: Cole's version was so distinctive and so popular that "Unforgettable" in effect became *his* song, not Gordon's. It was among the first songs of the 1950s and 1960s to be identified more strongly with the singer than the songwriter.

During the 1950s, Cole was a frequent guest on the Ed Sullivan show and became the first black star to host a network television show. His *Nat King Cole Show* ran for a year in 1956 and 1957 before being canceled because of the lack of national sponsors. Cole would die of lung cancer in 1965.

Frank Sinatra

Frank Sinatra (1915–1998) was the dominant pop singer of the postwar era. He got his first major break in 1939, when Harry James hired him. Within a few months, he left James for Tommy Dorsey's band, where he recorded the first of his big hits, "I'll Never Smile Again" (1940). By 1942 he had become the first of the teen idols—anticipating Elvis by almost fifteen years—and during the 1950s, he became one of the biggest stars in the entertainment industry—as a singer, actor, and all-around celebrity.

Sinatra did not have Cole's jazz background but, like Bing Crosby, listened carefully to jazz and was comfortable in a jazz setting. His ease is evident in his rendition of Cole Porter's "You Do Something to Me," which was included on a 1950 album. Porter wrote the song for his 1929 musical *Fifty Million Frenchmen.* As presented in the music, it is a moderately slow foxtrot. It gained life outside of the show, with numerous recordings during the 1930s. Marlene Dietrich's sultry version, recorded in 1939, stands out.

Sinatra's rendition transforms Porter's foxtrot into a swinging jazz tune. Both Sinatra's singing and the instrumental accompaniment make clear that when the swing era ended, swing musicians simply gravitated from the bandstand to the recording studio. The arranger for this recording session was Alex Stordahl. Tommy Dorsey's chief arranger when Dorsey hired Sinatra; he became Sinatra's musical director when Sinatra left Dorsey. The musicians support Sinatra with a more polished and subtle version of big-band swing: A buoyant rhythm section underpins the horns, while Sinatra dances over the flowing pulse. What began as a seductive foxtrot has become a bouncy, brassy swing tune. It is a thorough remake of the song.

LISTENING CUE • "You Do Something to Me" (1929), Cole Porter. Frank Sinatra, vocal (1950).

STYLE Jazz-influenced song interpretation • **FORM** Three statements of the form: A, A^1, B, A^2

Listen For . . .

INSTRUMENTATION
Voice plus swing-era-style big band: saxes, trumpets, trombones, plus full rhythm

PERFORMANCE STYLE
Sinatra's gritty crooning, like talking in song

RHYTHM
Bright swing (four-beat) rhythm, clearly marked in rhythm section; several kinds of rhythmic play, including strong syncopations in horns and Sinatra's subtle beat-defying timing

TEXTURE
Rich texture: voice/lead instrument plus secondary horn parts (riffs, sustained chords) and rhythm section

Remember . . .

SINATRA'S STYLE
Sinatra personalizes songs through distinctive, slightly edgy sound and reshaping of melody

NEW TAKE ON AN OLD SONG
Porter's sedate foxtrot redone as swing-style song

VOCALS IN FOREFRONT
Two vocals frame instrumental chorus.

SWING LIVES ON
Almost every feature of this recording comes from swing era; biggest difference is Sinatra's jazzier singing style.

Listen to this selection in CourseMate.

NAT KING COLE and FRANK SINATRA sing into an NBC microphone, Los Angeles, California, 1946.

Sinatra would leave Columbia records, for which he had been recording since 1943, shortly after making this recording. He moved to Capitol records, where he joined Nat Cole as a top star. By 1960, he was secure enough in his status to form his own record company, Reprise. Beginning in 1961, he flooded the market with his own albums, all of which charted.

Sinatra, Cole, and a handful of other top singers, most notably Ella Fitzgerald, would set a new standard for pop singing. Their work from this period remains the reference point for the interpretation of modern-era popular song.

UNIT 9

LOOKING BACK, LOOKING AHEAD

DURING THE 1950s, pop was on top of the musical world. Television gave performers unprecedented exposure. Pop singers performed frequently, and a few, most notably Perry Como, had their own television shows, in which they often featured other pop performers. Advances in recording improved sound quality, and the long-playing record removed the three-minute constraint on performance length. Pop hits poured out of radios as stations hired disc jockeys to play recorded music as television replaced radio as the all-purpose entertainment medium.

Musical theater had become a popular, sophisticated entertainment. Many shows ran for years; the top shows soon made their way onto the screen. What modern jazz lost in popularity it gained in hipness; it was, literally, the "cool" music of the 1950s, even when it was hot.

However, there were signs that the modern era had run its course. Most central was simply the fact that the evolutionary momentum that had shaped modern-era popular music between the wars had stalled. Much musical theater turned back the clock musically. Jazz-influenced pop, exemplified here by Cole and Sinatra, solidified the advances of swing but did not point to further change, and too much of the popular music of the 1950s was simply silly: mindless, meretricious music. Modern jazz veered away from pop to chart its own path. Another sign was the growing diversity of the popular music landscape.

The Diversity of Popular Music at Mid-Century

By the early 1950s, popular music—and less popular music connected to the mainstream popular styles—covered an enormous amount of musical territory. Consider that in New York alone, one could hear:

- Mambos and other Afro-Cuban music in ballrooms uptown and downtown
- Bebop in many of the several jazz clubs on 52nd Street
- Song interpreters singing standards in swanky cabarets
- Folk groups like the Weavers in Greenwich Village clubs
- Aspiring doo-wop groups on street corners throughout the city
- Musicals on Broadway
- Black gospel in Harlem churches

This burgeoning variety was replicated on a smaller scale throughout the United States, often with a regional accent: electric blues in Chicago, Latin-tinged rhythm and blues in New Orleans, cool/West Coast jazz in southern California.

The following chart, which lists music, discussed in the text, produced between 1945 and 1954, gives some sense of this diversity.

Even this small sampling of music, which does not include either downtown or uptown Latin music, hints at the unprecedented diversity of popular music at mid-century. This diversity is the product of a fragmented musical landscape. Much of the music on the playlist—honky-tonk, folk, electric blues, rhythm and blues—had little common ground with pop, in intent or musical result. The thorough makeovers given pop remakes and covers of rhythm and blues, folk, and country songs simply highlight the contrasts between pop and "outsider" genres.

However, the growing market presence of these outsider styles, evidenced by the growth of the folk/country and western and race/rhythm-and-blues charts in the 1940s and 1950s, portended a disruptive change in the popular-music landscape. It gathered momentum during the 1950s and overturned the pop world in the 1960s.

Year	Track	Artist	Style
1945	"Salt Peanuts"	Charlie Parker	Bebop
1946	"Choo Choo Ch'Boogie"	Louis Jordan	Jump-band song
1947	"Move On Up a Little Higher"	Mahalia Jackson	Black gospel
	"It's Mighty Dark to Travel"	Bill Monroe	Bluegrass
1949	"Some Enchanted Evening"	Ezio Pinza	Musical theater song
	"Lovesick Blues"	Hank Williams	Honky-tonk
1950	"You Do Something to Me"	Frank Sinatra	Swinging version of foxtrot standard
	"Goodnight Irene"	The Weavers	Folk/pop fusion
1951	"Unforgettable"	Nat Cole	Distinctive interpretation of pop ballad
1952	"It Wasn't God Who Made Honky Tonk Angels"	Kitty Wells	Honky-tonk
1954	"Hoochie Coochie Man"	Muddy Waters	Electric blues
	"Django"	Modern Jazz Quartet	Modern jazz
	"Mystery Train"	Elvis Presley	Rockabilly
	"Sh-Boom"	The Chords	Doo-wop

Classic Styles

Even as rock was coalescing in the late 1950s and early 1960s, many pre-rock genres crystallized into what would become their classic form. In popular song, it was jazz-influenced song interpretation; in jazz, it was modern jazz; in Afro-Cuban music, it was mambo; in country music, it was honky-tonk; and in blues, it was electric blues. After the dust from the rock revolution of the 1960s settled, these became the referential styles. Veterans of the 1950s and early 1960s, such as pop singer Tony Bennett and jazz saxophonist Dexter Gordon, revived their careers. Their music became an inspiration for several generations of artists, such as singers Michael Buble, Jane Monheit, and Diana Krall, jazz artists Wynton and Branford Marsalis, salsa pianist Eddie Palmieri, bluesmen Robert Cray and Stevie Ray Vaughan, and country singers Merle Haggard and George Strait, whose music has kept these genres vital. Musical theater of the Rodgers and Hammerstein era has become classic in much the same way that opera is classic: an established repertoire that is periodically revived by professional, educational, and amateur companies. All of this music remains the heart of the legacy of popular music in the United States from the first half of the twentieth century.

Rhythm and Blues, 1946–1954

UNIT 10

In January 1922, Okeh Records placed an advertisement in the *Chicago Defender*, a black newspaper, that announced, "All the greatest race phonograph stars can be heard on Okeh records. . . . Ask your neighborhood dealer for a complete list of Okeh race records."

Okeh had recorded Mamie Smith's "Crazy Blues" at the end of 1920; its success opened the door for other classic blues singers, most notably Bessie Smith. "Down Hearted Blues," Smith's first recording for Columbia Records (now Sony), in 1923, reputedly sold over 1 million copies.

During the 1920s, recordings by black musicians mainly for a black audience occupied a small but important niche within the recording industry. Other major companies, most notably Victor and Columbia, created branches of their catalog to serve the "race" market. Joining them in catering to the black community were small labels like Paramount and W. C. Handy's Black Swan, which was bought by Paramount in 1924. However, the race record part of the music industry almost went under during the first years of the Depression. Sales of race records, which had been as high as 5 percent of total sales at the end of the 1920s, dropped to only 1 percent in the early 1930s, and several record companies went out of business or stopped recording black musicians.

Business began to pick up toward the end of the 1930s; by 1942, *Billboard,* then and now the bible of the music industry, began charting "race record" hits. The magazine dubbed the chart the "Harlem Hit Parade"; reportedly chart position was determined by an informal poll of a handful of record stores in Harlem. After World War II, *Billboard* reverted to "Race Records," but in 1949, Jerry Wexler, then a staff writer at the magazine, suggested the more politically correct and musically appropriate term: *rhythm and blues.*

Jerry Wexler pretty much got it right. **Rhythm and blues,** the term that he coined to replace *race records,* highlights the most significant change in blues-based music after World War II: more rhythm. Rhythm and blues (or simply R&B) was not one style, but several, the majority of which had strong beats and made extensive use of blues style and form. The differences among them were, for the most part, more a matter of emphasis and provenance. The roots of electric blues are in the Delta blues of Robert Johnson and others; much of the "big-beat" music of the postwar era built on the rhythms, riffs, and sounds of big-band swing. The one important exception was slow doo-wop, which mixed black gospel and pop. In this unit, we sample rhythm-and-blues styles in the decade after World War II.

CHAPTER 37

The Emergence of Rhythm and Blues

By the time *Billboard*'s renamed chart made its first appearance on June 25, 1949, rhythm and blues had become a small but significant part of the record industry. During World War II, what we now call **rhythm and blues** was just an occasional blip on the radar screen of popular music. After the war ended, rhythm and blues took off—maybe not as fast as Jackie Brenston's "Rocket 88"—but quickly enough to get the attention of *Billboard*'s staff. However, it was in the 1950s that rhythm and blues began to expand its niche in the pop marketplace, even as it carved out its distinctive sound identity. In less than a decade, rhythm and blues became an integral part of a new pop world.

The commercial growth of rhythm and blues during the 1950s was mainly a product of three factors: the economic and social empowerment of blacks, the growing interest of whites in black music, and the crossover appeal of the music itself.

Black Social and Economic Issues in the 1950s

The central issue for blacks after World War II was equality: racial, economic, and social. Black and white soldiers had fought for the United States during World War II, sometimes side by side, but more often in segregated units. The irony of blacks fighting to defend freedom in a country that did not treat them as free men was not lost on President Truman. In 1948, he signed an executive order demanding an end to discrimination in the armed services. This was one of numerous postwar developments that moved the United States—however painfully—closer to an integrated society.

If World War II brought the question to the fore, the postwar economic boom, the massive emigration of blacks from the rural South, and the Cold War gave the United States the reasons to respond to it. The flourishing postwar economy meant more and better-paying jobs. It put more money in the pockets of blacks, although not at the same rate as whites, and it reduced competition for jobs, which was one reason for trying to maintain the racial status quo, especially in the South. The migration of blacks to the North and West, which had begun in earnest after the turn of the century, accelerated during and especially after World War II. There they had the right to vote, which enabled them to exert pressure on politicians.

Another factor was the evident hypocrisy between the United States presenting itself to other nations as a defender of freedom and denying it to some of its citizens. During the Cold War, schoolchildren recited the Pledge of Allegiance every day, reiterating that the republic was "one nation under God, indivisible, with liberty and justice for all." Observers outside of the South, as well as those in other countries, were increasingly reminded that so long as all Americans were not equal under the law, this pledge—what the nation professed to believe and practice—was in fact a lie.

The two events that catalyzed the civil rights movement occurred within a year of each other. The first was the Supreme Court's 1954 decision, *Brown v. Board of Education of Topeka,* which rescinded the "separate but equal" policy sanctioned by the Court's 1896 decision in *Plessy v. Ferguson*. In *Plessy,* the Court had held that blacks could be educated in separate (or segregated) schools as long as they were "equal" in quality to the schools whites attended. Now, the Court said that there could be no equality unless blacks and whites had equal access to all schools.

Following this decision, the civil rights movement gained momentum in the courts and on the streets. In 1955, Montgomery, Alabama, native Rosa Parks refused to give up her bus seat to a white person. When she was arrested and sent to jail, blacks in Montgomery boycotted the municipal bus service for a year. Two years later, Dr. Martin Luther King Jr. organized the Southern Christian Leadership Conference, which advocated nonviolent protest modeled after that used by Mahatma Gandhi in India. All of this laid the foundation for the major advances in civil rights during the 1960s.

LOUIS JORDAN and His Tympany Five in the film *Caledonia*, 1942

Unlike jazz musicians such as Charles Mingus, rhythm-and-blues artists did not lift their voice in support of the civil rights movement during the 1950s. Their contribution was indirect: the appeal of their music helped heighten awareness of black culture. At the same time, rhythm and blues benefited from the increased attention given to race relations in the media; it was a two-way street. The first R&B style to emerge in the postwar era was the up-tempo music of the jump bands, and especially the music of Louis Jordan.

Jump Bands

Jump bands stripped down and souped up the sound of big-band swing. They kept the rhythm section but reduced the horn sections drastically, typically paring down three full sections to a couple of saxophones and a trumpet. Often, they strengthened the beat by converting the four-beat swing rhythm to a shuffle. They built songs on repeated riffs, usually over a blues or blues-based form. The songs typically took a medium tempo, because shuffle rhythm put the more frenetic swing tempos out of reach. Jump bands also emphasized singing more than swing had. The vocalist was the key figure in the group, and the lyrics typically told a funny story or allowed the singer to brag a little, or both. A blend of hokum, boogie-woogie, and big-band swing, jump-band music was different from all of them.

"Choo Choo Ch'Boogie"

"Choo Choo Ch'Boogie," was a big hit in 1946 for the jump band Louis Jordan and His Tympany Five. Louis Jordan (1908–1975) first made his mark as a saxophonist in Chick Webb's fine swing band. He played for Webb from 1936 through 1938, then formed his own smaller group a year later. Unlike many later rhythm-and-blues artists, Jordan got a record deal with a major label, Decca, with whom he signed a contract in 1939. This undoubtedly helped build his audience.

The song begins with the pianist laying down a medium-tempo boogie-woogie bass while the horns play a simple riff. The first part of Jordan's vocal is a series of six short phrases, all of which rhyme and all of which develop from a simple repeated riff. Although the words happen over a blues harmonic progression, they do not follow the standard form of the blues lyric. Instead, they serve as a storytelling verse to the catchy chorus that follows. The theme, of course, is life on the railroad—certainly a common topic for songs of that era. (Note the reference to "ballin' the jack," that is, getting the train moving.) Like numerous other uptempo blues songs, "Choo Choo Ch'Boogie" adapts the conventional blues form to a verse/chorus pattern; the hook of the chorus provides an easy point of entry into the song.

In a jump band like Louis Jordan and His Tympany Five, the roles of the musicians are clearly defined: the

LISTENING CUE • **"Choo Choo Ch'Boogie" (1946),** Louis Jordan. Louis Jordan and His Tympany Five.

STYLE Jump-band song • **FORM** Blues-based verse/chorus form. Verse contains six 2-bar phrases over blues progression; chorus is last eight bars of blues progression.

Listen For . . .

INSTRUMENTATION
Vocal, rhythm section (piano, bass, drums—using brushes—and guitar), and small horn section

RHYTHM
Shuffle rhythm (intensified four-beat rhythm), with a light backbeat
Vocal and horn parts move in tandem with shuffle rhythm, with occasional strong syncopation.

HARMONY
Blues progression in verse; chorus = last two-thirds of a blues chorus (IV-I-V-I)

TEXTURE
Melody plus background riffs and rhythmic accompaniment during vocals

Remember . . .

JUMP BAND
Essentially a streamlined swing band: a full rhythm section plus a mixed horn section—trumpet(s) and saxophones

SHUFFLE RHYTHM
Long/short division of each beat intensifies swing rhythm.

RIFF-HEAVY MELODY
Both vocal line and solos are built mainly from riffs.

FLEXIBILITY OF BLUES FORM
Another verse/chorus blues: blues progression in verse; last two-thirds of progression in chorus

TRAINS
Popularity of trains in black music reflects not only the useful sounds but also their importance to transportation at mid-century.

Listen to this selection in CourseMate.

bass walks; the drummer plays a shuffle beat; the guitar and/or the piano also helps keep the beat—the pianist may also play fills and solo; the saxophone honks riffs, either behind the vocalist, in response to him, or in a solo; and the other horns join the sax in creating harmonized response riffs.

The tone of the lyric is humorous and self-deprecating; we sense that the "I" in the song is a happy-go-lucky kind of fellow. (The wanderer has pretty much disappeared from our twenty-first-century lives, but even a half century ago, hoboes—men who "rode the rails" from place to place [stowed away on trains], working odd jobs in exchange for food, a roof, and maybe a little cash, or simply begging—were more common. Their mystique, a holdover from the Great Depression, was still powerful in the years after World War II.) The music—with its bouncy shuffle beat, catchy riffs (not only in the vocal parts but also in both the piano and the sax solos), and pleasant vocal style—helps capture the mood of the lyric.

This became the formula for Jordan and many of the jump bands that followed him. One reason for the increasing appeal of these songs, to black Americans and gradually to whites as well, was the easy points of entry: upbeat lyrics; repeated riffs, either sung or played on a honking saxophone; a clear beat, usually in a shuffle rhythm; and a chorus-based form.

Big-Beat Rhythm and Blues

During the early 1950s, the rhythmic foundation of the most rhythmic rhythm and blues did not change, but it did get stronger, more active and louder. With the aid of amplification and an amplified guitar, the increased prominence of rhythm section instruments, and a fair amount of muscle, the rhythms of the rhythm section came out from behind the rest of the band, as we hear in "Rocket 88."

Jackie Brenston's "Rocket 88" (1951) was a big rhythm-and-blues hit with a big beat. Although Brenston was the singer on this date, it was pianist Ike Turner's band that Brenston fronted, and the most distinctive sound on this recording is Willie Kizart's distorted guitar, not Brenston's singing. The story of how it found its way onto a record is the stuff of rock-and-roll legend.

According to most accounts of the making of this record, the band was driving from Mississippi to Memphis, with their instruments strapped on top of the car. At some point, the guitar amp fell off, or was dropped, and the speaker cone was torn. As a result, the guitar produced a heavily distorted sound, even after Kizart

LISTENING CUE • **"Rocket 88" (1951),** Jackie Brenston and Ike Turner. Jackie Brenston and his Delta Cats.

STYLE 1950s big-beat rhythm and blues • **FORM** twelve-bar blues

Listen For . . .

INSTRUMENTATION
Vocal, saxophone, electric guitar, piano, bass, drums

PERFORMANCE STYLE
Severe distortion in the electric guitar

RHYTHM
Strong shuffle rhythm with occasional triplets layered in pounded out by prominent rhythm section

HARMONY
Prototypical blues progression outlined by guitar riff

TEXTURE
Thick sound, with guitar in low register (covering bass), sax riffs in low middle register, Brenston's vocal in mid-range, and Turner's piano in a higher range

Remember . . .

SHUFFLE BEAT
A strong shuffle rhythm with occasional triplets adding to rhythmic activity; the interaction between layers clarifies the long–short pattern of the shuffle rhythm.

DISTORTED GUITAR
Kizart's busted amplifier leads to a novel sound: the severely distorted guitar is a happy accident!

BASIC BLUES
The guitar line clearly outlines the most basic version of the twelve-bar blues progression and blues form.

JUMP-BAND HEAVY
This recording features standard jump-band instrumentation—rhythm section with electric guitar plus saxophones, with the saxophone in the spotlight, but the rhythm instruments are prominent.

A SONG ABOUT CARS
Like trains, cars were an appealing topic during the postwar years in transportation-happy America.

Listen to this selection in CourseMate.

had stuffed it with paper. When recording engineer Sam Phillips heard it, he decided to make an asset out of a perceived liability, so he made the guitar line, which simply adapts a shuffle-style boogie-woogie left hand to the guitar, stand out.

Active Rhythms in Postwar Rhythm and Blues

The rhythm of "Rocket 88" sounds more active mainly because of two features, the use of triplets and the increased prominence of the shuffle rhythm. The term **triplet** identifies a rhythmic pattern that divides each beat into three equal parts. Before the early 1950s, triplets were seldom used in blues, jazz, and pop, and when they were used, it was mainly in slower tempos. After 1950, triplets became a staple in slow rhythm and blues and were also used to add rhythmic energy in medium-tempo songs.

Kizart's guitar line provides an explicit outline of the shuffle rhythm. In Figure 37.1, we see represented the relationship among the beat; the guitar part, which lays down the shuffle rhythm; and the piano part, which plays triplets intermittently. (At this tempo, it would be very challenging physically to play triplets all the way through the song!)

Notice the way in which the shuffle rhythm lines up with the triplets: The long note in each beat lasts as long as the first two notes of the triplets, whereas the short note lasts as long as the third triplet. The triplets enable us to hear precisely the 2:1 ratio between the long and short notes of a shuffle rhythm.

The shuffle rhythm is *not* the characteristic rhythm of rock, although it was occasionally used as an alternative to rock rhythm in rock-era songs. However, as it is heard here—played loudly on a guitar with a distorted sound—it conveys the kind of energy that we associate with rock, because there are insistent rhythms that move faster than the beat. This rhythm is in the foreground throughout the song; it is this feature—loud, insistent, active rhythms—that seemed to attract teens, both black and white, and repelled so many adults, who wanted such rhythms heard gently in the background.

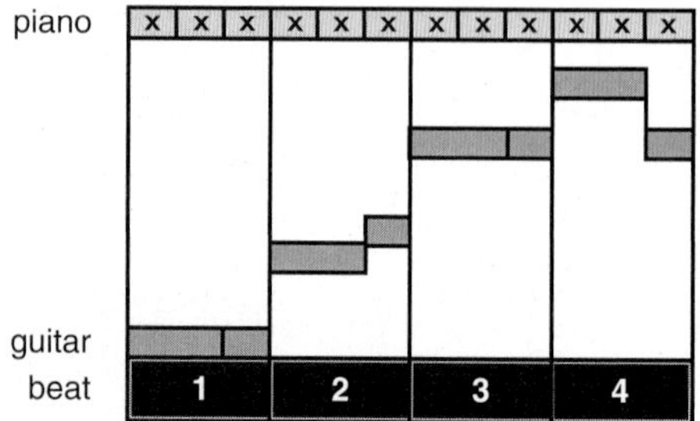

FIGURE 37.1 Rhythmic relationship between shuffle and triplet rhythms, as demonstrated in "Rocket 88."

© Michael Ochs Archives/Getty Images

"Rocket 88" poster showing Jackie Brenston, with Ike Turner at the piano, 1952

The Sound of 1950s Rhythmic Rhythm and Blues

In other respects, the song is right in step with the up-tempo songs of postwar rhythm and blues; rhythmic rhythm-and-blues bands were as consistent in their approach to instrumentation as they were in their approach to rhythm and harmony. "Rocket 88" is typical: The band behind Jackie Brenston consists of a full early-1950s-style rhythm section—electric guitar, piano, bass, and drums—plus two saxophones, one of which takes an extended solo. In 1950s rhythm-and-blues song, we expect to hear bands with a rhythm section and at least one saxophone; the saxophone will be a solo instrument as well as an accompanying instrument, and both accompaniments and solo passages will feature repeated riffs.

The lyric tells a story over a blues progression. Its subject touches on a recurrent theme: cars. "Rocket 88" was inspired by Joe Liggins' 1947 recording, "Cadillac Boogie," and it is one link in a chain that passes through Chuck Berry's "Maybellene" to the Beach Boys' "Little Deuce Coupe." There is the obligatory honking sax solo—a good one—and a nice instrumental out-chorus (the final statement of the blues progression) that's straight out of the big-band era.

Both the distortion and the relative prominence of the guitar were novel features of this recording—these are the elements that have earned "Rocket 88" so many nominations as "the first" rock-and-roll record. From our perspective, "Rocket 88" wasn't the first rock-and-roll record, because the beat is a shuffle rhythm, not the distinctive rock rhythm heard first in the songs of Chuck Berry and Little Richard. Still, the distortion and the central place of the guitar in the overall sound certainly anticipate key features of rock style.

CHAPTER 38
Electric Blues

Attend any of the many blues festivals throughout North America and you will hear band after band take the stage. Most will feature a full rhythm section with one or more electric guitars; horns are optional. For most contemporary listeners, this is the sound of the blues, the classic blues style that has remained largely unchanged for over half a century. The basic sound of these bands is unlike the blues of the twenties and thirties, and it's different from the rhythm and blues that we've just heard. It came together in the early fifties, when deep blues moved north from Mississippi to Chicago and went electric.

The electric guitar, already a common sound in country music and jazz by the early forties, soon began to find its way into the blues. Muddy Waters began playing electric guitar in 1944 so that he could be heard over the crowd noise in the bars where he performed; others followed suit. At the same time, bluesmen like Waters surrounded themselves with other instrumentalists—usually another guitarist and/or a pianist, a drummer, a bassist, and in Waters' case, Little Walter, the soulful master of the harmonica. This new sound has been called electric blues; now it is just the blues.

Electric blues came of age in the fifties. It completed its transformation from a rural to an urban music and its migration from the juke joints and street corners of Mississippi to the bars of Chicago's South Side. Blues kept its soul through the journey, most notably in the music of Muddy Waters.

© Steve Dibblee/iStockphoto

"It's real. Muddy's real. See the way he plays guitar? Mississippi style, not the city way." —Big Bill Broonzy

Muddy Waters

Muddy Waters (1915–1983), born McKinley Morganfield, grew up in Clarksdale, Mississippi, the northwest part of the state, in the heart of what is called the Delta region. The population was mostly black, and for the vast majority, life was brutal. Both males and females worked as sharecroppers, often from childhood; Waters was a farm laborer as a boy. Most lived at subsistence level, trapped in an unending cycle of economic dependence. From this harsh and isolated environment came what Robert Palmer called **deep blues,** a powerful music that gave expression to, and release from, the brutal conditions of the Delta.

Waters heard this music while he was growing up and began to play it in his teens. He started on the harmonica, then took up the guitar, because, "You see, I was digging Son House and Robert Johnson." By his late twenties, Waters had become a popular performer in the region.

Like many other southern blacks, Waters moved north during World War II, settling on Chicago's South Side. He continued to play, first at house parties, then in small bars, and recorded for Columbia in 1946. (The recordings were not released until many years later.) Still, it was not enough to pay the rent, and Waters was working as a truck driver when he approached Aristocrat Records about recording for them. Aristocrat, which had just been bought by the Chess brothers, would soon become the Chess label, and Waters would become their biggest star before Chuck Berry.

The Sound of Electric Blues

Muddy Waters' singing and playing retained its earthiness and passion after he moved north; he added the power of amplification and a full rhythm section during his first years in Chicago.

In the music of Waters and other like-minded Chicago bluesmen, electric blues found its groove during the fifties. By the end of the decade, it had settled into its classic sound. Its most consistent features include:

- Regular blues form (or an easily recognized variant of it)
- Rough-edged vocals
- Vocal-like responses and solos from the lead guitar or harmonica
- A dense texture, with several instruments playing melody-like lines behind the singer

© John Cohen/Getty Images

MUDDY WATERS (left) and harmonica player Isaac Washington, performing in New York, 1959.

- A rhythm section laying down a strong beat, usually some form of the shuffle rhythm popularized in forties rhythm and blues

Its stars attracted a loyal following, mostly in the black community. Records by Muddy Waters, B. B. King, Howlin' Wolf, Lowell Fulson, Elmore James, and Bobby Bland consistently found their way onto the R&B charts. They were not as well-known as the pop-oriented groups, but far better known—within and outside the black community—than their country kin from previous generations.

"(I'm Your) Hoochie Coochie Man"

"(I'm Your) Hoochie Coochie Man," the 1954 recording that was Waters' biggest hit, epitomizes the fully transformed electric blues style. It retains the essence of country blues in Waters' singing and playing. Blues singer Big Bill Broonzy described Waters' appeal in this way:

> It's real. Muddy's real. See the way he plays guitar? Mississippi style, not the city way. He don't play chords, he don't follow what's written down in the book. He plays notes, all blue notes. Making what he's thinking.

Willie Dixon's lyrics make references to love potions and voodoo charms, sexual prowess and special status; Waters' singing makes them credible. It is easy to conjure up such a world and envision him as the hoochie-coochie man. That much remained virtually unchanged from the rawest country blues of the twenties and thirties. Plugging in and adding a rhythm section simply amplified the impact of the message.

The song alternates between two textures: the stop time of the opening, where instrumental riffs periodically punctuates Waters' vocal line, and the free-for-all of the refrain-like finish of each chorus. The stop-time opening contains two competing riffs—one played by the harmonica, the other by the electric guitar. In the chorus, everybody plays: harmonica trills; guitar riffs; piano chords; thumping bass; shuffle pattern on the drums underpin Waters' singing. Each of the melodic and rhythmic strands is an important part of the mix, but none is capable of standing alone. The dense texture they produce, with independent but interdependent lines, was almost unprecedented in small-group music before rock.

The electric blues of the fifties brought nastier guitar sounds into popular music. The overdriven guitar sounds that jumped off numerous blues records were intentional. Almost as soon as they went electric, blues guitarists began to experiment with distortion in order to get a guitar sound that paralleled the rawness of singers like Muddy Waters and Howlin' Wolf. Among the leaders in this direction were Buddy Guy and Elmore James, both based in Chicago through much of the fifties.

The influence of electric blues on rock came in two installments, first in the music of Chuck Berry, then in the blues-based rock of the 1960s.

LISTENING CUE • "(I'm Your) Hoochie Coochie Man" (1954), Willie Dixon. Muddy Waters, guitar and vocal; Little Walter, harmonica; Willie Dixon, bass; Jimmy Rogers, guitar; Otis Spann, piano; and Fred Below, drums.

STYLE Electric blues • **FORM** Modified blues form: First phrase is doubled in length; it serves as a verse; last two phrases are the refrain.

Listen For . . .

INSTRUMENTATION
Vocal, electric guitars, harmonica, piano, bass, and drums

PERFORMANCE STYLE
Waters sings passionately, with great rhythmic freedom, over both the stop time and strong, active rhythm.

RHYTHM
Strong contrast between stop time in verse section and shuffle+ triplet rhythm in the refrain segment, all at slow tempo

HARMONY
Blues progression with first phrase expanded to eight bars on I chord

TEXTURE
Dense, dark sound, from several instruments active in low and mid register

Remember . . .

EXPANDED BLUES FORM
The first phrase is twice as long as in a conventional blues; the last two phrases serve as a refrain.

VOCAL-LIKE INSTRUMENTAL RESPONSES
Both the guitar and harmonica answers sound almost vocal in style: Harmonica player Little Walter almost sings through his instrument.

RHYTHMIC CONTRASTS
Stop-time at beginning of each chorus; rhythm guitar and drums lay down a strong shuffle rhythm, piano adds triplets, over which Waters' vocal and Walter's harmonica soar freely.

BLUES AS "REAL" MUSIC
Waters' singing is especially passionate in the refrain-like part of the song; Little Walter's harmonica mimics vocal style; rhythm instruments add to impact.

Listen to this selection in CourseMate.

CHAPTER 39

Early Doo-Wop

After World War II, pop, gospel, and rhythm and blues came together in a new family of styles that featured male or mostly male singing groups. The styles ranged from gospel-tinged pop ideally suited for slow dancing to up-tempo numbers and novelty songs. The common threads seem to be the gospel and pop influences (the male gospel quartets and pop vocal groups like the Mills Brothers) and the names, which identify the groups as a unit: the Platters, the Penguins, the Cadillacs, the Drifters, and countless others. The first recordings of these new sounds appeared in the late forties, many by "bird" groups such as the Ravens and the Orioles.

The Orioles' 1953 hit, "Crying in the Chapel," blazed the trail. Its history highlights the blurred genre boundaries in the early rock era: "Crying in the Chapel" was a country song that crossed over to the pop charts, which was covered by an R&B group whose version also made the pop charts!

The breakthrough hit "Sh-Boom" came the following year. The original R&B version by the Chords hit both pop and rhythm-and-blues charts the same week: July 3, 1954. Other doo-wop hits, such as the Penguins' "Earth Angel" and the Moonglows' "Sincerely," soon followed. For whites, doo-wop put a fresh coat of paint on familiar-sounding material. For the majority of white teens who had heard their parents' Tin Pan Alley pop growing up, the familiar elements must have made the music more accessible.

The Sound of Upbeat Doo-Wop

The Chords' eye toward the pop charts is clearly evident in "Sh-Boom," which we might describe as "jump-band lite." Because many of these groups developed their songs a capella and were given backup studio musicians—many of them jump-band performers—they took on the jump-band's shuffle rhythm and instrumentation: rhythm section plus saxophone. But the beat is discreet—very much in the background—and the good saxophone solo straddles the boundary between jazz and honking R&B. Moreover, the song is not a blues; its form and underlying harmony use "Heart and Soul," a familiar pop standard, as a model.

The song focuses on the voices; the instrumental accompaniment is very much in the background. The Chords' sound is typical: a lead singer (Carl Feaster) with a pleasant but untrained voice, plus four backup singers, including the requisite bass voice (William "Ricky" Edwards), who steps into the spotlight briefly. When singing behind Feaster, the backup singers alternate between sustained chords and the occasional rhythmic interjection—"Sh-Boom." During the saxophone solo, the voices mimic a big-band horn section playing a riff underneath a soloist.

Doo-Wop: Voices as Instruments

"Life could be a dream, life could be a dream"; "doo, doo, doo, doo, Sh-Boom." The first part of the lyric is typical of the romantic pop of the era; the second is the defining feature of **doo-wop.** As the song unfolds, the lyric alternates between explaining why life could be a dream and nonsense syllables

LISTENING CUE • **"Sh-Boom" (1954),** Edwards, Feaster, Feaster, Keyes, McRae, the Chords.

STYLE Doo-wop • **FORM** One statement of AABA form, plus introduction, interlude, and ending

Listen For . . .

INSTRUMENTATION
Male vocal group plus full rhythm section (electric guitar, bass, piano, drums) and saxophone

PERFORMANCE STYLE
Pleasant but untrained voices; honking saxophone style

RHYTHM
Shuffle rhythm at moderate tempo

HARMONY
Use of "Heart and Soul" progression

TEXTURE
Either call and response between lead and backup singers or close harmony (sung chords in a narrow range)

Remember . . .

JUMP-BAND LITE
The Chords backed by a standard R&B band: horns and + rhythm instruments; song has shuffle rhythm, like most 1950s R&B songs, but at moderate tempo and with a less aggressive sound.

DOO-WOP VOCAL SOUND
Pleasant, but not sweet, vocal timbre, with lead singer, bass soloist (in the bridge), and close harmony behind the lead

NONSENSE SYLLABLES FOR RHYTHM
The use of "nonsense" syllables to inject energy into performance harks back to the gospel quartets (for example, Golden Gate Gospel Quartet) and big-band horn sections, which backup vocalists emulate.

Listen to this selection in CourseMate.

© Gilles Petard/Redferns/Getty Images

The Chords (clockwise from bottom left) Claude Feaster, William Edwards, Carl Feaster, Jimmy Keyes, Buddy McRae, and Rupert Branker (front), 1954.

like "hey, nonny ding dong, shalang alang alang." "Sh-Boom" returns regularly between phrases of the lyric; it is like a gentle prod that keeps the rhythmic momentum going. Significantly, the title of the song comes from one of these nonsense syllables, not from the first phrase of the lyric.

The practice of using the voice to imitate instruments, especially percussive-sounding instruments, is a distinctively black practice. Before doo-wop, it was evident in such diverse music as Louis Armstrong's jazz-like scat singing, the rhythm section-like support of backup singers in male gospel quartets, and the nonsense syllables used in 1940s rhythm and blues, in such hit songs as "Stick" McGhee's "Drinking Wine Spo-Dee-O-Dee." With doo-wop, the practice became so integral to the music that it gave the style its name. The term *doo-wop*—borrowed from songs that used the phrase—was applied retrospectively to this music to acknowledge its most salient feature.

The function of the nonsense syllables is to inject rhythmic energy into the song. The syllables are typically rich in consonant sounds that explode (*b*) or sustain (*sh* or *m*). In the "Sh-Boom"–like parts of the song, the voices become instruments. They are not percussive instruments per se, because they have pitch, but the vocal sounds have a percussive quality, like the plucking of a string bass or the slapping of an electric bass.

Cover Versions and Commercial Success

A cover version of "Sh-Boom" by the Crew Cuts reached No. 1 on the pop charts just a week after the Chords' original. Their remake was a white take on a black song (inspired in part by white pop).

The film *Dreamgirls,* set during the years of early doo-wop and R&B, was in part the story of a "stolen" cover of

© DreamWorks/Courtesy Everett Collection

James "Thunder" Early's (played by Eddie Murphy) first single, which flops when recorded successfully by a white pop group.

The notion of a cover version is a rock-era concept; it signals the shift of song identity from an almost abstract entity that can exist in multiple versions to a particular performance captured on record. White covers of black songs occurred frequently in the early years of rock and roll. Pat Boone's covers of Little Richard's "Tutti Frutti" and Fats Domino's "Ain't That a Shame," both of which outsold the originals, are particularly notorious examples. Because white covers often outsold the black versions, cover versions have acquired racial baggage; some commentators have viewed them as white acts riding on the coattails of black acts and enjoying the success that should have gone to the black acts.

The injustice of covers is not so much a musical issue. The blacks who sang doo-wop were borrowing liberally from white pop. The greatest musical injustice in white covers of black recordings is bad taste: the pop music establishment superimposing their conception of a sound with mass appeal, and enervating the music as a result.

Rather, it's mainly a financial and racial issue: that blacks did not have easy access to the pop market, that many were naive about the music business and never saw the money that their records made, that the labels that signed and recorded them could not compete with the majors, and that white versions sold better than the black originals. Covers became less common as white audiences opened up to black music of all kinds. Perhaps the best evidence for this shift in consciousness would be the Marcels' raucous version of the standard "Blue Moon," which topped the pop charts in 1961. It was a sound that no white group could imitate.

"Sh-Boom" has also received numerous nominations for the first rock-and-roll record. It was not the sound that would soon define rock and roll, but it did bring a fresh pop-oriented rhythm-and-blues style to a mainstream audience. Its popularity was evidence that rock and roll was getting ready to explode.

UNIT 10

LOOKING BACK, LOOKING AHEAD

In the decade after World War II, rhythm and blues got a name, a host of new styles, and a much bigger audience. Electric blues, jump bands, and doo-wop were among the new sounds of the decade. All these new styles sounded black, but they covered a lot of territory: There's a big gap between doo-wop ballads and electric blues. Still, there was also a lot of interplay among the styles. From one perspective, the blues got rhythm and rhythm got the blues, and uptempo doo-wop mixed pop, black gospel, and jump-band R&B.

In the early 1950s, rhythm and blues acquired a second name: rock and roll. After 1955, the two would diverge racially and rhythmically, principally through the innovations of two black men, Little Richard and Chuck Berry, and a "white man with the negro feel."

Rock and Roll

UNIT 11

UNIT 11

By the time "Maybellene" hit the charts late in the summer of 1955, DJ Alan Freed was in New York, and "rock and roll" was on the air and in the air. Freed had moved to New York the previous year in order to offer his rock-and-roll radio show on WINS.

For the first part of the 1950s, rock and roll was simply another term for rhythm and blues, but in 1954, white artists began to cover R&B hits. A year later, Chuck Berry and Fats Domino had songs on the pop charts, Bill Haley's "Rock Around The Clock" rose to the top of the charts, and Domino's song, "Ain't That a Shame," also reached No. 1 in a cover version by Pat Boone.

By 1956, rock and roll was for real. Little Richard woke the nation up with "Tutti Frutti." Elvis Presley had eleven Top 40 hits that year; four reached Number 1. By the end of the year, "rock and roll" was a household word and Elvis was a household name. During these early years, almost any music by and for teens was considered rock and roll.

Rock and roll began as an outsiders' music. Its first stars were mostly African Americans or Southern whites. The music resonated with many teens. Rock and roll helped them create an identity; indeed, it was part of their identity, as much as their dress, their speech, their cars.

Because both performers and audience had such recognizable identities, it was easy—even natural—to lump all the music that teens (and many African Americans) listened to under one banner. However, during the latter half of the 1950s, rock and roll and rhythm and blues diverged. The first—and easiest—distinction between them was racial: Rock and roll usually featured white performers and catered to a white audience; rhythm-and-blues artists were black, and so was their core audience. But this method, although accurate up to a point, was fundamentally flawed. Several important rock and roll artists—above all Chuck Berry, the architect of the sound of rock and roll—were African Americans. By 1957, it was possible to make a clear musical distinction, one that helps explain why we consider the music of Berry and Little Richard to be rock and roll, not rhythm and blues. In this unit, we trace the musical evolution of rock and roll.

CHAPTER 40
Rock and Roll Begins

When did rock and roll begin? The answer depends a great deal on the context in which the question is asked. Was it when people labeled rhythm and blues "rock and roll"? Or when young white singers began covering rhythm-and-blues songs? Or when the media acknowledged a new kind of music and its new stars? Or when what was called rock and roll brought new sounds to the pop charts?

The term itself dates back to at least the 1920s. It came into popular music via blues lyrics. In these songs, "rockin'" and "rockin' and rollin'" were euphemisms for sexual intercourse. One of the first "race record" hits was Trixie Smith's "My Man Rocks Me (With One Steady Roll)." The lyrics to Wynonie Harris's 1948 R&B hit "Good Rockin' Tonight" make the sexual reference as explicit as it could be and still get the record in the stores and on the jukeboxes in the late 1940s: "I'm gonna hold my baby as tight as I can, tonight she'll know I'm a mighty man." A few years later, "rock and roll" was used to refer to music, not sex, although sex remained an undercurrent for both teens and their horrified parents.

Teens in the 1950s

After the war, the economy continued to boom. Economic growth meant more disposable income, some of which was spent on entertainment. America's newfound prosperity trickled down to a newly enfranchised segment of society, the teenager. No longer burdened by farm chores or the work-to-survive demands of the Depression, teenagers had far more leisure time than their predecessors. They were also better off. Parents gave them allowances, and many found after-school jobs. More time and more money inevitably led to the emergence of the new teen subculture.

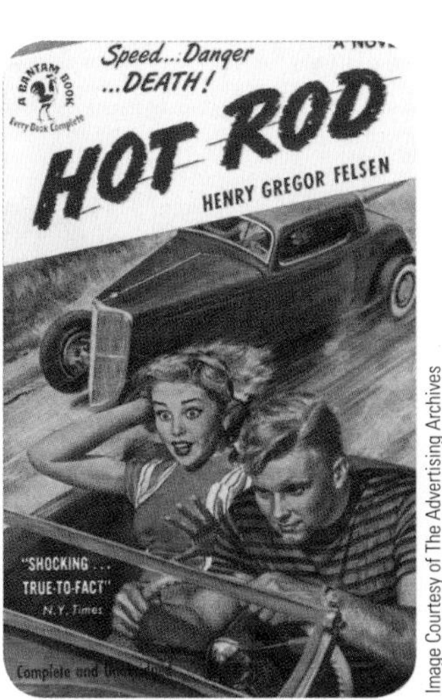

Image Courtesy of The Advertising Archives

Teens defined themselves socially, economically, and musically. "Generation gap" became part of everyday speech; so, unfortunately, did "juvenile delinquent." Teens put their money where *their* tastes were, and many had a taste for rock and roll. They rebelled by putting down high school; idolizing Marlon Brando, James Dean, and other "rebels without a cause"; and souping up cars (celebrated in the rock and roll of this era, from Chuck Berry's "Maybellene" to the Beach Boys' "Little Deuce Coupe" and "409"). However, the most obvious symbol of their revolt against the status quo was their music.

Rock and roll and rhythm and blues epitomized this new rebellious attitude. The music was, by contemporary pop standards, "crude" and obviously black or black inspired. Some songs were blatantly sexual: Jerry Lee Lewis's "Great Balls of Fire" was a prime offender. Elvis and his fellow rock and rollers talked differently, wore their hair differently, dressed differently, danced and walked differently. All of it—the music, the lyrics, the look—horrified teens' parents; that was part of the appeal. More than any other aspect of American life in the 1950s, music preference demarcated the boundary between teens and adults.

The Beginnings of Rock and Roll

It was disc jockey Alan Freed who attached "rock and roll" to a musical style. Freed was an early and influential advocate of rhythm and blues. Unlike most of the disc jockeys of the era, he refused to play white cover versions of rhythm-and-blues hits, a practice which gained him respect among black musicians but made him enemies in the business. While broadcasting over WJW in Cleveland in 1951, he began using "rock and roll" as code for rhythm and blues.

Freed's "Moondog's Rock and Roll Party" developed a large audience among both whites and blacks, so he took his advocacy of rhythm and blues one step further, into promotion. He put together touring stage shows of rhythm-and-blues artists, which played to integrated audiences. His first big event, the Moondog Coronation Ball, took place in 1952. Twenty-five thousand people, the majority of them white, showed up at a facility that could accommodate only a small fraction of that number. The ensuing pandemonium was the first of many "incidents" in Freed's career as a promoter.

Freed linked the term *rock and roll* to rhythm and blues, so it's no wonder that Fats Domino and Dave Bartholomew, the mastermind of so many New Orleans rhythm-and-blues hits, commented that rock and roll was rhythm and blues. Bartholomew said, undoubtedly with some bitterness, "We had rhythm and blues for many, many a year, and here come in a couple of white people and they call it rock and roll, and it was rhythm and blues all the time!" As rhythm and blues began to find a white audience, white acts began to tap into this new sound. Among the first was Bill Haley and His Comets.

Bill Haley's "Rock Around the Clock"

One of the first big rock and roll hits came from an unlikely source, by way of an unlikely place, and took an unlikely path to pop success. Bill Haley (1925–1981), who recorded it, grew up in Pennsylvania listening to the *Grand Ole Opry* and dreaming of country music stardom. By the late 1940s, he had begun fronting small bands—one was called the "Four Aces of Western Swing"—and enjoyed some local success. Over the next few years, he began to give his music a bluesier sound and chose—or wrote—songs with teen appeal. "Crazy, Man, Crazy" (1953) was his first hit. In 1954, he had some success with a song called "Rock Around the Clock."

A year later "Rock Around the Clock" resurfaced in the soundtrack to the film *The Blackboard Jungle*. The connections among film, song, and performer were tenuous. The film portrays juvenile delinquents in a slum high school, but "Rock Around the Clock" is exuberant rather than angry, and Haley, at almost thirty, looked nothing like a teenaged rebel. But it was music for and about teens (parents weren't likely to rock around the clock), and that was enough for the producers. With the release of the film, the song skyrocketed to No. 1. It was Haley's big moment. He had a few other minor hits, but he never repeated his chart-topping success.

The First Rock and Roll Record?

"Rock Around the Clock" is often identified as the first rock-and-roll record because it was the first big hit clearly associated with rock and roll. And it was a different sound—at least for pop. The sound is a light version of jump-band rhythm and blues. Haley's voice is bright, but it has little of the inflection that we associate with blues singing. The band supports Haley's voice with a small rhythm section that includes a guitar played in a high register and drumsticks tapping out a brisk shuffle rhythm. The band plays riffs underneath Haley, then alone. In retrospect, we consider this energetic, upbeat music to be not rock and roll, but rockabilly, a country take on postwar rhythm and blues.

Even as Haley's record zoomed to the top of the charts, Elvis Presley was recording a grittier kind of rockabilly at Sam Phillips's Sun records. We consider the relationship between Elvis, rockabilly, and rock and roll next.

LISTENING CUE • **"Rock Around the Clock" (1954),** Max Friedman and James Myers. Bill Haley and His Comets.

STYLE Rockabilly • **FORM** Verse/chorus blues form

Listen For . . .

INSTRUMENTATION
Voice, electric guitar, acoustic bass, drums, and saxophone (accordion)

PERFORMANCE STYLE
Haley's voice is light and friendly but not bluesy or country—and not pop crooning either.

RHYTHM
Shuffle rhythm at a fast tempo
Syncopation in vocal line, guitar riff, and instrumental riff in sixth chorus

TEXTURE
Light, layered texture with most instruments and voice in a high mid-range contribute to bright sound.

Remember . . .

LIGHT-HEARTED LYRIC
"Rocking" here is simply about dancing the night away; nothing suggests a more intimate involvement between partners.

LIGHT-HEARTED MUSIC
The brisk tempo, discreet shuffle beat, and generally high register of Haley's voice and the guitar give the song a bright feel.

SOUND OF ROCKABILLY
A "lite" version of rhythmic R&B: faster tempo, higher register, less rough-edged vocal

Listen to this selection in CourseMate.

CHAPTER 41
Elvis Presley

In the summer of 1953, a young truck driver named Elvis Presley walked into the Sam Phillips Recording Service in Memphis to make a demo record. Phillips wasn't in, so his assistant, Marion Keisker, handled the session. Perhaps to make him feel at ease, she asked him about himself. The conversation went something like this:

Marion: "What kind of singer are you?"

Elvis: "I sing all kinds."

Marion: "Who do you sound like?"

Elvis: "I don't sound like nobody."

Marion: "Hillbilly?"

Elvis: "Yeah, I sing hillbilly."

Marion: "Who do you sound like in hillbilly?"

Elvis: "I don't sound like nobody."

This now-legendary encounter gives us some insight into Elvis's success. Imagine yourself—barely out of high school and with no professional experience—having such a clear sense of who you are and what you can do. Elvis truly didn't sound like anyone else. Less than three years later, he would be a household name.

Elvis Presley: The First Rock-and-Roll Star

Elvis Presley (1935–1977) recorded his first local hit for Phillips's Sun Records in 1954. The record, a cover of bluesman Arthur Crudup's "That's All Right," sparked interest on country-western radio (although some stations wouldn't play it because Elvis sounded too black). Within a year he had reached No. 1 nationally on the country-western charts with "Mystery Train"—one of Elvis's most enduring early hits. In late 1955, he signed a personal management contract with Colonel Tom Parker (actually Andreas van Kuijk, an illegal immigrant from Holland), who arranged a record contract with RCA. RCA quickly got Elvis in the studio. "Heartbreak Hotel," his first No. 1, topped the charts in March 1956. Soon, Elvis was a national phenomenon. By 1957, he had recorded several No. 1 hits and made numerous television appearances, most notably on *The Ed Sullivan Show*.

Elvis quickly became the symbol of rock and roll for millions, for both those who idolized him and those who despised him. With his totally uninhibited stage manner, tough-teen dress, greased pompadour, and energetic singing style, Elvis projected a rebellious attitude that many teens found overwhelmingly appealing. To the audiences of today, Elvis may seem almost wholesome. However, his seeming lack of inhibition when performing contrasted sharply with white pop singers who stood in front of microphones and crooned. In his day, this was bold stuff, and he took a lot of heat for it because he refused to tone down his style despite the criticism. In sticking to his guns, he gave rock and roll a sound and a look—both of which immediately set the style apart from anything that had come before. Elvis was rock and roll's lightning rod. For teens he was all that was right with this new music; for their parents he symbolized all that was wrong with it. And for all intents and purposes, he stood alone.

ELVIS performs on *The Milton Berle Show*, April, 1956.

The *Billboard* charts reflect his singular status. Except for Elvis's hits, rock and roll represented only a modest segment of the popular music market. The top-selling albums during this time were mostly soundtracks from Broadway shows and film musicals. Even sales of singles, which teens bought, show that rock and roll did not enjoy the unconditional support of America's youth. The top singles artists during the same period were either pre-rock stars (Frank Sinatra and Perry Como), younger artists singing in a pre-rock style (Andy Williams or Johnny Mathis), teen stars like Pat Boone, who covered early rock-and-roll songs, or vocal groups like the Platters, whose repertoire included a large number of reworked Tin Pan Alley standards. Among the lesser figures—from a commercial perspective—are such important and influential artists as Buddy Holly, Chuck Berry, Little Richard, and Ray Charles. Elvis was, by far, the most important commercial presence in rock and roll; no one else came close.

Elvis at Sun

Elvis could not have picked a better place to start his musical career than at Sam Phillips's studio. By the time, Elvis arrived at his door, Phillips had been operating his recording service for over three years and had recorded numerous blues-based acts, including Jackie Brenston, Junior Parker, and Bobby Blue Bland. Elvis brought only himself, his rudimentary guitar skills, and his remarkable voice. Although he didn't play much guitar, he played the radio really well. He was an equal-opportunity listener with an insatiable appetite for music. And what he heard, he used: Elvis could emulate almost any style—pop, country, gospel, R&B—and still sound like himself. For Sam Phillips, he was the "white man with the Negro feel" that he had been searching for. Phillips recruited guitarist Scotty Moore and bassist Bill Black to back up Elvis, and advised him on what songs to record. Several were covers of rhythm-and-blues songs: "Mystery Train" was a cover of a 1953 recording by bluesman Junior Parker, who also recorded for Sun. Elvis's version transforms rhythm and blues into rockabilly.

Rockabilly

Carl Perkins, perhaps the truest of the rockabilly stars, once explained his music this way: "To begin with . . . rockabilly music, or rock and roll . . . was a country man's song with a black man's rhythm. I just put a little speed into some of the slow blues licks."

Rockabilly began as a white southern music. Its home was Memphis, more specifically Sam Phillips's Sun Records, which would also record Perkins and Jerry Lee Lewis. Even today the style retains this strong southern identity. The sound of rockabilly, however, was not confined to Memphis or even the South: "Rock Around the Clock" is a familiar example.

Elvis's Sun sessions are quintessential rockabilly. In Junior Parker's 1953 version, "Mystery Train" is a boogie-based rhythm-and-blues song; it chugs along at a slow pace underneath Parker's bluesy vocal and the occasional saxophone train whistle. Elvis's version is brighter and more upbeat, and it uses a modified honky-tonk beat: two-beat bass alternating with a heavy backbeat on the electric guitar that is modified with a quick rebound that begins alternately on, then off, the beat. In form, the song is a modified blues; it has the poetic and melodic form of a blues song, but its harmony and phrase length are slightly irregular.

Elvis's singing is the magical element. In both its basic timbre and its variety, his sound is utterly unique—the purest Elvis. It ranges from a plaintive wail on the opening high notes to the often-imitated guttural singing at the end of each chorus. Elvis positions himself not only between country and rhythm and blues, but beyond them. We don't hear the nasal twang so common in country music, nor do we hear the rough-edged sound of a blues singer. Elvis draws on both but sounds like neither ("I don't sound like nobody").

LISTENING CUE • **"Mystery Train" (1955),** Elvis Presley.

STYLE Rockabilly • **FORM** Blues form with modified harmony (both first and second phrases start on IV) and phrases of variable length

Listen For . . .

INSTRUMENTATION
Voice, electric guitar, acoustic bass, drums

PERFORMANCE STYLE
Elvis's high, lonesome sound, plus occasional special effects in vocal asides

RHYTHM
Two-beat rhythm with "rebound" backbeat at fast tempo

HARMONY
Different take on blues harmony: start on IV chord

TEXTURE
Open sound, with light bass and drums, guitar just under Elvis's voice

Remember . . .

FAST TEMPO WITH A MODIFIED TWO-BEAT RHYTHM
Drums maintain a light, fast rhythm very much in the background; the distinctive feature is the "rebound" backbeat in the guitar, which comes with, then ahead, of the backbeat.

ELVIS'S SOULFUL SINGING AND UNIQUE SOUND
Elvis's singing is bluesier than traditional country singing, and without a twang. At the same time, it is distinct from the timbres of 1950s R&B singers.

MODIFIED FORM OF THE BLUES PROGRESSION
Each chorus starts on a IV chord instead of a I chord; in the vocal sections, the first two phrases are of variable length instead of the customary four bars.

Listen to this selection in CourseMate.

Elvis in Hollywood

Elvis's sound brought him radio attention, but it was his looks and his moves that propelled him to stardom. Shortly after breaking through with "Heartbreak Hotel," he made his first Hollywood film, *Love Me Tender*. He would make three more, including *Jailhouse Rock,* before his induction into the army. Among the songs featured in the film was "Jailhouse Rock." Jerry Leiber and Mike Stoller, an up-and-coming songwriting/producing team, wrote the song for Elvis. Released in conjunction with the film, it went to No. 1 in the fall of 1957. In the film, it serves as a soundtrack to an extended dance number.

We get some sense of his presence and his appeal in the scene from his 1957 film *Jailhouse Rock* where he sings the title song. In staging the scene, choreographer Alex Romero wisely asked Elvis to perform some of his songs, then choreographed the movements of the other dancers to mesh with Elvis's moves. In the scene, we see that for Elvis, all of this is fun. He moves freely, spontaneously; the other dancers seem routine by comparison. Elvis's uninhibited movement, evident in film and television clips, contrasts sharply with pop singers—white and black—who simply stand in front of microphones and croon their songs.

"Jailhouse Rock" highlights the qualities that made Elvis so appealing and evidences the craft of Leiber and Stoller, who wrote and produced the song. The song begins with guitar and drums marking off a stop-time rhythm, which continues as Elvis begins to sing. The beginning of the song is, practically speaking, all Elvis, and he makes the most of it. There is an exuberance and a lack of inhibition in his singing that jumps out of the speakers. In this song, Elvis communicates fun—the exhilaration of moving to the beat (even when it can only be felt)—in a way that was unprecedented in pop. There is an emotional honesty to Elvis's singing that transcends the staginess of the scene in the film. The story may be fake, but Elvis's enthusiasm is real. Elvis found this kind of realness in the blues, and in songs like "Jailhouse Rock" he brought it into the mainstream.

Rhythmically, "Jailhouse Rock" shows rock and roll in transition. The most rocklike feature is the guitar pattern, which divides the beat into two equal parts. By accenting and slightly lengthening the first note of each pair, Elvis creates a rhythmic feel (evident especially in the stop-time verse sections) that is somewhere between a standard rock rhythm and a shuffle rhythm. And even though the bass player is playing an electric bass, he is still walking—one note on each beat, like a swing-era or jazz bassist. Most strikingly, the band switches to a swing rhythm in the instrumental interlude; we can almost hear a sigh of relief from the guitarist and drummer as they let go in a rhythm that they know how to feel. Because of the rhythmic inconsistencies, "Jailhouse Rock" is rock and roll commercially, but not quite rock and roll rhythmically.

The musically significant part of Elvis's career lasted only three years. It ended in 1958, when he was inducted into the army. Although still a major public figure in the sixties and seventies, he seldom recaptured the freshness of his earlier years, and he seemed out of step with 1960s rock and rhythm and blues. Still, during his ascendancy, he was crowned the king of rock and roll. What justified his coronation?

The King of Rock and Roll?

Here's a heretical thought: Elvis Presley, the king of rock and roll, sang very little rock and roll. Such a statement would have been literally incredible to teenagers living in 1956 or 1957; for them, and their parents, Elvis embodied rock and roll. As Carl Belz, the first important rock historian, noted in *The Story of Rock:*

> Elvis Presley is the most important individual rock artist to emerge during the music's early development between 1954 and 1956. His extraordinary popularity surpassed that of any artist who appeared in those years, and it remained as a standard for almost a decade. . . . For the music industry, Presley was "king" for almost ten years. He was the first rock artist to establish a continuing and independent motion picture career, the first to have a whole series of million-selling single records—before 1960 he had eighteen—and the first to dominate consistently the tastes of the foreign record market, especially in England, where popularity polls listed him among the top favorites for each year until the arrival of the Beatles.

Belz equates importance almost exclusively with popularity. His list of Elvis's firsts contains no musical innovations; importance is strictly numbers and visibility. However, Elvis's contributions to rock history extend beyond his remarkable commercial success. He brought a fresh look, a fresh attitude, and a fresh sound to popular music. All three proved to be enormously influential.

Elvis gave rock and roll its most memorable visual images. His looks sent girls into hysteria and guys to the mirror, where they greased their hair and combed it into Elvis-like pompadours. His uninhibited, sexually charged stage persona scandalized adults even as it sent teen pulses racing. These images endure, as the legion of Elvis imitators reminds us. There had been flamboyant black performers, like T-Bone Walker, whose stage antics included playing his guitar behind his head while doing the splits, but no popular white entertainer had ever moved like Elvis did, and no one had ever looked like he enjoyed it as much. Even now, when we watch clips of Elvis performing,

LISTENING CUE • **"Jailhouse Rock" (1957),** Jerry Leiber and Mike Stoller. Elvis Presley, vocal.

STYLE Rock and roll • **FORM** Verse/chorus blues form in which the first phrase is doubled in length

Listen For . . .

INSTRUMENTATION
Voice, electric guitar, piano, bass, and drums

RHYTHM
Primitive rock rhythm, kept mainly in guitar during refrain; Elvis and band not sure whether to rock or swing
Nice contrast between syncopated stop time in verse and rocking/walking in refrain

MELODY
"Talking blues" in verse; simple riff in refrain

TEXTURE
Wide spacing: guitar low, just above bass, Elvis in the middle, piano high

Remember . . .

ELVIS'S SINGING
It's exuberant and uninhibited, influenced by blues and country, but a completely new vocal sound.

FULL RHYTHM SECTION WITH PROMINENT ELECTRIC GUITAR
The rhythm section includes drums, bass, piano, and electric guitar; the guitar stands out in both its accompanying and solo roles.

EXPANDED VERSE/CHORUS BLUES FORM
The verse-like section is extended to eight measures; the chorus remains eight measures in length.

RHYTHMIC VARIETY
Stop time in the verse versus consistent timekeeping in the choru

MULTIPLE RHYTHMIC CONCEPTIONS
Rock rhythm in the band during the chorus, swing during the instrumental interlude (one can almost hear the band relax back into a rhythm they're familiar with), and Elvis somewhere in between: not really swing or the even beat division of rock.

Listen to this selection in CourseMate.

we sense that he is having fun. This was an extraordinarily liberating presence for a new generation of pop stars.

His musical contributions were less influential. Certainly, he brought a new vocal sound into popular music. In his various blends of blues, R&B, country, gospel, and pop, Elvis summarized the musical influences—and epitomized the musical direction—of this new music. But his musical significance stops there. He neither wrote his own songs nor consistently used the rock-and-roll rhythm and sound copied by so many late-1950s and early-1960s bands. The road from rock and roll to rock would follow a different path.

CHAPTER 42
The Architects of Rock and Roll

In the latter part of the 1950s, the most apparent distinction between rock and roll and rhythm and blues was racial: Most of the prominent rock-and-roll stars were white; R&B stars were black. So if one simply extrapolated the history of rock and roll from what had developed through the end of 1956, it would be reasonable to assume that rock and roll was simply white takes on black music, like rockabilly and the pop covers of R&B hits.

In fact, however, the crucial difference between rhythm and blues and rock and roll was not race, but rhythm. Most of the R&B acts from the late 1950s continued to build their songs on the shuffle rhythms used so extensively in postwar rhythm and blues or on modified pop rhythms. By contrast, white rock and rollers were drawn to a more active rhythm, which was assembled over a two-year period by two black musicians: Little Richard and Chuck Berry.

Little Richard

Little Richard, born Richard Penniman (1932) in Macon, Georgia, was on the road in black vaudeville shows by the time he was fourteen. He made a few records in the early fifties, but none of them did much. In 1955, Lloyd Price (of "Lawdy Miss Clawdy" fame) suggested that Little Richard send a demo to Art Rupe, who ran Specialty Records, one of the many independent labels recording rhythm and blues. He did, and a few months later Bumps Blackwell set up a recording session at Cosimo Matassa's J&M studio in New Orleans. The house band included some of the legends of New Orleans rhythm and blues, including drummer Earl Palmer and saxophonist Lee Allen. The session got off to a slow start because Little Richard sang mostly slow blues songs, which were not his strength. During a break in the recording session, they went to a local club, where Little Richard began to sing a "blue" song, a naughty novelty number that he'd featured in his act. Blackwell realized that that was the sound they wanted, so on the spur of the moment they recruited local songwriter Dorothy LaBostrie to clean up the words. Her new lyrics didn't make any more sense then than they do now, but they were enough to get Little Richard his first hit, "Tutti Frutti."

© Pictorial Press Ltd/Alamy

LITTLE RICHARD CA. 1958

Little Richard made his mark in a series of songs released between late 1955 and early 1958. Many of them were about girls: "Long Tall Sally," "The Girl Can't Help It" (the girl in this case was blonde bombshell Jayne Mansfield, the star of the film for which the song was written; Little Richard also appeared onscreen), "Lucille," "Good Golly, Miss Molly," and "Jenny, Jenny" stand out.

He found his sound right away in "Tutti Frutti" and kept it pretty much the same throughout his three years in the limelight. His songs seem to offer little variation, mainly because his vocal style is so consistent but also because they are fast and loud and rely so heavily on standard blues form. "Long Tall Sally" could be grafted onto "Tutti Frutti" without dropping a beat—they are that much alike.

"Lucille" and a New Orleans Conception of Rock and Roll

The changes in Little Richard's music are due mainly to the musicians behind him. Unlike Chuck Berry's backup band, they quickly adapted to Little Richard's new rhythm. In his first hits, such as "Tutti Frutti," the band plays in a conventional rhythm-and-blues style: walking bass, heavy backbeat on the drums, and so on. However, in some of his later hits, such as "Lucille" (1957), the entire band is thinking and playing rock rhythm. Bass, guitar, and sax play a repetitive riff in a low register, while Little Richard hammers away, and the drummer taps out a rock beat and a strong backbeat. The contrast with Berry's songs from the same year is clear: Berry is single-handedly trying to establish the new beat; in songs like "Lucille," the entire band is on the same page as Little Richard.

The low register riffs and the interplay between them and a strong, active, and steady beat are among the most

LISTENING CUE • **"Lucille" (1957),** Little Richard.

STYLE Rock and Roll • **FORM** Large-scale form: verse/chorus; both verse and chorus use blues progression

Listen For . . .

INSTRUMENTATION
Voice, saxophones, piano, guitar, bass, drum

PERFORMANCE STYLE
Loud, abrasive vocal sound

RHYTHM
Clean rock rhythm, understood by Little Richard and the entire rhythm section

HARMONY
Standard blues progression, outlined by the bass/guitar line

TEXTURE
Thick sound because of prominent bass/guitar line in a low register

Remember . . .

LOUD SOUND
Little Richard's abrasive vocal sound, complete with whoops, is the most uninhibited vocal sound of the early rock era.

REAL ROCK RHYTHM
The entire band understands rock rhythm: even division of the beat in the bass line; reinforcement of rock rhythm by drummer.

DARK SOUND
Rhythm section and saxophone operate in low mid-range, which darkens the sound. The prominent sounds in a lower register foreshadow one of the defining features of 1960s rock.

Listen to this selection in CourseMate.

distinctive elements in the music coming from New Orleans during the 1950s, whether heard in rhythm and blues or Little Richard's rock and roll. In particular, the heavy bass line, locked-in rock beat, and slower tempo forecast the feel of 1960s rock.

Like so many early rock-and-roll songs, "Lucille" is a verse/chorus blues. The scene-setting sections feature stop-time breaks (when the band stops playing underneath Little Richard) and no change in harmony. The lyric tells the tale of the wayward "Lucille," but the song is really about Little Richard's voice and the beat. We don't listen to Little Richard songs for the lyrics, as we do with Chuck Berry. It would seem that they're there simply because he has to sing *something.*

Little Richard and Rock and Roll as Outrageous Music

Little Richard sang with a voice as abrasive as sandpaper. He hurled his lyrics at the microphone, periodically interrupting them with his trademark falsetto howls and whoops. His singing, like his piano playing, is more percussive than anything else: We are more aware of rhythm than melody, which in most cases is minimal. His music started loud and stayed that way. It was a conscious decision, as he acknowledged:

> I came from a family where my people didn't like R&B. Bing Crosby and Ella Fitzgerald was all I heard. And I knew that there was something that could be louder [*sic*] than that, but I didn't know where to find it. And I found it was me.

Little Richard embodied the new spirit of rock and roll more outrageously and flamboyantly than any other performer of the era. He gave it one of its most identifiable and influential vocal sounds. And he blazed its rhythmic trail. In his sound and persona, Little Richard officially put rock and roll over the top. He was flagrantly gay in an era when gay meant only "happy" and the vast majority of homosexual men were locked tight in the closet. And he was black. When Little Richard performed, he made the outrageous seem routine. In a favorite pose—one leg up on the lid of the piano, hands beating out a boogie beat, and a smirk on his face—there was no way you could avoid noticing him. Generations of rockers—gay, straight, androgynous, and cross-dressing—have followed his example.

Little Richard has claimed that he was responsible for the new beat of rock and roll. He was right, up to a point. However, it didn't become a rock-defining sound until Chuck Berry showed how it could be played on the guitar.

Chuck Berry

Chuck Berry (b. 1926) was the ultimate architect of rock and roll. More than any other musician of the 1950s, he crafted the style that would soon lead to rock.

"Maybellene," Berry's first big hit, gave little rhythmic hint of the direction in which his music would evolve. However, he quickly found his new direction: Berry's hit recordings between "Roll Over, Beethoven" (1956) and "Johnny B. Goode" document the synthesis that eventually produced rock and roll's beat and texture.

Berry's instrumental contribution was twofold: He provided both the first important model for lead guitar playing and the first definitive rock rhythm guitar style. The lead guitar style came first. In "Roll Over, Beethoven," the guitar introduction builds on the thick double-note style that Berry used in "Maybellene." It becomes even more insistent because it is now based on rock rhythm. Berry was not a virtuoso guitarist, like many of those who followed him, such as Jimi Hendrix or Eric Clapton. But his playing was perfectly suited to broadcast the new rhythm that would define rock and roll: the repeated notes made the rhythm insistent; the double notes gave it density.

In the long nights at the Cosmopolitan Club, Berry must have heard hours and hours of Johnny Johnson's boogie-woogie. What Berry did was transfer boogie-woogie left-hand patterns, similar to the ones heard on "Roll 'Em, Pete," to the guitar. The repetitive boogie-woogie patterns became, in Berry's adaptation, the first authentic rock rhythm guitar style; even in medium-tempo songs, he typically divides the beat into two equal parts. In "Roll Over, Beethoven," this pattern is very much in the background. In "Rock and Roll Music," it is more prominent, but there is no lead guitar.

Finally, in "Johnny B. Goode" (1958), he put all the pieces together. In this song, we can hear how Berry forged this revolutionary new style. Berry's voice is neither bluesy nor sweet, but it's well suited to deliver the rapid-fire lyrics that are a trademark of his songs.

The basic instrumentation of "Johnny B. Goode" is conventional enough. It is Berry's **overdubbing**—recording an additional part onto an existing recording—that is the breakthrough and the key to the sound of rock and roll. (We can assume that one of the guitar parts was overdubbed because both lead and rhythm guitar styles are Berry's and no other guitarist is credited in the album notes.) The two guitar lines, the rhythm section—a walking bass, drums (here adding a heavy backbeat), and a steady rhythm guitar—and an active piano **obbligato** (second melody playing under the main melody) create a dense texture. Berry's rhythm guitar line is heard throughout; the lead guitar line includes both solo choruses and instrumental responses during the vocal sections.

Berry's influence and appeal went beyond the music: the lyrics of his songs captured the newly emerging teen spirit. He talked about them ("School Days" and "Sweet Little Sixteen"), to them ("Rock and Roll Music"), and for them ("Roll Over, Beethoven"). His music defines the core elements that make rock and roll stand apart not only from pop and country, but also rhythm and blues.

How did a black man speak so easily to white teens without either compromising his dignity or threatening the establishment during a period of real racial tension? (The year that Berry recorded "Rock and Roll Music," 1957, was also the year that President Eisenhower forcibly integrated the Little Rock schools.) Perhaps it's because the lyrics speak with such detachment and humor about their subjects. Berry is usually an impersonal commentator. Johnny B. Goode is a country boy;

LISTENING CUE • "Johnny B. Goode" (1958), Chuck Berry.

STYLE Rock and roll • **FORM** Large-scale form: verse/chorus; both verse and chorus use blues progression

Listen For . . .

INSTRUMENTATION
Vocals, plus two guitars (overdubbed), piano, bass, drums

PERFORMANCE STYLE
Berry's singing neither pop-pretty nor bluesy—it is too light and friendly; his guitar playing has an edge—in its basic sound, his use of double notes in solo and rhythm lines, and the occasional bent notes.

RHYTHM
Steady eight-beat rhythm in vocals, lead and rhythm guitar; rest of band in four

HARMONY
Blues progression used in verse and chorus

TEXTURE
Strong rhythmic layer, with rhythm guitar, bass, and drums, underpins vocal lines and solos.

Remember . . .

ROCK RHYTHM GUITAR PATTERNS
Berry adapts the boogie-woogie left-hand patterns to the guitar; they become the foundation for rock rhythm guitar.

ROCK LEAD GUITAR PATTERNS
The double notes, bent notes, and syncopated patterns were features of the first important rock lead guitar style.

VERSE/CHORUS BLUES FORM
Verse and chorus (both over the 12-bar blues progression) alternate throughout the song.

Listen to this selection in CourseMate.

his race is not mentioned. Even when Berry himself is (presumably) the subject of the song, he deflects attention away from himself toward events (the car chase in "Maybellene") or activities (going dancing in "Carol"). Even in "Brown-Eyed Handsome Man," possibly his most autobiographical song, he writes in the third person.

Chuck Berry Merges the Roots of Rock and Roll

In "Johnny B. Goode" we hear the three main influences on rock and roll come together. From electric blues Berry took the instrumentation, the thick texture, and the prominent place of the guitar. From boogie-woogie he took the eight-beat rhythm. From more rhythmic and uptempo R&B styles, he took the blues-based verse/chorus form and the heavy backbeat.

At the same time, it's clear that the song is more than just the blending of these influences. The guitar work, Berry's voice, the content and style of the lyrics—all of these features were new elements, and all would prove extraordinarily influential. Berry's guitar breaks and solos were on the must-learn list of every serious rock guitarist. His lyrics, among the first to discuss teen life, are humorous, irreverent, and skillful.

Both the content and the style of his songs were widely copied. The surfing songs of the late fifties and early sixties are an especially good example of Berry's influence on song lyrics and musical style. No rock-and-roll artist was more covered by the creators of rock—the Beach Boys, the Beatles, the Rolling Stones, et al.—than Chuck Berry.

In 1959 Berry was arrested on a Mann Act violation and eventually sentenced to a two-year jail term, even as a new generation of rock musicians on both sides of the Atlantic were going to school on his music. Since the 1960s, he has toured the globe with only his guitar ("he used to carry his guitar in a gunny sack"), replaying his hits for the umpteenth time. Onstage, he often makes little attempt to hide his bitterness: he will stop in the middle of a performance if necessary to correct his pickup band. There have been moments of vindication: Berry seemed genuinely happy in his triumphal performance of "Johnny B. Goode," backed by Bruce Springsteen's E Street Band, at the 1995 concert celebrating the opening of the Rock and Roll Hall of Fame.

The Evolution of Rock and Roll

Recall that the musical term "rock and roll" surfaced first as Alan Freed's code for the rhythm and blues that he played on his radio program. It was a simply a new label for an existing sound, not a new style. Between 1954 and 1956, rock and roll began to develop an identity. It represented new looks, in the appearance and movements of Elvis, Little Richard, Chuck Berry, and others. It offered new sounds, in the music of rockabillies like Bill Haley, Carl Perkins, and Elvis, white cover acts like the Crew Cuts and (yes) Pat Boone, black crossover acts like the many doo-wop groups and Fats Domino, and in the initial rock-defining songs of Little Richard and Chuck Berry. It projected a fresh, impudent, attitude, expressed in image, lyrics, and sound that teens found appealing. And it gained a commercial presence, most prominently in the overwhelming success of Elvis Presley.

However, it wasn't until the late 1950s that rock and roll developed a musical identity that distinguished it not only from pop but also rhythm and blues. Most crucially, the music of Little Richard and Chuck Berry defined a new more active rhythm—the rhythm that would define rock when it became common currency and its most pervasive feature—and Berry's approach to lead and rhythm guitar playing became the primary reference point for the sound of rock. It is mainly in their music that we hear the kind of rock and roll that led directly and inevitably to rock.

CHAPTER 43

Buddy Holly and the Viral Evolution of Rock and Roll

In the 1978 film, *The Buddy Holly Story,* there is a scene where Buddy, played by Gary Busey, and his girlfriend Cindy, are in his car late at night listening to a song by the Five Satins on the car radio, which was being broadcast by KWKH, a clear channel radio station from Shreveport, Louisiana, that programmed rhythm and blues after prime time on Saturday night. In this scene at least, the film is true to life: According to a friend, Holly often drove around until he found a location where he could pick up the station. It was one of the few ways that Holly could hear rhythm and blues in west Texas during the early 1950s.

The Viral Evolution of Rock and Roll

The passion of Holly and his fellow rock-and-rollers was the driving force behind the rapid evolution of rock and roll. But there were two other contributing factors: a shorter and more direct path between inspiration and result, and the novelty of the style. The contrast with the production path of pop is striking. A pop song, even a cover of a rhythm-and-blues or country song, typically involved input from several sources: the artist, the songwriter, the arranger, the musicians, the producer, the industry people, and more. Moreover, the result would be compared against three decades of popular song. In this context, novelty was not a virtue; change came slowly or not at all. By contrast, rock and roll musicians could listen to a recording or a performance—of any style—find something they liked, and copy it or use it as inspiration for something new, often with some help from a like-minded producer.

A second wave of rock-and-roll stars, including Eddie Cochran, Gene Vincent, and the Everly Brothers, did just that. The most imaginative was Buddy Holly, the most creative mind in rock and roll's second generation.

Buddy Holly

Born Charles Hardin Holly, Buddy Holly (1936–1959) grew up in a musical family and appeared on local radio while in high school. After graduating, Holly formed the Crickets. They were a big enough hit locally that they opened a show for Elvis when he came through Lubbock in 1955, but their early records went nowhere. Holly scored his first hit late in 1957 with "That'll Be the Day." It would be his biggest hit, but not his most interesting.

© Michael Ochs Archives/Getty Images

BUDDY HOLLY on the Ed Sullivan Show, 1958

When Holly began to play around with the still-brand-new elements of rock and roll, he found a helpful collaborator in an unlikely place. Norman Petty ran a recording studio in Clovis, New Mexico, a small town about 100 miles from Lubbock. Petty encouraged Holly and the Crickets to go for new sounds, some of which Petty created himself (he was a master of echo and reverb). Still, it was Holly's imagination that took rock and roll to a new level. We can hear this on one of his less popular but more enduring songs from 1957, "Not Fade Away."

As in several of Holly's songs, the lyrics introduce a new persona into rock and roll: the "I" in the song is not the big man on campus, but the gawky guy who loses his girl or who never had her in the first place. Holly wrote and sang for the rest of us; in his music and his appearance, he was rock and roll's first everyman. However, it is the music, and in particular the beat, that makes the song so innovative.

Beyond the Dance Floor in Holly's "Not Fade Away"

The first sounds we hear are the offbeat rhythms of the guitar and the bass, soon reinforced by the backup vocals. Even as the song gets underway, with guitar, bass, drums, and Holly's vocals all present, there is no instrument marking a steady beat. Instead, Holly borrows the "Bo Diddley beat" (virtually the same as the clave pattern

LISTENING CUE • **"Not Fade Away" (1957),** Buddy Holly and Norman Petty. Buddy Holly and the Crickets.

STYLE Latin-tinged rock 'n' roll • **FORM** Strophic: same melody sets multiple verses.

Listen For . . .

INSTRUMENTATION
Lead and backup vocals, lead guitar, acoustic bass, and percussive sounds.

PERFORMANCE STYLE
Holly's hiccuppy vocal style is a rock-and-roll trademark; drummer Jerry Allison played on a cardboard box instead of a drum set.

RHYTHM
The dominant rhythm—heard at first just by itself—is the Bo Diddley beat.
Fast tempo, but no steady timekeeping; only Bo Diddley beat measures time.

TEXTURE
Rich texture: voice/lead instrument plus secondary horn parts (riffs, sustained chords) and rhythm section

Remember . . .

TEEN LYRICS WITH FEELING
Lyrics like these project a more vulnerable image than the "mighty, mighty man" lyrics heard in so many rhythm-and-blues songs.

BEYOND DANCE MUSIC
In a single stroke, Holly opens the door to a new world of musical possibilities—he elevates rock and roll from the dance floor to music just for listening.

THE RAPID EVOLUTION OF ROCK AND ROLL
Holly's apparent adaptation of the Bo Diddley beat suggests that recordings sped up the evolutionary pace: musicians would listen to a song, then use it as a point of departure for a new direction. "Bo Diddley" was a hit two years earlier.

Listen to this selection in CourseMate.

of Afro-Cuban music), introduced by Bo Diddley in his song "Bo Diddley" about two years earlier, and the drum style associated with it, and uses it as the rhythmic reference point. The end of the song offers an ironic touch, fading away slowly even as Holly proclaims that his love will never fade away.

Most rock-and-roll songs begin by laying down a clear, steady beat. Even Bo Diddley meshes the "Bo Diddley beat" with a steady rhythm in the maracas and drums. By contrast, the beat in "Not Fade Away" is hard to find. It is clearly not music for social dancing. We can understand why "Not Fade Away" was not as popular as some of Holly's other songs; most teens still wanted to dance to rock and roll. But we can also understand why songs like this one so profoundly influenced the Beatles and other 1960s rock groups. "Not Fade Away" is a great example of how creative minds like Holly's recycled the sounds of first-generation rock and roll and sent a message that it could be more than dance music.

The Day the Music Died

On February 3, 1959, Buddy Holly died in a plane crash while en route from Iowa to North Dakota. As Don McLean noted in "American Pie," it was "the day the music died." The crash that killed Holly, Ritchie Valens, and J. P. "the Big Bopper" Richardson was one in a string of calamities that seemed to end rock and roll as suddenly as it had begun. The previous year, Elvis was drafted into the army. When he resumed his career two years later, he had lost the cutting edge that had defined his earlier work. Little Richard gave up his career to become a preacher. Jerry Lee Lewis married his thirteen-year-old cousin without divorcing his previous wife, and the ensuing scandal seriously damaged his career. In 1959, Chuck Berry was arrested on a Mann Act violation and eventually sentenced to a two-year jail term.

The **payola scandal** of 1959 also contributed to the apparent decline of rock and roll. Because they controlled airplay of records, disc jockeys wielded enormous power. Some, like Alan Freed, used it to promote the music they liked. But many, including Freed, accepted some form of bribery in return for guaranteed airplay. The practice became so pervasive that it provoked a government investigation. Also at issue was the question of licensing rights. ASCAP, the stronger licensing organization, reportedly urged the investigation to undermine its major competitor, BMI, which was licensing the music of so many black and country performers. Establishment figures viewed the investigation results as proof of the inherent corruption of rock and roll.

By the early 1960s, it seemed as if rock and roll were just a fad that had run its course. In retrospect, it was just getting its second wind.

CHAPTER 44
Doo-Wop in the Late 1950s

Muddy Waters once remarked that "the blues had a baby and they called it rock and roll." We might add that if rock and roll was the baby of the blues, 1950s rhythm and blues was its older brother. Although it had been around longer, it gained a firm toehold in the pop market only in the latter part of the fifties—about the same time rock and roll caught fire.

One reason was more variety. Late 1950s rhythm and blues encompassed a broader range of music, and most of the top acts—such as Fats Domino, Sam Cooke, the Coasters, the Platters, and Ray Charles—projected distinct musical identities. Many had crossover appeal, and appeared consistently on the pop charts—the Platters had four No. 1 pop hits—and R&B acts in general had a stronger market presence in the latter part of the decade.

Gospel's Influence on Rhythm and Blues

Perhaps the primary source of this increased variety was the deepening influence of black gospel music. Since its emergence in the late 1940s, rhythm and blues had been more than big-beat rhythm and blues; gospel and pop were often part of the mix. After 1955, however, gospel supplanted both big-beat rhythms and blues as the primary influence in the rhythm and blues that crossed over to the pop charts. Its impact is most evident and most pervasive in the vocal sounds and styles.

Gospel became a training ground for both doo-wop groups and solo singing stars like Sam Cooke and Ray Charles. The influence of gospel singing style was especially apparent in new versions of pop standards or new songs in a pop style; the vocal timbre of gospel singers is different from the pop and jazz singers of the 1950s, and the call and response exchanges between lead and backup singers are different from backup singing in pop.

As a result, the gospel influence stands out even in recordings that feature then more elaborate production techniques of pop, such as richer instrumental accompaniment and more complex arrangements. Even one- or two-hit wonders like the Marcels invested their recordings of pop material with a distinct personality.

The most commercially successful rhythm-and-blues style in the latter part of the 1950s was the music of vocal groups, retrospectively titled **doo-wop.** Doo-wop was not one sound, but several. Probably the most popular were slow romantic ballads. Some were radical remakes of modern-era pop standards; others were newly composed songs in a similar style. But there was also the dark humor of the Coasters, raucous remakes of pop standards by groups such as the Marcels ("Blue Moon") and Cleftones ("Heart and Soul"), the upbeat puppy love of groups like Frankie Lymon and the Teenagers, and much more. We sample two contrasting doo-wop sounds in the tracks discussed next.

Slow Doo-Wop

It has been a given that there is no "right" way to perform a modern-era pop song. Recall that when a song became a hit, bands rushed to record their version, and if it became a standard, the top pop interpreters strived to put their personal stamp on it. Even still, there was no real precedent for the radical reshaping of popular song by doo-wop groups. The Flamingos' 1959 recording of the 1934 hit "I Only Have Eyes for You" is an exceptionally fine example of this practice.

The Flamingos were a Chicago-based vocal quintet: two pairs of cousins and a lead singer. They were among the more successful doo-wop groups in the late 1950s, charting steadily on the R&B charts and occasionally crossing over to the pop charts.

As originally conceived in 1934, "I Only Have Eyes for You" is a beautiful foxtrot ballad. The Flamingos' version is a thorough reconception of the song, with several obvious differences from conventional pop. The sound of lead singer Sollie McElroy and the close harmony of the Flamingos as a group are different from the pop singers of the 1930s and 1940s; so are the frequent exchanges between lead and backup singers.

The tempo of the performance is much slower, so slow in fact that the recording, which lasts more than three minutes, includes only one statement of the chorus. Like the vocal styles and call and response between singers, the slow tempo has its roots in gospel style: It was common for black gospel musicians to perform conventional hymns like "Amazing Grace" at a markedly slower tempo than their white counterparts. Gospel-trained doo-wop singers simply transferred the practice to pop.

To energize this slow tempo, the pianist plays repeated chords in a triplet rhythm. The "doo-wop-sh-bop" riffs of the backup vocalists during the verse are the kind that earned doo-wop its name. The riff stands out in two ways: It is the main source of rhythmic energy in the song, and it replaces even the

LISTENING CUE • **"I Only Have Eyes for You" (1934, recorded1959),** Harry Warren and Al Dubin. The Flamingos.

STYLE Pop ballad sung doo-wop style • **FORM** Pop song form (AA^1BA^2), with verse and long tag

Listen For . . .

INSTRUMENTATION
Lead/backup vocals, plus full rhythm, with electric guitar prominent at beginning and drummer using brushes

RHYTHM
Extremely slow tempo, with piano triplets providing momentum

HARMONY
Static in verse; rich in chorus

MELODY
Pop song: melody built from opening riff

TEXTURE
Rich sound: low guitar, high piano, close harmony or lead and doo-wop in middle

Remember . . .

DOO-WOP VOCAL TIMBRE
The pleasant blend of a doo-wop singing group replaces the smooth crooning of a pop singer in the performance of pop standards.

HALF-SPEED TEMPO
The song moves at about half the typical speed of a foxtrot: We hear the chorus of the song only once rather than two or three times.

BIPOLAR HARMONY
Long stretches of a single chord contrast with lush harmonies, most notably on the title phrase.

INSISTENT TRIPLET RHYTHM
Triplets inject rhythmic energy into the song, helping to balance out the slow tempo.

Listen to this selection in CourseMate.

title phrase ("I only have eyes for you") as the song's melodic signature. In this respect it anticipates an important rock-era development: the distribution of melodic interest among several parts rather than concentrating it in the lead vocal line.

The harmony in this performance is bipolar. For long stretches, such as the opening verse and the first part of the chorus, there is no harmonic change. Upon arriving at the title phrase, the harmony suddenly becomes lush, with new chords on almost every syllable of the lyric. This kind of harmonic practice is unique to doo-wop.

All four style features—the timbre of the singers, the slow tempo, the signature vocal riffs, and the static harmony—give the recording a distinctive identity; it's not just another version of the song.

The Producer in the Early Rock Era

"We don't write songs, we write records," said producers Jerry Leiber (b. 1933) and Mike Stoller (b. 1933). Leiber and Stoller's remark sums up the new reality of music making in the rock era. Increasingly, a song was not just a melody, which singers could perform "their way," but the entire sound world captured on disc.

With this shift, the producer assumed an increasingly important role. The first producers wore several hats—artist and repertoire (A&R) man, songwriter, arranger, contractor—as well as recording engineer, in several cases. Because producers controlled so many elements, they often put their own stamp on the sound of a recording. For example, the New Orleans sound was the product of a distinctive arranging style played by the same nucleus of musicians. Dave Bartholomew at Imperial Records (who produced Fats Domino's sessions) and "Bumps" Blackwell at Specialty Records (who produced so many of Little Richard's hits) favored a heavy sound. To achieve this, they would often have saxes, guitar, and bass all play a low-register riff. Little Richard's "Lucille" is a clear example. It could be part of the sound, regardless of the featured artist. Indeed, behind virtually all of the major fifties stars was an important producer. Sam Phillips oversaw Elvis's early career and Jerry Lee Lewis's rock-and-roll records, while Leonard Chess produced Chuck Berry's hits, and Norman Petty, most of Buddy Holly's.

Leiber and Stoller

Leiber and Stoller stand apart from the others because they wrote so many of the songs their acts recorded and in general exerted more control over the final product. Knowing that they operated within strict time constraints—by their measure, no more than

3 minutes 40 seconds (3:40) and no less than 2:20 (the upper and lower time limits of a 45 single)—Lieber and Stoller wrote a song with the recording session in mind. They crafted every aspect of the song—not only the words and melody but also the sax solos, the beat, the tempo, and just about every other element of the recorded performance.

They began as songwriters in love with the sound of the new black music. Among their first hits was "Hound Dog," originally written for Big Mama Thornton and covered a few years later by Elvis Presley. For Presley, they wrote and produced such hits as "Jailhouse Rock." However, they left their imprint most strongly on the recordings of the Coasters and the Drifters.

Leiber and Stoller were among the first to elevate record production to an art. They were meticulous in both planning and production, often recording up to sixty takes to obtain the result they sought. Their most distinctive early songs were what Leiber called "playlets"—songs that told a funny story with serious overtones; Stoller called them "cartoons." As with print cartoons, the primary audience was young people—of all races—who identified with the main characters in the story. These were humorous stories, but with an edge.

The Coasters

The Coasters—so named because they came from the West Coast, unlike most of the other doo-wop groups—were really doo-wop in name only, because their music was so different from that of almost all the other groups of the time. They had formed as the Four Bluebirds in 1947 and became the Robins in 1950, singing backup behind Little Esther. They reformed in late 1955, renaming themselves the Coasters.

The group's fortunes changed when they began working with Leiber and Stoller in 1954. The following year, Atlantic signed Leiber and Stoller as independent songwriters and producers. Together, they and the Robins/Coasters ran off a string of hits: "Smokey Joe's Cafe," "Charlie Brown," "Yakety Yak," and "Young Blood," which topped the R&B charts and reached the Top 10 in the pop charts in 1957.

The story told in "Young Blood" deals with youthful infatuation, but it is a far cry from the starry-eyed romance found in songs like "Sh-Boom." As "Young Blood" shows, the Coasters' songs were the opposite of most doo-wop: steely-eyed, not sentimental, and darkly humorous. The Coasters' singing sounds slick, but not sweet. Although the Coasters have a black sound, the theme of the song is universal. Teens of all races could relate to it, and did.

The musical setting is a distinctive take on fifties rhythm and blues. The core instrumentation is typical: full rhythm section plus saxophone behind the vocal group. A shuffle rhythm with a heavy backbeat provides the underlying rhythmic framework. But the most prominent rhythm is the repeated guitar riff, which has a distinct rhythmic profile, and there are numerous shifts in the rhythmic flow—breaks that showcase the Coasters' trademark humorous asides that drop down the vocal ladder, with bass singer Bobby Nunn getting in the last word, and sections where the rhythm players sustain long chords instead of marking the beat. These and other features separate "Young Blood" musically from more straightforward R&B songs, just as the lyrics separate the song from both blues-oriented lyrics and romantic doo-wop.

Leiber and Stoller laid the groundwork for subsequent generations of producers. Such major figures as Phil Spector, Berry Gordy, George Martin, and Quincy Jones trace their roles back to Leiber and Stoller and the other producers of the 1950s who helped transform the making of popular music.

Doo-Wop and Black Pop

Doo-wop was unique among the rock and roll and rhythm-and-blues styles that emerged during the late 1940s and 1950s because it was both old and new at the same time. Unlike electric blues, big-beat rhythm and blues, rockabilly, and the high-intensity rock and roll of Elvis, Chuck Berry, Little Richard, and so on, doo-wop was strongly connected to—even dependent upon—the pop music that rock and roll and rhythm and blues were reacting against. At the same time, however, it presented pop in a radically new way: different vocal sounds, new tempos, different rhythmic foundations, richer textures, plus the frequent nonsense syllables that became the signature of the style.

Doo-wop died out suddenly around 1960, as new and more up-to-date kinds of black pop emerged: girl groups such as the Shirelles and the Crystals, and slickly produced vocal groups like the second incarnation of the Drifters.

Listening to doo-wop is often an exercise in nostalgia. Because its sounds are so distinctive and its peak period of popularity is so clearly circumscribed, it easily evokes a keen sense of time and place. However, doo-wop also served as the bridge between pre-rock pop and the black pop of the 1960s and beyond. It preserved the romance of earlier pop styles through the emphasis on tuneful melody and rich textures, while simultaneously introducing features that anticipated the black pop of the 1960s. More than any other music of the 1950s, it helped bring new sounds and new faces to rock-era pop.

LISTENING CUE • "Young Blood" (1957), Jerry Leiber and Mike Stoller. The Coasters.

STYLE Doo-wop • **FORM** Large-scale AABA form, with A = verse/chorus

Listen For . . .

INSTRUMENTATION
Vocal group (solo and together), plus electric guitar, bass, drums, and saxophone

PERFORMANCE STYLE
Contrast in vocal timbres an effective device, especially when voices heard in sequence

RHYTHM
Swing/shuffle rhythm at moderate tempo with strong backbeat
Repeated riffs and stop time in rhythm section in lieu of steady timekeeping

MELODY
Both verse and chorus-like sections built from short, slightly varied riffs

Remember . . .

WRY TONE OF LYRICS
A story of youthful infatuation that leads nowhere but trouble

DISTINCTIVE SHUFFLE RHYTHM
The loping guitar/bass riff and heavy backbeat give this shuffle-based rhythm a more open sound. There is no instrument consistently marking the shuffle rhythm.

SOUND OF THE COASTERS
The Coasters use the "down-the-ladder" breaks to showcase all of the voices, not just the lead singer and the bass.

PRODUCERS' IMPACT
Leiber/Stoller input is evident not only in song, but in setting: varied supporting rhythms and textures, including stop-time effects and strong contrasts.

Listen to this selection in CourseMate.

CHAPTER 45
R&B Solo Singing in the Late 1950s

Among the songs that topped the R&B charts in 1955 was Ray Charles's first hit, "I Got a Woman." Charles did not write the song; rather, he gave the gospel hymn "Jesus Is All the World to Me" new words and a new beat. His transformation of the sacred into the profane scandalized members of the black community. The blues singer Big Bill Broonzy summed up what Charles had done and why it outraged so many when he said, "He's crying, sanctified. He's mixing the blues with the spirituals. He should be singing in a church."

Solo Singers

Charles was the most important and influential of the black solo singers who fueled the growth of rhythm and blues in the late 1950s. Many, like Clyde McPhatter and Jackie Wilson, launched solo careers after starting as lead singers in doo-wop and R&B singing groups. (Both McPhatter and Wilson sang with Billy Ward's Dominos.)

Sam Cooke, the golden boy of black pop, bypassed doo-wop, going directly from gospel to a solo career. Jerry Wexler, who by this time was a partner in Atlantic Records—the label that had Charles, the Coasters, and several other top R&B acts on their roster—commented on Cooke's singing:

> Sam was the best singer who ever lived, no contest. . . . he had control, he could play with his voice like an instrument, his melisma, which was his personal brand—I mean, nobody else could do it—everything about him was perfection.

Cooke seemed to have it all: looks, charm, and one of the truly superb voices in popular music history. Recognizing this in 1960, RCA brought him to their label, where he produced a stream of hits. But his career ended abruptly one night in 1964 when he was shot and killed by a woman in a Los Angeles hotel room.

Cooke, like Elvis, made his contribution mainly with his remarkable singing. That was not the case with Ray Charles.

RAY CHARLES

Ray Charles

Ray Charles (born Ray Charles Robinson, 1930–2004) lost his sight at age seven to an undiagnosed case of glaucoma. The onset of blindness may well have stimulated his voracious appetite for music. Charles grew up listening to and playing everything: blues, gospel, country, jazz, classical, pop. He launched his professional career in the late 1940s; in his first recordings, he emulated the style of Nat Cole, the most popular black vocalist of the era and a fine jazz pianist. In 1952, Atlantic Records bought his contract from Swingtime, the label that had released his first recordings. For about two years, he recorded rhythm-and-blues songs distinguished mainly by the unique quality of his voice.

He broke through as a rhythm-and-blues artist in 1955 with "I Got a Woman" and followed it with several No. 1 R&B hits, including "A Fool for You," "Drown in My Own Tears," and "What'd I Say," which also reached No. 6 on the pop charts. During this time, he also gave expression to his interest in jazz, performing at jazz festivals as well as R&B events and recording with major jazz artists like vibraphonist Milt Jackson. In this respect, he was the main rhythm-and-blues link to jazz's "return to roots" movement.

Like many R&B artists of the period, Charles included a few Latin numbers in his act and helped bring Latin music into rhythm and blues. The Latin numbers had an obvious effect on songs like "What'd I Say."

"What'd I Say"

"What'd I Say" is not one song, but three: an instrumental, a solo vocal, and a rapid-fire call and response dialogue between Charles and The Raelettes. The instrumental section features Charles's take on Latin rhythm.

LISTENING CUE • "What'd I Say" (1959), Ray Charles.

STYLE 1950s R&B gospel/blues/Latin fusion • **FORM** Twelve-bar blues

Listen For . . .

INSTRUMENTATION
Solo singer, backup vocals (at end), electric piano, bass, drums, horn section (trumpets, saxophones)

PERFORMANCE STYLE
Charles's vocal style fuses blues and impassioned gospel.

RHYTHM
Americanized Latin rhythm (no clave pattern)

HARMONY
Blues progression used throughout

TEXTURE
Frequent call and response at the end: first horns, then backup vocalists

Remember . . .

FROM INSTRUMENTAL TO VOCAL
Full version of "What'd I Say" begins as instrumental featuring Charles; middle section = solo vocal; end features full band, backup vocalists.

AMERICANIZED LATIN RHYTHM
Drumming, Charles's *montuno*-like opening riff show adaptation of Latin rhythm to R&B. Rhythms less insistent, more complex alternative to rock rhythm.

BLUES + GOSPEL + JAZZ
Charles brings together several streams in black music: jazz-like improvisation in opening, blues theme, style, and blues harmony, gospel-like call and response and screams, moans, and so on, in Charles's singing

Listen to this selection in CourseMate.

The opening piano line sounds like an American cousin of the piano *montunos* of Afro-Cuban music, and the drum part is much closer to Americanized Latin drumming than it is to standard rock drumming, ca. 1959. In most other respects, the song is straight rhythm and blues.

The solo vocal section alternates between stop time and the instrumental riffs, which are now part of the background. Although the solo vocal section uses the by-now venerable verse/chorus blues form, it does not tell a story. Instead, it offers a series of images, mostly of dancing women. The sequence of the images in the live recording differs from the studio version, further suggesting that the real message is in the feeling behind the words, not the words themselves. The final section, where Charles's moans often transcend verbal communication, confirms this impression.

Charles's late 1950s music, and "What'd I Say" in particular, marked a crucial juncture in the relationship between gospel and blues. The song revisits a blues tradition—in subject matter (the joy of sex), narrative style (pictures, not a story), upbeat mood, and form (verse/chorus blues)—that began with songs like Thomas A. Dorsey's "It's Tight Like That." Dorsey brought the blues into African-American sacred music. Charles closes that particular circle by bringing gospel music into an upbeat blues song.

After establishing himself as the most important, innovative, and influential rhythm-and-blues artist of the 1950s, Charles abruptly switched gears—not once, but three times—with excursions into pop (1960), jazz (1961), and country music (1962). These new directions brought him unprecedented success. Although his gospel/blues fusions made him a top artist among blacks, his gospel/blues/jazz/pop/country fusions made him one of the most successful and influential artists in all of popular music during the early 1960s.

Charles's influence on rock-era music is substantial and diverse. His country recordings influenced a number of important country musicians, including Merle Haggard and Willie Nelson. He was the first major rock-era performer to record an album of standards, a practice that subsequent generations of singers, such as Linda Ronstadt, Willie Nelson, and Rod Stewart, have followed.

However, his most far-reaching contribution was his fusion of blues and gospel. In his late 1950s hits, Charles merged rhythmic and blues-drenched R&B with the most fervent kind of gospel singing, the kind one might hear in black Pentecostal churches. The use of the fervent gospel style is functional; it adds a dimension to the blues that was not there before. Sexual relations (and the lack of them) have been the most recurrent theme in blues, as we have noted. The infusion of ecstatic gospel style enabled him to communicate the agonies and ecstasies of love so characteristic of the blues with even more deeply felt emotion. His music, and particularly his singing, would become the most important influence on the soul music of the 1960s.

CHAPTER 46
Rock and Rhythm and Blues in the Early 1960s

> It was a unique fusion that Wilson had been tinkering with in the family garage where, inspired by The Four Freshman and their complex vocal blends, and armed with a multitrack tape recorder, he'd spent hours exploring the intricacies of harmony and melody. By overlapping his own dynamic voice (which peaked in a soaring falsetto) and various instruments, he could create the effect of a full group.

This third-person account, from a previous iteration of his website, describes Brian Wilson's initial experiments in multitrack recording. In the early 1960s, multitrack recording was a still new technology that enabled a new creative process. Previously, musicians typically had to imagine the sounds they wanted, write them down in musical notation, then rely on their fellow musicians to realize their musical conception. By contrast, in **multitrack recording,** musicians like Wilson were working with actual sounds throughout the entire creative process. Further, they are able to experiment with their work at every stage of the process; they can add a part, and if it is not the desired result, they can remove it. Today, creating music in a sound-only environment is commonplace; fifty years ago, Wilson was on the cutting edge.

Wilson would use this new technology to glorify the surfer's fun-in-the-sun lifestyle. Such contrasts between musical and technological sophistication and the seemingly simpleminded results it produced are often evident in rock and rhythm and blues in the early 1960s.

The Adolescence of Rock: The Early Sixties

Rock and roll and rhythm and blues grew up quickly. Both were music mainly for teens through the fifties; in the early sixties, both music and audience matured. The difficult adolescence of rock and rhythm and blues is evident in virtually every aspect of the music—its diversity, its themes, its lyrics, and in the music itself. Suddenly, rock-related music covered much more musical territory: the high-minded and idealistic music of the folk revival and the barbed commentaries on the inequities of contemporary society by Bob Dylan and others; Roy Orbison's one-man rockabilly revival; the slickly produced music of the Drifters; the garbled garage-band sounds of the Kingsmen; the seeming hedonism of surf music; the sophisticated silliness of Phil Spector's music (what does "Da Doo Ron Ron" mean anyway?) and much more.

The complement to this broadening of rock's base was more thorough integration: white songwriters writing songs for black girl groups, whose recordings of them had widespread appeal; Dick Clark, a white promoter/television show host, enlisting Chubby Checker, a black performer, to teach Americans how to "do the Twist," which seemingly everyone from the president on down did; and *Billboard* suspending the rhythm-and-blues chart from late 1963 through early 1965 because there had been so little difference between the R&B and pop charts.

Songs from rock's musical adolescence typically feature an often appealing mix of innocence and immaturity with innovation and sophistication, as is evident in songs by the Shirelles and the Beach Boys.

The Shirelles and the Rise of Girl Groups

The Shirelles were a female vocal quartet—Shirley Owens, Micki Harris, Beverly Lee, and Doris Coley—who formed as the Poquellos in 1958 while still in high school. Their rise to the top of the charts is another of the happy accidents of the rock era. The group had won over the crowd at a high school talent show with a song they wrote themselves, "I Met Him on a Sunday." A classmate, Mary Jane Greenberg, introduced them to her mother, Florence, who, after some haggling, signed them to record the song for her fledgling label, Tiara Records. It was a local hit—big enough to be picked up by Decca. When released by Decca, the song charted nationally; it was the Shirelles' first hit.

Image courtesy of The Advertising Archives

In songs like "Will You Love Me Tomorrow," the Shirelles sang peer to peer about a meaningful issue.

After a few more Decca-released recordings that went nowhere, Greenberg re-formed Tiara as Scepter Records and brought in Luther Dixon to produce the group. From 1960 to 1963, the Shirelles were almost always on the charts. Their biggest hit came in 1960 with "Will You Love Me Tomorrow," a song written by Carole King and Gerry Goffin, her husband at the time. The song, written and performed by women, gives a woman's perspective on the fragility of new love.

Carole King's song gives us the other side of boastful, male R&B songs ("Good Rockin' Tonight"). The man thinks only of tonight; the woman worries about tomorrow. There is no mistaking the message of the song—the lyrics are simple and clear. In its frankness and distinctively female point of view, the song had no significant precedent in pop. Its most direct antecedents were the classic blues of Bessie Smith and others, and country "response" songs like Kitty Wells' "God Didn't Make Honky Tonk Angels."

The music reinforces the message of the lyrics, not because it presents a coherent setting, but because its main components send such different messages. There are three groups of sounds: the rhythm section, the string section, and the Shirelles. The rhythm section lays down a rather mundane rock beat, one that was fashionable during these years in rock-influenced pop. It remains constant throughout the song; there is almost no variation. But the string writing is bold and demanding—the most sophisticated part of the sound. The intricate string lines stand in stark contrast to the Shirelles' vocals, especially Shirley Owens's straightforward lead.

And therein lies the charm. The instrumental backup, and especially the skillful string parts, contrasts with the naïve schoolgirl sound of the Shirelles (none of whom was yet twenty years old when the song was released). All of this meshes perfectly with King's lyrics, the song's simple melody, and the group's look. Shirley sounds courageous enough to ask the question and vulnerable enough to be deeply hurt by the wrong answer. She, like the lyric, sounds neither worldly nor cynical.

The song and the singers reflect the changing attitudes of the early 1960s. It was written by a white woman, produced by a black man, supported with white-sounding string writing, and sung by young black women. The Shirelles crossed over consistently partly because of the changing racial climate (the civil rights movement was gathering steam) and partly because they were teens like their audience. In songs like "Will You Love Me Tomorrow," the Shirelles sang peer to peer about a meaningful issue. The message of the song is color-blind: teens of all races could relate to it.

LISTENING CUE · **"Will You Love Me Tomorrow" (1960),** Carole King and Gerry Goffin. The Shirelles.

STYLE Early 1960s girl group • **FORM** Considerably expanded AABA form

Listen For . . .

INSTRUMENTATION
Lead and backup vocals, full rhythm (piano, bass, electric guitar, and drums), and full strings (violins and cellos)

PERFORMANCE STYLE
The Shirelles' singing has a girl-next-door quality: their voices are not classically trained or modeled after mature pop, blues, or jazz singing.

RHYTHM
Moderate tempo; straightforward rock rhythm, with rebound backbeat (two taps on the snare drum rather than just one)

MELODY
A section grows out of the opening riff-like phrase, forming an arch, with the peak on "so sweetly"; strong push toward the title phrase.

TEXTURE
Distinct layers: lead vocal, backup vocal, violins playing an obbligato, and low strings and rhythm instruments laying down steady patterns

Remember . . .

VULNERABLE LYRICS, VULNERABLE GIRLS
Innocent-sounding girls' No. 1 question; the Shirelles' vocal style and look enhance the question in the lyric.

DRESSING UP
String writing adds a layer of sophistication to simple vocal sounds and rhythm-section accompaniment.

SIMPLE ROCK RHYTHM
The state of rock rhythm ca. 1960: straightforward rock beat in drums, slightly liberated bass line

BETWEEN ROCK, R&B, AND POP
Teen-themed song, black pop vocal style, simple rock rhythm, pop-like string writing

Listen to this selection in CourseMate.

Surf Music

For teens who had grown up with snowy winters and dreary, late-arriving springs, the beaches of southern California seemed like a hedonist's paradise: sun, surf, cars, babes—the endless summer. They learned about the surfing lifestyle through films like *Beach Party* and the lyrics of songs by the Surfaris, the Ventures, Jan and Dean, and—above all—the Beach Boys.

Surf music added two immediately recognizable sounds to rock's sound world. High-register close harmony vocals were a trademark of the Beach Boys and, to a lesser extent, Jan and Dean. An array of new guitar sounds found wider traction; they included intense reverb, single line solos in a low register (most famously in the Ventures' "Walk, Don't Run"), and down-the-escalator tremolos and other virtuosic effects popularized by Dick Dale, the "king of the surf guitarists" and one of rock's first cult figures, and those who imitated him.

In large part because of these distinctive sounds, surf music acquired an indelible regional identity. A single vocal harmony or descending tremolo was all that was needed to put a listener on a Malibu beach, watching the waves or cruising along the strip. This was the first time in the short history of rock where the music evoked a strong sense of place.

Rock and roll developed first in the center of the country, from Chicago through Memphis to New Orleans, but the music did not evoke these locales. By contrast, surf music is a sound about a place and a lifestyle. It would not be the last. The new sounds coming out of California were the first clear signal of the geographic diffusion of rock. The British invasion would be a far more potent sign, because it made an American music international. It is in this early sixties development that we see the first stages in what would become the global reach of contemporary rock-era music.

Surf music is a sound about a place and a lifestyle.

The Beach Boys

The most important and innovative of the surf music bands was the Beach Boys. Their band was a family affair. The original group consisted of three brothers, Carl (1946–1988), Dennis (1944–1983), and Brian Wilson (b. 1942); their cousin, Mike Love (b. 1941); and a friend, Al Jardine (b. 1942).

The Beach Boys' first recordings point out their debt to rock's first generation, and particularly the music of Chuck Berry. It's blatantly evident in their hit "Surfin' USA," which is such a faithful reworking of Berry's "Sweet Little Sixteen" that Berry sued Wilson for writing credit. At the same time, they transformed the sound and updated the rhythmic conception: Their reworking of Berry's riffs and rhythms are rock, not rock and roll. In their recordings released between 1963 and 1965, they glorified the surfer lifestyle in songs that subtly varied their innovative, immediately recognizable sound.

"I Get Around," a song that reached the top of the charts in June 1964, shows key elements of their style and the variety possible within it. The song begins with just voices, presenting the essence of the Beach Boys' vocal sound. In order, we hear unison singing, tight harmonies, and a soaring single line melody layered over harmonized riffs—all sung with no vibrato.

The refrain follows, its split melody supported by a driving rock rhythm played by the entire band. Unlike this rhythm, the distinctive vocal sound of the Beach Boys came from outside rock. Its source was the Four Freshmen, a slick, skilled, jazz-flavored vocal group who navigated complex harmonies as nimbly as Count Basie's saxophone section. Wilson, who admired the group and acknowledged them as a source of inspiration, used their sound as a point of departure. The song goes well beyond the blues-based harmony of most rock and roll. Wilson charts a distinctly new path in the fresh new chord progressions underneath the vocal.

The scene-painting verse sections are set off from the chorus by the substitution of an open-sounding, loping rhythm for the straightforward rock rhythm of the refrain. Even the instrumental solos have a characteristic, clearly defined sound. The short interlude in the verse combines a doubled organ and bass line with double-time drums, while the guitar solo is supported with sustained vocal harmonies.

LISTENING CUE • "I Get Around" (1964), Brian Wilson. The Beach Boys.

STYLE Rock • **FORM** Verse/chorus form, with first statement of chorus framing first verse

Listen For . . .

INSTRUMENTATION
Lead and backup vocals; electric guitar, electric bass, drums, organ

PERFORMANCE STYLE
High lead singing plus closely spaced vocal harmony

RHYTHM
Basic rock beat, reinforced by guitar, bass, and drums, predominates.

HARMONY
Rich harmony: well beyond I-IV-V

TEXTURE
Considerable variation in texture: a cappella vs. full band, steady timekeeping vs. loping rhythm or stop time, melodic interplay between lead and backup vocals

CLEAR ROCK RHYTHM WITH CONSIDERABLE VARIATION
Strong rock beat in chorus, with bass, drums, and rhythm guitar moving at rock beat speed. An open, loping long–short rhythm in verses provides contrast, as does the lack of an underlying rhythm during the a cappella introduction.

SOUND VARIETY IN INSTRUMENTATION AND TEXTURE
Overall low register of the instruments balancing high-register vocals; innovative sound combinations such as the organ doubling the guitar in the verse

STRONG BASS LINE THROUGHOUT THE SONG
The bass moves at rock-beat speed in the chorus and lopes along in the verses. This is the development that, more than any other, effects the musical transition from rock and roll to rock.

Remember . . .

DISTINCTIVE VOCAL SOUND
The high lead singing with intricate, important backup vocal parts gave the Beach Boys' songs an unmistakable and virtually inimitable sound.

Listen to this selection in CourseMate.

The "fun in the sun" lyrics belie the considerable sophistication of the music, in harmony, rhythm, and texture. This sophistication was mainly the work of Brian Wilson; in their peak years, the sound of the Beach Boys was Brian Wilson's conception. Wilson's conception would continue to evolve through the 1960s, reaching a peak with the release of the landmark 1966 album *Pet Sounds*.

UNIT 11

LOOKING BACK, LOOKING AHEAD

From Rock and Roll to Rock; From Rhythm and Blues to Motown and Soul

IN 1954, ROCK AND ROLL was on the verge of national recognition; in 1964, rock was on the verge of a revolution. During that same period, rhythm and blues crossed over to the pop charts so thoroughly that *Billboard* merged the pop and R&B charts for over a year.

The intervening decade divides almost evenly into two 5-year spans demarcated by points of reckoning for both rock and roll and rhythm and blues. In the case of rock and roll, it was mainly the devastating string of disasters and defections that involved most of the important acts: Elvis's post-Army gravitation to Hollywood and Las Vegas; Jerry Lee Lewis's scandal; Little Richard's call to the ministry; Chuck Berry's conviction; and above all, Buddy Holly's death. The payola scandal was salt in the wound. For rhythm and blues, the point of reckoning was mainly musical: How does this music leave the past behind and move into a new era?

From these pivotal points, both rock and roll and rhythm and blues moved forward. Despite the sometimes-jarring contrasts between music and message, there is overall a sense of growth, of coming together into a new kind of music. And despite the significant differences in style, there are common musical features in much of this that stamp it as from the early sixties, not the fifties. Two stand out: the liberation of the bass line and the collective adoption of rock rhythm.

The switch from acoustic to electric bass began in earnest during the late 1950s; by the early 1960s, the electric bass was the bass instrument of choice in both rock and rhythm and blues because amplification made it much easier to match the volume level of guitarists and drummers. This in turn freed the bass player from working hard simply to produce even a simple walking bass line. Rock and R&B bass players could now take a more flexible approach—active or laid back, on the beat or rhythmically independent. This was the key step in the collective embrace of rock rhythm.

The one musical feature that most consistently distinguishes the rock and R&B of the early 1960s from the music of the previous decade is a collective conception of rock rhythm. Chuck Berry had shown how rock rhythm should sound. However, it wasn't until the early 1960s that bassists and drummers routinely aligned with this more active rhythm. The initial efforts resulted in basic—even awkward—versions of rock rhythm, as the tracks discussed in this chapter exemplify. But in both cases, and in much of the music of the early 1960s, the entire rhythm section is playing a rock beat, rather than the shuffle rhythms used almost universally in 1950s R&B, or the conflicting rhythmic approaches heard in so much rock and roll.

Moreover, once musicians got on the same page rhythmically, the music evolved quickly. By 1964, the British were invading, Motown acts were charting regularly, James Brown was getting his brand new bag together, and Dylan was thinking about going electric.

The Rock Revolution: 1964–1970

© Exactostock/SuperStock

UNIT 12

UNIT 12

If it were possible to encapsulate the rock revolution in a single sound, it could easily be the opening chord of the Beatles' "A Hard Day's Night." In a single strum, George Harrison broadcast a new sound world, new freedoms, a new attitude, and a new way of creating music. The dissonant clangor was intentional: According to producer George Martin (the "fifth Beatle"), the group wanted a bold beginning because the song was the title track for the film of the same name.

The chord symbolized the search for new sounds and new ways of making them. Harrison played the chord on a Rickenbacker twelve-string guitar; underneath his sound is McCartney's bass note and Martin's supporting piano chord. The thoughtfully planned instrumental mix suggests that the quest for distinctive sounds was part of the new aesthetic of rock.

The chord symbolized harmonic freedom: It is more about sound than about structure. It relates tangentially to the key of the song but is not part of the standard progressions for that key. As a result, it previews the mix of conventional, blues, and modal harmonies that underpin the melody of the song—and in the rock of the 1960s and beyond.

The chord rings for an indeterminate time—about three seconds—before the band launches into the song proper, with Lennon's melody supported by a driving rock beat. As such, it implies that the more aggressive rhythms may be the heart of the new music, but that rock is not bound by its new rhythm.

The chord resonated not only at the beginning of the song (and the film) but also throughout the rapidly evolving world of rock. In effect, the Beatles threw down the gauntlet, even as they announced a new direction in their music that would ultimately lead to *Sgt. Pepper's Lonely Hearts Club Band*, their supreme accomplishment.

In the process, they would spearhead the rock revolution. Their stunning achievements in a too-brief career together were one aspect of the most eventful time in the history of popular music. In this unit, we touch on several important developments in 1960s rock: Dylan's role in making rock music that matters, the Beatles and their musical evolution, the new black pop coming from Motown, the consolidation of the core rock style, soul, and the diverse musical scene in San Francisco during the late 1960s.

CHAPTER 47
The Rock Revolution: A Historical Perspective

Among the musicians knighted by the Queen of England are the esteemed conductors Sir Thomas Beecham and Sir Georg Solti, the opera star Dame Kiri Te Kanawa, violinist Sir Yehudi Menuhin . . . and Sir Paul McCartney. Other key figures in 1960s rock elevated to the peerage include Mick Jagger, Eric Clapton, Roger Daltrey of The Who, and Ray Davies of the Kinks. These venerable and venerated rock stars are the old guard of rock-era music, and their music fills classic rock playlists. It is comfortable music now, not cutting edge, because of decades of familiarity. But when it came out, it disrupted an industry and fueled a cultural and social revolution.

To this day, the rock revolution still seems like the most momentous change in the history of popular music. In the fall of 1963, who could have predicted the extraordinary developments of the next four years, capped by the release of *Sgt. Pepper?* Nothing since has transformed popular music to such a degree in such a short time, and only the modern-era revolution of the 1920s has had a comparable impact.

The new music of the 1960s—an extraordinary range of rock substyles, Motown, soul—was both the soundtrack and an agent of change for a decade of turmoil. A generation eager to overturn the values of their parents found verbal and musical messages that embodied their radical ideas.

Social and Cultural Change in the 1960s

Those who came of age during the latter half of the sixties grew up in a world far different from the world of their parents. A decided majority experienced neither the hardships of the Great Depression nor the traumas of World War II and the Korean War. They were in elementary school during the McCarthy witch hunt; in most cases, it had far less impact on them than it did on their parents. A good number came from families that were comfortable financially, so as teens they had had money to spend and time to spend it.

A sizeable and vocal segment of these young people rejected the values of the group they pejoratively called the "establishment." They saw the establishment as excessively conservative, bigoted, materialistic, resistant to social change, obsessed with communism and locked into a potentially deadly arms race, and clueless about sexuality. Fueled by new technologies and drugs—both old and new—they incited the most far-reaching social revolution since the twenties. For college-age youth of the mid-1960s, there were four dominant issues: minority rights, sexual freedom, drug use, and war.

Civil Rights

A generation that had grown up listening to rock and roll, rhythm and blues, and jazz found it difficult to comprehend the widespread discrimination against blacks that they saw as legitimized in too many segments of American society. They joined the drive for civil rights—through demonstrations, sit-ins, marches, and, for some, more direct and potentially violent support, such as voter registration in the South. The successes of the civil rights movement created momentum for other minority rights movements: women, Chicanos, gays, Native Americans.

Sexual Freedom

Commercial production of an effective oral contraceptive—the Pill—began in the early sixties. For some women, this was the key to sexual freedom; it enabled them to be as sexually active as males, with virtually no risk of pregnancy. It precipitated the most consequential change in sexual relations in the history of western culture. Moreover, it extended the drive for equal rights from the voting booth—in the United States, women were granted the right to vote only in 1920—into the bedroom and sparked a revival of feminism, which sought, among other things, to extend these rights into the workplace.

Drugs

During this same period, the recreational use of mind-altering drugs spread to large segments of the middle class. Previously, drug use had been confined to small subcultures; for example, many jazz musicians in the post–World War II era were heroin addicts. Marijuana, always a popular drug among musicians and minorities, became the most popular drug of the sixties among young people, and especially the counterculture. However, the signature drug of the sixties was D-lysergic acid diethylamide, a semisynthetic drug more commonly identified as LSD or acid. The drug was developed in 1938 by Albert Hoffman, a Swiss chemist; Hoffman discovered its psychedelic properties by accident about five years later. Originally, psychiatrists used it therapeutically, and during the Cold War, intelligence agencies in the United States and Great Britain apparently ran tests to determine whether the drug was useful for mind control. The key figures in moving LSD from the lab to the street

MARIJUANA, the drug of choice during the sixties.

were two Harvard psychology professors: Timothy Leary and Richard Alpert. They felt that the mind-expanding capabilities of the drug should be open to anyone. In reaction, Sandoz, Dr. Hoffmann's chemical firm, stopped freely supplying scientists with the drug, and the U.S. government banned its use in 1967. Underground use of the drug has continued despite this ban.

Vietnam

In the latter part of the sixties, the Vietnam War replaced civil rights as the hot-button issue for young people. In 1954, Vietnam, formerly French Indo-China, was divided—like Korea—into two regions. The north received support from the USSR and communist China, while the southern region received the support of western nations, especially the United States. A succession of American presidents saw a military presence in South Vietnam as a necessary buffer against communist aggression.

As a result, U.S. military involvement gradually escalated over the next decade. Finally, in 1965 the government began sending regular troops to Vietnam to augment the special forces already there. This provoked a hostile reaction, especially from those eligible to be drafted. Many recoiled at the prospect of fighting in a war that seemed pointless; a few fled to Canada or elsewhere to avoid the draft. Massive antiwar demonstrations became as much a part of the news during the late sixties as the civil rights demonstrations were in the first part of the decade. The lies and deceptions of the government and military, which among other things reassured the American people that the war was winnable and that the U.S. forces were winning, coupled with news reports of horrific events such as the My Lai massacre, in which U.S. soldiers killed close to 500 unarmed civilians in a small village, further eroded support for the war.

The gulf between the older establishment positions and attitudes of young Americans on civil rights, sex, drugs, and war widened as the decade wore on. Still, there was a major shift in values: Civil rights legislation passed, the role of women in society underwent a liberating transformation, recreational drug use became more common and socially acceptable in certain circles (although it was still illegal), and the war eventually ended in failure. As a result of this revolution, ideas and practices that seemed radical at mid-century—such as multiculturalism and equal opportunity in the workplace—are accepted norms in contemporary society, in theory if not always in practice.

The Counterculture

A small but prominent minority of young people chose to reject mainstream society completely. They abandoned the conventional lifestyles of their parents and peers; some chose to live in communes. They followed Timothy Leary's advice to "turn on, tune in, drop out." They dressed differently, thought differently, and lived differently. They were the ideological heirs of the Bohemians of nineteenth-century Europe and the Beats of the late 1940s and 1950s. Members of the group were known as hippies; collectively, they formed the heart of the counterculture. Many gravitated to the San Francisco Bay Area.

Throughout the sixties, the Bay Area was a center for radical thought and action. The free speech movement led by Mario Savio got started at the Berkeley campus of the University of California in 1964; it led to confrontations between student protesters and university administrators over student rights and academic freedom. In 1966, in Oakland—next to Berkeley and across the bay from San Francisco—Huey Newton, Bobby Seale, and Richard Aoki formed the Black Panthers, a radical black organization dedicated to

© Jim Jurica/iStockphoto

THE INTERSECTION OF HAIGHT AND ASHBURY, the countercoulture destination in San Francisco.

revolutionary social reform by any means necessary, including violence. Hippies generally followed a less confrontational path.

For hippies, Mecca was San Francisco; their counterpart to the Sacred Mosque was Haight and Ashbury, an intersection in what had been an ordinary neighborhood in San Francisco, near Golden Gate Park, the largest public park in the city. The area became a destination for those who wanted to "make love, not war" and travel the fast route to higher consciousness by tripping on psychedelic drugs. Migration to San Francisco peaked during the 1967 "summer of love," when an estimated 75,000 young people flocked to the city.

In San Francisco, Memphis, Detroit, London, and elsewhere, the new music of the 1960s, from acid rock to southern soul, was both a soundtrack for social change and a voice to articulate the new values that transformed life in America and abroad.

Rock: A Revolutionary Music

Why did the new music of the 1960s connect so powerfully with this generation? There are at least three key reasons: the sheer novelty of the music, the power of the words, and the messages embodied in the music. The music of the rock revolution was novel because the innovations were comprehensive, not cosmetic. Every aspect of the music—its influences, creative process, authorship, sound, musical message, and end product—evidences the impact of new ideas and resources. The music took advantage of brand new and still evolving technology in both performance and production.

Song lyrics spoke to and for the audience, in language that was often frank, personal, topical, and occasionally challenging, but the more powerful message was in the music itself. We highlight significant changes that made rock decisively different from the popular music of the previous generation.

A Fully Integrated Music

Rock is an integrated music. It isn't just that the music of the sixties was more profoundly influenced by black music than any earlier mainstream style. It's also that the influence went both ways—we hear black influences in music by white bands and white influences in music by black performers. And, most important, these various influences are assimilated into a new sensibility and a new sound. Embedded in the music is the idea that integration is about not only being together but also blending together.

Song Ownership and the Creative Process

From the outset, rock changed the relationship between composer and performer. Most of the early rock stars, such as Chuck Berry, Buddy Holly, and Little Richard, performed original material—Elvis was an interesting exception to this trend. In their music, the song existed as it was recorded and performed, not as it was written, if indeed it was written down at all. With rock, a song was no longer just the melody and the harmony, but the total sound as presented on the record—not only the main vocal line but also guitar riffs, bass lines, drum rhythms, and backup vocals.

Increasingly, rock musicians took advantage of multitrack recording, an emerging new technology, to shape the final result even more precisely. Multitrack recording made it possible to record a project in stages instead of all at once. Strands of the musical fabric could be added one at a time and kept or discarded at the discretion of the artist or the producer.

This ability to assemble a recording project in layers fostered a fundamental change in the creative process. It was possible to experiment at every stage of a project, and it was normal for one person or group to stay in creative control of the project from beginning to end.

Because the composers were typically among the performers on the recording and maintained control throughout the creative process, the artistic vision of the act and the message of the music reached its audience more directly. This in turn strengthened the bond between act and audience.

The New Sounds of Rock

The sounds of rock were startlingly new. Rock and roll and rhythm and blues had laid the groundwork, but when these new sounds arrived—with Dylan and the folk rockers, the ascent of Motown, the British invasion, the "guitar gods," soul, and more—the impact was stunning.

The core of the rock band—electric guitar, electric bass, and drums—was in place by the early 1960s, and by the latter half of the decade, rock and soul musicians had developed new ways of playing these instruments, for example, the sonic flights of Jimi Hendrix and Motown bassist James Jamerson's reconception of the role of the bass.

Moreover, electric instruments benefited from a huge boost in amplification. Marshall stacks, the amps used by the Who, Cream, and so many other rock bands, weren't even available in 1960, but by the end of the decade their sound was filling arenas. Other companies kept pace, replacing tubes with transistors and boosting output many times over. A performance at Candlestick Park in San Francisco, at the time an outdoor baseball stadium with a capacity of almost 50,000, would have been a bad idea in 1960, the year it opened; in 1966, however, it was the venue for the Beatles' last public performance.

With increased amplification and a balance of power among the instruments, what had been the background component of a band in modern-era pop became, in many cases, the whole band, or at least the center of the action. This shift flipped the balance between horns and rhythm instruments. Horns, when used, were usually an extra layer; they were no longer in the limelight except for the occasional saxophone solo. And particularly in white rock, they were no longer an integral part of the band.

Rock Rhythm

This core nucleus laid down a new beat: a **rock beat.** The defining characteristic of a rock beat is the layer than moves twice as fast as the beat. Played forcefully, this faster, more insistent rhythm is far more assertive than shuffle, swing, or two-beat rhythms.

In the rock of the sixties, producing a rock beat became a collective responsibility. With the liberation of the bass line to play a truly creative role, the instruments became both more independent and more interdependent. No instrument, not even the rhythm guitar, was absolutely locked into a specific pattern, like the bass player's walking pattern, the banjo player's "chunk" on the backbeat, or the drummer's ride pattern in pre-rock music. The distinctive groove of rock was the end product of the interaction of all the rhythm instruments. Take one away, and the groove was gone.

Sharing Melody

This sharing of responsibility also applied to melody. Up to this point, the main source of melodic interest in the songs we've heard was, appropriately enough, the melody—the vocal line when it was sung and the lead instrumental line when it was played. That changed with rock: Melodic interest was spread out to the other instruments. In many of the songs we hear in this unit, the song is immediately identifiable from an instrumental riff, generally the first of several melodic hooks. The hook identifies the song well before the singer enters. Typically, other instruments also had parts with some melodic interest. One result was a greater variety of texture, from delicate tapestries with a few well-spaced parts to densely packed free-for-alls.

All of these changes—in instrumentation, rhythmic and melodic approach, and texture—applied to both white rock and the black music called "soul," through the mid-seventies. The difference from one style to the next was usually a matter of emphasis or interpretation; indeed, new ideas flowed freely in both directions.

Rock Attitudes and the Musical Message

These innovations give us a musical perspective on the wholesale shift in attitude that was at the core of the revolution. Three qualities of this new attitude stand out: Sixties rock was egalitarian, it was eclectic, and it was real. Until 1960, most groups had a leader, who fronted the band, or a featured performer. In the thirties it was Benny Goodman with his orchestra. After the war, it was Muddy Waters, or Louis Jordan and His Tympany Five. Even Buddy Holly fronted the Crickets. Vocal groups—from the Mills Brothers, a popular black vocal group from the 1930s through the 1950s, to the girl groups—were the almost singular exception.

By contrast, most sixties rock bands took group names: the Beatles, the Beach Boys, the Who, Jefferson Airplane. In so doing, they projected a collective identity. There was nothing in their name that said one member was more important than the others. The interplay among voices and instruments was another key. In hooking the listener with a catchy riff or in laying down the beat, no one person was consistently in the spotlight.

The sources of the new rock style, and the way in which they made their way into rock and soul, also evidenced this new attitude. Rock took a pragmatic approach to musical borrowing: Musicians took what they needed, no matter what its source, and transformed it into something new.

Contrast that with music before 1960. Pop artists gave country songs a shower and a shave before putting them on record, as a pop cover of any Hank Williams song will attest.

Most sixties rock bands projected a collective identity. There was nothing in their name that said one member was more important than the others.

© Ace Create/iStockphoto

If the recordings are any indication, neither the singers nor the arrangers made much of an effort to understand either the sound or the sensibility of country music. Similarly, rhythm and blues hit usually got a bleach job when covered by pop acts: the Chords' cover of "Sh-Boom" is one example among too many. Even many of the teen idols, from Pat Boone to Fabian and Frankie Avalon, dressed the part but neglected the sound and the style of rock and roll.

In the sixties, sounds came from everywhere: Delta blues, East Indian music, symphonic strings, jazz, music hall, folk, country—if it was out there, it was available for adoption. More important, rock musicians didn't necessarily privilege any particular style or family of styles. There is no sense of connection between the social standing of a style and its use in rock, unless it's an inverted one: The grittier the source, the more it was admired, as in the case of Delta blues. The Beatles' music epitomizes this egalitarian, eclectic approach: One track can be sublime, the next can sound like a children's song.

There was a hierarchy of importance within rock, especially in the wake of the Beach Boys' *Pet Sounds* and the Beatles' *Sgt. Pepper's Lonely Hearts Club Band*. The possibility of making an artistic statement in rock has been part of its collective understanding since Dylan went electric. But these artistic statements were typically crafted out of seemingly ordinary materials. Even when rock emulated classical music and other established traditions, it did so on its own terms; the Who's *Tommy* was a rock opera but a far cry from conventional opera. For the best rock bands, the sound world of the sixties was like a well-stocked kitchen; bands simply took what they needed to create the feast.

Finally, rock was *real* in a way that earlier generations of pop had not been. Rock formed a bond with its audience that was different from the connection between Tin Pan Alley popular song and its audience. Tin Pan Alley songs offered listeners an escape from reality, whereas rock songs often intensified the reality of life in the present. Songs were not written so much *for* something—such as a musical or a film—as *to say* something.

Rock's concern with the present, combined with its direct and often personal communication between song, singer, and audience, elevated the role of the music for many members of that audience from simple entertainment to, in the words of noted rock critic Geoffrey Stokes, "a way of life." Sixties rock and soul was a revolutionary music; the rock revolution is, in fact, the only widely acknowledged revolution in the history of popular music.

The Ascendancy of Rock

During the latter half of the 1960s, rock swept away the modern-era pop that had dominated the music industry for decades. By 1970, rock music had become the new mainstream, a new family of styles. Virtually every other kind of music that was not rock or rock-influenced was out of fashion. In this respect, the rock revolution and its reverberations paralleled the coming together of popular music in the late twenties: the blend of fox trot song, jazz, and blues. But the range of styles within this new mainstream was much broader than in that earlier time. This is a reflection of the openness of rock musicians toward music of all kinds—and the openness of the rock audience toward musicians and music of many different kinds.

The Beatles were the poster boys of the rock revolution. Their invasion of America sparked it: their commercial and musical impact was crucial to rock's ascendancy. By the time they disbanded, the revolution was complete.

More important, the Beatles played a key role in reshaping the music and the industry that supported it. Among the most significant developments to which they contributed substantially were establishing rock as the new popular music, making rock an international musical language, creating a new kind of popular song, proposing rock as art, confirming the recording as the primary musical document, and expanding the range of musical influences and sounds, from sitars and calliopes to tape loops and crowd noises. These and other changes helped reshape popular music in the sixties.

The death of the Beatles as a group and the tragic deaths of so many important rock stars, including Jimi Hendrix, Janis Joplin, Brian Jones, and Jim Morrison, might superficially seem to have echoed the troubles that plagued rock and roll at the end of the fifties. Although the losses were significant and tragic, rock didn't miss a beat. The revolution that had toppled pop was over. Rock was now big business and would grow even bigger in the coming decade.

CHAPTER 48

Bob Dylan Makes Rock Matter

For those who have grown up with digital downloading and compact discs, playing a long-playing record might seem like a labor-intensive task. You have to remove the disc from its sleeve, place it on a turntable, which is probably located on shelving containing the speakers, amplifier, and other hi-fi equipment, and then place the stylus at the beginning of the disc, or let the turntable do it automatically. Only then can you return to where you were sitting or lying, to listen to about 30 minutes of music. When one side was finished, you have to get up, flip the disc and place it on the turntable with the other side up, and once again place the stylus at the beginning of the disc.

So it's easier to listen to Bob Dylan's 1965 album *Bringing It All Back Home* on a CD or iPod than it is on vinyl, but these newer formats obscure the message implicit in the layout of the original LP. On one side of the album was acoustic material. The other side was electric: Dylan performing with a large backup band. The first side documented where he was coming from, and the other side revealed where he was going.

Through high school, Dylan (b. 1941) was a rock-and-roll musician. He played locally in several bands during high school and declared in his high school yearbook that his ambition was "to join the band of Little Richard." However, he quickly gravitated to folk music after enrolling at the University of Minnesota. He dropped out of school after only one year and relocated to New York, where he soon became the most influential figure on the emerging Greenwich Village folk scene.

Dylan moved forward by returning to his rock-and-roll roots. For his folk followers, going electric was the beginning of the end. But viewed in relation to the rest of his career, it was the end of the beginning. From that point on, Dylan was a rock musician, not a folksinger. Still, the folk phase of his career was crucial to his development.

From Folk to Rock

The folk revival that began in the late fifties had a short lifespan, even by pop standards. As a movement with mass appeal, it began in 1958, when the Kingston Trio's recording of "Tom Dooley" topped the pop charts. It ended seven years later, when Dylan went electric at the Newport Folk Festival, and folk fathers Alan Lomax and Pete Seeger went ballistic.

In its revived form, folk music was an urban music. Recall that the earlier folk revival of the forties and early fifties, sparked by the work of the Lomaxes, Woody Guthrie, and—most popularly—the Weavers, had brought folk music into the city. The second revival, which began in the late fifties, made the separation between country roots and contemporary urban performance even wider. By 1960, this old/new folk music was flourishing in coffeehouses, often located in the more bohemian parts of major cities (Greenwich Village in New York, North Beach in San Francisco) or near college campuses.

The folk revival was apolitical at first. Its audience seemed to like folk's tuneful melodies, pleasantly sung. That soon changed, as this new folk revival quickly rediscovered its activist past.

Bob Dylan as Folksinger

Dylan's music from the early sixties recaptures the substance and spirit of the songs of Woody Guthrie. His eponymous debut album contained mostly traditional songs, but his three subsequent acoustic albums featured original material, which ranged from "Talkin' John Birch Paranoid Blues," which he delivered in the "talking blues" style often used by Woody Guthrie—resonant speaking over a strummed guitar accompaniment, with an occasional harmonica interlude—to anthem-like songs like "Blowin' in the Wind." In either case, the words were preeminent; the guitar accompaniment typically consisted of simple strumming of the I, IV, and V chords. The main musical variable was the melody—including whether there was one.

© Pictorial Press Ltd/Alamy

BOB DYLAN, 1965. "I knew they were pointing the direction where music had to go"—Bob Dylan on the Beatles.

Adding Instruments

However, by 1964 Dylan's lyrics were becoming more surreal and stream of consciousness. He had written "Mr. Tambourine Man" in February 1964 and performed it at the Newport Folk Festival that summer. Perhaps to counterbalance the more abstruse lyrics, Dylan added rock-oriented instrumental accompaniment to his music, to help communicate the general mood of the song. The impact of the additional instruments is evident on the electric tracks from *Bringing It All Back Home,* which was released in March 1965.

Among the most provocative tracks on the album was "Subterranean Homesick Blues." The lyric is proto-rap: A stream of obscure references, inside jokes, stinging social commentary, and cinéma vérité–type images—all delivered much too fast to understand in a single hearing.

The density of the lyric and the speed of Dylan's delivery challenged listeners to become engaged; one could not listen to him casually and expect to get much out of the experience. For this track, Dylan added a full rhythm section behind his acoustic guitar and harmonica. The band sets up a honky-tonk feel with a clear two-beat rhythm. At the same time, it's a free-for-all for the guitarists; their interaction evokes electric blues. The ornery mood it sets up right at the start is an ideal backdrop for Dylan's words and voice.

What's so remarkable and significant about this song and others like it is that it simultaneously elevates popular music to a higher level of seriousness and brings it down to earth by wiping away traditional forms of pretentiousness. Dylan's lyric is far more complex than anything that had been done before. Similarly, his singing is not pretty by any conventional standard—it was ordinary enough to convince Jimi Hendrix that he could start singing—but it's certainly appropriate for the song. And Dylan embeds his words and singing in a down-home setting.

Dylan's unprecedented combination of words and music reverses the traditional pop approach to artistry. Before, those who wanted to create artistic popular music emulated classical models: George Gershwin's *Rhapsody in Blue* or musical theater productions like *West Side Story*. Dylan's music sends a quite different message: One can be sophisticated without being "sophisticated"; that is, without taking on the conventional trappings of sophistication, such as symphonic strings.

"Subterranean Homesick Blues" was Dylan's first single to chart. His earlier folk songs had enjoyed success, but through others: Peter, Paul and Mary's version of "Blowin' in the Wind" had reached No. 2 in 1963. Dylan was not averse to commercial success, although he wanted it on his own terms. The Byrds, a Los Angeles-based group that

LISTENING CUE • "Subterranean Homesick Blues" (1965), Bob Dylan.

STYLE Blues/country/rock synthesis • **FORM** Blues form with expanded first phrase

Listen For . . .

INSTRUMENTATION
Voice, harmonica, acoustic and electric guitar, electric bass, piano, drums

PERFORMANCE STYLE
Dylan's raspy voice was a drastic departure from almost any other kind of popular singing—pop, R&B, folk, country, or blues.

RHYTHM
Strong two-beat rhythm with emphatic backbeat; fast delivery of words

MELODY
Not a conventional melody: rather, streams of words on a single note, occasionally interrupted by a riff-like idea ("Look out, kid")

HARMONY
Stretched-out blues progression

Remember . . .

CONFRONTATIONAL TONE
Provocative lyrics, delivered very quickly

RAISING THE BAR
Street poetry with a bluesy, hard-country accompaniment = serious musical statement without classical sounds

BLUES/COUNTRY/ROCK FUSION
Honky-tonk beat, blues sounds and form, contemporary folk lyric, blended together

ROCK ATTITUDE VS. STYLE
Rock in attitude but not in style features (no rock beat or rock band instrumentation)

Listen to this selection in CourseMate.

helped create folk rock, provided additional motivation. Their radically reshaped revision of "Mr. Tambourine Man," a cover of an acoustic track from *Bringing It All Back Home,* topped the singles chart in June 1965.

Dylan Rocks

Dylan officially entered the rock era with his next album, *Highway 61 Revisited.* Recorded in August, 1965, the album brought into full flower the power latent in the electric side of *Bringing It All Back Home*. The songs mix blues, country, rock—and even pop, in "Ballad of a Thin Man"—into a new Dylan sound. The title of the album suggests this roots remix. *Highway 61* runs through the heart of the Mississippi Delta, and the title track is a hard shuffle with strong echoes of "deep blues."

"Like a Rolling Stone," the first track to be recorded, shows how he harnessed his verbal virtuosity to write an accessible rock song. The words still have sting: The song paints an "I-told-you-so" portrait of a young girl who's gone from top to bottom. But they tell a story that we can follow, even on the first hearing.

The song sounds like a rock song from the start: A free-for-all of riffs overlay Dylan's vigorous electrified strumming and a straightforward rock beat on the drums. This sound is maintained throughout the song, with Dylan's harmonica competing with Mike Bloomfield's guitar in the instrumental interludes.

The body of the song consists of four long sections. Within each section, verse and refrain alternate, as they do in many rock songs. However, Dylan immediately puts his own spin on this rock convention: Each section has, in effect, two verses and two hooks. The first verse of each section consists of two rapid-fire word streams, saturated with internal rhymes—typical Dylan. But each word stream paints only one picture, and each phrase ends with a short, riff-like idea (such as "Didn't you, babe? . . ."), followed by a long pause. The slower pacing of the images and the break between phrases help the listener stay abreast of Dylan's lyric.

The second verse serves as a long introduction for the first of two melodic hooks: Dylan's voice drips scorn as he sings "How does it feel?" followed by a memorable organ riff; this is repeated, the question left hanging in the air. Dylan then gives a series of equally scornful responses that fill out our picture of the girl's plight. These culminate in the title phrase. By expanding each section internally, Dylan also expands the dimensions of the song; it lasts over 6 minutes, twice the length of a typical song.

"Like a Rolling Stone" established Dylan's rock credentials and his originality as well as any one song could. Despite its length, the song would become one of Dylan's most successful singles, briefly reaching No. 2 in the summer of 1965.

LISTENING CUE • "Like a Rolling Stone" (1965), Bob Dylan.

STYLE Rock • **FORM** Blues; expanded verse/chorus, with both verse and chorus containing two sections

Listen For . . .

INSTRUMENTATION
Voice, electric guitars, electric bass, piano, organ, tambourine, drums

PERFORMANCE STYLE
Dylan's gritty voice usually finds a midpoint between speaking and singing.

RHYTHM
Loose rock rhythm at a medium tempo

MELODY
Melody has lots of repeated pitches and a narrow range
Melodic peak at end of the chorus

TEXTURE
Thick texture, with multiple instruments in mid range supporting and surrounding Dylan's voice

Remember . . .

PRIMACY OF THE WORDS
The words are the primary focus; the story makes the song special. There is minimal melodic interest, especially in the almost monotonic verse.

ROCK ENHANCING THE MESSAGE
At the same time, the spontaneous interaction of the band behind Dylan—who was extremely casual about the accompaniment—gives the music an edge that enhances the lyric and the grating sound of Dylan's voice. The overall impact of the song is far greater than it would have been with just an acoustic guitar accompaniment.

EXPANDED RANGE OF ROCK
By integrating thought-provoking lyrics into a rock song, *and* scoring big with it, Dylan essentially freed rock. After songs like this, rock could be anything; it could say anything, as the Beatles and others would soon prove.

Listen to this selection in CourseMate.

However, it was the album taken as a whole that would fully reveal what Dylan would bring to rock. The next five tracks on the album are extraordinarily diverse:

- "Tombstone Blues," an uptempo song with a hard honky-tonk beat
- "It Takes a Lot to Laugh, It Takes a Train to Cry," a Dylanesque transformation of the blues, set to a medium groove shuffle rhythm
- "From a Buick 6," a blues-form song with piles of riffs and a honky-tonk beat
- "Ballad of a Thin Man," a ballad with slithery pop-ish harmony and a light shuffle beat
- "Queen Jane Approximately," an early 1960s-style rock ballad

There are no recurrent stylistic conventions, such as a basic beat, harmonic approach, or formal plan. Instead, Dylan used these and the other songs on the album to invest rock with a freewheelin', anything-goes attitude.

In the process, Dylan thumbed his nose at the conventions of pop music, and the pop music business. Songs ranged in length from just over 3 minutes to well over 11 minutes; most were 5 minutes or more. The song titles could be descriptive, evocative—or not: the title of one song, "From a Buick 6," has no apparent connection to the song itself. These are outward signs that the songs themselves are unconventional: shockingly original, despite their deep roots in rock and roll, blues, folk, country, and Beat poetry.

The songs seem to have come about almost by spontaneous combustion. They would take shape in the recording studio, with seemingly arbitrary decisions—such as guitarist Al Kooper playing organ on "Like a Rolling Stone"—crucially shaping the final result. The songs juxtapose the sublime and the ridiculous and package elusive ideas in images that brand themselves on your brain. Above all, they democratize popular music while elevating its message in a way that had never been done before: With Dylan, high art did not have to be high class.

Dylan's most far-reaching musical innovation was the evocative use of musical style. He used beats, instruments, harmonies, forms, and the like to create an atmosphere: in "Highway 61 Revisited," the title track from the album, the rough-and-tumble ensemble sound recalls Delta blues, which contextualizes the title. Earlier generations of pop artists had used style evocatively, but no one before Dylan had let it penetrate so deeply into the fabric of the music. *Highway 61 Revisited* became one of the most influential rock albums of all time.

Following that album, Dylan gravitated toward country music. His next three studio albums—*Blonde on Blonde* (1966), *John Wesley Harding* (1967), and *Nashville Skyline* (1969)—were recorded with Nashville session musicians. His country excursion strengthened the connection between rock and country, just as his earlier work helped link folk and rock. This was another of Dylan's major contributions to rock in the sixties: He played the key role in bringing both folk and country into rock.

The Importance of Bob Dylan

Dylan raised the level of discourse in rock in a completely original way. Drawing on blues and folk, the topical songs of Woody Guthrie, and the Beat poets—after hearing Dylan, Allen Ginsberg said, "The world is in good hands"—he synthesized all of this into something radically new. The contrast between Dylan's lyrics and what had come before is so pronounced that it is hard to conceive of them as part of the same musical tradition.

Similarly, Dylan's musical settings opened up new sound worlds, and—more important—new possibilities for the integration of words and music. Precisely because the lyrics were often so provocative and challenging, Dylan used musical settings to evoke mood—to convey the general character of the song without overpowering the words.

Dylan made his music important completely on its own terms, rather than by emulating an established style. By not only giving rock credibility but also redefining what credibility in popular music was, Dylan raised the bar, for rock and for popular music. Overnight the music grew up. It was no longer possible to mock rock—or at least Dylan's music—as mindless music for teens.

Dylan challenged his audience to meet him at his level, rather than playing down to them. As a result, he never enjoyed broad commercial success. However, his music profoundly influenced many of the important acts of the 1960s and beyond. Nowhere is Dylan's influence more evident than in the music of the Beatles.

CHAPTER 49
The Beatles

On August 28, 1964, Bob Dylan and the Beatles met face to face for the first time. The Beatles were on tour in the United States and staying at the Delmonico Hotel in New York. They had acquired *The Freewheelin' Bob Dylan* album while in Paris in January 1964; according to George Harrison, they wore the record out, listening to it over and over. John Lennon, in particular, seemed drawn to Dylan's gritty sound and rebellious attitude. Somewhat later that same year, Dylan was driving through Colorado when he heard the Beatles for the first time on the radio. Later he would say, "I knew they were pointing the direction where music had to go." Each had something that the other wanted, and perhaps found intimidating: The Beatles, especially Lennon, wanted Dylan's forthrightness; Dylan responded to the power of their music and envied their commercial success.

Whatever initial uneasiness Dylan and the Beatles may have felt with each other went up in smoke. Upon learning that none of the Beatles had tried marijuana, Dylan promptly rolled a couple of joints and passed them around. As Paul McCartney later recalled, "'Til then, we'd been hard Scotch and Coke men. It sort of changed that evening."

The Beatles' encounter with cannabis is credited with helping to change the course of their music. Ian McDonald, author of *Revolution in the Head,* a track-by-track account of the Beatles' recordings, observed, "From now on, the superficial states of mind induced by drink and 'speed' gave way to the introspective and sensual moods associated with cannabis and later LSD."

Still, there was more to this meeting than turning the Beatles on. It seemed to further motivate both parties to learn from the other. For Dylan, it was yet another reason to go electric. For the Beatles, Dylan elevated the standard to which the Beatles would hold their music. More specifically, his music occasionally served as a model for their songs, especially those in which Lennon provided the more significant creative input. Later, in explaining their musical breakthrough in the mid-sixties, McCartney said, "We were only trying to please Dylan." Without question, the music they created after the meeting, especially from *Rubber Soul* on, represents a far more substantial legacy than their earlier work. Still, the Beatles and their music had already had a commercial and cultural impact.

Beatlemania and the British Invasion

By the time the Beatles got together with Dylan, they were riding the crest of Beatlemania. The band had scored their first U.S. No. 1 hit, "I Want to Hold Your Hand," in January 1964 and appeared on *The Ed Sullivan Show* for the first time in February. In little more than a month, the band developed a passionate following, one that would surpass Elvis's; the media dubbed it "Beatlemania."

Other British bands followed the Beatles to the United States, and within a year the **British invasion** was underway. The first wave, in 1964, included the Beatles, the Rolling Stones, the Kinks, the Animals, the Dave Clark Five, and several others.

The sudden popularity of British bands in America abruptly reversed the flow of popular music between the United States and the rest of the world. Up until the early sixties, popular music had been largely an American export. Before the sixties, few European musicians performing popular music enjoyed much of a following in the United States. All that changed with the British invasion.

Of course, the music that they played had deep American roots. Many of the bands began their careers by covering songs by Chuck Berry, Buddy Holly, and other

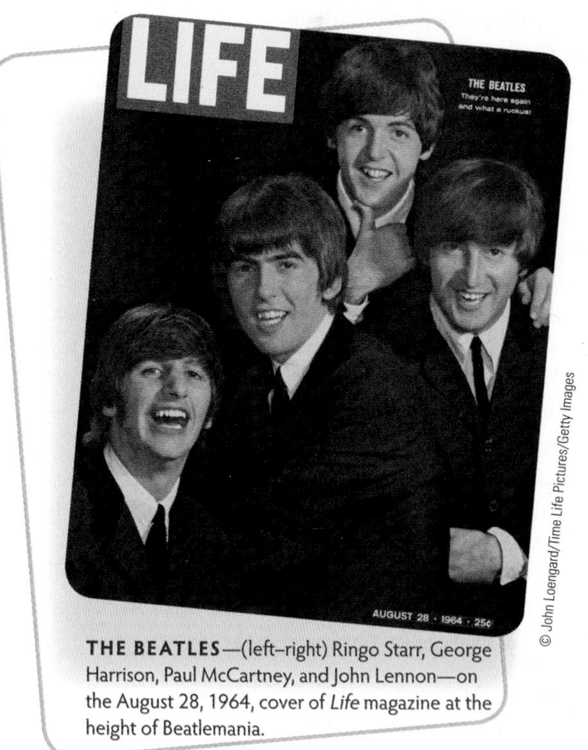

THE BEATLES—(left–right) Ringo Starr, George Harrison, Paul McCartney, and John Lennon—on the August 28, 1964, cover of *Life* magazine at the height of Beatlemania.

rock-and-roll acts. The Rolling Stones' name underscores the musical impact of bluesmen like Muddy Waters and Robert Johnson. But what they brought back to the United States was an altogether new music. What's more, it was never viewed as exotic, and it soon became mainstream. Indeed, the British invasion, more than any other event, fueled the ascendancy of rock in the United States during the sixties.

What is surprising is the ease with which rock—and by extension popular music—became an international music. Up to this point, popular music *in* America and popular music *from* America were pretty much the same thing. After the Beatles, that was no longer true. Although Americans acknowledged, even celebrated, the Britishness of the Beatles and the other invading bands, there was no sense that their music was foreign. Perhaps it was because the sounds were at once familiar (because they were so deeply rooted in American culture) yet fresh (because they represented a new way of interpreting American music). Perhaps it was the open-minded spirit that seemed to pervade the sixties. Whatever the reason, their nationality was a nonissue.

The Musical Evolution of the Beatles

We can trace the beginning of the Beatles back to the summer of 1957, when John Lennon (1940–1980) met Paul McCartney (b. 1942) and soon asked him to join his band, the Quarrymen. George Harrison (1943–2001) joined them at the end of year; the group was then known as Johnny and the Moondogs. They went through one more name change, the Silver Beetles, and one more drummer, Pete Best, before settling on the Beatles and Ringo Starr (b. Richard Starkey, 1940), who joined the group after they had signed a recording contract.

The major phase of the Beatles' career lasted just under eight years. For all intents and purposes, it began on June 6, 1962, when they auditioned for George Martin, the man who would produce most of their records. It ended on April 10, 1970, when Paul McCartney announced that the Beatles had disbanded.

The Beatles' musical growth was unparalleled in popular music; the suddenness with which their music matured remains an astounding development. Among the most important reasons for the exceptional quality and appeal of their music are these three:

- *Knowledge of styles.* They had firsthand familiarity with a broad range of styles. In their dues-paying years, the band performed not only rock-and-roll covers and original songs but also pop hits of all kinds. From their years of apprenticeship, they had a thorough knowledge of pop before rock, and they absorbed styles along with songs.
- *Melodic skill.* Along with the Motown songwriting teams, the Beatles were the first important rock-era musicians to write melody-oriented songs that were in step with the changes in rhythm, form, and other elements that took place during this time. No one since has written so many memorable melodies.
- *Sound imagination.* Aided by the development of multitrack recording and the consummate craftsmanship of their producer, George Martin, the Beatles enriched their songs with startling, often unprecedented, combinations of instruments and—occasionally—extraneous elements, such as the crowd noises and trumpet flourishes of "Sgt. Pepper."

The Beatles' music went through four phases, each lasting about two years:

- Beatlemania: from 1962 to the end of 1964
- Dylan-inspired seriousness: 1965–1966
- Psychedelia: late 1966–1967
- Return to roots: 1968–1970

Not surprisingly, transitions from one phase to the next were gradual. Still, the differences between representative examples are easily heard. As their music matured, it became bolder and more individual. The songs are more clearly the work of the Beatles—no one else could have made them—and less like each other. The contrast from song to song had clearly deepened. One can almost reach into a bag filled with song titles, pull out any five, and marvel at the distinctive identity in meaning and sound of each song and the pronounced differences from song to song. To convey some sense of their growth from a rock band with a difference into one of the creative forces of the twentieth century, we consider tracks from the first three phases.

"A Hard Day's Night"

"A Hard Day's Night" was a feature film shot in March 1964 and released that summer, first in England, and then in the United States. It is about fans' hysterical response in both countries to the Beatles' live performances, and an attempt to capitalize on it—the more cynical parties in the production process expected the Beatles' star to fall as quickly as it had risen. The film came early in their career; the soundtrack was their third American album. Despite their relative inexperience, the Beatles had significant input into the film, choosing both the screenwriter and the director, Richard Lester. They also chose the title, which came from an off-hand remark by Ringo that caught their fancy.

LISTENING CUE • **"A Hard Day's Night" (1964),** John Lennon and Paul McCartney. The Beatles.

STYLE Rock • **FORM** AABA

Listen For . . .

INSTRUMENTATION
Lead, backup singers, twelve-string electric guitar, electric guitar, electric bass, drums, and bongos

PERFORMANCE STYLE
Both vocal sounds and instrumental support have an edge.

RHYTHM
Straightforward rock rhythm, but with double-time (twice as fast as rock rhythm) rhythm on bongos; syncopations in the melody

MELODY
Pop-style AABA song in which A section grows out of a riff

HARMONY
Basic harmony with occasional modal chords mixed in

Remember . . .

FROM ROCK AND ROLL TO ROCK RHYTHM
Aggressive rock rhythm in guitars, drums, and free-moving bass line confirm collective conception of rock rhythm.

FROM ROCK AND ROLL TO ROCK SOUND
Aggressive vocal sound, innovative opening chord, dense texture presage new sonic directions in 1960s.

MODAL AND TONAL
Beatles interpolate modal harmonies into standard pop harmony, e.g., under "working like a dog." Mix of tonal pop and modal chords expands rock harmonic vocabulary.

POP MELODY
Although a rock song, melody and form are more typical of pre-rock pop: AABA form, plus phrases developing from title-phrase riff.

DISTINCTIVE FEATURES
Opening chord/outro, vocal harmony, double-time bongos, shift in texture at bridge all show Beatles' keen ear for distinctive elements.

Listen to this selection in CourseMate.

As they did in so many other areas, the Beatles confounded the experts with a film that broke new ground in almost every important respect. The film was quasi-autobiographical. Shot documentary-style in black and white, it purports to present a "day in the (incredibly hectic) life" of the band. It captured their cheeky good humor—Paul's cinematic grandfather was a running gag—even as it dramatized the relentless pressures of stardom, which would compel them to retire from public performance less than three years later. The group's naturalness in front of the camera, coupled with *cinéma vérité,* resulted in a film far different from standard commercial fare and the rock-and-roll films of the 1950s.

The title track from the album reveals the qualities that made their music stand out right from the start and anticipates the directions that it would soon take. In its sound and rhythmic approach, the band is leading the way in the transformation of rock and roll into rock. The band is locked into a rock beat (which Ringo enhances with double-time rhythms on bongos); the interplay among the rhythm instruments goes well beyond basic rock timekeeping. The sound of the band has an edge—the ring of the opening chord, the vocals, the strident guitar sound, and the relentless drumming. Compared to 1950s bands, and even the Beach Boys' sound, it is aggressive. At the same time, it is friendly: Lennon's song recalls pre-rock pop; so does the vocal harmony. The lyric is innocent enough, at least on the surface; in tone, it is more like "Sh-Boom" than the Rolling Stones' "Satisfaction," which would appear within a year. There are numerous innovations: the search for new sounds, the extensive use of multitrack recording, the opening and closing sounds, and use of modal harmony. (**Modal harmony** consists of chords built from modal scales, rather than the major and minor scales used in nineteenth- and early-twentieth-century pop. Like major and minor scales, modal scales also have seven notes per octave, but in a different arrangement. Modal scales are common in British folk music; "Greensleeves" is a familiar example.) The mix of conventional, modal, and blues chords brought a fresh sound to rock harmony.

Like the film itself, the mix of old and new shows the Beatles beginning their move away from convention. Teen-themed songs would soon disappear, as both the band and their audience quickly grew up.

Dylan-Inspired Seriousness (and Humor) in "Eleanor Rigby"

The Beatles' maturation in the wake of their encounter with Dylan is evident in *Rubber Soul* (December 1965), *"Yesterday" . . . and Today* (June 1966), and especially

Revolver (August 1966). Dylan's influence is evident in the lyrics, which were more meaningful, less teen oriented, and wider ranging in subject matter and tone. It is also evident in the music, although it takes a quite different form. Like Dylan, the Beatles were expanding their sound world but in a more adventurous and more encompassing way. Dylan drew mainly on existing popular styles and used them evocatively. By contrast, the Beatles reached farther afield, into musical traditions far removed from rock and its roots, such as classical Indian music (for instance, the sitar and finger cymbals heard in "Norwegian Wood") and string playing reminiscent of classical music. Moreover, they synthesized these extraneous sounds seamlessly into their music; they became part of the fabric of sound behind the vocals.

As their music matured, it became bolder and more individual. The songs are more clearly the work of the (new) Beatles—no one else could have made them—and less like each other. The contrast from song to song had clearly deepened. Among the most distinctive tracks is "Eleanor Rigby."

A song about the unlamented death of a relationship is unusual enough in popular music. A song about an unlamented death was unprecedented. "Eleanor Rigby," recorded in June 1966, for the album *Revolver,* broke sharply with pop song conventions in both words and music. McCartney relates the story of Eleanor Rigby with a detachment rare to this point in popular music. There is no "you" or "I," even of the generic kind. The story is told strictly in the third person. Her tale is as gloomy as a cold, damp, gray day. Even the refrain is as impersonal as a Greek chorus. They simply observe: "Ah, look at all the lonely people." There's no particular empathy for either Eleanor Rigby or Father McKenzie.

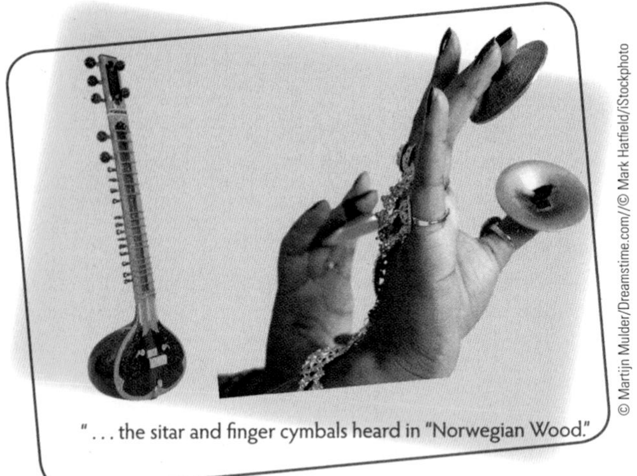

"... the sitar and finger cymbals heard in "Norwegian Wood."

The musical setting is as bleak as the words. A string octet (four violins, two violas, and two cellos), scored by George Martin from McCartney's instructions, replaces the rock band; there are no other instruments. The string sound is spare, not lush—the chords used throughout emulate a rock accompaniment, not the dense cushions of sound heard in traditional pop. Like Eleanor Rigby herself, the melodies of both chorus and verse don't go anywhere. Set over alternating chords, the chorus is just a sigh. The melody of the verse contains longer phrases, but they too mostly progress from higher to lower notes. The harmony shifts between chords; there is no strong sense of movement toward a goal. Lyric, melody, harmony, and the

LISTENING CUE · "Eleanor Rigby" (1966), John Lennon and Paul McCartney. The Beatles.

STYLE Art rock • **FORM** Verse/chorus, with the chorus framing verses

Listen For . . .

INSTRUMENTATION
Voice, string octet (violins, violas, cellos)

PERFORMING STYLE
Vigorous, rhythm-section-like string playing, not lush cushion of pop

RHYTHM
Rock-like rhythm implied in string accompaniment; some syncopation in melody

MELODY
Arching phrases with long descent in chorus

HARMONY
Oscillation between two chords: no sense of direction

Remember . . .

BLEAK LYRICS
A song about seemingly pointless lives, told in an emotionally detached manner

STRING OCTET AS ROCK GROUP
For rock, this is a completely novel instrumentation; for popular music, this is a completely novel way of playing strings

PORTRAYING MISERY MUSICALLY
The long melodic sighs, static harmony, and restless string accompaniment amplify the mood of the lyric; it captures the desperate lives of Eleanor Rigby and Father McKenzie

Listen to this selection in CourseMate.

repetitive rhythm of the accompaniment convey the same message: time passes, without apparent purpose.

With "Eleanor Rigby," the Beatles announced that their music—and, by extension, rock—was, or could aspire to be, art. The most obvious clue was the classical-style string accompaniment. However, the subject of the song and the detachment with which it is presented have more in common with classical art songs than pop or rock songs. Having recorded rock's answer to the **art song,** the Beatles soon created rock's answer to the art song *cycle:* the **concept album.**

The Sound World of the Beatles in "A Day in the Life"

Increasingly during the course of their career, the Beatles' "style" was not so much a particular set of musical choices, as was the case with Motown recordings heard next, but an *approach* to musical choices: Write tuneful melodies and embed them in evocative sound worlds. Settings—instruments, textures, rhythms, even form—were purposeful; their function was to amplify and elucidate the message of the lyrics.

In *Sgt. Pepper's Lonely Hearts Club Band,* released in June 1967, there are not only strong contrasts from song to song, but also occasionally within a song, as in "Lucy in the Sky with Diamonds" and the even more remarkable "A Day in the Life."

In "A Day in the Life," the Beatles create two opposing sound worlds that highlight the contrast between the mundane, everyday world and the elevated consciousness of an acid trip. The distinction is projected by the most fundamental opposition in music itself, other than sound and silence: music with words versus music without words. The texted parts of the song are everyday life, while the strictly instrumental sections reflect the influence of tripping—they follow "I'd love to turn you on" or a reference to a dream.

This contrast is made even more striking by the nature of the words and music. The text of the song and the music that supports it paint four scenes. The first scene is the singer's response to a newspaper account of a man who dies in a horrible automobile accident while, one suspects, he was tripping. The second portrays Lennon attending a film—perhaps an allusion to the film *How I Won The War,* in which he had acted a few months prior to recording the song. The third depicts the singer in the workaday-world

LISTENING CUE · **"A Day in the Life" (1967),** John Lennon and Paul McCartney. The Beatles.

STYLE Art Rock · **FORM** Imaginative hybrid form: elements of AABA form (the pattern of the mundane sections) and verse/chorus (mundane = verse, string blob = chorus)

Listen For . . .

INSTRUMENTATION
Simple rock band instrumentation: acoustic guitar, electric bass, drums, maracas, alternating with orchestral strings performing slow glissandos (gradual changes in pitch); orchestral winds and brass in "dream section"

RHYTHM
Strong contrasts in tempo: slow rock tempo; double-time; pulse gradually disappears in instrumental sections.

MELODY
Tuneful melody with short phrases in narrative sections, which expand, then dissolve into trill, which dissolves into indeterminate pitch

HARMONY
Simple harmony with occasional modal chords in vocal sections; dissonant blob of sound in instrumental section; simple tonic chord at the end

TEXTURE
Open texture in vocal sections: voice, light guitar, and maracas in mid-range, bass and drums in a lower range; thick texture in instrumental sections

Remember . . .

CONTRASTING LEVELS OF CONSCIOUSNESS
Underlying message of song is contrast between everyday "reality" and altered consciousness. Expressed most fundamentally by opposition of words/no words. Shift from pop to orchestral instruments and tuneful to avant-garde music underscores shift in consciousness.

NOVEL FEATURES
Song begins simply: strummed chords. It ends on an "OM" chord that lasts for over 30 seconds. In between are slowly elevating globs of string sounds, shifts in tempo, trills that dissolve into completely new music, and more. All are novel effects for rock (and the pop that preceded it) ca. 1967.

STYLISTIC DIVERSITY
Stylistic diversity of the song, so essential to its meaning, stretches boundaries of rock. The "altered consciousness" music has virtually no connection to rock, and even the ordinary music is some distance from conventional rock.

Listen to this selection in CourseMate.

rat race. The last one is a commentary on another even more mundane news article. It is news reporting—and, by extension, daily life—at its most trivial: Who would bother counting potholes? The music that underscores this text is, in its most obvious features, as everyday as the text. It begins with just a man and his guitar. The other instruments layer in, but none of them makes a spectacular contribution. This everyday background is opposed to the massive orchestral blob of sound that depicts, in its gradual ascent, the elevation of consciousness. The dense sound, masterfully scored by George Martin, belongs to the world of avant-garde classical music—it recalls Krzysztof Penderecki's *Threnody for the Victims of Hiroshima* (1960) and other works of that type.

The apparent simplicity of the vocal sections obscures numerous subtle touches. Starr's tasteful drumming and McCartney's inventive bass lines are noteworthy. So is the doubling of the tempo in the "Woke up . . ." section. What had previously been the rock beat layer is now the beat. This expresses in music the narrator's frantic preparation for work, without disturbing the underlying rhythmic fabric of the song. Perhaps the nicest touches, however, are found in the vocal line: the trill heard first on "laugh" and "photograph," then expanded on "nobody was really sure . . .," before floating up to its peak on "Lords." It is precisely this melodic gesture—the trill, now set to "turn you on"—that presages the move from the vocal section to the orchestral section, and by extension the beginning of an acid trip. When the trill/leap material returns in the film-viewing vignette, this connection becomes explicit; the melodic leap is followed by the trill, which blends seamlessly into the orchestral texture. As a melodic gesture, the trill/leap sequence is also a beautiful surprise, strictly on its own terms.

The final chord is an instrumental suggestion of the clarity of enlightenment after the transition, via the orchestral section, from mundane life in the "normal" world. It is a striking ending to a beautifully conceived and exquisitely crafted song.

"A Day in the Life" encapsulates the art and achievement of the Beatles as well as any single track can. It highlights key features of their music: the sound imagination, the persistence of tuneful melody, and the close coordination between words and music. It represents a new category of song—more sophisticated than pop, more accessible and down-to-earth than classical, and uniquely innovative. There literally had never before been a song—classical or vernacular—that had blended so many disparate elements so imaginatively. Critics searched for a way to describe the song and the album. They labeled it a "concept album" and declared it the rock-era counterpart to the song cycles of nineteenth- and twentieth-century art music.

For Beatles historian Ian McDonald, the opening chord of "A Hard Day's Night" and the final chord of "A Day in the Life" frame the group's "middle period of peak creativity." Certainly, Harrison's chord announces that the group isn't just another rock band, and the seemingly endless chord at the end of "A Day in the Life" has a sense of finality, not just for the song, or even the album, but also the most creative period in their career. The Beatles recorded much memorable music after *Sgt. Pepper,* but none of it stretched boundaries and expanded possibilities to the extent that music of *Sgt. Pepper* did.

The Legacy of the Beatles

The Beatles remain rock's classic act, in the fullest sense of the term. Their music has spoken not only to its own time but also to every generation since. Their songs are still in the air; they remain more widely known than any other music of the rock era. The Beatles' music is a cultural artifact of surpassing importance. No single source—of any kind—tells us more about the rock revolution of the 1960s than the music of the Beatles.

The Beatles had begun their career by affirming what rock was, in comparison to rock and roll and pop. As they reached the zenith of their career, they showed what it could become. Their contributions played a decisive role in reshaping rock, the music industry, and Western culture.

CHAPTER 50
Motown

When Berry Gordy Jr. (b. 1929) got out of the army in 1953, he returned to his hometown of Detroit and opened a record store. He stocked it with jazz, a music he loved, but he refused to carry rhythm-and-blues records in spite of a steady stream of customers asking for them. Two years later he was out of business. He would learn from the experience.

After a couple of years working on an assembly line at the Ford plant, Gordy returned to the music business, first as a songwriter, then as the founder of yet another independent record company. This time around, his goal was to create the first black pop style to cross over completely—to find a large audience among blacks, whites, and everyone else. He would succeed.

The Motown Pyramid

Gordy's Motown empire blended careful planning and tight control over every aspect of the operation with inspiration and spur-of-the-moment decisions. As it developed during the early sixties, Motown's organizational structure was a pyramid. At the top of the pyramid was Gordy. Underneath him were songwriters and producers like Smokey Robinson and the Holland/Dozier/Holland team. Underneath them were the house musicians. Berry recruited his core players from Detroit's jazz clubs. He relied on the skill and inventiveness of musicians such as bassist James Jamerson (the man most responsible for liberating the bass from its pedestrian four-to-the-bar role), keyboardist Earl Van Dyke, and guitarist Joe Messina to bring to life the songs brought by the arrangers to the garage-turned-recording studio christened Hitsville U.S.A. The fourth level were the acts themselves: Stevie Wonder, Mary Wells, the Supremes, the Temptations, the Four Tops, Martha (Reeves) and the Vandellas, (Smokey Robinson and) the Miracles, and Marvin Gaye.

The Motown sound grew out of this pyramid structure. At its core was Gordy's guiding principle: to create music with the widest possible appeal. To that end, he focused on the most universal of all subjects—love won and lost—and required songs that told the tales in everyday language. Smokey Robinson recalls that Gordy told him early in their association that a song should tell a story; Robinson (and the other Motown songwriters) followed that advice.

Gordy's songwriters followed his plan, not only in words but also in music. Motown songs set the story to a melody with memorable hooks. The songs usually unfolded according to a proven strategy: part of the story building to the chorus containing the hook; more of the story, followed by the repetition of the chorus; still more story—if there's time—followed again by the chorus. This template was easy for listeners to follow.

The house band created the beats, the grooves, the memorable instrumental riffs—within seconds we know both of the songs discussed below, before the vocalists begin singing—and the colors. These musicians, so essential to Motown's sound and success, were virtually anonymous. Often they would go to bars after a recording session and hear on the jukebox songs that they'd helped create; few if any of the patrons would know how much they had contributed.

It was the singers who took turns in the spotlight. Not surprisingly, they received the lion's share of Gordy's attention. He determined what songs they recorded, what clothes they wore, their stage routines, and almost everything else related to their professional lives. Many artists came from disadvantaged circumstances, and Motown ran what amounted to a charm school to polish the public personas of its stars. Gordy did everything he could to have them project a smooth, cultivated image, both on stage and off.

The Motown Sound

The product of this multidimensional interaction among Gordy, the songwriters and arrangers, the house musicians, and the acts was the **Motown sound.** Among its most consistent and outstanding features were these four:

- *Melodic saturation.* Songs are full of melodic fragments. The lead vocal line is the most prominent, but there are many others: backup vocals, guitar and keyboard riffs, horn fills, string lines. The presence of so much melody, all of it easily grasped, helped ensure easy entry into the song; it also was a good reason to listen over and over again.
- *A good, but unobtrusive beat.* Motown songs typically feature a strong backbeat and an understatement of other regular timekeeping. In particular, timekeeping in the mid-range register is subdued to give greater prominence to the voices.
- *A broad sound spectrum.* Motown recordings gave listeners a lot to listen for. The instrumental and vocal sounds cut across all social, racial, and economic lines. In the forefront are the relatively untutored singing styles of the vocalists, both lead singers and backup vocalists. There are sounds as simple as a tambourine and as sophisticated as French horn swoops and orchestral string sounds. The rhythm section typically included more than the minimum number of players;

usually there were at least two guitars, several percussionists, and keyboards. With all of this richness, there were sounds for everyone, regardless of background.

- *A predictable form.* From the two songs discussed next, one could construct a pretty reliable template for a Motown song: layered instrumental introduction, solo two-phrase verse, bridge, title phrase, and commentary. There is enough variation in the form and in the other features of the song to keep it fresh, but we can certainly anticipate the events in the story.

These features were designed to engage listeners and keep them listening again and again. All four features offer basic points of entry: melodic hooks, a clear backbeat, interesting and varied instrumental sounds, and an easy-to-follow form. The combination of easy entry and rich texture was a key element in Motown's success. We hear the Motown sound realized in two No. 1 Motown hits, the Supremes' "Come See About Me" and Marvin Gaye's memorable version of "I Heard It Through the Grapevine."

The Supremes

The Supremes—Florence Ballard (1943–1976), Diana Ross (b. 1944), and Mary Wilson (b. 1944)—went from a Detroit housing project to international celebrity in the space of a few years. The group was originally a quartet, the Primettes, the female counterpart to the Primes, who would soon become the Temptations. As the three-singer Supremes, they signed with Motown in 1961, started charting in 1964, and soon had five consecutive No. 1 singles. They became the most popular female vocal group of the 1960s and the main reason that Motown kept challenging the Beatles for chart supremacy.

© Pictorial Press Ltd/Alamy

The Supremes, (*l–r*) Mary Wilson, Florence Ballard, and Diana Ross, the group that embodied the whole Motown package.

The Supremes embodied the whole Motown package. In the television performances from their peak years, they appear in performance dressed in matching dresses or gowns, and with matching wigs. They move gently to the beat or step lightly; the athletic movements of today's divas are still well in the future. It's all slick and wide-eyed at the same time: the look, the gestures, the moves that match the vocal exchanges. The impression is of a more sophisticated version of the Shirelles, yet they still project the innocence of youth and inexperience. The visual impression of the group was one key to their success. It is also evidence of Gordy's overriding control in all aspects of performance.

The sounds of their voices match the look. Ross is clearly the most skilled of the three, but her vocal quality has a naturalness and naiveté that rigorous training would have disguised. The other two Supremes were less distinctive; by 1967, the group was called Diana Ross and the Supremes. (The name change may have had as much to do with Ross's favored status as Gordy's mistress as with her singing ability.)

The third hit in the string of five No. 1 singles was "Come See About Me," which topped the charts at the end of 1964 and the beginning of 1965. The song explores the plight of the jilted lover.

The lyrics present Ross's plea in everyday, if somewhat melodramatic, language. The song and the Supremes' singing of it suggest that the Ross's imaginary partner is a passing fancy; the song is relentlessly upbeat, as are the exchanges between the singers.

The musical setting follows the Motown template: instrumental introduction with catchy sound (the drums) and catchy riff; verse over static harmony; bridge to the hook; melodic hook repeated several times; repetition of the form two more times with an instrumental interlude. All of this takes place over an unobtrusive, bass-heavy accompaniment that lets the spotlight shine on the Supremes. And, as with so many Motown hits, there are features that deviate enough from the template to give the song a distinctive stamp: the handclaps on the beat, the "extra" phrase in the bridge, the other Supremes completing Ross's phrases.

By the time "Come See About Me" topped the charts, the Motown hit factory was a well-oiled machine. Songs from Motown acts such as the Supremes, the Temptations, and the Miracles poured out of car radios, jukeboxes, and fraternity houses. By 1966, three of every four Motown releases hit the charts, an astonishing percentage. Two years later, Motown released one of the

LISTENING CUE • **"Come See About Me" (1964),** Holland-Dozier-Holland. The Supremes.

STYLE Motown • **FORM** Verse/chorus, with bridge split between verse (new lyrics) and chorus (repeat lyrics)

Listen For . . .

INSTRUMENTATION
Lead and backup vocals; full rhythm, with electric bass, electric guitar, piano, drums, vibraphone, hand claps; horn section (trumpets, saxes) briefly between choruses

PERFORMANCE STYLE
Ross's wispy-voiced singing; untutored sound of other Supremes

RHYTHM
Light rock rhythm: beat keeping in handclaps, backbeat on guitar, rock layer in background, more varied rhythm in bass

MELODY
Vocal melody consists of short phrases—exchanged between Ross and Supremes.

TEXTURE
Vocals in the forefront, strong bass, open sound in mid-range behind vocals

Remember . . .

MOTOWN SOUND
Typical Motown sound: open mid-range and light marking of rock rhythm to highlight voices; strong, free-moving bass line anchors sound.

MOTOWN TEMPLATE
Individual realization of Motown formal template: verse/bridge/chorus; chorus includes second part of bridge and title-phrase melodic hook.

SOUND OF THE SUPREMES
The Supremes offer a more refined and mature version of the girl-group sound. Ross's wispy-voiced singing mixes innocence and worldliness.

Listen to this selection in CourseMate.

great songs of the rock era, Marvin Gaye's version of "I Heard It Through the Grapevine."

Marvin Gaye

Of all the Motown artists, none sang with more emotional intensity than Marvin Gaye (1939–1984). His turbulent life—stormy relationships with his wife and other women, drug and alcohol abuse, and his death at his father's hand—seemed to find expression in his music. Whether singing about love, as in "Grapevine," or contemporary life, as in several songs from his groundbreaking 1971 album *What's Going On,* he communicated an extraordinary range of feeling: pain, hope, joy, and frustration.

"I Heard It Through the Grapevine" is a drama in miniature. It is beautifully integrated: Every element blends seamlessly to convey the sense of the text, in which story of love gone wrong gradually unfolds. The opening keyboard riff, harmonized with open intervals, immediately establishes a dark mood. Other instruments enter in stages, leading to the entrance of the voice. Each statement of the melody of the song contains four sections. The first two are blues-like in that they generally stay within a narrow range and go down more than up. The third builds to the final section for the hook of the song, "I heard it through the grapevine." It is the emotional center of each statement. A Greek chorus–like commentary by the backup singers ends each section.

It's worth noting how well the musical setting of "Grapevine" helps project the lyric. From the first ominous keyboard notes, the instrumental backing matches Gaye's despair. (Another version by Gladys Knight and the Pips, which charted the previous year, projects an altogether different mood.) Some have accused Motown of being formulaic—pop music's answer to the Detroit auto assembly lines; but emotional, as well as musical, variety was possible within a consistent overall plan.

Motown: Updating Black Pop

Motown updated black pop. From Louis Armstrong and Ethel Waters through Nat "King" Cole and the Mills Brothers, into doo-wop and the girl groups—one direction in black music had been a distinctly African-American take on popular song. Motown continued that tradition but went well beyond it: It was not just a new take on pop but a new, black popular style—and a new kind of romantic music.

In its pop orientation, Motown was heading in the opposite direction from rock. Rock tended to look at

LISTENING CUE • **"I Heard It Through the Grapevine" (1968),** Barrett Strong and Norman Whitfield. Marvin Gaye, vocal.

STYLE Motown • **FORM** Verse/chorus

Listen For . . .

INSTRUMENTATION
Lead and backup vocals. Rhythm section with extra percussion (electric piano, electric guitar, electric bass, drums, tambourine, and conga), and orchestral instruments (violins and the French horn just before the voice enters)

RHYTHM
Moderate tempo; rock rhythm with strong backbeat but subdued marking of the rock rhythmic layer—mainly drums and conga on deep-sounding drums

MELODY
Vocal melody consists of short phrases—longer than the opening riff. Bluesy quality because of downward direction.

HARMONY
Minor key version of I-IV-V with a few additional chords (minor keys have often been associated with sad moods)

TEXTURE
Layered texture, distributed over wide range: Bass and percussion are low, voices and keyboard in the middle, strings usually in a high register. Considerable variation from the empty sound of the opening to the full ensemble in the chorus.

Remember . . .

DEPICTING MOOD MUSICALLY
The dark mood of the song is established at the outset by such features as the ominous opening riff, the choice of an electric keyboard to play it, the open harmony, and the subtle, open-sounding rhythm. The melody of the song, which moves mainly from high to low, reinforces the mood.

FLEXIBLE TEMPLATE
The Motown template is predictable in its general features but accommodates considerable variation in detail and mood, as a comparison of "Come See About Me" and "Grapevine" reveals.

GAYE'S SINGING
The strained sound of Gaye's high-register singing also helps communicate the despair described in the lyrics.

Listen to this selection in CourseMate.

love cynically (the Beatles' "Norwegian Wood" comes to mind), lustfully (the Rolling Stones' "Satisfaction"), or not at all. Motown songs preserve the romance in earlier popular songs even as they bring both lyrics and music into the present. Romance is evident not only in the sound—the rich string writing, the understated playing of the rhythm section—but also in the look. The groups wore tuxedos and gowns, like Las Vegas acts, not tie-dyed T-shirts and jeans, like the Woodstock crowd.

Motown was one of the remarkable success stories of the sixties. For the first time in history, a black style was on equal footing with white music. Motown would lose its toehold at the top in the seventies; the Jackson 5 was Motown's last big act. Stevie Wonder gained artistic freedom as a condition of his new contract, and he used it. Marvin Gaye also sought and got independence, eventually leaving Motown altogether. The company has remained an important player in pop music, and though it is no longer the dominant and innovative force that it was in the sixties, its legacy is still very much with us.

CHAPTER 51
Rock

In 1969, the Rolling Stones began to be billed as the "world's greatest rock and roll band." Whether the label came from the band itself or—as Jagger claimed—from an enthusiastic master of ceremonies is open to debate. Regardless of who used it first, the label has stuck; it has become as much as a part of their brand as Jagger's tongue. One can attribute some of its staying power to the Stones' longevity—who would have predicted in 1969 that they would be a hot ticket in the twenty-first century?—and some more to media hype. But at the heart is their mastery of rock's core sound.

Implicit in the billing is the assumption that in the space of five years, rock had evolved from a brand new sound to a timeless style. In 1964, the rules were just being written; by 1969, the essence of rock style had been worked out. From this point on, rock becomes, in effect, a timeless style. For the Stones and others, "rock and roll" is not a revival of Chuck Berry, but the purest form of rock.

When we think of timeless rock, we expect to hear bands with a core of electric guitar, electric bass, and drums playing songs with heavy riffs over a rock beat at a loud volume. Within these general parameters, there are two primary options: solo-oriented versus group-oriented rock. In this chapter, we trace rock's progress toward its timeless form through tracks by the Rolling Stones and Jimi Hendrix.

Group-Oriented Rock and the Rolling Stones

The Rolling Stones grew out of a chance encounter in 1960, when Mick Jagger (b. 1943) saw Keith Richards (b. 1943) standing in a train station with an armful of blues records. It was not their first meeting; both had grown up in Dartford, England, and had attended the same school for a year, when they were six. Their meeting eleven years later would be the beginning of their band.

Both spent a lot of time at the London Blues and Barrelhouse Club, where they met Brian Jones (1942–1969) and Charlie Watts (b. 1941). At the time, Watts was the drummer for Alexis Korner's Blues Incorporated, which would also include Jagger after 1961. The Rolling Stones came together in 1962 when they added bassist Bill Wyman (born William Perks, 1936) after an audition. Keyboardist Ian Stewart (1938–1985) was also a member of the band at the time. Stewart stopped performing with the group soon after their career took off

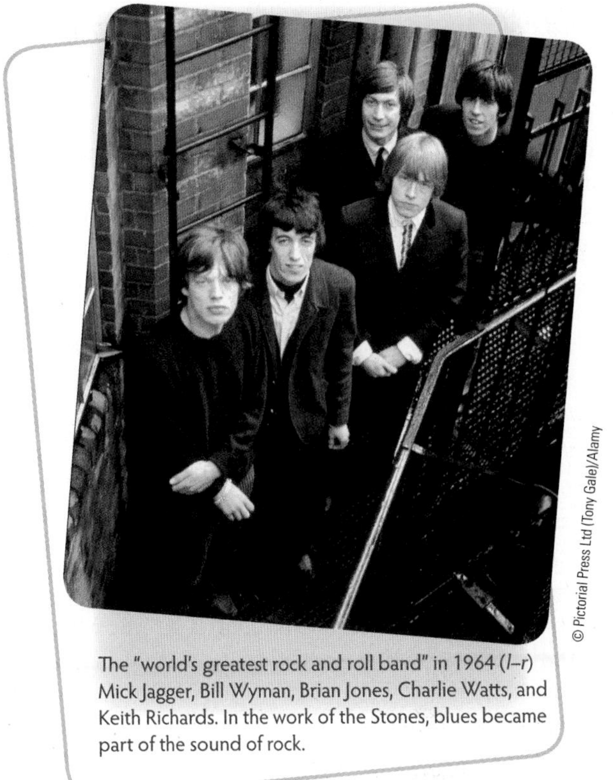

The "world's greatest rock and roll band" in 1964 (*l–r*) Mick Jagger, Bill Wyman, Brian Jones, Charlie Watts, and Keith Richards. In the work of the Stones, blues became part of the sound of rock.

but retained a close connection with the Stones and performed on many of their recordings.

Like other British bands, the Rolling Stones began by covering blues and rock-and-roll songs. Within a year, Jagger and Richards, inspired by the success of Lennon and McCartney, started writing original songs for the band. They broke through in 1965: "(I Can't Get No) Satisfaction" and *Out of Our Heads,* the album from which it came, topped the charts that summer. By the time they recorded the song, they had pretty well defined their sound, style, and image.

Their conception of rock began with an attitude: sexually charged, down and dirty, swaggering, real. All of this was an extension of the bluesman's persona, and it is embodied most powerfully in Mick Jagger. Although he came from a comfortable middle-class family and was attending the London School of Economics in the early sixties, Jagger didn't simply imitate the bluesmen he admired—he forged his own identity, one that reverberated with their influence but was also different and credible. The rest of the band also assumed this attitude; Keith Richards's sneer is the visual counterpart to the nasty riffs for which he is so well-known. Andrew Loog Oldham, who became their manager in 1964, actively promoted this image. By his own admission, he wanted them—or at least their public image—to be the opposite of the Beatles. Their music matched their image.

The Rolling Stones "(I Can't Get No) Satisfaction"

"(I Can't Get No) Satisfaction," the Rolling Stones' first major hit, acknowledges the enormous influence of the blues, and Muddy Waters in particular, on the group. Both the band's name and the song title trace back to two of Waters' early recordings: a 1950 recording entitled "Rolling Stone" and a 1948 recording entitled "I Can't Be Satisfied."

As this track evidences, the Rolling Stones built a new sound from rock and roll, blues, and their own inspiration. From Jagger's sound to Wyman's bass lines, it was all of a piece. We highlight two of its qualities, the rhythmic groove and the dark, nasty sound.

- *The groove.* Like many other Rolling Stones songs, "(I Can't Get No) Satisfaction" starts with a syncopated riff; Watts enters only after the song is pretty well under way. Rock's characteristic groove grows out of the interplay between the basic rock rhythm, the backbeat, and the layers of syncopated riffs and lines, much as the swing in swing is the product of riffs over a four-beat rhythm.
- *A dark, nasty sound.* Jagger's singing—rough, highly inflected, almost drawled, and more speech-like than sung—is the most obvious expression of the nasty Stones sound. Complementing it is the thick, dark texture produced by Richards's low-register rumblings, Wyman's bass, and Watts' use of the bass drum. Typically, the highest sound in a Stones song is Jagger's voice, which stays in a mid-range. Both Jagger's singing and the thick texture come directly from the blues; in the work of the Stones, blues becomes part of the sound of rock.

The compelling rhythms and the dense, riff-laden texture set the tone for the stories told in the songs. "(I Can't Get No) Satisfaction" is a study in sexual frustration: The music says what the words do not. As Jagger vents his sexual frustration with harangues about petty matters, the opening guitar riff never changes. It embodies Jagger's frustration because it tries (and tries) to go somewhere but never does. The form of the song also reinforces Jagger's frustration, because the sequence of verse and chorus are switched. What is usually the verse is the part that returns again and again. It builds to a peak, at which point Jagger begins to rant. There is no release, and the section ends futilely in a drum break.

To an audience raised on pop, all of this had the taste of forbidden fruit—it was a far cry from the teen-themed rock and roll songs of the fifties or the early Beatles, or the

LISTENING CUE · "(I Can't Get No) Satisfaction" (1965), Mick Jagger and Keith Richards. The Rolling Stones.

STYLE Rock · **FORM** Verse/chorus

Listen For . . .

INSTRUMENTATION
Lead vocal, electric guitar, acoustic guitar, electric bass, drums, tambourine

PERFORMANCE STYLE
Fuzztone guitar sound, Jagger's vocal sounds, from title-phrase whisper to verse-like rant: aggressive, edgy sound

RHYTHM
Rock rhythm, with strong beat keeping and even stronger syncopations

MELODY
Vocal melody constructed from simple riffs; verse-like section on one note; guitar riff most memorable melodic idea

TEXTURE
Thick texture: low-register electric guitar, low-tuned drums, electric bass, all under Jagger's vocal most of the time

Remember . . .

MEMORABLE GUITAR RIFF
Richards's fuzztone guitar riff sets mood for song and returns periodically throughout the song—one of several signature guitar riffs appearing ca. 1965.

BEAT-ORIENTED ROCK RHYTHM
Watts plays rock rhythm with heavy emphasis on the beat. The other rhythms—guitar riff, bass line, and Mick's tambourine and vocal line—weave around the strong beat.

DARK TEXTURE
Most of the sounds, including Richards's guitar riff, are in a low register; Jagger's singing is the highest sound = a dark-sounding texture, which helps convey mood of the song.

INVENTIVE FORM
The inversion of verse and chorus is an innovative twist on conventional verse/chorus form; it seems to help project the message of the song: Jagger's inability to get satisfaction.

BLUES INFLUENCE
The impact of blues style is evident in dense, heavy texture, with interplay among the instruments, reliance on repeated riffs, Jagger's vocal style, aggressive sound, and subject of song.

Listen to this selection in CourseMate.

surf music of the Beach Boys. The Stones' lives mirrored their public personas: Brian Jones's death "by misadventure," the Altamont riot, the occasional brushes with the law—all were real-life analogues to the world depicted in their songs. In effect, the Rolling Stones helped bring a blues sensibility into the mainstream. Both words and music thrilled a new generation and repulsed an older one.

The group followed *Out of Our Heads* with *Aftermath* (1966). It was their first album to feature only original songs by Jagger and Richards. The group briefly fell under the spell of the Beatles: Their *Their Satanic Majesties Request* was an ill-advised answer to *Sgt. Pepper*. They soon returned to rock and roll, recording such rock-defining hits as "Jumping Jack Flash" (1968) and "Honky Tonk Women" (1969). With songs like these, the group refined its groove and defined its place in the history of popular music.

Solo-Oriented Rock and Jimi Hendrix

Among the most compelling new sounds of the late sixties were power trios. These were bare-bones bands—just guitar, bass, and drums—set up to showcase the skills of their exceptionally able guitarists, most notably Jimi Hendrix and Eric Clapton. These musicians took one additional element from blues—the guitar as the bluesman's "second voice." With the aid of the solid-body guitar, they used it as a point of departure as they introduced a new element into rock: virtuosic soloing.

The Solid-Body Electric Guitar

The solid-body electric guitar dates back to 1948, the year in which Leo Fender, a radio repairman turned instrument maker, introduced his Broadcaster. Fender's Broadcaster, which became the Telecaster, and his Stratocaster, introduced in 1954, became standards by which other solid-body guitars were measured. The sudden increase in amplification in the sixties made the instrument far more powerful. An array of sound modifiers, such as the wah-wah pedal, made the instrument more versatile. It remained for Jimi Hendrix to use these new resources to effectively turn the electric guitar into a new instrument. Hendrix drew deeply on the blues for inspiration.

JIMI HENDRIX, 1969

Blues Guitar and Rock

Throughout the recorded history of deep blues, the guitar had been a melody instrument as well as a harmony and rhythm instrument in support of the voice. From Blind Lemon Jefferson on, bluesmen would answer sung phrases with vocal-like guitar lines, double the vocal line, or showcase the guitar's melodic capabilities in an instrumental solo. While Berry and others were creating rock guitar styles, electric bluesmen such as Guitar Slim and Buddy Guy were playing the guitar in a style that paralleled their raw, earthy singing, exploiting such novel effects as severe distortion. Their style served as a model for a new generation of rock guitarists. The most important was Jimi Hendrix.

Jimi Hendrix Going Beyond the Blues

Hendrix grew up with the blues, hearing it as part of a broad spectrum of black music that also included jazz and rhythm and blues. He used electric blues as a point of departure, but he greatly increased the range, volume, and variety of sounds, even as he helped morph blues guitar styles into the dominant rock solo style. Hendrix was the trailblazer in both his expanded vocabulary of riffs, scales, and bent notes and his use of electronics. His playing opened up a world of new sound possibilities. As described by the *Rolling Stone Encyclopedia of Rock & Roll,*

> Hendrix pioneered the use of the instrument as an electronic sound source. Rockers before him had experimented with feedback and distortion, but he turned those effects and others into a controlled, fluid vocabulary every bit as personal as the blues he began with.

His transformation of blues into rock is evident in "Voodoo Child (Slight Return)," a track from his 1968 recording, *Electric Ladyland*. "Voodoo Child (Slight Return)" is a blues-inspired song, on several levels. The vocal sections of the song inflate and reshape the twelve-bar blues form. The lyric begins as if it were a conventional rhymed couplet with the first line repeated. But Hendrix adds a refrain-like fourth line to the lyric, which contains the title phrase of the song. Hendrix also modifies the musical features of blues form by extending the length of the phrases and by using a strikingly different harmonization: static in the first part of the song, then

LISTENING CUE • "Voodoo Child" (1968), The Jimi Hendrix Experience.

STYLE Power-trio rock • **FORM** Modified blues form in vocals; open form over one chord in solos

Listen For . . .

INSTRUMENTATION
Electric guitar, electric bass, drums, maracas

PERFORMANCE STYLE
Hendrix's varied array of new sounds: pitchless strumming, bent notes, etc., that exploit the full range of the instrument

RHYTHM
Medium-slow rock rhythm with considerable syncopation, activity, and rhythmic play from guitar, bass, and drums; maracas maintain rock rhythmic layer.

MELODY
Guitar solo features instrumental-style melody: wide range, fast-moving notes, complex riffs.

HARMONY
Augmented blues form in vocals; static harmony in solo passages

Remember . . .

VIRTUOSITY
Hendrix's virtuosity involves sound as well as speed. Both are unprecedented in rock.

BEYOND BLUES
The vocal section is a modified twelve-bar blues: The last phrase is repeated with different harmony. As in electric blues, the guitar lines pair with the voice and answer the voice, but the solos go well beyond the typical blues guitar solo.

OPEN TEXTURE
Typical sound of Hendrix-style power trio—strong bass and wide-ranging guitar; no consistent middle register sound

Listen to this selection in CourseMate.

fresh-sounding chords in the latter part. The relationship between voice and guitar recalls the Delta blues of Robert Johnson and Muddy Waters in the passages where the guitar line parallels the vocal line (the guitar version of the melody is usually far more elaborate) and the call-and-response between voice and guitar. The vocal sections serve as formal pillars, supporting what is in essence an unbroken five-minute improvisation. Hendrix ignores the harmony of the vocal section in his solos; they take place over one chord.

Hendrix's brilliant improvisations are the expressive focus of the performance. The variety is astounding: He roams over the entire range of the instrument, interweaving sustained bent notes, rapid running passages, riffs, and chords in a dizzying sequence. He draws a dazzling array of sounds from his guitar, ranging from the pitchless strummings of the opening to the sustained high-note wails, distorted chords, and hyper-vibrated notes in his solos. And he mixes them together in dazzling sequences that seem completely spontaneous in their unpredictability. It is, in effect, an inventory of the sound possibilities of the instrument.

Hendrix's solos represent a new kind of genius, one that emerges from the particular demands of rock improvisation. In them, he elevated sound variety to a level of interest comparable to pitch and rhythm, and he enormously expanded the vocabulary of available sounds: Hendrix plays in Technicolor. In a Hendrix solo, *how* a note sounded became just as important as its pitch and rhythmic placement. In so doing, he built on the expressive sounds of the blues and the artistry and melodic inventiveness of jazz, merging and transforming them into a definitive improvisational style in rock.

Hendrix's playing helped define rock-based improvisation more than the work of any other artist, but it also helped redefine the possibilities of improvisation within popular music. It echoes through much of the music of the 1970s and 1980s, especially heavy metal and hard rock. Others have built on it, but none have surpassed it in imagination and originality. It remains the standard of rock guitar playing.

Like too many of his musical contemporaries, Hendrix was a drug casualty. He died after a drug–alcohol interaction in September 1970 in the midst of plans for new projects that reportedly would have taken his music in quite different directions. Although we regret his premature death, we remain grateful for his substantial legacy, made all the more impressive because it took only three years to compile.

Hendrix's improvisations set up a powerful dialectic within hard rock: how to balance individual brilliance with group impact. The tradeoff is between the groove produced by the interplay of several lines (as we heard in the music of the Rolling Stones) versus the expressive power of a soloist's inspiration and virtuosity. The influence of Hendrix and the Rolling Stones echoes through much of the music of the early seventies and beyond. Among the most important bands of the era are those, like Led Zeppelin and Deep Purple, that found a balance between group interplay and solo brilliance.

CHAPTER 52
Soul

For much of the 1960s, "soul" was the umbrella term for black popular music. Indeed in 1969, almost after the fact, *Billboard* changed the name of its rhythm-and-blues chart to "Soul." And much of it was popular, by any measure. The Motown success story was the most spectacular evidence of the ascendancy of black music, but Motown artists were not alone: Twelve of the top twenty-five singles acts during the decade were black. It was a diverse group that included James Brown, Aretha Franklin, Ray Charles, Dionne Warwick, and the Supremes; they represented not one style but several.

Soul and Black Consciousness

Soul was more than a musical term. It came into use as an expression of the positive sense of racial identity that emerged during the decade. "Black is beautiful" was the slogan of many politically active members of the African-American community. This shift in attitude, among blacks and some whites, was the social dimension of the relentless pursuit of racial equality. It went hand in hand with the enfranchisement of so many African Americans through the Civil Rights Act of 1964 and the Voting Rights Act of 1965.

As the drive for racial equality peaked, then deflated in the wake of the assassination of Martin Luther King, Jr., black music occasionally became a vehicle for social commentary. James Brown released a series of exhortations, beginning with the 1968 song "Say It Loud—I'm Black and I'm Proud." Marvin Gaye's landmark album *What's Going On* appeared in 1971. But most of the music did not contain overt references to social conditions or racial issues. More often it dealt with the subjects that so frequently transcended race: love won and lost, and the good and bad times that resulted.

Soul Music

Black music charted a musical path different from white rock. There are three main reasons for the divergent paths. The first and most significant is the strong gospel tradition. Most of the major African-American performers of the sixties had grown up singing in church. There is no better example than Aretha Franklin, the "Queen of Soul": Aretha's father was pastor of one of the largest churches in Detroit, and she sang at his services from early childhood.

Another was the difference in rhythm (a more open, syncopated, and less emphatic approach to rock rhythm), instrumentation (horn sections were the rule in R&B, but not in rock and roll), and texture (the bass was in the foreground, the guitar typically more in the background).

A third reason for the array of distinctly black styles in the sixties was the artistic control of a few key producers. Berry Gordy was one. Another was Jerry Wexler, who had helped build Atlantic Records into a major pop label. Memphis-based Stax Records relied more on the musical intuition of its house musicians, who included Booker T. and the MGs, and the Memphis Horns, to create a "house" sound.

Although, in the 1960s, virtually all of the new black music was called "soul," **soul** really refers to the emotionally charged black music of the sixties that draws deeply on gospel and blues. It is best exemplified by the music that came from two southern cities—Memphis, Tennessee, and Muscle Shoals, Alabama—and two performers—Aretha Franklin and James Brown. This was music of real commitment: Percy Sledge bares his soul when he sings "When a Man Loves a Woman," and James Brown was, among other things, the "hardest-working man in show business." The music expressed deep feelings, with little or no pop sugarcoating; when Aretha asks for respect, she spells it out.

The soul music of the mid- and late sixties came in two speeds: fast and slow. In either case, the music was raw. There was nothing particularly pretty about the voices of Otis Redding, Sam and Dave (Sam Moore and Dave Prater), Percy Sledge, or James Brown, but there was no mistaking the energy or the emotion. The instrumental sounds were painted in primary colors: strong bass at all times, powerful horns, vibrant sax solos, drums, guitar, and keyboard. Power won out over finesse.

The soul band of the sixties was an updated version of the jump bands of the late forties and the early fifties and Ray Charles's bands of the late fifties. Fast songs, propelled by agile bass lines, had a relentless rhythmic drive, the product of rhythmic play: a decisive backbeat, steady timekeeping, and lots of syncopated riffs. The balance within the band is different from rock: Most of the syncopation comes in the bass line and the horn parts; compared with rock, the guitar part (usually there's only one guitarist) is typically less prominent. By contrast, slow songs provided a more subdued accompaniment; they surrounded the singer with a rich halo of sound.

Vocalists like Redding rose to the challenge of singing over this powerful and relentless backing. They sang, shouted, growled, moaned, and groaned. Their singing—laced with explosive consonants and short vowels—is almost percussive.

The songs continue to mine a familiar vein in rhythm and blues: In his sexual potency and his willingness to brag about it, Sam and Dave's "Soul Man" is a direct descendant of Roy Brown's "mighty, mighty, man" and so many other rhythm-and-blues heroes.

James Brown

James Brown (1933–2006) at once epitomized the "soul man" and stood apart from the other male soul singers. Not shy about positioning himself in the popular-music pantheon, Brown billed himself as "Soul Brother Number 1" and the "Godfather of Soul." As with the Rolling Stones' claim to be the world's greatest rock-and-roll band, Brown's claim was based on fact: He *was* the most important male soul artist of the sixties.

The innovations that transformed Brown's music (and catapulted him to stardom) happened almost overnight. He had been working actively since the mid-fifties—his first R&B hit came in 1956—but he did little to set himself apart from other R&B artists until his breakthrough 1965 hit, "Papa's Got a Brand New Bag." (In sixties slang, a bag is an area of expertise.) Brown's new bag was a breakthrough in rhythm.

Brown created his unique rhythmic approach by addition and subtraction. He had a good-sized band—drums, bass, guitar, and keyboards (when Brown chose to play on recordings)—plus a full horn section: trumpets, saxophones (including a baritone sax), and trombone. This is the addition: His backup band is larger than most rock bands. Except for the bass, however, all the instruments have a reduced role. Guitar and drums are in the background, and often only the drummer supplies any kind of steady rhythm. The bass line is typically the most active and varied. The horns play riffs; the baritone sax part is usually just a note or two every eight beats. Brown sings only now and then; we imagine his footwork in the silences. This is the subtraction: less vocal and less involvement from most of the instruments.

All of this—more instruments doing less—creates an irresistible rhythm and an airy, open texture. There is no melody to speak of; Brown's voice becomes a percussion instrument—especially in the nonverbal sounds. (Try to emulate his singing and you'll find that your voice will explode and die away quickly, like many percussion sounds do.)

The interest comes in the interaction among the instruments. The beat and the rock rhythm are felt more than

LISTENING CUE · **"Papa's Got a Brand New Bag" (1965),** James Brown. Brown, vocal.

STYLE Soul · **FORM** Verse/chorus blues form, with one-chord interludes

Listen For . . .

INSTRUMENTATION
Lead vocal, electric guitar, electric bass, drums, trumpets, trombone, saxophones

PERFORMANCE STYLE
Brown's singing is percussive.

RHYTHM
Light rock-beat timekeeping in drums only regular rhythm; strong backbeat, other parts (bass, vocal, horn riffs) mainly syncopated

HARMONY
Either blues progression or static harmony (in verse sections)

TEXTURE
Open

Remember . . .

EMPHASIS ON RHYTHM
Song is about rhythm. No continuous melody, just fragments tossed back and forth between Brown and the horns. Harmony is basic blues progression or one chord. Absence of melodic and harmonic interest directs our attention to groove.

PERCUSSIVE SOUNDS
All of the instruments and Brown's singing are percussive: emphatic consonants (papa, bag), explosive single note on baritone saxophone, guitar chord, fingered electric bass sound, in addition to drums.

TEAMWORK
None of the parts is interesting enough to stand alone. Brown's voice stands out mainly because of the words and distinctiveness of sound, but it is not dominant. Collectively, the parts—vocal and instrumental—interlock to create a seamless flow.

OPEN SOUND
Because there is just enough activity to maintain groove, the musical flow is buoyant—no thick guitar chords or heavy bass lines to weigh it down. Brown's trademark groove was one of most distinctive and influential sounds of the 1960s.

Listen to this selection in CourseMate.

heard; everything else is over or against the time. It is a complex, if repetitive, rhythmic texture. And it is very close in principle to the rhythms and textures of West African music.

Brown's subsequent music brought popular music closer to its African roots than it had ever been before. Indeed, John Chernoff reported in his 1971 book, *African Rhythm and African Sensibility,* that African musicians felt more at home with James Brown's music than with that of any other popular musician of the time.

Brown's music has been profoundly influential. With its emphasis on intricate rhythms and de-emphasis of melody and harmony, it would create the blueprint for funk and rap. With deep roots in gospel, blues, rhythm and blues, and jazz, and its blending and modernizing of these styles, it represents a unique soul synthesis. In its originality and individuality, it stands apart from all the other music of the sixties. It remains one of the most influential styles from that decade.

Aretha Franklin

If James Brown was the godfather of soul, Aretha Franklin (b. 1942) was its reigning queen and one of the singular talents of popular music. Aretha grew up in a privileged yet painful environment. Her father was C. L. Franklin, pastor of one of the largest churches in Detroit and one of the most admired preachers in the African-American community. Through him she came in contact with some of the great names in music: For example, gospel great Mahalia Jackson was a family friend. Aretha grew up in a hurry—singing in her father's church and then on the road as a child; a mother at sixteen; a pop/jazz singer on Columbia Records at nineteen (which turned out to be a dead end); and a series of abusive relationships.

© Val Wilmer/Redferns/Getty Images

ARETHA FRANKLIN, the first woman to be inducted into the Rock and Roll Hall of Fame, performing in 1968.

Jerry Wexler jump-started her career in 1967 when he signed her to Atlantic Records and took her to Fame Studios in Muscle Shoals, Alabama, where Rick Hall had previously recorded such soul hits as Percy Sledge's "When a Man Loves a Woman." From the first note, Wexler knew he had something special. When the recording session ended disastrously (because of an alcohol-fueled fight between one of the session musicians and Ted White, Aretha's husband and manager at the time) and Aretha went into hiding, he tracked her down, brought her musicians to New York, and finished the album. It was a huge success; it established her reputation as one of the supreme talents in popular music.

Many of Aretha's first hits talked about heartbreak, like most soul ballads of the time. However, her first uptempo hits, most notably her cover of Otis Redding's "Respect" and her own "Think," emotionally redefined "fast soul." What had frequently been a forum for men to boast about their sexual prowess became the backdrop to a demand for dignity in "Respect" and a tongue-lashing in "Think." In both songs, the groove is as good as it gets, but it supports a call to arms rather than an invitation to sensual pleasure. "Respect," in fact, took on a meaning beyond the intent of its lyric: It became an anthem for the women's movement, which was just gathering momentum.

The musical formula for "Respect" is typical for 1960s soul: interlocked rhythm section, with horns playing riffs or sustained chords. The two major differences are Aretha's singing and the backup vocals, which give the song a churchier sound. The most memorable and individual section of the song is the stop-time passage when Aretha spells out what she wants—"R-E-S-P-E-C-T"—so that there's absolutely no misunderstanding. What had been a straightforward verse/chorus song suddenly shifts up a gear. The remainder of the song features the dense texture previously heard in the chorus: a series of riffs from the backup vocalists—"sock it to me," "just a little bit," and finally the repeated "Re-re-re-re" (not only the first syllable of "respect" but also Aretha's nickname)—piled on top of the beat and horn riffs, with Aretha commenting on it all from above.

Having quickly established her credentials as the queen of soul, Aretha began to explore other musical territory She has been one of the very few artists of the rock era who can cover songs convincingly. Her versions of Burt Bacharach's "I Say a Little Prayer," Sam Cooke's "You Send Me," Nina Simone's "Young, Gifted, and Black," and Paul

LISTENING CUE • **"Respect" (1967),** Otis Redding. Aretha Franklin, vocal.

STYLE Soul • **FORM** Verse/chorus, with interlude and stop-time section at the end

Listen For . . .

INSTRUMENTATION
Lead and backup vocals, electric guitar, electric bass, drums, tambourine, trumpets, saxophones

PERFORMANCE STYLE
Aretha's edgy gospel/blues mix; aggressive guitar sound; loud horns

RHYTHM
Rock rhythm with strong backbeat at moderate tempo; syncopation prominent in vocal, bass line, sax solo

MELODY
Melody = series of short riffs

TEXTURE
Thick texture = Aretha high, horn, guitar, piano, bass, drum parts fill in middle/ lower range

Remember . . .

CHANGE GENDER, CHANGE MEANING
Aretha's presence brings woman's point of view to fore.

ARETHA'S SINGING
Unmatched in expressive range, power, sensitivity, and emotional impact

SOUTHERN SOUL PLUS
Song adds backup vocal group to typical soul instrumentation of vocalist plus rhythm section and horns. They are integral to the impact of the song, especially in call-and-response sections.

Listen to this selection in CourseMate.

Simon's gospel-influenced "Bridge over Troubled Water" are all standouts. Several of her own songs give further evidence of her expressive range: in "Rock Steady," she tips her hat to James Brown, while "Daydreaming" is as tender and romantic a song as any released in the early seventies.

Aretha's music is deeply personal and, at the same time, universal. The responsive listener feels her communicate one-on-one, yet her message transcends such a relationship. The best of Aretha's music seems to demand both empathy and ecstasy. We can give ourselves up to the groove even as we listen to her tough-time tales. No one in the rock era has fused both qualities more powerfully and seamlessly than she.

The Decline and Legacy of Soul

The soul movement went into a slow decline with the assassination of Martin Luther King Jr. in 1968. James Brown and Aretha Franklin continued to perform and record successfully, but racial tension seemed to affect the chemistry within the interracial house bands at Stax in Memphis and Fame in Muscle Shoals, and between the bands and the performers they backed. There were still successes: Isaac Hayes produced "hot buttered soul" in Memphis, and Al Green, another exceptional voice, enjoyed considerable success in the early seventies. Green, who had grown up singing gospel, became an ordained minister shortly after a friend flung hot grits on his back, then killed herself. He finally left the pop world behind altogether in 1979, after injuring himself during a performance.

Soul music lasted less than a decade on the charts. The first soul hits appeared in 1965; by 1975, only James Brown was still carrying the soul banner. Its influence, however, has been evident ever since. Soul brought a more contemporary version of the deep feeling of the blues into black music. In this respect, it is the insider's counterpart to the British blues bands: a new view of blues sensibility by those who grew up with it.

CHAPTER 53
San Francisco and the Diversity of Rock

From the start, rock has been not a single style, but a heterogeneous mix of styles linked by common musical features and shared attitudes. This became even more apparent during the latter part of the sixties, when rock became the dominant popular music and simultaneously went in several different directions, musically and geographically.

We may perceive the diversity of rock through geography in two ways. One is to note the numerous regional dialects of rock that surfaced in the sixties. In the United States, there was surf music from southern California, soul music from Memphis, Motown from Detroit, in addition to the music coming from England.

The other way is to observe the activity within a geographical region. During the latter part of the sixties, one good place to do this was the San Francisco Bay Area. Because of Haight-Ashbury, "flower power," LSD, and the other trappings of the hippie scene, the music most associated with the Bay Area during the late sixties was acid rock. However, the notoriety of the counterculture masked the diversity in the Bay Area music scene. Many of the important acts active during that time and place went beyond acid rock or had no connection with it. They included the Grateful Dead, whose music embraced much more than the drug culture; Creedence Clearwater Revival playing down-to-earth rock and roll; Santana's Latin rock; and the proto-funk of Sly and the Family Stone. The two examples discussed next hint at this diversity.

Acid Rock and Jefferson Airplane

As tripping on acid became more widespread, artists used words, images, and music to capture the psychedelic experience. Psychedelic art—rich in color, dense and distorted, and often suffused with religious and mystical images—became an important new direction in the visual arts; among the most famous and memorable visual images of the psychedelic sixties was "Further," Ken Kesey's old school bus painted in a rainbow of colors.

Music was even more integral to the psychedelic experience because it was used not only to evoke but also to enhance tripping on acid. Music could contribute to the experience, depict the experience, and be a product of it. The Jefferson Airplane's "White Rabbit" does all three.

The band that first directed the spotlight to San Francisco and to acid rock was Jefferson Airplane. Vocalist Marty Balin (b. 1942) and guitarist Paul Kantner (b. 1941) formed Jefferson Airplane in 1965; the next year, Grace Slick (born Grace Wing, 1939) replaced Signe Anderson as the female vocalist with the group and soon became the face as well as the dominant voice of the group. Her good looks and extroverted and uninhibited stage personality were key elements in the success of

LISTENING CUE • **"White Rabbit" (1967),** Grace Slick. Grace Slick, vocal, with Jefferson Airplane.

STYLE Acid rock • **FORM** Modified AABA form

Listen For . . .

INSTRUMENTATION
Vocal, electric guitar, electric bass, drum

RHYTHM
Shifts between Spanish-flavored march rhythm and rock rhythm; little syncopation

MELODY
Slowly rising melody, built around long notes

HARMONY
Spanish modal harmony at start; rock modal harmony at ends of phrases

TEXTURE
Muted sound: vocal highest and strongest, guitar, bass in low register

Remember . . .

IMPORTANCE OF WORDS
Message of the song is mainly in the words; the melody is not a stand-alone melody, like those found in Motown or Beatles songs, nor is the accompaniment interesting enough to stand alone.

SPANISH FLAVOR
Spanish rhythms and harmonies connect to rock mainly by association; they are certainly not typical in rock music.

BIG CRESCENDO
Gradual crescendo makes final line of song sound like a call to action—an emphatic exhortation to take an acid trip.

Listen to this selection in CourseMate.

the group. The rest of the group during the late sixties included lead guitarist Jorma Kaukonen (b. 1940), bassist Jack Casady (b. 1944), and drummer Spencer Dryden (1938–2005).

Slick brought two songs with her from the Great Society, the band she had formed with Jerry Slick, her husband at the time. As reworked by Jefferson Airplane, they became the group's two Top 10 singles: "Somebody to Love" and "White Rabbit." Both songs appeared on *Surrealistic Pillow* (1967), the first album the group recorded with Slick.

Of the two, "White Rabbit" connects more directly to the drug experience. The title of the song refers to the white rabbit in Lewis Carroll's *Alice in Wonderland*. In Carroll's tale, the rabbit, dressed in a waistcoat, leads Alice into a hole and into a fantasy world where she has all manner of strange experiences. The lyric comments on a scene in the story where she meets a caterpillar that seems to be smoking opium. Slick would later remark that the song was an indictment of parents who read stories like *Alice in Wonderland* to their children and then wonder why the children do drugs. However, the connection with LSD was oblique enough that the song made it past the censors, although the drug references (such as "feed your head") seem quite clear in retrospect.

In "White Rabbit," the lyrics (and Slick's singing) are primary; the music plays a supporting role. Among the defining features of the song are the flamenco-inspired instrumental accompaniment (adapted for a rock band) and the sustained crescendo to the final "Feed your head." Slick remarked that the inspiration for the accompaniment came from her repeated listening to *Sketches of Spain* while tripping on LSD. *Sketches of Spain* was an adventurous album by the jazz trumpeter Miles Davis; the most extended track was a drastic reworking of a guitar concerto by the Spanish composer Joaquin Rodrigo. Another remarkable feature of the song is its slow, steady crescendo (a gradual increase in volume). The song begins quietly with an extended instrumental introduction in which the instruments enter one by one—bass, drums, then lead and rhythm guitars. Both the rhythm and the chord progression evoke Spanish music. Slick also enters quietly. The music gets louder as the song proceeds, reaching a climax on the line "Feed your head." As Slick belts out the lyric, the band shifts from the Spanish-flavored rhythm with which the song began to a straightforward rock rhythm; it is as if music, like the mind and Slick's voice, has been set free from the restrictive Spanish rhythm.

Jefferson Airplane remained one of the leading psychedelic rock bands into the early seventies, when the group reconstituted itself with Slick and Kantner as Jefferson Starship. Although their new name implied that they had become even more adventurous—starships fly higher than airplanes—the band actually became more mainstream and enjoyed even more commercial success during the seventies and eighties.

The Decline of Psychedelia

Both the psychedelic scene and psychedelic rock lost their potency around 1970. The 1967 "summer of love" devolved into a bad trip as the decade drew to a close. Haight-Ashbury went into decline; it would become gentrified a decade later. For many, LSD lost its status as the mind-expanding drug of choice.

The absence of a distinct musical identity made it difficult to sustain acid rock as a vital rock substyle; the style neither evolved (like heavy metal or country rock did) nor achieved a more or less permanent stasis (like hard rock). It was—and remains—very much a period piece, a sound of a particular time and place.

Acid rock lacked a distinct musical identity in large part because the drug experience was an overlay; it was not an integral element of the style. It was the connection to LSD and the environment in which it was used extensively, rather than a specific musical feature, or set of features, that linked the widely varied music identified as **acid** or **psychedelic rock.** The musical products were seemingly as varied as the acid trips themselves. The connection could be in the music, in the words, or both.

Most of the major acid-rock acts rooted their style in folk and blues. The Grateful Dead began as a jug band; the members of Jefferson Airplane had prior experience in folk, blues, and R&B; and both Jimi Hendrix and Eric

Whereas Grace Slick took her listeners into a fantasy world in songs like "White Rabbit," Janis Joplin got real by drenching herself in blues and soul.

Clapton, who were also associated with acid rock, had deep blues roots. For many of the top San Francisco–based acts, this connection with American roots music was a stronger musical bond than the drugs. Perhaps the clearest example of this came in the music of Janis Joplin.

Down to Earth: Janis Joplin and the Blues

The only female performer in the San Francisco rock scene with a more commanding presence than Grace Slick was Janis Joplin (1943–1970). Like Slick, Joplin fronted a band, had a let-it-all-hang-out stage personality, and wrestled with a severe substance abuse problem. Both looked the part of the counterculture diva—both dressed and undressed. But there were differences. Slick had a striking appearance and had come from a high-class background. Before joining Jefferson Airplane, she had modeled for three years at a high-end San Francisco department store and had begun her undergraduate education at Finch College, a finishing school for young ladies. Joplin had grown up a social outcast in a Texas oil town; music was her escape. Joplin sipped while Slick tripped; Janis's taste for Southern Comfort was legendary. (Ironically, it was Slick who later developed an alcohol abuse problem, while Joplin died of a heroin overdose.) And while Slick took her listeners into a fantasy world in songs like "White Rabbit," Joplin got real by drenching herself in blues and soul.

Like many other young musicians of the time, Joplin migrated to San Francisco during the mid-sixties. Born in Port Arthur, Texas, Joplin began performing in coffeehouses in her native state before traveling to California in 1965. There, she began performing with a local blues band: Big Brother and the Holding Company. The group made an enormous impact at the 1967 Monterey Pop Festival, thanks mainly to Joplin's dynamic stage performance. Signed to Columbia Records, they recorded only one album with Joplin, the 1968 release *Cheap Thrills*. Critics praised Joplin's singing but criticized the band for its ragged playing. Joplin soon separated from the band and became an important solo act for the rest of her brief life.

Joplin was rock's original blues diva. Before Joplin, few women sang with anything approaching the supercharged passion and freedom inherent in her singing, and all of them were black. Indeed, Joplin's singing seems to owe more to Otis Redding and other male southern soul singers than to any woman, because what distinguishes Joplin's singing from that of other female singers is the rawness of her sound and the sheer exuberance of her performing style. She had a voice that often sounded like she had gargled with broken glass, although she could also sing as tenderly as any crooner. She combined that with a unique kind of vocal virtuosity. With its stutters, reiterations, rapid-fire streams of words, melismas, interpolations, and the like, her singing style is almost operatic in its exhibitionism.

LISTENING CUE • **"Piece of My Heart" (1968),** Jerry Ragovoy and Bert Russell. Janis Joplin, vocal, with Big Brother and the Holding Company.

STYLE Acid rock • **FORM** Verse/chorus form

Listen For . . .

INSTRUMENTATION
Lead, backup vocal, electric guitars, electric bass, drums

PERFORMANCE STYLE
Joplin's raspy voice and vocal pyrotechnics—stutters, and so on; blues-influenced guitar style

RHYTHM
Rock rhythm in slow tempo, with frequent double-time rhythms; contrast between leisurely verse, busy verse, rock-rhythm chorus

MELODY
Active, almost instrumental melody because of Joplin's elaborations

TEXTURE
Strong contrasts: thin texture in verse, thick texture around Joplin's singing in bridge and chorus; all instruments active, mainly with riffs and busy lines, plus high backup vocals

Remember . . .

BLUES-INFLUENCED ACID ROCK BAND
The standard instrumentation, blues-inspired riffs, and effects—such as the distortion and the spacey sounds and feedback at the end of the song—all connect the song to blues-oriented acid rock.

PASSIONATE SINGING
Joplin's singing is unique, not only for its basic quality, which recalls the voices of the great male soul singers, but also for its uninhibited use of an array of vocal devices and many shifts of mood.

ROCK THAT IS REAL
There were dozens of bands that dug into the blues in order to invest their music with the kind of emotional honesty heard in the music of the best blues artists. Few white singers, male or female, could match Joplin's intensity or emotional commitment.

Listen to this selection in CourseMate.

Although Joplin thought of herself as a blues singer, most of the songs that she recorded were not blues, at least in the formal sense. Unlike the classic female blues singers of the twenties, who recorded mainly conventional blues songs, Joplin recorded a wide range of material. However, she brought blues feeling and style into everything she recorded, blues or not.

"Piece of My Heart," a track on *Cheap Thrills*, was the only song of hers to reach the singles charts during her lifetime, and the album topped the charts for eight weeks in 1968.

"Piece of My Heart" remains the song most closely associated with her; two biographies include it in the title. The song had been a modest R&B hit the previous year for Erma Franklin, Aretha Franklin's younger sister. Her version was a solid and straightforward slow soul song. Characteristically, the lyric tells the story of a troubled relationship, here from a woman's point of view: She is at once vulnerable and—as the lyric says—tough. Given Joplin's history and personality, it is easy to understand why she would be eager to cover it.

The thorough transformation of the song begins with the band; the instrumental accompaniment features the kind of blues-tinged rock that was often a part of the San Francisco psychedelic scene, rather than a bass-heavy R&B sound. The instrumentation is standard: two guitars, with some distortion in the lead guitar, plus bass and drums. The rhythms are more active and freer than in a straightforward rock song.

All of this is a foil for Joplin's soulful singing. There is enormous contrast, in volume and vocal quality, from the almost screamed opening ("Come on") to the almost whispered verse ("Didn't I make you feel") to the half-spoken/half-sung ("Each time I tell myself") and the wailed chorus. As she delivers the song, she lays herself emotionally bare—as if she had stripped off all of her clothes. Few singers of any era were willing to throw themselves into a performance the way Joplin did, and fewer had the vocal agility and range to carry it off successfully.

Janis Joplin defined a new role of women in rock. It was no longer simply being a pretty face in front of the band; Joplin matched men—black and white—in power and presence. In this respect, she paved the way for others: Patti Smith, Annie Lennox, Bonnie Raitt, Madonna, are among those who benefited from her trail-blazing efforts.

She paid a price for her passion. With her premature death, she joined the not-exclusive-enough club of rock icons who lived too hard and died too young. Ironically, she did not live long enough to enjoy her biggest hit; "Me and Bobby McGee," written for her by Kris Kristofferson, one of her ex-lovers, appeared on *Pearl*, an album released after her death. She left the album incomplete; she was to have added vocals to a track entitled "Buried Alive in the Blues" on the day she died.

Joplin and her music embody the tensions of the new womanhood that emerged in the sixties. On stage and in the studio, she is the equal of men, yet vulnerable in a specifically feminine way; she is modern in her sensibility, yet deals with timeless issues in her songs. For a new generation of women, she showed both what they might aspire to and the dangers of getting it.

The dramatic differences between "White Rabbit" and "Piece of My Heart" only hint at the diversity of the music scene in the San Francisco Bay Area, which clearly evidences the stylistic explosion of the late sixties. As late as 1964, even an astute observer of rock music would have needed superior foresight to predict the many directions that rock-era music took in the latter part of the decade. The differences among songs and styles touch every aspect of the music—what songs are trying to communicate and how they communicate their message in words and music. No region more clearly exemplified this trend.

UNIT 12

LOOKING BACK, LOOKING AHEAD

IN LESS THAN FIVE YEARS, rock fomented a musical, cultural, and social revolution. It got underway in earnest early in 1964, with the British invasion and the ascent of Motown. By the time all of the music discussed in this unit had been released, rock had reshaped popular music and the music industry that supported it. Chart dominance tells only part of the story. Even more telling was its impact on established styles. Pop, musical theater, and jazz that sounded current—even cutting edge—in the early 1960s was out of date by the end of the decade, and those working in these styles hopped on the rock bandwagon, creating rock musicals, pop rock, and jazz/rock fusion.

Rock and rhythm and blues forged a different relationship with its audience. It introduced new sensibilities that were often more direct, more personal, and more real, and created new lyrical and musical approaches to convey them. In the process, this revolutionary new music helped change cultural attitudes in the United States and abroad and effect significant social change.

Rock lost its revolutionary fervor in the 1970s; for many of the top acts, calculation and craft replaced the excitement of experimentation. The rock and rhythm and blues of the early 1970s was often more polished and in many ways more appealing, but less adventurous and surprising.

Rock and R&B after 1970

UNIT 13

© iStockphoto

UNIT 13

On May 13, 1971, the day he turned twenty-one, Stevie Wonder's contract with Motown Records expired. Up to that point, the arrangement had been good for both parties: Wonder was a child star, and both he and Motown reaped the rewards. However, when he came of age, Wonder took the $1 million in royalties that Motown had been holding in trust for him, formed his own record and publishing companies (Taurus and Black Bull, respectively), and negotiated a new record deal with Motown. For Wonder, the crucial clause in the contract was complete artistic control. In effect, he made his records and Motown sold them.

Wonder assumed artistic control in an unprecedented way. He immersed himself in electronics, learning how to use synthesizers and electronic keyboards, a new and rapidly evolving technology at the time. With these newly developed skills, he played most—and sometimes all—of the parts on many of his recordings. On Wonder's recordings, a single artist with a lot of equipment replaced the multilevel Motown production pyramid. The string of albums that he produced in the early seventies did well enough that he was able to renegotiate his contract with Motown in 1975. The new deal gave him a $13 million advance and a 20 percent royalty rate.

Wonder's emancipation from Motown and his subsequent contractual arrangements illustrate three key features of rock and R&B after 1970. First, this new music had become a big business. Second, important artists were determined to go their own way, no matter where it took them. Third, technology would play an increasingly important role in shaping the sound of popular music. We encounter all three features in the chapters that follow.

CHAPTER 54
Commerce and Technology in 1970s Rock

By the early 1970s, the rock revolution was over. It was evident on the charts and in corporate offices, and in the flurry of hastily arranged musical marriages among rock and pre-rock styles: pop rock, rock musicals, and jazz fusion. Rock and R&B were now driving the music industry, so the industry made rock and R&B its business.

By the early 1970s, spectacle had become part of the business of rock.

The Business of Rock

In the seventies, rock traded tie-dyed T-shirts for three-piece suits. In so doing, it turned its core values upside down. From the beginning, rock had portrayed itself as music of rebellion. But as the market share of rock and R&B grew, so did the financial stake. It cost more to create and promote a record, put on a concert, and operate a venue. There was more money to be made but also more to be lost. Not surprisingly, a corporate mentality took over the business side of rock. It was evident to some extent in the music itself, in that some artists seemed to make commercial success their highest priority and let that shape their music: Elton John, the bestselling rock star of the seventies, was the poster boy for this path. However, the impact of profit-oriented thinking was far more telling behind the scenes. It determined to a great extent which music would get promoted and how. Its impact was most evident in the media and in the use of new market strategies designed to maximize sales.

Cross-Marketing

A major business innovation of the seventies was **cross-marketing.** In pursuit of greater financial rewards, record companies used tours to help promote record sales. The stadium or large-arena concert became commonplace. More ritual than musical event, these concerts usually confirmed what the audience already knew about the music of a particular act. As a rule there was little, if any, spontaneity in performance, as acts drew their set list from current or recent albums.

Often the performances were more about show than sound, although there were plenty of both. Flamboyance had been part of rock from the start, and by the early seventies, spectacle had become part of the business. Lights, fog, costumes, makeup, pyrotechnics, and the like were now the norm at rock concerts. Such productions were almost a necessity because performers had to seem larger than life in such huge venues. At its most extreme, outrageous dress, makeup, and stage deportment replaced musical substance as the primary source of interest. Acts like Kiss epitomized this theatrical aspect of seventies rock.

Rock as Big Business

The seventies proved that there was money to be made in rock and R&B on a scale that was hard to imagine even a decade before. Record sales had increased enough that the Recording Industry Association of America (RIAA) created a new category in 1976, the platinum record, which signified the sale of 1 million units. (The gold record represented sales of 500,000 units.) Moreover, the album had replaced the single as the primary unit, so revenues were even higher.

The increased sales, which occurred during a long economic recession, certainly reflect the deeper bond between music and listener, the "rock as a way of life" state of mind. But there were other causes. The ever-growing diversity of the musical landscape meant that there was music for almost every taste. Technology reinforced the personalization of musical taste: The development of cassettes meant that one's music became increasingly portable and customizable.

Tape Players

In the sixties, two important tape-based consumer formats emerged. One was the four- or eight-track tape. These tape players began to appear in cars (and Lear jets—Bill Lear had the technology developed for his line of corporate jets) in 1965 and remained popular through the seventies. The other, more enduring playback device was the audiocassette. A number of manufacturers, most

13, 14, 17, 18, 19

notably Philips, Sony, and Grundig, worked to develop cassettes and cassette players and to come up with an industry standard. By the seventies, this new technology had caught on: Cassette sales grew much faster than LPs (vinyl) and by 1982 exceeded them.

This new format had many advantages. The units were smaller, and so were the playback devices. Some were portable; others went into car consoles. By the mid-seventies, boom boxes had appeared, offering a portable and low-priced alternative to the home stereo. The first Walkman came from the Sony factory in 1979; other companies quickly followed suit. All of these devices made listeners' personal recordings as accessible as the radio.

Moreover, cassette players also made it possible for consumers to assemble their own playlists, using blank tapes. With improvements in recording quality, most notably Dolby noise reduction technology, there was less loss in fidelity during copying. People could now take their music with them wherever they went.

Media and Money

However, no medium showed the impact of the big-business mindset more than radio. In the early years of rock, radio had been an important part of the music's outsider image—Alan Freed in the fifties and "underground" FM stations in the sixties. In the seventies, however, the most significant new trend was **AOR (album-oriented radio).** In this format, disc jockeys could no longer choose the songs they played. Instead, program directors selected a limited number of songs designed to attract a broad audience while offending as few as possible. Often stations bought syndicated packages, further homogenizing radio content. Free-form radio all but disappeared, and so did the adventurous spirit that it symbolized. As a result, distortion was out; tunefulness was in. Acts like Barry Manilow, the Carpenters, Stevie Wonder, Chicago, the Eagles, Fleetwood Mac, Paul McCartney and Wings, and, above all, Elton John got a lot of airplay and topped the charts.

The New Mainstream

Rock not only reshaped the mainstream, it reshaped the *idea* of a mainstream. The term implies a single dominant trend. However, as the list of AOR and chart-topping acts suggests, the mainstream in the 1970s was instead a diverse array of melodically oriented styles. This is an expected consequence of the inherent diversity of rock.

If one had to reduce the relationship between sixties and early-seventies music to a single word, that word might well be *more*. Whatever happened in the sixties happened more in the seventies. Rock became diverse in the sixties; it became more diverse in the seventies as styles and substyles proliferated. Sixties musicians found the new grooves of rock and soul. Seventies musicians found them more easily; rhythms were often freer and more daring, or more powerful. The sounds of bands got even bigger in the seventies through more powerful amplification and additional instruments. Contrasts between styles and the attitudes that they conveyed also became more pronounced. The seventies both heard the intimate confessions of the singer-songwriters and witnessed the bombast of David Bowie's grand spectacles. Sometimes these contrasts even appeared in the same song; Led Zeppelin's "Stairway to Heaven" is a memorable example. Some artists, such as Joni Mitchell, created highly personal music. Other acts hid behind a mask: David Bowie is an extreme example.

The breakup of the Beatles symbolized the fragmentation of the new mainstream of the rock era. After they dissolved in 1970, each of the band members went his own way. Paul McCartney was the most active and the most commercially successful; Wings, the group that he formed in 1971, was one of five 1970s acts to reach the Top 20 in both singles and album sales. Another was Elton John, the top pop artist of the decade.

Elton John and the Expansion of Mainstream Rock

The career of Elton John (born Reginald Dwight, 1947; his stage name came from the first names of fellow band members in his first band, Bluesology) is a testimony to the power of personality. Off stage, he is an unlikely looking rock star: short, chunky, balding, and bespectacled. On stage, his costumes and extroverted style made him larger than life; it rendered his everyday appearance

On stage (here in 1975), Elton John's costumes and extroverted style made him larger than life.

irrelevant. He was one of the top live acts of the seventies and the best-selling recording artist of the decade.

John's first hits were melodic, relatively low-key songs like "Your Song," but his albums also contained harder-rocking songs like "Take Me to the Pilot." As he repositioned himself in the mainstream, he retained his ability to tell a story in song, largely due to his partnership with lyricist Bernie Taupin, while infusing his music with pop elements that helped expand the range of his music. He followed "Crocodile Rock," a fun take on fifties rock and roll and his first No. 1 hit, with "Daniel," a sensitive ballad. For the remainder of the decade, he veered from style to style. At the center of his music was his husky voice, which changed character from the soul-tinged sound in songs like "The Bitch Is Back" to a much more mellow sound in songs like "Little Jeannie." Moreover, because of his considerable skill as a songwriter, he was able to fold external elements into his own conception, rather than simply mimic an existing sound.

In "Tiny Dancer," a track from his 1971 album *Madman Across the Water,* demonstrates both the craft and the range of his music at the start of his career. The lyric, written by his longtime collaborator Bernie Taupin, begins as if it is going to tell a story. However, as it develops, it resolves into a collage of vivid images. It is as if we see short video clips that quickly cut away to another scene. There are oblique first-person references; some of the scenes seem to describe a relationship between John and the tiny dancer ("Piano man, he makes his stand"). But it is not a direct narrative.

John's setting of the lyric begins simply with John playing syncopated piano chords, first to get the song underway, then to accompany his singing of the melody. Through most of the opening statement of the verse, it is as if the song will be set simply and intimately. However, other instruments enter in stages: steel guitar at the end of the first large section, other rhythm instruments at the repetition of the opening section, then a choir at the end of the repeated section. At that point, John shifts gears, using the piano to give a stronger, more marked rhythm and shifting the harmony into uncharted waters. This builds toward the chorus, which adds a string countermelody to the many instruments and voices already sounding.

As recorded, "Tiny Dancer" takes over 6 minutes to perform: even at this length, there are less than two complete statements of the song. (In "Tiny Dancer," a complete statement consists of two verse-like sections that are melodically identical, a transition and a chorus.) This expands the verse/chorus template used, for example, in so many Motown songs. We can gauge the degree of expansion by noting that one verse-like *section* is equivalent to a complete chorus of a "Heart and Soul"–type *song.* To realize this larger form, John uses a huge ensemble: his voice and piano, plus bass, drums, guitar, steel guitar,

LISTENING CUE • "Tiny Dancer" (1971), Bernie Taupin and Elton John. John, vocal and keyboard.

STYLE 1970s mainstream rock • **FORM** Expansive verse/chorus form

Listen For . . .

INSTRUMENTATION
Vocal, piano, steel guitar, electric guitar, electric bass, drums, strings, choir

RHYTHM
Slow sixteen-beat rhythm in verse; shift to rock beat in bridge; back to sixteen-beat rhythm in chorus; syncopation, especially in piano part

MELODY
Verse melody grows from short riff; title-phrase hook in chorus is longer

HARMONY
Dramatic shifts in harmony: verse = I-IV-V; bridge = new key; chorus = looping chord progression with delayed return to home key

TEXTURE
Texture "crescendos" through layering in of instruments, from just voice and piano to orchestral richness

Remember . . .

ARTY LYRIC
Taupin's arty, cinematic lyric shifts from image to image: There is no central narrative holding the lyric together. Even the chorus is deliberately obscure.

EXPANSIVE FORM
Form of "Tiny Dancer" follows a predictable verse/chorus pattern but unfolds on a much grander scale than a typical sixties rock or Motown song.

LAVISH INSTRUMENTATION
Piano, rhythm-section instruments, steel guitar, strings, and voices added layer by layer for maximum impact

RHYTHMIC CONTRAST
Rhythmic shifts, from active sixteen-beat rhythm of verse, through clearly marked rock rhythm in bridge, back to sixteen-beat rhythm; help outline form.

Listen to this selection in CourseMate.

backup vocals, rich strings, and choir. The result is, when desired, a denser and fuller-sounding texture. Moreover, John adds and subtracts instruments to outline the form and accumulate musical momentum through the verse sections to the climax of the song in the chorus.

In the four albums following *Madman Across the Water,* John often integrated catchier riffs and rhythms into his songs. All four were No. 1 albums; so was a subsequent "greatest hits" compilation. John remained active through the eighties and nineties, despite his short and difficult marriage to recording engineer Renate Blauel, acknowledgement of his sexual preferences, and numerous substance abuse issues. In the early nineties, he cleaned up his life and directed his energy to film and stage. He won his first Grammy in 1994 for one of the songs from the Disney animated film *The Lion King,* written in collaboration with lyricist Tim Rice. Another of their successful projects was what one reviewer called a "camp" remake of Giuseppe Verdi's famous opera *Aida.*

Two of the most impressive and fascinating aspects of John's career are its longevity—he is still an active performer—and the range of his collaborations. John Lennon's last public appearance came at an Elton John concert in 1974; about three decades later, John performed with Eminem at the Grammy awards ceremony. The list of those whom Elton John has performed with and befriended reads like a rock-era *Who's Who.* This speaks not only to his musical flexibility but also his generous nature.

John's career path epitomizes the trade-off between artistic integrity and commercial success that was a common theme in the 1970s. His early albums showed him to be a singer-songwriter of considerable gifts. As his star rose, he immersed himself in the Top 40, while adopting a Liberace-like stage persona, eventually donning elevator shoes, flamboyant costumes, and outlandish eyewear. His songs found the middle of the road, and he found megastardom. Somewhere along the line, he lost some of his musical individuality, trading it for familiarity and accessibility, and his visual identity at times deflected attention away from his real talent. John was not alone in this regard; others went down his yellow brick road to superstardom.

CHAPTER 55

Rock in the Early 1970s

It took rock musicians about fifteen years to really get it—that is, to completely assimilate the numerous musical influences that fed into rock, transform them into the dominant style, and become comfortable with its conventions. Most fundamentally, this is evident in the top bands' approach to rhythm. As the 1970s began, musicians approached rock rhythm with unprecedented freedom because they had reached a comfort zone with its essential elements.

Two landmark recordings from the early 1970s, The Who's "Won't Get Fooled Again" and Led Zeppelin's "Black Dog," show in quite different ways the rhythmic independence achieved by elite rock musicians when they felt comfortable with the rhythmic foundation of rock.

The Who

The Who came together as a group in 1964. Vocalist Roger Daltrey (b. 1944), guitarist Pete Townshend (b. 1945), and bassist John Entwistle (1944–2002) had been part of a group called the High Numbers. They became The Who when drummer Keith Moon (1947–1978) joined them. A year later, their music began to appear on the British charts. Their early hits, most notably "My Generation" and "Substitute" (both 1966), speak in an ironic tone. Indeed, "My Generation" became the anthem for the "live hard, die young, and don't trust anyone over 30" crowd. Musically, they were a powerhouse band with a heavy bass sound that displayed the strong influence of 1960s rhythm and blues. Townshend's power chords, Entwistle's agile and imaginative bass playing, and Moon's flamboyant drumming gave Daltrey's searing voice a rock-solid foundation. Still, it seemed that they were no more than a singles band, incapable of anything more than a series of good 3-minute songs. That perception began to change with the release of the album *Happy Jack* (1967), which included an extended piece, "A Quick One While He's Away," and it was dramatically altered with the release of the rock opera *Tommy* in 1969.

© Michael Ochs Archives/Getty Images

THE WHO (*left to right,* bassist John Entwistle, singer Roger Daltrey, drummer Keith Moon, and guitarist Pete Townshend), onstage here in 1973, never forgot how to rock and roll.

Townshend conceived of a sequel to *Tommy,* called *Lifehouse,* which was to be even grander. He eventually put the project aside but incorporated some of the material into an album of singles, entitled *Who's Next*. Among the most novel features of the album was Townshend's extensive use of the brand new ARP synthesizer.

Synthesizers

In 1969, Alan R. Pearlman founded ARP Instruments in order to produce **synthesizers** capable of creating a variety of electronic sounds. His first synthesizer, released in 1970, was a fairly large machine. His second model, the ARP 2600, which was released in 1971, was portable and flexible enough to be used in live performance.

The first synthesizers were cumbersome machines: The Moog synthesizer used by Wendy Carlos in her landmark 1968 recording *Switched-On Bach* looked like an old-fashioned telephone switchboard, with plugs connecting the various oscillators. By contrast, the ARP 2600 was one of the first to use transistors instead of tubes, which made the synthesizer smaller and lighter. It was limited, in that it was capable of producing only one sound at a time. However, as transistors became smaller and more powerful, improved models capable of simultaneously playing several sounds began to appear.

To promote his new instruments, Pearlman gave units to some of the top rock and R&B musicians of the era, in return for permission to use their names in advertising his product. Among his first clients was The Who's Pete Townshend. Judging by the almost immediate results, Townshend was fascinated by the synthesizer and the cutting-edge technology it represented. The synthesizer played a central role in "Won't Get Fooled Again," a track from *Who's Next*.

In "Won't Get Fooled Again," Townshend uses the synthesizer as a futuristic rhythm guitar, pitched in a high register instead of the more characteristic mid-range, but providing steady reinforcement of the rock rhythmic layer throughout the song. The insistent rhythm of the synthesizer chords seems to liberate the rest of the band. Townshend's power chords and riffs, Entwistle's active and free bass lines, and Moon's explosive drumming all play off this steady rhythm. It is this interplay between the steady rhythm of the synthesizer and the rest of the group that gives the song its extraordinary rhythmic energy.

LISTENING CUE • **"Won't Get Fooled Again" (1971),** Peter Townshend. The Who.

STYLE Hard rock • **FORM** Expansive verse/bridge/chorus form, with long introduction and extended vocal and instrumental interludes

Listen For . . .

INSTRUMENTATION
Vocal, ARP synthesizer, electric guitar, electric bass, drums

RHYTHM
Complex, highly syncopated rock beat at moderately fast tempo, with synthesizer marking rock rhythm, and Moon's manic drumming playing against the beat

MELODY
Vocal line assembled mainly from short riffs

HARMONY
Harmony built around I-IV-V but colored with modal chords and complex, shifting harmonies on synthesizer-only sections

TEXTURE
Dramatic shifts in density, with long synthesizer-only stretches contrasting with thicker sections featuring full band.

Remember . . .

SYNTHESIZERS IN ROCK
Innovative use of ARP synthesizer as rhythm instrument: In its steady rock-beat speed timekeeping, synth effectively assumes role (if not the sound and register) of rhythm guitar.

EXPANSIVE FORM
Extended form, with strong contrasts among synthesizer alone, vocal sections, and instrumental sections. More than half the song comes from long instrumental sections.

RHYTHMIC LIBERATION
Steady timekeeping in synthesizer part liberates band rhythmically. All three instrumentalists are free to keep time or play against the time. The result is an extraordinarily varied rhythmic texture, from heavy timekeeping by everyone, to the open sound of the synthesizer alone or the band playing riffs, lines, and rhythms that conflict with beat.

Listen to this selection in CourseMate.

"Won't Get Fooled Again" is a sprawling song—well over 8 minutes of music. The long synthesizer introduction and even longer interlude toward the end provide a dramatic contrast to the vocal sections, and its steady rhythm underpins the electrifying group jams in the extended instrumental passages. In "Won't Get Fooled Again," innovative technology enhances the basic sound and rhythm of a rock band. Despite the new sound source, the result is classic rock and roll.

Led Zeppelin

Although often cited as a seminal heavy metal band, Led Zeppelin ultimately defies categorization. From *Led Zeppelin* (1969), the group's first album, it was clear that heavy metal was just one aspect of their musical personality. Their center is clearly the blues; their version of heavy metal evolved from it. At the same time, there seems to be nothing in their musical world that is not fair game for appropriation. What's particularly interesting in their music is the way in which influences bleed into one another. Their music may cover a lot of stylistic territory, but it is not compartmentalized.

The range of their music came mainly from guitarist Jimmy Page (b. 1944), whose curiosity led him not only to immerse himself in the blues but also to seek out exotic musical styles (e.g., flamenco and East Indian music). Led Zeppelin's front man was vocalist Robert Plant (b. 1948), who was Page's second choice as lead singer but turned out to be an ideal voice for the group. Bassist John Paul Jones (b. 1946) had been, with Page, part of the British music scene in the late 1960s; drummer John Bonham (1948–1980) was a friend of Plant's from their Birmingham days. Page also produced their albums. His production skills were as important a component of their success as his guitar playing; he brought a wonderful ear for sonority and texture to their music.

Page and Plant shared a deep interest in the mystic, the mythical, and the occult. This interest would increasingly inform their work, from untitled albums to cryptic covers, sparse liner notes, nonreferential lyrics, and numerous archaic musical influences.

Another quality that sets their music apart from almost every other group of the era is their ability to establish, then reconcile, extremes. The extremes are evident in virtually every aspect of their music making. Plant sang higher than most other male vocalists (and many females too). Their ensemble playing was more daring, their riffs more elaborate and beat defying, the contrasts within and between songs deeper and more striking.

Their untitled fourth album, known variously as *Led Zeppelin IV, Zoso,* and the Runes LP gives a clear sense of the breadth of their expressive range—from the unbridled power of "Rock and Roll" to the delicacy of the acoustic "The Battle of Evermore." "Stairway to Heaven," perhaps the best-known song on the album, merges both.

"Black Dog," another track from the album, demonstrates Led Zeppelin's connection to heavy metal and their role in the continuing evolution of rock rhythm. From the very beginning of the song, it's clear that they've internalized the feel of rock rhythm. The beat is implied under Plant's unaccompanied singing, the silence, and the extended, blues-based instrumental line, but there is not the kind of comfortable timekeeping heard in so many good rock songs. Even the chorus-like riff under Plant's "Oh, yeah" is completely syncopated. What timekeeping there is in this song is purposeful and specific, rather than routine. In terms of freeing rhythm while still retaining the groove, "Black Dog" goes about as far as is possible. The track makes clear that Led Zeppelin became so comfortable with the rock groove that they could play with it—boldly.

The extended instrumental lines in "Black Dog" also point out another feature of Led Zeppelin's approach to rock—one that would profoundly influence heavy metal bands. In effect, they harness solo-like lines within a tight group conception. In rock, guitar solos can be spectacular displays, but they can also undermine the collective conception that is at the heart of a rock groove. Page's solution was to work out solo-like parts and integrate them into a group conception. For future heavy metal bands, this aspect of the recording was key: One of the marvels of good heavy metal performances is the tight ensemble of a band as they negotiate challenging and intricate passages. We can hear its roots in recordings like this.

© Laurance Ratner/WireImage/Getty Images

PLANT AND JIMMY PAGE of Led Zeppelin on stage in 1975 at the Chicago Stadium.

Led Zeppelin gained a large, loyal audience. They were also one of the first British bands to concentrate on the United States as a fan base because of its huge population compared to Britain's; they toured the United States far more than most of their peers. Their tours sold out and broke attendance records, and all of their recordings went platinum. They're still popular more than three decades after they disbanded. There is no ambiguity about why: Their music is a rare combination of almost

LISTENING CUE · **"Black Dog" (1971),** John Paul Jones, Jimmy Page, and Robert Plant. Led Zeppelin.

STYLE Early heavy metal · **FORM** Multisectional

Listen For . . .

INSTRUMENTATION
Vocal, electric guitar, electric bass, drums (guitar overdubbed during solo)

PERFORMANCE STYLE
Plant's singing in extreme high range; moderate distortion in guitar and bass parts

RHYTHM
Highly syncopated rock rhythm at moderate tempo with long sections without steady timekeeping

MELODY
Contrast between opening, with long vocal and instrumental exchanges, and other sections, with rapid exchange of short riffs

TEXTURE
Contrast between open, voice-alone sound and dark, dense instrumental response; thick sound, with low-register guitar + voice in chorus

Remember . . .

RHYTHMIC PLAY
From very beginning to final fadeout, rock rhythm is implied but never clearly marked. Instead, Plant hints at it in his unaccompanied singing, and instrumental responses soar over it with long lines or bounce off it with syncopated riffs. Only Bonham marks the beat and rock rhythm consistently.

COMPLICATED LINES
Long instrumental responses in verse sections suggest solo-like lines worked out by entire group. Considerable expansion of typical answering riff in more conventional rock song.

VOCAL/INSTRUMENTAL BALANCE
Musical interest divided between Plant's abnormally high singing and more complex and melodically interesting instrumental parts. There is also more strictly instrumental music than vocal or vocal/instrumental music, both within verses and overall, because of Page's extended solo.

Listen to this selection in CourseMate.

unrestrained power and subtle artistry, of raw emotion and superbly calculated craft. For some, the mix was too heady; the band never attracted the broad-based audience of the Beatles or Elton John. But for a large core, it was just the right strength. Millions of loyal fans remain unsatiated. Many were aspiring heavy metal musicians.

Heavy Metal and Early 1970s Rock

Joe Elliot, lead vocalist for Def Leppard, was quoted as saying, "In 1971 there were only three bands that mattered. Led Zeppelin, Black Sabbath, and Deep Purple." The differences among the three bands make clear that **heavy metal** was anything but a monolithic style. Their similarities highlight the qualities that set heavy metal apart from other hard rock styles.

Power and craft are two outstanding qualities of heavy metal. Most of its musical conventions—distortion; massive amplification; use of modes, pentatonic scales, and power chords; basic rhythms; power trio instrumental nucleus—were also part of the vocabulary of all hard rock music in the early 1970s. What metal bands did was to take these features and streamline or amplify them to give them more impact. Metal bands used *more* distortion and played *more* loudly. They took rock's shift away from traditional harmony several steps further by using conventional chords sparingly or, in some cases, abandoning harmony altogether. There is little harmony in "Black Dog" and it is based on modes instead of conventional harmony. Metal guitarists played power chords with *more* "power"—that is, greater resonance—and used them almost exclusively, and they developed more flamboyantly virtuosic styles. Metal's riffs and rhythms were stronger and more pervasive: at times, vocal lines seemed to ride on the riffs like a whitewater raft.

All of this supported nonmusical manifestations of power. Heavy metal evoked supernatural, or at least paranormal, power, especially in the group personas of Black Sabbath and Led Zeppelin. Even as the women's rights movement was in the ascendancy, metal bands projected masculine power, to the point where performers could sport skillfully styled long hair, wear makeup, and sing higher than many women without fear of abandoning their sexual identity.

The other was the mastery of craft. Like the alchemists of old, heavy metal performers diligently studied ancient formulas, from the modes of medieval music to the musical patterns of Bach and Vivaldi. These they adapted to rock, then juxtaposed them with elemental musical material. Guitarists like Page and Ritchie Blackmore of Deep Purple spent countless hours mastering their instruments. As a result, heavy metal has been, almost from the start, rock's most virtuosic substyle. It is evident not only in the individual brilliance of the many technically fluent performers but also in the complex and intricate ensemble playing, often at breakneck speeds. Both individual and group virtuosity are evident in "Black Dog."

Power and craft put the focus on the music. The music is *there* more; one of the qualities that distinguishes heavy metal from most other styles is the sheer amount of nonvocal music. Even more important, music is the primary source of heavy metal's overwhelming impact and expressive power. Words serve a largely explanatory role. Most of the audience at a metal concert will know the lyrics to songs, but not from the vocal, which is often unintelligible.

In its emphasis on instrumental virtuosity and power, its distance from more mainstream practice (including intelligible, conventional lyrics), and its cult-like environment, heavy metal represents a more extreme point along the continuum of hard rock styles. This is evidenced in its reception during the 1970s: the relatively small but fervent audience, hand in hand with limited airplay on mainstream radio and negative press from rock critics. Still, it was one of the most influential and distinctive hard rock styles of the era.

A Timeless Music

"Won't Get Fooled Again" and "Black Dog" exemplify a key moment in the history of rock. It is around this time that rock emerged as a fully developed style; what makes rock rhythm rock becomes common currency. Up to this point, we hear rock musicians restlessly seeking to discover the optimal approach to rock rhythm; they found it around 1970. From this point on, rock becomes a timeless music, in the sense that its conventions are clear and widely understood, and that musicians feel comfortable enough with them to play rock with great freedom. The rhythms and sounds of rock-era music would continue to develop beyond this point, as we will discover. But the rock that emerged around 1970 defines the core values of rock in a way that neither the rock that preceded it nor the rock that evolved beyond it does.

CHAPTER 56
Black Pop in the 1970s

Among the people of the African diaspora, the impulse to play with sound seems almost as strong as the impulse to play with rhythm. Two aspects of this impulse that seem especially persistent are the discovery of found sounds and the quest to make multiple sounds at the same time. Found sounds have taken many forms: making instruments out of everyday materials, like the cowbell in Cuban music, the steel drums of calypso, or the turntables of rap DJs; using everyday objects—a toilet plunger, the neck of a wine bottle—to modify the sound of a conventional instrument; or simply inventing new ways of making sound from an instrument, like "patting juba" by tapping out rhythms on various parts of one's body or slapping an electric bass.

The most familiar instance of the impulse to play multiple instruments simultaneously is the drum kit. More complex expressions of this practice range from jazz multi-instrumentalist Rahsaan Roland Kirk's ability to play the saxophone and two other instruments simultaneously to one-man bands like the obscure Abner Jay, the self-styled "last great southern black minstrel show," who accompanied himself with an electric guitar, bass drum, and hi-hat while he sang or played harmonica.

With his emancipation from Gordy's tight control, Stevie Wonder was able to combine both of these practices and take them high-tech. Both the electronic instruments—especially keyboards—that Wonder used on recordings like "Superstition" and the twenty-four-track mixing boards that made the recording possible were new, rapidly developing technologies. Wonder was the first major artist, black or white, to take them to their logical extreme: make a complete recording by not only assembling it track by track but also recording each track himself.

Wonder's high-tech one-man band was one of several important new directions in black pop during the early 1970s. Motown continued turning out hits. The Jackson 5 was their biggest new act of the 1970s, but Motown was losing its dominant position in the marketplace. Former Motown acts like Marvin Gaye and Gladys Knight and the Pips enjoyed significant success. A diverse group of solo singers, including Roberta Flack and Bill Withers, offered mature expressions of love, whereas Barry White offered love without limits. Philadelphia superseded Detroit as the main hit-making locale in black pop. We sample this music through tracks by Stevie Wonder and the O'Jays, one of the top Philadelphia acts.

Stevie Wonder

There's a certain irony that Motown's most powerful and original talent, and its longest running success story, is in many ways the antithesis of the Motown image and sound. Stevie Wonder is a solo act; most Motown acts were groups. The visual element was crucial to Motown's success: Its groups, dressed in gowns or tuxedos, moved through stylized, carefully choreographed routines as they sang their songs. Our enduring image of Stevie Wonder: a blind man with sunglasses and long braided and beaded hair, sitting behind a keyboard and rocking from side to side in a random rhythm. Motown recordings were collective enterprises; behind the groups were largely anonymous songwriters and studio musicians. Wonder created his own recordings from soup to nuts, not only singing and playing all the instruments at times but also performing the technical tasks—recording, mixing, mastering, and so on.

There are also differences in subject and attitude. In the mid-sixties, Motown song lyrics talked mainly about young love, usually in racially neutral, often-idealized language. Only reluctantly did they begin to address "real life" in songs like the Supremes' "Love Child." By contrast, Stevie Wonder took on social issues from his self-produced first album; the vignette of an innocent man's arrest in "Living for the City" is chilling. Stevie Wonder has advocated a long list of causes, from his firm push for a national holiday for Martin Luther King, Jr., to rights for the blind and disabled.

Stevie Wonder was born Steveland Morris (some accounts say Steveland Judkins) in 1950. A hospital error at birth left him blind. By ten, he was a professional performer, singing and playing the harmonica (he also played piano and drums). Within two years, he had

STEVIE WONDER

signed a Motown contract and was being billed as "Little Stevie Wonder, the 12-Year-Old Genius." (The "little" disappeared two years later, but the "Wonder" stuck.) He had a number of hits in the sixties, including "Uptight" (1966) and the beautiful love song "My Cherie Amour" (1969), but emerged as a major force in popular music only when his contract with Motown guaranteed him complete control over his work.

Wonder was the most popular black artist of the seventies. A series of albums, beginning with *Music of My Mind* (1972), established his unique sound and cemented his reputation as a major player in popular music. Each album release was a major event, especially within the black community, and his recordings also enjoyed enormous crossover success.

The widespread popularity of Wonder's music grows out of a style that is broad in its range, highly personal in its sound, and universal in its appeal. His music is a compendium of current black musical styles. In his songs are the tuneful melodies and rich harmonies of black romantic music, the dense textures and highly syncopated riffs of funk, the improvisatory flights of jazz, and the subtle rhythms of reggae and Latin music. Yet, even though he absorbs influences from all quarters, his style is unique.

"Superstition," a No. 1 single from the 1972 album *Talking Book,* is a funky up-tempo song with a finger-wagging lyric; in it, Wonder chastises those who would let their lives be ruled by superstitious beliefs. The melody that carries the lyric grows slowly out of a simple riff. Like so many Motown (and rock-era) songs, it builds inexorably to the title phrase.

The harmony shows the two main sources of his style: The verse sits on a bed of riffs, all built from the African-American pentatonic scale; there is no harmonic change. By contrast, the transition to the hook is supported by rich, jazz-like harmonies.

Most distinctive element of Stevie Wonder's sound, however, is the rich texture that flows underneath the vocal line. The song begins simply enough, with a rhythmically secure drum part. Onto this, Wonder layers multiple lines: the signature riff, a repeated-note bass line, plus several more riffs in the background, all highly syncopated. Stevie played all the lines on synthesizers, overdubbing until he produced the dense, funky texture that became one of his trademarks. (Wonder was one of the first musicians to develop a sound based almost completely on synthesizers.)

"Superstition" shows us the rhythmic side of Wonder's musical personality; there is also a romantic side, as evidenced in songs like " You Are the Sunshine of My Life." In either mode, Stevie Wonder is an optimist, a "glass is half full" person. Even in his darkest songs, hope is implicit, if not in the lyric, then in the bounce of the beat: How can you be down if your hips are shaking and your foot is tapping? Wonder's optimism is remarkable in light of numerous personal problems. Not only has he been blind from birth, but he also suffered a devastating automobile

LISTENING CUE · "Superstition" (1972), Stevie Wonder. Wonder, vocal and keyboard.

STYLE 1970s black pop · **FORM** Verse/chorus

Listen For . . .

INSTRUMENTATION
Vocals, drums, percussion, electric keyboards and synthesizers, trumpet/sax horn section, electric bass

RHYTHM
Rock beat at moderate tempo with multiple syncopated double-time riffs

MELODY
Both vocal line and instrument figures are based on repeated riffs

HARMONY
Oscillation between static harmony on pentatonic scale (verse) and rich harmony leading up to hook

TEXTURE
Thick texture, with several keyboard patterns and horn riffs weaving around timekeeping and vocal

Remember . . .

DARK LYRICS, UPBEAT GROOVE
Lyrics sermonize on real-life concern, but Wonder's singing and song's rhythm project optimism.

DENSE, RIFF-RICH TEXTURE
Dense texture woven together by multiple repeated riff figures in low and mid-range

NOVEL ELECTRONIC SOUNDS
Numerous synthesizer sounds replace conventional instruments.

FUNKY RHYTHMS
Layers of active, syncopated rhythms at sixteen-beat speed over rock beat create funky groove.

Listen to this selection in CourseMate.

accident in 1973 that left him in a coma for several days. He followed this adversity with some of his best music. He remains one of the icons of rock-era music.

The Sound of Philadelphia

In the early seventies, it seemed as if Motown had opened a branch office in Philadelphia. The most Motown-like records of the period appeared on Gamble and Huff's Philadelphia International label, not Gordy's. The basic formula was the same: lush orchestrations, solid rhythms coming from a rhythm section that had played together for years, jazz-tinged instrumental lines—all supporting vocal groups singing about the ups and downs of love. Only the details were different.

Three men engineered the **Philadelphia sound:** Kenny Gamble (b. 1943), Leon Huff (b. 1942), and Thom Bell (b. 1941). All were veterans of the Philadelphia music scene; they had worked together off and on during the early sixties in a group called Kenny Gamble and the Romeos. A few years later, Gamble and Huff began producing records together. They enjoyed their first extended success with Jerry Butler, who revived his career under their guidance. Their big break came in 1971, when Clive Davis, the head of Columbia Records, helped them form Philadelphia International Records. The connection with Columbia assured them of widespread distribution, especially in white markets.

The artist roster at Philadelphia International included the O'Jays, Harold Melvin and the Blue Notes, Teddy Pendergrass (who left the group to go solo), Billy Paul, and MFSB, which was the house band. Their competition came mainly from Thom Bell, who produced the Stylistics and the Spinners, a Detroit group that went nowhere at Motown but took off when paired with Bell in 1972.

The O'Jays

In the early 1970s, the O'Jays included Eddie Levert (b. 1942), William Powell (1942–1977), and Walter Williams (1942). Formed as a quintet in 1958, the group languished on the fringes of the R&B scene throughout the 1960s, with only a few hits. The turning point in their career came in 1968, when they met Gamble and Huff. Chart success came in 1972, shortly after Columbia Records created the Philadelphia International subsidiary for Gamble and Huff. Their first hit, "Back Stabbers," began a run of forty hit singles over the next fifteen years; nine of them topped the R&B charts and five reached the pop Top Ten.

"Back Stabbers" shows how the Philadelphia-based producers extended and updated the black pop style developed at Motown. The instrumental introduction

LISTENING CUE · **"Back Stabbers" (1972),** Leon Huff, Gene McFadden, and John Whitehead. The O'Jays.

STYLE Philadelphia sound · **FORM** Verse/chorus

Listen For . . .

INSTRUMENTATION
Lead and backup vocals, plus large rhythm section (piano, electric guitar, electric bass, drums, extra percussion), vibraphone, strings, horns

RHYTHM
Brisk rock rhythm clearly marked by percussion instruments, with double-time riffs in vocal line, free rhythms in bass, syncopated riffs in melodic instruments

MELODY
Chorus = chain of riffs; verse and bridge have longer phrases; melodic material

HARMONY
Minor key supports dark theme of song: like Marvin Gaye's "I Heard It Through the Grapevine"

TEXTURE
Rich texture, with strong bass, active mid-range percussion, low/mid-range horns, high strings behind vocals, often in harmony

Remember . . .

RHYTHMIC EFFECTS
Syncopated orchestral riffs and stop time dominant when they occur, overpowering steady rock rhythm in percussion

MULTIPLE MELODIC HOOKS
Motown influence evident in multiple melodic hooks, heard in vocal line, strings, and rhythm instruments

RICH ORCHESTRATION
Large, percussion-enhanced rhythm section, plus full string section and horns, support vocals

SPRAWLING FORM
Expansion of Motown-type form: big multistage, jazz-influenced instrumental introduction; chorus framing verse, extended bridge

Listen to this selection in CourseMate.

of "Back Stabbers" runs for 40 seconds—far longer than any of the Motown intros. It begins with a quasi-classical piano tremolo, an ominous rumble that helps establish the dark mood of the song. The unaccompanied piano riff that follows simply hangs in sonic space; there is still no regular beat keeping. Finally, the rest of the rhythm section enters, with the guitarist playing a jazz-style riff.

The rhythm sound is fuller than late sixties Motown records, not just because of the addition of Latin percussion instruments (Motown had been using them for years) but because there are more of them, and the reinforcement of the beat and the eight-beat layer is more prominent. After the conclusion of the opening phrase, the strings and, later, brass enter; all combine to create a lush backdrop for the O'Jays.

The song, cowritten by Huff, advises an unnamed man to guard against "friends" who are out to steal his woman. Like so much black pop, the song is about love, or at least a relationship. What's different about the lyric is that the narrator is an observer, rather than the person in the relationship. In effect, it's "I Heard It Through the Grapevine" told from the other side of the grapevine, but up-close and personal. It was the first of a series of such songs by the O'Jays.

As typified in this song, the Philadelphia sound is the Motown formula revised, expanded, and modernized. The instrumental introductions are more elaborate; the texture is richer; the songs themselves are more complicated; the spotlighted instruments are more contemporary sounding (in the case of the guitar); and there is greater rhythmic freedom, not only in the opening but also in the syncopated riffs that are the instrumental hooks of the songs.

For Stevie Wonder, the Philadelphia stars like the O'Jays, and many other black acts, the early and mid-1970s were their commercial and artistic peak. Wonder's most valued albums come from this time; they have assured his iconic status. The formula behind the Philadelphia sound worked well for the better part of the decade. However, toward the end of the decade, the Philadelphia sound was supplanted by disco, in many ways a more obvious version of the style. The Jackson 5 enjoyed their greatest success at Motown in the early 1970s; a shift to Philadelphia International did not spark a resumption of their earlier success. Other Motown artists followed a similar career trajectory, even though some, like the Jackson 5 and Marvin Gaye, left Motown altogether.

Much of the romantically-oriented black pop of the 1970s was a continuation of the Motown-dominated black pop of the 1960s—not surprising, because many of the acts were Motown veterans or modeled their sound on the Motown style. Wonder's music was exceptional in its willingness to address social issues, its more complex rhythms, and extensive use of electronics. Still, it is typically tuneful music. This tunefulness would give way to more rhythmic styles—funk, disco, and rap—as the decade drew to a close.

CHAPTER 57
Gender, Art, and the Boundaries of Rock

In the decade between 1965 and 1975, one of the primary sources of creative energy in rock was the tension between its core and its boundaries. Rock's core look and sound has been four or five aggressively heterosexual males singing and playing electronically amplified instruments loudly, to a driving rock beat. However, even as acts like the Rolling Stones consolidated this core style, others—most notably Dylan, The Beatles, Frank Zappa, and Brian Wilson—were leaving it behind. Among the important new directions of the early 1970s, two—singer-songwriters and glam rock—explored questions of art, artifice, and gender in rock-era music from radically different perspectives. We consider these questions through the music of Joni Mitchell and David Bowie.

The Singer-Songwriters

The term **singer-songwriter** came into use during the early seventies to identify those solo performers who made personal statements in song. Their songs were typically supported by a subdued, often acoustic, accompaniment that put the vocal line in the forefront.

Within these general parameters, there has been astonishing variety: autobiographical confessions, *cinéma vérité* portraits or acerbic social commentary, cryptic accounts that leave the identity of the narrator in question. Most are songs in a restricted sense of the term, in that they have coherent melodies that help tell the story and make musical sense through an inner logic. They are seldom formulaic; formal and melodic imagination finds its greatest outlet in these songs.

Among the first wave of singer-songwriters were established acts who went solo: Neil Young left Crosby, Stills, Nash, and Young, and Paul Simon dissolved his long-time partnership with Art Garfunkel. They were joined by a new generation of folk-inspired performers, most notably Joni Mitchell and James Taylor. Randy Newman, by contrast, came from a family heavily involved in traditional pop and film music; Carole King had been writing hit songs for over a decade.

The music of the singer-songwriters of the late sixties and early seventies represents the continuing evolution of the folk/country/pop fusions of the mid-sixties. The dominant influences were Bob Dylan and The Beatles, but other influences were also evident—folk and country especially, but also jazz, blues, pop, gospel, and Latin music.

Elevating the Feminine

The folk revival provided women with the most accessible point of entry into rock. With its intimate environment, emphasis on words and melody, and understated acoustic accompaniment, the urban folk music of the postwar era was far less macho than rock and roll, jazz, or blues. Indeed, young women folksingers were fixtures in coffeehouses throughout the sixties; Joan Baez was the most notable.

During the sixties, the repertoire of many female folksingers mutated from reworked folksongs to contemporary songs in a similar style. Judy Collins's work in the sixties embodies this transition; Janis Ian's "Society's Child" (1965–1967), her first hit, helped mark this new direction.

Among the new voices of the early 1970s were Carole King and Joni Mitchell. Both enjoyed success as songwriters before breaking through as performers. After a decade of working behind the scenes writing songs for others, Carole King began a solo career after her divorce from Gerry Goffin in 1968. She broke through in 1971 with *Tapestry,* which remained on the charts for almost six years and eventually sold over 22 million units. Similarly, Mitchell's first foray onto the charts came as a songwriter: Judy Collins's version of "Both Sides Now" reached No. 8 in 1968.

Joni Mitchell

Joni Mitchell (b. 1943) was born Roberta Anderson in Fort Macleod, Alberta, Canada, and grew up in Saskatchewan, the neighboring province. As a young girl, she had equally strong interests in art and music. After high school, she enrolled in the Alberta College of Art and Design and played folk music in the local coffeehouse. Like many Canadians in search of a career, she gravitated to Toronto, where she met and married Chuck Mitchell, also a folksinger, in 1966. The couple moved to Detroit. After her divorce a year later, she moved to New York, where she

JONI MITCHELL

connected into the folk scene, mainly as a songwriter, and then to Southern California the following year.

Mitchell began recording under her own name in 1968. She found her musical voice, and her audience, in a series of albums released between 1969 and 1974. In them, Mitchell uses the folk style of the early sixties as a point of departure, but she transforms every aspect of it—lyrics, melody, and accompaniment—into a highly personal idiom. We hear this in "All I Want," a track from her milestone 1971 album *Blue*.

Although it deals with a relationship, "All I Want" is a distinct departure from conventional songs about love. Most love-related songs present their situation in a coherent narrative. Typically, both words and music follow a predictable path toward a goal that serves as the expressive high point of the song. By contrast, Mitchell's songs disdain the conventions of rock and pop. In her songs, ideas shape the forms, not vice versa. Melodies respond to the words, yet follow their own internal logic. Other aspects of the setting—most notably harmony, instrumentation, and rhythm—are individual to a particular song. They remain in a supporting role; the focus is squarely on the words and melody.

By contrast, Mitchell's lyrics seem to open the door to her subconscious. There are mercurial shifts in mood. One moment she's high on love ("Alive, alive . . . juke box dive"), the next, she's licking her emotional wounds ("Do you see . . . both get so blue"). The only consistent feature of the lyric is the emotional inconsistency of her relationship ("Oh I hate you some . . . I love you some"). Thoughts and images tumble over each other in a stream of consciousness. There is no story; indeed, there is no sense even of time passing.

The music amplifies the temporal and emotional ambiguity of the lyric. The accompaniment begins with Mitchell playing an ostinato—a note repeated over and over—on an Appalachian dulcimer and James Taylor playing guitar. They deliberately avoid establishing a key or even marking the beat clearly. The song itself is strophic: The same melody serves three stanzas of poetry. It begins tentatively, echoing the indecision of the lyric. The most intense point comes in the middle. Shorter phrases and a more active, wide- ranging melodic contour echo the more active and frequent images in the text. They in turn lead to the heart of the song: "Do you want." Like smoke rising from one of Mitchell's ever-present cigarettes, the melody gradually drifts up, reaching its peak on the words "sweet romance," the real issue of the song. It drops down quickly, but not to rest; the final sustained note is not the keynote. The instrumental introduction returns as the outro; the song ends limply, as if it is a musical question mark.

All of this underscores the message of the lyrics. Mitchell describes a complex, difficult relationship and the emotional rollercoaster that it puts her through; there is no change in it during the course of the song, no resolution at the end. In "All I Want," Mitchell opens herself up, so that we can experience the turmoil in her troubled relationship. It is an emotional breakthrough—for her, for rock, and for popular music.

LISTENING CUE • **"All I Want" (1971),** Joni Mitchell. Mitchell, vocal and dulcimer; James Taylor, guitar.

STYLE Singer-songwriter • **FORM** Strophic, open-ended

Listen For . . .

INSTRUMENTATION
Voice, acoustic guitar, Appalachian dulcimer

RHYTHM
Subtle eight-beat pulse supports syncopated guitar chords, melody with varied rhythm

MELODY
Melody spins out from long idea; forms a long curve peaking toward end.

HARMONY
Ambiguous harmony frames song; accompaniment outlines key with rich harmony.

TEXTURE
Subdued but rich, rhythmically active accompaniment under melody

Remember . . .

CONFESSIONAL LYRICS
Words reflect the turbulent state of mind of narrator by jumping from image to image.

OUTPOURING OF MELODY
Melody spins out from the opening phrase, finally peaking toward the end.

INDECISIVE HARMONY
Instrumental intro and outro that frame melody are harmonic question marks; harmony that supports melody is also unpredictable and unstable at times.

OPEN-ENDED FORM
Form of "All I Want" consists of three distinct sections; there is no sense of resolution at the end.

Listen to this selection in CourseMate.

After 1974, Mitchell turned in other directions. Through the rest of the seventies, she connected with jazz and the avant-garde. This culminated in a collaboration with jazz great Charles Mingus, which was cut short by Mingus's death in 1979. Her seventies experiments anticipated the world music movement of the eighties. In the eighties, she continued to explore what some called "jazz/folk" fusion, as well as to develop her career in the visual arts as a photographer and painter.

Glam Rock: Rock as Spectacle and Artifice

Rock has had a strong visual element ever since Elvis first combed his hair into a pompadour and curled his lips into a sneer. By the late sixties, the visual dimension of rock had become, in its most extreme manifestations, far more flamboyant and outrageous: flaming or smashed guitars, provocative gestures and body movements. This outrageousness was in part a consequence of larger venues. With arena concerts now increasingly common, performers had to appear larger than life to have visual impact.

Among the most spectacular expressions of theatricality in rock was **glam** (or **glitter**) **rock.** It emerged in the early seventies, mainly in the work of David Bowie and T Rex, a group fronted by Marc Bolan.

As it took shape in the mid-sixties, rock prided itself on being real. It confronted difficult issues, dealt with real feelings, looked life squarely in the eye. This realism provoked a reaction. The Beatles followed *A Hard Day's Night,* a documentary-style film of their life on the run from fans, with *Help!* a psychedelic fantasy, in which they assumed personas, visually and musically.

Rock as artifice—rock behind a mask—found its fullest expression in glam rock, most spectacularly in David Bowie's first public persona, Ziggy Stardust. In portraying Ziggy Stardust, Bowie stripped identity down to the most basic question of all: gender. Was Ziggy male or female, or something in between? With his lithe build, flamboyant costumes, and heavy makeup, Bowie as Ziggy was a mystery. Particularly because he was not well known prior to Ziggy, there was no "real" Bowie to compare with his Ziggy persona. As Bowie pranced around onstage, he rendered his gender—or at least his sexual preference—ambiguous. Add to that a fantastical story, and—when performed live—a spectacular production: Glam rock, as exemplified by Bowie, was the opposite of real.

David Bowie/Ziggy Stardust

Bowie (born David Jones, 1947) began his career in the sixties as a British folksinger. Influenced by Iggy Pop, Marc Bolan, and the Velvet Underground, he began to reinvent his public persona. In 1972, he announced that he was gay.

DAVID BOWIE performing as Ziggy Stardust at the Hammersmith Odeon, 1973.

(However, he commented in an interview over a decade later that he "was always a closet heterosexual.") Later that year, he put together an album and a stage show, *The Rise and Fall of Ziggy Stardust and the Spiders from Mars*. It featured Bowie, complete with orange hair, makeup, and futuristic costumes, as Ziggy, a rock star trying to save the world but doomed to fail.

The songs from *Ziggy Stardust* provide the musical dimension of Bowie's role-playing. Their effect is not as obvious as his appearance, but without them, his persona would be incomplete. The three components of the songs—the words, Bowie's singing, and the musical backdrop—all assume multiple roles, as we hear in "Hang On to Yourself," one of the tracks from the album. The lyric is laced with vivid images: "funky-thigh collector," "tigers on Vaseline," "bitter comes out better on a stolen guitar." These arrest our ear, without question. But Bowie continually shifts from person to person as he delivers them. He "reports" in the verse—"She's a tongue-twisting storm"—and entreats in the chorus—"Come on, come on, we've really got a good thing going." His voice changes dramatically from section to section. It's relatively impersonal in the verse and warm, almost whispered, in the chorus. The music is both obvious and subtle in its role-playing. Bowie embeds instrumental and vocal hooks into the song: the guitar riff and the whispered chorus, a shock after the pile-driving verse. Both make the song immediately accessible and memorable.

But there are also subtle clues woven into the song that seem to tell us that, for Bowie, the hooks are the dumbed-down parts of the music. With such features as the extra beats after the first line of the verse ". . . light machine" and elsewhere, Bowie seems to be hinting that he's capable of a lot more sophistication than he's showing on the surface. Indeed, the spare style of the song was one of the freshest and most influential sounds of the seventies. Like Ziggy, he is descending down to the level of mass taste (even as he's reshaping it) because he wants the effect it creates, not because that's all he can do.

In Ziggy Stardust, Bowie creates a persona that demands attention but is shrouded in mystery. What makes his persona so compelling, both in person and on record, is not only its boldness but also its comprehensiveness. Precisely because accessibility and ambiguity are present in every aspect of the production—the subject of the show, Bowie's appearance, the lyrics, his singing, the music—Bowie raises role playing from simple novelty to art. This quality has made him one of the unique talents of the rock era. Bowie was also one of the most influential musicians of the decade. The "lean, clean" sound of "Hang On to Yourself" was a model for punk and new wave musicians; indeed, Glen Matlock of the Sex Pistols remarked that "Hang On to Yourself" influenced "God Save the Queen."

Ziggy was Bowie's first and most outrageous persona. For the rest of his career, he has continually reinvented himself in a variety of guises, all markedly different from the others, including "plastic soul" man and techno-pop avant-gardist. Bowie has been rock's ultimate poseur. And that has been his art: assuming so many different personas—not only in appearance and manner, but also in music—that he has made a mystery of his real self. Given Bowie's constantly changing roles during the course of his career, it is small wonder that he has been the most successful film actor among post-Elvis rock stars.

Stretching Rock's Boundaries

Mitchell and Bowie approach art from two different directions: intimate, personal music versus gaudy theater. In Mitchell's case, the art grows out of her gifts as both lyricist and songwriter: the imagination and individuality of words and music and their synergistic integration. Her work ranks with the best popular songs of the century, and they invite comparison with the art songs of classical music. Although Bowie's music also displays craft and imagination, what stands out with *Ziggy Stardust* is the boldness of the premise and the theatricality of the result.

Rock's deepest immersion in art lasted about a decade, from 1966 (the year in which the Beach Boys' *Pet Sounds* and Frank Zappa's *Freak Out* were released) to the mid-seventies, when enthusiasm for the various **art rock** explorations seemed to wane. It was as if once rock had established its cultural credibility, it was time to move in other directions.

LISTENING CUE · **"Hang On to Yourself" (1972),** David Bowie. Bowie, vocal.

STYLE Glam rock · **FORM** Verse/Chorus

Listen For . . .

INSTRUMENTATION
Lead and backup vocals, lead and rhythm guitar, electric bass, drums, handclaps, synthesizer

PERFORMANCE STYLE
Bowie's varied vocal timbres; heavy distortion on rhythm guitar, whiney lead guitar sound on riff

RHYTHM
Fast, insistent rock beat periodically reinforced by guitar and drums; rhythmic play = syncopated guitar chords, active irregular bass line, occasional "extra" beats

MELODY
Abundance of riffs in verse and chorus

TEXTURE
Sharp contrasts in texture between verse and chorus, mainly because of shift in dynamics, timekeeping, contrasting riffs, different timbres, and busy bass line in chorus

Remember . . .

PROTO-PUNK
Loud, repeated power chords played on guitar with some distortion, in a basic rock rhythm and at a fast tempo; these are salient features of punk style. They inform basic feel of song throughout.

HOOKS
Loaded with instrumental (e.g., whiny guitar riff) and vocal hooks, which serve narrative of album/stage show (making the band appealing).

SOPHISTICATED FEATURES
Several sophisticated features not customarily found in straightforward rock (frequent shifts in mood, occasional addition of extra beats, sporadically active bass lines, and Bowie's ever-shifting vocal timbres) = song about a rock band rocking out, rather than simply a good rock song.

Listen to this selection in CourseMate.

CHAPTER 58
Steely Dan and the Art of Recording

In 1959, the National Academy of Recording Arts and Sciences began presenting a Grammy Award for the "Best Engineered Album, Non-Classical." The award is given to one or more engineers for their work on a particular record date. The first winner of the award was Ted Keep, for his work on the novelty hit "The Chipmunk Song." Subsequent winners include the engineers responsible for *Sgt. Pepper* and *Abbey Road.* The only act whose recordings have won four awards is Steely Dan: Their engineers won the award in 1978, 1979, 1982, and 2001.

STEELY DAN

© Michael Ochs Archives/Getty Images

Steely Dan

The pursuit of studio perfection is just one of the qualities that distinguishes Steely Dan. Although it began as a band, Steely Dan became a popular and critically acclaimed act only after its two creative minds, keyboardist Donald Fagen (b. 1948) and bassist Walter Becker (b. 1950), dissolved the group and retained the name to label their studio-driven brainchild.

Becker and Fagen met at Bard College, where they played together regularly in a number of bands, including the Leather Canary. After Fagen graduated, they moved to New York, where they joined the backup band for Jay and the Americans. While in New York, they met producer Gary Katz, who would eventually invite them to Los Angeles to sign them up with ABC Records—first as songwriters, then as a working band. At ABC, they met recording engineer Roger Nichols; Nichols would record all of their music. On recordings, Becker and Fagen began using the cream of Los Angeles studio musicians, most of whom had extensive jazz experience. After 1974, Steely Dan became a studio band, in order to better realize Becker and Fagen's distinctive musical vision.

LISTENING CUE · "Peg" (1977), Walter Becker and Donald Fagen. Steely Dan.

STYLE Jazz-influnced pop rock • **FORM** Verse/chorus (with two statements of verse)

Listen For . . .

INSTRUMENTATION
Lead and backup vocals, electric guitars, keyboards, lyricon, electric bass, drums, extra percussion

RHYTHM
Sixteen-beat rhythm at bright tempo; highly syncopated riffs in both vocal and instrumental sections

MELODY
Riff-based vocals; angular lines in instrumental intro and interludes

HARMONY
Sophisticated version of twelve-bar blues progression

TEXTURE
Dense texture, with numerous melodically interesting parts behind vocal

Remember . . .

WORDS VS. MUSIC
Clever, ironic lyrics with virtually no apparent connection to the music

FORMAL IMAGINATION
Conventional verse/chorus form, but verse is hip twelve-bar blues form and chorus has rich harmony, in instruments and backup vocals.

INFUSION OF JAZZ VALUES
Evident in rich, varied harmony; rhythmic play; angular instrumental lines; virtuosic playing

Listen to this selection in CourseMate.

It's difficult to describe their "style," because each of their songs seems so different from the next. Among their hits is an electronically enhanced "cover" of Duke Ellington's 1927 recording of "East St. Louis Toodle-oo." The three constants in their music seem to be impeccable production, stream-of-consciousness lyrics that offer slices of life in Los Angeles, and sophisticated, distinctive musical settings. There is often a jarring incongruity between the lyrics and the often-complex music to which they are set. It is apparent in songs like their 1977 hit "Peg," one of the tracks from *Aja,* their sixth album and one of the first recordings to be certified platinum; *Aja* would win a Grammy for best engineered nonclassical recording.

The lyric of "Peg" presents a fragmentary account of a film star on the rise, told by someone who knew her when, but who is probably on the outside looking in now. It conveys a bittersweet mood; whatever connection he had with Peg has dissolved now that her career is on the way up.

Although many of their fans have spent long hours trying to decode the lyrics to Steely Dan songs, the exercise seems ultimately beside the point, because the songs are mainly about the music. More than anything else, the lyrics serve as window dressing, to entice those listeners who find lyrics important, or at least a necessary point of entry into the song. The lyrics are hip and provocative—Fagen was an English major, and he and Becker shared a strong interest in Beat literature. But there is not the sense of connection between words and music that has informed so much of the music that we have heard.

The reason may well be Becker and Fagen's abiding interest in jazz, a largely instrumental music. Jazz values, such as melodic and harmonic complexity, rhythmic play, virtuosity, imagination, permeate their music, independently of the lyrics. In "Peg," the instrumental introduction evokes the angular lines and rich harmonies of bebop, while the harmony under the verse of the song is a clever reworking of a twelve-bar blues progression. Throughout the song, there is extensive rhythmic play among the rhythm instruments, especially the bass. At the same time, in its overall design the song follows the familiar rock-era verse/chorus pattern, and the chorus has a hook carved from a single, richly harmonized melody note: "Peg."

With their particular mix of provocative lyrics, accessible sounds, rhythms, and riffs, jazz influence, and perfectionist approach to recording, Steely Dan was one of a kind. In their music and their attitude toward music making, they were without any real precedent, and no band has really followed their lead. Becker and Fagen parted ways in 1981. Twelve years later, they came together, resurrected the Steely Dan name, and began recording and touring again. They remain active and productive through the early years of the twenty-first century: *Two Against Nature* won four Grammy Awards in 2001, including top album.

UNIT 13

LOOKING BACK, LOOKING AHEAD
A Decade of Transition

THE MUSIC PRESENTED in this unit has at least two things in common. It was created in the early and mid-1970s, and it charted. Only *Ziggy Stardust* and Joni Mitchell's *Blue* failed to reach the top ten. *Blue* reached No. 15 and eventually went platinum. *Ziggy Stardust* reached No. 5 in the United Kingdom, although it barely made the charts in the states; it too would go platinum.

From this short list, we can infer some of the major changes in rock and the industry that supported it. First, and in many ways most important, rock had become a bigger business. Listeners bought more albums (on vinyl, cassette, or eight-track) than singles, which meant that the potential profits were greater, but so were the potential risks. Recording became an art, a craft, and an expensive process: higher quality, higher risk, and higher reward. The platinum record (1,000,000 units sold) became an industry yardstick in 1976. Similarly, concerts were often spectacular events; stadiums and arenas were common venues.

Those making money in the music business worked to reduce risk. Album-oriented radio was an attempt to homogenize musical taste in an increasingly diverse environment. Cross-promotion between touring and recording packaged the artist and his product. Safety (performing the songs on the current recording) replaced spontaneity, except in the case of the Grateful Dead and a few other acts.

The commercially dominant music lost its cutting edge. Evolution—the continuing development of the breakthrough advances of the 1960s—replaced revolution; craft replaced discovery. The results were in some ways more satisfying. Typically, the songs and their settings are more polished; the performances are more skilled. But the excitement of encountering something startlingly new occurred far less frequently in the early 1970s than it did just a half-decade earlier.

The edge in the music of the seventies came from outside: funk, reggae, disco, and punk would reshape the music scene in the latter part of the decade.

New Trends of the Late 1970s

UNIT

14

UNIT 14

CBGB was a small club located in the Bowery section of New York City. Originally, it was the bar in the Palace Hotel. By 1973, the year that CBGB opened, the hotel had gone from palatial to poverty stricken. It had become a cheap rooming house for the alcoholics and druggies who inhabited the neighborhood.

The full and creative name of the club is CBGB & OMFUG—Country, Blue Grass, and Blues, and Other Music for Uplifting Gormandizers. Owner Hilly Kristal's original plan was to book those kinds of acts into his new club. However, one day Patti Smith, who had heard about the club from some of her biker friends, went over to ask Hilly to book her boyfriend Tom Verlaine's band. Kristal hired the band—Richard Hell, Richard Lloyd, and Tom Verlaine of Television—for a gig, followed by another with another newly formed band, the Ramones. Neither date attracted much of a crowd.

Nevertheless, Kristal persevered and promoted. After some success with Patti Smith early in 1975, he decided to present "A Festival of the Top 40 New York Rock Bands." He spent a lot of money on advertising and scheduled it in the summer to coincide with the Newport Jazz Festival, a big-time event. It was a gamble that paid off. Critics came to hear the bands, and the audience for punk exploded overnight.

Venues like CBGB recalled the early years of rock and roll, when crowds typically numbered in the hundreds rather than the thousands drawn by the top rock and rhythm and blues acts of the seventies. The punk and new wave music that came from such clubs represented a grassroots movement that hearkened back to rock's early years. It was also one of the most influential new directions in rock.

Punk was one of several outsider styles that emerged in the 1970s. Disco, like punk, took shape in New York clubs; reggae became the new sound of Jamaican music in the early 1970s; funk could be heard wherever George Clinton landed his mothership.

The images we have of these styles—the Ramones, with T-shirts and sunglasses, making a big noise in a small club; the glitter of the disco ball and the platform shoes of disco dancers; Rastafarian dreadlocks; the outrageous outfits worn by George Clinton and the members of his bands, Parliament and Funkadelic—parallel the considerable musical differences.

None of these styles carved out and kept a dominant share of the popular music market. Disco was the most commercially successful style, but among disco acts, only the Bee Gees and Donna Summer sustained any kind of chart presence. For the most part, all of these styles were outside the commercial loop. Nevertheless, all profoundly influenced the music of the late 1970s, 1980s, and beyond.

CHAPTER 59
Funk

Like *blues, jazz, rock, soul,* and *rap, funk* is a one-syllable word from African-American culture that began as nonmusical slang, then found its way into music, and eventually became a style label.

"Funk" originally targeted not the ears but the nose. As far back as the late eighteenth century, *funky* meant foul or unpleasant; a person who neglected to bathe for several days usually gave off a funky odor. Over time it acquired another meaning: hip. Stylish clothes were "funky threads." When James Brown sings, "Ain't It Funky Now," he is referring to the ambience, not the smell.

The terms "funk" and "funky" came into popular music through jazz. Beginning in the mid-fifties, *funk* referred to a simpler, more blues-oriented style—a "return to roots" and a departure from the complexities of hard bop. By the sixties, it had also come to mean soulful. (It also retained the other meanings; context and delivery determined which meaning was appropriate.) By the early seventies, **funk** had come to identify a particularly rhythmic strain of black music.

From Soul to Funk: Sly and the Family Stone

The path from soul to funk went through James Brown; Brown was the "father of funk" as well as the "godfather of soul." Funk musicians built their music on both the basic concept of Brown's music and many of its key features. However, it was Sly and the Family Stone who played the key role in the transition from soul to funk.

The band was the brainchild of Sly Stone (born Sylvester Stewart, 1944), a disc jockey turned producer and bandleader. More than any other band of the era, Sly and the Family Stone preached integration. The lineup included two of Stone's siblings (his brother Freddie and sister Rosie), Cynthia Robinson on trumpet, and several others, including trend-setting bassist Larry Graham. There were blacks and whites, and women as well as men.

In a series of hits spanning a five-year period (1968–1972), Sly and the Family Stone created an exuberant new sound. We hear it in "Thank You (Falettinme Be Mice Elf Agin)," which reached the top of the charts in January 1970. The music of James Brown is the direct antecedent of this song and this style. Like Brown's music, there is a groove built up from multiple layers of riffs, played by rhythm and horns. There is no harmonic movement—everything

LISTENING CUE • **"Thank You (Falettinme Be Mice Elf Agin)" (1970),** Sylvester Stewart. Sly and the Family Stone.

STYLE Proto-funk • **FORM** Open, with chorus

Listen For . . .

INSTRUMENTATION
Vocals (group singing most of the time), electric bass, electric guitar, drums, keyboards, and horns (trumpet and saxophone)

RHYTHM
Moderate tempo; rock rhythm with sharp backbeat; many layers of rhythmic activity, including several double-time (based on rhythm twice as fast as rock beat) rhythmic figures. Almost everything is syncopated.

MELODY
Repetitive melodies made up of short riffs in both the verse and the chorus

HARMONY
One chord throughout the entire song

TEXTURE
Dense, layered texture, made up of riffs in rhythm instruments and horns underneath the vocal. Texture remains much the same throughout the song.

Remember . . .

DARK LYRICS, UPBEAT MUSIC
Words and music = conflicting messages? Party-time groove versus sobering portraits of ghetto life

EMPHASIS ON THE GROOVE
Focus on rhythm and texture; harmony = one chord; melody = repeated riffs

NEW BASS SOUNDS
New, more percussive style: string plucked, slapped, or thumped

BRIDGE FROM JAMES BROWN TO FUNK
Common threads include the great groove, static harmony, and percussive sounds.

Listen to this selection in CourseMate.

Sly & The Family Stone perform on the TV show *The Midnight Special*, 1971.

happens over one chord, and the vocal part is intermittent, with long pauses between phrases.

The most direct antecedent for complex rhythms over static harmony is found in James Brown's music. However, the sound is much denser and more active than that heard in "Papa's Got a Brand New Bag." Although the drummer marks off a rock beat along with the backbeat, the underlying rhythmic feel of the song is twice as fast. This new rhythmic foundation is what is now often called a **sixteen-beat rhythm.** We sense this faster-moving layer in virtually all the other parts: the opening bass riff, the guitar and horn riffs, and—most explicitly—in the "CHUCK-a-puck-a" vocalization. The more active texture opens up many more rhythmic patterns that can conflict with the beat.

There is a spontaneous aspect to the sound, as if it grows out of a jam over the basic groove. It is this quality that gives the song (and Stone's music) its distinctive looseness—looseness that implores listeners to "dance to the music."

Social Commentary and Seductive Grooves

If we just listen to Sly's music, it can hypnotize us with its contagious rhythm. However, when we consider the words—the opening lines of the lyric are "Lookin' at the devil, grinnin' at his gun/Fingers start shakin', I begin to run"—we sense that the band is laughing to keep from crying, or burning down the house. As with many other Sly and the Family Stone songs, there is a strong political and social message. We sense that the music is the buffer between the band and society, a restraint against violent activism.

This is our first example of what would become a growing trend in Afro-centric music, from the United States and abroad: powerful lyrics over infectious rhythms. There is an apparent contradiction between the sharp social commentary in the lyrics and the seduction of the beat. They seem to be operating at cross-purposes: full attention and response versus surrender to the groove. Perhaps that's so, but it's also possible to interpret this apparent conflict in other ways. One is to view the music as a tool to draw in listeners, to expose them to the message of the words. Another is to understand the music as a means of removing the sting of the conditions described in the lyrics: Lose yourself in the music, to avoid simply losing it.

Sly and the Family Stone became popular after the assassination of Martin Luther King, Jr., and after the backlash from the civil rights movement had built up steam. Although civil rights legislation removed much of the governmental support for the racial inequities in American life, it did not eliminate prejudice or racial hatred. The lyrics of this and other songs by Sly and the Family Stone speak to that.

The music provided one way to escape the pain of prejudice. Drugs were another. Sly Stone used them to excess and torpedoed his career in the process. He became increasingly unreliable, often not showing up for engagements; promoters stopped booking his band. Once again, drugs had silenced a truly innovative voice.

The influence of Stone's innovations is evident in a wide range of music from the seventies and beyond—directly in styles like the art/funk jazz fusion of Herbie Hancock and the film music of Curtis Mayfield, and indirectly in styles like disco. However, it led most directly to funk, especially the music of George Clinton.

George Clinton and Funk

George Clinton (b. 1940) was the mastermind behind two important funk bands, Parliament and Funkadelic. While still a teen, he formed the Parliaments, but as a doo-wop group. They signed with Motown in 1964 but did not break through. When Clinton left Motown, he had to relinquish the Parliaments name, so he formed Funkadelic while battling Motown to reclaim the name. Funkadelic represented a major change of direction. As the group's name implies, it brought together funk and psychedelic rock: James Brown and Sly Stone meet Jimi Hendrix. When Clinton regained control of the Parliament name in 1974, he used two names for the same band.

He recorded guitar-oriented material under the Funkadelic name and more polished horn-section material with vocal harmonies under Parliament's. This enabled the two "bands" to perform on one stage at one time.

The formation of Funkadelic signaled Clinton's transformation into Dr. Funkenstein (he also referred to himself as Maggot Overlord); the title of his 1970 album *Free Your Mind . . . And Your Ass Will Follow* shows another side of his funky sense of humor.

Although Clinton certainly enjoyed being provocative and playing with words, there is in many of his songs a sense that he too is laughing to keep from crying. He tucks his darker messages inside humorous packages set to a good-time groove. When he tells listeners to "Tear the roof off the sucker," he could be urging them to party hard—or to riot.

Without question there's an escapist aspect to his work: Clinton's many aliases, the flamboyant costumes he and his bands wore in performance, and the sci-fi world he created (the "Mothership Connection") evidence that. Clinton seems to invite listeners to become "one nation under a groove"; surrendering to the rhythm offers momentary relief from the pain of daily life as a black person in the United States. We experience this in his 1976 hit "Tear the Roof Off the Sucker (Give Up the Funk)," which his band Parliament recorded.

The song shows Clinton's debt to James Brown and Sly and the Family Stone, and the ways in which his music went beyond theirs. Clinton's most obvious debt to Brown is in personnel. After 1975 his roster included three significant James Brown alumni: bassist Bootsy Collins, saxophonist Maceo Parker, and trombonist Fred Wesley. They were key members of his large band, which included as many as twelve musicians at a time. As a result, the sound of Clinton's bands is fuller than either James Brown's or Sly Stone's because there are more instruments and all of them are busy.

Like Brown and Stone, Clinton creates the groove over static harmony: this is a one-chord song. The texture is dense: there are riffs and sustained chords from both horns and keyboards, high obbligato lines from a synthesizer, an active but open bass line, lots of percussion, and voices—both the choral effect of the backup singers and Clinton's proto-rap. Clinton gives Bootsy Collins a chance to stretch out. Collins's lines are active, syncopated, and melodic, calling attention to the increasingly prominent role of the bass in this branch of black music.

The rhythm has a sixteen-beat feel over the eight-beat rhythm laid down in the drum part. Clinton's rap-like introduction moves at this faster rhythm, and so do the horn riffs, the bass line, and the guitar parts. This is a denser version of Stone's proto-funk style. It is a darker sound as well, mainly because of Clinton's voice and the prominence of the bass.

Clinton's various bands ran into trouble in the late seventies, primarily because of bad money management, sloppy business practices, and drug abuse. By 1981, Clinton had consolidated the two versions of the band under one name, the P-Funk All Stars.

In its purest form, funk never crossed over to the pop mainstream. "Tear the Roof Off the Sucker," which was Parliament's highest-charting song, only reached No. 15. It was more successful commercially in pop/funk fusions, such as those by Earth, Wind & Fire.

LISTENING CUE • **"Tear the Roof Off the Sucker (Give Up the Funk)" (1976),** George Clinton, Bootsy Collins, and Jerome Brailey. Parliament.

STYLE Funk • **FORM** Open

Listen For . . .

INSTRUMENTATION
Voices, electric bass, drums, conga drum, electric guitars, synthesizers, and horns

RHYTHM
Moderate tempo; basic beat is a rock rhythm, but many parts move twice as fast as rock (the opening "rap," the bass patterns, and the conga part). Lots of syncopation in the instrumental background.

MELODY
Melody derived from blues-inflected modal scale. First melody: long, unbroken descending line. Second melody: short riffs. Third melody: long sustained phrase. All three melodies are simply repeated several times; there is no development.

HARMONY
No harmonic change: decorative harmonies (in voices and synthesizer) derived from modal scale

TEXTURE
Dense texture, with voices, percussion, bass, sustained chords on horns and synthesizers, and high synthesizer lines and chords.

Strong contrast from section to section ("Give up the funk" = voices, bass doubling the melody, and percussion)

Remember . . .

RHYTHM OVER MELODY
The rhythm, which features complex interactions among the various instruments, is more interesting than the melody, which doesn't develop at all.

THE BASS AND BLACK MUSIC
Completely liberated bass: little timekeeping; instead, intricate patterns and riffs, occasional doubling of melody

IN THE GROOVE/IN THE MOMENT
The only focus is to give up the funk. No story, no musical journey toward a goal.

ROAD TO RAP
The emphasis on rhythm and the chantlike melodies are a prelude to rap and techno.

Listen to this selection in CourseMate.

Earth, Wind & Fire and a Black Music Synthesis

From the time Jerry Wexler coined the term, "rhythm and blues" has also embraced not only rhythmic and bluesy music but also black pop, which emphasizes melody and harmony over strong rhythm and deep blues feeling. During the 1950s and 1960s, black pop and rhythmic and bluesy R&B inhabited largely discrete worlds: doo-wop and Motown versus big beat music, electric blues and soul. James Brown didn't sing black pop; Diana Ross didn't sing soul.

Few artists have successfully fused these two streams. Among the few are two truly great performers: Ray Charles and Aretha Franklin. Both brought soul into pop, and vice versa. In the early seventies, Marvin Gaye and Stevie Wonder moved easily between funk and romantic pop. In the latter part of the decade, Earth, Wind & Fire joined them.

Maurice White (b. 1941), the founder and leader of Earth, Wind & Fire, named the group after his astrological sign. He is a Sagittarian: the sign contains three of the four elements—earth, wind, and fire—but not water.

After a successful career as a session drummer at Chess Records and with jazz pianist Ramsey Lewis, White set out in 1969 to create a new kind of group. By 1971, they were Earth, Wind & Fire. The next year, they moved to Columbia (now Sony) Records and continued to climb up the charts. By 1975, they had become one of the elite groups of the decade, both on record and in live performance, and remained a top act through the end of the decade.

Earth, Wind & Fire was a big group. In this respect, they were in step with other black acts, such as George Clinton's funk bands, Barry White's Love Unlimited Orchestra, and the various Philadelphia groups. As many as fourteen musicians could be on stage. The nucleus of the band was White, who sang and played a kalimba, an African thumb piano; his brother Verdine (b. 1951) on bass; and singer Philip Bailey (b. 1951). In words and music, the group projected a positive attitude, as we hear in their first No. 1 single, the Grammy-winning 1975 hit "Shining Star."

In "Shining Star," Earth, Wind & Fire juxtapose funk and more melodious music within a single song: the verse sets up a complex funk-style groove over a single chord, while the refrain underpins a more coherent, riff-based melodic line with rapidly changing harmonies. Rich harmony helps project the optimistic, hopeful mood of the title and refrain: "Shining star for you to see, what your life can truly be."

Earth, Wind & Fire's ability to meld funk-like grooves with more melodious material is one key to their crossover success. This versatility is evident in the range of their hit songs, from soulful ballads like "That's the Way of the World" to funkish grooves like "Serpentine Fire." Few seventies acts were at home in both funk and black pop styles; fewer still succeeded in blending the two. Earth, Wind & Fire was one of them.

The influence of funk was far more extensive than its market share. Its more active and complex rhythms bled into much of the new music of the latter part of the 1970s and early 1980s. It's apparent in much pop-oriented black music, and even more in disco. Much disco employed a more obvious form of funk rhythms. However, it was rap that was most directly influenced by funk; indeed, with the advent of digital technology, rappers sampled Clinton's music mercilessly.

LISTENING CUE · **"Shining Star" (1975),** Maurice White, Larry Dunn, Philip Bailey. Earth, Wind & Fire.

STYLE: Funk/black pop fusion • **FORM:** Verse/chorus

Listen For . . .

INSTRUMENTATION
Lead and backup vocals, trumpets, saxophones, keyboards, electric guitars, bass, drums, additional percussion

RHYTHM
Extensive syncopation over active sixteen-beat rhythm, mainly in guitar and drums

MELODY
Both verse and chorus built mainly from repeated riffs

HARMONY
One chord in the verse, quickly changing percussion in chorus

TEXTURE
Dense, with numerous active syncopated lines

Remember . . .

INSPIRATIONAL MESSAGE
Both words and music emphasize the power of positive thinking.

FUNK/POP MIX
The verse of this song is Earth, Wind & Fire's take on funk. By contrast, the chorus is more melodic and has active harmony, although it retains the groove.

SIXTEEN-BEAT RHYTHM
It is marked in the guitar and conga drum. Other rhythms map onto this faster rhythm; most are syncopated.

STACKS OF RIFFS
Numerous riffs in the horns and rhythm instruments help create a dense texture.

Listen to this selection in CourseMate.

CHAPTER 60

Reggae

Reggae is Jamaica's best-known music. It took shape in Jamaica around 1970 and found a second home in the United Kingdom by mid-decade. Since its emergence, reggae has spoken to and for Jamaicans. Its most powerful messages reverberated with the legacy of colonialism following political independence. By the end of the seventies, reggae was known throughout the world.

In this chapter, we explore the place of reggae in Jamaican culture, highlight the influence of Rastafarianism and rhythm and blues on the style, and identify key musical features of reggae through the music of Jimmy Cliff and Bob Marley.

Jamaican Independence and Social Unrest

Most Jamaicans are of African descent—about 90 percent at the turn of the twenty-first century—and most trace their roots back to slavery; like the United States, Cuba, and Brazil, Jamaica was a destination for the slave traders. More than 600,000 slaves arrived in Jamaica between 1665 and 1838, the year in which the slave trade ended. British colonial rule continued for more than a century. Great Britain gradually transferred authority to Jamaicans, with the final step—independence—taken in 1962. Redress of the economic and social inequities of colonialism, however, did not keep pace with the political changes.

One result was a great deal of social unrest in the sixties. "Rude boys," disenfranchised young black Jamaicans who grew up in the most disadvantaged sections of Kingston, personified the violent dimension of this unrest. They were sharp dressers and often carried sharp knives and guns. For many Jamaicans, including the police, they were outlaws. Others, however, saw them as heroes, much as the James Brothers and Billy the Kid were heroes to earlier generations of Americans or as today's gangsta rappers are to some young people. Another group with a much longer history of confrontation with white authorities were Rastafarians.

Rastafarianism

Rastafarianism was an important consequence of Marcus Garvey's crusade to elevate the status of people of African descent. Garvey, born in Jamaica, agitated for black power in the United States during the 1920s in response to the dire poverty and discrimination that the vast majority of blacks living in the Americas faced. His efforts blended church and state; even as he pressed for an African homeland to which former slaves could return (it never materialized), he prophesied that Christ would come again as a black man. After serving half of a five-year sentence in an Atlanta prison, he was exiled from the United States and returned to Jamaica.

Rastafarians claimed that Garvey's prophesy had been fulfilled. Jesus had indeed come again, in the person of Haile Selassie (Prince Ras Tafari), the emperor of Ethiopia. Selassie claimed lineage back to King Solomon, which Rastafarians have taken as further proof of Selassie's divine status. In line with Selassie's personal genealogy, Rastafarians also claim to be descendants of the twelve tribes of Israel.

These beliefs, which have never come together as "official" doctrine—as has happened in organized religions—are the religious dimension of Rastafarians' efforts to promote a more positive image of Africa and Africans. This has largely come from within the movement.

For those on the outside, the most vivid impressions of Rastafarianism are images, smells, and sounds: dreadlocks, ganja (marijuana, which they ingest as part of their religious practice), and music. To Jamaican music, they gave a sound—Rastafarian drums—and reggae superstar Bob Marley.

Rhythm and Blues and Jamaican Popular Music

The influence of rhythm and blues on Jamaican music is in part a matter of geography. Kingston, the capital city, is just over 500 miles from Miami as the crow flies and about 1,000 miles from New Orleans. Stations from all over the southern United States were within reach, at least after dark. So it should not surprise us that Jamaicans tuned in their radios to American stations in the years after World War II. For many young Jamaicans, rhythm and blues replaced **mento,** the Jamaican popular music of the early fifties.

Sound systems, the mobile discos so much a part of daily life in Jamaica, offered another way to hear new music from America. Sound systems were trucks outfitted with the musical necessities for a street party: records, turntables, speakers, and a microphone for the DJ. Operators would drive around, pick a place to set up, and begin to play the R&B hits that the enterprising DJs had gone to the United States to fetch.

From Ska to Reggae

By the end of the 1950s, Jamaican musicians had begun to absorb rhythm and blues and transform it into new kinds of music. **Ska,** the first new style, emerged around 1960;

it would remain the dominant Jamaican sound through the first part of the decade. Ska's most distinctive feature is a strong afterbeat: a strong, crisp *chunk* on the latter part of each beat. This was a Jamaican take on the shuffle rhythm heard in so much fifties R&B. It kept the long/short rhythm of the shuffle but reversed the pattern of emphasis within each beat. In the shuffle rhythm, the note that falls on the beat gets the weight; the afterbeat is lighter. In ska it is just the opposite, at times to the extent that the note on the beat is absent—there is just the afterbeat. It remains the aural trademark of early ska.

As ska evolved into **rock steady** in the latter half of the sixties, musicians added a backbeat layer over the afterbeats. This created a core rhythm of afterbeats at two speeds, slow and fast: which soon became the characteristic off-beat *ka-CHUN-ka* rhythm of **reggae.** Because the bass had no role in establishing and maintaining this rhythm, bass players were free to create their own lines, and the best ones did. As rock steady evolved further into reggae, other rhythmic layers were added. The absence of beat marking, the mid-range reggae rhythm, the free-roaming bass, and the complex interplay among the many instruments produced a buoyant rhythm, as we hear in Jimmy Cliff's "The Harder They Come."

Jimmy Cliff and the Sound of Reggae

Jimmy Cliff (born James Chambers in 1948) was one of reggae's first stars. By the time he landed the lead role in the 1972 film *The Harder They Come,* he had gained an international reputation as a singer-songwriter. His appearance in the film and the songs that he recorded for the soundtrack cemented his place in popular music history. In *The Harder They Come,* Cliff plays Ivan O. Martin, a musician who becomes a gangster. Although his character is loosely based on a real person from the 1940s, Cliff's title song brings the story into the present. The lyric resonates with overtones of social injustice and police oppression and brutality even as it outlines how the character will respond: "I'm gonna get my share now of what's mine."

The music sends a different message. Behind Cliff's vocal is a large rhythm section, with organ playing on the backbeat, another keyboard playing afterbeat chords, guitar and drums marking the rock rhythmic layer, and the bassist playing an active, bouncy, line. Their interaction produces the rich, complex, buoyant reggae rhythm, its most distinctive feature.

In "The Harder They Come," we are again faced with the seeming contradiction between words and music. The lyrics are dark, even menacing, but the music nevertheless brings a smile to one's face and a body movement somewhere. This is happy music, in its rhythm, in the lilt in Cliff's voice, in the form (a carbon copy of Motown's verse/bridge/chorus formula), and in the gently undulating melody. We are left to ponder: Is the music the candy that entices us to listen to the message of the lyrics, or a way to forget for the moment the situation that the lyrics depict? What we do know is that many of the songs that put reggae on the international musical map embedded hard messages within the music's infectious rhythms and sounds.

LISTENING CUE · "The Harder They Come" (1972), Jimmy Cliff. Cliff, vocal.

STYLE Reggae · **FORM** Verse/chorus

Listen For . . .

INSTRUMENTATION
Lead vocal, two keyboards (with organ sounds), piano, electric bass, drums, electric guitar

PERFORMANCE STYLE
Cliff's vocal style, with its use of falsetto and melisma, seems inspired by sixties American music. Choked guitar sound.

RHYTHM
Moderate tempo; rock-based rhythm with distinctive reggae feel; considerable syncopation and lots of activity, some of it double-time (moving twice as fast as the rock rhythm)

MELODY
Long phrases, which are repeated, in the verse and the first part of the chorus (bridge); the title phrase is a short riff.

TEXTURE
Densely layered, with several chord instruments, plus busy bass and drums behind the vocal

Remember . . .

REGGAE AS PROTEST MUSIC
Jamaican people's music: It came from them, and it spoke to them and for them, in direct, uncompromising language.

REGGAE RHYTHM
The interaction of the two organs produces the distinctive ka-CHUN-ka rhythm of reggae heard mainly in two organ parts.

WORDS AND MUSIC/WORDS VS. MUSIC
Combines lyrics that describe the harsh conditions in which the black underclass lives with irresistible, joyous music

Listen to this selection in CourseMate.

Like the music of Sly and the Family Stone and George Clinton, reggae contrasted hard lyrics with happy music. However, reggae was different in that it first became known outside of Jamaica as music with a message. The music of Bob Marley, Jimmy Cliff, Peter Tosh, and other early reggae stars called attention to the social inequities in Jamaica. Moreover, it came at a time when rock had largely forsaken its role as a vehicle for social commentary. Marley would help fill that void, becoming a powerful voice on social issues.

Bob Marley and 1970s Reggae

Bob Marley (1945–1981) began his recording career in the early 1960s; it took off in 1964, after he formed the first edition of his backup group, the Wailers. By the early 1970s, he was extremely popular in Jamaica. A recording contract with Island records propelled him to global stardom.

His success on record and in concert gave him and his country's music unprecedented exposure. For many outside of Jamaica, Bob Marley *was* reggae. Worldwide, he was its most popular artist. His popularity gave him the leverage to work for meaningful change in Jamaican society. He became the decade's most visible spokesperson for peace and brotherhood, carrying the torch of sixties social activism and idealism into the seventies. Much of Marley's music was political: Songs like "I Shot the Sheriff" and "Get Up, Stand Up" are familiar examples.

BOB MARLEY, 1978

However, he periodically displayed a more intimate side. In "Is This Love," Marley speaks one-on-one with a special woman. In keeping with the content and tone of the lyric, the form of this song sprawls lazily through time. The slower layer (marked by a sharp guitar "chunk") is the reference tempo, as it is in most rock steady and reggae songs. The vocal line implies the primacy of slower tempo, especially when Marley sings the title phrase over and over: "Is this love, is this love, is this love, is this love that I'm feelin'?"

The gentle pulsations of the drum and tambourine, prompted by the fast shuffle afterbeat rhythm in the organ

LISTENING CUE • **"Is This Love" (1978),** Bob Marley.

STYLE Reggae • **FORM** Verse/two-part chorus (first part contains title phrase)

Listen For . . .

INSTRUMENTATION
Lead, backup vocals, several percussion instruments, including Rastafarian drums, bass, guitars, horns (at end) and keyboards

RHYTHM
Shuffle-based reggae rhythm at moderately slow tempo: light beatkeeping and ka-*chun*-ka pattern formed by offbeat/backbeat keyboard chords
Slow-moving vocal line, free bass line over characteristic reggae rhythm

MELODY
Memorable extended instrumental riffs recur throughout; vocal line has widely spaced repeated riff in verse; flowing

TEXTURE
Rich texture, concentrated in mid-range (bass moves freely)

Remember . . .

LOVE SONG
Song about love, not politics, sung at a leisurely tempo

REGGAE RHYTHM
Rich rhythmic texture with light percussive beat keeping, flowing melody, distinctive backbeat/afterbeat ka-*chun*-ka rhythm in keyboards, free bass line

BUOYANT SOUND
Activity concentrated in mid-range, with keyboard and percussion providing steady but not beat-heavy rhythm, serves as musical cushion for vocal line.

Listen to this selection in CourseMate.

(rather than the even, rock-like afterbeats in "The Harder They Come"), keep the rhythm afloat, while the vocal parts—Marley's slow-moving melody and the sustained harmonies of the "I-Threes"—and in-and-out bass slow the beat down to a speed below typical body rhythms—even the heartbeat at rest or the pace of a relaxed stroll. As a result, the rhythm of the song is buoyant and lazy at the same time. All of this evokes a feeling of languid lovemaking in the tropics, a perfect musical counterpoint to the lyric of the song.

Reggae as an International Music

Reggae's popularity outside of Jamaica owed much to the heavy concentrations of Jamaicans in England. As part of the transition from colonialism, Great Britain opened its doors—or at least its ports—to people from its colonies. More arrived from the Caribbean than from any other former colony—around 250,000 in the late fifties and early sixties. By the end of the sixties, the British government had put into effect legislation that severely restricted immigration. By that time, however, those Jamaicans already in England re-created much of their culture. All the Jamaican music of the sixties and the seventies found a supportive audience in England, among Jamaicans eager for this link to their homeland and among British whites intrigued by this quite different music.

For a new generation of British musicians in search of "real" music, reggae (and ska) provided an at-home alternative to the blues. Eric Clapton, who had immersed himself so deeply in the blues during the sixties, led the way with his cover of Marley's "I Shot the Sheriff"; the recording topped the charts in 1974. A wave of new British acts, among them the Clash, Elvis Costello, UB40, and the Police, wove the fresh sounds of reggae into their music.

Reggae's path to America seems unnecessarily roundabout. The music didn't find an audience in the United States until after it had become popular in England. Once known, however, its influence was even more diverse—and more divorced from the music's social context. For example, we hear echoes of the distinctive reggae rhythm in the Eagles' huge 1977 hit "Hotel California."

Jamaican music influenced African-American music in two markedly different ways. Black pop musicians used the rhythmic texture of reggae to further liberate the bass from a timekeeping role, beyond advances of Motown and the Philadelphia sound. Because reggae embedded the pulse of a song in its distinctive mid-range rhythms, bass players were free to roam at will, largely independent of a specific rhythmic or harmonic role. Its influence was evident in such songs as "Sexual Healing," Marvin Gaye's 1982 ode to carnal love, and "What's Love Got to Do with It," Tina Turner's 1984 cynical rejection of it.

The other source of influence was not reggae, per se, but a characteristic element of the sound system–based Jamaican street parties. Between songs, DJs delivered a steady stream of patter. Much of it was topical, even personal: They would pick out, and sometimes pick on, people in the crowd that had gathered around. This practice was called **toasting.** It became so popular that Jamaican record producers like Lee "Scratch" Perry began releasing discs in which the B side was simply the A side without the vocal track. The instrumental track would then serve as the musical backdrop for the DJ's toasting—and save the producers some money.

Toasting is a direct forerunner of rap. Kool Herc, a Jamaican who moved to the Bronx as a young teen, brought toasting from Kingston to the streets of New York, where it quickly evolved into hip-hop: Grandmaster Flash, one of the seminal figures in early rap, described Kool Herc as his hero. Rap's first hit, the Sugar Hill Gang's 1979 "Rapper's Delight," is a classic example of the practice: extended raps over a loop of Chic's "Good Times."

CHAPTER 61
Disco

Disco is short for *discothèque. Discothèque* is a French word meaning "record library" (by analogy with *bibliothèque*, meaning "book library"). It came into use during World War II, first as the name of a nightclub—Le Discothèque—then as a code word for underground nightclubs where jazz records were played. Because of the German occupation, these clubs were run like American speakeasies during the Prohibition era.

From Discothèques to Disco

Discothèques survived the war, and after the war became increasingly popular in France. The first of the famous discos was the *Whisky à Gogo* in Paris, which featured American liquors and American dance music, both live and on record. Others sprung up in the postwar years, eventually becoming a favored destination of jet-setters. Discothèques began to open in the United States around 1960. The first was Whisky a Go Go in Chicago, in 1958. The Peppermint Lounge, which Joey Dee and the Starlighters called home and where the rich and famous did the Twist, opened in 1961 in New York City.

"Disco is the best floor show in town."
—Truman Capote

As dance fads like the Twist moved out of the clubs and into mainstream society, the original audience sought out new dance music in different, less exclusive, and less pricey venues. By the end of the sixties, a new club culture was thriving. It was an egalitarian, nonrestrictive environment. The new, danceable black music of the late sixties and early seventies provided the soundtrack: Sly and the Family Stone, Funkadelic, Stevie Wonder, Marvin Gaye, Curtis Mayfield, Barry White, and above all the Philadelphia acts, such as the Spinners, the Stylistics, the O'Jays, and Harold Melvin and the Blue Notes. Clubbers included not only blacks but also Latinos, working-class women, and gays, for whom clubbing had become a welcome chance to come out of the closet and express themselves. Despite the gains of the various "rights" movements in the sixties and seventies, these were still marginalized constituencies.

The Mainstreaming of Disco

By mid-decade, however, **disco** had begun to cross over. Integrated groups like KC and the Sunshine Band, which exploded onto the singles charts in 1975, began making music expressly for discos. *Saturday Night Fever* was the commercial breakthrough for the music. Almost overnight, what had been a largely underground scene briefly became the thing to do.

In New York, the favored venue was Studio 54, a converted theater on 54th Street in Manhattan. It became so popular that crowds clamoring to get in stretched around the corner. It was the place to see and be seen. Writing about Studio 54 at the end of the seventies, Truman Capote noted, "Disco is the best floor show in town. It's very democratic, boys with boys, girls with girls, girls with boys, blacks and whites, capitalists and Marxists, Chinese and everything else, all in one big mix."

Disco and Electronics

Meanwhile, the discothèque scene continued to flourish in Europe. The new element in the music there was the innovative use of synthesizers to create dance tracks. Among the most important musicians in this new domain were Kraftwerk, a two-person German group, and Giorgio Moroder, an Italian-born, Germany-based producer and electronics wizard who provided the musical setting for many of Donna Summer's disco-era hits.

Kraftwerk and Moroder exemplified the increasingly central roles of the producer and of technology. Disco became a producers' music, even more than the girl groups of the sixties. Just as Phil Spector's "wall of sound" was more famous than the singers in front of it, so did the sound of disco belong more to the men creating and mixing the instrumental tracks than the vocalists in the studios. Here, the wall of sound was laced with electronic as well as acoustic instruments. Singers were relatively unimportant and interchangeable; there were numerous one-hit wonders. Donna Summer was an exception.

Donna Summer: The Queen of Disco

If there's one performer whose career embodies disco—its brief history, its geography, and its message—it is Donna Summer (born Donna Adrian Gaines, 1948). Summer grew up in the Boston area and moved to Europe, while in her teens, to pursue a career in musical theater and light opera. While working as a backup vocalist, she met Giorgio Moroder (b. 1940), who would collaborate with her on her major seventies hits. Her first international hit, "Love to Love You Baby," was released in 1975; it was a hit in both the United States and Europe. Summer's erotic moans were the most striking feature of the song. In its graphic evocation of the bedroom experience, it is in spirit an answer to Barry White's seductive songs.

As the song title suggests, "I Feel Love," her next big American hit, also explores the erotic dimension of love, although not as blatantly as the earlier song. Here Summer's deliberately wispy voice floats above Moroder's sea of synthesized sound. Summer's vocal may be the most prominent element of the music, but the background is certainly the more innovative. The innovation begins with Moroder's use of electronic counterparts to a traditional drum set; there isn't one conventional instrument on the track. Even more noteworthy is the idiomatic writing for synthesizers. Moroder creates a rich tapestry of sound by layering in a large quantity of repetitive patterns, some constantly in the foreground, others in the background and often intermittent. None of them really corresponds to traditional rock guitar or bass lines. It is not only the sounds that are novel but also the lines that create the dense texture behind Summer's vocal.

Rhythmically, the song converts the sixteen-beat rhythms of funk and black pop into an accessible dance music by making the beat and the sixteen-beat layer more explicit. From the start, we hear the steady thud of a bass drum–like sound on every beat and an equally steady synthesized percussion sound moving four times the speed of the beat in a mid-range register. Other parts, most obviously the synthesized ascending pattern that runs through the song, also confirm regular rhythms. Compared to previous examples that used this more active rhythm, "I Feel Love" is far less syncopated and much more obvious in its timekeeping. This is certainly due in large part to its use as dance music. The busy rhythms of the accompaniment contrast sharply with Summer's leisurely unfolding vocal line and the slow rate of harmonic change. These two seemingly conflicting messages about time in fact invoke two aspects of the disco scene: the activity of the dancers to the throbbing beat and the endlessness of the experience, as one song mixes into the next. (The abrupt ending of the song suggests its use in a disco: The DJ would fade it away before the end as he brought up the next song.)

Summer's career started before disco went mainstream, then crested during the late seventies. Perhaps anticipating the imminent commercial decline of disco, she took her music in new directions in songs like "Bad Girls." This helped sustain her popularity through the end of the seventies; her last three albums of the decade went No. 1.

Among the most loyal members of Summer's fan base were gays. Their connection to disco took on a public face in the music of the Village People.

The Village People: Disco out of the Closet

The Village People was the brainchild of Jacques Morali, a French producer living in New York. Morali's various accounts of the formation of the Village People are

LISTENING CUE • **"I Feel Love" (1977),** Donna Summer, Giorgio Moroder, and Peter Bellotte. Donna Summer, vocal.

STYLE Disco • **FORM** Two statements of verse/chorus form

Listen For . . .

INSTRUMENTATION
Voice and array of synthesized sounds: bass, percussion, chords, and so on

PERFORMANCE STYLE
Summer's wispy voice vs. bright electronic sounds

RHYTHM
Regular timekeeping at three speeds: beat, 2× beat, and 4× beat; other rhythms unfold slowly.

MELODY
Repeated riff in accompaniment; slow, narrow-ranged vocal line

TEXTURE
Rich texture made up of electronic sounds envelops Summer's vocal.

Remember . . .

ELECTRONIC SOUND WORLD
No conventional instruments; electronic substitutes for percussion, bass, and chord instruments

OBVIOUS RHYTHM
Beat marking in electronic bass drum, low synthesizer riff produces relentless timekeeping at three levels.

WOMAN VS. MACHINE
Contrast between Summer's gradually unfolding vocal line and slow harmonic change and active rhythms in many parts

Listen to this selection in CourseMate.

Portrait of the original members of The Village People (*l–r*) Randy Jones (the cowboy), David Hodo (the construction worker), Felipe Rose (the American Indian), Victor Willis (the cop), Glenn Hughes (the leather man), and Alexander Briley (the G.I.).

conflicting, but what is certain is that he recruited the men who fronted his act literally off the street and in gay clubs.

The public image of the Village People was six guys dressed up as macho stereotypes among gays: the Indian (in full costume, including headdress), the leather man (missing only the Harley), the construction worker, the policeman, the cowboy, and the soldier. These expressions of hyper-maleness were, in effect, gay pinups. Their look was more important than their sound, although after a disastrous appearance on *American Bandstand,* Morali fired five of the six men and replaced them with new recruits.

The whole Village People act was an inside joke. Morali and gay audiences laughed behind their hands while straight America bought their records by the millions and copied the look—mustaches, leather jackets, and the like. Many listeners were not aware of the gay undertone to the lyrics—or if they were, they didn't care.

The group's song "Y.M.C.A.," their biggest hit on the singles charts (No. 2 in 1978), shows the macho men at work. In most cities and towns around the United States, a YMCA (established by the Young Men's Christian Association) is a place for families to participate in an array of activities. Some are athletic—basketball, swimming, and gymnastics—others are social and humanitarian, such as meals for senior citizens. In larger cities YMCAs can also accommodate residents. In cities like New York, these became meeting places for gays.

The lyrics of the song have fun with this situation. Seemingly innocuous lines like "They have everything for men to enjoy/You can hang out with all the boys" take

LISTENING CUE • **"Y.M.C.A." (1978),** Jacques Morali, Henrio Belolo, and Victor Willis. The Village People.

STYLE Disco • **FORM** Verse/Chorus

Listen For . . .

INSTRUMENTATION
Voices (a lead vocal, plus others occasionally reinforcing the lead line), drums, tambourine, handclaps, electric bass, keyboard, violins, and brass (especially trumpets)

RHYTHM
Disco tempo (about 120 beats per minute). Bass drum thuds out the beat; backbeat is also strong.
Melody moves at a moderate pace with some syncopation.
String and brass figurations often move four times as fast as the beat (sixteen-beat speed)

HARMONY
Updated versions of the "Heart and Soul" progression (verse and chorus are slightly different). The progression cycles through the entire song; it never resolves.

TEXTURE
Rich, layered texture: low = bass and bass drum; mid-range = voices, sustained strings, some brass riffs, and percussion sounds; high = brass riffs and string figuration. Always a thick sound.

Remember . . .

CODED LYRIC
NYC YMCA = gay meeting place. Lyric full of inside jokes.

DISCO, A MULTIPLE-MINORITY MUSIC
Disco's original audience included gays, blacks, and Latinos; provoked homophobic and racially prejudiced reactions.

SLICK DANCE MUSIC
Amateurish singing, relentless dance beat, and fancy strings

FUNK, DISCO, AND THE BEAT
Funk and disco are close musical relatives, but the more obvious beat in disco made it more popular.

CONTROL OF THE PRODUCER
With disco the producer assumed the main creative responsibility. Singer(s) were primarily for image.

Listen to this selection in CourseMate.

on a quite different meaning when understood in the context of the Y as a gay gathering place.

The music is quintessential disco. It's apparent in the march-speed tempo, with the beat marked by the bass drum; active rhythms, especially the bass in the chorus and the string figuration; rich orchestration, with strings, oversize rhythm section, and electronic instruments; catchy chorus melody; and repetitive harmony.

Disco: Culture, Reception, and Influence

Although most disco artists came and went—Donna Summer was the biggest star, Chic the most successful band—disco was widely popular during the latter part of the seventies. During that three-year window, it spread from urban dance clubs to the suburbs, and its audience grew considerably. Disco had clear and strong gay associations, as "Y.M.C.A." makes clear, but it was more than music for gays and blacks. In this respect, *Saturday Night Fever* was a slice of life. There were many working-class urban youth who used disco dancing as an outlet.

Disco was more than the music or even the culture that had produced it. For many it became a lifestyle. It was hedonistic: Dancing was simply a prelude to more intimate forms of contact. It was exhibitionistic: Fake Afro wigs; skin-tight, revealing clothes; flamboyant accessories; platform shoes; everything glittering. And it was drug-ridden: With disco, cocaine and Quaaludes became mainstream drugs; the logo for Studio 54 showed the man in the moon ingesting cocaine from a silver spoon.

Reactions against Disco

All this, plus the inevitable stream of mindless disco songs (the ratio of chaff to wheat in any genre is high; disco was no exception), gave disco's detractors plenty of ammunition. They trashed the music and the culture. Ostensibly, it was simply a reaction against disco's many excesses, but there was also a strong homophobic undercurrent. Perhaps the most notorious disco-bashing incident occurred in Chicago during the summer of 1979. Steve Dahl, a disc jockey at a local rock station, organized Disco Demolition Night. Fans who brought a disco record to a Chicago White Sox doubleheader got into the park for 98¢. They spent the first game chanting, "Disco sucks"; after the first game, they made a pile of records in centerfield. An attempted explosion turned into chaos.

Disco and Dance Fads

When disco disappeared from the charts and the radio, there was an "I told you so" response from those who hated it. But in retrospect, it would have been surprising if it had lasted much longer. All the major dance fads in the twentieth century have had short life spans: the Charleston and the Black Bottom in the early 1920s, jitterbugging and Lindy hopping around 1940, the Twist and other rock-and-roll dances around 1960. The Charleston and the Twist were dance fads that caught on somewhat after the introduction of new rhythms: the two-beat foxtrot in the teens and early twenties and the eight-beat rhythm of rock and roll in the fifties. Disco, like the jitterbug, was a dance fad that emerged with the division of popular music into two related rhythmic streams. In the thirties, it was sweet (two-beat) and swing (four-beat). In the seventies, it was rock (eight-beat) and disco (sixteen-beat). The swing and disco eras were brief periods when the more active rhythms of black and black-inspired music became truly popular. In both cases, much of the music was rhythmically more obvious than the music that had spawned it. Many of the hits of the swing era, especially by the white bands, laid down a strong beat but lacked the rhythmic play of music by Count Basie, Duke Ellington, or Benny Goodman. Similarly, disco was more rhythmically straightforward than funk or black pop. This made it accessible to a greater number of dancers but sacrificed musical interest in the process.

The Influence of Disco

It shouldn't be surprising that disco faded away so quickly. It was following much the same path as the other dance fads that signaled the arrival of a new beat. And it should not be surprising that a new beat took root in the music of the 1980s, following disco's demise. In this way, disco was influential, far more so than its brief life span would suggest.

Disco has also had a more underground influence—on two levels. It was, more than any other popular style, the gateway for the wholesale infusion of electronica. And it created a new kind of underground dance-club culture, which would continue through the eighties and flower in the nineties.

CHAPTER 62
Punk

Among Hilly Kristal's first customers at CBGB was Malcolm McLaren, who came to New York in 1974 to attend a boutique fair. Three years earlier, McLaren had opened a clothing boutique in London called Let It Rock, with Vivienne Westwood; it featured vintage and retro styles, as well as custom-made theater costumes. However, McLaren saw himself as a political provocateur. He wanted to be able to thumb his nose at the establishment and make money on it at the same time. McLaren viewed rock music as a vehicle for his politics; bands would make a statement with images as well as sound.

While in New York, McLaren persuaded the New York Dolls, who had just been dropped by Mercury Records, to let him manage them and design their outfits. He costumed them in red leather and had them perform in front of a hammer and sickle. For the Dolls, the shock strategy backfired. The blatant nod to the Soviet Union apparently turned off other labels, and the band broke up the following year. For McLaren, it was simply the prelude to an even bolder statement. After hearing early **punk** bands like the Ramones and the Neon Boys (who would become Television) and after seeing Richard Hell's torn clothing and studded collars, McLaren returned to England, changed the name of his boutique to SEX, and started carrying fetish clothing and original punk-inspired items. This in turn attracted a clientele from which McLaren would eventually assemble the Sex Pistols.

That a boutique storeowner and fashion designer would form and manage the U.K.'s seminal punk band says a lot about the movement. At least in McLaren's realization of it with the Sex Pistols, punk was part of a larger package. It was only one component of a presence designed to stand out, outrage, and affront those on the outside. Hand in hand with the noise of punk went the hostile attitude and—even more obvious from a distance—the look: spiked hair in a rainbow of colors, tattoos and body piercings, torn clothes ornamented or even held together with safety pins.

Punk sought to recapture the revolutionary fervor and the relative simplicity of early rock. In this sense, it was a reactionary movement—a counterrevolution against what its adherents saw as the growing commercialism of mainstream rock. However, in its reconception of these values, it established an important and influential new direction in rock, which continues to the present.

The Roots of Punk

Punk took shape in New York. Much like the folksingers of the sixties, bands performed in small clubs located in Greenwich Village and Soho. CBGB, the most famous of these clubs, launched the careers of a host of punk and new wave bands. Among the CBGB graduates were Patti Smith, Richard Hell (in the Neon Boys, then Television, and finally as Richard Hell and the Voidoids), the Ramones, and Talking Heads. Ohio was another spawning ground: Pere Ubu, from Cleveland, and Devo, from Akron, both had careers under way by 1975.

Among the major influences on punk in New York were the Velvet Underground and the New York Dolls. The Velvet Underground embraced the New York City subculture sensibility and nurtured it in their music. Their songs (for example, "Heroin") were dark, which foreshadowed punk's "no future" mentality, and the sound of their music was often abrasive and minimalist. They presented an anti-artistic approach to art, a rejection of the artistic aspirations of the Beatles and other like-minded bands. Moreover, their impresario was an artist, Andy Warhol, who packaged them as part of a multimedia experience (the famous Exploding Plastic Inevitable); this anticipated McLaren's vision of punk as a fusion of image and sound in the service of outrage.

The New York Dolls, led by David Johansen, were America's answer to David Bowie, Marc Bolan, and the rest of the British glam bands. They lacked Bowie's musical craft and vision; their musical heroes were not only the Velvet Underground but also the MC5 and Iggy Pop and the Stooges. In effect, they dressed up the latter groups' proto-punk and made it even more outrageous, wearing makeup and cross-dressing outlandishly—they out-Bowied Bowie in this respect—and in taking bold risks in performance. Brinksmanship came easily to them, as they were, in the words of one critic, "semi-professional" at best.

Patti Smith, a rock critic turned poet-performer, was the first major figure in the punk movement to emerge from the New York club subculture. Smith was its poet laureate, a performer for whom words were primary. There is nothing groundbreaking in the sound of her music. Indeed, she wanted her music to make a statement, not create a spectacle. Her work had much of the purity and power of punk: purity in the sense that it returned rock to its garage-band spirit, and power in the outrage. But it was not outrageous, at least not by the Sex Pistols' standards. Smith was also important because she was a woman in charge; she played a pivotal role in the creation of this new/old style. Partly because of her presence, punk and new wave music were much more receptive to strong women than conventional rock.

In the United Kingdom, punk was a music waiting to happen. All the components were in place, except for the sound. Disaffected working-class youth wanted an outlet for their frustration: pierced body parts, technicolor hair, and torn clothes made a statement, but they weren't loud enough, and they didn't articulate the message. Following McLaren's return to London and the Ramones' 1976 tour, punk took off in England as well as in the United States, most notably in the music of the Sex Pistols. Elvis Costello quickly became the bard of the new wave. The Clash, the Pretenders (fronted by Akron, Ohio, native Chrissie Hynde), and the Buzzcocks were among other leading U.K. bands in the late seventies.

The attitudes expressed in the punk movement reflected deeply rooted contradictions in everyday life during the seventies. The "we" mind-set of the sixties—the sense of collective energy directed toward a common goal—gave way to a "me" mindset, where people looked out for themselves. The various rights movements and the move toward a more democratic society eroded class distinctions at a rapid rate. Still, there was a strong conservative backlash in both Britain and the United States. At the same time, a prolonged recession, fueled in part by the absence of fuel due to the Arab oil embargo, gave working- and middle-class people little opportunity to take advantage of their new social mobility. And sky-high interest rates and inflation created the fear that today's savings would be worth far less in the future. "No Future," the nihilistic battle cry of the Sex Pistols, was in part a product of this bleak economic outlook.

The Power of Punk

Although the look screams outrage and the words scream rebellion, the power of punk comes through mainly in the music; it is the sounds and rhythms of punk that most strongly convey its energy and attitude. Especially when experienced in its native environment—a small club overflowing with people—the music overwhelms, injecting the crowd with massive shots of energy.

Punk is to rock and roll what heroin is to opium: It gains its potency by distilling its most potent elements and presenting them in concentrated form. "Pure" punk songs are short; they say what they have to say quickly and move on. In their mid-seventies heyday, the Ramones would play 30-minute sets in which all of the songs lasted about 2 minutes. Within such brief time spans, punk offers songs that intensify the dangerous aspects of rock and roll: the volume, the sounds, the rhythms.

Punk is loud. Subtlety is not part of the equation; typically, it's full-bore from beginning to end. Punk is noise: guitarists and bassists routinely use heavy distortion. Punk singing is the triumph of chutzpah over expertise. Indeed, the lack of vocal skill or sophistication was a virtual requirement; one couldn't credibly croon a punk song. Part of the message was that anyone could front a band if he or she had the nerve. Punk is fast: Tempos typically exceed the pace of normally energetic movement—walking, marching, disco dancing. However, the most compelling feature of punk is its approach to rock rhythm.

Saturated Rock Rhythm

A brief recap of twenty years of rock rhythm: Recall that what distinguished rock and roll from rhythm and blues was the eight-beat rhythm. We heard it in the guitar lines of Chuck Berry and the piano playing of Little Richard and gradually in other rhythm instruments, as musicians caught on to this new rhythmic conception. Move ahead to the late sixties and early seventies: as rock musicians became comfortable with rock rhythm, the basic rock beat became a springboard for rhythmic play, as we heard in the music of The Who, Led Zeppelin, and others.

Punk restored the essence and power of rock rhythm by isolating it, saturating the rhythmic texture with it, and speeding it up. In punk, the "default" way of playing the rock rhythmic layer was simply to repeat a note, a chord, or a drum stroke over and over at rock-beat speed. Musicians could graft riffs onto this rhythm to create variety and interest, but this was an overlay; typically, the eight-beat rhythm continues through the notes of the riffs. By contrast, Chuck Berry's rhythm guitar patterns typically oscillate every beat between two chords. This oscillation creates slower rhythms that attenuate the impact of the faster rhythm. Punk strips away these slower rhythms, presenting rock rhythm in a purer form.

Punk made this "purer" form of rock rhythm stand out through a two-part strategy. First, the entire rhythm section typically reinforced it: Guitar(s), bass, and drums all hammer it out. Indeed, depending on the speed of the song and the skill of the drummer, the reinforcement could be heard on the bass drum as well as the drums or cymbals. Second, it favored explicit timekeeping over syncopation and other forms of rhythmic play. We sample the power of punk in a song by the Sex Pistols.

The Sex Pistols

We think of rebels as independent figures standing apart from the crowd. So there is an uncomfortable irony to the fact that the most rebellious act in the history of rock music was part of an extraordinarily complex and manipulative artist/manager relationship. Malcolm McLaren made the Sex Pistols: vocalist Johnny Rotten (born John Lydon, 1956), guitarist Steve Jones (b. 1955), bassists Glen Matlock (b. 1956) and Sid Vicious (born John Ritchie, 1957–1979), and drummer Paul Cook (b. 1956);

he also made them an instrument that enabled him to realize his own provocative ends.

McLaren found the Sex Pistols in his shop. Matlock, the original bassist with the group, worked for McLaren. When he let McLaren know that he and two of his friends, guitarist Steve Jones and drummer Paul Cook, were putting together a band, McLaren found them rehearsal space, took over their management, and recruited a lead singer for them. John Lydon, who became Johnny Rotten (allegedly because of his less than meticulous personal hygiene), had been hanging around SEX for a while. McLaren had gotten to know him and felt that he had the capacity for outrage that he'd been looking for. (Another SEX shop hanger-on, Sid Vicious [John Ritchie], would eventually replace Matlock.)

In fact, none of the four had much musical skill at the time they formed the band. Jones was more adept at thievery than guitar playing: He stole the group's first sound system. McLaren booked the group into small clubs, where they acquired more of a reputation for outrageous conduct than for musicianship. Word spread about the group through word of mouth, newspaper reviews, and subculture fanzines.

The Sex Pistols found their musical direction after hearing the Ramones and learning the basics of their instruments. What they had from the beginning, however, was the ability to shock, provoke, confront, and incite to riot. Indeed, their sets often ended in some kind of fracas; their attitude was more than words and symbols. When they added the musical energy of the Ramones, they were ready to overthrow the ruling class, a stance that is evident in two of their best-known songs, "Anarchy in the UK" and "God Save the Queen." Johnny Rotten opens "Anarchy in the UK" with "I am an Antichrist; I am an anarchist" and ends with a drawn out "Destroy." The opening line lances both church and

THE SEX PISTOLS walk down the street in 1977 (*l–r*) Paul Cook, Sid Vicious, Johnny Rotten, Steve Jones.

LISTENING CUE • **"God Save the Queen" (1977),** Cook, Jones, Matlock, and Rotten. The Sex Pistols.

STYLE Punk • **FORM** Verse/chorus

Listen For . . .

INSTRUMENTATION
Vocal, guitar, bass, drums

PERFORMING STYLE
Abrasive vocal style: loud speech; less than singing; heavy distortion in guitar and bass

RHYTHM
Distilled, intensified rock rhythm at moderately fast tempo

MELODY
Most distinctive melodic material = guitar riffs; vocal not distinct melodically, even in chorus

TEXTURE
Thick, heavy sound; low-range power chords stand out.

Remember . . .

INCENDIARY LYRICS
Song lyrics slam British royalty, establishment; "no future" = hard times for underclass

SOUND WITH AN EDGE
Abrasive vocal, distilled, aggressive, saturated rock rhythm, distorted power chords produce classic punk rock sound

POWER OF PUNK
Inflammatory message in lyrics reinforced by aggressive musical setting

Listen to this selection in CourseMate.

state; the final word makes clear their agenda. Rotten, a skinny kid who knew no bounds, sings/screams/snarls the lyrics. In "God Save the Queen," we can imagine the sneer on Rotten's face as he delivers the opening line, "God Save the Queen, the fascist regime." And although Rotten railed against the "fascist regime," punk's use of the swastika image evoked the ultimate fascist regime.

The music amplified the message of the lyrics. It wasn't just that it was loud—particularly when heard in the small venues where the punk bands played. Or simple—power chords up and down the fretboard. It was the beat. Punk fulfilled the confrontational promise of the very first rock-and-roll records. It was the subversive element that got the revolutionary message across loud and clear, even when the lyrics didn't. In "God Save the Queen," guitar and bass move in tandem to hammer out a relentless rock rhythm almost all the way through; only the periodic guitar riffs that answer Rotten's vocals give it a distinctive shape. The drummer reinforces this rock rhythm by pounding it out on the bass drum and either a tom-tom or hi-hat. Like the Ramones, the band distilled and intensified rock and roll's revolutionary rhythmic essence. There is no way that a rock beat could be more pervasive or powerful.

The power of the song comes from its stylistic coherence. Every aspect of the song—the lyrics, Rotten's vocal style, the absence of melody, simple power chords, the heavily distorted sounds, and the relentless, fast-paced beat—conveys the same basic message: They are mutually reinforcing.

The message of the Sex Pistols resonated throughout the United Kingdom. Many working- and middle-class youths were tired of the rigid class system that they inherited and foresaw a bleak future. The Sex Pistols' songs encapsulated the frustration and rage they felt.

The Sex Pistols embodied the essence of punk in every respect. No one projected its sense of outrage and its outrageousness more baldly. Despite their meteoric rise and fall (Lydon announced the breakup of the group in January 1978), the Sex Pistols were enormously influential. No group in the history of rock had more impact with such a brief career.

CHAPTER 63
Punk Reverberations

In November 2003, *Rolling Stone* published a special issue entitled "The 500 Greatest Albums of All Time." The list was compiled from the nominations of 273 musicians, writers on music, and industry figures. At No. 8, ahead of Dylan's *Blonde on Blonde* and The Beatles' *White Album* is the double album *London Calling,* which was recorded by the Clash in 1979. It is the only album by a band formed after 1970 to make the top ten. The contrasts among the nineteen tracks on the album evidence that the Clash were among the new rock acts of the late 1970s that went beyond the monothematic message of the Sex Pistols' music. So were the New Wave bands in both the United States and United Kingdom. We explore these parallel-to-punk paths through the music of Talking Heads and the Clash.

New Wave

New wave was the umbrella term used to identify the music that emerged in small clubs, mainly in New York and London, during the mid-seventies. It embraced not only punk acts but also other bands seeking a similar audience. Among the more important were Talking Heads and Devo in the United States and Elvis Costello and the Attractions in England.

These diverse acts shared considerable common ground. Both bands and audience assumed an anti-mainstream position. With few exceptions, their music, whatever form it took, was a reaction against prevailing tastes. The reaction could be rage, weirdness, cleverness, humor, and more; but it was typically a reaction.

As this new music emerged, it was labeled "punk" or "new wave" more or less interchangeably. In retrospect, one of the significant distinctions between punk, or at least the "pure" punk of the Ramones and Sex Pistols, and the new wave styles that emerged at the same time is the aim of the music. Punk aims for the gut; new wave aims for the brain, or perhaps the funny bone. The songs of new wave acts such as Talking Heads and Elvis Costello demand attention to the words, and the musical setting puts the lyrics in the forefront.

To support clear delivery of the lyrics, new wave bands favored a stripped-down, streamlined sound: guitar(s), bass, and drums, with the occasional keyboard. (Elvis Costello seemed fond of cheesy-sounding synthesizers.) The rhythmic texture was relatively clean, with little syncopation or rhythmic interplay. This energized the songs without overpowering or deflecting attention from the vocals. Instrumental solos were at a minimum; the primary role of the music was to enhance the words.

The Talking Heads

The Talking Heads started out in art school. Lead singer David Byrne (b. 1952) and drummer Chris Frantz (b. 1951) attended the Rhode Island School of Design together before moving to New York. They formed the group in 1975, with Tina Weymouth (b. 1950), Frantz's then-girlfriend (and later wife), playing bass, and added guitarist/keyboardist Jerry Harrison (b. 1949) two years later.

Although they operated in the same CBGB milieu as the Ramones and other similar punk bands, the Talking Heads came from an opposite place conceptually. Where the Ramones' sound remained remarkably consistent from song to song, the Talking Heads' music, beginning with their debut album *Talking Heads '77* and continuing throughout their sixteen-year career together, offers considerable variety. In their earlier albums, this is especially remarkable, given their limited instrumental resources and Byrne's vocal limitations.

Many of their early songs drew on the rock and rhythm and blues with which they were surrounded in

DAVID BYRNE of Talking Heads in 1980

their formative years. However, they processed these influences in their songs, much as cubist painters like Picasso and Braque processed the scenes and objects that they portrayed in their paintings. These once familiar sounds often occured as distorted or fragmented in the Talking Heads' music, to the extent that the connection with an earlier style is all but broken. This manipulation of familiar sounds provided an instrumental setting that enhanced the impact of Byrne's quirky lyrics and quavery voice, which was ideally suited to convey a person who has drunk way too much coffee or is simply over the edge.

"Psycho Killer," a surprise hit from their first album, evidences salient features of their sound: lyrics and Byrne's singing in the forefront, varied accompaniment, with several subtle features in support. Rhythm and texture are simple and clean; the bass line marks the beat with a repeated note, while guitar and keyboard move at rock-beat speed. The jangly guitar—first in the arpeggiated accompaniment of the verse, then in the chords under the chorus—echoes Byrne's words and sound. This spare backdrop—perhaps a musical counterpart to the white cell of the psycho ward—is an ideal foil for Byrne's vocal.

The lyric is inflammatory. Byrne announces quite clearly that he's crazy ("a real live wire"), and his neutral delivery makes his portrayal especially effective—as if he's a time bomb waiting to explode. In contrast to "God Save the Queen," which goes full bore from beginning to end, there are numerous changes in accompaniment, from the edgy beginning to the brutal beat-by-beat chords in the interlude where Byrne shifts to French.

As "Psycho Killer" demonstrates, the sound of Talking Heads was fueled more by imagination than by craft. There's nothing particularly challenging in any of the instrumental parts, nor is Byrne a vocalist with a wide expressive range. There is no obvious virtuosity or lavish instrumentation. Yet the Talking Heads created one of the most innovative sound worlds of the seventies.

In "Psycho Killer," Talking Heads explored a dark and difficult theme. The song illustrates how new wave often projected rage or frustration, but with more finesse: a sharp stick instead of a bludgeon.

The music of the Talking Heads reflects their seemingly insatiable curiosity regarding the world of music. During the 1980s, Byrne would become one of the leaders of the world music movement; *Naked*, their last studio album, released in 1988, featured African musicians.

The Clash and the Evolution of Punk

Like the Rolling Stones, the Clash grew out of a chance encounter. However, the meeting between guitarists Mick Jones and Joe Strummer took place not in a train station over an armful of blues records, but while waiting in line for an unemployment check. As in the United

LISTENING CUE • **"Psycho Killer" (1977),** David Byrne, Chris Frantz, and Tina Weymouth. Talking Heads.

STYLE New wave • **FORM** Verse/chorus, with a long, multipart chorus, and a contrasting section in the middle and long instrumental ending (onset of madness?)

Listen For . . .

INSTRUMENTATION
Vocal, guitar, bass, drums, keyboard

PERFORMANCE STYLE
Byrne's quavery vocal sound, which gets more intense as song progresses

RHYTHM
Understated rock beat: more emphasis on beat than rock rhythm; little syncopation

MELODY
Mainly repeated phrases in narrow range in verse and chorus; wider ranging as song unfolds

TEXTURE
Widely spaced, open sound, with variety from section to section

Remember . . .

PROMINENT LYRICS
Byrne's lyrics describe a person in the process of losing it; his depiction of a serial killer. Switch to French in chorus a distinctive touch.

PORTRAYING A DEMENTED PERSON
Byrne's untutored and uninhibited singing and melody grow more unrestrained from verse to chorus; dynamic depiction of madness.

INSTRUMENTS IN BACKGROUND
Modest instrumentation, understated rhythm, spare texture provide neutral background, like sterile room in psycho ward, for Byrne's vocal

Listen to this selection in CourseMate.

States, rampant inflation in the United Kingdom had had a devastating effect on the economy. An influx of people from the former British colonies (Jamaicans, East Indians, Nigerians, and others) strained social services and heightened racial tension. At the same time, the class distinctions that had been part of British life for centuries were under assault—as was made manifest in "God Save the Queen."

The Clash came together in 1976 when Strummer (1952–2002) and Jones (b. 1955) teamed up with bassist Paul Simonon (b. 1955) and drummer Terry Chimes (b. 1955). Topper Headon (b. 1955) soon replaced Chimes. Simonon gave the group its name, which suited the confrontational personality of the group and their on-stage persona. In the summer of 1976, Strummer and Simonon found themselves in the middle of a riot between Jamaican immigrants and police. "White Riot," the song that they wrote in response to the incident, was the group's first major hit. It not only got the group noticed but also set the tone for their career: Many of their songs railed against political and social injustices. "White Riot" and many other early songs follow the lead of the Ramones; they are fast, loud, and crude. However, the group quickly evolved into a much more skilled and versatile band. By 1979, the year when they released *London Calling*, the Clash were at home in a variety of styles. However, they never lost the passion that informed their first work. It is evident in virtually all of their music, regardless of subject.

"Death or Glory," a track from *London Calling*, comments on a central issue for the group: whether money will motivate a group to sell out. The lyric oozes attitude. The cast of characters includes a "cheap hood" and a "gimmick hungry yob" ("yob" is British slang for a young working-class thug). The images are brutal: The hood beats his kids; bands that haven't got it should give it up. The chorus sums up the disillusionment that pervades the song.

The music that supports it is simply good rock, rather than high-energy pure punk. The song uses the conventional verse/chorus form; the chorus features catchy melodic hooks that embed themselves in listeners' ears. Once under way, the song maintains a driving beat enriched with rhythmic interplay among the rhythm section players, except for an adventurous interlude that spotlights Headon. The texture is dense in a way that is typical of rock, with melodic lines in both guitars and bass, and there is an array of timbres, from the distorted chords that announce the chorus to the more mellow bass and guitar sounds in the introduction.

"Death or Glory" is not representative of *London Calling*, nor are any of the other tracks. Each song has a distinct character and musical setting; they range from swing-evoking "Jimmy Jazz" and reggae-inspired "Revolution Rock" to the clever punk-style "Koka Kola." However, throughout the album the Clash infuse their music with the power and passion of punk. Regardless of the style or

LISTENING CUE • **"Death or Glory" (1979),** Mick Jones and John Mellor. The Clash.

STYLE Punk-influenced rock • **FORM** Verse/chorus form

Listen For ...

INSTRUMENTATION
Lead and backup vocals, lead and rhythm guitar, electric bass, drums, keyboard

RHYTHM
Clean, active rock rhythm at moderately fast tempo, with most parts moving at eight-beat speed except during interlude, when activity doubles
Distinctive, often syncopated rhythm in guitar accompaniment

MELODY
Contrast between rapid rhythm, flat contour in verse, hooks in chorus, musing instrumental riffs in intro/interludes

TEXTURE
Thick texture, with much melodic interest in guitar parts underneath plain vocal line and in instrumental sections

Remember ...

LYRICS IN FOREFRONT
Both verse and chorus put words in forefront; lyrics laced with brutal images of wannabes who fail as musicians and people.

ROCK SONG CONVENTIONS
Verse/chorus form and melodic hooks make the song easy to follow and appealing.

STRONG SECTIONAL CONTRASTS
Musing introduction, straight-ahead verse, chorus with can't-miss hook, instrumental interludes shift to more or less relaxed rhythms.

Listen to this selection in CourseMate.

influences of the music, the songs matter—because of the lyrics and because the music backs up the lyrics.

More than any other group of the late seventies, the Clash demonstrated by example how to revitalize rock with words and music that mattered, because, unlike the "gimmick hungry yob," they refused to compromise. (Interestingly, their record company undermined their integrity by marketing them as the "The Only Band That Matters," a phrase created by their fans.)

The Reverberations of Punk

Punk and new wave restored the soul of rock and roll. The important bands resurrected rock's sense of daring and amped it up well beyond what had gone before. Their music contains powerful messages: political, social, and personal. However, in punk, the rock can be as brutally blunt in its musical message as in the lyrics. There is a synergy among attitude, words, and music that gives both punk and new wave unprecedented impact. Once again, this is rock music that sought to change the world, or at least shake it out of its complacency.

In punk, the message is primary, whether it is expressed directly or obliquely. This helps account for the relative simplicity of the musical materials—whether presented as a sound blitz (as in the Sex Pistols' music) or with imagination (as in the music of the Clash and Talking Heads). If the musical setting were too elaborate, it would deflect attention away from the underlying intent of the song.

As with any significant new music, punk and new wave would reverberate through the music of the next generation. Punk, and especially the music of the Clash, served as a bridge between the significant rock of the sixties and the significant rock of the eighties, most notably the work of U2.

It introduced a new conception of rock rhythm that would filter into numerous mainstream and alternative styles. This was one reason why much of the rock from the eighties sounds as though it is from that decade and not from an earlier time. It sharpened the edge of much rock-era music, even the pop of Michael Jackson and Madonna. It opened the door for those outside corporate rock; the alternative movement that began in the early eighties continues the independent spirit that typified the punk and new wave music of the late seventies. That spirit lives on most fully in the post-punk bands that have emerged since 1980.

UNIT 14

LOOKING BACK, LOOKING AHEAD

The Influence of Funk, Reggae, Disco, and Punk

FUNK, REGGAE, DISCO, AND PUNK were the styles that would shape the forward-looking music for the rest of the twentieth century. Like much of the music that had shaped previous generations of popular music, all began as styles outside the mainstream. However, unlike earlier generations, all four styles developed from rock-era music. Punk was in many ways a retro rock style; funk was one continuation of James Brown's distinctive approach to rhythm and sound; reggae evolved from the mixing of Jamaican music with rhythm and blues; and disco drew on black pop and the new electronic sound world.

The new music from the early eighties to the present sounds like it was created after 1980, rather than the sixties or seventies, for a number of reasons: new electronic sounds and effects, new voices, outside influences, and the like. Most fundamentally, however, there is a new approach to rhythm. Rock rhythm got a makeover from punk; reggae's multilayered rhythms introduced new levels of complexity and subtlety; sixteen-beat rhythms became the dominant style beat; and even more active rhythms surfaced in rap, techno, and related styles. These rhythmic innovations help place the music chronologically after 1980.

By the eighties, rock-era music had evolved well past the rock-defining music of the late sixties and early seventies. Rap and techno, punk/funk/disco fusions, the new pop of Michael Jackson and Madonna, and the significant rock of U2 and Springsteen—all evidenced the new attitudes, sounds, and rhythms. Indeed, the rock styles that remained truest to the spirit and sound of the 1960s were mainly "alternatives."

Latin Music since 1960

UNIT 15

UNIT 15

To celebrate its fortieth birthday, the National Academy of Recording Arts & Sciences went international. NARAS was formed in 1957; a year later, it awarded the first Grammys. In 1997, the academy formed a separate branch for Latin music, the Latin Academy of Recording Arts & Sciences (LARAS), which the parent organization describes as "a unique, multinational membership-based association composed of music industry professionals, musicians, producers, engineers and other creative and technical recording professionals who are dedicated to improving the quality of life and the cultural condition for Latin music and its makers both inside and outside the United States."

Three years later, LARAS sponsored the first Latin Grammy Awards. The event took place at The Staples Center in Los Angeles and was broadcast over CBS. It was the first prime-time programming in which Spanish and Portuguese were used extensively. In keeping with its international orientation, awards are given for Latin recordings made both inside and outside the United States.

Between 2000 and 2010, Mexican and Brazilian artists dominated the awards, with 109 and 106 artists, respectively. Artists from Spain were third, with fifty-one awards. Artists from Cuba and the United States were seventh and eighth, with thirty-two and twenty-three artists. For American listeners, the number of Brazilian winners might not be surprising, given the familiarity of Brazilian music since the 1960s. By contrast, Mexican music in the United States is a more regional phenomenon, although Mexican and Mexican-American music accounted for over half of Latin-music sales in 2007.

In this unit, we sample widely contrasting examples of Latin music since the 1960s, whose roots trace back to Brazil, Mexico, and Cuba.

CHAPTER 64
The Bossa Nova and Brazilian Music

In 1959, *Black Orpheus,* a film that retold the Orpheus legend in Rio de Janeiro during Carnaval (the Brazilian Mardi Gras), won first prize at the Cannes Film Festival. The soundtrack for the film introduced **bossa nova,** a new Brazilian popular style, to new audiences in both Europe and North America. In the wake of its success and the collaboration of Brazilian musicians and American jazzmen during the early 1960s, Brazilian music quickly became part of American musical life.

Music from Brazil

Before 1960, Brazilian music was exotic and largely apart not only from American popular music but also Cuban-derived Latin music. Indeed, it was more familiar as a look—the fruit-basket headdresses and platform shoes of Carmen Miranda—than as a sound through the 1930s and 1940s. The *maxixe,* a Brazilian tango, had a brief vogue in the teens, then disappeared. Brazilian music's first international ambassador was an Afro-Brazilian flutist/saxophonist/composer named Alfredo da Rocha Vianna Filho, better known as Pixinguinha ("Pee-shun-geen-a"). After he and his group Os Oito Batutas (literally "the eight batons"; a more apt translation might be "the eight masters"—the group was formed from the elite members of a group of black musicians based in Rio de Janeiro) developed a strong local following and delighted visitors from abroad, including Belgian royalty, they traveled to Europe amidst opposition from white Brazilian journalists, who railed against "arrogant and ridiculous blacks" representing Brazil with their "barbaric and primitive music." In fact, Pixinguinha was a skilled instrumentalist, and his music was far from barbaric. The group's stay in Paris was a tremendous success, and it made the samba a popular social dance in Europe. Although the samba was not as sensationally received in the United States, it was still familiar enough to musical insiders to inspire "The Carioca," a song by American songwriter Vincent Youmans that accompanied Ginger Rogers and Fred Astaire's big dance number in the 1933 film *Flying Down to Rio.*

Brazil's musical emissary to the United States was Carmen Miranda. Miranda (1909–1955), a Portuguese-born Brazilian entertainer, came to America in 1939 and soon became a film star, appearing in fourteen films between 1940 and 1953. Through her performances in film and on recordings, she would embody the sound of Brazilian music for Americans. (Brazilians were not as enthusiastic about her American work; they accused her of Americanizing her sound.)

Despite Miranda's success, Brazilian music, unlike Cuban music, failed to enter the mainstream during her career. The main musical reason seems to be the lack of common ground between her Brazilian music and the American popular music of the time. Most of Miranda's songs were *choros,* a song style developed most notably by Pixinguinha; by the 1930s, it had become the dominant popular style in Brazil. A *choro* was originally a lament. However, in the 1910s and 1920s, Afro-Brazilians infused it with the active rhythms of the samba; skilled performers brought virtuosity at breakneck tempos.

There was little about the choros that American musicians could easily adapt to mainstream popular music or jazz. The typical choros group included several guitar-like instruments, unfamiliar percussion instruments, and the flute. The underlying samba rhythm typically moved four times the speed of the beat (not twice as fast, as in Cuban music). In songs like "Tico-Tico" (one of the most popular Brazilian songs of the era), the melody moved at this faster speed—the lyrics stream out at this fast speed, much as they do in rap—although here they are attached to a melody.

The unfamiliarity of the sounds and rhythms kept Brazilian music on the fringes of American musical life until the early 1960s. By that time, American popular music had acquired the more active rhythms of rock, and Brazilian musicians had created bossa nova, a new samba-influenced song style.

Bossa Nova and Its Impact

Bossa nova is Brazilian slang for "something new and different." The music emerged in Rio de Janeiro during the late fifties as a sophisticated, more melodic, and rhythmically less complex samba-inspired popular song style. A small nucleus of musicians, notably songwriters

© Michael Ochs Archives/Getty Images

STAN GETZ QUARTET and **ASTRUD GILBERTO** performing "Girl from Ipanema" in the 1964 film *Get Yourself a College Girl.*

Antonio Carlos Jobim (1925–1994), Luis Bonfa (1922–2001), singer/guitarist João Gilberto (b. 1931), and songwriter/guitarist Baden Powell (1927–2000), fell in love with American jazz, especially jazz-influenced pop singing and West Coast–based cool jazz. They blended the harmonic sophistication and cool of West Coast jazz with the rhythms of Brazil, to produce this new style.

The bossa nova craze peaked in the mid-sixties with authentic music by Jobim and Gilberto, Sergio Mendes's Brazilian crossover music, and the inevitable travesties, such as "Blame It on the Bossa Nova." The landmark bossa nova recording appeared in 1964; it was a collaboration between singer/guitarist João Gilberto and jazz saxophonist Stan Getz. The signature track was "The Girl from Ipanema," which charted as a single later that year.

The recording featured not only Getz and João Gilberto but also Astrud Gilberto, his wife at the time, singing an English translation of the lyric. The opening of the song contains two keys to the style and the sound of bossa nova: João Gilberto's cool, flat, low-pitched voice and the complex off-beat rhythms of the guitar chords. Bass and drums flesh out the rhythmic texture, with bass on every slow beat and drums marking a steady rhythm four times as fast as the bass. Jobim plays the occasional fill on piano and takes a brief solo toward the end.

Jobim's song has the AABA form heard in so many pop songs of the twenties, thirties, and forties. The first phrase of the melody is deceptively simple—a simple riff that gently slides down over smoothly shifting chords. The bridge is more complex: Bold harmonies support a sinuous melody. Jobim's songs favored both subtly shifting melodies and exotic, jazz-derived harmonies that were an ideal complement to the subtle rhythm of the guitar and Gilberto's low-key, almost monotonic singing. Getz's playing is straightforward and lyrical; his sound has the restrained quality and smooth edge that the Brazilians admired so much. His contribution underscores the affinity between jazz and bossa nova.

The bossa nova fad lasted only a few years, but its impact touched American music in several important ways. Bossa nova rhythms became a pop alternative to rock rhythm, and Brazilian rhythms, from both bossa nova and samba, helped shape the rhythms of several new jazz styles that emerged after 1970. More generally, bossa nova reintroduced American listeners to the sixteen-beat rhythms of the samba, active patterns that move four times as fast as the beat. This time they took. Though there is no clear causal relationship between the rhythms of the samba and the active rhythms heard in the black music and jazz/rock fusions of the late 1960s and early 1970s, there is a decided similarity. Because of the bossa nova, these more active rhythms had been in the air since the early 1960s.

LISTENING CUE • **"The Girl from Ipanema" (1963),** Antonio Carlos Jobim. Astrud Gilberto, vocal; João Gilberto, vocal and guitar; and Stan Getz, saxophone.

STYLE Bossa nova • **FORM** Four choruses of an AABA-form song

Listen For . . .

INSTRUMENTATION
Voices, acoustic guitar, saxophone, piano, bass, and drums

PERFORMANCE STYLE
Both Gilbertos, but especially João, sing with flat, uninfected voices

RHYTHM
Bass and drums establish a sixteen-beat rhythm at moderately slow tempo. Highly syncopated guitar chords conflict with this rhythm.

MELODY
A section spins out from three notes repeated several times. The B section repeats a long, winding phrase three times before closing with a new idea.

HARMONY
Rich chords shift underneath repetitive melody; far removed from I-IV-V in bridge.

Remember . . .

BOSSA NOVA AND JAZZ
Jazz, especially jazz harmonies, influenced Jobim and Gilberto.

COOL LATIN MUSIC
Hot Latin music is loud, fast, dense, and busy; bossa nova is slower, softer, and leaner.

SAMBA, BOSSA NOVA, AND AMERICAN ACCEPTANCE
Carmen Miranda was an exotic; bossa nova fit better with rock-era music.

BRAZILIAN MUSIC AND SIXTEEN-BEAT RHYTHMS
The first sixteen-beat rhythms popular in the United States; "lite" alternative to rock rhythm

Listen to this selection in CourseMate.

CHAPTER 65
Tejano Music

A *tejano* is a male Texan of Mexican descent. It is also the name for the music that *tejanos* developed. ***Tejano*** music is a hybrid, blending Mexican music with outside influences—at first local, but more recently wide ranging.

Tejano music is a good candidate for the Latin counterpart to country music. Its home is south Texas with its wide-open spaces. The country connection is more than a matter of geography; there are numerous close parallels between *tejano* music and American country music. Like early country music, and very much *unlike* Cuban music, early *tejano* music seldom featured percussion, drums, or complex rhythms. Like the cowboy songs of the 1930s and 1940s, early *tejano* songs featured tuneful melodies and simple accompaniments. The most obvious differences were the language and the instruments.

The Characteristic Instruments of *Tejano* Music

The two most characteristic instrumental sounds of early *tejano* music were the accordion and the *bajo sexto*. The ***bajo sexto*** is an oversized Mexican twelve-string guitar that typically served as a bass instrument in small groups (or *conjuntos*). (In recent *tejano* music, it more often serves as an extra rhythm instrument.) The accordion has its roots in central Europe. Its use in *tejano* music tells us something about immigration patterns in Texas.

Mexicans are the most visible ethnic group in Texas, in part because so many have retained their language and much of their culture. People of German descent are a less widely acknowledged but still significant ethnic group; today, people of German descent comprise about one-sixth of Texas's population. From about 1830 through the end of the nineteenth century, a steady stream of German immigrants settled in Texas. They created enclaves and established towns—New Braunfels, for example—across south central and southeast Texas. Even today, there are still a few parts of Texas where German (that is, Texas German) is still spoken in everyday conversation.

The Germans who settled in Texas ranged from farmers (the majority) to middle-class businessmen and craftsmen, to a few professionals. They were drawn by the promise of cheap land and the chance to escape the political upheavals of nineteenth-century Germany. Upon arrival, they re-created the lifestyle they had enjoyed in their homeland—to the extent that they could. This included such German staples as beer (Texas Germans founded the breweries that make Pearl and Shiner, two popular Texas beers) and polkas, a popular dance in central Europe. Polka bands, then as now, included an accordion, an instrument that developed in German-speaking Europe during the middle of the nineteenth century.

Instruments tend to travel from one culture to the next; the steel guitar's path from Hawaii to Nashville via vaudeville is a spectacular example. So it is not surprising that the accordion found a home among Spanish-speaking Texans from Mexico.

In the early years, the accordion was the key instrument in *tejano* music. It went out of favor in the 1960s and 1970s, as *tejano* began to incorporate contemporary influences, especially country, rock, and—later—disco. The music of Little Joe Y La Familia, one of the leading *tejano* bands of the sixties and seventies, typified this approach. Their music includes a full, and modern, rhythm section; full horn section; and, at times, rhythms from other kinds of music. But by the mid-1970s, *tejano* music also experienced a "return-to-roots" movement. Among the leading figures in this revival of traditional *tejano* music was Flaco Jiménez.

Flaco Jiménez

Accordionist Flaco Jiménez (b. 1939) is typical of this more recent generation of *tejano* musicians. He is the son, and student, of Santiago Jiménez, Sr., one of the pioneers of *tejano* music (who learned accordion from his father, who in turn learned it from a German immigrant). As a young man, Jiménez mastered the traditional *tejano* accordion style. His musical curiosity led him to explore other styles, and he was in turn brought to a larger audience by Ry Cooder, a fine rock guitarist with a deep interest in the traditional music of many cultures. Jiménez and Cooder recorded together in 1976. Since that time, he has recorded with a host of pop music stars, most notably on the 1992 album *Partners*. On the album, Jiménez performs with Los Lobos, Cooder, rock stars John Hiatt and Stephen Stills, country singers Emmylou Harris and Dwight Yoakum, and Linda Ronstadt.

Ronstadt and Jiménez perform "El Puente Roto" (the broken bridge), a song about both a broken bridge and a broken heart. The song has a traditional sound, with strong German and Mexican connections. The German influence is evident in the prominent place of the accordion and the polka rhythm (OOM-pah), with a light afterbeat played on guitar and drums. The Mexican influence is most prominent in the paired vocal and instrumental lines and the long, lightly syncopated melodic lines. The affinity with country music, rather than rock or Cuban music, is apparent in the focus on the story, which rides on the prominent melody, the spare rhythm section with only unamplified guitar, bass, and drums, and the straightforward timekeeping and simple rhythms of the melody.

Jiménez melds these influences into a sound that is recognizably *tejano:* Spanish-language story-telling lyrics, the paired vocal and instrumental lines, the sound of the accordion, and the polka-like rhythmic foundation marked out simply by the guitar, bass, and drums combine to give "El Puente Roto" an immediately identifiable identity.

The Range of *Tejano* Music

Tejano music is not one style, but several. As Jiménez's career attests, both traditional and more modern *tejano* styles have coexisted, often side-by-side, for several decades. There are the traditional waltz songs, polkas, and foxtrots, and the traditional instruments, *bajo sexto* and accordion; both reflect the mixed heritage of the music. There are outside influences, coming from both Anglo and Hispanic sources. These can mix in varying proportions, as our single example can only begin to suggest. An album by Selena (Quintanilla), *tejano* music's biggest star—posthumously if not before—may contain both pop covers (a 1970s disco medley) and a Spanish-language waltz song straight out of the 1950s. *Tejano* music has a clear regional identity; as its name implies, its locus is Texas. However, the sales figures for the Mexican branch of Latin music suggest that its appeal extends beyond Texas and the southwest.

LISTENING CUE • **"El Puente Roto" (1992),** Jiménez. Linda Ronstadt, vocal; Flaco Jiménez, vocal and accordion.

STYLE Tejano • **FORM** Verse/chorus

Listen For . . .

INSTRUMENTATION
Twin lead vocals, accordions, saxophone, bajo sexto, guitar, bass, drums

RHYTHM
Bright polka/two-beat rhythm with crisp afterbeat on drums; only light syncopation

MELODY
Long phrases with long pauses for instrumental interludes

HARMONY
Mostly I-IV-V

TEXTURE
Voices and featured instruments in pairs, with straightforward polka rhythm (OOM-pah) in guitar, bass and drums, plus occasional running figures on bajo sexto

Remember . . .

THE SOUND OF THE ACCORDION
The accordion is the dominant instrument; one, then two, accordion lines fill the space between vocal phrases with fast-moving runs.

COUNTRY PARALLELS
The affinity with country music is evident in focus on the story, which tells a love-gone-wrong tale; the polka rhythm with a strong afterbeat, similar to the two-beat rhythm of honky-tonk; the long phrases of the melody; the harmony, which relies mainly on I, IV, and V; and the straightforward, lightly syncopated rhythms.

EVERYTHING IN PAIRS
Voices and instruments moving in tandem is characteristic of a wide range of Mexican music. Here both voices (Ronstadt and Jiménez) and instruments (accordion and saxophone) move in lockstep at a close interval.

Listen to this selection in CourseMate.

CHAPTER 66

Salsa and Tropical Latin Music

In 1959, Fidel Castro toppled the United States-friendly regime of Fulgencio Batista, the dictator who had ruled Cuba for the second time since 1952. In the wake of the Cuban revolution, a flood of refugees emigrated from Cuba to the United States. The flood of refugees soon diminished to a trickle. Relations between Cuba and the United States deteriorated quickly, and in 1962 Castro banned travel between the countries.

Deprived of continuing contact with Cuban musicians, U.S.-based Latin musicians during the 1960s and 1970s followed two paths. One was to create hybrid styles, such as the short-lived ***bugalú,*** Latinos' version of "soul music." The other, more significant response was the development of salsa.

Salsa began as an American-based Latin "return to roots" movement. It was effectively an affirmation of the distinctly Afro-Cuban identity of the uptown mambo style popular during the late 1940s and 1950s. Salsa updated the uptown mambo mainly by assimilating elements of other styles, both Latin (Puerto Rican music, for example) and American (jazz, R&B). Nevertheless, according to accounts by both older and younger musicians, it retained its Afro-Cuban core, even though few of the first-generation salsa musicians were Cuban or of Cuban descent. The dominant figures in salsa during the late 1960s and 1970s were Latino, but not Cuban. New York–born Puerto Rican (Newyorican) musicians, like pianists Charlie and Eddie Palmieri, trombonist Willie Colón, and the Panamanian-born singer Ruben Blades, were especially influential.

The Sound of Traditional Salsa in the 1970s

Among the landmark salsa recordings of the 1970s was Willie Colón's *Siembra,* released in 1978; it is one of several collaborations between Colón's band and Blades. "Ojos," a track from the album, demonstrates how traditionally-oriented salsa updated the Afro-Cuban/American synthesis first heard in the mambo and ultimately connected back to the Cuban *son*. Among the characteristic features of the style are these four:

1. *Dense, percussion-rich texture.* A dense rhythmic texture featuring several characteristic Cuban percussion instruments. The most prominent are the conga, timbales, and bongos.
2. *Clave rhythm.* As in other Afro-Cuban music, the clave pattern serves as the rhythmic reference point. Other regular rhythms, such as the *montuno* patterns played by the pianist and the *tumbao* bass pattern, coordinate with it or add a layer of complex activity. The trombone melody right after Blades' verse-like canto conforms to the clave rhythm.
3. *Tumbao bass.* Salsa bassists play a clave-derived pattern that comes on offbeats, rather than marking the main beats, as in American rhythms. This is one feature that usually distinguishes salsa from other Latin styles and Americanized Latin music.
4. *Montuno piano patterns.* The pianist in a salsa band plays active, syncopated patterns over and over. Many of them are reminiscent of ragtime.

The form of this song expands on two-part structure typical of the Afro-Cuban mambo. The first part is the canto, the second—and longer—part is the *montuno.* Canto and *montuno* function much like the verse and chorus in much popular song, but there are significant differences.

The canto proper begins after an extended instrumental introduction. This is the narrative section of a salsa song, much like the verse in a verse/chorus song, but this material is only presented once; there are no subsequent verses.

After the canto ends decisively, the *montuno* begins with a coro. Typically, the coro consists of a short riff, followed by silence. In this recording, it is played first by instruments, then sung at least partially to the title words. Its brevity gives the *sonero* ample opportunity for solo flights. An *inspiración,* which is an extended jam for the percussionists, follows. In the mambo and salsa, this is analogous to the improvised solos in jazz performances. In this section, the trombones repeat a riff, while percussionists break out of their more restricted patterns to play in a rhythmically freer style. The coro then returns; as before, an instrumental statement of the riff precedes a vocal version. The two are combined with an active piano *montuno* pattern before a reprise of the vocal part of the coro. The song ends with a reprise of the brass introduction.

"Ojos" exemplifies the most traditional approach to salsa in rhythm, instrumentation, melody, texture, and form, "Ojos" is remarkably similar to the mambos of the 1950s. The most striking differences are the horn section—all trombones, instead of a mix of brass and saxophones—and the electric bass, which gives the group a firmer foundation.

LISTENING CUE • **"Ojos" (1978),** Johnny Ortiz. Willie Colón and Ruben Blades, vocal.

STYLE Salsa • **FORM** *Canto/montuno* (similar to but more expansive than verse/chorus)

Listen For . . .

INSTRUMENTATION
Vocal, four trombones, piano, electric bass, congas, timbales, claves, and other Afro-Cuban percussion instruments

PERFORMANCE STYLE
Blades sings boldly, with expressive nuance in the *canto* and agility in a high register in the responses in the *coro.*

RHYTHM
Complex rhythms with abundant syncopation, especially in bass *tumbao* pattern and piano *montuno* figures, all at a moderately fast tempo

MELODY
Coro melody built from "in-clave" riffs; Blades' vocal lines more active and elaborate

TEXTURE
Dense, deep texture because of the strong electric bass, trombones in mid-range, active piano patterns, and numerous percussion instruments

Remember . . .

SIGNATURE AFRO-CUBAN RHYTHM
The clave pattern is inherently asymmetrical, and both the *tumbao* pattern of the bass and the piano *montuno* are typically completely syncopated. When combined with the multiple layers of activity in the percussion section and the "in-clave" melodic figures, the rhythm is complex, buoyant, and distinctively different from American and Americanized Latin rhythms.

FOCUS ON PERCUSSION
Extensive percussion throughout, with timbales, bongos, and conga, and cowbell prominent in the "inspiración" percussion jam

TRADITIONAL SALSA
"Ojos" retains the core features heard in the mambo: sonero supported by piano, bass, horns, and multiple percussion instruments; canto/*montuno* form; clave-based rhythmic organization; frequent call and response; percussion jam. The electric bass (and better recording) give the piano and bass a more prominent and supportive role.

Listen to this selection in CourseMate.

Salsa, Tradition, and the Marketplace

Like so many other outsider styles—jazz, country, blues—salsa has wrestled with the conflict between fidelity to core values, artistic freedom, and commercial success. Musicians like Colón, vocalist Celia Cruz (the reigning queen of salsa until her passing in 2003), and pianist/bandleader Eddie Palmieri have remained true to the Afro-Cuban roots of salsa even as they absorb other influences. Palmieri has been especially bold in his exploration of new possibilities: He has blended jazz-like improvisation and the harmonic complexity, rhythmic freedom, and formal richness of jazz and contemporary classical music with this Afro-Cuban core sound. His music has enjoyed the acclaim of both critics and aficionados. Rhythmically authentic salsa/jazz fusions came from jazz musicians such as Chick Corea, who worked with Latin percussionists Willie Bobo and Mongo Santamaria early in his career.

During the late 1960s and early 1970s, the salsa closest to the music's Afro-Cuban roots had a limited audience: mainly Latinos and a small minority of non-Latinos drawn to the music. Salsa began to cross over to a more mainstream audience in the mid-1970s, particularly with the emergence of disco. Latinos were among the early patrons of discothèques, so it's not surprising that it exerted some influence on this new dance music. However, in this context, salsa acquired a more generic connotation, referring to music with a Latin flavor, but not distinctively Afro-Cuban. For example, "Salsation," one of the songs used in the *Saturday Night Fever* soundtrack, has a Latin sound because of the brass riffs, the Latinish rhythm, and Latin percussion. But its rhythmic foundation owes more to disco than Afro-Cuban music. This gave the song more crossover appeal but removed several features that defined authentic salsa. The contrast between authentically Afro-Cuban salsa, as heard in "Ojos," and the pop/Latin fusion heard in "Salsation" updates the uptown/downtown dichotomy in the Latin music of the 1940s and 1950s.

As salsa grew in popularity during the latter part of the twentieth century, artists with a connection to Afro-Cuban music sought to incorporate the core features of salsa into a Latin style that was less restrictive and more broadly accessible. Among the most successful has been Gloria Estéfan.

Tropical Latin and Gloria Estéfan

The winners of the first Latin Grammy for Best Short Form Music Video were Gloria Estéfan and her producer/husband Emilio Estéfan, Jr., for the song "No Me Dejes de Querer." The song topped three Latin music charts and was Estéfan's first Spanish-language song to reach the *Billboard* Hot 100 charts. For Estéfan, the song and *Alma Caribeña* (2000), the album on which it appeared, represented another return to the Spanish language; the majority of her recordings have been in English. Musically "No Me Dejes de Querer" exemplifies what is now called **tropical Latin.**

Both Gloria (Fajardo) Estéfan (b. 1957) and her husband Emilio Estéfan Jr. (b. 1953) fled with their families to Miami in the wake of the Cuban revolution. The couple met in 1975 when Emilio, who was moonlighting as a musician from his job as a sales manager, heard Gloria sing and asked her to join his band, which would quickly evolve into Miami Sound Machine. They married three years later.

Miami Sound Machine made seven studio albums between 1977 and 1983, playing what amounted to contemporary American music sung in Spanish and intended primarily for a Spanish-speaking audience: disco, pop, ballads, and the occasional Latin number. They became a mainstream pop act in 1984 with the release of *Eyes of*

GLORIA ESTÉFAN performing in Australia, 1991

LISTENING CUE • **"No Me Dejes de Querer" (2000),** Gloria Estéfan, Emilio Estéfan, Jr., and Robert Blades. Gloria Estéfan, vocal.

STYLE Tropical Latin • **FORM** Verse/chorus

Listen For . . .

INSTRUMENTATION
Lead/backup vocals; piano; guitars; electric bass; Afro-Cuban percussion; brass, with trumpet featured; saxophone

PERFORMANCE STYLE
Estefan's passionate singing, always with a slight edge

RHYTHM
Alternates between Latin rhythms not in clave and Afro-Cuban rhythms in clave at a moderate tempo

MELODY
Verse contains moderate-length phrases in narrow range; chorus exchanges short riffs sung by chorus with longer responses.

TEXTURE
Dense texture, especially thick in middle, with guitars, voices, and horns

Remember . . .

SALSA LOVE SONG
Flowing rhythms at moderate tempo ideal for salsa song about love

FROM "LATIN" TO SALSA
Song shifts back and forth between generic "Latin" rhythm and authentic salsa/mambo rhythms.

LA CANTANTE
Estefan's rich voice, which verges on cracking at passionate moments, clearly conveys the emotions in the lyric.

Listen to this selection in CourseMate.

Innocence, their first English-language album. They would follow it with two others before Gloria started to receive top billing. In many of the group's early hits, like "Dr. Beat," their style was indistinguishable from American/international pop.

A broken vertebra suffered in an accident involving the band's bus during a 1990 tour kept Gloria at home for a year. Upon her return, she began recording in both Spanish and English; *Mi Tierra* (1993), her first Spanish-language album as a headline act, drew much more deeply on her Cuban heritage, in words and music. So did *Alma Caribeña.*

The set for the "No Me Dejes de Querer" music video is a posh Mediterranean-looking nightclub, with arched entries and palm trees. Estéfan begins the video leaning alluringly against a column; in the course of the video, she flits from table to table and takes a turn on the dance floor, leaving a string of men pining after her. Most of the men, including the musicians, are dressed in white suits and are wearing fedoras; most of the women wear clingy dresses. There is dancing throughout. The scene evokes pre-revolutionary Havana, or Rio or Buenos Aires, as seen in numerous films of the pre–World War II era, but the look is up to date, with black, brown, and white dancers moving sinuously over the dance floor.

The music clearly derives from salsa. The verse is a Cubanized Caribbean sound—Latin rhythms and instruments, plus guitars strumming. During the instrumental break before the chorus, the traditional salsa sounds and rhythms kick in: piano *montuno*, bass playing the offbeat *tumbao* pattern, vocal line in clave. There is a modern-sounding solo in the middle of the song by Puerto Rican pianist Papo Lucca. The blazing trumpet solo at the end underscores the affinity between salsa and jazz. In all of this, the connection between tropical Latin and the Afro-Cuban mambo and more traditional salsa of Willie Colon is apparent.

There is a striking difference in intent, however. "No Me Dejes de Querer" is not only dance music but also a love song: the title phrase is usually translated as "Don't Stop Loving Me." The lyrics are intensely romantic: The opening line, translated into English, reads "I don't ever want to imagine/That your eyes will not gaze upon me," and it goes on from there.

Estéfan's rich, expressive voice is an ideal complement to the lyrics; the melody, built from short phrases and featuring exchanges between a male chorus and Estéfan, floats over the pulsating salsa rhythms. It inverts the Latin lover stereotype: a sultry woman on a sultry evening promising unending love as she leaves one man for another.

"No Me Dejes de Querer" is salsa-inspired song—danceable song, to be sure, but song in which the focus is on the words, the melody, and the singer. In this respect, it compares to mambo much as bossa nova compares to samba. In this way, Estéfan expands the expressive range of this hybrid Cuban-American music.

UNIT 15

LOOKING BACK, LOOKING AHEAD
The Diversity of Contemporary Latin Music

THE 2010 LATIN GRAMMYS—the eleventh annual ceremony—presented awards in eighteen categories. Eight were American/international/Latin fusions: pop, urban, rock, alternative, singer/songwriter, Christian, jazz, and classical. Four were regional: tropical (five subcategories, including salsa); regional Mexican (five subcategories, including tejano), traditional (three subcategories), and Brazilian (seven categories). *Billboard* lists five album charts, including Regional Mexican Albums and Tropical Albums.

These and other industry sources highlight the diversity of Latin music. The diversity comes from two sources. One is the significant contrast in style among Latin genres. The four examples discussed in this unit, admittedly a miniscule sampling, nevertheless offer aural confirmation of the range of Latin music. The differences between bossa nova, tejano, and salsa and salsa-influenced music are comprehensive: different—indeed, almost mutually exclusive—approaches to instrumentation, rhythms, melody, and harmony.

The other is the extensive cross-pollination within Latin music, among Latin genres, and between Latin and American/international styles. Salsa remains the most influential Latin style. One occasionally hears Cuban percussion instruments in regional Mexican music, but the accordion and bajo sexto are not part of the sound of salsa. And it is arguably the most distinctive sound as well; the full battery of percussion and the complex, asymmetrical, clave-based rhythms of salsa immediately distinguish it from music that simply borrows elements of the style.

The popularity of Latin music in the United States continues to grow. The first Latin charts debuted on *Billboard* in 1985; several more were added in the 1990s and 2000s. This growth reflects not only the increase in Spanish-speaking residents of the United States but also the greater openness of non-Hispanic listeners to Latin music.

Country Music in the Rock Era

UNIT 16

In the United States, Elvis is the best-selling solo act of all time, having sold close to 130,000,000 units as of December 2010. A quick question: Who is second? The answer isn't Michael Jackson or Madonna, Billy Joel or Elton John, or any pop, rock, or R&B act. It's Garth Brooks, who has sold over 128 million units since beginning his recording career in 1989.

For country music, Brooks's spectacular sales figures are neither an aberration nor an isolated instance. The RIAA publishes a list of acts whose albums have sold 10 million units. Of the 100 best-selling acts of all time, 24 began their recording careers in the 1990s or later. Of these, eight are country acts: Brooks and Dunn, Kenny Chesney, Dixie Chicks, Faith Hill, Alan Jackson, Toby Keith, Tim McGraw (Faith Hill's husband), and Shania Twain.

Joining them in the Top 100 were five country acts whose careers began in the 1980s: Brooks, Alabama, Vince Gill, Reba McIntire, and George Strait. All remained active through the 1990s, and all but Alabama are still active performers. Newer artists like Taylor Swift and Dierks Bentley, as well as *American Idol* winners Kelly Clarkson and Carrie Underwood, routinely join them on *Billboard's* comprehensive album charts. For country, the Top 100 is end weighted: Only two other country singers, Willie Nelson and Kenny Rogers, appear on the list.

One reason for country music's recent surge in popularity is the use of a more accurate and efficient method of calculating sales. Toward the end of 1991, *Billboard* began using Nielsen SoundScan, an information system that tracks sales through the use of barcodes scanned at registers in retail centers and record stores throughout the United States. Around the same time, the music industry started using computers to track radio airplay. In combination, the two information sources provided much more precise—and eventually more reliable—data about popularity.

Not coincidentally, the market share of country music just about doubled between 1990 and 1993, from 9.6 percent to 18.7 percent. This alerted industry executives on both coasts to something that country fans had known for decades: Country music was much more popular than the music industry thought it was.

The dramatic jump in market share was just one indication that country music had become a major player in the popular music industry. Country music television networks, country stars in advertisements, the emergence of Nashville as an important music center, crossover chart success—these also show the growing presence of country music.

In this unit, we sample country music from the 1960s to the 2000s. We take a country perspective on rock, encounter the music of several of the top acts, consider why country music's share of the popular music business has grown so significantly since the 1980s, and revisit the central tension in country music between identity and commercial success.

CHAPTER 67
Countrifying Rock

During the 1950s, the connection between country music and rock and roll only went in one direction, from country to rock. Chuck Berry's "Maybellene" is a remake of the country song "Ida Red." Elvis, Carl Perkins, and the other rockabillies brought a country flavor to rock and roll. The Everly Brothers grew up singing country music. However, mainstream country music remained largely unaffected by rock and roll.

In the early 1960s, rock came to country. Ray Charles's two best-selling country and western recordings, both released in 1962, were radical reinterpretations of country hits. They brought country music to a new audience and influenced generations of country singers. Joan Baez, Bob Dylan, and their likeminded peers revived the songs of the Carter Family, which would ultimately lead to the folk-rock fusion of the Byrds and others, and Bob Dylan's Nashville sessions, which brought folk, country, and rock together. However, the most influential synthesis of rock and country during this time came from Roy Orbison.

Roy Orbison

In 1964, Roy Orbison (1936–1988) scored his only No. 1 hit with "Pretty Woman." Orbison, who was born in Vernon, Texas, started his recording career as a rockabilly artist. In the mid-1950s, he worked with Norman Petty (Buddy Holly's producer), then Sam Phillips. He had little success with either of them, so he moved to Monument records, an independent label based near Nashville.

Many have called Orbison the last rockabilly. The case can also be made that he was the first country rocker. More than Jerry Lee Lewis, he brought a country sensibility to rock and showed country musicians how to blend rock with country. His "Mean Woman Blues," a cover of Elvis's 1957 version, is a superb illustration.

"Mean Woman Blues" brings together blues, rhythm and blues, rock, and country, all supporting Orbison's splendid singing. The form of the song is a conventional twelve-bar blues, and the lyric begins with a rhymed couplet. The riffs sung by the backup vocalists and the honking saxophone solo derive from 1950s/early 1960s rhythm and blues. The drummer taps out a relentless rock rhythmic layer. What gives the song a country tinge is the alternation of a strong bass note and comparably strong backbeat. In effect, this approach to rock rhythm layers the rock rhythmic layer onto a honky-tonk–style two-beat rhythm. This would become the default approach to rock rhythm not only in the country rock of the 1970s but also in rock-era country music.

Country and Rock in the 1960s

Orbison's country-flavored rock, evident in hits like "Blue Bayou," also a huge hit for Linda Ronstadt in 1977, and even "Pretty Woman," was one of several intersections between rock, country, and rhythm and blues. Country became the key ingredient in differentiating "American" rock from the music of British bands during the late 1960s. It is apparent in the music of the Band, the Grateful Dead,

LISTENING CUE • **"Mean Woman Blues" (1963),** Claude Demetrius. Roy Orbison.

STYLE Early country rock • **FORM** Twelve-bar blues

Listen For . . .

INSTRUMENTATION
Lead and backup vocals, electric guitar, electric bass, drums, piano, saxophone

PERFORMANCE STYLE
The extraordinary range and warmth of Orbison's singing. Honking saxophone riffs and surf-guitar style solo.

RHYTHM
Straightforward rock rhythm: rock layer mainly on hi-hat, bass alternating with backbeat, other patterns reinforcing rock pattern

TEXTURE
Extensive call and response and background riffs

Remember . . .

ROCKING A TWELVE-BAR BLUES
Orbison updates Elvis's version by trading the 1950s R&B shuffle/rockabilly rhythm for a clean rock beat.

ORBISON'S GREAT VOICE
Orbison's rich high tenor is one of the great voices of the rock era.

COUNTRY ROCK BEAT
The rhythmic foundation is essentially a rock beat layered over a honky-tonk beat. It is a very early instance of what would become the most common approach to uptempo rock rhythm in country music.

Listen to this selection in CourseMate.

and Creedence Clearwater Revival and, more regionally, in the Southern rock of the Allman Brothers. The most comprehensive attempt to bring country into rock came from Gram Parsons, a singer and songwriter from the Southeast, who engineered the Byrds' transition from folk rock to country. During their brief time together, then left to form the Flying Burrito Brothers, the leading country-oriented rock band of the late 1960s. Other late 1960s country/rock intersections included the country/pop/rock fusions of singer/guitarist Glen Campbell and the subtle incorporation of rock elements into country music from Nashville and elsewhere.

By the early seventies, a true country/rock synthesis was evident in songs in which the lyric told a story in everyday language. The lyric was set to a tuneful melody and supported by an understated accompaniment, often featuring instruments with a country association. An early example of country rock is the Eagles' "Take It Easy."

The Eagles and the Rise of Country Rock

Formed in 1971 mainly from Linda Ronstadt's backup band, the Eagles became one of the most successful rock groups of the seventies. The original Eagles were Don Henley (b. 1947), drums; Glenn Frey (b. 1948), guitar; Bernie Leadon (b. 1947), country instruments—banjo, steel guitar, and others; and Randy Meisner (b. 1946), bass. Don Felder (b. 1947), who also played an assortment of country instruments, joined the group in 1974.

The song that put both the Eagles and **country rock** on the map was their first single, "Take It Easy." It demonstrates their effective fusion of rock and country. The lyric is all country: women trouble, trucks, small towns (Winslow is east of Flagstaff), but the music smoothly blends rock and country. The song begins with a low-wattage power chord, then settles into a nice rock groove.

This particular interpretation of a rock beat is a more relaxed version of Orbison's honky-tonk/rock beat synthesis. As in "Mean Woman Blues," the rhythm has two distinct layers. One is a straightforward rock rhythm, played on the drums and acoustic guitar. The other is in essence a modified honky-tonk two-beat rhythm: bass and bass drum mark the first and third beats, in alternation with the backbeat on the second and fourth beats. Almost everything else also has a country flavor.

As their career gained momentum, the Eagles moved toward the mainstream, often shedding country elements along the way. Still, songs such as "Lyin' Eyes" (1975) retain a strong country flavor. The band shifted direction rather abruptly in 1975, when guitarist Joe Walsh replaced Bernie Leadon. "Hotel California" (1977), their big hit from this later period, borrows from a "southern" sound of a quite different kind: reggae. It's a skillful adaptation of the reggae feel—as skillful as their earlier assimilation of country—but the Eagles sound like a different band altogether. It was a complete makeover. Although the Eagles went far beyond their country rock beginnings, part of their legacy was the "countrification" of rock rhythm.

LISTENING CUE • "Take It Easy" (1972), Jackson Browne and Glenn Frey. The Eagles.

STYLE 1970s country rock • **FORM** Verse/chorus

Listen For . . .

INSTRUMENTATION
Lead and backup vocals, electric guitar, acoustic guitar, electric bass, drums, banjo

PERFORMING STYLE
Beautiful close harmony in chorus

RHYTHM
Classic country-rock rhythm; double-time banjo over guitar solo

MELODY
Long narrative phrases in verse; sustained riff-like phrases in chorus

TEXTURE
Rich texture, with close harmony vocals in chorus and banjo line

Remember . . .

COUNTRY-THEMED LYRICS
A contemporary take on the free-lovin' ramblin' man

COUNTRY ROCK BEAT
Rock rhythmic layer over modified honky-tonk beat

BLUEGRASS SOUNDS
Double-time banjo figuration and guitar patterns add to country flavor

COUNTRY VOCAL SOUNDS
Close harmony on the chorus, verse harmonized from above another country element

Listen to this selection in CourseMate.

CHAPTER 68

The Outsiders

Bakersfield, California, in the heart of the San Joaquin Valley may seem an unlikely home for a country music rebellion, if only because it's over 2,000 miles from Nashville. However, because of the influx of families from the South and Southwest during the Dust Bowl in the 1930s, its population quadrupled between 1930 and 1960. By the 1960s, these families supported a thriving country music scene in Bakersfield. The key figure early on was Buck Owens; he and his band played a much harder country than the music coming out of Nashville. However, Bakersfield's biggest country music star would soon be Merle Haggard.

Inside and Outside in Country Music

As country music began to cross over to the pop charts more consistently in the years after World War II, pop artists began to cover country songs—Patti Page's version of Pee Wee King's "Tennessee Waltz" is an outstanding example. Nashville's tastemakers noted how the pop versions sold much better than the country originals. Their response was to make country more like pop. The result was the Nashville Sound, the dominant sound in country music during the late 1950s and early 1960s. The singing of Jim Reeves and Eddy Arnold was closer to pop than it was to Hank Williams or Lefty Frizzell, and the background, with sumptuous strings and smooth-voiced choirs, smacked more of easy-listening music than country.

Although Reeves and Arnold were among the most successful country performers of their time, there were those who felt—and rightly so—that country music was losing its identity in its quest for crossover success. The most prominent were the "outlaws," most notably Johnny Cash, Merle Haggard, Willie Nelson, and Waylon Jennings. They made their case away from Nashville: Cash in Memphis, Haggard in Bakersfield, California, and Nelson and Jennings in Austin, Texas.

Merle Haggard

The family of Merle Haggard (b. 1937) was among those who migrated west early on, in 1934. Haggard was born there three years later. After the death of his father when he was nine, Haggard ran wild and was more in trouble than out of it until he went to prison in 1958 on a burglary conviction. Inspired by a performance by Johnny Cash at San Quentin, the prison where he was incarcerated, he worked on his music. After being paroled in 1960, Haggard returned to Bakersfield and got involved with Owens' music and with Owens' ex-wife, whom he soon married.

© Time Life Pictures (Lynn Pelham)/Getty Images

MERLE HAGGARD, 1970

Haggard soon carved out his niche, as the spokesman for the working class and champion of middle-American values. Haggard has said that his songs come out of his life; he sings them as if he's talking about it. The song that resonated most deeply with his audience was his huge 1969 hit "Okie From Muskogee." Haggard has claimed that he wrote the song as a joke, but he has sung it with no trace of sarcasm. Regardless of Haggard's intent, the lyric seemed to speak for America's "silent majority."

His sound is gritty, not pretty, with an unmistakable country edge. "Okie from Muskogee" paints a vivid, if stylized, picture of life in America's heartland, far removed from the excesses of the San Francisco hippies. The musical setting is more contemporary, with an understated rock rhythm replacing the hard two-beat of honky-tonk. But the spirit is much the same: a plainspoken lyric set to a simple melody, with a no-frills, well-played backdrop.

"Okie From Muskogee" was the first of many Haggard forays into social commentary. When released, it was as current as the six o'clock news. And Haggard played a key role in establishing what was soon called "hard country" as a commercially and critically viable alternative to the music coming from Nashville. The outlaws would soon join him.

LISTENING CUE · **"Okie from Muskogee" (1969),** Merle Haggard, Roy Burris. Merle Haggard.

STYLE Hard country • **FORM** Verse/chorus, but with verse and chorus sharing the same melody

Listen For . . .

INSTRUMENTATION
Electric guitar, electric bass, acoustic guitar, piano, drums played with brushes

PERFORMANCE STYLE
Haggard's straight vibrato-less vocal sound

RHYTHM
Understated rock and honky-tonk rhythm with little syncopation

MELODY
Moderate-length phrases

HARMONY
Two-chord song, in two keys

Remember . . .

MESSAGE SONG
Serious or not, Haggard spoke for the "silent majority" in this song.

PURE COUNTRY VOCAL STYLE
Haggard's vocal sound is unadulterated country: flat, hard, no vibrato, no histrionics

MUSIC IN THE BACKGROUND
Simple song with understated accompaniment gets out of the way of Haggard's vocal and the message of the song

Listen to this selection in CourseMate.

The Outlaws: Waylon Jennings and Willie Nelson

Tradition-oriented country found another home in the 1970s: Austin, Texas. Willie Nelson, who had tired of the Nashville treadmill, moved to Austin in 1971. He loosened up his image—wearing jeans onstage and letting his hair grow long—and started a Fourth of July festival that brought together, according to one commentator, "the hippie and the redneck."

Nelson and Waylon Jennings started the "outlaw" movement, so called because of its defiance of Nashville's calculated commercialism, and not because of any criminal wrongdoing on their part. As it turned out, Nelson and Jennings were more in tune with public taste than Nashville. Their 1976 album, *Wanted: The Outlaws,* was the first million-selling country album. Their collaboration continued most noticeably on tour and in a series of "Waylon and Willie" albums.

WILLIE NELSON AND WAYLON JENNINGS, 1978

One of their biggest hits was "Mammas, Don't Let Your Babies Grow Up to Be Cowboys," a Grammy-winning hit in 1978. The song shows the independent spirit of the two men in both words and music. It's most obvious in the words. The "cowboys" that Nelson and Jennings sing about are, according to Bill Malone, "the free-living, good-timing good old boys that figure so prominently on southern backroads and in southern folklore." The portrait they paint is far from flattering and full of contradictions: Their cowboys like "clear mountain mornings" as well as "smoky old poolrooms," "little warm puppies and children" as well as "girls of the night." It's a mixed message: Like them, but don't trust them.

The music that supports this message is just as independent: It is a modern version of the traditional cowboy song of the 1930s and 1940s, like Eddy Arnold's theme song, "Cattle Call"—or such standbys as "Home On The Range." This basic conception is flavored with the sounds of an up-to-date honky-tonk band: full, mostly electric rhythm section, steel guitar, and background vocals support Waylon and Willie's narrative.

LISTENING CUE • **"Mammas Don't Let Your Babies Grow Up to Be Cowboys" (1978),**
Ed and Patsy Bruce. Willie Nelson and Waylon Jennings

STYLE Hard country • **FORM** Verse/chorus, but with verse and chorus sharing the same melody

Listen For . . .

INSTRUMENTATION
Duet vocal, steel guitar, electric and acoustic guitars, electric bass, drums

PERFORMANCE STYLE
Jennings has typical country vocal sound; Nelson's quavery voice is a distinctive sound.

RHYTHM
Slow tempo, with beats divided into three parts; little syncopation

MELODY
Long phrases, with considerable repetition

HARMONY
Three-chord song, with progression repeated

Remember . . .

EVOKING COWBOY SONG
Triple beat division recalls cowboy songs of 1930s/1940s

STORY IN FOREFRONT
Simple repetitive melody and harmony, unobtrusive accompaniment with steel guitar comments, carry story, but stay out of the way.

FLAWED HERO
The Bruces' portrait of a cowboy is far different from the cowboys portrayed in classic westerns.

Listen to this selection in CourseMate.

By simultaneously evoking the cowboy song in the music and painting a less-than-flattering portrait of him in the words, they debunk the mythical cowboy seen in the films and television shows of earlier generations. It has the same cold-shower effect as learning that Wayne McLaren, the rugged Marlboro man in Philip Morris's cigarette ads, died of lung cancer at age fifty-one.

Nelson has sung the music he likes. This has included not only traditional country material and his own music in a traditional style, but also Tin Pan Alley standards (his 1978 *Stardust* album) and blues-flavored rock songs in collaboration with rock star/songwriter Leon Russell. This eclectic approach broadened his, and country's, audience considerably; it made him the most successful country crossover artist of the 1970s.

CHAPTER 69
Country Royalty

One doesn't usually take a rider-mower on the open road. However, for George Jones, there was no other alternative. He was a full-blown alcoholic during his marriage to Shirley Ann Corley, his second wife, often going on benders that lasted for days. At the time, they lived 8 miles outside of Beaumont, Texas. During one of his days-long drunks, Shirley decided to make it impossible for George to drive into town to get more liquor, so she hid the keys to all of their cars. She didn't think of the lawn mower, but George did, and rode the mower into town to slake his seemingly unquenchable thirst for bourbon.

The lawn-mower trip was not an isolated event. He did it again when married to Tammy Wynette, his third wife. She recalled in her 1979 autobiography *Stand by Your Man* that she had to go hunt for him late one night. When she got to the nearest bar, which was miles from home, she found the mower by the entrance. When he saw her come in, he laughed and said, "Well, fellas, here she is now. My little wife. I told you she'd come after me." For Wynette, however, Jones's alcohol abuse was no laughing matter; she divorced him after six years of marriage.

TAMMY WYNETTE AND GEORGE JONES performing in happier times.

George Jones and Tammy Wynette

Almost from the start, country music has chronicled the good times and the bad times of men and women, together and apart. Songs have expressed almost every conceivable point of view: the faithful wife, the wandering wife, the faithful husband, the philandering husband. Often songs seemed as though they were airing dirty linen in public; in 1952, Kitty Wells answered Hank Thompson's "The Wild Side of Life" with "It Wasn't God Who Made Honky Tonk Angels."

George Jones (b. 1931) and Tammy Wynette (1942–1998) embodied this dimension of country music so fully that it was difficult to discern where life ended and art began. Both were major stars. Jones's career had begun in the late forties. His hits started coming in 1955; by the sixties, he was charting regularly, both as a solo artist and in duets, mostly with women.

Wynette (born Virginia Wynette Pugh; she made Tammy Wynette her stage name at the suggestion of Nashville producer/songwriter Billy Sherrill) began her career while working as a beautician to pay the bills. She had left her first husband, who discouraged her from pursuing a career as a country singer. After being turned down repeatedly, she impressed Sherrill enough that he offered her a contract with Epic Records in 1966. Within a year she was on her way, and by 1968 she had three No. 1 country hits, including "Stand by Your Man." The next year, she married George Jones (they claimed to have married the year before). It was her third marriage—her second lasted less than a year and was annulled.

Her marriage to Jones was a disaster, which Wynette alluded to in songs that barely disguised their real-life troubles. Jones had been an alcoholic for years, and his drinking ruined their marriage and nearly ruined his career. Jones went through the seventies in a drunken stupor; as he said in his 1997 autobiography, if he was sober, he was asleep. By 1979, he was bankrupt and his career was in jeopardy. He missed so many engagements that he became known as "No Show Jones." By his own account, it took much too long to record the narration at the end of "He Stopped Loving Her Today," his comeback hit, because he couldn't talk without slurring his words when he was drunk, and he couldn't get to the studio sober.

Both Wynette and Jones found some stability in their personal lives around 1980. In 1978, Wynette married songwriter George Richey, with whom she remained married until her death twenty years later. Jones married Nancy Sepulvado in 1983, and with her help finally freed himself from dependence on alcohol and drugs. He has been sober for decades.

Despite the issues in their personal lives, together and apart—and perhaps partly because of them—Wynette and Jones were a perfect match musically. Both sang with real feeling and empathy; their duet recordings like "Take Me" and "Let's Build a World Together" document this. The emotional impact of their singing was, if anything, even more evident in their solo work. We hear it in two of their biggest hits: Wynette's "D-I-V-O-R-C-E," which topped the country charts in 1968, and Jones's "He Stopped Loving Her Today," which reached No. 1 on the country singles chart in 1980.

Singing with Feeling

Make up a short list of singers who stand out because of the emotional power and conviction of their singing, and it may very well include Billie Holiday, Bessie Smith, Frank Sinatra, Muddy Waters, Hank Williams, Ray Charles, and just a few others. There is no obvious art in their singing. None sings with the refined quality of a classically trained vocalist, nor do they display the vocal agility of a gospel or jazz singer, or a contemporary diva.

Although they come from different genres, their singing shares certain qualities: It is personal, honest, straightforward, and intensely emotional. Because of this, these singers can transmute even a mundane song into a moving experience.

We hear these same qualities in the singing of Tammy Wynette and George Jones. Both excelled at expressing in song the anguish of love gone wrong. They had experienced this pain firsthand and were able to translate it into music that touched listeners deeply. In Wynette's "D-I-V-O-R-C-E" (1968) and Jones's "He Stopped Loving Her Today" (1980), we encounter the heartbreak of the end of a relationship. "D-I-V-O-R-C-E" tells the story in the present tense; we learn about the breakup of the marriage as it's happening. In "He Stopped Loving Her Today," the parting happened long ago (the love letters in the song are eighteen years old).

Wynette's vocal style is, on one level, so everyday that she sounds as though she could be singing along with the radio while doing someone's hair. But there is passion in her singing: She sounds strong and vulnerable at the same time. When she sings in "D-I-V-O-R-C-E," her voice sounds as though it's on the verge of breaking. The intensity of her singing tells us she has been through the experience she's singing about: In fact, her firstborn was only two and she was carrying her third child when she divorced for the first time only three years earlier. She is able to draw on that experience, then use the song to convey it to us. Her performance is emotionally naked because it is both plain and passionate. She is at once the neighbor next door and larger than life.

"He Stopped Loving Her Today" was the song that turned George Jones's career around and helped turn his life around, as well. Despite his substance-abuse problems, he delivered a performance of real conviction. The lyric strains our credulity: In this day and age, it is hard to imagine anyone carrying an unrequited love to the grave. But Jones's performance, which builds slowly to the climax, makes it credible. When he opens up on the chorus, he makes us feel how deeply the anonymous "he" felt about the woman who left him behind. There is not a trace of sentimentality in his singing. There is only

---

LISTENING CUE • **"D-I-V-O-R-C-E" (1968),** Tammy Wynette, Bobby Braddock, and Claude Putman. Wynette, vocal.

STYLE Rock-tinged country • **FORM** Verse/chorus: verse and chorus almost identical melodically

Listen For . . .

INSTRUMENTATION
Voice, choir, electric guitar, steel guitar, acoustic guitar, electric bass, drums

PERFORMANCE STYLE
Wynette's heartfelt singing a classic country vocal sound

RHYTHM
Gentle rock rhythm at moderate tempo

MELODY
Four long phrases in verse and chorus (almost identical)

TEXTURE
Voice(s) dominant, bass next strongest voice, middle lighter; variation from solo voice (thinner) to chorus (thicker)

Remember . . .

MODERN COUNTRY THEME
Song updates personal themes of country music.

WYNETTE'S IMPASSIONED SINGING
Wynette's style—subtle timing, change in quality from strong to whispered—gives emotional credibility to lyric.

DOMINANT COUNTRY SOUNDS
In addition to Wynette's singing, steel guitar main obbligato instrument, guitar with reverb (borrowed from early 1960s rock)

COUNTRY ROCK BEAT
Rock rhythm on top of honky-tonk–style two beat: bass alternating with crisp backbeat

Listen to this selection in CourseMate.

LISTENING CUE • **"He Stopped Loving Her Today" (1979),** Bobby Braddock and Claude Putman. George Jones, vocal.

STYLE Contemporary country ballad • **FORM** Verse/chorus; verse and chorus have the same harmony and phrase structure.

Listen For . . .

RHYTHM
Slow tempo. Soft country rock beat; backbeat strong at high points in the song. No strong syncopation, but subtle rhythmic play in Jones's singing.

MELODY
The verse features four medium-length phrases with pauses in between. The chorus has the same phrase structure and harmony, but the melody is higher.

INSTRUMENTATION
Jones's voice; backup choir; acoustic, electric, and steel guitars; electric bass; drums; full string section (violin, not fiddle, sound); harmonica, and piano

PERFORMANCE STYLE
Jones's singing has subtle timing and warmth within the straight (no vibrato) country sound.

TEXTURE
Melody is dominant. Rhythm section is in the background with a relatively simple accompaniment. Other instruments and sections (strings) play melodic background parts: figuration and sustained chords.

Remember . . .

TELLING A STORY SIMPLY
The ballad is about the story; everything else—Jones's emotionally credible sing, the gentle background—supports that.

NASHVILLE PRODUCTION
Mix of country (harmonica and steel guitar) and commercial (choir and rich string writing) sounds.

EVOLUTION OF COUNTRY MUSIC
Archetypical contemporary country song derives more directly from story-telling songs of Vernon Dalhart and Jimmie Rodgers than old-time music of 1920s and before.

Listen to this selection in CourseMate.

the pain, plainly yet artfully expressed in subtle timing and—at the climax—deep inflection that says more than just the words could ever say.

Unlike Wynette, Jones is not singing this song from direct personal experience—indeed, he could not without the intervention of a medium. At best, we sense the empathy of the friend who is unable to console the "he" in the song while he's alive. Perhaps Jones felt the parting from a different mistress: the bottle. Around this time Jones began to dry out and put his life back together. In effect, he died and was reborn—sober this time.

Both Wynette and Jones sing simply and directly; there is nothing mannered in their singing. Their art is in expressive nuance and timing, not histrionics. Because of their emotional power, the best recordings of Wynette and Jones are evergreens—still as vital today as they were when they were released and a continuing affirmation of the expressive essence of so much country music. Their singing remains a standard for those who have followed in their path.

The Nashville Sound

Both of the songs were written by Bobby Braddock and Curly Putman, who were veteran Nashville songwriters, produced by Billy Sherrill, recorded in Nashville, and released on Epic Records. They were the product of a well-oiled musical machine used for manufacturing an unending string of hits.

The music is essentially emotionally neutral: There is nothing in the melody of the song that tells us about the pain—except when the singers reshape it. The accompaniments are tasteful and very much in the background. In both songs, we hear steel guitar and a discreet rhythm section playing a subdued rock rhythm at a slow tempo. It's a rhythmic foundation that helps maintain momentum at a slow tempo and keeps the songs in step with the times. "D-I-V-O-R-C-E" also has a choir very much in the background, which surfaces only during the chorus. In Jones's song, a string section creates a lush cushion of sound.

Both songs show Nashville at its most efficient: The songs are simple songs that are good vehicles for good singers, and they feature professional musical settings appropriate to the mood of the song. In songs like this, the story and the singers' telling of it are the expressive focus. Everything else should be in the background, and it is.

There would seem to be a purpose to the neutrality of the song and the setting. Nashville has many skilled songwriters capable of much more than three-chord songs. The producers, arrangers, and studio musicians are also highly skilled, even though they seldom flaunt it. Although the fruit of their work is far more involved and elaborate than "This Land Is Your Land," it seems to embody much the same philosophy as Woody Guthrie's: Don't let the tune or the accompaniment get in the way of the words. In country music, however, it's not just what you say, but how you say it.

The songs are similar in approach: The story unfolds gradually, describing a painful situation in plain language. Each has a gimmick—the spelling out of words in "D-I-V-O-R-C-E"; the fact that we learn toward the end that only death can end his (unrequited) love. The emotional impact of these songs comes almost exclusively from the singing of Wynette and Jones. Performed by less gifted performers, they could easily slip into soap-opera sentimentality.

The Growth of Country Music

The crossover success of Wynette, Jones, and many other acts from the late 1960s and 1970s signaled the continued growth of the audience for country music. For the first time in its history, country music attracted a large enough audience beyond its traditional constituency to make substantial inroads into the pop charts.

Two of the reasons for country music's increased popularity involved politics: Both the conservative backlash from the sixties and the election of Jimmy Carter gave country music a boost. Haggard's song was the tip of the iceberg; country music seemed to stand hand in hand with conservative points of view. Ironically, it also began to attract a young, non-southern, post-hippie audience—the very group that prompted the conservative backlash—at about the same time. Carter's election stirred southern pride; he was the first president from the Deep South elected in the twentieth century. The White House became a major venue for country performers during his presidency.

There was broad support for virtually the entire spectrum of country music: updated versions of traditional styles (Johnny Cash, Merle Haggard, and Willie Nelson), country-flavored pop (Glen Campbell and Kenny Rogers) and the commercially oriented contemporary country coming from Nashville, and rock/country fusions (the early Eagles, Kris Kristofferson, and Linda Ronstadt). The clearest indicator of the strength of country's newly won popularity was the commercial success of hard-country acts. Haggard, Nelson, and other like-minded artists defied the conventional Nashville wisdom that commercial success requires diluting country with pop. More than any other trend, their broad appeal signaled country's entry into the musical mainstream.

As a result, many of its stars gained national recognition: Merle Haggard, Johnny Cash, Tammy Wynette, George Jones, Loretta Lynn, and Willie Nelson all became household names. Dolly Parton went beyond that: She became a pop icon, one of the handful of celebrities whose every move is grist for the tabloid mill.

CHAPTER 70
The Explosion of Country Music

In 1999, Larry Cordle and Lonesome Standard Time released an album entitled *Murder on Music Row*. The title track spelled out the divide between traditionalists and those in the country music industry who would sell out in pursuit of fame and fortune. The lyrics don't mince words: "But someone killed country music/Cut out its heart and soul/They got away with murder/Down on music row." (Music Row is the Tin Pan Alley of country music, in Nashville.)

George Strait and Alan Jackson covered Cordle's song, first in a performance at the 1999 Country Music Association awards ceremony, then on Strait's *Latest Greatest Straitest Hits* (2000). The track won the 2000 CMA Vocal Event of the Year award.

The New Traditionalists

About twenty years earlier, Ricky Skaggs had issued a more metaphorical warning when he covered Lester Flatt and Earl Scruggs's "Don't Get Above Your Raisin" in 1981. The song is ostensibly about a social-climbing girl, who is described unflatteringly by the boyfriend she's left behind. However, many in country music took the song as an allegory for country's loss of traditional values in its romance with pop and rock and its need to reconnect to its roots: The "gal" in the song is country music.

Strait, Jackson, Skaggs, Randy Travis, Vince Gill, and Dwight Yoakum were among those "new traditional" country artists whose careers took off in the 1980s. All sought to put country music's old wine into new bottles. All have enjoyed commercial success, but none more than George Strait, the "King of Country."

George Strait

If the tabloids in the checkout line are any indication, good news is not particularly newsworthy. That's not the case for George Strait: The almost unbroken good news of his personal and professional life has not hampered his career. According to the RIAA, he has sold about 70 million units; among country artists, only Garth Brooks has sold more.

Unlike the idols that he sings about in "Murder on Music Row" Strait (b. 1952) has had few bumps in the road: no substance abuse issues, women problems, or jail terms. He grew up near San Antonio, Texas; his mother left him with his father and brother when he was in third grade; he dropped out of college to elope with his wife Norma in 1971 and enlisted in the U.S. Army shortly after; returned to college in 1975 and started performing locally. Shortly after signing with MCA records, he released his first single: "Unwound" (1981) reached the country singles Top 10. Since that time, he has had an unbroken string of hits, and has received dozens of awards.

Among his No. 1 singles was "Check Yes or No" (1995), which won several awards as top country single of the year. In the song, a guy tells how he met his sweetheart

LISTENING CUE • **"Check Yes or No" (1995),** Danny Wells and Dana Hunt. George Strait.

STYLE New traditional country • **FORM** Verse/chorus

Listen For . . .

INSTRUMENTATION
Vocal, steel guitar, guitars, bass, drums

RHYTHM
Discrete rock rhythm with some syncopation in melody

PERFORMING STYLE
Strait's classic country style: unaffected singing with no vibrato

MELODY
Verse has moderately long phrases; chorus contains several hooks, including the title phrase.

TEXTURE
Thin and understated in verse; richer, with full band in chorus

Remember . . .

COMFORTABLE COUNTRY
Strait's singing style, the featured steel guitar and fiddle, and the discreet and skillful support from the rhythm instruments are among the most familiar and enduring features of country music.

STORY IN THE FOREFRONT
The novel element in the song is the story; the musical setting is designed to enhance it, rather than deflect attention from it.

THE APPEAL OF COUNTRY MUSIC
For the many listeners who want no-frills songs with accessible, easily grasped words and music, country is the first place to go.

Listen to this selection in CourseMate.

in third grade, married her, and is still in love with her twenty years after the wedding. Its feel-good storyline is a different side of country music—there's no dirty linen, demon rum, divorce, or death. Strait's singing is direct and unmannered, the song builds nicely to the chorus, and the instrumental accompaniment, which features steel guitar and fiddle, provides skilled, yet unobtrusive support. There are no surprises, and that is a large part of the song's appeal.

Strait's music is firmly rooted in the past. The music of Alabama enhances traditional country themes and sounds with a more contemporary setting.

Alabama

When Teddy Gentry, the bassist with the country group Alabama, received his first royalty check from RCA, he bought his grandfather's farm, where he had been raised. The following year, he bought his great-grandfather's farm, which was adjacent to his grandfather's. The combined properties are now the Bent Tree Farms; the name refers to the trees used by the Cherokees on their Trail of Tears.

This sense of place, and the culture that has emerged from it, is central to Alabama's music. Gentry (b. 1952) and his two partners—Gentry's cousin and lead vocalist/rhythm guitarist Randy Owen (b. 1949), and Jeff Cook (b. 1949), the lead guitarist, fiddler, and musical driving force—grew up in Ft. Payne, Alabama, not far from Lookout Mountain. The three of them formed Alabama in 1969, plunged full-time into the music business in 1973, and spent the rest of the 1970s as a bar band, mainly along the South Carolina coast. After a disastrous record deal with a small label that went bankrupt, the group decided to limit partnership in the band to the three of them. Other musicians who played with them were salaried.

In songs like the group's 1992 hit "Born Country," country themes and sounds predominate. For Gentry, the lyric could be autobiographical. Traditional country elements dominate the music as well: Owen's vocal style and the close harmony of all three in the chorus, the honky-tonk–based rhythm in the chorus, the fiddle solo and guitar licks. However, more modern sounds—the array of synthesizer timbres underneath the vocals and in interludes, and the widely varied textures—complement the country elements without obscuring them. The result is a track that is clearly country, but with a more up-to-date sound. This skillful mix of old and new helps account for Alabama's extraordinary success and the broadened demographic that they brought to country music.

Putting the New in New Traditional Country

The relationship between country traditionalists and more pop-oriented country acts is not black versus white but different shades of grey. "Tradition" in country music has always been relative: Hank and the Hag would not have been allowed on the *Grand Ole Opry* in the 1930s, and the steel guitar came from Hawaii. So selling out has more to do with the balance between country and outsider elements. At one extreme is music that is indistinguishable from mid-1950s hard country; at the other is music that is country in name only. In between, and unmistakably country, are groups like Alabama.

LISTENING CUE · **"Born Country" (1991),** Byron Hill and John Schweers. Alabama.

STYLE Contemporary country • **FORM** Verse/chorus

Listen For . . .

INSTRUMENTATION
Vocals, plus fiddle, drums, tambourine, electric bass, acoustic and electric guitars, keyboard, synthesizers, and strings

RHYTHM
Contrast between offbeat accompaniment in verse and honky-tonk rock beat in chorus

PERFORMING STYLE
Close harmony in chorus

HARMONY
Contrast between open, power chord-like harmonies in verse and full harmonies in chorus

TEXTURE
String/synthesizer cushion enrich conventional vocal/fiddle/country rhythm section

Remember . . .

COUNTRY THEME
"Born Country" celebrates country lifestyle

ENHANCED SOUND
Modern pop instruments discreetly support vocals and country instruments: fiddle, guitar.

COUNTRY BALANCE POINT
Electronic instruments modernize, but do not undermine, country theme or musical setting.

Listen to this selection in CourseMate.

CHAPTER 71
Country, Pop, and Glamour

In the 1980 film *9 to 5*, Dolly Parton portrays Doralee Rhodes, a country girl who has moved to the city with her husband and taken a position as a secretary to Franklin Hart, a male chauvinist pig of a boss, who is portrayed perfectly by Dabney Coleman. Hart has been trying to seduce Doralee without success and has bragged that he is in fact sleeping with her, which initially makes Doralee a pariah among her female coworkers. As the film progresses, Parton's co-stars Lily Tomlin and Jane Fonda discover that Hart has been lying and that there's a brain underneath Doralee's blonde wig and a good heart underneath the ample bosom.

9 to 5 was Parton's first film role. In addition to her starring role, she also wrote and recorded the title track, which topped both the country and pop charts and received Academy Award and Golden Globe nominations for best song. Her success on screen and in the studio completed her transformation from Porter Wagoner's sidekick to pop culture icon.

DOLLY PARTON

© Pictorial Press Ltd/Alamy

Dolly Parton and the Pursuit of Pop Success

Dolly Parton (b. 1946) grew up dirt poor on a tobacco farm in east Tennessee. In her 1971 hit "Coat of Many Colors," she recounts how her mother sewed a coat out of scraps of cloth because they didn't have enough money to buy her even a second-hand coat. Parton's talent and ambition more than made up for her family's poverty. She made her first appearance on the *Grand Ole Opry* at thirteen years old, and moved to Nashville to pursue a music career after graduating from high school. In 1967, she released her first album and joined Porter Wagoner on his long-running television show. More determined than any of

LISTENING CUE • **"9 to 5" (1980),** Dolly Parton. Parton, vocal.

STYLE Country pop • **FORM** Open-end verse/chorus

Listen For . . .

INSTRUMENTATION
Lead and backup vocals, horn section, big rhythm section (drums, keyboards, guitar, bass)

PERFORMING STYLE
Parton's singing has a decided country twang.

RHYTHM
Moderately slow, clear rock rhythm with strong backbeat, double-time activity, and frequent syncopation

MELODY
Riff-based chorus with three-note title phrase hook

TEXTURE
Dense, multilayered texture with horn riffs and keyboard and guitar fills over steady rhythm

Remember . . .

POP SONG/POP SETTING
With its syncopated riff-based melody, Parton's song has more in common with pop than country, and her musical support has no obvious country elements. It's a "city" song, not a country song.

COUNTRY CONNECTION
Parton's singing is the only clear connection with country music.

COUNTRY, POP, AND CROSSOVER SUCCESS
Although the success of "9 to 5" was due in part to the success of the film, it's clear that Parton's heavy infusion of pop elements played a large role.

Listen to this selection in CourseMate.

her peers or predecessors to "get above her raisin'," she left Wagoner in 1974; signed with Katz-Gallin-Morey, a Los Angeles–based public relations firm in 1976; began covering pop and R&B songs; and achieved her commercial breakthrough a year later with the album *Here You Come Again*. The film *9 to 5* was the first of several starring roles during the 1980s; they cemented her status as one of the few celebrities identified by a single name.

Parton's title track hit parallels her role for the film. The lyric describes the grind and frustrations of city-style work in direct, everyday language. The musical setting is urban—R&B-flavored pop; there is no obvious evidence of countrifed rhythms, instrumentation, or melody. Parton's twang and pure country vocal timbre embedded in a pop setting depict musically Doralee's situation in the film: a country girl in the city. The song and its success aligned perfectly with Parton's professional ambitions; it was a certified pop/country hit.

Parton not only brought glitz into country but also blazed a trail for other women with talent, ambition, and a good business sense (as a businesswoman, Parton is often referred to as the "Iron Butterfly"). Among the beneficiaries of Parton's success are Trisha Yearwood, Shania Twain, Faith Hill, and Carrie Underwood. And like Parton, most of these female country stars have blended country with pop and rock. We consider two contrasting approaches to country fusions in the music of the Dixie Chicks and Taylor Swift.

The Dixie Chicks and a Country Perspective on Rock

In 2002, the Dixie Chicks—at the time Natalie Maines (b. 1974), Martie Maguire (b. Martha Erwin, 1969), and Emily Robison (b. Emily Erwin, 1972)—released a cover of Fleetwood Mac's 1975 hit "Landslide." The music video of "Landslide" alternates between Maines standing in surreal settings; Robison, who is proudly pregnant, lying in a stylized grassy field with a house that grows roots; and Maguire walking through an urban neighborhood. All three women project down-home glamour: Maines and Robison wear long gowns but are barefoot; Maguire is wearing a sexy pantsuit. They are clearly worldly women, and the backgrounds have more to do with the art of Salvador Dali than with actual farms and forests. At the same time, we hear and see Robison play the dobro and Maguire play mandolin—after she plucks it out of midair.

In its mix of traditional and modern, rural and urban, and real and surreal, the video seems to encapsulate the creative tension between then and now that characterizes much contemporary country music, and the music of the Dixie Chicks in particular. Both the video and their version of the song highlight the group's independent career path.

The Dixie Chicks began as a four-person, all-girl bluegrass group busking on Dallas street corners. The sisters are excellent instrumentalists: Maguire on violin and mandolin; Robison on banjo and dobro. As their career

LISTENING CUE • "Landslide" (2002), Stevie Nicks. The Dixie Chicks.

STYLE Contemporary country • **FORM** Verse/bridge/chorus

Listen For . . .

INSTRUMENTATION
Lead and harmony vocals, banjo, mandolin, acoustic guitar, dobro, bass

PERFORMANCE STYLE
Country twang in lead and harmony vocals: no vibrato, pure sound

RHYTHM
Bluegrass-type activity over two-beat rhythm at a moderate tempo; not much syncopation

MELODY
Moderate-length phrases in narrow range unfold gently, peaking to the title word.

TEXTURE
Rich texture concentrated in mid-range, with several melodically interesting accompaniment figures; vocal, with and without harmony, in the forefront

Remember . . .

TRADITIONAL SOUND, MODERN SONG
Remake of AOR rock hit given a fresh sound with bluegrass instrumentation

CLOSE HARMONY
Dixie Chicks' distinctive vocal sound comes from Maguire and Robison's harmonizing above and below the melody.

COUNTRY CROSSOVER
Huge success of song is evidence of enduring appeal of tuneful melody presented directly, freshly, and skillfully.

Listen to this selection in CourseMate.

took off, they moved away from bluegrass toward contemporary country. The pivotal point in their career came in 1995, when Maines, the daughter of top-session steel guitarist Lloyd Maines, joined the group, now down to just three, as lead vocalist. Maines' singing gave the group a more mainstream sound; they quickly became a top country act, with multiple multiplatinum albums.

Home (2002), their third album with Maines, simultaneously looked back to the past and ahead to the future. Unlike the previous two albums, it was an all-acoustic recording. In addition to the traditional bluegrass instruments—fiddle, banjo, dobro, mandolin, bass—there were steel guitar and Celtic instruments on several tracks. Despite this traditional orientation, the group scored a huge crossover hit with their cover of Fleetwood Mac's "Landslide."

For the Dixie Chicks, adapting "Landslide" was a relatively straightforward task. Maines' vocal style isn't that far removed from that of Fleetwood Mac lead singer Stevie Nicks, and the original version of the song features an intricate acoustic guitar accompaniment. The group simply adapted the guitar accompaniment to banjo and mandolin, added acoustic bass, guitar, and dobro, and sang the chorus in their trademark three-part close harmony. The two versions of "Landslide" sound like not-too-distant points on a continuum. The song would serve as a prelude to the group's more thorough embrace of rock, a career direction precipitated in part by their controversial political positions.

Taking the Long Way from Country to Rock

In April 2003, the Dixie Chicks launched their Top of the World tour, in support of *Home,* in London. During the concert. Maines remarked, "Just so you know, we're ashamed the president of the United States is from Texas." She would later apologize for disrespecting the president, but not for her antiwar position. It was not her first antiwar statement; previously, she had taken fellow country star Toby Keith to task for his ardent support of the war and the president. The remark provoked death threats and boycotts, and another thinly veiled barb at Keith continued to erode their support among country fans, to the point that Martie Maguire told a German reporter later that year, "We don't feel a part of the country scene any longer; it can't be our home any more." Despite a disappointing tour, the group refused to back down from their earlier position.

For their next album, the group worked with superproducer Rick Rubin, who had overseen projects by such diverse acts as Run-D.M.C., Metallica, the Red Hot Chili Peppers, and Johnny Cash. Martie Maguire recalled Rubin telling her, "I think this should sound like a great rock act making a country album, not a country act making a rock album." The result was *Taking the Long Way,* which entered the Top 200 album charts at No. 1 and won several Grammys. What might have been professional suicide in an earlier time redefined their career and broadened their audience, even as it left some of their country core behind. In the lyrics to "Not Ready to Make Nice," a single from the album, they recounted their ordeal—the death threats, a mother telling her child to hate a stranger—and made clear that they would continue to stand by their principles.

After concluding their Accidents and Accusations tour, which was poorly attended in country music strongholds, the group took a break from recording and touring. In June 2010, they briefly joined the Eagles' Summer 2010 tour.

Four days after the Dixie Chicks began their Accidents and Accusations tour, Taylor Swift released her first single, "Tim McGraw." It marked the beginning of her swift ascent to stardom.

Taylor Swift and "Cosmetic" Country

If Larry Cordle, George Strait, and Alan Jackson wanted to locate the murderers of country music, they could find culprits in the offices of Scott Borchetta's Big Machine Records, located along Nashville's Music Row. Borchetta founded Big Machine Records in 2005 and signed Taylor Swift after hearing her sing at a local club. Her self-titled first album followed quickly on the heels of "Tim McGraw." Two years later, Swift released *Fearless,* which became the best-selling album of 2009.

The prosecutors of the Music Row murderers might well try to convict Swift and Borchetta on the *lack* of evidence: songs that aren't about common country themes, a vocal style that does not have that immediately identifiable country sound, rhythms that are not countrified. There are traditional country instruments, but they are part of the mix rather than in the forefront. Swift's strongest defense would be her passionate love of country music.

Taylor Swift (b. 1989) grew up in Wyomissing, Pennsylvania, a comfortable small town about 60 miles northwest of Philadelphia and just under 800 miles from Nashville. Her interest in country music began early. Among the country artists she has cited as influences are Patsy Cline, Dolly Parton, Shania Twain, and the Dixie Chicks, whom she credits for "stretching boundaries." The granddaughter of an opera singer, she began performing in grade school, made her first trip to Nashville at age eleven, where she tried without success to secure a recording contract, and started writing songs at twelve, shortly after learning three chords on the guitar. To support her intense desire for a career as a country musician, her family relocated to Hendersonville, Tennessee, a suburb of Nashville, when she was fourteen, and she signed a contract as a songwriter with Sony/ATV shortly after the move. By sixteen, she had recorded her first album, which went multiplatinum; she was a star before she graduated from high school.

Country music may have been Swift's first and deepest love, but her music also has much in common with the singer-songwriters of the early 1970s and the tuneful rock and roll and rhythm and blues of the late 1950s. Like the singer-songwriters, Swift's music is drawn so directly from her own experience that some of her ardent fans have attempted to match the stories in her songs to real-life incidents. And both words and music can evoke 1950s teen-themed music: "Tim McGraw" describes the painful end to a summer relationship; its melody is set over a four-chord progression that is reminiscent of the "Heart and Soul" chords so common in doo-wop and rock-and-roll ballads. We discover another chapter in her high school life in "You Belong with Me," a track from *Fearless*.

In "You Belong With Me," Swift seems to be channeling Buddy Holly. Her lyric tells a story of teen angst, and in the music video, until her glamorous appearance at the dance, she wears big-rimmed glasses that are only slightly more stylish than Holly's thick frames. (In a nice touch, she also portrays the drama queen with whom she competes for the star wide receiver.) The song is by a high school student about the kind of crisis that seems so much a part of high school life. The locale could be anywhere in the United States where football is played; there's nothing that suggests country life. The musical setting is only cosmetically country. We hear banjo and steel guitar in the verse of the song, but they disappear in the chorus. Stylistically, "You Belong with Me" has more in common with the punk-tinged pop rock of the 1980s than it does with any of the music in this unit.

LISTENING CUE • **"You Belong With Me" (2009),** Taylor Swift and Liz Rose. Taylor Swift.

SYLE Country pop • **FORM** Verse/chorus with contrasting section before final chorus

Listen For . . .

INSTRUMENTATION
Lead vocal, banjo, steel guitar, acoustic guitar, electric guitar, electric bass, drums, synthesizers

PERFORMING STYLE
Swift's singing devoid of traditional country twang; banjo used like rhythm guitar

RHYTHM
1980s pop punk rock beat, especially in chorus; some syncopation in verse and chorus

MELODY
Long phrases in both verse and melody

HARMONY
Beyond the typical three chords of country music

Remember . . .

MUSIC FOR TEENS
The lyric is about teen life and love in mainstream America.

TUNEFUL CONTEMPORARY POP
A long-phrased melody over a bouncy rock beat

WHERE'S THE COUNTRY?
The country connections are tenuous at best: mainly banjo and steel guitar at the beginning of the song. Story, vocal style, and rhythm have no apparent connection to country music.

Listen to this selection in CourseMate.

UNIT 16

LOOKING BACK, LOOKING AHEAD

The Murder of Country Music?

CONSIDERED FROM A TRADITIONALIST'S PERSPECTIVE, "You Belong with Me" and the other tracks on *Fearless* do in fact sound the death knell of country music. The country elements are at best part of the mix and at worst completely absent. However, the focus on traditional country music values may obscure the larger and more important question, which is: How well do Swift's songs succeed at what they set out to do? A traditional country music setting would not serve the stories that Swift tells in her songs very well. Her country-flavored pop/rock mix does, as millions of fans who relate to her words and music have discovered. From a country perspective, Swift is indeed "stretching boundaries," but from a popular music perspective she's imaginatively bringing together disparate styles into a pleasing synthesis.

Country music won't die because of her music and the music of like-minded acts—there will almost certainly be another generation of George Straits and Alan Jacksons, and an audience for their music. Instead, Swift's songs bring a new dimension to country music, and to popular music.

The overwhelming success of *Fearless* is yet another reminder of the central place of country music in the popular music landscape. There is a sound musical reason for its increased presence: Country music fills the "accessibility void" in contemporary popular music. For listeners who want songs with easy-to-understand words set to a tuneful melody, country music is a consistently better source than rap, dance music, alternative rock, heavy metal, or pop.

Electronica and Rap

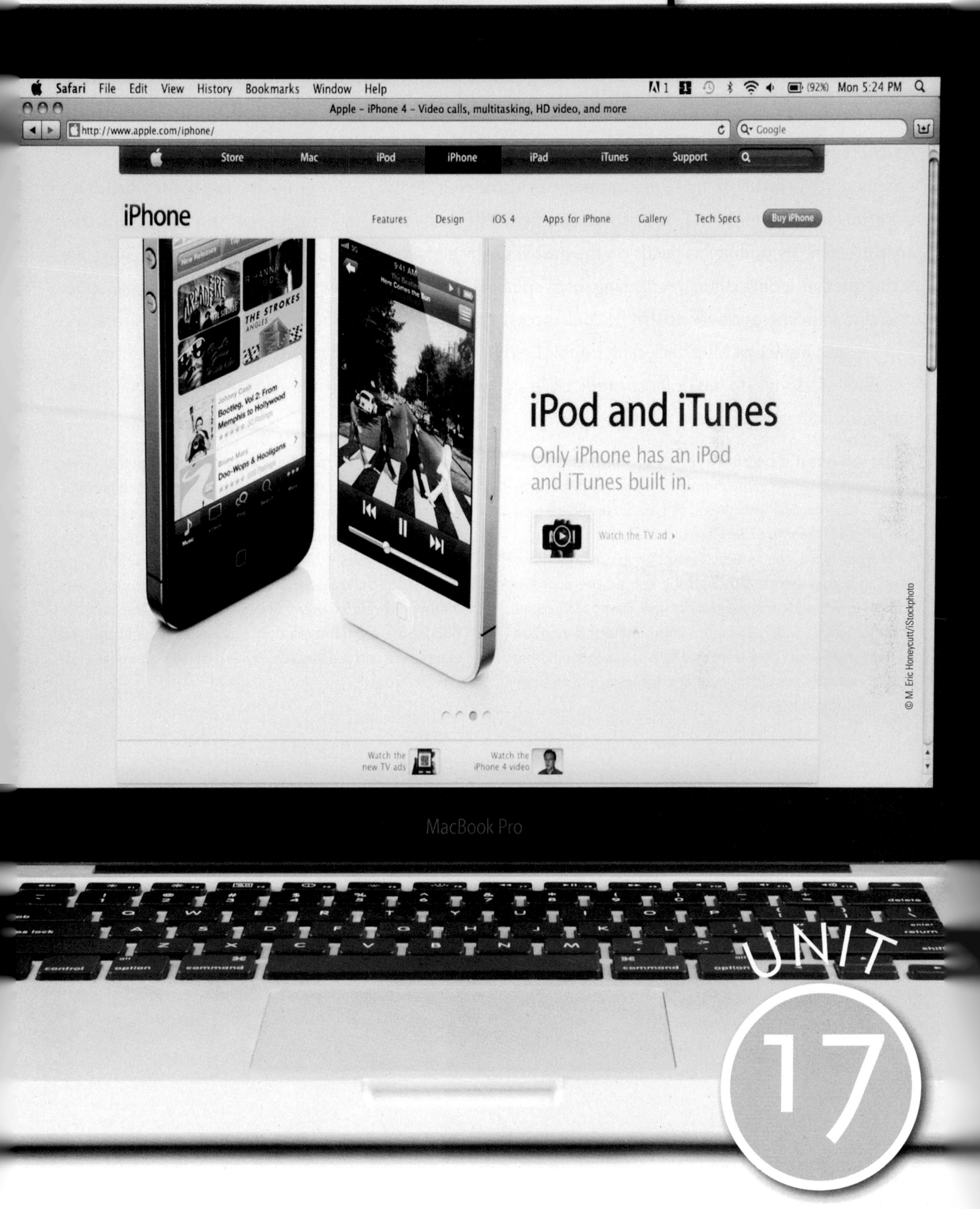

© M. Eric Honeycutt/iStockphoto

UNIT 17

UNIT 17

At the top of the welcome page of Joseph Saddler's website (www.grandmasterflash.com) is the statement: "The first DJ to make the turntable an instrument." In the seventies, DJs never put their hands on the grooves of the vinyl discs they played. Saddler, better known as Grandmaster Flash, made the turntable an instrument by putting his hands on the grooves, which enabled him to develop an array of innovative techniques, including cutting, scratching, back spinning, and flaring. Soon, he would mark particular spots on a disc with tape or crayon so that he could access a particular spot on the fly. Armed with two turntables, a mixer, and a stack of discs, including doubles of the tracks he planned to use, Flash could transform the playback of a song—to this point as predictable an event as the sun rising in the east—into a unique, spontaneously crafted experience.

In the sense that it became a device in which one could shape musical sound in the moment, Flash turned the turntable into a musical instrument. But because the sounds had already been recorded, the turntable was different in kind from more conventional instruments such as those used in a rock band. Although the use of prerecorded sounds in live performance was not new, Flash's techniques brought a new, richer, and more improvisatory dimension to the experience. They were one sign of a movement that would radically transform cutting-edge rock-era music in the eighties and beyond.

It should be noted that there was a good reason that other DJs handled recordings by the edge: Bringing the grooves into contact with anything—fingers, crayons, errant tonearm needles—would damage the disc and eventually render it unplayable. While Grandmaster Flash was perfecting his novel techniques, another revolution was under way that would render them all but obsolete. In this unit, we discuss the digital revolution and consider its impact on electronica and rap, the two styles that would benefit most directly from it.

CHAPTER 72
The Digital Revolution

The Ocean House is a luxurious beachfront hotel in Watch Hill, Rhode Island. It opened in June, 2010, on the site of the first Ocean House, a grand Victorian hotel that had become dilapidated; the owners replicated the look and ambience of the old Ocean House as closely as possible. On many evenings, especially in the summer, guests might hear a pianist playing a Chopin waltz, a Joplin rag, a Gershwin song, or a number from a Sondheim musical as they enter the hotel. The piano, a beautiful seven-foot Steinway grand, is situated in the "living room" of the hotel, just past the front desk. The sound of the piano does not carry into the dining areas in the hotel, but state-of-the-art digital technology offered a way to transmit live piano music to those parts of the hotel out of earshot.

The Steinway was retrofitted with a device that turned it into a MIDI keyboard controller. The controller is connected to a computer containing samples of a Steinway concert grand, so that when the pianist plays on the Steinway, the computer can stream audio that sounds like a high-end recording of what the pianist is playing in real time. The audio signal is transmitted over the hotel WiFi to an iPod touch that's one of the sound sources for the hotel's music system. To hear the piano music beyond the "living room" in the hotel, a staff member has only to select the iPod touch as the sound source.

MIDI, sampling, and streaming audio are among the digital technologies that have revolutionized every aspect of the music industry: creation, storage and preservation, dissemination, and consumption. In 1981, the year that the Ocean House Steinway was built, digital audio technology was in its infancy. Today, it is developing so rapidly that the technology that you've just read about will probably have been superseded by something even more sophisticated. In this chapter, we explore these and other music-related developments in the digital revolution.

Digital Audio

Digital audio introduced a fundamentally new and different process for the manipulation of sound. Electronic technologies convert sound waves into electrical signals, process the signals, then convert them back into sound. Digital technology adds an extra step: It encodes the waveform generated by the electrical signal into a binary format, then reverses the process for output. This encoding is accomplished by **sampling** the wave at regular intervals, with several possible gradations. On a standard

© Perry Kroll/iStockphoto

CD, the wave is sampled 44,100 times a second; there are 65,536 (16 × 16 × 16 × 16) possible gradations of the wave. This high sampling rate, coupled with the thousands of gradations, makes it possible to simulate the shape of the wave so closely that the original waveform and the digital sampling of it are virtually identical.

Digital audio fools our ears in much the same way that digital images fool our eyes. In introducing what Apple calls the "Retina Display" on the iPhone, Steve Jobs said, "there's a magic number around 300 dpi (dots per inch), if you hold something about 10–12 inches away from your eye, it's the limit of the human retina to distinguish pixels." When magnified, what seems to be a smooth image a foot away is actually a grid of squares, each a single color or shade of gray. However, the size of each square is so small that our eyes are fooled into seeing color blends, curves, and other continuous images. In much the same way, our ears are fooled by digital sampling.

This ability to encode waveform data digitally has had several benefits. First, it eliminates signal degradation. In analog tape recording, there were inevitably some unwelcome sounds: One can hear tape hiss on predigital recordings that have not been remastered or on cassette copies of recordings. The more a tape is copied, the more pronounced the extraneous sounds become. By contrast, digital information can be copied an infinite number of times, with no loss of audio quality, as anyone who has burned a CD or used a file-sharing service knows.

Second, it became possible to maintain quality despite unlimited use. Previously, the quality of sound degraded over time because of the physical contact of a stylus with a record groove, or tape with the tape head. A recording played for the one-hundredth time on a turntable or cassette player will sound worse than the first time, no matter how much care is taken. This problem disappeared with digital audio.

Third, the high sampling rate has enabled those working with computer audio to isolate musical events with a precision that earlier generations could only dream about. Instead of shuttling a tape head back and forth to find the right starting point, those working in the digital domain can quickly identify and mark the beginning and end of a musical event. Once isolated, they can manipulate it at will—compressing or expanding it, changing its pitch higher or lower, changing its timbre, or enhancing it with special effects.

The New Digital Technologies

It was one thing to have the capability of using digital technology; it was quite another to actually have the hardware that made it possible. After years of research and development, three crucial technologies emerged in the early eighties: the audio CD, MIDI, and sampling. Two others, computer audio and the Internet, took off around the turn of the century.

For just a few thousand dollars, anyone can create a home studio that can do just about anything that could have been done only in a million-dollar studio less than a generation ago.

© Chris Schmidt/iStockphoto

Audio CD

The **audio CD** (compact disc) required more than the ability to convert sound into digital data; it was also necessary to apply laser technology to encode data to and decode it from the storage medium (hence "burn" a CD). Research on the laser dates back to a 1958 paper by a physicist at Bell Labs. By the early seventies, lasers were being used to read digital data stored on discs. By 1980 Philips and Sony, two of the leaders in audio research, had agreed on a standard for CD audio: 16-bit sampling and a 44.1K sampling rate.

In 1984 the first CD pressing plant in the United States—in Terre Haute, Indiana—started producing CDs. The first CDs were expensive because the production process was seriously flawed; only a relatively small percentage of the CDs produced were good enough for release. As a result, the cost of a CD was high—higher than cassette or vinyl. Not surprisingly, given the nature of the music business, the cost of a CD remained higher than that of a cassette, even though production costs were soon much lower.

MIDI

Musical Instrument Digital Interface, or simply **MIDI,** is an industry standard that allows electronic instruments to communicate with one another and with a computer. In theory, this seems like a natural and modest step. In practice, it was a tremendous breakthrough for two main reasons. First, it enabled a single person to simulate an orchestra, a rock band, or a swing band, using just one instrument. Using a MIDI-enabled electronic keyboard or other similarly configured device, musicians could choose from an array of MIDI-out sounds—usually no less than 128. They could perform the passage as if playing a piano or organ, but the sound coming out would be like a trumpet, or bells, or violins, or a host of others.

Second, MIDI devices could interact with sequencers. A **sequencer** is a device that enables a person to assemble a sound file, track by track. Using a sequencer that can store eight tracks, a person can re-create the sound of a band: one track for the bass, another for the rhythm guitar, and so on.

Sequencers can also be used to create loops. A **loop** is a short sound file—such as a drum pattern or a bass line—that can be repeated and combined with other loops or freely created material to create a background for a song, whether it's rap, pop, techno, house, or something else. To make this process easier, loops are usually a standard length: eight beats (two measures), sixteen beats (four measures), and so on. With these kinds of resources, assembling the rhythm track to a song can be like building with Legos®. Users simply snap them into a track in their digital audio software.

Sampling

A **sample** is a small sound file. (Please note that this meaning of *sample* is different from the sample of a waveform; the two meanings are related but different.) There are two basic kinds of samples in common use. One is the recorded sound of a voice or group of voices, an instrument (e.g., the Steinway grand piano) or group of instruments (such as a violin section), or some other sound. This sound can then be activated through some other device. For instance, one can buy a disc with the sampled sound of several cellos playing every note on the usable range of the instrument, recorded in many different ways. Then the buyer can install it on a computer, activate it inside the appropriate software, and produce a passage that sounds like a recording of the cello section of a first-rate symphony orchestra.

Primitive forms of this technology have been available since the sixties. The first commercial "sampler" to achieve any kind of currency was the Mellotron®. It was a keyboard instrument in which depressing a key would activate a looped tape of a string sound. It was not very flexible, but it was a cost-efficient alternative to hiring violinists. However, sampling didn't really become practical until digital technology.

Now, sampling has reached such a level of sophistication that it is often impossible to determine whether a passage was recorded live or created using samples. In effect, this kind of sampling is a more advanced version of MIDI playback because the sounds are rendered more accurately.

The other primary kind of sampling involves lifting short excerpts from existing recordings to use in a new recording, much like a visual artist will use found objects to create a collage or assemblage. It has been a staple of rap background tracks since the technology became available in the mid-eighties.

Computer Audio

In 1965 Gordon Moore, one of the founders of Intel, predicted that the number of transistors on a computer chip would double every couple of years. Moore's law, as it has been called, has largely held true. What this has meant is that the amount of computing power one can buy for $1,000 has doubled every eighteen months or so.

Because CD-quality digital audio requires over 1 million samples per second, the first personal computers could not handle audio processing in real time. Fast-forward to the turn of the century, though, and it's a different story. One can burn CDs at . . . I hesitate to write a number here, because by the time you read this, the number will be out of date. Digital audio workstations, sequencers, special effects plug-ins, notation software—there is almost nothing in the process of creating and producing a recording that cannot be done on a computer equipped with the right software and peripherals.

The Internet and Its Impact

The first attempts to create an Internet, or network of networks, date back to the seventies. By 1980, a protocol that enabled different networks to communicate with one another was in place. During its early years, the Internet was mainly under government supervision and control; the National Science Foundation managed it in the United States. However, in 1993, the Internet backbone was opened to the private sector in the United

An iPhone 4G from 2010 has quadruple the RAM, a CPU that's twice as fast, more storage, and a display with almost as many pixels as an iMac from 2000. It fits in the palm of your hand and enables you to access the Internet from almost anywhere. And in the United States, it costs less than half as much as the iMac in inflation-adjusted dollars.

States, and Mosaic, the first browser, became available. (Mosaic became Netscape the following year.) Browsers simplified access to the Internet by providing a graphical user interface, similar to those found on Windows and Mac operating systems.

By 2000, the mechanics of the now-familiar Internet experience were in place. Since then, the pace of innovation and evolution has been breathtakingly fast and remarkably comprehensive. Driving this growth were astounding technological advances, in computing power, storage, portability, access, and more. By way of example: An iPhone 4 from 2010 has quadruple the RAM, a CPU that's twice as fast, more storage, and a display with almost as many pixels as an iMac from 2000. It fits in the palm of your hand and enables you to access the Internet from almost anywhere. And in the United States, it costs less than half as much as the iMac in inflation-adjusted dollars.

Internet access and speed have grown at a comparable pace. Between 2000 and 2010, Internet access almost quintupled. In 2000, less than 6 percent of the world's population could go online; in 2010, almost 29 percent could. In 2010, over three people in four in North America have Internet service; in Europe and Australia/Oceania, about three out of five do. Internet access in Africa has grown by almost 2,400 percent in a decade! With the increasing penetration of broadband coverage, the speed of data transfer has also accelerated. Viewing video online was a rarity in 2000; it was routine in 2010.

Numerous new businesses and services have leveraged these technological advances to open up all aspects of commence: as author Craig Anderson has discussed in depth, "free" is now an option. Consider the cumulative impact on the music industry of these developments:

- **Napster:** Napster went public in 1999 as a peer-to-peer file sharing application. By 2001, Shawn Fanning, its creator, had closed down the service after several artists sued the company. However, BitTorrent sites continue to make music available (illegally) for free. Legal and ethical issues aside, such peer-to-peer networks can function much like a greatly enhanced version of the preview clips on digital download sites such as iTunes and Amazon. They give enthusiastic listeners with more time than money the opportunity to sample a large body of music by a particular act before deciding whether to buy one or more albums.
- **iTunes/iPod:** iTunes appeared in 2001 as an application for organizing and playing back audio files on a Mac computer; the first iPod was introduced a few months later. The iTunes Music Store opened in April 2003, offering tracks from the top record companies and, somewhat later, numerous independent labels. In less than five years, the iTunes Store had become the number one music retailer in the United States; by late 2010, Apple had sold 10 billion tracks.
- **Facebook/MySpace:** Social networks such as Facebook and MySpace took off in the latter half of the decade. Users shared their tastes in music on both; MySpace has become a useful promotional outlet for acts at all levels, from high school garage bands to top acts.
- **YouTube:** YouTube, founded in 2005 and bought by Google a year later, has made everyone a potential video producer or distributor. Users of the site have uploaded not only their own music but also music videos, footage from live events, and audio recordings from their favorite acts, without much regard for copyright infringement. Copyright holders must police YouTube themselves, so much of the material remains available. Some acts have embraced YouTube as an additional promotional tool; one can watch the video of Lady Gaga's "Poker Face" after sitting through a 15-second advertisement (and also watch Korean singer/iPhonist Kim Yeo Hee, aka Applegirl002, cover the song, using four iPhones to accompany herself).

A Digital Democracy

These technologies have made music production available to the masses. The advances in computer-based digital audio have put high-end music production within almost everyone's budget. For just a few thousand dollars, anyone can create a home studio that can do just about anything that could have been done only in a million-dollar studio less than a generation ago. For the aspiring creative artist, the financial investment is a small fraction of what it once was.

The larger investment is time—not only to develop the necessary musical skills but also to master the applications necessary to create the desired result. There are plenty of role models, from Stevie Wonder, Brian Eno, and Grandmaster Flash, to Trent Reznor, Moby, Juan Atkins, Richard James, and hundreds more. And it will only get better.

Digital technology has made it easier to make well-crafted music, both for those with well-developed musical skills and those with little or no skill. But it has also allowed for a less immediate kind of music making. In performance or recording, there can be a world of difference between having a drummer playing and having a drum loop playing, simply because the drummer can respond in the moment. For creative artists, one challenge is to use the technology in ways that enhance the personal dimension of their music rather than undermine it. Another is to create a radically new esthetic, one that builds naturally on the innovations of digital technology. We explore this new esthetic in a discussion of electronica.

CHAPTER 73
Early Electronica

Among the most enduring sound worlds in twentieth-century music is the one created by the singer with guitar: Blind Lemon Jefferson, Jimmie Rodgers, Gene Autry, Maybelle Carter, Robert Johnson, Woody Guthrie, Bob Dylan, Joan Baez, Joni Mitchell, and countless others—country and city, traditional and topical. This sound world transcends style, race, gender, locale, or theme.

Now imagine a sound world that is almost completely opposite. There's little or no singing—and what vocals there are have been filtered through an electronic device. There's no melody with accompanying chords; instead there might be wisps of riffs or some sustained notes. Instead of the simple rhythm of the accompaniment, there is the thump of a low percussion sound marking the beat, several fast-moving patterns, plus other electronically generated loops. Instead of the strumming of an acoustic guitar, there's an array of electronic sounds, complete with special effects (fx). Instead of a story with a beginning and an end, there's total immersion in a sound world with no apparent time boundaries. Instead of a single performer singing and playing while a few others listen, there's a DJ in a booth, surveying a dance floor filled with bodies moving as he mixes the music.

You'll find examples of this totally opposite sound world in the dance/electronica section of your favorite music store—on the street, in the mall, or online. **Electronica** has become the umbrella term for a large and varied family of styles: house, techno, trance, ambient, jungle, drum 'n' bass, industrial dance, and many more.

The almost total contrast between electronica and the folk/blues/country singer underscores how radically different the electronic-based music of the eighties, nineties, and the twenty-first century is from so much earlier music, including much of the music of the early rock era. The differences begin with its origins and continue with its venues, its performance, and ultimately its intent.

The Antecedents of Electronica

In the twentieth century, most popular music genres have evolved through the influence of music from "below"—that is, music from "plain folk" who live outside and beneath the realm of high culture. We often use the word *roots* to convey this. Electronica is different. Its origins are in the most cerebral and esoteric music of the mid-twentieth century, the classical music avant-garde.

During the middle of the twentieth century, composers in Europe and the United States, using equipment as sophisticated as the first tape recorders and synthesizers and as everyday as nuts and bolts, explored virgin musical territory. Shortly after World War II, French composer Pierre Schaeffer began creating music using recorded sounds, rather than musical ideas inside his head, as raw material. The recordings could be of any sounds at all, and they could be modified or transformed before being assembled into a music event. Schaeffer called this process ***musique concrète*** ("concrete music").

Others—among them German composer Karlheinz Stockhausen, French-American composer Edgard Varèse, and American composer John Cage—assembled compositions completely from synthesized sounds, recorded, then spliced together to form a complete composition. In 1958, Lejaren Hiller set up the first computer music studio at the University of Illinois. Among these new electronic works were the first examples of the recording as the creative document—with no performer involved in the creative process.

Much of this music was conceptual: It grew out of a particular idea that the composer wanted to explore. The results probed every possible extreme. American composer Milton Babbitt created works in which every musical parameter was regulated by a predetermined mathematical series, a process called total serialism. At the other end of the spectrum were works by John Cage, in which events were determined by chance. One famous work required the performer to sit in front of a piano without playing it for 4 minutes and 33 seconds; the composition was the ambient sounds in the performing space. Stockhausen composed a work for piano in which fragments of music were printed on an oversized score; the performer determined the sequence of the fragments during the performance. Varèse created *Poème électronique,* an electronic piece that mixes synthesized and *concrète* sounds, for the 1958 World's Fair in Brussels, where it played over 425 loudspeakers.

All of these concepts have found their way into the various electronica styles. For example, the loudspeaker setup for *Poème électronique* anticipates the "total immersion" sound systems of dance clubs. Stockhausen's piano piece, where the performer switches arbitrarily from fragment to fragment, anticipates the DJ mixing on the fly. *Musique concrète* anticipates the found sounds that appear in so much electronica and related styles like rap. And totally electronic pieces anticipate the millions of synthesizer-generated dance tracks.

This isn't to say that there's a straightforward causal connection between mid-century avant-garde music and the electronica of the last twenty-five years. Rather, it should suggest three things. First, even the most esoteric ideas and concepts have a way of filtering down; in this case, they made it all the way to the underground—the club scene that has nurtured this music. Second, electronica could blossom only when the necessary equipment became accessible and affordable. Third, electronica involves more than simply making dance music on computers. Its most imaginative creators have radically altered or overturned conventional assumptions about music making.

A rave is a huge dance party conducted in a large space: outdoors, an abandoned warehouse, or even a large club.

© iStockphoto

Ambient Music, the First Significant Electronic Style

Ambient music, the first significant electronic style to emerge in popular music, dates back to the seventies. Its early history includes Pink Floyd, Kraftwerk, and Tangerine Dream. The father of ambient music, though, is Brian Eno; his recording *Ambient I: Music for Airports* (1978) is seminal. Eno's early music, which shares common ground with the classical minimalist composers, was a bridge between the more esoteric world of classical electronic music and electronica in the popular tradition.

As its name suggests, ambient music is more atmospheric than dance oriented, with more attention to texture and less emphasis on rhythm. As a genre within electronica, it hasn't had a home, but it has merged with both house and techno, introducing a more varied sound world into both. In these hybrid genres, it began to catch on in the late eighties and early nineties.

Music for Dancing, Places to Dance

The dance club is the home of electronica. The dance scene that has nurtured the music since the early eighties has been an underground continuation of disco. The songs produced by Donna Summer and Giorgio Moroder were among the best and most successful examples of early electronica. In essence, there were people who still wanted to dance after disco declined in popularity; the club scene, and the music created for it, gave them the outlet.

During the eighties, two major club scenes emerged in the Midwest: **house music** in Chicago and **techno** in Detroit. Both would have a profound influence on dance music throughout the world. House music was a low-budget continuation of disco. DJs like Frankie Knuckles would use bare-bones rhythm tracks as part of mixes that included disco hits and current disco-inspired songs. The Detroit scene was almost exclusively the work of three friends and colleagues—Juan Atkins, Derrick May, and Kevin Saunderson—who had known one another since junior high. Despite their Detroit base, they were drawn to techno pioneers like Kraftwerk rather than Motown acts. As Atkins said in an interview, "I'm probably more interested in Ford's robots than in Berry Gordy's music." As DJs and producers, they delivered a stark, dark kind of dance music under numerous guises, including Atkins's Model 500 and May's Rhythim Is Rhythim.

By the mid-eighties, the music had migrated to Great Britain. The event that brought the music, the culture, and the drugs up from the underground and into the public eye was the 1988 "Summer of Love," a rave that went on for weeks. A **rave** is a huge dance party conducted in a large space: outdoors, an abandoned warehouse, or even a large club. Ecstasy and other designer drugs were very much part of the scene; they suppressed the need to eat or sleep. (Never mind that the drugs are dangerous—even deadly—especially when consumed with alcohol.) Indoors or out, however, electronica offered a novel musical experience.

Mixes

Dance music has defined a new performance paradigm for popular music. The nature of the venue—the dance club, rather than the arena, auditorium, night club, or coffeehouse—has fundamentally altered what is performed, how it's performed, how it's created, and how it's experienced.

The obvious difference, of course, is the use of recordings, rather than live musicians, to produce the music being heard. That doesn't mean that there isn't the spontaneity and performer–crowd interaction that can be part of a live performance; it's just that it comes from a different source—the DJ—and it occurs mainly

It was the DJ who transformed the practice of connecting songs into an art. A DJ with a two-turntable setup was able to mix a series of songs into a set, an unbroken string of songs.

in the sequencing of tracks rather than within an individual song.

The idea of stringing together a series of songs has a long history in popular music. From the thirties on, dance orchestras and small dance combos would occasionally play a **medley,** a group of songs connected by musical interludes. Often medleys were slow dance numbers; bands would play one chorus of each song rather than several choruses of one song. But they could be any tempo.

During the early years of the rock era, medleys were harder to create in the moment, because the identity of a song was more comprehensive. More than just the melody and harmony, it included every aspect of the song as preserved on the recording. It was more difficult to alter songs so that one would flow easily into the next. Still, the idea of connecting songs did not disappear, as landmark albums such as *Sgt. Pepper* and *The Dark Side of the Moon* evidence. However, it wasn't until disco that the idea of creating medleys resurfaced, in a much-updated form.

It was the DJ who transformed the practice of connecting songs into an art. A DJ with a two-turntable setup was able to **mix** a series of songs into a **set,** an unbroken string of songs that could last longer than even the most extended Grateful Dead jam.

The art of the DJ begins with music that he or she selects. For this reason, many DJs create their own music; it helps them develop a signature style. In the dance club, skilled DJs string together a series of dance tracks with seamless transitions. It is not just that they blend one record into the next without dropping a beat—unless they plan to. They orchestrate the sequence of songs, how much they'll use of each song, and the kind of transition they'll use to give a sense of architecture to the set. It is in this context that they can respond to the dancers' energy, building to a climactic moment or moments as the set unfolds.

In the discussion of rock and rhythm and blues in the sixties, we noted that the record had become the document, the fullest and most direct expression of the musicians' creative intent. This changes in dance music. The musical unit is no longer the *recording*—which is seldom if ever played in its entirety—but the *set*. The recording is the raw material for the set; recordings are the building blocks—much as riffs are the building blocks of so many songs.

This in turn changes the nature of a dance track. It isn't just that it's music for dancing. Instead, the dance track is often created with the idea that it is a component of a larger structure—the set—rather than an entity complete unto itself—the song. This is a radical departure from mainstream rock; rock gave the song an integrity that it could not have had in earlier generations.

Moreover, music for club use employs a different sonic spectrum. During the sixties, popular music designed for airplay concentrated on mid-range frequencies because these come across better on radio than high or low frequencies do. By contrast, dance clubs typically have good sound systems, so producers can take advantage of the entire range of audible frequencies. Electronica styles typically make full use of this, especially low-end frequencies.

This combination of a full sonic spectrum and relentless dance beat, all in an enclosed space, produces a kind of sensory inundation. It is virtually the opposite extreme of sensory deprivation, and it seems to have many of the same mind-altering consequences.

Early Electronica "No UFO's"

Around 1985, "No UFO's" by Model 500 (Juan Atkins, b. 1962) might have been part of a DJ's mix; it is a good early example of Detroit techno. Characteristically, the EP on which "No UFO's" was released contains two versions, "vocal" and "instrumental." The main differences are the length—the instrumental version is almost 3 minutes longer—and voices on the vocal version, although what passes for singing on the track bears no resemblance to Motown. Both versions are constructed mainly from loops. Most are one of four kinds. At the heart is the beat: a bass drum-like sound on every beat and a strong backbeat, marked by several percussive sounds. These persist throughout almost the entire track. The most common are an array of aggressive high-pitched percussive sounds that establish or line up with a sixteen-beat rhythm. There are a few pitched loops: mainly a fast-moving pattern built on four pitches in a low register and sustained chords. Occasionally, there is a cross rhythm: percussive or vocal sounds that sound three times in the space of two beats. The vocal version overlays a story chanted in five-syllable increments; the instrumental version has very little voice, of any kind. In both the texture is active and complex; typically, there are at least four layers of activity in addition to a vocal part.

This example can only hint at the range of sounds, rhythms, and textures possible within the world of electronica. Still, it highlights key features of the genre: a steadily marked beat at about 120 beats per minute; rich, complex textures featuring electronically generated percussive and pitched sounds; very little singing; subtle changes within a generally repetitive, modularly constructed form; and little sense of beginning or end.

Early electronica was the most faceless music of the last part of the twentieth century. Its creators worked anonymously in studios—often alone—and assumed aliases: Aphex Twin is Richard James; Rhythim Is Rhythim is Derrick May. The music they produced—largely instrumental and without the melodic points of entry common to other kinds of popular music—did little to encourage the listener to identify with them in the same way that they would identify with the lead singer or lead guitarist of a rock band. In many ways, this recalls the structure of the music business at the turn of the previous century, when largely anonymous songwriters turned out reams of songs for Tin Pan Alley publishers. For the most part, DJs are the stars of electronica, but it is a very localized form of stardom. However, in the latter half of the 1990s, electronica began to develop a larger audience and a more mainstream presence.

LISTENING CUE · "No UFO's (Instrumental)" (1985), Juan Atkins. Model 500.

STYLE Early electronica dance music · **FORM** Irregularly repetitive

Listen For . . .

INSTRUMENTATION
All sounds except for vocal fragments are generated electronically: drum machines and synthesizers use a variety of timbres.

RHYTHM
Moderately fast beat (about 120 beats per minute); sixteen-beat rhythm with a strong beat (bass drum-like sound) and a stronger backbeat
Most other rhythms (pitched and percussive synthesized sounds) move at sixteen-beat speed; riffs and patterns map onto a rhythm moving four times the beat speed. Lots of syncopation; variation in beat keeping.

MELODY
Pitched lines are melodic in the sense that they have a contour and do not outline chords. They are not tuneful: The low pattern is too fast and syncopated to sing easily, and simply repeats.

TEXTURE
Dense, layered texture is made up of percussive and pitched patterns. Variation in texture as parts leave and return is a main source of interest.

Remember . . .

WHERE'S THE BAND?
Except for voice clips, all sounds are electronically generated; no one "plays" an instrument.

MIXING
In a dance club, the instrumental version of "No UFO's" would be part of a seamless mix; neither beginning nor end would be heard.

NEW WAY OF MAKING MUSIC
No one has to perform in real time at any stage in the creation of the music.

BUSY RHYTHMS
"No UFO's" mixes obvious beat keeping and the backbeat with several layers of active, often complex rhythms.

MANIC MINIMALISM
"No UFO's" is high-energy music with little significant variation or change.

Listen to this selection in CourseMate.

CHAPTER 74
Electronica and the Mainstream

In a 1993 review, Jon Pareles, the contemporary popular music critic of the *New York Times,* wrote:

> If techno music is going to make the leap from dance clubs to the pop charts, its starkly propulsive dance rhythms are going to need melodies, identifiable stars or both. Moby, a one-man band from New York City, could be the techno performer whose showmanship carries him to a wider audience without turning techno tracks into pop songs.

If subsequent developments were any indication, Pareles was preaching to the choir. By mid-decade, electronica began to chart, in the music of acts such as Björk, Chemical Brothers, and Moby, and the resources of electronica were integrated into other non-pop styles, such as the industrial music of Trent Reznor, the mastermind behind Nine Inch Nails. A commercial breakthrough came shortly after the turn of the millennium. In 2002, Moby made the front covers of *Spin, Wired,* and the *New York Times Magazine*.

Electronica as a *Popular* Music: Moby

In the United States, Moby (born Richard Melville Hall, 1965—he took his professional name from the famous novel *Moby Dick,* by Herman Melville, a distant relation) has put a face on electronica, in part by bringing his music closer to a mainstream pop style. This, of course, has provoked cries of outrage from hardcore clubbers who feel that he's selling out. Nevertheless, his music has helped the genre significantly broaden its audience base.

© Pictorial Press Ltd/Alamy

MOBY (Richard Melville Hall) performing in 2002. In Moby's music, the electronic elements—including the rhythm track, the orchestral strings-inspired sound cushion under the chorus, and numerous other subtle effects—merge with rock and rap elements to create a new fusion for the new millennium.

Moby began his professional career in 1982, playing guitar in a punk band called the Vatican Commandos; he left a year later. By 1989, he had redirected his energies to electronic music. Over the next decade, he attracted a loyal following, first in Great Britain, then in the United States, among dance club audiences as a recording artist and DJ. His first hit was "Go," a single from his 1993 album *The Story So Far.* His breakthrough came in 1999, with the release of the album *Play.* Although sales started slowly, by 2002 the album had sold over 10 million units, earning it diamond album certification. Several singles, including "South Side," also charted. More tellingly, every one of the eighteen tracks on the album has been licensed for commercials, films, and soundtracks. With this album, electronica, as represented by Moby's music, found mainstream success.

Moby originally recorded "South Side" with Gwen Stefani (b. 1969), the vocalist with No Doubt, a Jamaican-influenced alternative band. The version that featured her did not appear on the first release of the album. However, the single version and the reissue of the album did include her. That she was present, and a key component of the song, indicates a significant difference between "South Side" and "No UFO's." "South Side" assimilates the electronic elements into a traditional rock song format: The song has a beginning and an end; an instrumental introduction; a (rap-inspired spoken) verse; a sung chorus with a can't-miss hook; and a vintage-style guitar solo. In this format, the song is clearly directed toward radio airplay instead of being confined to use within a club. Indeed, the song reached No. 3 on *Billboard*'s Modern Rock Tracks and No. 14 on their Hot 100 chart.

The electronic elements—including the rhythm track, the orchestral strings-inspired sound cushion under the chorus, and numerous other subtle effects—are merged with rock and rap elements to create a new fusion for the turn of the millennium. However, the song follows a time-honored pattern in popular music that we first observed in the music for the minstrel show: Create a new sound by assimilating outsider styles (fiddle music/techno) into the prevailing style.

It is clear that "South Side" owes much of its success to the incorporation of rock and rap elements. Historically, when a new sound emerges, audiences have first embraced versions of it that contain familiar elements—the cover versions of R&B songs in the fifties are a noteworthy example. However, it is also clear that by incorporating these familiar elements into "South Side," Moby has abandoned the esthetic of techno, as exemplified in tracks such as "No UFO's." It is a song, not a dance track. Whether this is good or bad—or neither—depends on your point of view. Those who preferred their techno "pure" would be turned off by the song (and many of Moby's longtime fans felt betrayed by his move to the

LISTENING CUE • **"South Side" (1999),** Moby.

STYLE Crossover electronica • **FORM** Verse/chorus, with spoken verse, different versions of the chorus

Listen For . . .

INSTRUMENTATION
Spoken and sung voices, electric guitar, synthesized percussion, bass, and sustained sounds

PERFORMANCE STYLE
Verse is spoken, not rapped; rock-like guitar solo

RHYTHM
Dense sixteen-beat rhythm underpins slower moving rhythms in instrumental breaks and chorus

MELODY
Chorus is simple, narrow-range phrase repeated over and over

HARMONY
One chord hinted at in verse; repeated chord progression in chorus

Remember . . .

BUSY RHYTHMS
Active, funky rhythms, with the sixteen-beat layer clearly marked by percussion sounds

ROCK/RAP ELEMENTS
Verse/chorus form, with rap-influenced spoken verse, sung chorus; guitar solo

ELECTRONIC ELEMENTS
Synthesized sounds include not only Latin-flavored percussive sounds but also sustained sounds behind vocals in chorus and elsewhere

Listen to this selection in CourseMate.

mainstream); those who were not ready to take their electronica straight welcomed the more familiar features.

Deconstructing Popular Song

When the album version of "South Side" was released as part of a "single" in England on Mute Records, it was one of seven versions of the song on the CD. The others were:

- The single version
- The "Hybrid Dishing Pump Remix" version
- The "Peter Heller Park Lane Vocal" version
- "Ain't Never Learned" version
- The "Hybrid Dishing Pump Instrumental" version
- "The Sun Never Stops Setting" version

The many versions of the song highlight one of the most fascinating digital-era developments in popular music: the **deconstruction** of a song. Recall that one of the significant developments of the early rock era was the emergence of the "record as document." That is, the song was what was recorded on the album or single. However, even then multiple versions of songs occasionally appeared: the single version of the Doors' "Light My Fire" is much shorter than the album version, which features long instrumental solos by Ray Manzarek and Robby Krieger. As mentioned earlier, Jamaican record companies took this a step further when they would issue the instrumental backing of a song as the "B" side of the record so that DJs could toast over it. Still, musicians and producers were limited because of the relative difficulty in isolating and recombining tracks and song components and segments in analog mixing.

Digital technology liberated music creators from both the signal degradation and ease-of-use issues in analog recording. As computers gained speed and audio workstation software developed, it became possible to construct a song out of several components, which could be modified, added to, and otherwise manipulated to create other versions of the song, some of which can be quite different. For example, the "Peter Heller Park Lane Vocal" version of "South Side" is 5 minutes longer than the album track, and one track is an instrumental.

Because the track or song's components for "South Side" were in digital format, it was possible to, in effect, assemble them into different forms. Increasingly, releasing multiple versions of a song or track, either simultaneously or in subsequent remixes, is now common practice in techno, rap, and pop. As a result, what a song is has become far more fluid than it was in the sixties and seventies.

In electronica, multiple versions of a song do not multiply sales. Moby's *Play* has been a rare exception. The large family of electronica styles commands a relatively small market share. Nevertheless, its influence on popular music has been profound. Rap, pop, rock, world music—there is hardly a contemporary sound that does not show at least some influence of the technology and tools of dance music.

CHAPTER 75
Early Rap

Several years ago, students at the university where I used to teach asked me to participate in a discussion titled "Is rap music?" To get the discussion started, one of the students read a definition of music from a dictionary, by which measure rap was not music. What did *not* emerge from the subsequent discussion was a challenge to the question itself. Whether rap is dictionary-definition music ultimately has no bearing on its importance as an expressive art. So the answer to the question "Is rap music?" is neither "yes" nor "no," but rather "It doesn't matter."

Rap

Rap is a form of creative expression that uses musical sounds to help get its message across, but music is typically only one of several elements. Its most consistent features are poetry delivered intensely and rhythmically over a spare, rhythmically active musical accompaniment, usually generated by electronic sounds. But it can be more: One could argue convincingly that a well-done rap video is the first total-arts genre, because it often combines poetry, drama, visual arts, dancing, and music.

Forerunners of Rap

The practice of talking over a musical accompaniment has a long history in popular music. Al Jolson used to talk over instrumental statements of the melody in the twenties; bluesmen and contemporary folk artists like Woody Guthrie would routinely strum and talk. Within the popular tradition, the practice of reciting poetry over a musical accompaniment goes back to the fifties, when Beat poets like Kenneth Rexroth presented their work backed by a jazz combo. Somewhat later, black poets like Amiri Baraka (LeRoi Jones) often delivered their work with jazz in the background. In the sixties, acts as different as Bob Dylan and James Brown delivered words that were both rhymed and rhythmic, using a vocal style that fell somewhere between everyday speech and singing. However, the most direct antecedent of rap was the toasting of the Jamaican DJs who ran mobile sound systems and kept up a steady stream of patter as they changed discs. Another antecedent of rap, one closer to home, was George Clinton's funk.

RAP emerged as one artistic dimension of the hip-hop culture, along with break dancing and graffiti.

Rap and African-American Culture

There are numerous parallels between the Mississippi Delta in the first half of the twentieth century and the South Bronx in the latter half. Both regions are heavily black. Both are heartbreakingly poor; there is either no work or work at such low pay that one cannot make ends meet. They are violent, even lawless places. Health and living conditions are closer to life in a Third World country than the suburbs of New York or Memphis: out-of-wedlock children born to young teens; rats and roaches everywhere; segregated, underfunded schools, where the playground may become a battleground.

There are differences, of course. The Delta was—and is—rural. Geography, prejudice, and poverty kept the people who lived there thoroughly isolated from mainstream culture. The South Bronx is urban. Fifth Avenue in Manhattan is a short subway ride away. But it might as well have been another world for those who lived in the ghetto. In effect, there has been, in both cases, an invisible barrier that has severely constrained meaningful contact between blacks and whites. However, television brought the rich and famous into the living rooms of South Bronx residents; they had a much sharper sense of what they didn't have than their Delta counterparts.

Both are depressing, demoralizing environments, environments that can suck hope out of one's mind, body, and spirit. So it is a testament to the resiliency of African Americans and the vitality of their culture that the Delta and the South Bronx have been home to two of the most vital, important, and influential forms of artistic expression to emerge in the twentieth century. Just as the Delta is the spiritual home of the blues, the South Bronx is home to rap.

Ask those who listen to rap what draws them to it. Chances are they'll say, "It's real." Like the blues, the realness of rap is not just in what it says, but in how it says it. Rap gives us a window into life in the ghetto: the good, the bad, the ugly . . . and the beautiful. There is humor; bleak visions of the past, present, and future; posturing; misogyny and responses to it; slices of gang life and pleas to bring an end to it; brutal depictions of current conditions; and forceful demands for action. Like other roots music—blues, folk, country—this is music by and for its constituency. That rap has found a much wider audience is incidental to its original mission. The power comes from its emotional urgency: As with the blues, we can feel it's real. It has an edge, in words and sound.

Rap is a contemporary instance of a popular style's speaking to and for its audience. In a 1992 *Newsweek* article, Public Enemy's

Chuck D called rap "Black America's CNN." In his view, it provides information and opinions for the inner city, viewpoints not available through conventional media. Chuck D feels that rap and rap videos give whites exposure to a side of black life that they could not get short of living in a ghetto.

Rap and Hip Hop

Rap emerged as one artistic dimension of **hip-hop** culture, along with break dancing and graffiti. All three were unconventional forms of expression that required considerable skill and preparation. **Break dancing** is extremely athletic; its vigorous moves parallel the energy of the music to which it's performed. Graffiti artists prepared their work much like a military campaign. They would plan the graffito through a series of sketches, scout out the train yards, sneak in and paint the cars, then sneak out. Their use of trains and buses as "canvases" suggests that graffiti was another way to get their message out of the ghetto.

There is a kind of defiance built into all three: rap, graffiti art, and break dancing. The implicit message is "You can put us down, but you can't keep us down." You—the man, the establishment—can subject us to subhuman living conditions. You can ignore us. But you can't break our spirit. We can create something that comes from us, not you, and you can't do what we do, even though you want to.

Grandmaster Flash: Messages and Techniques

Among rap's pioneers was Grandmaster Flash. Flash (born Joseph Saddler, 1958) was born in Barbados but moved with his family to the Bronx at a young age. He grew up with passionate interests in his father's jazz records and electronics, which he merged as a budding DJ at block parties and in public parks.

Inspired by Kool Herc, the first great hip-hop DJ, Flash developed the array of turntable techniques that would revolutionize rap. Even more significantly, he translated these techniques into a radically new musical conception: the **sound collage.** In the visual arts, an artist creating a collage assembles found materials (artifacts such as print materials, photographs, or machine parts) or natural objects (such as seashells, flowers, or leaves) into a work of art. The collage can consist exclusively of the preexisting materials, or it can be integrated into the work of the artist. What the visual artist does with found materials, Flash did with sound. In effect, he cut and pasted sound clips from recordings into his music. The clips could range in length from a fraction of a second to several seconds; in either case, Flash completely recontextualized them.

The first track in which he showcased these skills was "The Adventures of Grandmaster Flash and the Wheels of Steel," which he recorded with the Furious Five, featuring Melle Mel (Melvin Glover) and ex-Sugarhill Gang percussionist Duke Bootee (Ed Fletcher). The track, a minor R&B hit in 1981, included excerpts from Chic's "Good Times," Blondie's "Rapture," and Queen's "Another One Bites the Dust," as well as samples from other songs and sources; it would become a textbook for the creative possibilities of sampling. As practiced by Flash, sampling was a radical transformation of the age-old practice of musical quotation. Instead of inserting snippets of melody, Flash mixed in the entire musical event as preserved on record.

Another of Flash's early and important contributions was "The Message," which reached No. 4 on the R&B charts in 1982 and also crossed over to the pop charts. It was innovative in both subject and setting.

"The Message" presents a brutal picture of life in the ghetto. Its impact begins with the rap itself, which describes the oppressive and parlous circumstances of everyday life for those who live there. Another noteworthy feature was the "arrest" at the end of the track, a "slice of life" interpolation that interrupts the musical accompaniment for several seconds. When the accompaniment resumes, it is as if the arrest were barely a blip on the radar screen—a virtual nonevent in the ongoing misery of life in the ghetto. Both the rap and the arrest scene convey a much more serious message. With "The Message," rap graduated from party music to serious social commentary.

The other major innovation in "The Message" is the coordination of the musical setting with the message of the rap. There are many layers of activity, most of it generated on synthesizers and drum machines. The most prominent are the strong backbeat and the high synthesizer riff, the closest thing to melodic material on the entire track. However, none of the many layers establishes a consistent, active rhythm. The bass part, percussive guitar-like midrange part, and the multiple percussion parts dart in and out of the texture; the overall effect evokes James Brown's music, but it is much emptier sounding than the textures typically heard in his music. The sixteen-beat rhythm that is implicit in the instrumental sections becomes explicit only when the rap begins. An abrupt change in the rhythm of the rap, from the sixteen-beat–based stream to a variant of the clave pattern, signals the arrival at the "chorus": "Don't push me cuz I'm close to the edge."

The spare, widely spaced sounds and the way the synthesizer riff trails off seem to communicate the desolation of the ghetto environment; the lack of change in the setting seems to imply the difficulties faced in improving this depressing environment.

Rap crossed over to the mainstream with Run-D.M.C.'s version of "Walk This Way." As with earlier rap songs, "Walk This Way" built the rap on a preexisting musical foundation, in this case, Aerosmith's 1976 hit "Walk This

LISTENING CUE · **"The Message" (1982).** Grandmaster Flash.

STYLE Rap · **FORM** Rap-style verse/chorus

Listen For . . .

INSTRUMENTATION
Rapping (no singing) plus electronically generated pitched and percussive sounds

RHYTHM
Sixteen-beat rhythms kept mainly in the rap; no consistent time keeping in the instrumental setting except for strong backbeat
Clave-like syncopation in rap "chorus"

MELODY
Melodic material: repeated synthesizer riffs

TEXTURE
Open texture with wide registral gaps between bass and high synthesizer riff

Remember . . .

DEPRESSING ACCOUNT
Lyrics paint a dismal picture of ghetto life.

EMPHASIS ON RHYTHM
Rap plus repetitive riffs and percussion sounds; no melodic development but rhythmic interest

BLEAK MUSICAL SETTING
Open texture—high synth riff, low bass, other percussion/riffs/rap in mid-range; repeated riffs (they go nowhere musically) reinforce bleak message of rap.

Listen to this selection in CourseMate.

Way." The new twist was that Aerosmith members Steven Tyler and Joe Perry participated in the recording session. This new version made the charts exactly a decade after the original, in 1986. A year later, LL Cool J and the Beastie Boys (who were signed to Def Jam Records, the most prominent rap label) found the charts; with their emergence, rap burst out of the ghetto and into the 'burbs.

Public Enemy: Rap as a Political Music

Among the major rap acts of the late eighties and nineties was Public Enemy. The group's key figures were Chuck D (born Carlton Ridenhour, 1960), Flavor Flav (born William Drayton, 1959), and DJ Terminator X (born Norman Rogers, 1966). They surrounded themselves with a substantial posse, some of whom contributed to their work.

Public Enemy was the most political of the rap acts to emerge during the late eighties. Their look rekindled memories of the black radicals from the sixties: paramilitary uniforms, Black Panther evocations, fake Uzis carried by their entourage as they appeared on stage. The look supported the message of the raps.

In "1 Million Bottlebags," a track from their 1991 album *Apocalypse 91 . . . The Enemy Strikes Black*, Public Enemy takes on everyone. The rap is an indictment of alcohol abuse. It takes on all of those responsible for the problem—not only those who consume it and can't stop, but also the companies that prey on blacks by advertising their liquor products heavily in the ghetto. The language is powerful and direct; it is from the street. The frustration and anger behind it are palpable.

The rap begins with a collage of sounds: a bottle breaking, a "news bulletin" about target advertising by liquor companies in the black communities, the rhythm track, the sound of beer (or malt liquor) being poured, a beer belch, then horn-like synthesizer chords. The rap begins. Sirens and more prominent rhythm sounds signal the arrival of a chorus-like section. The end of the track simulates changing stations on a radio. Juxtaposed are a long statement about the immorality of making money off the impoverished and a scathing critique of the way in which racist corporate types dismiss the problem.

There are five kinds of sounds on the track: the rap, the spoken elements, the real-world sounds (for example, the bottle breaking), the rhythm tracks, and the pitched sounds, such as the siren screeches that mark the chorus. The siren screeches are at once a musical sound—a two-note riff—and an evocation of a too-familiar real-life sound. There is complexity in the density of information, which matches the multiple levels of commentary.

The rhythm track, which combines a strong backbeat with interlocked patterns that collectively mark the sixteen-beat rhythm, serves several purposes. It is the glue that holds the track together, through the changes of voice, the spoken clips, and other sounds. It reinforces the delivery of the rap. Because both move at sixteen-beat speed, the percussion sounds give the rap support and strength. And it creates a groove: even more than in funk, you can move to the groove even as you take in the message.

LISTENING CUE • **"1 Million Bottlebags" (1991),** Ridenhour/ Robertz/ Rinaldo/ Depper. Public Enemy.

STYLE Rap • **FORM** Rap-style "verse/chorus"

Listen For . . .

INSTRUMENTATION
Rap, electronic percussion, synthesizer, "found" sounds

RHYTHM
Aggressive sixteen-beat rhythm, reinforced by rap and percussion
Syncopated synthesizer chords and riffs, mainly in chorus

MELODY
Melodic fragments highlight chorus-like sections

TEXTURE
Main focus rap and percussive sounds; other sounds, low and high, are intermittent

Remember . . .

EQUAL-OPPORTUNITY DENUNCIATION
Rap indicts both the abusers and the producers of alcohol: the former for their unwillingness to clean up, the latter for targeting the black community in their advertising.

RICH SOUND WORLD
Five different sound sources: rap, spoken elements, real-world sounds, percussion sounds, and pitched sounds—the siren-like sounds and the synthesizer chords

RAP, RHYTHM, AND MESSAGE
Rap delivery and rhythm create a sixteen-beat rhythm at a fast tempo, which conveys the anger and frustration of the rap; so do aggressive sounds (percussion sounds, siren).

Listen to this selection in CourseMate.

"1 Million Bottlebags" is even less melodic than "The Message." The only easily identifiable melodic elements are the siren-like sound and the repeated chord; in both cases, the same pitch is repeated again and again. The absence of melody is a strength, not a shortcoming. Its presence would dilute the impact of the rap. It would soften the edge that is present everywhere else: in the delivery of the rap, in the rhythm track and other musical sounds, and in the sound clips.

The moral high ground staked out by Public Enemy in tracks like "1 Million Bottlebags" was undermined by incidents such as the 1989 *Washington Post* interview with Professor Griff (born Richard Griffin, 1960), Public Enemy's "minister of information," in which he made numerous provocatively anti-Semitic remarks, including claiming that Jews were responsible for the majority of wickedness that goes on throughout the world. It was the most flagrant of several anti-Semitic public incidents in Public Enemy's career; others included an endorsement of Nation of Islam leader Louis Farrakhan. The controversy surrounding such incidents created dissension within the group and a sudden decline in their fortunes. By 1993, Chuck D put the group's career on hold; he would revive Public Enemy later in the decade, when they recaptured some of the success that they had previously enjoyed. Still, their most substantial contribution came in the late eighties and early nineties; more than any other group of the era, they made rap relevant—the black CNN—to both blacks and non-blacks, and created sound worlds that amplified the impact of the lyrics. It remained for a new generation of rappers to bring it into the mainstream.

CHAPTER 76
Mainstreaming Rap

As the 1980s began, the audience for rap was small and almost exclusively black. As the 1990s began, the audience was much larger. It has continued to grow through the 1990s and into the twenty-first century; during the 2000s, the market share of the rap/hip-hop was larger than the market share for traditional R&B. The main *musical* reason for the expanded audience for rap would seem to be the incorporation of melodic material. We explore this idea in music by 2Pac and Eminem.

The Case of Gangsta Rap

In rap, the boundary between life and art is all but invisible. The work of rappers often comes directly from their life experiences; the raps may simply document them. Nowhere has this been more evident than in gangsta rap.

Gangsta rap, which emerged in the latter part of the eighties, brought the violence of inner-city life into the music and out into the world. A visual image of this life was the 1988 film *Colors,* starring Robert Duvall and Sean Penn as police officers trying to control violence between the Bloods and the Crips, two rival Los Angeles gangs. Ice-T, among the first of the gangsta rappers, recorded the title track of the film.

Although Schoolly D, a Philadelphia-based rapper, is credited with the rap that sparked the genre (the 1986 single "P.S.K."), gangsta rap has been perceived as a West Coast phenomenon because of the success of rap artists and groups such as N.W.A. and Ice-T, then Dr. Dre (a former N.W.A. member), Snoop Doggy Dogg, MC Hammer, and 2Pac (Tupac Shakur). The success of these artists escalated the territorial animosity from rival gangs within a community to the communities themselves. Bad blood developed between West Coast gangsta rappers and New York hip-hop artists; both groups used lyrics to dis the opposing camp. The violence portrayed in the lyrics often spilled over into real life. Snoop Doggy Dog and Tupac Shakur were among the notable gangsta rap artists who served jail time; the shooting deaths of Shakur and Notorious B.I.G. are commonly regarded as gang retribution.

Violence was not the only controversial aspect of the music. Raps were often pornographic and misogynistic, and richly scatological. Most recordings routinely earned the "parental advisory" label from the RIAA. For suburban whites, gangsta rap must have seemed like forbidden fruit; the genre would enjoy a large following among whites, most of whom experienced the rappers' world only vicariously.

Although its audience had grown steadily throughout the late eighties and early nineties, gangsta rap crossed over to the mainstream in large part because of a musical decision: to work pop elements into hardcore rap. It first appeared in the music of New York hip-hop artists such as Notorious B.I.G. and Nas, and quickly spread to the west coast: Tupac Shakur's "California Love," which topped the pop, R&B, and rap charts in 1996, epitomizes this new approach.

Tupac Shakur

If ever an artist seemed destined to live and die by the sword, it would be Tupac Shakur (1971–1996). His parents were active in the Black Panthers; his mother was acquitted on a conspiracy charge only a month before Shakur's birth; his father is currently incarcerated in Florida; and others close to his mother during his childhood were either in and out of prison or fugitives.

What made his too-short life doubly tragic was the terrible conflict between the sensitive and violent sides of his personality. He was intelligent and curious—reading Machiavelli during his prison term—and creative and multitalented, with obvious gifts as an actor, poet, dancer, and musician. Yet in his personal and professional lives, he gave vent to the violent side: run-ins with the law, a sexual abuse lawsuit, and scandal. "Hit 'Em Up" was a personal attack on Notorious B.I.G.; in it, he claimed to have slept with B.I.G.'s wife. That his life would end prematurely as a result of the ultimate violent act seems in retrospect almost a foregone conclusion.

Shortly before his death, Shakur recorded "California Love" with Dr. Dre for Death Row Records, the label headed by Suge Knight, who was also repeatedly in trouble with the law. The opening scene of the music video of the track and the action during the song itself seem inspired by the Mad Max films: They purport to present a desolate, lawless world a hundred years in the future. Although it is skillfully produced, the video has no obvious thematic connection with the song, which is very much in the present—the "'95" that Dr. Dre mentions is clearly 1995, and Tupac's first words are "out on bail/ fresh outta jail," which happened to be true. Both the video and the song evidence the mutation of rap from an outsiders' music flourishing in inner-city parks to a big business.

The track shows how rap found a mainstream audience in part by bringing in non-rap elements. It begins with a striking processed vocal riff; the instrumental

LISTENING CUE • **"California Love" (1996),** Tupac Shakur. Tupac Shakur and Dr. Dre.

STYLE Gangsta rap • **FORM** Verse/chorus, with the chorus framing the rapped verses, and with an introductory title phrase and numerous interludes

Listen For . . .

INSTRUMENTATION
Vocals, raps, synthesized percussion, bass and chord-instrument sounds, "natural" percussion sounds (cowbell, whistle)

PERFORMANCE STYLE
Electronic modification of sung vocal parts

RHYTHM
Sixteen-beat rhythm kept in percussion and rap; other rhythms moving more slowly.

MELODY
Sung chorus built from repetitive riff frames raps

TEXTURE
Rhythmically dense, melody-rich texture with heavy bass, high mid-range percussion and synth chords, vocal in between, plus active high-range synthesizer riffs

Remember . . .

RAP + MELODY = CROSSOVER SUCCESS
Sung chorus plus instrumental melodic fragments underneath sung vocals and raps

SLICE OF CALIFORNIA LIFE
Raps mix a salute to California with personal remarks: jail, jewelry, clothes, and the obligatory commentary on street life.

RICH SOUND WORLD
Imaginative instrumental and vocal sounds, collage-like melodic fragments, and dense, active rhythms create rich, constantly varying sound world.

Listen to this selection in CourseMate.

introduction that follows spotlights the bass. The next section features a tuneful melody with a rich accompaniment that becomes the main chorus of the song. The chorus returns after Dr. Dre's rap, followed by another sung section, "Shake it," which gives way to Tupac's rap.

The rap lyrics offer a sizeable dose of gangsta rap posturing. There are references to violence, gangs, prostitution, money, clothes, and jewelry. But the prevailing mood, in both words and music, is party hard, because "we keep it rockin'!" Especially in the chorus, it sounds more like a promo for the chamber of commerce than an incitement to riot.

Compared to early rap, its most surprising feature, and undoubtedly one of its most appealing features, is its melodic and textural richness. The vocal melodies are the most apparent evidence of this, but woven into the texture behind both the sung sections and the raps are lush synthesizer harmonies and multiple fragments of melody. The return of the chorus features even more supplementary melodic activity, both vocal and instrumental. Almost all of this activity, and especially the synthesizer chords and lines, occurs in middle and high register, above the vocal range of the rap. This counterbalances the characteristic dark bass sound that runs throughout the song.

Additionally, several layers of percussion sounds mark the backbeat, rock beat, and sixteen-beat rhythms or play against these regular rhythms; the whistle stands out as a source of rhythmic play. The rhythmic texture of the song is even denser than that heard on "1 Million Bottlebags," although the tempo is considerably slower.

The rich texture created by the numerous melodic fragments and sustained chords are an important source of the enormous crossover appeal of the song. It makes the song more accessible and more familiar, and there is more to connect to—not only the two raps and the beat, but also the melodies and the sound variety. The strategy to mainstream rap through melody succeeded on both coasts, and it has remained a common practice up until the present.

Fortunately for Death Row Records, Shakur had recorded a substantial amount of unreleased material. Six albums were released posthumously, the last in 2004. All went platinum. His legacy extends beyond his recordings. Following his death, his mother, Afeni Shakur, established the Tupac Amaru Shakur Foundation to "provide training and support for students who aspire to enhance their creative talents."

In the 2000s, rap would gain an even larger commercial presence. One important reason was the work of Eminem.

Eminem and the Mainstreaming of Rap

A quick glance at Eminem's record sales might lead one to think history was simply repeating itself: White musicians co-opt a black music and popularize it without

© Trinity Mirror/Mirrorpix/Alamy

EMINEM performing on stage in Glasgow, 2001

really understanding the style. It was a recurring pattern in the twentieth century, most notoriously in the 1950s, when pop singers tried to cover rhythm-and-blues songs. The reality in this case is far more complex.

There is no doubt about Eminem's commercial success. He is among the most successful artists of the 2000s. All of his studio albums have gone multiplatinum, and all but the first peaked at the top of the album charts. He has had numerous chart-topping singles, including "Lose Yourself" and "Love the Way You Lie."

However, Eminem (born Marshall Mathers, 1972) has paid his dues along the way. As a teen, he participated in battle raps with black rappers and eventually earned the respect of African-American hip-hop audiences. Early in his career, he teamed with black rapper Royce da 5′9″ to form Soul Intent. His mentor has been Dr. Dre, who has provided the musical context for his raps. And he could easily have been a child of the ghetto: raised by a single mom; moving around constantly; dropping out of school; devastated by an uncle who committed suicide; fathering a child out of wedlock; dealing with substance abuse issues; trying to hold together a tumultuous relationship with his longtime partner, Kimberly Scott, whom he met in 1989, married in 1999, divorced in 2001, remarried and divorced again in 2006; fending off lawsuits; and picking public spats with other celebrities. As with other rappers, his life has spilled over into his art: Among the numerous lawsuits that have been filed against him are those by his mother and ex-wife, who have sued him for defamation of character. Many of his songs, including "Love the Way You Lie," are or could easily be autobiographical.

Eminem recorded "Love the Way You Lie" for his 2010 album *Recovery*. Both the album and the single quickly went to the top of the charts. In this track, he partnered with R&B star Rihanna; she sang the chorus, and his raps provided the verse. (Interestingly, she recorded another version of the song with sung verse and chorus and with a rap by Eminem interpolated.) The track exemplifies the synergy that can result when rap and song are combined. Rihanna's sung chorus, which opens the track and is repeated throughout, is the hook that anchors the track in listeners' ears. The unvarying repetition serves at least two purposes: It lodges the hook more deeply even as it underscores the main theme of the track, and it doesn't deflect attention away from the rap by introducing variety. The four-chord accompaniment that is also recycled under both chorus and rap helps glue the two together.

Eminem's rap is musical Everclear—the 190-proof kind. It is an intense, condensed account of a tumultuous relationship. The juxtaposition of sung and rapped content highlights the power of rap: Words sung to music typically take much longer to deliver, and even when they are delivered rapidly, the musical setting can attenuate the impact of the words. The high pitch of Eminem's delivery energizes the violent contrasts in his rap, which in turn resonates with the violence in the relationship. His vivid images flash by (in words and also in the video) like a film on fast forward. The track and the video are a gripping 4½-minute reality show.

Eminem's overwhelming commercial success—he was the top R&B/hip-hop artist on *Billboard*'s 2010 year-end chart, critical acclaim, and his widespread acceptance within the music industry and by black and white audiences evidences his almost unique position in contemporary musical life: he is a highly skilled performer in an almost exclusively black genre, who happens to be white.

In the twenty-first century, rap—in all of its manifestations and combinations—is an enduring and significant part of the rock-era musical world. The numerous rap/R&B syntheses—and rap/rock hybrids such as rapcore, rap rock, and rap metal—offer further evidence of its strong presence in popular music.

LISTENING CUE • **"Love the Way You Lie" (2010),** Marshall Mathers, Alexander Grant, Holly Hafermann, Makeba Riddick. Eminem, with Rihanna.

STYLE Crossover rap • **FORM** Verse/chorus (with the raps as verses)

Listen For . . .

INSTRUMENTATION
Sung vocal, rap, piano, acoustic guitar, synthesized bass, percussion, string-like sustained sound

RHYTHM
Slow-moving melodic rhythm in chorus, faster rhythm in rap, sixteen-beat rhythmic foundation under both

MELODY
Repetitive melody consisting of a single high–low phrase repeated several times

HARMONY
Unusual four-chord progression underpins both chorus and rap

TEXTURE
Strong contrasts in texture between spacious-sounding chorus (wide registral differences) and more lightly accompanied rap (mainly guitar and percussion)

Remember . . .

LOVE PROBLEMS
"Love the Way You Lie" is about a relationship on the rocks. The title phrase highlights a central problem; the raps vividly describe the tempestuous times of a "tornado" and a "volcano." The rap presents the problems more explicitly, more violently, and in greater detail than in pop.

MIXING IN MELODY
Part of the success of the track is the sung chorus—and Rihanna's singing of it.

CONTRASTING SOUND WORLDS
Vocal chorus has much richer accompaniment—sustained chords, more percussion—than rap verse. Chord progression helps connect them.

Listen to this selection in CourseMate.

17

UNIT 17

• • • •

LOOKING BACK, LOOKING AHEAD
Moving Beyond Rock

ALTHOUGH THEY ARE ONLY A MINISCULE SAMPLING of the available music, the six tracks considered in this unit highlight key features and important trends regarding electronica and rap. The early tracks offer compelling evidence of the electronica and rap, arguably the two most progressive musical styles since 1980, moved beyond rock. Here are key differences:

- Sixteen-beat rhythms, instead of a rock beat
- More active and complex rhythmic textures
- Electronic instruments and samples instead of a core rhythm section of guitar, bass, and drums
- Few if any sung riffs and no melody to speak of; no hooks in a sung chorus or in a lead guitar part

Moreover, the very *idea* of a song as a fixed, discrete document contained on a recording comes under attack in both styles. Tracks like "No UFO's" are just a single element in a DJ's mix, and one of several possible remixes.

The post-1990 tracks show how both expanded their audience in part by including more melodic material. Both, and particularly rap, remain important components of the contemporary musical scene.

Beyond Rock in the 1980s

UNIT 18

UNIT 18

Joel Whitburn is the guru of the *Billboard* charts. He heads Record Research, a company he founded to collect and publish chart information, and has published about 100 reference books. Whitburn developed a complex rating system to evaluate commercial success of rock-era acts based on chart performance. By his measure, the top ten acts on the album charts of the seventies and eighties were as follows:

	1970s	**1980s**
1	Elton John	Prince
2	Chicago	Michael Jackson
3	Paul McCartney and Wings	Bruce Springsteen
4	The Bee Gees	Whitney Houston
5	The Rolling Stones	Madonna
6	Eagles	The Rolling Stones
7	Fleetwood Mac	Billy Joel
8	Led Zeppelin	The Police
9	Carole King	U2
10	Bob Dylan	John Mellencamp

Whitburn's system is only one way to measure popularity. Still, his data prompt us to ask: Where's the rock?

The seventies list is dominated by white male acts. The only exception is Carole King, and there are no minorities. By contrast, only one of the top five acts of the eighties is a white male. The Rolling Stones are the only act to appear on the list for both decades—improbably, not because of the music, but because of their lifestyle. The music of Billy Joel ranges far beyond conventional rock. U2 and the Police created new sounds based on the sounds and rhythms of late 1970s music. The new act closest to the core rock sounds of the late sixties and early seventies was John Mellencamp; even Springsteen consistently incorporated the new sounds of the eighties into his music.

In this unit, we sample a wide range of rock, pop, and rhythm and blues to explore how the dominant music of the 1980s largely moved beyond the core sounds of the late 1960s and 1970s.

CHAPTER 77
Beyond Rock

Perhaps it's karma. Coincidence or not, it is certainly intriguing that the three biggest pop acts of Ronald Reagan's presidency were Michael Jackson, Prince, and Madonna. In an era of political and social conservatism, all three presented complex, provocative, and at times confusing images of race and gender.

New Directions in the 1980s

The eighties brought new sounds as well as new looks to rock-era music. Much of the commercially dominant music of the eighties sounds as if it could not have been created before 1980, for at least two reasons. One was the use of sounds and rhythms that were not common currency, or even available through much of the 1970s. The other was the integration of style elements from what had been "outsider" styles in the 1970s.

New Sounds and Rhythms

Advances in electronic synthesis opened up a broad new palette of sounds to the musicians of the 1980s. Digital technology made both the replication of existing timbres and the creation of new timbres easier; it also streamlined the enhancement of conventional sounds through various effects. As a result, music that did not incorporate synthesized sounds became the exception rather than the rule. These sounds are integral to the distinctive styles of acts as diverse as U2 and Madonna.

The music of the 1980s also stands out because of new rhythms. Three were widely used: the energized rock beat derived from punk; adaptations of the afterbeat rhythms of reggae; and, most commonly, the sixteen-beat rhythms first heard in funk, black pop, and disco. These took various forms, often in combination, as in the relentlessly pulsing rhythms in the music of U2 and the syncopated, dance-oriented rhythms in Madonna's music. As a result, the timeless rock groove of the Stones and others was less common in the middle-ground music of the eighties than these new, more active rhythms.

"Insider/Outsider" Fusions

Punk and disco seem about as easy to blend as oil and water. As they emerged in the late seventies, they seemed to demarcate contrasting ideologies and musical approaches. Punk was real, whereas disco, as experienced in a club, was an escape into a timeless world. Punk was about grit; disco was about glitter. Punk bands hammered out a concentrated rock rhythm on conventional rock instruments; disco featured DJs mixing a string of recordings, most of which combined a strong beat with active sixteen-beat rhythms. The lyrics of punk songs usually said something; disco lyrics often descended into banality.

However, in *Christgau's Record Guide,* a 1990 survey of 3,000 recordings from the eighties, Robert Christgau, the "dean of American rock critics," cited "post-punk/post-disco fusion" as a key development of the decade. He described a synthesis of the two in **DOR,** or **dance-oriented rock,** an umbrella term used by DJs in 1980s disco pools to identify an array of eighties styles. Because pools helped spur the sale of nonradio records, some acts made sure there were dance-oriented tracks on their albums.

The fusion of disparate inside/outside styles was nothing new in rock; it had been common practice from the start. However, the innovations resulting from the fusions of the eighties were different from those of the previous generation, for at least three reasons. First, the eighties was the first generation of rock music (and, for that matter, twentieth-century popular music) that was not nurtured by the blues. Second, the outside styles came from *within* rock-era music. Third, because of the blending of rock styles, the boundaries between rock, rhythm and blues, and pop became more fluid and transparent; the list of the top artists of the eighties hints at that.

Finally, another fusion profoundly affected the dissemination of music: Sound, image, and movement came together in a newly emergent genre—the music video—that became a staple on a new network—MTV—in a new medium, cable television.

MTV and Music Videos

Those who have grown up with hundreds of networks may find it difficult to imagine a time when television viewing options consisted almost exclusively of three networks: NBC, CBS, and ABC. Larger metropolitan areas had public television and a few independent stations, but until the early seventies most viewers had only the three major

networks from which to choose. That changed radically when cable TV became commercially viable.

Cable TV is almost as old as commercial broadcasting. The first cable TV services were launched in 1948; a well-situated antenna brought television signals to homes in remote rural regions. There was some growth during the fifties and sixties, but cable TV as we currently know it didn't get off the ground until the latter part of the seventies. Two key developments—the launching of communications satellites and significant deregulation of the broadcast industry—made cable television economically feasible, and the Cable Act of 1984 effectively deregulated the television industry. In its wake, the cable industry wired the nation. With new revenues came new and more varied programming.

Cable changed the economics of the television industry and transformed it in the process. Networks relied exclusively on advertising for their revenue; the signal was free. Cable TV services charged subscribers a fee and passed on a percentage of that fee to the channels that they offered their subscribers. This new source of revenue made possible the fragmentation of the television market. A network that could command only 1 or 2 percent of the market would have no chance for success against the major networks; but that same 1 or 2 percent of the cable market could provide enough income to make the network viable.

Among the first of these new cable networks was **MTV.** The network began broadcasting in 1981. Symbolically, the first music video that MTV broadcast was "Video Killed the Radio Star." The original format of the network was analogous to Top 40–style radio stations. Videos replaced songs, and VJs (video jockeys) assumed a role similar to radio disc jockeys.

Perhaps because cable originally serviced mainly rural parts of the country, MTV took an AOR-type approach to programming. For the first couple of years, programming targeted a young, white audience. Bands were almost exclusively white—Duran Duran, a British pop group with a keen visual sense, was one of the early MTV bands. Black acts cried "racism" with some justification.

It was Michael Jackson who broke MTV's color barrier. The demand for his spectacular music videos was so overwhelming that the network changed its policy. MTV started VH1 in 1985 and diversified its programming in several ways, adding documentaries, cartoons, and talk shows. In particular, its segments on rap helped bring that genre out of the inner city.

MTV has affected both consumers and creators. The network became a key tastemaker for young people around the world. It has influenced not only what they listen to but also many other aspects of youth culture: dress, looks, body language, vocabulary, and attitudes. However, its most significant contribution was providing an outlet for music videos.

Rock had been a look as well as a sound from the start, but it wasn't until the late sixties that the idea of using videos as a promotional tool took hold. At the same time, live performances were captured on video or film. Documentaries of the 1967 Monterey Pop Festival and Woodstock in 1969 remain treasures. Further experiments, especially by new wave acts like Devo, moved closer to the integration of sound and image that characterizes contemporary music video. With the arrival of MTV, the music video became a key component of the music industry.

The music video inverted the conventional relationship among story, image, and sound. In musical theater and film musicals, songs were written for the story, ideally enhancing those moments when the emotions a character felt were too much for mere words. In earlier music videos, the relationship was the opposite: The visual element was designed to enhance the song. Now the music video is such an essential component of pop success that acts create song and video as an integrated whole. In either form, it is a relatively new expressive medium.

The most obvious, and most widely discussed, consequence of music videos was the suddenly increased emphasis on the look of an act, and the look of the video, as a determinant of success. The two artists who leveraged this new, integrated medium to gain overwhelming commercial success were Michael Jackson and Madonna.

CHAPTER 78
Pop in the Eighties

To celebrate the twenty-fifth anniversary of Michael Jackson's *Thriller*, Sony prepared a *Thriller 25 Super Deluxe Edition*. This greatly expanded version of the original album—released a year late in 2008—included not only the nine original tracks but also remixes of five tracks, with contributions from will.i.am, Fergie, Kayne West, and Akon. The remixes, especially those by will.i.am, radically reconceive the songs: adding extra percussion layers and the dark bass sounds customary in rap, electronica, and much contemporary R&B and pop; simplifying the harmony or even eliminating it altogether; and chopping up the form. In some cases, all that's left from the original is Jackson's singing. These thorough transformations make clear the ways in which pop changed since the original *Thriller* was released. But they do not—indeed they cannot—demonstrate how fresh Jackson's music sounded in 1982.

Pop in the 1980s

The early eighties ushered in a new generation of pop stars. The stars and their music were dramatically different from the music of the previous decade in several respects. Race, gender, and even sexual preference were nonissues. The leading pop acts of the 1980s were Michael Jackson, Prince, and Madonna. None of them is a white male. Both Jackson and Madonna were multifaceted entertainers. After them, it was no longer enough to be just a good singer or musician; one had to be able to move well, although no one topped Michael Jackson in skill or imagination. Video and film became essential components of stardom. Michael Jackson's videos broke the color barrier on MTV, and video and film were essential in boosting both Prince and Madonna to superstardom. The three set the tone for the pop music videos of the next decades. Their music was a melting pot: Although the new pop of the eighties and beyond connects most directly to the black pop tradition of the sixties and seventies, the music was certainly open to other influences: disco, punk, reggae, funk, Latin music, dance music, and rap. Synthesizer played an increasingly important role, as rhythm instruments, extra percussion, and string and horn analogues.

This new pop was unprecedentedly popular. Michael Jackson's *Thriller* album easily surpassed the sales of the previous best-selling album. As Robert Christgau pointed out, the sheer sales volume of *Thriller* was part of its significance. Prince and Madonna also had impressive sales figures.

Precisely because its artists drew from so many sources, there has been no single "middle ground" style. It has not been defined by a distinctive kind of beat keeping, like punk; or a rhythmic feel, like funk; or a special sound quality, like the distortion of heavy metal. Instead, a set of principles, rather than specific musical features, defined the music that topped the charts during the eighties. The songs typically have intelligible lyrics that tell a story—usually about love or its absence or about a slice of life. They are set to a singable melody. The melody in turn is embedded in a rich, riff-laden texture; most layers—if not all—are played on synthesizers. The songs typically have a good beat—easy to find and danceable, neither too monotonous nor too ambiguous. These features are embodied in the music of Michael Jackson, and especially the nine tracks on *Thriller*.

Michael Jackson

Berry Gordy's vision was a black pop style whose appeal transcended the black community. One branch of its legacy was the post-eighties pop middle ground marked out by Michael Jackson (1958–2009). Jackson is the most direct link between Motown and 1980s pop. As a member of The Jackson 5, he was part of Motown's last great act. As a solo performer in the late seventies and early eighties, he went beyond Motown by helping to define the new pop middle ground musically, reviving the all-around performer and establishing the music video as a new, integrated mode of expression. Most spectacularly, his dancing went far beyond the stylized choreography of the Motown acts.

Although only twenty-four when *Thriller* (1982) was released, Michael Jackson had been a professional entertainer for three-fourths of his life and a star for half of it. He had released solo singles in the early seventies, but Jackson's solo career didn't take off until 1978, when he starred in the film *The Wiz*. During the filming, he met composer/arranger/producer Quincy Jones, who collaborated with him on *Off the Wall* (1979), his first major album, and *Thriller*. Jones's skill and creativity proved to be the ideal complement to Jackson's abilities.

Jackson was fortunate to be in the right place at the right time. MTV had gone on the air in 1981; *Thriller* was released a year later. Jackson helped transform the music video from a song-with-video into a mini-film that used a song as the focal point; for example, the video of "Thriller" is over twice the length of the track on the album. Jackson made it work through his exuberant dancing.

The title track to *Thriller* shows the musical side of these changes. It is a long song by pop standards, in part because of the long buildup at the beginning and the voiceover at the end by Vincent Price, one of Hollywood's masters of

LISTENING CUE • **"Thriller" (1982),** Rod Temperton. Michael Jackson, vocal.

STYLE 1980s middle-ground pop • **FORM** Verse/chorus

Listen For . . .

INSTRUMENTATION
Lead and backup vocals, electronic analogues to conventional instruments (bass, horns, percussion, chord instruments) percussion, guitar; nonmusical sounds, spoken commentary

PERFORMANCE STYLE
Jackson's light, not-scary voice balanced by Price's macabre "rap"

RHYTHM
Active rhythms at march/disco tempo: bass riff at rock-beat speed; busy sixteen-beat percussion parts, fast horn riffs; many riffs syncopated

MELODY
Short title-phrase riff at chorus; verse = longer phrase

TEXTURE
Dense texture formed mainly from layers of riffs: bass, mid-range, vocal, higher range horn-like riffs; sustained sounds behind riffs

Remember . . .

EXTENSIVE ELECTRONICS
Electronic versions of conventional instruments: bass riff throughout, plus horn-like riffs, sustained chords

EXPANSIVE FORM
In both audio track and video, instrumental interlude; in video, allows the action/dance scene to unfold

MOTOWN INFLUENCE
Bright rhythms, bass-heavy texture, melodic saturation, and verse/chorus form build on Motown formula

Listen to this selection in CourseMate.

the macabre. But the heart of the song is a Disneyesque version of scary. Michael's voice, the skillful orchestration, the security of the four-on-the-floor bass drum and heavy backbeat, and the busy rhythms all ensure a cartoonish kind of spooky music more reminiscent of *Scooby Doo* than of *Friday the 13th*. The video reinforces this as each of the nightmarish scenes dissolves into fiction, except for Price's last laugh and Jackson's cat's eyes.

"Thriller" exhibits several distinctive characteristics of post-1980 pop. One is the extensive use of electronic instruments in combination with conventional instruments. Among the most prominent electronic sounds are the repeated bass riff, the sustained harmonies behind Michael's vocals, and the brash chords of the opening, all played on synthesizers. The basic rhythm grows out of disco: We hear a strong backbeat, a relentless bass-drum thump on each beat, and several layers of percussion marking off a sixteen-beat rhythm. However, the other instrumental parts, especially those played on rhythm section instruments or their electronic counterparts, create a texture that is denser and more complex than that heard in a conventional disco song. Jackson's vocal line is simply one strand in the texture; in the verse, it is in the forefront, but in the chorus sections the backup vocals and instruments playing the title-phrase riff all but drown him out. It floats on the busy rhythms and riffs that provide much of the song's momentum—indeed, in the video, the basic rhythm track sustains the flow through the graveyard scene, and, after a short break, through the first part of the extended dance number that is the heart of the video.

Although only three of the tracks were shot as music videos, all of the songs on *Thriller* have a distinct identity. There is considerable contrast from song to song, as the musical settings capture the tone and content of the lyric. For example, the hard-edged riffs that open "Wanna Be Startin' Somethin'" anticipate the lyric's schoolyard-style provocation. The punk-inspired beat and Eddie Van Halen's guitar underscore the message of "Beat It." The loping rhythm (a shuffle beat on top of a rock beat), the use of pre-rock pop harmony, and the soft synth sounds reinforce the friendly rivalry between Michael and Paul McCartney in "The Girl Is Mine," and a setting that mixes an open middle range—just a simple synthesizer riff—with the irritation of a persistent bass riff and percussion sound characterizes the emptiness of the groupie-style relationship in "Billie Jean." Both the songs and Quincy Jones's masterful settings give the album an expressive range that compensates for the one-dimensional quality of Jackson's singing.

There is no doubt that *Thriller* would have been a successful album without the videos. But it also seems certain that the videos, and the fact that the songs were so "video-ready," played a crucial role in its overwhelming success.

Thriller was the crowning achievement of Jackson's career; nothing before or since matched its success.

Madonna

In Renaissance-era Italian, *madonna* was originally a variant of *mia donna,* or "my lady." The term eventually came to refer more specifically to Mary, the mother of Jesus. For example, the phrase "madonna and child" identifies those works of art that depict Mary with the infant Jesus. In the eighties, "Madonna" acquired a more contemporary image: the pop star whose given name soon was enough to identify her to the world at large.

Madonna (born Madonna Ciccone, 1958) was born the same year as Michael Jackson. In 1978, while Jackson was starring in *The Wiz,* Madonna moved to New York to further her career as a dancer. She soon became active in the club scene, while she struggled to pay the rent. However, her star rose quickly. Her first records, released in the early eighties, gained her a following, mainly among clubbers. Although these songs didn't cross over, they created enough of a buzz that she received a contract to record her first album, *Madonna,* which was released in 1983.

In 1984, she took one of the many bold steps that have characterized her career, releasing the video of "Like a Virgin." Shot in Venice, Italy, the video rapidly juxtaposes images of Madonna in a white wedding dress with her in street clothes and a provocative evening dress—attire that suggests she is anything but a virgin.

MADONNA combined provocative, shocking and controversial themes and images with bright, accessible music.

The video established a formula that would set the tone for her subsequent work: combine provocative, shocking, and controversial themes and images with bright, accessible music.

LISTENING CUE • **"Like a Prayer" (1989),** Madonna, Patrick Leonard. Madonna, vocal.

STYLE 1980s middle-ground pop • **FORM** Verse/chorus

Listen For . . .

INSTRUMENTATION
Vocal, choir, organ, guitar, multiple percussion instruments, bass, keyboards

PERFORMANCE STYLE
Madonna's straightforward, plain singing; guitar distortion

RHYTHM
Busy sixteen-beat rhythms at dance tempo

MELODY
Abundance of riffs in verse and chorus

TEXTURE
Contrast between sustained harmonies under vocal and active, dense, percussion-rich texture

Remember . . .

SIMPLE SONG/POP HOOK
Simple melody offers easy point of entry.

CONTRASTS
Striking contrasts in sound, rhythm, and texture: melody plus sustained chords form dense texture, with Madonna, choir, and lots of rhythm, including distorted guitar

FROM PRAYER TO POP
Melody, choir, organ connect to religious service; pop sections have no religious overtones musically.

Listen to this selection in CourseMate.

Among her most controversial projects of the eighties was the video for "Like a Prayer." The song was the title track from her 1989 album of the same name. The video conflates religious images (e.g., a scene in which she grasps a knife, and it cuts her in a way that evokes the stigmata of the crucified Christ); symbols of racism (burning crosses); numerous incongruities and impossibilities (a black gospel choir in a Catholic chapel; the statue of a black saint who comes to life, then doubles as the black man wrongly accused of murdering a woman); and the one constant—Madonna in a revealing dress. All of this outraged numerous religious groups, who threatened to boycott Pepsi, which had recruited Madonna as a spokesperson. The controversy served as free publicity—the album topped the charts.

The video for "Like a Prayer" dramatically evidences the emergence of the music video as an entity distinct from the song that spawned it and from other expressive forms that merge song, image, and movement. The messages of the song—among them, that racism is wrong, that we are all brothers and sisters in Christ, and Madonna is sexy—come through mainly in the rapid-fire series of images/scenes/song fragments. There is little sense of continuity in the narrative, visually or in the lyric, and there are long stretches where Madonna makes no attempt to sing in the video, even as we hear her voice in the song. This shows the rapid evolution of the music video, not only in Madonna's own work but also in the medium overall. It has moved well beyond simply capturing a live performance, as was the case in "Everybody," her first video; at this point in her career and in the brief history of the medium, such videos seem a distant memory.

Musically, Madonna's winning formula has been to combine a simple, catchy melody with trendy sounds and rhythms and skillful production. The melody of "Like a Prayer" flows in gently undulating phrases, with little or no syncopation. When isolated from its setting, the melody bears a closer resemblance to a children's song or a folk melody than to a dance-inspired song from the eighties. And like a folk melody, it is easily absorbed and remembered. The support for this melody oscillates between sustained chords sung by a choir and played on an organ, and a Caribbean-flavored background that bears a striking resemblance to Steve Winwood's 1986 No. 1 hit "Higher Love." As with much post-1980 pop, the active accompaniment is dense, rhythmically active, and rich in both electronic and conventional instrumental sounds. The steady flow of Madonna's melody connects the dance-like sections with those sections containing only sustained harmonies and extremely light percussion sounds. "Like A Prayer" breaks no new ground musically, but it does merge disparate and seemingly contradictory musical features into an effective song, just as the video does.

The most ground-breaking aspect of Madonna's career has been her ascension to a position of complete control of her career: writing her songs, producing her recordings, choreographing her performances, and making the key decisions about every aspect of production and promotion. This owes more to her ambition, business acumen, and chutzpah than it does to her musical talent. In achieving elite celebrity status—single-name recognition, tabloid fodder for the better part of two decades—as she directed her career, she has become a role model for a new generation of women performers.

Many have found her public persona liberating. Without question, her success added a new dimension to sexual equality within the pop music business. Women, or at least women like her, no longer had to be front persons for men. Cynical observers have dismissed the provocative images that she presents, such as those encountered in the "Like a Prayer" video, as attention-getting stunts whose shock value obscures a lack of talent and imagination. It is true that Madonna is not spectacularly creative in any artistic dimension of the music business: She is not Michael Jackson's equal as a dancer, Prince's equal as a songwriter or an instrumentalist, or Tina Turner's equal as a vocalist. However, to dismiss her talents out of hand would be to ignore the sense of conviction with which Madonna presents these controversial juxtapositions and to dismiss their role in challenging value systems that have grown rigid over time.

Neither Jackson nor Madonna has been a musical innovator. Their most influential and innovative contributions have come in other areas: the reintegration of song and expressive dance; their role in establishing the music video as a new expressive medium; their sheer star power; and in Madonna's case, her business acumen. All have become key components of popular music since the mid-1980s.

CHAPTER 79

Post-Punk/Post-Disco Fusions: The Music of Prince

It would be difficult to find any rock artist who embodies more confluences and contradictions than Prince (born Prince Rogers Nelson, 1958). His music is a rock and rhythm-and-blues melting pot. One hears elements of funk, punk, hard rock, disco, black and white pop, and more, in varying proportions. His touring bands have included blacks and whites, women and men. His particular syntheses came to be known as "the Minneapolis sound," after the city where he was born and where he has continued to make his home base (he opened Paisley Park Studios there in 1987). The confluences extend to his personal life; the unpronounceable symbol that he used in lieu of his name from 1993 to 2000 (when he became "the artist formerly known as Prince") reputedly represents a merging of the symbols for male and female.

The contradictions are present in his life and his music. He created a public persona so blatantly erotic at times that his music sparked the campaign to put parental advisory labels on recordings, but he has led an extremely reclusive private life, which reportedly has a strong spiritual dimension. (He claimed that God directed him to change his name to a symbol.) He has been an artist sufficiently drawn to the spotlight that he co-authored and starred in a quasi-autobiographical film (*Purple Rain*), and he is a musician who willingly and anonymously writes for, produces, and accompanies other artists. (Prince often uses aliases when he appears on others' recordings.) His music has been deeply rooted in the valued music of earlier generations. In a 1985 *Rolling Stone* interview, he acknowledged artists as diverse as Stevie Wonder, Joni Mitchell, Miles Davis, Santana, and George Clinton. Yet his music has grown by absorbing numerous contemporary influences some distance from his musical roots—such as new wave—and by blending sounds produced by cutting-edge technology—for example, drum machines in the early eighties—with more conventional instruments, all of which he plays masterfully.

One measure of Prince's greatness as an artist has been his ability to reconcile the contrasting, even contradictory, elements of his musical life into a personal style that retains its identity despite its great stylistic and emotional range. Listening to a Prince album can be like taking a course in rock history. Prince has mastered virtually all rock-era styles. For Prince, style mastery isn't simply the ability to cover a style; he seldom does

© Frank Micelotta/Getty Images

PRINCE performing in 1990

just that. Instead, he draws on disparate style elements and mixes them together to evoke a particular mood. For him, beat patterns, sounds, and rhythmic textures are like ingredients in a gourmet dish; they are used to flavor the song. More important, he also adds original ideas to create the nouvelle cuisine of eighties pop.

Prince is the son of musicians: jazz pianist John Nelson and singer Mattie Shaw. To escape his parents' troubled relationship (they divorced when he was ten), Prince sought refuge in music. By his teens, he had not only mastered the full array of rhythm instruments but also begun writing his own material and learning production skills. Although not a child star, he was more precocious in some respects than Michael Jackson as both musician and producer. He played all the instruments on his first five albums and produced the albums as well. Stevie Wonder had pioneered this electronic version of the one-man band in the early seventies; Prince grew up with it.

He secured his first recording contract, which gave him total freedom in the studio, in 1977. The hits began coming two years later, beginning with "I Wanna Be Your Lover." *Purple Rain* (1984) brought him commercial success (sales of 13 million units; three hit singles) and critical recognition (the soundtrack won three Grammy awards). In its wake, he became one of the few superstars of the eighties. His subsequent work continued to explore new territory. As he remarked in the *Rolling Stone* interview, "I always try to do something different and conquer new ground." He reached what many commentators feel was an artistic high point in 1987 with the release of the double album *Sign 'O' the Times.*

LISTENING CUE • **"Sign 'O' the Times" (1987),** Prince.

STYLE 1980s post-punk/post-disco fusion • **FORM** Verse/chorus

Listen For . . .

INSTRUMENTATION
Vocal, electric guitar, synthesizers (riffs, percussion, sustained chords)

RHYTHM
Sixteen-beat rhythm at moderate tempo implied throughout by interaction of layers, percussion parts

MELODY
Mainly long phrases in verse and bridge; no hook at chorus

HARMONY
No harmony in verse; sustained, slowly changing chords in bridge

TEXTURE
Spare texture: no bass, chord instrument much of the time; mainly repeated riffs

Remember . . .

DARK SONG
Loud, repeated power chords played on guitar with some distortion, in a basic rock rhythm and at a fast tempo; these are salient features of punk style. They inform the basic feel of song throughout, although Bowie adds a number of sophisticated touches.

UNDERMINING POP FORM
Verse/chorus form that subverts the arrival at the chorus by subtracting instruments and returning to bleak opening texture

DARK SETTING
Music reinforces mood of lyrics through empty-sounding texture, form without conventional hook, absence of conventional rock band sounds (no bass, rhythm guitar, steady timekeeping in drums).

Listen to this selection in CourseMate.

"Sign 'O' the Times"

"Sign 'O' the Times," one of three singles from the album to chart, presents a bleak vision of contemporary life: gangs, AIDS, drugs, and natural disasters, interlaced with anecdotal accounts of the fallout from drug use. The music is correspondingly bleak. The track begins with an intricate rhythm formed from a syncopated synthesizer riff and two electronically generated percussion sounds, and this texture continues throughout the song. The repetition seems purposeful; it seems to suggest a despair that knows no end. It substitutes for a standard rhythm section and supports Prince's vocal in the verse section. Other consistent elements include a strong backbeat and a synthesized bass riff that often provides a response to the vocal line. Funky, jazz-influenced guitar figures, then sustained synthesizer chords, which provide the first harmonic change, highlight the buildup to the crux of the song: One finds release only in death. To underscore this difficult idea, Prince brings the music back to the empty sound of the opening—an abrupt and disconcerting return to reality. Only a blues-tinged guitar solo, again over the relentless synthesizer riffs and intricate percussion rhythms, provides relief from the misery portrayed in the lyric; this is interrupted by percussion sounds that evoke the fire of a machine gun.

"Sign 'O' the Times" gains its impact as much from what's missing as from what's present. There is no rhythm guitar, no bass line, and no routine timekeeping on a drum set. There is no hook at the highpoint of the chorus to latch onto. There are no familiar chord progressions and few other clues that help us navigate through the song. The rhythms are complex, as in funk, but disciplined; the texture is spare, not dense. These features help create a sound world that is as vivid and powerful as a black and white photograph of a gray day in the ghetto.

"Sign 'O' the Times" shows how Prince mixes disparate elements into a coherent and effective whole. From punk, via rap, he took realness—there is no fantasy, or escape, in this song. From funk, he took complex layered rhythms, which he pared down to convey the mood of the song. He adapts blues-influenced rock guitar to the context, supporting it unconventionally with the minimalist synthesizer riffs and rhythms.

Almost any other Prince song will sound quite different in many respects; that is one reason for his commercial and critical success. The most consistent elements are likely to be the mix of synthesized and conventional instruments; an open-sounding, intricately worked-out texture that puts a different spin on the conventional interplay between regular timekeeping and syncopated patterns; and a few distinctive features that help set the song apart from the sources that inspired it. In this song, it is the absence of bass and drum set and the rich sustained harmonies in the first part of the chorus. But the distinctive element can be anything: "U Got the Look," another top hit from *Sign 'O' the Times,* offers a radically transformed version of the twelve-bar blues progression.

Even by rock standards, Prince is an eccentric. Still, the odd, often contradictory aspects of his personal life cannot obscure or diminish Prince's remarkable musical achievement. He remains one of the most multitalented, multidimensional musicians in the history of rock.

CHAPTER 80
The Maturation of Black Pop

In the music video of her 1984 No. 1 hit "What's Love Got to Do with It," Tina Turner strides confidently through the streets of New York as she sings the song and occasionally dispenses advice with a gesture or two. Eight years earlier, she was running; in July 1976, she left her husband, Ike Turner, after a violent argument in the middle of a tour. For the next two years, she was in hiding because she feared retribution from him. When she left, she had only 36¢ and a gas credit card, and was reduced to living off friends—even doing housekeeping. "What's Love Got to Do with It" and *Private Dancer,* the album from which it came, confirmed her return to pop stardom.

At the time of the album's release, Turner was forty-four. She was the oldest of several black pop stars from the 1960s and 1970s who continued to make great music and enjoy commercial success. Marvin Gaye (until his untimely death in 1984), Aretha Franklin, Stevie Wonder, and Diana Ross are others who stand out. A new generation of singers—among them Lionel Richie, Natalie Cole (daughter of the great Nat Cole), Whitney Houston, and Luther Vandross—were some of the brightest stars of the eighties and nineties.

The New Black Pop

The sound of the eighties black pop resulted mainly from two significant changes: the use of synthesized sounds to replace most, if not all, of the traditional instruments; and more adventurous rhythms. The sumptuous backgrounds that were so much a part of the sound of later doo-wop, Motown, Philadelphia, and Barry White are part of this updated black pop sound. The difference is that producers often use electronic analogues to the strings, horns, and even rhythm instruments. Their function is much the same, but the sounds are new. This fresh sound palette gives the music a more contemporary flavor. So did the 1980s-style rhythms featured in so many of the songs, including the pop-punk rock beat, sixteen-beat rhythms, and reggae-tinged rhythms. All were filtered through a Motown-like approach to time-keeping. Regular timekeeping was generally in the background, and at times it was dispensed with altogether; dominant rhythms moved either much more slowly (for instance, sustained chords) or faster than the beat; and the faster rhythms typically played against the beat, with irregular patterns or syncopations. We hear both innovations in Turner's hit song.

Tina Turner

If anyone were entitled to be cynical about love, it would be Tina Turner (born Annie Mae Bullock, 1939). In 1956, as a young woman still in her teens, she connected with Ike Turner, eight years her senior and already a music business veteran. The connection soon became personal as well as professional. They married in 1962, and for more than a decade they prospered professionally as the Ike and Tina Turner Revue; they had a huge hit in 1971 with a cover of Creedence Clearwater Revival's "Proud Mary."

However, for much of their relationship, Ike abused Tina emotionally and physically. The abuse grew worse as their career declined; Ike's alleged drug use and almost paranoid distrust of outside management were main factors. Their professional relationship complicated any personal breakup. When she finally broke free of Turner—in the middle of a tour—she also broke contractual obligations. Because of this, the divorce settlement devastated her financially; she retained only her name.

It took Tina half a decade to get her solo career on track. Her break came in 1983, when she covered Al Green's "Let's Stay Together" for B.E.F. (British Electric Foundation), the production side of a synth-pop group doing some serious soul searching. (B.E.F. would eventually record not only with Turner but also Chaka Khan, Mavis Staples, and other major black artists.) The next year saw the release of *Private Dancer;* "What's Love Got to Do with It" was one of three singles from the album that charted. The song would win three Grammys the following year. It was Turner's first No. 1 hit as a solo act.

The song and Turner's singing project an embittered view of love; any excitement found in the physical aspects of a relationship is tempered by the foreknowledge that the relationship will never mature into love. She sings from the heart; close to two decades of pain spill out in her soulful singing.

IKE AND TINA TURNER

LISTENING CUE • **"What's Love Got to Do with It" (1984),** Terry Britten and Graham Lyle. Tina Turner, vocal.

STYLE 1980s black pop • **FORM** Verse/chorus

Listen For . . .

INSTRUMENTATION
Vocal, bass, drums, percussion, synthesizers (sustained chords, riffs)

PERFORMANCE STYLE
Turner's soulful, passionate singing

RHYTHM
Slow rock beat, more active rhythms in background, including reggae-like rebound backbeat

MELODY
Long phrases in verse; repeated title-phrase riff highlights chorus

TEXTURE
Several layers, but open sound (sustained chords, subtle riffs) encases Turner's rich voice

Remember . . .

ANTI-LOVE SONG
Lyric speaks directly and honestly about the hurt of a broken heart.

TURNER'S PASSIONATE SINGING
Turner's singing is comparably direct; it makes the lyric emotionally credible.

1980s POP SOUND
Instrumental accompaniment dominated by synthesized sounds; rhythm features open texture with light rock-rhythm timekeeping, more active rhythms darting in and out.

Listen to this selection in CourseMate.

The song uses the verse/chorus template as a point of departure. The verse builds inexorably to a magnetic hook, which Turner's gritty voice invests with deep feeling. By contrast, the musical setting is muted—almost arid. Synthesizer sounds are prominent: sustained synthesizer chords and obbligatos. The rhythm shows the influence of reggae in the persistent rebound pattern on the offbeat, the open texture, and a free-roaming bass in the chorus. The accompaniment never matches the intensity of Turner's singing; it is almost as if the accompaniment is indifferent to her despair. This has the effect of casting Turner's pain into relief; in the song, she grieves alone.

Race and Romance in Popular Music

The rebirth of Turner's career was not only a personal triumph but also a symbolic milestone for mature women of all races, and especially black women. Only four decades earlier, Ethel Waters, then forty-seven, portrayed Petunia in the 1943 all-black film *Cabin in the Sky.* From the late 1920s, she was one of the top black pop singers. She could sing, "My man and I ain't together" (from Harold Arlen's bluesy standard "Stormy Weather") to Cotton Club audiences and on disc, but she couldn't act it out on screen. In *Cabin in the Sky,* she sings another great pop standard, "Taking a Chance on Love," to Eddie Anderson, who would later become famous as Jack Benny's servant Rochester. But she is dressed dowdily and simply rolls her eyes back and forth as she sings. The song and the singing are great, the message is romantic, but their interaction is anything but. Indeed, the scene reminds contemporary viewers that minstrelsy was not ancient history in 1943; Hollywood refused to portray blacks in a romantic relationship. In the late forties and fifties, Nat Cole thrilled black and white audiences with beautiful love songs like "Unforgettable," but his appeal was limited to his voice, at least among white audiences.

The personification of romantic song in popular music began to transcend race in the sixties, with the popularity of the girl groups and Motown acts. By the time Turner recorded "What's Love Got to Do with It," her sex appeal was certainly not delimited by her age or her ethnicity in North America. This was even more the case in Europe, where she has had an ardent fan base (and where she currently resides). By the end of the century, race and ethnic heritage were nonissues in romantic music, as a parade of contemporary pop divas evidences.

The grittiness of the lyric and of Turner's singing was exceptional in the black pop of the 1980s and 1990s. Younger stars like Whitney Houston favored love-related themes closer in tone to typical Motown and Philadelphia songs. However, the musical changes, especially in sound and rhythm, were widespread throughout the 1980s and into the 1990s.

The 1980s were the final flourishing of post-Motown black pop. As the century drew to a close, R&B in general and black pop in particular acquired a harder edge, mainly through the infusion of themes and sounds from rap and electronica.

CHAPTER 81
Punk-Inspired Pop

Rock got a "beat lift" around 1980. The new sound was lean, clean, vibrant, and colored with an array of synthesizer timbres and effects. It harnessed the energy of punk, but its most direct antecedent was the music of David Bowie, himself one of punk's seminal influences. From these sources, it distilled a purer form of rock rhythm, typically spread throughout the texture, from bass and kick drum to high-pitched percussion and synth parts. Its leanness and cleanness came in large part from an open-sounding mid-range. Crisp single-note lines and sustained chords replaced thick guitar chords and riffs.

Bowie himself was a major contributor to this new sound. So were new wave artists such as Elvis Costello, Blondie, the Pretenders, Talking Heads, Devo, and the B-52s. However, there were also groups that had neither punk's rage nor new wave's weirdness.

The Go-Go's' "We Got the Beat" (1981) could easily be the signature song of this new rock sound. Like a typical Ramones' song, it has a simple lyric, mostly the repeated title phrase. And it has punk's saturated rock rhythm—not only in the drum part but also in repeated notes and chords from top (high piano chords) to bottom (bass and low guitar). But the spirit of the song is completely different. It is almost mindlessly happy—much closer to fifties rock and roll than it is to punk or new wave. However, the rhythmic approach clearly places it in the eighties. So does the makeup of the band. The Go-Go's were among the first of the all-girl rock groups.

"We Got the Beat" also shows how the point of punk's rhythmic innovation had been turned completely on its head within five years. In the Sex Pistols' music, the rhythm was aggressive and confrontational. Here it's simply bouncy. Lead singer Belinda Carlisle (b. 1958) had been a cheerleader in high school; it was as if someone put a yellow smiley face on Johnny Rotten.

Van Halen

Among the bands to utilize this new approach was Van Halen, an excellent second-generation heavy metal band. Two brothers, drummer Alex (b. 1953) and guitarist Eddie (b. 1955) formed the band with bassist Michael Anthony (b. 1954) and lead vocalist David Lee Roth (b. 1954). Their 1978 debut album, simply titled *Van Halen,* showcased Eddie Van Halen's breathtaking virtuosity. The appropriately titled "Eruption," a free-form solo by Van Halen, immediately raised the bar for guitarists. The album was an immediate success and one of the

LISTENING CUE · **"Jump" (1984),** Alex Van Halen, Eddie Van Halen, and David Lee Roth. Van Halen.

STYLE Punk-influenced pop rock • **FORM** Mainly opening section (A). which serves as intro, first vocal statement, and outro. Vocal bridges and guitar and synth solos interpolated.

Listen For . . .

INSTRUMENTATION
Vocal, synths, electric guitar, drums

RHYTHM
Basic rhythm: bouncy rock beat at moderate tempo; time kept in bass; signature riff syncopated

MELODY
Instrumental riffs most prominent melodic strand; different versions of same rhythm

HARMONY
Fresh approach to I-IV-V throughout most of song; bridge uses more wide-ranging harmony

TEXTURE
Open sound: strong bass, high synth riff, vocal, drums in middle; bridge = sudden shift in texture—more fluid rhythm, thicker texture in mid-range

Remember . . .

HAPPY SONG
Good mood in lyrics echoed by syncopated riff, guitar and synth solos, and clearly outlined rhythm at a moderate tempo

FROM PUNK TO POP
"Saturated" rock rhythm (bass repeated note/drums) recontextualizes more aggressive punk approach to rock rhythm.

1980s POP ROCK SOUND
Prominent synths: main solo voice, as well as bass line support, dominant riff, and background color augment traditional rock instrumentation.

Listen to this selection in CourseMate.

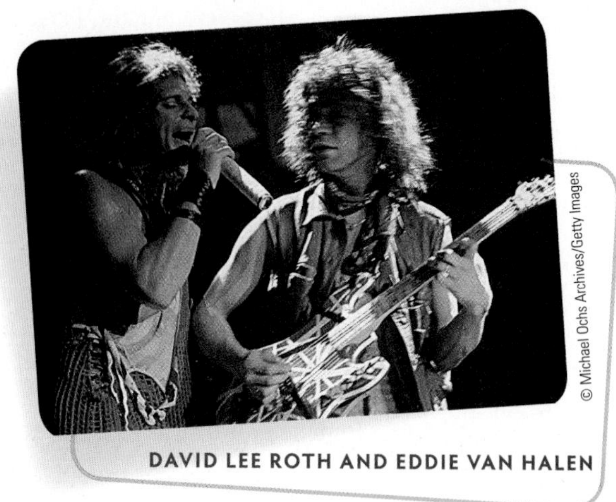

DAVID LEE ROTH AND EDDIE VAN HALEN

most spectacular debut albums in rock history. It would be the first of an almost unbroken string of platinum albums by the band.

Although associated with heavy metal because of the guitar-centric songs and Eddie Van Halen's playing, Van Halen was, from the start, more than a heavy metal band. During the early eighties, in the latter part of Roth's tenure with the band, Eddie Van Halen sought to move more toward the mainstream, in part by incorporating synthesizers into their sound—he is also a skilled keyboardist. Among the fruits of this particular direction was "Jump," from their sixth album, *1984;* it was the band's first No. 1 single.

"Jump" exemplifies the new sound of punk-inspired and pop-oriented rock that emerged in the early eighties. Among the features that most clearly identify this sound are prominent synthesizer parts, an open texture, and the contemporary approach to rock rhythm. For most of the song, including the opening signature riff, synths rule. In addition to replacing the lead guitar as the source of the opening instrumental hook, they provide most of the accompaniment for Roth's vocal. Van Halen plays guitar only in the contrasting section and in a brief tantalizing solo, which only hints at his technical mastery and sonic imagination. This soon gives way to a synthesizer solo that is more extended but less virtuosic. The synth riff lies mainly in a medium-high register; it is in a higher range than Roth's vocal line much of the time. By contrast, the bass line, played by Anthony (on bass) and Van Halen, is in a low register. What's missing—or very much in the background—most of the time are chords played by a rhythm guitarist. By omitting this typically prominent part of the texture, Van Halen gives the song a more spacious sound.

Underpinning Roth's vocal and the synthesizer and guitar parts is a bass line that is mostly a single note repeated at rock-beat speed. It changes infrequently in the heart of the song—mainly at the end of phrases, in the contrasting section, and during Van Halen's guitar solo. By presenting the rock-rhythm layer most prominently in a repeated-note bass line, Van Halen (and the other eighties bands that also used this strategy) further concentrates this already distilled form of rock rhythm. Here, the bass part turns rock rhythm into a musical trampoline on which the rest of the texture bounces. In this form, the rhythm is vibrant, not aggressive. Indeed, "Jump" is a good-humored song; we can almost see Roth smirking as he sings the song. Shortly after recording *1984,* Roth left the band. Sammy Hagar (b. 1947) replaced him for the better part of a decade. He too left, in 1996. Gary Cherone (b. 1961) then began his brief tenure as lead vocalist. The band, inactive since 2004, undertook a reunion tour with Roth in 2007.

The sounds and rhythms popularized in songs like "Jump" were one of the freshest trends in rock during the eighties. Other acts—including the Eurythmics, Cyndi Lauper, and the Smiths—also featured it in their music. The livelier, cleaner rhythmic textures and the expanded sound palette created by the new synth timbres make the music sound distinctly different from almost all of the music of the seventies and before. A similar approach underpins some of the most significant rock of the decade.

CHAPTER 82
Significant Rock

In Ethiopia, a country in northeast Africa, the vast majority of people depend on farming for their livelihood. In the seventies, the Soviet-backed government instituted a land-reform program that limited the acreage that individuals could farm. In 1984, drought, overcultivation, and the government's poorly conceived and ineptly executed marketing program created a famine that devastated the country.

British journalist Michael Buerk, aided by Kenyan cameraman and journalist Mohammed Amin, traveled to Ethiopia in the fall of 1984. On October 24, the BBC broadcast a 7-minute film that showed thousands of people dying from starvation. The other major news agencies quickly picked up the film. Over a billion people around the world soon saw Buerk and Amin's account of the Ethiopian famine.

Making Rock Relevant

Among those who saw Buerk's broadcast was Bob Geldof (b. 1954), the lead singer with the Irish new wave band the Boomtown Rats. Geldof was so moved that he resolved to organize a musical event to raise money for famine relief and to raise people's awareness of the crisis; he would call his project Band Aid. He enlisted the help of Midge Ure (born James Ure, 1953), a member of Ultravox, another U.K. new wave band. Together they wrote the song "Do They Know It's Christmas?" then recruited an all-star cast to perform it, and obtained 24 hours of free studio time to record it. Among the guest performers on the recording were Paul McCartney, Bono, Sting, Boy George, and Phil Collins. The recording was released on December 15, less than two months after Geldof viewed Buerk's broadcast. It quickly topped the charts in the United Kingdom. Geldof donated all the revenues from its sale to assist the Ethiopian people through the Band Aid Trust, which he formed for that purpose.

Around the time "Do They Know It's Christmas?" was released in Great Britain, another equally bleak news report of the famine aired in the United States. After viewing the broadcast, Harry Belafonte (b. 1927), a singer and actor who had parlayed his spectacular success as a calypso singer in the fifties into a long and distinguished career in entertainment, called his manager Ken Kragen, who also managed several other top entertainment stars, about organizing a project for famine relief. Within short order, Lionel Richie, Stevie Wonder, and Michael Jackson were on board; Jackson and Richie wrote the song "We Are the World." The principals scheduled a recording session right after the American Music Awards ceremony. An all-star cast—including Paul Simon, Tina Turner, Diana Ross, Willie Nelson, Bruce Springsteen, Bob Dylan, and Ray Charles—recorded the song on January 28, 1985; Quincy Jones produced the session. The single came out in March. On Good Friday (April 5 that year), 5,000 radio stations played the song simultaneously. The single, and an album spun off from the single, both went multiplatinum. The project, called USA (United Support of Artists) for Africa, raised over $50 million for famine relief.

Capitalizing on the goodwill generated by the Band Aid project, Geldof organized Live Aid, the most massive fund-raising event in the history of the music business. His idea was to create a "global jukebox" with broadcasts of concerts from stadiums in London and Philadelphia. The concerts—over 22 hours between the two venues—and live performances from other venues throughout the world—for example, Moscow, Sydney, the Hague—would be broadcast throughout the world via satellite. The roster of acts performing at the multiple venues reads like a Who's Who of rock. Live Aid, performed July 13, 1985, drew a worldwide audience estimated at over 1 billion viewers. At one point during the broadcast, Billy Connolly, a Scottish comedian and actor who was opening for Elton John, announced that he had been informed that 95 percent of the world's television sets were watching the event. Live Aid eventually raised over $260 million for famine relief in Africa. Even more important, the events and the recordings called attention to the plight in Africa. Shipments of grain surpluses from the United States and elsewhere soon alleviated the suffering in Ethiopia.

These events and others like them (such as Farm Aid) put the "we" back in rock. In the sixties, rock had defined itself as a "we" music: first in the bands themselves (names like the Beatles, the Beach Boys, the Who, the Rolling Stones gave bands a collective identity), then in the bond between music and audience. The "we" in rock was a generation that didn't trust anyone over thirty. The seventies, by contrast, have been dubbed as the "me" decade; in music, self-involvement (what about me?) and the pursuit of success seemed to negate the sense of community created in the sixties.

The massive fund-raising events of the eighties signaled the return of rock's conscience, but with a huge difference. In the sixties, rock gave voice to a generational revolution. It provided the soundtrack for an assault on the establishment and, by overthrowing the pop music establishment, it led by example. In the eighties, rock *was* the establishment, the dominant segment of the music industry. As a result, it could leverage the celebrity of its artists in projects that served a greater good. In the eighties, "we" in rock not only included the musicians, the music industry, and the audience, but also those whom they sought to help.

Through a series of spectacular "-Aid" events, altruism returned to rock in the mid-1980s. We might think of these events as a successful response to a mid-life crisis, as if a man asked himself where the idealism of his youth had gone and resolved not only to recapture it but also to convert those ideals into positive actions. The sense of purpose that these events symbolized was one sign of a renewal in rock. Leading this renewal were Bruce Springsteen and U2.

Bruce Springsteen

Asbury Park is a New Jersey beach town about an hour's drive from New York City. Bruce Springsteen (b. 1949) grew up in and around the town. Early on, he forged the musical split personality that has been his trademark. He worked with bar bands close to home and also played solo gigs in Greenwich Village clubs, where he mingled with Patti Smith and other early punk rockers. This helps account for the huge swings in his music, from the all-acoustic *Nebraska* album to the hard-rocking *Born in the U.S.A.*

His enormous success comes in part from his ability to integrate seemingly contradictory aspects of his life and work. He is a superstar and a man of the people, a musician who plays to sold-out arenas and shows up unannounced to sit in with local bands. Throughout his career, he has stayed close to his working-class roots and has written songs that reflect their concerns. At the same time, he is larger than life—the "Boss" to his fiercely loyal fans.

BRUCE SPRINGSTEEN, 1985

In 1974, rock critic Jon Landau went to a Springsteen concert at the Harvard Square Theatre. In a long, rambling review, he wrote, "I saw rock and roll's future and his name is Bruce Springsteen." Landau turned his words into action, becoming Springsteen's manager.

Landau's evaluation was right on the mark in the sense that Springsteen became the biggest star of the next two decades to consciously continue the core tradition of rock. While others branched off in new directions, Springsteen stayed close to his rock-and-roll roots, even as he updated and expanded the sound. For example, his first big hit, the 1975 song "Born to Run," features an oversized band (several guitars, saxophone, keyboards, bass, and drums), an extended guitar hook, a sprawling form, and a powerful, obvious beat.

After "Born to Run," Springsteen's career was primed for takeoff. However, a drawn-out legal battle involving Landau and Springsteen's first producer, Mike Appel, kept Springsteen out of the studios for about three years. He returned with a string of critically acclaimed and mildly (for 1980) popular albums: *Darkness on the Edge of Town* (1978), *The River* (1980), and the acoustic *Nebraska* (1982). He finally broke through to a mass audience in 1984 with *Born in the U.S.A.* It was in this album that Springsteen fully realized the big conception first expressed in songs like "Born to Run."

In the title track, Springsteen mixes a strong story line, simple riffs and rhythms, and subtle details. The lyric paints a brutal portrait of a Vietnam War veteran through powerful, almost posterized images: "sent me off to a foreign land/to go and kill the yellow man." The verses telegraph defining moments in the protagonist's life, from early childhood to his inability to get a job and the insensitivity of the government in supporting veterans. Springsteen's words put an ironic spin on the title phrase. In this context, what could be a prideful affirmation of patriotism becomes a jingoistic mantra—a badge of shame for a country that sends its less fortunate off to fight in a senseless war, then does little to help those who return.

Springsteen sets his trenchant lyric in an almost minimalist musical environment. The song begins with only a single octave on the piano, a heavy backbeat, and a synthesizer riff. The spacing of these three elements—low, middle, high—and a judicious amount of reverb (which makes the backbeat sound uncomfortably close to a rifle shot) give the introduction a big sound by defining a wide open space waiting to be filled in. As the song unfolds, Springsteen fills in the middle; the most prominent of the additional parts either strengthen the bass or fill in the upper range—most notably, the piano part presents a more active version of the synthesizer riff. These and other instruments weave in and out of the texture, but

LISTENING CUE • **"Born in the U.S.A." (1984),** Bruce Springsteen. Bruce Springsteen, vocal, with the E Street Band.

STYLE 1980s serious rock • **FORM** Verse/chorus, but with the instrumental accompaniment keeping the same riff throughout

Listen For . . .

INSTRUMENTATION
Vocals, synthesizers, drums, keyboard, bass

PERFORMANCE STYLE
Springsteen's strained vocal sound = intense conviction

RHYTHM
Rock rhythm at moderate tempo with overpowering back beat; rock timekeeping off and on

MELODY
Main melodic feature: title-phrase riff, played, then sung, dominates song.

TEXTURE
Open sound dominated by high riff, strong backbeat, low sustained bass notes

Remember . . .

ANTIWAR SONG
Lyric a scathing indictment of war and its costs

SIGNIFICANT ROCK
Open texture with Springsteen's raspy voice in the middle conveys a sense of importance

SPRINGSTEEN STRATEGY
Combine easily grasped features (riff, backbeat) with subtle touches (piano doubling synth riff)

SYNTHS AND 80s ROCK
Dominant presence of synthesizer sounds = fresh sound in 1980s rock

Listen to this selection in CourseMate.

the riff and backbeat are constants—even through Max Weinberg's "war zone" drum solo.

Springsteen is at once simple and subtle. The prominent elements in "Born in the U.S.A." stand out vibrantly, whereas the spacing of the texture and the balance between the prominent features and background support is more sophisticated. Springsteen has maintained this strategy in his subsequent music, most notably in *The Rising,* his response to 9/11. He remains one of the few artists in rock music with a truly powerful presence.

Springsteen's "significant" sound, as evidenced in "Born in the U.S.A.," was one of several musical options that he would employ in his music from the early eighties on. Other tracks on the album range from the punk-drenched "No Surrender" and the country-flavored "Darlington County" to the synth rock of "Dancing in the Dark" and the moody ballad "My Hometown."

In similar fashion, another significant band of the eighties would define themselves musically by developing and refining one of the truly distinctive styles of the decade.

U2

From the start, U2—lead vocalist Bono (born Paul Hewson, 1960), guitarist-keyboardist The Edge (born David Evans, 1961), bassist Adam Clayton (b. 1960), and drummer Larry Mullen (b. 1961)—have had a sense of their destiny. In 1981, three years after the group came together, Bono told *Rolling Stone,* "Even at this stage, I do feel we are meant to be one of the great bands. There's a certain spark, a certain chemistry, that was special about the Stones, The Who, and the Beatles, and I think it's also special about U2." They have fulfilled their destiny because they have stayed together and because they have never lost their passion for rock and what it can be. As recently as 2000, after more than two decades of touring, recording, and sending their message out into the world, Bono told *USA Today* that "There is a transcendence that I want from rock. . . . I'm still drunk on the idea that rock and roll can be a force for change. We haven't lost that idea."

U2 soon made Bono a prophet. In their first two albums, *Boy* (1980) and *October* (1981), the group addressed personal issues, among them relationships and their faith. By 1983, the year that they released *War,* their third album, the band had defined its purpose, found its audience, and begun to define its sound. With this album, their music took on the politically and socially aware edge that would characterize it through the rest of the eighties. "Sunday Bloody Sunday," a track from *War* and their first No. 1 hit in the United Kingdom, for example, recounts an especially bloody incident in the ongoing strife between Catholics and Protestants in Northern Ireland, and the musical setting reinforces the message of the lyrics; the five-note bursts played by the entire band underneath Bono's vocal line evoke the sound of gunfire.

The following year, U2 began their long and fruitful collaboration with Brian Eno (b. 1948)—a founding member of Roxy Music, an electronica pioneer, the father of ambient music, and by 1984, a much-in-demand producer. (More recently, Eno has identified himself as a "sonic landscaper," a label that applies readily to his work with U2.) Eno brought a polish to U2's music while preserving the distinctive sound world that they had begun to create. Their first album together was the 1984 release *The Unforgettable Fire;* he would collaborate on four of their albums. By 1985, *Rolling Stone* had dubbed them the band of the eighties, but it wasn't until *Joshua Tree* (1987) that they achieved the overwhelming commercial success to match their critical acclaim.

Virtually from the start of their career, U2 cultivated a sound world that made their music sound significant. They put the essential components in place in their first albums, enhanced them with the help of Brian Eno, and maintained them through the eighties. The sound grows out of punk but already has a distinct identity in songs like "Gloria" (1981) from their second album. Surrounding Bono's vocals is a four-strand texture, separated into low, middle, and high:

- Two low-range sounds: repeated notes at rock-beat speed in the bass and beat keeping on the bass drum
- A mid-range percussion sound: a rock-rhythm layer on the sock cymbal
- A medium-high–range sound: the angular guitar line, also moving at rock-beat speed

The insistent rock rhythmic layer, played by the entire band, derives from punk, but U2 has already put their personal stamp on it in the spacing of the instruments and in The Edge's asymmetrically patterned single-line guitar figures. Because of the registral openness and the angular guitar lines, the effect is quite different from punk. Whereas the sound of Ramones-style punk rams the listener head on, the sound of U2, even at this early stage, envelops the listener.

This distinctive sound world is built on contrast: between high and low and between slow and fast. As the band's music evolved during the eighties, the contrast deepened. One significant change came from within the band. The active rhythms doubled in speed, from rock rhythm to a sixteen-beat rhythm, while such features as chord rhythm often moved at even slower speeds. In his work with U2, Eno enriched the "sonic landscape" by deepening the contrast between slow and fast with sustained synthesizer sounds and by introducing stronger textural contrasts. These changes gave U2's music an even more sharply defined profile, as we hear in "Where the Streets Have No Name," a hit track from their 1987 album *Joshua Tree.*

"Where the Streets Have No Name" continues U2's predilection for meaningful words encased in meaningful-sounding music. The lyrics describe a universal longing for the harmony that can be created when divisions by class, race, and wealth disappear. They are general enough to have spawned multiple interpretations. Some connect the song's message to Ethiopia, where Bono and his wife had done relief work. Others link it to Los Angeles, where the video of the song was filmed. Still others associate it with Dublin, where the street one lives on could identify one's social and economic status. And most connect it to the world beyond.

Bono presents the lyric through a melody whose simplicity is obscured by the rich instrumental backdrop. If we tune out the instruments and simply listen to Bono's voice, we hear a folksong-like tune: short phrases that gently rise and fall within a narrow range. Like folksongs from the British Isles, this melody is coherent even without accompaniment, and it would work with a simple folk guitar accompaniment.

It is U2 and Eno's grand setting that relocates this simple melody from the front porch to the stage. The extended instrumental introduction—almost 2 minutes in length—begins with sustained organ and synthesizer sounds. The Edge's busy guitar pattern slowly emerges out of this sound cushion. At first it is in a rhythm that oscillates once for every six notes, like a jig in slow motion. Imperceptibly, he converts the pattern to the sixteen-beat rhythm that is sustained through the rest of the song. The rhythmic patterns range from the sustained synthesizer chords, which may last four measures before changing, through the beat-speed thump of Mullen's bass drum, Clayton's rock-beat–speed repeated note, and the sixteen-beat rhythms of the guitar(s)—there are two guitar sounds much of the time—and drums. All of this encases Bono's singing in a musical halo.

The sound world that U2 created in "Where the Streets Have No Name" was the band's musical signature during the eighties. It is heard in many of their hits during that decade, and it becomes progressively more sophisticated from album to album. It has the effect of elevating the simple melody that lies at its center, investing it with a power and impact that it could not have had in a simpler setting. In this sense, the music of U2 is the ultimate folk rock, one in which the power of the words is matched by the power of the music.

LISTENING CUE • **"Where the Streets Have No Name" (1987),** Adam Clayton, Dave Evans, Paul Hewson, and Larry Mullen, Jr. U2.

STYLE 1980s significant rock • **FORM** Verse/chorus, but with extended instrumental intro and outro

Listen For . . .

INSTRUMENTATION
Vocal, synths, guitar, bass, drums

RHYTHM
Steady timekeeping at moderate tempo in bass (eight-beat) and drums (sixteen-beat); steady rhythm in guitar but irregular patterns; contrast with slow-moving vocal line, sustained chords

MELODY
Tuneful, simple melody

HARMONY
Slow-moving melody

TEXTURE
Open sound: low bass, bass drum, mid-range timekeeping on cymbal, guitar upper mid-range, vocal in center

Remember . . .

POSITIVE MESSAGE
Lyrics that send a message of hope: for a world that is not divided by class, wealth, race, or any other arbitrary criterion

IRISH BARD
Simple, folklike melody; Bono's singing: Irish tenor with blues-like grittiness

U2 SOUND
Characteristic 1980s U2 sound: slow-moving, tuneful vocal melody, steady rock-speed bass line; sixteen-beat rhythm on drums; complex patterns at sixteen-beat speed in guitar; sustained synth harmonies in background

SIGNIFICANCE AND SYNCOPATION
Persistent rhythms at several speeds, with very little syncopation (except in melodic pattern of guitar part) plus spacious texture send message that this is important music.

Listen to this selection in CourseMate.

Significant-Sounding Rock

For many, Bruce Springsteen and U2 were the only two truly important acts of the eighties. Both confronted difficult problems in which they had a deep personal involvement: the Vietnam War, the conflict in Northern Ireland, and the suffering in Africa. And both wore their hearts on their sleeves—they would rather be too passionate than too reserved.

In the two examples discussed above, the power of their music comes from applying two principles: simplifying and highlighting basic rhythms and creating a full, yet open sound. By emphasizing regular timekeeping over syncopation, and maintaining the same basic texture with only subtle variation through long stretches of time, the instrumental settings convey both simplicity and seriousness. Their function is to enhance the power and presence of the lyric.

The rhythmic approach used by both Springsteen and U2, although realized in strikingly different ways, has the same effect: It cuts the cord with good-time rock. As we have noted in earlier chapters, the rock groove that makes people want to get up and dance grows out of the interplay between regular rhythms and rhythms that conflict with it or transcend it. Both of the songs discussed in this section minimize or all but eliminate this interplay. In "Born in the U.S.A.," it is confined almost exclusively to the dominant riff and the backbeat; in "Where the Streets Have No Name," it occurs only in the irregular *patterns* of The Edge's active accompaniment, not in the rhythm itself, which is regular. It is as if both Springsteen and U2 are saying that they want listeners to hear the message in the lyrics. Listeners can draw power from the music, but they should not be distracted by rhythms that are too playful for the lyric. In post-punk rock, a serious message virtually demands music with minimal syncopation.

CHAPTER 83
Renewing Rock and Roll

Among the most important acts to debut in 1988 was a group known as the Traveling Wilburys. The group presented themselves as half-brothers who were all sons of the late Charles T. Wilbury Sr.: Lucky, Otis, Charles T. Jr., Nelson, and Lefty. In fact, the Traveling Wilburys were one of the great supergroups of any era. On their first album, released in the fall of that year, the Wilburys included Bob Dylan, Jeff Lynne, Tom Petty, George Harrison, and Roy Orbison. This recording was the only one to include all of the original members; Orbison passed away later that year.

Lynne (b. 1947) was the catalyst for the formation of the group. After leading the Electric Light Orchestra throughout the seventies and into the eighties, Lynne dissolved the band in 1986 to move into solo work and production. While at lunch, Harrison and Lynne called Bob Dylan to ask whether they could use his home studio to record a song. Orbison was in town and agreed to sing on the track. Petty (b. 1950) and Dylan joined in. The good times led to an album assembled over a ten-day period.

There is symbolic significance to the coming together of Dylan, Orbison, and Harrison just before Orbison's death. The path from Anglo-American folk music to rock forked with the birth of country music in the twenties and split even farther apart with the reclamation of the folk heritage and the emergence of contemporary folk music in the thirties. Until the sixties, they evolved along largely separate paths. Rock-and-roll acts found little common ground with folk counterparts other than their shared heritage and a mostly young audience; Buddy Holly and The Kingston Trio were in different worlds musically. Their intersection with—and through—rock began in the early sixties, in large part because of the work of Orbison and Dylan. By the late eighties, the schism was ancient history; the formation of the Wilburys celebrated that fact.

Neo-Traditional Trends of the Eighties

The Wilburys' collaboration was one branch of a neo-traditional movement within rock during the eighties and nineties. The Rolling Stones breathed life into their career in the early eighties, while boogie bands such as ZZ Top kept trucking along. Also, many newer rock acts—such as John Mellencamp, Tom Petty and the Heartbreakers, and Dire Straits—carved out a niche in the rock marketplace.

Flashing back to an even more distant past was a jump-band revival led by the Stray Cats; it would gain momentum in the nineties in the music of groups such as the Brian Setzer Orchestra. Fresh voices breathed new life into two of rock's most influential antecedents: the blues and the socially conscious song. The blues revival that began in the mid-eighties gave a boost to the careers of established bluesmen and introduced new stars, such as Stevie Ray Vaughan and Robert Cray. Later in the decade, a new generation of socially aware female singer–songwriters, among them Tracy Chapman and Suzanne Vega, would evoke the spirit of early Bob Dylan.

John Mellencamp

Perhaps the most down-to-earth of the newer rock acts was John Mellencamp—literally: "Rain On The Scarecrow" (1986), one of his most powerful songs, presents the plight of the small-time farmer through a tale about a family that's losing their farm. So it's not surprising that Mellencamp was one of the main forces behind the Farm Aid benefits.

Mellencamp, known as John Cougar at the beginning of his career ("Cougar" was his first manager's invention; Mellencamp learned about it only after seeing the name on the cover of his debut album), began his career in the mid-seventies, but it didn't take off until the early 1980s. His breakthrough album was *American Fool* (1982), which included the No. 1 single "Jack & Diane." It was the first of five Mellencamp albums released in the 1980s to reach the Top 10 on the album charts and go platinum. Mellencamp's "Paper in Fire," a hit single from the 1987 album *The Lonesome Jubilee,* shows his connection with, and expansion of, the American rock-and-roll tradition exemplified by Creedence Clearwater Revival, the Grateful Dead, and the Band. Mellencamp encases an excellent story, which unfolds slowly and suspensefully, in a well-grooved rock-and-roll setting. The lyric tells a cautionary tale about the fate of those who get but don't give. Mellencamp sets up the chorus beautifully by presenting the verse with a subdued, static accompaniment, then exploding with siren-like syncopated chords at the chorus.

Through the instrumentation of the song, Mellencamp deepens the country/blues fusion that typified the "American" sound, ca. 1970 by drawing on both sound worlds. Among the backup instruments are a banjo (bluegrass), slide guitar (deep blues), fiddle (country), and accordion (zydeco); the tambourine shaking out a

LISTENING CUE • **"Paper in Fire" (1987),** John Mellencamp. Mellencamp, vocal.

STYLE Neo-traditional 1980s rock • **FORM** Verse/chorus

Listen For . . .

INSTRUMENTATION
Lead and backup vocal, lead guitar, slide guitar, violin, harmonica, accordion, electric bass, banjo, drums, tambourine

PERFORMANCE STYLE
Mellencamp's husky voice ideal for storytelling

RHYTHM
Rock rhythm at fast tempo, with double-time rhythm in tambourine and abundant syncopation, especially "fire siren" riff

MELODY
Abundance of riffs in verse and chorus

TEXTURE
Sharp contrast between verse and chorus, mainly because of subtraction/addition of instruments

Remember . . .

COMPELLING STORY
Three vignettes relate in different ways how those who take without giving get burned.

SOUND PAINTING
Musical setting amplifies impact of lyric: verse = suppressed energy; chorus explodes, with siren-like sounds.

AMERICAN SOUND
Mellencamp's down-home vocal style, solid rock rhythm, bluegrass and blues instruments (banjo, slide guitar, fiddle, and so on) all project an "American" rock sound, ca. mid-1980s.

Listen to this selection in CourseMate.

double-time rhythm throughout the song was a staple in the minstrel show and in numerous rock bands of the 1960s.

"Paper in Fire" is an especially successful continuation of the storytelling tradition within rock that dates back to Bob Dylan. Like Dylan, Mellencamp uses the musical setting to amplify the sense of the text; the music behind the words and melody are integral to the impact of the song. It demonstrates that fresh approaches to the by-now-timeless rock style produce memorable music.

UNIT 18

LOOKING BACK, LOOKING AHEAD

Rock, Pop, and R&B in the 1980s

IN THE EIGHTIES, pop, rhythm and blues, and rock reinvented themselves. Of the eight tracks presented in this unit, only one—Mellencamp's "Paper in Fire"—could reasonably have been created before 1980. The others belong to the 1980s, mainly because of the increased prominence of synthesized sounds and new punk/funk/disco/reggae-influenced rhythms. Also evident in several of these tracks is a return to relevance; the songs by Madonna, Prince, Turner, Springsteen, U2, and Mellencamp have meaningful messages, although they convey them in markedly different ways.

Among the most outstanding developments of the decade was the modernizing of pop and its emergence as a new middle ground in popular music. Pop stars, and particularly Michael Jackson and Madonna, led the way in reconceptualizing the music video as an integrated expressive form rather than a visual accompaniment to the song.

With the introduction of the CD, music-related cable TV channels, and the overwhelming popularity of music videos, the music industry continued to expand during the 1980s. The top pop, rock, and rhythm-and-blues acts achieved unprecedented commercial success. However, even as more middle-ground acts co-opted the cutting-edge music of the 1970s, alternative sounds emerged in towns and cities like Athens, Georgia, and Aberdeen, Washington.

Alternatives

UNIT 19

UNIT 19

Aberdeen, Washington, a town of about 16,000 people, is situated at the eastern end of Grays Harbor, an inlet along the Pacific Coast in the west-central part of the state. The town bills itself as the gateway to the Olympic Peninsula, a beautiful temperate rainforest. However, timber, not tourism, is the main industry. It is not a wealthy town. Unemployment runs high, especially among younger residents.

The dominant colors in Aberdeen are green and gray. As in other towns along the coast in northern California and the Pacific Northwest, the climate is relatively mild—not too cold in the winter and not too warm in the summer. Trees and other plants thrive there. However, it rains frequently—about 85 inches a year—and fog and overcast skies are far more common than sunshine, especially in winter.

Though it's hard to establish a causal connection between artists and the environment in which they were raised, one can't help wondering whether Kurt Cobain's music would have taken a radically different form had he been born in Miami, Florida, which is about as far southeast as Aberdeen is northwest. As it happened, grunge, the alternative music that Cobain and Nirvana helped bring to a mass audience, seems to reflect the depressed circumstances and depressing weather that one encounters in Aberdeen.

Grunge brought alternative music into the mainstream and made Seattle a rock hotspot during the nineties. However, by the time Nirvana crossed over in 1992, the alternative movement was a decade old and rapidly diversifying from its punk base.

Alternative first surfaced as an umbrella term for a large family of rock-related, punk-inspired styles that began to develop in the early eighties. Bands and their fans saw themselves as a musical alternative to 1980s pop and MTV-oriented rock. By the end of the 1980s, "alternative" was defined as much by what it wasn't as by what it was. The striking musical differences among the musical examples discussed in this unit highlight the broad range of musical alternatives to the middle ground of the 1980s and 1990s.

CHAPTER 84

From Punk to Alternative

The elevator-trip version of alternative rock: In the sixties, rock mattered; in the seventies, it sold out—except for punk; in the eighties, alternative bands mattered; in the nineties, they sold out. Such a simple paradigm necessarily distorts the reality of the situation. Integrity is not incompatible with popular success, as the Beatles and many other acts have demonstrated. Nor is all pop necessarily bad. But there's no question that the bottom-line mentality of the major players in the music business has made mainstream pop more calculating and less daring. In this respect, the paradigm rings true.

What the paradigm does describe, with greater accuracy, is the us-versus-them attitude of those who inhabited the world of alternative rock. As the movement took shape, musicians and audiences believed passionately that their music mattered. For them, rock was a way of life, as it had been in the sixties. Like the punk and new wave music from which it developed, early alternative flourished in a largely closed ecosystem. Control was the key. Alternative bands sought the artistic freedom to make the music they wanted to make, uncorrupted by a corporate mind-set.

The Alternative Movement

Alternative was a grassroots movement to restore integrity and importance to rock. Bands toured relentlessly, going from one small club to the next. (The Bird, Seattle's first punk rock club, had an official capacity of ninety-nine people, although twice that many routinely crowded into the club.) They recorded low-budget albums on their own or on independent labels and sold many of them at performances. Some got airplay on college radio stations; during the eighties, commercial stations seldom programmed songs by alternative bands. Many developed loyal, even fanatic, followings; some fans published or wrote for fanzines. Occasionally, bands attracted attention from outside critics and fans: *Rolling Stone* selected *Murmur,* R.E.M.'s first album, as the best album of 1983.

Because it started out on such a small scale, the world of alternative music was far more personal. Fans, writers, and others who supported the music felt a sense of ownership. Usually, they had gone the extra mile or two to seek out bands to follow. They bought their recordings. Perhaps they had gotten to know members of the band, done some of the grunt work, or written for a fanzine. The sense of connection went beyond the music; as the Minutemen, one of the pioneer alternative bands, sang, "Our band could be your life." So when a band caught on—signed with a major label; played on big, well-organized tours; made videos; appeared on MTV—fans felt betrayed, or at least marginalized.

Success was also a concern for the musicians. The experience of becoming a rock star helped drive Kurt Cobain to suicide. His suicide note alludes to this.

> I feel guilty beyond words about these things, for example when we're backstage and the lights go out and the manic roar of the crowd begins. It doesn't affect me in the way which it did for Freddie Mercury, who seemed to love and relish the love and admiration from the crowd, which is something I totally admire and envy. The fact is, I can't fool you, any of you. It simply isn't fair to you, or to me. The worst crime I can think of would be to pull people off by faking it, pretending as if I'm having one hundred percent fun. Sometimes I feel as though I should have a punch-in time clock before I walk out on-stage. I've tried everything within my power to appreciate it, and I do, God believe me, I do, but it's not enough. —Kurt Cobain

It is painful to read how fame caused Cobain to lose the thing that he valued the most. In 1994, he cancelled Nirvana's appearance at Lollapalooza, the Woodstock-like touring festival that helped catapult alternative into the mainstream, then took his life.

It's ironic that "rock that mattered" became an alternative to mainstream music, rather than the heart of it, in less than two decades. Even though many of the sixties artists whose music mattered the most—artists such as Bob Dylan, Frank Zappa, the Velvet Underground—were never mainstays on the singles charts, there was a sense of common purpose between them and acts such as the Beatles and the Rolling Stones that did have a real pop presence. Moreover, they had the support of those behind the scenes, from major labels eager to book the next important act to free-form radio and festivals like Woodstock.

That wasn't the case in the eighties. For the most part, the mainstream had evolved away from this change-the-world attitude. Acts like Springsteen and U2—acts that said something important to a lot of people—were the exception, not the rule. Most of the other integrity-first bands were simply an alternative to the mainstream.

Alternative: A Neo-Traditional Trend

Alternative began as a neo-traditional movement: Recapturing the sense of importance that characterized rock in the sixties and punk and new wave music in the seventies was its primary goal. However, the message was different. Alienation replaced the heady optimism of the sixties as the dominant theme. Musically, alternative derived most directly from punk and new wave. Tempos were fast, rhythms were busy, sound levels were generally loud—and sounded louder because of the small spaces in which they played. The point of departure was the garage band. The core instrumentation was typically vocals, a guitar or two, bass, and drums, although bands often went beyond this basic lineup.

As the movement gained momentum in the latter part of the eighties, it diversified by infusing elements of other rock-era substyles—such as funk, metal, and electronica—into its punk core or by imparting a more modern sensibility to genres that had come and gone, such as ska and the music of the early seventies singer-songwriters. Common ground became more a matter of attitude and commercial presence (or lack of it—bands flew under the radar of big music) than musical similarity. The first **Lollapalooza** tour (1991)—an important outlet for alternative music in the nineties—featured such diverse acts as Jane's Addiction (the festival was band member Perry Ferrell's idea), Nine Inch Nails, and Ice-T and Body Count. None of these is a "pure" post-punk band.

With the sudden and surprising success of grunge in the early nineties, alternative music wrestled with the tension between high-mindedness and commercial success. In the early twenty-first century, alternative is as much a music industry label as it is a statement of purpose.

From Punk to Alternative

The boundary between punk and new wave on the one hand and alternative on the other seems more geographic than temporal or musical. The formation of the first alternative bands occurred around 1980, when the careers of bands like the Clash, Elvis Costello and the Attractions, and Talking Heads were at a high point. Their music represents a stylistic continuation of punk and new wave; there is no radical difference between the two at the beginning.

However, alternative took root in college towns throughout the United States rather than in major metropolitan areas. The size of the town wasn't as important as the size of the university; it was the student body that provided the most enthusiastic support for these bands. Active regional scenes, in the United States and ultimately throughout the world, would become a hallmark of alternative music.

Early Alternative Rock

The two bands most responsible for starting the alternative music movement were Hüsker Dü, based in St. Paul, Minneapolis (home of the University of Minnesota), and R.E.M., formed in Athens, Georgia (home of the University of Georgia). Both locales were well outside the New York–London axis where punk and new wave flourished. Hüsker Dü (the group took their name from a Swedish board game whose name means "Do you remember?") began as a hardcore punk band trying to out-Ramone the Ramones. Their music occasionally ventured beyond this frenetically paced music toward a more moderate and melodic style.

R.E.M. (*l–r*, Mike Mills, Peter Buck, Michael Stipe, Bill Berry), 1986

Although admired as an important influence on the new alternative movement, Hüsker Dü never crossed over to a more mainstream audience. That wasn't the case with R.E.M. R.E.M. was formed in 1980 by guitarist Peter Buck (b. 1956) and vocalist Michael Stipe (b. 1960). Buck and Stipe recruited bassist Mike Mills (b. 1958) and drummer Bill Berry (b. 1958), agreed on a name (REM is the acronym for "rapid eye movement," a defining characteristic of the lightest stage of sleep), then performed relentlessly. They quickly became favorites of the local underground rock scene, playing college bars and parties while waiting for their big break, which came quickly.

"Radio Free Europe," their first hit, helped put the band on the rock music map and establish the essentially retrospective orientation of alternative music. It has the bright tempo, clean rhythm, and lean sound associated with David Bowie and new wave bands. The texture is spare in the verse; by contrast, the chorus features a much richer texture because of the jangly, reverberant guitar figuration and the active bass line underneath Stipe's vocals.

Characteristically for R.E.M., the lyric is as elliptical as the music is clear. The words are intelligible, but what do they mean? By their own admission, the band has deliberately written nonspecific lyrics. As Michael Stipe said in a late-eighties interview, "I've always left myself pretty open to interpretation."

The sharp and sudden contrasts between verse and chorus provide a foretaste of what would become a defining feature of alternative music: dramatic, often jarring contrasts within songs. And Buck's flashback to a guitar sound directly descended from the Byrds' Roger McGuinn provides an early instance of the infusion of alternative's punk base with elements from other retro styles.

LISTENING CUE • **"Radio Free Europe" (1981),** Bill Berry, Peter Buck, Mike Mills, Michael Stipe. R.E.M.

STYLE Early alternative • **FORM** Verse/chorus

Listen For . . .

INSTRUMENTATION
"Radio" noises: vocals, guitars, bass, drums

PERFORMANCE STYLE
Nice contrast between detached guitar sound in verse, more resonant and sustained sound in chorus

RHYTHM
Punk-influenced fast, basic rock beat, with strong backbeat, repeated notes in bass/guitar in verse; chorus adds sustained vocal sound.

MELODY
Verse = short, separated statement on repeated melodic phrase; chorus = string of long notes in different key

TEXTURE
Shift in texture underscores verse/chorus contrast: spare sound in verse; richer sound, with moving bass line, guitar figuration in chorus

Remember . . .

WHAT IS THE SONG ABOUT?
Nonnarrative lyrics whose meaning is at best abstruse

POST-PUNK ROCK
Clean, prominent rock rhythm in drums and bass at fast tempo, but active bass line; harmonies in different key departure from conventional punk approach: less aggressive, subtler

SHARP CONTRASTS
Open sound of the verse and warmer, guitar-enriched texture of the chorus, with more melodic bass line

Listen to this selection in CourseMate.

By the late eighties, R.E.M. had begun to bring alternative into the mainstream: "The One I Love" (1987) was their first Top 10 single. They would remain a popular band through the nineties, although Berry retired from performing in 1997.

In their determination to follow their own creative path, even if it circled back to the past instead of moving toward the future, the group set the tone for the alternative movement. And the simplicity of their sound—basic instrumentation, clear textures, little if any electronic wizardry—was a model for the alternative bands that followed. Among them was Sonic Youth.

The Persistence of Punk

Even as reverberations from the punk movement touched much of the new music of the eighties, "pure" punk—that is, the music that was most in tune with the attitude and sound of late seventies punk—went underground. With its breakneck tempos, screamed-out vocals, loud and crude riffs, and confrontational, politically charged lyrics, hardcore punk (or simply hardcore) was the most direct continuation of the punk esthetic established by the Sex Pistols.

The movement known as post-punk identifies a family of styles that merged the aggressive elements of punk with more experimental elements and outside influences, such as synthesizers. Joy Division, which dissolved in 1980 after the suicide of lead singer Ian Curtis, is generally regarded as a seminal post-punk band. The early industrial group Throbbing Gristle is often associated with post-punk. Other noteworthy bands include Public Image, Ltd. (fronted by John Lydon), Sisters of Mercy, and Sonic Youth.

From the start, the fundamental creative tension in punk has been power versus expressive range. The challenge for bands was to broaden the range without dampening the impact. In the seventies, this tension was manifested in the different paths of punk and new wave music. In the eighties, it was evident in the numerous punk offshoots, most notably in the numerous post-punk substyles, such as **no wave.** The most successful no wave band, critically and commercially, is Sonic Youth.

Sonic Youth

Sonic Youth is a four-person band formed in 1981. During the peak of its career in the latter part of the eighties and early nineties, the band members were guitarists Thurston Moore (b. 1958) and Lee Ranaldo (b. 1956), bassist-guitarist Kim Gordon (b. 1953), and drummer Steve Shelley (b. 1963).

Like other no wave bands, Sonic Youth brought a rock-as-art sensibility to their work. Using the basic instrumentation, fast tempos, and clear timekeeping as a point of departure for their style, they overlaid it with unusual guitar sounds, noise, exotic harmonies, and sharp contrasts in texture. This sound world supported lyrics that put a fresh spin on familiar themes, sung/shouted accessibly to a simple melody. We hear these qualities in "Hey Joni," a track from their critically acclaimed double album *Daydream Nation* (1988).

"Hey Joni" begins with low synthesizer drone that is gradually surrounded by extraneous noises. This abruptly gives way to the refrain of the song, in which both the connection and the distance from punk are evident. Drummer Shelley raps out a fast, straightforward rock rhythm—the kind that one expects to hear in a typical punk song. However, both guitarists alternate between conventional power chords and more dissonant and intricate figuration. An alternative effect comes to the forefront during the interlude between refrain and verse. Syncopated riffs in one guitar part compete with high-register figuration that use the more delicate sound of **harmonics** (musicians create the sound of harmonics on a stringed instrument by depressing the string only partway at certain points; this creates higher-pitched sounds with a distinctive ring). Other similar effects, such as the "Wipeout"-inspired glissando, follow in the verse and subsequent instrumental interludes. The changes in texture, which are concentrated in the middle registers, create a kaleidoscopic effect.

For Sonic Youth, sonic variety is key. Although they start from a basic rock-band instrumentation, they create magical sounds with the interplay of often discordant riffs and figuration and by employing special effects, such as the harmonics used here. The song melds the energy of punk with the glorious guitar sounds and noises for which the group is known.

Although *Daydream Nation* remains their most respected and best-known album, Sonic Youth has continued to evolve and explore new directions. Their tour with then barely known Nirvana was captured on the DVD *1991: The Year Punk Broke*. Their work, and especially the innovative guitar sounds and noises, have influenced more recent alternative bands.

LISTENING CUE • "Hey Joni" (1988), Gordon, Moore, Ranaldo, Shelley. Sonic Youth.

STYLE No wave • **FORM** Verse/chorus based–lyrics repeat, but no real melody; spoken sections and extended instrumental interludes

Listen For . . .

INSTRUMENTATION
Vocals, synthesizer, guitars, bass, drums

PERFORMANCE STYLE
Monotone singing/speaking; array of magical guitar sounds, e.g., harmonics

RHYTHM
Fast tempo with punk-like rock beat is the norm, but with considerable variation in instrumental interludes, such as double-time drums, and less marking of the rock beat.

MELODY
No melody to speak of in the vocal line: mainly sung on one note or spoken. Guitar figuration melodically interesting

TEXTURE
Dramatic contrasts between loud, punk-like textures in vocals vs. more delicate and rhythmically subtle texture in instrumental interludes.

Remember . . .

PUNK INFLUENCE
Punk tempo and rhythm, marked clearly by the drummer in vocal sections

UNUSUAL TEXTURES
Dense in the middle range because of multiple riffs and figuration, often with little or no bass; strong contrasts between vocal and instrumental sounds

AN ARRAY OF GUITAR EFFECTS
From conventional distortion to harmonics and the "noise halos" that surround guitar pitches

MELODY VS. HARMONY
Single-pitch "melody" supported by jarring, often discordant harmonies, often layered on top of each other

Listen to this selection in CourseMate.

CHAPTER 85
Other Alternatives: Heavy Metal and Alternative Fusions in the 1980s

The rock critic Lester Bangs is often credited with naming heavy metal and was one of the few important rock critics to initially support the genre. However, toward the end of the 1970s, he did an about face, writing:

> As its detractors have always claimed, heavy-metal rock is nothing more than a bunch of noise; it is not music, it's distortion—and that is precisely why its adherents find it appealing. Of all contemporary rock, it is the genre most closely identified with violence and aggression, rapine and carnage. Heavy metal orchestrates technological nihilism.

Bangs's opinion was in step with prevailing view. Most critics, commentators, and the media denounced it, dismissed it, or ignored it altogether. However, metal didn't go away; it simply went on the road. Despite this neglect and scorn—mainstream exposure on radio and MTV was minimal during the early 1980s—heavy metal developed a loyal and steadily increasing fan base through the late seventies and eighties through frequent touring. Fans packed venues to hear their favorite bands, bought their recordings, and kept up to date through fanzines.

In the sense that it stayed below critics' radar (except when metal bands became more pop oriented), attracted a fervent following that grew during the 1980s, and offered a sound and look that was decidedly different from MTV fare, heavy metal was as alternative as alternative. And even as heavy metal grew in popularity, other alternative styles emerged, such as the rock/rap/funk/metal fusion of the Red Hot Chili Peppers.

The Revival of Heavy Metal

In the 1980s, heavy metal gained momentum through an influx of new bands—Megadeth, AC/DC, Motörhead, Judas Priest, Slayer, Iron Maiden, Twisted Sister, Scorpions, and Metallica—and a new generation that responded to their music. Young males made up most of the heavy metal fan base in the eighties. In the wake of the economic hard times in both Great Britain and the United States, many faced a bleak future. They felt out of the loop, especially during the eighties, when the gap between rich and poor widened so dramatically. They responded to the recurrent themes in heavy metal: the occult, sexual dominance (often to the point of misogyny), rage, frustration, protest, and—above all—power.

And it was the music above all that conveyed the power. Most characteristically, heavy metal was loud to the point where a listener *felt* it as much as heard it. The sound was heavily distorted, a sign both of power (distortion originally came from overdriving amplifiers) and defiance (distortion was originally an undesirable byproduct of amplification, to be avoided if possible).

Performances were a communion between musicians and their audience. Bands preached to the converted. Fans knew the words to songs (from liner notes), even though they were often unintelligible in performance. Stage shows were typically spectacles on a grand scale, comparable to an elaborate pagan ritual. In response, metalheads engaged in **headbanging,** heavy metal's version of dancing. In the familiarity of the audience/congregation with the songs, their involvement in the performance, and the sense of power that they experienced during the event, a heavy metal concert was more like a religious rite than a conventional concert.

The Sounds of 1980s Heavy Metal

Heavy metal was never a monolithic style, but in the eighties it became even more diverse. Substyles, often based on a single feature, proliferated. By the end of the decade, there was speed metal, thrash metal, death metal, industrial metal, and more. Its diversity was also due to its blending with other styles; during the eighties, heavy metal came in several grades of purity. Distortion remained metal's sound signature, but "pure" heavy metal was far more than a rock song played with distortion.

As evidenced in the music of top eighties bands such as Metallica and Megadeth, a heavy metal song is a far cry from standard rock, rhythm and blues, or pop fare. Here are some of the most striking differences:

- *Distortion is typically more extreme than in conventional hard rock.* Metal bands compensated for nonmetal bands' use of distortion by increasing distortion to the point that it obscured pitches.
- *Instrumentation is basic:* Metal bands use core rock instrumentation. Synths, saxes, and other sounds are stylistic impurities.
- *It is not tuneful music.* Vocal lines tend to be more incantation than melody.
- *The ratio of instrumental sections to vocal sections is much higher than in most other rock-based styles.* In addition to extended solos, where lead guitarists show off their prowess, there are also long passages with no vocal lines. These typically consist of a series of intricate riffs.

- *It typically avoids conventional harmony.* Power chords rule, but complete harmonies and chord progressions are the exception rather than the rule.
- *The best metal bands are virtuosic.* In solo and group playing, metal bands create and perform intricate riffs, often at breathtakingly fast tempos, with a level of precision comparable to that of a fine string quartet or tight jazz combo.
- *Metal "songs" tend to be long, sprawling, multisectional works.* Blocks of sound, often in different tempos and with different key centers, all arranged in complex, unpredictable sequences, often replace the verse/chorus pattern of more conventional rock.

These features occur in heavy metal tracks undiluted with other stylistic elements. What passed for heavy metal in the eighties ranged from mainstream rock covered with a metal sheen (for example, Def Leppard's "Photograph") to the music of such conscientious bands as Metallica. We consider "One," a track from their 1988 album *And Justice for All.* The song was released as a single during the following year; it was also the song used for the band's first music video.

Metallica

Metallica began the eighties, toiling in relative obscurity. The group, formed in 1981 by guitarist-vocalist James Hetfield (b. 1963) and drummer Lars Ulrich (b. 1963), built an ardent cult following during the first part of eighties even as it burned through a string of guitarists, including Dave Mustaine (b. 1961), who would later form Megadeth. In 1983, Hetfield and Ulrich recruited Kirk Hammett (b. 1962); Hammett remains the lead guitarist with the group. Cliff Burton (1962–1986), the bassist for Metallica's first three albums, died in a freak accident during a 1986 Swedish tour. Jason Newsted (b. 1963) replaced him; he would remain with the group through 2001.

Metallica's record sales were brisk, although the band got almost no exposure on radio or television. The group eventually broke through on radio in 1988 with "One," a single from their fourth album (and first with Newsted), *And Justice for All,* which peaked at No. 6 on the charts. Even a cursory listening to "One" makes clear that the market came to Metallica, not the other way around. "One" is a grim antiwar statement that unfolds on a large scale: The work is well over seven minutes long. It makes few concessions to mainstream rock—in lyrics, music, or length. The form of the song takes its shape from the images in the lyrics; it is an especially graphic depiction of the horrors of war, as experienced by one of its many casualties.

In its sprawling form—from the gentle, almost flamenco-like opening to the abrupt ending; relatively little emphasis on vocal lines; musical sophistication (e.g., there are several shifts from four-beat to three-beat measures); and deep contrast from dark and moody beginning to powerful conclusion—"One" demands a lot

LISTENING CUE • "One" (1988), James Hetfeld and Lars Ulrich. Metallica.

STYLE 1980s heavy metal • **FORM** Multisectional

Listen For . . .

INSTRUMENTATION
War sounds; vocal, guitars, bass, drums

PERFORMANCE STYLE
Growling vocal, extreme distortion in guitars, bass in latter part of track

RHYTHM
Frequent shifts between four-beat and three-beat measures; rock rhythm implied throughout

MELODY
Multiple melodies in vocal sections: verse deliberately flat—several repeated notes—chorus short, simple

TEXTURE
Numerous textures ranging from guitar solo/duet to full band in low register: massive dark sound

Remember . . .

PROTEST SONG
Lyrics and music send grim, powerful antiwar message.

SPRAWLING FORM
"One" unfolds slowly with Spanish-flavored guitar intro, dramatic shifts in pacing, rhythm, texture, extended instrument sections: episodic form, with several "scenes."

UPDATED METAL SOUNDS
Intense distortion, tight ensemble (especially in the latter half of the song), fluent guitar solo

STRONG CONTRASTS
Shifts from section to section amplify "flashback" elements in lyrics.

Listen to this selection in CourseMate.

from its listeners. The music is as uncompromising and grim as its message.

"One" has more in common with a film soundtrack than a conventional rock song. Indeed, after recording the song, Metallica discovered the similarities between their song and *Johnny Get Your Gun,* a 1939 antiwar novel that author Dalton Trumbo later turned into a film. The music video of "One" juxtaposes scenes from Trumbo's film with footage of the band and adds dialogue from the film to the music. Curiously, many of Metallica's fans objected to the video, the band's first. Perhaps it was the fact of the video that troubled them, because the video, with its skillful mixing of band scenes with film footage, makes the antiwar message of the track even more compelling.

Metallica's "One" is significant rock. With its long, narrative-based form; dramatic shifts in mood; masterful playing; and vivid sound images, "One" exemplifies Metallica's principled approach to music making—there is nothing in the track that suggests any effort to accommodate more mainstream tastes.

Despite its growing popularity, no rock music of the eighties was less understood or less appreciated than heavy metal. However, even though critics and audiences may have scorned it early on, musicians didn't. Not only did it develop into one of the important directions of the late eighties and nineties, it also bled into the exciting new fusions of the alternative bands that began to surface at the end of the decade. It remains a significant part of the rock music scene.

Alternatives beyond Punk: Infusions of Funk, Rap, and Heavy Metal

Among the most eclectic and electric new sounds of the late eighties and early nineties alternative scene was the music created by bands such as Red Hot Chili Peppers, Primus, Jane's Addiction, Living Colour, and the Spin Doctors. Like the music of the pop middle ground, this alternative music thoroughly integrated black and white music. But all of it was almost militantly anti-pop.

The songs expressed wildly different attitudes, from rage to razor-sharp humor. However, they shared stylistic common ground, which comes mainly from two features. One was deep roots in soul and sixties hard rock. This connection is evident in the complex, active, syncopated rhythms and the reaffirmation of the basic rock-band instrumentation. The other was the infusion of elements from important non-pop styles of the late seventies and eighties, most commonly funk, heavy metal, and rap. From funk, they took complex, active sixteen-beat rhythms and strong bass lines. From heavy metal, they took extreme distortion and virtuosity. They occasionally overlaid these mixes with rap-inspired voice parts, more spoken than sung.

RED HOT CHILI PEPPERS performing in 2006

In 1985, none of these sources was new. Neither was the idea of forging new styles by mixing black and white sources, which is rock's most time-honored tradition. What gave the music a late eighties sound was its thorough integration of rock and soul, and punk and funk, and the currency of its sources. We hear this interplay in "Good Time Boys," a track from the Red Hot Chili Peppers' 1989 album *Mother's Milk.*

The Red Hot Chili Peppers

The Red Hot Chili Peppers (RHCP) was formed in 1983 by four alumni of Fairfax High School of West Hollywood, California. Two of the original four, bassist Michael "Flea" Balzary (b. 1962) and vocalist Anthony Kiedis (b. 1962), are still band members. Hillel Slovak (1962–1988), the original guitarist, died of a heroin overdose in 1988; his death prompted drummer Jack Irons (b. 1962) to leave the band. Drummer Chad Smith (b. 1961) and guitarist John Frusciante (b. 1970) replaced Irons and Slovak.

The Red Hot Chili Peppers received their training in funk from the highest authority. George Clinton produced their 1985 album *Freaky Styley,* which also featured Maceo Parker and Fred Wesley, both veterans of James Brown's band. Neither their self-titled debut album nor *Freaky Styley,* their second album, went anywhere commercially, but their next album, *The Uplift Mofo Party Plan* (1987), did. *Mother's Milk,* with new band members Smith and Frusciante, did even better. It would become the group's first platinum album, eventually selling over 2 million units.

In "Good Time Boys," a track from *Mother's Milk,* the Red Hot Chili Peppers blend the edge of punk with the strong bass lines of funk, the distorted guitar sounds and prominent and complex riffs of hard rock and heavy metal, and rap-like vocals. Among the most innovative

LISTENING CUE • **"Good Time Boys" (1989),** Flea, Frusciante, Kiedis, Smith. The Red Hot Chili Peppers.

STYLE 1980s rock/funk fusion • **FORM** Verse/chorus with solos and "radio dial" interlude

Listen For . . .

INSTRUMENTATION
Vocalists, guitar, bass, drums

PERFORMING STYLE
Funk-like "popped" bass sound, heavy distortion in guitar, rapped vocal sections

RHYTHM
Highly syncopated rhythms based on sixteen-beat rhythmic foundation, with active vocal, guitar, and bass lines

MELODY
Vocal lines in verse half-sung/half-rapped; chorus built from short rifffs; complex, extended instrumental riffs

HARMONY
Verse over one chord; chorus in a new key

Remember . . .

GOOD-TIME WORDS
Good-time lyrics, rapped in the verse, sung in the chorus

BEST OF TWO WORLDS
Both bass and guitar have prominent roles: fusion of R&B and rock instrumental roles.

DENSE SOUND
Thick texture because of active guitar and bass lines and low- or mid-register placement.

NEW ROCK RHYTHMS
Complex sixteen-beat rhythms over a rock beat in both vocal and instrumental sections

Listen to this selection in CourseMate.

features of the song is the presence of both a strong bass line and a prominent guitar part. In the music that we have heard, typically either guitar or bass is dominant—guitar in rock, bass in R&B. Here they are virtually equal partners. Flea's bass lines stand out beneath the rap-style verse; Frusciante's complex guitar riffs take over in the instrumental interludes. And with its chanted, pentatonic melodic line, sung in unison by the band and guest vocalist Randy Ruff and doubled on the bass, the chorus recalls Parliament-style funk. All this supports an upbeat, self-promoting lyric, much closer to rock and roll and early rap in style and spirit than it is to the anger of punk or the weirdness of new wave. A simulated spinning of the radio dial interrupts the song just after the midway point. The final radio clip ends with the phrase "She's a white girl . . ." sung to a vanilla accompaniment; the abrupt return to the funky groove underscores the strong black influence in this song.

The influence is especially evident in the rhythm. From the very opening riff to the end of the song, the rhythms are complex, active, and highly syncopated. Smith lays down a rock beat, but Frusciante's riffs, Flea's bass lines, and Kiedis's rap-style all move twice as fast.

"Good Time Boys" illustrates the punk/funk fusion of the latter part of the eighties and early nineties. The infusion of funk and rap elements helped introduce a different tone in alternative music and broaden its horizons. The success of the Red Hot Chili Peppers helped put alternative on the music industry's radar and blur the musical, commercial, ecological, and ideological boundaries that distinguished alternative from other genres.

The band's well-documented problems with drugs—Kiedis, Frusciante, and Flea were addicts—crippled the band during the nineties. Frusciante left the band in 1992 and was invited to return in 1998 after quitting drugs. At the turn of the century, they were the leading "modern rock" act in the music industry. Like other acts that have moved from the fringes of the industry to stardom, they have left the alternative world behind. And they were never at the center of it, as were R.E.M. and Nirvana during their early years. For the Red Hot Chili Peppers, "alternative" is increasingly just a label.

CHAPTER 86
Alienation

Generation X is a term popularized by Canadian novelist Douglas Coupland. It identifies the children of the baby boomers—those born mainly in the latter part of the sixties and the seventies. Most were born during the hangover from the sixties, with race riots, the squalid end to the Vietnam War, the rise of the "silent majority," the impeachment of Nixon, and rampant inflation all but obliterating the optimism with which the decade began. The members of Generation X, some of whom came from counterculture families, came of age during the "greed is good" eighties. Many, especially those stuck in service-industry "McJobs" (another term coined by Coupland), felt completely estranged from their baby-boomer parents and the world portrayed in the media. They saw little hope for advancement in their work; many felt that their odds of enjoying the lifestyle of the rich, if not the famous, were about as good as winning the lottery. They were more in tune with the "no future" mind-set broadcast by the disaffected youth in Great Britain and North America and the punk bands that set it to music. The "X" used to identify them underscored their lack of identity and power. As a result, they turned away from mainstream society and turned toward the music that expressed their anger, frustration, and alienation. Their theme song was Nirvana's 1991 hit "Smells Like Teen Spirit."

Grunge

The pivotal song in the history of alternative rock as a commercial music was Nirvana's "Smells Like Teen Spirit," from their 1991 album, *Nevermind*. For this recording, Nirvana consisted of singer-guitarist Kurt Cobain (1967–1994), bassist Chris Novoselic (b. 1965), and drummer Dave Grohl (b. 1969). Grohl replaced the drummers on Nirvana's first album, *Bleach* (1989), which the group made for just over $600. In the wake of its surprising success, Nirvana signed with Geffen Records. As a result, *Nevermind* was a far more elaborately produced album.

The album soared to No. 1, dethroning Michael Jackson's *Dangerous* album, which had been on top of the charts. "Smells Like Teen Spirit" got incessant airplay from MTV. All of a sudden the nineties had an anthem: It is still among the best-known songs of the decade. Alternative had crossed over.

Nirvana's particular brand of alternative came to be called **grunge,** though those involved in the scene hated the term. Grunge fused punk disaffection with the power and distortion of heavy metal. Like so many other alternative styles, it started on the fringes—literally: Aberdeen, Washington, is on the fringe of North America. The group's first single appeared on one of the many indie labels, the appropriately named Sub Pop, which was based in Seattle. Nirvana's sudden success made Seattle the mecca for grunge, but the sound had already surfaced in several locations around the United States.

In retrospect, it is easy to understand the enormous appeal of "Smells Like Teen Spirit," especially to its target

LISTENING CUE · "Smells Like Teen Spirit" (1991), Kurt Cobain. Nirvana.

STYLE Grunge · **FORM** Verse/chorus

Listen For . . .

INSTRUMENTATION
Vocal(s), guitar, bass, drums

PERFORMANCE STYLE
Screamed vocals, extreme distortion in loud section; modified vocal sound in "hello/how low"

RHYTHM
Active rock rhythm at moderate tempo

HARMONY
Distinctive progression cycles throughout song

TEXTURE
Dramatic contrasts between three sections: first section = empty sound, "hello" = reverberant guitar sound, third section = loud, with thick sound: vocal/ distorted guitar/drums/bass

Remember . . .

STRONG CONTRASTS
Three distinct sound worlds through most of song: empty verse, ringing bridge, screamed chorus

HARMONIC GLUE
Unresolved progression cycles throughout song, links contrasting sections.

SCHIZOPHRENIC SONG
Chord progression like depressed state impossible to shake; contrasting textures, sounds, dynamic levels suggest shift in mood.

Listen to this selection in CourseMate.

audience: angry young people who were not ready to buy into the system. The lyrics jerk from image to idea, like a trigger-happy video editor. Their power comes not from their coherence, but from the jarring juxtapositions—mulatto, albino, mosquito, libido; hello, how low.

The music amplifies this sense of dislocation. The song begins with a distinctive four-chord pattern. It is barely amplified; it sounds almost as if Cobain is trying it out for a song he's writing. Suddenly, we hear the same riff, this time with the whole band in heavy metal mode. Just as suddenly, the middle falls out—we are left with just bass, simple drum timekeeping, and a haunting two-note riff, which serves as an introduction to the verse; it continues underneath Cobain's singing. The two-note riff speeds up under the "hello/how low." The two-note vocal riff that sets "hello" then becomes the raw melodic material for the climactic section of the refrain. Here Cobain sings as if his throat is being ripped out. A short instrumental interlude, which interrupts the four-chord progression, bridges the chorus and the verse that follows. We hear this same sequence of events, then a loud instrumental version of the verse and "hello" section. Instead of the refrain, however, the song shifts to a third verse; we hear the entire verse/bridge/chorus sequence again, followed by primal screams on the word "denial."

"Smells Like Teen Spirit" is a dark song. Everything about it conveys that message; its enormous impact comes in part from the reinforcement of this mood on so many levels. The chord progression does not follow a well-established path; because of this we respond more to its rise and fall. It is like a hole that one cannot climb out of: every time the band arrives at the fourth and highest chord, they drop back down. Because the bass line/outline runs through almost all of the song, despite all of the contrasts, it seems to suggest a depressed state of mind that's impossible to shake. In this context, the instrumental break following the refrain sounds absolutely demonic; it is purposefully ugly, even mocking.

The big innovation—and perhaps the biggest stroke of genius—is the schizophrenic shift from section to section. Nirvana creates sharply defined sound worlds within each section of the song. They are haunting, mocking, and angry in turn. They create sharp contrasts from section to section—the kind one would more likely encounter between one song and the next, rather than within a song. When combined with the relentless chord progression and the repetition of the two two-note melodic fragments, they project a mood of utter despair. One can rage against the wind—or the machine—or fall into an almost apathetic state, but it is impossible to shake off the dark mood.

"Smells Like Teen Spirit" is a remarkable synthesis of several different, almost contradictory, elements. The melodic material—especially the several instrumental hooks, the "hello" section, and the vocal chorus—embed themselves in the listener's ear, offering immediate points of entry. At the same time, they don't sound like music calculated to be appealing. Rather, they seem to be a direct expression of the mood of the song; that they are catchy at the same time is a bonus.

KURT COBAIN OF NIRVANA, 1993

The sharp contrasts and abrupt shifts from section to section help "Smells Like Teen Spirit" portray the darkest depression: an oppressive weight that cannot be thrown off. And it makes Cobain's subsequent suicide even harder to take; it is as if he let us into his mind so that we can feel his despair.

"Smells Like Teen Spirit" is a punk song in spirit, expressing rage, alienation, and frustration in both words and music. But the eclectic mix of styles—power trio intro, understated verse, metal breaks—serves an expressive purpose here. It extends the emotional range of punk, if only because the quiet of the verse makes the louder sections, especially the chorus with its short vocal riffs, more powerful by contrast. Classic punk drove in only one gear; here, Nirvana shifts back and forth among several.

Radiohead: The New Art Rock of the Nineties

The members of Radiohead all went to the same high school, Abingdon School, a private institution outside of Oxford. Drummer Phil Selway (b. 1967), guitarist Ed O'Brien (b. 1968), guitarist-vocalist Tom Yorke

(b. 1968), bassist Colin Greenwood (b. 1969), and multi-instrumentalist Jonny Greenwood (b. 1971)—Colin's younger brother—formed the band On A Friday in 1986. They went to different universities but continued to practice together over vacations during their college years and came together again as Radiohead in 1992 (their name comes from a 1986 Talking Heads song, "Radio Head."). Their first album made it quite clear that the group would find their own direction. The album name *Pablo Honey* came from a bit by the Jerky Boys, a comedy group whose CDs consist of irritatingly funny phone calls. "Creep," the single that got them noticed, is very much in the spirit of the times: It is Buddy Holly, deeply depressed. Musically, however, it does little to predict the group's future.

The alienation that marked Radiohead's early work becomes even more apparent in subsequent albums. This is sometimes evident before the first sound: The booklet that comes with *OK Computer* (1997) contains the lyrics displayed almost randomly amid collage-like images. Both words and images are hard to decode. *Kid A* (2000) is even more frugal with content. There are simply fragments of images and no lyrics. It is as if the group were challenging its audience: We have something of value to say to you, but you have to work hard to discover what it is. This attitude extends to their songs, as we hear in "Paranoid Android," from *OK Computer*.

"Paranoid Android" was a boundary-stretching single. This is apparent on even the first hearing, because the song is almost 6½ minutes long, more than double the length of a typical single. The lyrics are at once unremittingly depressing and incoherent. We have the impression of someone (human or android) holding his head and screaming, "I can't stand this any more!" as he goes mad.

The song is profoundly disturbing, not because the music is as dark as the lyrics, but because it is often so beautiful. It begins with a pan-Latin sound: intricate guitar figuration outlining exotic harmony, plus the shaker associated with Brazilian music and the claves of Cuban music, then a higher-pitched classical guitarlike line. There is no bass yet; the music floats. Yorke delivers the lyric slowly and in measured fashion, which directs our attention more to the haunting, plaintive quality of his voice. The refrain of this part has only two syllables: "what's then." Because these are only two words, our attention goes even more to the sound of his voice. A beautiful halo of sound surrounds it, as bass and a high synthesizer part enrich the texture. All this seems to resonate with the melancholy that is so much a part of Latin culture. Radiohead seems to have captured its essence in this part of the song, although they apply it to a quite different end.

A long transition to a new section begins with a guitar riff set against the Latin percussion. The riff appears on

LISTENING CUE • **"Paranoid Android" (1997),** Ed O'Brien, Jonny Greenwood, Colin Greenwood, Phil Selway, and Thom Yorke. Radiohead.

STYLE 1990s prog rock • **FORM** Multisectional

Listen For . . .

INSTRUMENTATION
Vocal, Latin percussion, synthesizer, acoustic and electric guitars, bass, drums, keyboard

PERFORMANCE STYLE
Yorke's plaintive singing; sharp contrasts in instrumental timbre, from delicate acoustic guitar to heavily distorted sounds

RHYTHM
Latin-like rhythm in first part/rock rhythm in second section; occasional three-beat measures create imbalance; slow rock rhythm with sustained harmonies in third section

MELODY
Tuneful fragments in opening section

TEXTURE
Jarring contrasts in texture, but all are rich, with several melodically interesting layers; extended sections without vocal

Remember . . .

WORDS OF ALIENATION
Dark lyric, rich in obscure allusions, and as violently contrasting as the music

MUSIC OF ALIENATION
The contrast between sections shocks because the sections are so completely different in musical features such as instrumentation, rhythm and tempo, dynamics, and melodic style, and in the moods that they project. The opposition seems to be beauty vs. ugliness; the unifying element is the terrible sadness that runs through the entire track.

INTRASONG CONTRASTS: AN AESTHETIC FOR THE 1990s
In 1990s alternative music, jarring disjointedness often replaces internal coherence as an organizational principle.

ROCK AS ART REDUX
In their evocative use of rich, complex, contrasting sound worlds, Radiohead follows the lead of the Beatles.

Listen to this selection in CourseMate.

two levels and in two forms. The first statement lines up with four-beat measures. The higher-pitched restatement has one beat less (four beats plus three). The sense of imbalance that the foreshortened riff creates helps set up the next vocal section, which has no apparent connection to the previous section. We get a spark of distortion, then another statement of the riff with full-bore distortion. It gains in power because of the contrast with the two previous sections. After a brief guitar solo, we hear a sustained chord, then a slower section with wordless vocal harmonies. Yorke sings over these simple but beautiful harmonies. Little by little, other layers are added; by the time the guitar riff interrupts again, the sonority is rich with vocal parts and sustained string-like synthesizer sounds. The reprise of the guitar riff is strictly instrumental; with its abrupt ending, it seems to signal a descent into madness.

The facts of the song—its sprawling length; the three distinct sections and the reprise of the second section; the strong contrast in character within and between sections; the deliberate delivery of the lyrics—are there. The reading of it is necessarily subjective.

The more significant point is that the conflicts and discontinuities within the words, within the music, and between the words and music demand that listeners engage with the song in more than a casual way. In particular, the music is complex and rich enough—even though it is also quite accessible—to admit multiple levels of meaning. Not since the Beatles' demise has a group blended accessibility, challenge, sound imagination, and sound variety so artfully. This is rock aspiring to significance.

Alienation and Fragmentation

Although "Smells Like Teen Spirit" and "Paranoid Android" create dramatically different sound worlds, they share two common elements that place them in the nineties. One is the sense of alienation that the lyrics project. In both, there is palpable tension between the outside world and the world inside the protagonist's head. The other are sudden and jarring musical contrasts. In both tracks, the abrupt shifts from soft to loud seem to suggest a sudden loss of control—flying into a violent rage because one can't stand it anymore. These shifts magnify the message of the words; as used here, they provide the most consistent and powerful expression of the alienation depicted in the lyrics.

The strong sectional contrasts—sometimes to the point of discontinuity—describe a formal approach that is precisely the opposite of that used in more conventional rock songs. There, the chorus establishes the mood of the songs; the function of the verses is to amplify and explain that overall mood. Here, the various sections create their own moods; we are violently whipped from one to the next. This kind of sonic fragmentation within a song is common in alternative music since the early 1990s, in part because of the critical and commercial success of both bands.

CHAPTER 87
Women's Voices

Women quickly found a home in the alternative movement. Their growing presence can be understood as still another dimension of the more prominent place of women in popular music; the eighties were the decade not only of Madonna but also of Joan Jett, the Go-Go's, and the Bangles. What made the work of women in alternative music distinctive was that their voices were not constrained in any way by the expectations of more mainstream music. Alternative gave feminists a forum and enabled women of every persuasion to speak their mind.

The women's movement within alternative music took root in the latter part of the eighties and flourished in the nineties. Among the important trends was the **riot grrrl** movement, which supported a militant feminist agenda with post-punk music that favored confrontation over chops (that is, musical skill). The music was part of a self-contained subculture; Bands like Bratmobile and Bikini Kill played in clubs and at music festivals that promoted feminist solidarity. Feminist fanzines nurtured and promoted them and other acts, and independent labels released their recordings The **queercore** movement, which reacted against more mainstream gay and lesbian views, found a musical voice in the work of bands such as Sister George, Tribe 8, and Team Dresch, whose founder Donna Dresch also created the fanzine *Chainsaw,* which she spun off into a still active record label.

Alternative music also supported a revival of singer–songwriters, many of them women. Even as artists like Tracy Chapman, Suzanne Vega, k.d. lang, and Alanis Morrissette garnered major label contracts and the occasional Grammy award (Tracy Chapman's "Give Me One Reason" won a Grammy in 1996 for Best Rock Song), other singer–songwriters, such as Patty Larkin, Dar Williams, and Ani DiFranco, also toured and recorded extensively.

That the music of women within the alternative movement would take these two directions should not be surprising, because they have their roots in the two seventies styles most open to women. Patti Smith was a punk pioneer, and musicians like Talking Heads bassist Tina Weymouth made women instrumentalists less exceptional—Kim Gordon, the bassist with Sonic Youth, followed in her footsteps. Similarly, singer–songwriters like Joni Mitchell and Carly Simon brought a feminine perspective to the forefront of popular music; the music of contemporary artists such as Ani DiFranco continues that tradition.

Ani DiFranco

Although her music has evolved away from what she calls the "folk punk" of her early recordings, Ani Di Franco (b. 1970) embodies the entrepreneurial spirit of alternative music as fully as any artist. Rather than wait for a major label to offer her a contract, she started her own record company, Righteous Babe Records, in 1989 and put out her first album the following year. While in college at New York City's New School, she began touring actively, performing in small clubs and other venues, where she built up a loyal following. As she and her label grew more successful (it now offers all of her recordings, plus recordings by twelve other acts), she established the Righteous Babe Foundation, to give support to causes in which she believes, including queer visibility, opposition to the death penalty, and historic preservation. (The new headquarters of Righteous Babe is a formerly abandoned church in Buffalo.)

Like Joni Mitchell, whose music has reflected a similarly wide-ranging curiosity and a from-the-heart perspective, DiFranco's music has ranged from contemporary takes on the urban folk style to collaborations with major artists such as Prince, Janis Ian, Maceo Parker, and the Buffalo Philharmonic Orchestra. Three constants have been incisive lyrics, which usually speak either to social and political issues dear to her heart or the current take on her personal life; her affecting voice; and her fluent and imaginative acoustic guitar playing. We hear her mordant view on a failed relationship in "32 Flavors," a track from her 1995 album *Not a Pretty Girl.*

DIFRANCO'S enterprise and determination in charting her own career path, unbeholden to authority figures in any branch of the music industry, has been an inspiration to numerous young musicians.

LISTENING CUE • **"32 Flavors" (1995),** Ani DiFranco. DiFranco, vocals, guitar, bass; Andy Stochansky, percussion.

STYLE Alternative singer–songwriter • **FORM** Verse/chorus, but with a wordless chorus and an extended instrumental outro

Listen For . . .

INSTRUMENTATION
Lead/backup vocal, guitar, bass, percussion, drums

PERFORMANCE STYLE
Understated vocal, instrumental styles put lyrics in forefront

RHYTHM
Gentle sixteen-beat rhythm with persistent syncopation in accompaniment pattern

MELODY
Two repeated melodic ideas: stream of descending notes for verse; shorter wordless chorus

HARMONY
Vocal sections: cycling progression avoids conventional sequence.

Remember . . .

STORY OUT FRONT
Sharp-edged lyric that describes a relationship gone bad with vivid images and imaginative, occasionally humorous wordplay

BUOYANT UNOBTRUSIVE SETTING
Low-key vocal style, repetitious melody, and rhythmically active and melodically imaginative guitar/ percussion accompaniment create a buoyant cushion: melody, vocal style, and accompaniment an ideal foil for lyrics

RHYTHMIC NON SEQUITUR
Extended percussion jam = last half of song = no apparent relation to vocal section. Both project a sense of alienation that pours out of the lyrics and the music. And it comes from and speaks to a group dubbed Generation X.

Listen to this selection in CourseMate.

"32 Flavors" is the product of just two musicians: DiFranco and percussionist Andy Stochansky, a long-time collaborator. Together, they update the work of the great singer–songwriters of the early seventies. DiFranco's guitar accompaniment, which remains consistent throughout the song, is more elaborate and melodic than the accompaniments typically heard in the folk and folk-inspired music of the sixties and seventies. Guitar(s)—DiFranco added a discreet bass guitar part—and percussion provide a buoyant cushion for DiFranco's scathing indictment of a former partner. Lines like "cuz some day you are going to get hungry/ and eat most of the words you just said" cut like a scalpel because they are funny and true. DiFranco's warm, low-key vocal style in this song resonates with the gentle accompaniment; its understated quality gives the lyrics even more bite because of the contrast between the message and its delivery. The extended percussion outro is a nice bonus, although not connected thematically to the lyric.

The gently flowing music of Ani DiFranco heard here is some distance stylistically from the punk-inspired sounds that typify alternative music. However, her do-it-yourself approach to all aspects of her career—performing, recording, managing, promoting, and support for other grassroots efforts in causes that are important to her—embodies the spirit of alternative music. Her enterprise and determination in charting her own career path, unbeholden to authority figures, took the independence so prized by alternative acts to a new level.

UNIT 19

LOOKING BACK, LOOKING AHEAD
Three Decades of Alternative

THERE ARE NUMEROUS PARALLELS between the alternative movement and early rock. Both grew out of the most rhythmically aggressive music of its time: the eight-beat rhythms of rock and roll; the saturated eight-beat rhythms of punk. Both took shape on the fringes of the music industry, in out-of-the-way locales. Both were originally recorded on independent labels, then crossed over to the majors when the music gained commercial traction. Both developed passionate followings: Rock as "a way of life" evolved into "our band could be your life." Both diversified stylistically over time by drawing in a wide range of influences. By the 1990s, "alternative" was an umbrella term for a disparate family of styles, much as "rock" was in the 1960s. And both saw their market share grow over time. This comparison also largely applies to second-generation heavy metal, although it is not identified as an "alternative" music because of its direct connection to the heavy metal of the early 1970s.

Still, there are significant differences beyond the generation gap: 1950s–1960s, 1970s–1980s. Rock fomented a revolution. Punk, new wave, and alternative were, more than anything else, a counterrevolution, an attempt to reclaim the energy and attitude of early rock. To convey this musically, alternative bands often intensified those qualities that had distinguished rock from more established styles. They were often louder, more abrasive sonically, and aggressive rhythmically. Strong, almost schizophrenic, contrasts within songs, arguably the most widespread and significant musical innovation of alternative music, produced intensification by compression.

Unlike rock, alternative never became the dominant music of its time. It has remained a relatively small if vibrant segment of the industry despite the unquestioned critical and commercial success of acts such as Radiohead and the crossover success of pop-oriented "alternative" acts like Green Day.

A World of Music

UNIT 20

UNIT 20

They're found in museum stores, coffee shops, bookstores, and health-conscious groceries. They have bright, attractive covers that catch the eye. They offer sounds from around the world, from Asian Lounge music and African Grooves to zydeco. They are the CDs released by Putumayo World Music. Since its founding in 1993, Putumayo World Music has sold over 20,000,000 recordings, expanded its catalog (currently over 200 recordings), and given substantial sums from their sales to nonprofit organizations.

The idea to found a world music label came to Dan Storper in 1991, when he heard the Afropop group Kotoja while strolling through San Francisco's Golden Gate Park. He would start the company two years later. For millions of listeners around the world, Putumayo World Music has been the point of entry into other musical cultures. Their success points up the still small but vibrant and expanding market for what is commonly called "world music."

We live in a musically extraordinary time. For the first time in the history of civilization, there is a global expressive language. It is long been said that music is the universal language. There has been some truth to that: The fact that audiences in Beijing can enjoy and appreciate the music of Beethoven, and audiences in London can enjoy the music of Ravi Shankar suggest that music has the power to transcend geographical and cultural boundaries.

However, this kind of universality is akin to the study of Latin, classical Greek, or Sanskrit. Both classical music and classical Indian music are long-established traditions. In western culture, "classical" music is largely a fixed, or at best a slowly evolving, repertoire. Beethoven has been dead for almost 200 years. Although performances bring his music to life, they do not change what he wrote (travesties like Walter Murphy's "A Fifth of Beethoven" notwithstanding) or add to his output. Beethoven's music may speak to non-Western listeners, but it is not changed in the process.

By contrast, contemporary popular music is a **living** musical language. It is not just that Malaysians like Michael Jackson or that Russians respond to Radiohead; it is that regional dialects of contemporary music are emerging around the world, by combining electronic resources and the international (U.S./U.K.) rock/R&B/pop tradition with local music, and that artists from around the world are coming together to make new kinds of music by combining musical elements from different regions. In this unit, we consider intersections involving African music, the international rock-era popular style, and Celtic music.

CHAPTER 88
World Music

In discussing his involvement with World of Music, Arts, and Dance (WOMAD), Peter Gabriel, the lead vocalist in Genesis and an important solo artist since the late 1970s, noted:

> Pure enthusiasm for music from around the world led us to the idea of WOMAD in 1980 and thus to the first WOMAD festival in 1982. The festivals have always been wonderful and unique occasions and have succeeded in introducing an international audience to many talented artists. Equally important, the festivals have also allowed many different audiences to gain an insight into cultures other than their own through the enjoyment of music. Music is a universal language, it draws people together and proves, as well as anything, the stupidity of racism.

Gabriel was one of the founders of the World of Music, Art, and Dance. Since the first festival in the United Kingdom in 1982, WOMAD has grown into a multifaceted organization. Its festivals are huge events that take place around the world: In the 2001 Guinness Book of Records, it was cited as the biggest International Music Festival. It has provided a platform for numerous world music performers. Since its inception, its mission has been to use the arts to open minds and hearts to the world around us. As they state on their website (http://womad.org), "at festivals, performance events, through recorded releases and through educational projects, we aim to excite, to inform, and to create awareness of the worth and potential of a multicultural society."

The Roots of the World Music Movement

The roots of the world music movement that took shape in the early 1980s go back to the late 1940s, in the music of the Weavers. Among their biggest hits were songs from Israel ("Tzena, Tzena, Tzena") and South Africa ("Wimoweh"). In the latter part of the 1950s, Harry Belafonte would enjoy comparable success with his versions of calypso songs like "Banana Boat (Day O)." Although their music doesn't sound much like authentic versions of the songs, their advocacy of folk music from then-exotic locales and their effort to capture something of its spirit played a large role in creating the open-minded attitude that has characterized rock-era music. Belafonte also played a key role in introducing South African singer Miriam Makeba to United States audiences. She would enjoy a long run in the 1960s, but her success did not lead to widespread interest in South African music.

During the 1960s, the bossa nova craze and the Beatles played a big part in expanding the popular-music worldview. This Brazilian music was an international/regional fusion—jazz met samba in Brazil and returned as the bossa nova—that gained significant traction in the United States and elsewhere. The appeal of the music surmounted the language barrier. The Beatles spearheaded a more inclusive musical attitude on multiple levels. One was the simple fact of their success. The British Invasion of the mid-1960s made rock—and, by extension, popular music—an international music. The second level of influence was their musical daring: They were not afraid to try anything or use music from any source. By their example, they nurtured the open-mindedness of rock and folk artists. Most specifically, they helped bring Indian music to a much wider western audience. George Harrison's flirtation with the sitar and his use of it in songs like "Norwegian Wood" helped build a western audience for Indian musicians like Ravi Shankar.

The 1970s were the prelude to the world music explosion of the 1980s. The most significant development was the emergence of reggae. Reggae was an international/regional fusion with distinctive, easily recognizable sounds and rhythms. Its popularity and influence outside of Jamaica inspired artists and industry members in other Afrocentric styles, such as juju and calypso, to promote their music to a wider audience. Moreover, reggae's role as the conscience of popular music in the 1970s demonstrated once again that music could go beyond mere entertainment to be a force for social change. Artists in other Afrocentric styles also embraced this concept.

The Emergence of World Music

All of this laid the groundwork for the world music movement that flowered during the 1980s. Five key ingredients were in place: the use of music as an expression of national or cultural identity, the growing international recognition of regional popular styles, deep interest from a few mainstream popular musicians, the drive to reclaim folk heritages around the world, and audience interest.

In many cases, the revival and promotion of traditional music had a political dimension. This was particularly the case in Africa and the Caribbean. Almost all of the countries had formerly been colonies of England or France, and most had gained their independence only in the 1960s and 1970s. As the countries shook off colonial rule, traditional music became an expression of cultural identity and national pride, especially in Africa. For example, Kwame Nkrumah, Ghana's first president, made the restoration of traditional music a matter of governmental policy.

After independence, both England and France had liberal policies regard immigration from former colonies. Indeed, the Caribbean islands Guadeloupe and Martinique are *départements* of France. As a result, London and Paris became the centers of world beat because of the large expatriate colonies in both cities. These European capitals were homes away from home for both musicians and audience.

Reggae's popularity during the 1970s helped spark interest in other Afrocentric music. Among the regional styles to gain a toehold in the international market were calypso and soca (soul calypso, a regional/international hybrid that had emerged during the 1970s) from Trinidad, *zouk* and cadence from the French Caribbean, samba from Brazil, and Afropop styles like *juju* from Nigeria (King Sunny Ade was the best-known Nigerian musician).

None of these styles has succeeded on the same scale as reggae—many, especially the West African styles, must overcome the language barrier—but all have an international presence. Most were already in existence well before the 1980s (e.g., calypso dates back to the 1910s). Their emergence in the 1980s reflects both changes in the music—a more updated sound, through the addition of electronic instruments and the incorporation of elements from the international style—and the growing interest of musicians and audience from other parts of the world in new sounds.

The complement to regional musicians blending elements of the international style with their local music was mainstream musicians bringing these regional styles into their music. Three musicians stand out: Paul Simon, David Byrne of Talking Heads, and Peter Gabriel. All played an active role in promoting world music by using musicians on their recording dates (e.g., Youssou N'Dour with Peter Gabriel), and by seeking out and promoting regional music.

The 1980s also saw a revival of folk traditions around the world. Chief among them was Celtic music, but other regional folk and folk/international styles found enthusiastic international audiences, among them, music from Bulgaria (Le Mystère des Voix Bulgares, clarinetist Ivo Papasov), flamenco (the Gipsy Kings), contemporary Native American music, indigenous Australian music, and the chanting of Tibetan monks.

Technology played a crucial role in building audiences for this music. Affordable and portable recording equipment made it possible to record music almost anywhere in the world: folk musicians and those creating contemporary regional/international fusions benefited from this, just as rap and techno artists did.

Another factor in the broader acceptance of world music, and Afrocentric music in particular, was the rhythmic evolution of popular music. By the 1980s, much popular music—not only rap and electronica, but also the pop/rock/R&B middle ground—typically featured active rhythms and percussion-rich textures. As a result, international styles that featured similar rhythmic textures sounded more familiar than they would have in the 1950s or 1960s.

The world music movement includes a broad spectrum of musical styles and traditions. At one end of the spectrum is the preservation or replication of folk and regional traditions in as pure a state as possible. At the other are international/regional syntheses that feature collaborations between musicians from different cultures. Our miniscule sampling of world music focuses on four quite different syntheses.

CHAPTER 89
Afropop

All along the upper west coast of Africa, from Senegal to Zaire, native popular musics have flourished. Each country has its own popular style; indeed, many "national" styles actually emerge from a people within a country, such as the Wolof in Senegal. Nigeria is home to *juju* and Afrobeat; Ghana has highlife. *Makossa* is a popular local dance music in Cameroon; so is *soukous* in Zaire. *Gbegbe* grew up alongside other African popular styles in the Ivory Coast; *mbalax* is native to Senegal.

Some styles are updated versions of older popular styles. Highlife, for example, dates back to mid-century but was modernized with the addition of electric guitars and other changes. Other styles are transformations of traditional music: in the 1970s, Nigerian musicians created *gbegbe* to give their traditional music a modern sound.

National styles have moved freely from country to country. *Juju* has flourished in Ghana and Sierra Leone, as well as Nigeria. Not surprisingly, perhaps, the colonial language has had some effect on the dissemination of a style. Highlife is more popular in English-speaking countries; *soukous* more popular in French-speaking nations. But cross-fertilization transcends tribal, national, and linguistic barriers. In Africa and within the expatriate communities in Europe and the United States, musicians listen to and learn from each other. As a result, there are common elements in much West African music. Some of them distinguish it not only from U.S./U.K. rock era music but also Afrocentric Caribbean styles.

We hear the fruits of an African/international fusion in a track featuring two of Africa's musical ambassadors.

The Sound of Afropop

In 1991, Senegalese singer Youssou N'Dour (b. 1959) was appointed a Goodwill Ambassador for UNICEF. Eleven years later, Angélique Kidjo (b. 1960), a native of Benin, also became a UNICEF Goodwill Ambassador. Senegal and Benin are former French colonies in sub-Saharan Africa. Senegal is along the west coast: Dakar, the capital city and N'Dour's hometown, is the westernmost city on the African continent. Benin is a small country directly west of Nigeria and southeast of Senegal.

Kidjo and N'Dour are, respectively, the best-known African female and male singers. They have earned widespread critical acclaim: Both have won Grammys, and the *New York Times* labeled N'Dour "one of the world's greatest singers." Both have been extraordinarily active on behalf of causes that they believe to be important: Kidjo for education and human rights—she founded

YOUSSOU N'DOUR (left) and **ANGELIQUE KIDJO** in 2007

the Batonga foundation to provide young African girls with upper-level education to prepare them for leadership positions; and N'Dour for technology and health—N'Dour helped organize the 2006 Africa Live: The Roll Back Malaria Concert, which was given in Dakar.

Kidjo moved to Paris in 1983, where she obtained work as a backup vocalist. By 1989, she had a recording contract and a career in Europe. Within a few years, she had become the best-known African female vocalist since Miriam Makeba. N'Dour's international career also took off in the 1980s after Peter Gabriel recruited him for his first WOMAD concert.

In 2005, N'Dour's *Egypt* won a Grammy for Best Contemporary World Music Album; three years later, Kidjo received the same honor for *Djin Djin*. For Kidjo, *Djin Djin* was a conscious effort to return to her roots, to recapture and integrate into her music the rhythms and sounds of her home country. She had grown up listening to native musicians and rock, funk, and pop from abroad; the album is an expression of that rich heritage. The album features an impressive list of guest artists, including Peter Gabriel, Alicia Keys, saxophonist Branford Marsalis, Josh Groban, and Carlos Santana.

"Ae Ae" comes in two versions. The versions are identical except for the vocals: in the second version, N'Dour joins Kijdo and improvises a vocal obbligato over an otherwise instrumental interlude. "Ae Ae" features three of the most common features of African/international fusions: the extensive and prominent use of traditional African instruments; complete western rhythm sections, typically laying down a sixteen-beat rhythm; and melody and harmony that put a distinctively African spin on the major scales and three basic chords of European tonal harmony. In addition to a large array of unpitched percussion instruments, "Ae Ae" uses a *balafon,* a xylophone-like instrument, and a *kora,* a harp-lute made from a calabash.

LISTENING CUE • "Ae Ae" (2008), Angélique Kidjo. Kidjo and N'Dour, vocals.

STYLE Afropop • **FORM** Verse/chorus, with extended vocal solo interlude

Listen For . . .

INSTRUMENTATION
Lead and backup vocals, guitars, organ, bass, drums, extra percussion, African pitched instruments—balafon, kora

RHYTHM
Vibrant sixteen-beat rhythm at a bright tempo, with active timekeeping on several percussion instruments; persistent syncopations in chord instruments, bass

MELODY
Long phrases in verse, bridge; chorus (A-E, A-E) spun out from title-phrase riff

HARMONY
Song built mainly on I, IV, and V; shift to new key after false start in middle

TEXTURE
Rich texture, with multiple melodic strands in lead vocals, choir/backup vocals and African instruments; frequent call and response

Remember . . .

AFROPOP SOUNDS
The African instruments are one source; the distinctive guitar timbre is another.

INTERNATIONAL/REGIONAL FUSION
A seamless blend of international elements—core rhythm section, active rhythms, layered textures, verse/chorus form—with regional elements (language, native instruments)

UPBEAT SONG
Active, vibrant rhythms; basic three-chord harmony; frequent call and response; and tuneful chorus all project an upbeat mood.

COMMUNAL MUSIC MAKING
The extra percussion, African pitched instruments, and chorus behind Kidjo and N'Dour help convey an updated approach to African-style communal music making

Listen to this selection in CourseMate.

Both play moving lines behind the vocal throughout the song.

The rhythm section on "Ae Ae" includes drum set, electric bass, guitars, and organ, in addition to the African percussion instruments. The musicians lay down a vibrant groove based on the ubiquitous sixteen-beat rhythm, with an active bass line and a dense, percussive texture. The particular timbre of the electric guitar on this recording is distinctive to much West African music, and the African instruments, both pitched and unpitched, color the sound to give it a specifically African flavor. Still, it is a version of the international groove so popular around the turn of the century.

The approach to melody and harmony represent a common feature of pop styles throughout West Africa: an adaptation of European tonality in which melodies are constructed entirely from the seven notes of diatonic scales (rather than pentatonic scales) and harmony consists of progressions built from two or three chords that cycle with little or no change throughout the song. In "Ae Ae," there are three progressions, all built from I, IV, and V: one for the solo verse, the second for the bridge, and the third for the chorus.

This Afropop approach to melody and harmony has more in common with the hymns and other religious music brought to Africa by missionaries than with western popular music. The choral singing heard on this recording also highlights this European connection.

Weaving through the buoyant rhythms are the voices of Kidjo and N'Dour. Kidjo's lyric is part commentary on the plight of Africans who immigrate to Europe to escape the poverty, poor health, and political turmoil there and part exhortation to Africans to become self-sufficient. In this respect, the song continues the practice among members of the African diaspora (Kidjo now lives in New York) of sending a powerful message over a compelling groove. As Kidjo said in the video about *Djin Djin,* she wants to "entertain each other but learn at the same time."

In "Ae Ae," as in much of the music by African artists who have enjoyed international success, there is something of the atmosphere of a family reunion. It is not so much a coming together of people as of styles and cultures—music from the mother continent meeting up with its offspring in the Americas. What Africa had sent to the Americas via the slave trade came back to Africa transmuted but still compatible, so that they could be easily blended. A second wave of African music, mixed from traditional sounds and their evolutionary mutations among the diaspora, has found a welcome audience in America and around the world.

CHAPTER 90
Global/Pop Fusions

Ethan Zuckerman, a fellow at The Berkman Center for Internet and Society at Harvard Law and a cofounder of Global Voices, maintains the blog *My Heart's in Accra* (http://ethanzuckerman.com) to share his thoughts on "Africa, international development, and hacking the media." In an April 2009 entry entitled "From Protest to Collaboration: Paul Simon's *Graceland* and Lessons for Xenophiles," he discusses the creative process that eventually produced Simon's album in the context of the anti-apartheid movement. *Graceland* was ultimately a huge success for Simon and many of his fellow musicians, but its production and release generated considerable controversy.

Music, Race, and Cultural Change

Among the sources of increasing pressure on the South African government to eliminate apartheid was a widespread cultural boycott begun in 1961 by the British Musicians' Union and later overseen by the UN Centre against Apartheid. This boycott got a boost in 1985 when Steven Van Zandt, Bruce Springsteen's longtime on-and-off guitarist, created Artists United Against Apartheid and recorded "Sun City," a 7½-minute video with a simple message: Artists with a conscience don't perform in Sun City.

Sun City was a luxurious resort and casino built in 1979 in a *bantustan*—a black African homeland created by the South African government. Gambling, pornography, and other Las Vegas–type vices were illegal in white South Africa, so the government permitted the casino to be built in a black area. In response, Van Zandt mobilized an all-star aggregation of artists to promote a boycott of the resort. The video juxtaposes images of the casino, clips of police brutality in South Africa, and scenes from the American civil rights movement of the 1960s with cameos of the artists.

It was in this context that Simon recorded *Graceland*. Not surprisingly, he took an enormous amount of flak from several quarters, much of it misinformed. Among the most common criticisms involved "exploitation" and "musical colonialism." The facts tell a different story: Simon paid the musicians triple scale, shared songwriting credits, brought several musicians to New York to finish the album, and toured for a year with Miriam Makeba and Hugh Masakela, both South African exiles. That Simon would choose to go to South Africa to record was a logical step in his musical evolution.

Paul Simon

Paul Simon (b. 1941) has had a long history of collaboration that goes back to the beginning of his career, and as a solo artist he has been willing to integrate his musical identity with outside influences. His first professional success came from songs written with Carole King, and he first gained fame as a performer with Art Garfunkel (b. 1941). Their successes included the soundtrack for the (1967) film *The Graduate* (a rock first) and three chart-topping albums.

When Simon and Garfunkel dissolved their partnership in 1970, Simon immediately embarked on a solo career. The split seemed to liberate Simon musically: It was a case of addition by subtraction. Both Simon and Garfunkel have pleasant voices that do not project a strong and distinctive personality. Yet because there are two voices, usually in harmony, the vocal sound is typically the dominant element, even in a song like "The Boxer," which features a rich instrumental backdrop laced with unusual timbres.

However, in Simon's solo work, the musical settings became as important expressively as the words, melody, and Simon's singing, The settings often drew on a broad range of distinctive styles, for example, Latin music, both black and white gospel, and reggae. In this respect, Simon, more than any other post-1970 artist, has furthered the Beatles' revolutionary reconception of song, one in which setting, like words and melody, plays a key role in projecting meaning. In *Graceland,* he went beyond his work in the 1970s, geographically and musically.

In 1984, Simon was at a low point in his career. *Hearts and Bones,* released the previous year and his first album since 1975, had not done well. A friend shared a cassette of township jive (a popular style created by black South Africans) by the Boyoyo Boys. Inspired by this unfamiliar music, Simon sought out Hilton Rosenthal, the record's producer, about recording with South African musicians. Rosenthal assured Simon that collaboration was possible and sent him numerous recordings. However, because of the intense international opposition to apartheid, Simon consulted Quincy Jones and Harry Belafonte, who had been involved in the USA for Africa project, and received their assurance that his project was ethical. Encouraged, Simon went to South Africa, enlisted South Africans as cowriters, then had the black South African musicians record rhythm tracks. Only then did he begin to write the songs on top of tracks that he pieced together.

By reversing the conventional sequence of events in recording, Simon virtually guaranteed that the African element in the recording would be organic, not cosmetic. "Diamonds on the Soles of Her Shoes" exemplifies the extent of the African influence. It begins with the choral group Ladysmith Black Mambazo singing in Zulu; one translation of their lyrics is "Even though you saved that man today,/He will be ruined no matter what./Come on, girl." In the main section of the song, Simon describes the rich girl/poor boy relationship in a series of images as he rides the distinctively African sounds, rhythms,

LISTENING CUE • **"Diamonds on the Soles of Her Shoes" (1986),** Joseph Shabalala, Paul Simon. Simon, Ladysmith Black Mambazo, vocals.

STYLE South African Isicathamiya/Western pop fusion • **FORM** Two major sections. slow introductory section; fast section with instrumental interludes and no consistent formal plan

Listen For . . .

INSTRUMENTATION
Solo and choral vocals, guitars, bass, drums, multiple percussion, horns,

PERFORMING STYLE
Rich choral sound of Ladysmith Black Mamzabo; "African" guitar sonority

RHYTHM
Shift from slow unmeasured rhythm to buoyant sixteen-beat rhythm with light timekeeping and abundant syncopation

MELODY
Long phrases with gentle rise and fall and frequent pauses between vocal statements; melody-like instrumental parts

TEXTURE
Rich textures in slow opening, lead vocal with chordal support and/or call and response; in fast section, vocal plus percussion, guitar riffs, free-roaming bass line, horn riffs

Remember . . .

WORDS VS. MUSIC
No obvious connection between words and music, unlike Simon's music from the 1970s

THOROUGH FUSION
Seamless blending of pop and South African elements. African rhythms in step with 1980s practice.

SIMON'S SOUNDWORLD
Multiple African sonorities make wonderful complement to Simon's relationship song.

IMAGINATIVE SONG
From the slow beginning in Zulu to the cleverly crafted words and melody over the infectious South African background, and the call-and-response exchanges toward the end, Simon's song departs from the conventional verse/chorus paradigm of mainstream pop.

Listen to this selection in CourseMate.

and harmonies—in this case, a revolving three-chord progression. In effect, Simon merges his distinctive songwriting esthetic into the infectious music of his African collaborators.

The track and the album are a true global fusion, an outstanding example of the blending of regional and international music. *Graceland* was Simon's most successful album, commercially and critically, and the album and tour helped promote the careers of many of the artists involved, most notably Ladysmith Black Mambazo.

Music as a Force for Global Understanding

Apartheid was dismantled during the early 1990s, and in 1994 Nelson Mandela became the first South African president elected by a fully democratic vote. At Mandela's invitation, Simon became the first American to perform in post-apartheid South Africa. For Simon, it was not only a triumphant experience but also a moment of vindication in the wake of the controversy surrounding *Graceland*. As such, it is an object lesson on how complicated mixing art and politics can become.

Ethan Zuckerman's perspective on this matter is enlightening:

> Steven Van Zandt's position, a principled stance against engaging with South Africa under apartheid, is a cleaner, neater position than the complex compromise Simon chose, but I doubt it was as effective. Van Zandt helped call attention to a nasty situation in the waning days of the Botha regime—Simon introduced the wider world to a soundtrack for both a revolution and for a new South Africa.

As we listen to "Diamonds on the Soles of Her Shoes," it's easy to be caught up in the flow of the music and intrigued by Simon's quirky lyric. But the circumstances of its creation remind us how music is so much a part of our world even as it can carry us apart from it.

CHAPTER 91
Celtic Fusions

A crwth is a Welsh musical instrument that dates back to at least the eleventh century. (*Crwth* is also the killer "hangman" word.) It looks like a violin with a frame: It has a rectangular body with sound holes, a narrow neck, and a U-shaped rim that supports the neck and connects to the body. Its six strings can be bowed or strummed. The crwth made a modest comeback in the latter part of the twentieth century, as instrument makers replicated historical instruments and musicians reconstructed old performance traditions to the best of their ability. The revival of the crwth was one small part of the reclamation of Celtic culture.

Celtic Music and the Reclamation of Celtic Culture

During the early years of the Roman Empire, Celts (pronounced "Kelts," not "Selts") inhabited much of western Europe and were the original settlers of the British Isles, but by the seventh century C.E., their domain was reduced to Brittany, a region in the northwest of France, and parts of the British Isles. Over the next millennium, English and French governments largely succeeded in suppressing Celtic culture. The first seeds of a Celtic revival began toward the end of the nineteenth century. After growing steadily during the first part of the twentieth century, the movement gathered momentum after World War II. Celtic languages that had almost disappeared, like Irish and Scottish Gaelic, Manx (on the Isle of Man), Welsh, Cornish (in Cornwall, a region in Southwest England), and Breton were revived and taught to younger generations. Scholars took a fresh look at the history of their culture. People preserved or revived other aspects of their culture: food, dress, dance, and—of course—music.

The Chieftains and the Revival of Celtic Music

In Ireland, a man born in 1931 as John Reidy played a key role in bringing back, and bringing to light, Irish traditional music. While in his twenties, he began using the Gaelic form of his name: Seán Ó Ríada. During this time, he sought out Irish traditional musicians. In 1959, he went a step further and formed an Irish traditional band. Among the members was Paddy Moloney, a master of several traditional Irish wind instruments, among them uilleann pipes (an Irish bagpipe) and the tin whistle. In 1962, Moloney formed the Chieftains, using several other members of Ó Ríada's folk group, Ceoltóirí Cualann, in the group. The Chieftains worked semiprofessionally for over ten years; by 1975, they were well enough established to become full-time professional musicians.

The Chieftains first came to the United States in 1972, as part of an Irish festival. By 1979, they were the musical guests on *Saturday Night Live*. As their international reputation grew, the Chieftains undertook numerous collaborative projects, joining forces with musicians as diverse as the classical flutist James Galway and the Rolling Stones. Among the most interesting were sessions with American country musicians, including their 1992 album *Another Country* and *Down the Plank Road: The Nashville Sessions,* which was released in 2002.

Among the songs they recorded on *Another Country* was an exceedingly popular dance tune from the Southwestern United States, "Cotton Eyed Joe." In this recording, country traditionalist and multi-instrumentalist Ricky Skaggs joined them; he is the vocalist on this recording. The performance begins with Skaggs's vocal, then proceeds into the reel-like fiddle tune version of the song. For dancers in Ireland and the Appalachians, a good fiddler was the only musician necessary for dancing—and often he was alone.

Jig and reels—traditional folk dances in Ireland, Scotland, and Appalachia—are typically short, two-section pieces played at a brisk tempo (as is the case here). To create a longer number, musicians would string several jigs together, bringing one or more back in the course of the number. Here, the instruments enter in stages, joining in with each new phrase of the dance tune; they are a mix of new and old: electric bass and drums, plus traditional Irish instruments like the tin whistle and the bodhrán, the characteristic hand drum of Irish music (the drum has a single head that is played with a double-headed stick). During the reprise of the original dance tune, the performance becomes a free-for-all, with another fiddle and a banjo joining the group.

Fiddle and banjo, which made its way to Ireland during the nineteenth century, are part of the sound of traditional music in both Ireland and the United States. It is instruments like the tin whistle, uilleann pipes, and bodhrán that create the distinctive sound of Irish traditional music, when added to these others. The texture created by bands like the Chieftains—the melody played in a high range by the fiddle and a very high range by the tin whistle, the deep drumming sounds of the bodhrán, sustained sonorities on the uilleann pipes, and other melodic lines weaving in and out—is distinctive to this music.

The Chieftains' numerous recordings with American musicians are an affirmation of their common heritage. It is fascinating to hear what sounds like a distinctively American fiddle tune suddenly take on a different color

LISTENING CUE • **"Cotton Eyed Joe" traditional (1992),** Ricky Skaggs, vocal; the Chieftains.

STYLE Country/Irish fusion • **FORM** Multisectional

Listen For . . .

INSTRUMENTS
Voice, fiddles, drums, banjo, guitar, bass, bodhrán, flute, tin whistle, harp

PERFORMANCE STYLE
Skaggs's singing has a country twang.

RHYTHM FAST TEMPO
Dance-like rhythms—fast-moving melodic lines recall the reel, a folk dance from the British Isles that was also popular in the United States. A strong dance beat, with occasional syncopation.

MELODY
There are six melodies; only the first is "Cotton-Eyed Joe." It comes in two versions; only the first is really singable. The other melodies are for playing; their fast rhythm, rapid rise and fall, and infrequent pauses would make them challenging to sing.

DYNAMICS
Moderately loud for acoustic instruments.

HARMONY
I-IV-V, with long stretches on a single harmony at times. There is a shift to a new key in the middle and a return to the home key with the second vocal.

TEXTURE
Ranges from a single voice or instrument to a rich texture, with multiple versions of the melody, countermelodies (usually in the tin whistle or flute), sustained sounds, plus percussion and OOM-pah accompaniment.

Remember . . .

A SERIES OF DANCES/INSTRUMENTAL MELODIES
This performance features several melodies, of which "Cotton-Eyed Joe" is only the first. Dance numbers within in the Celtic tradition, in the British Isles and North America, typically feature a string of short dance tunes.

CELTIC INSTRUMENTS
Much of the character of Celtic music comes from such traditional instruments as the harp, uilleann pipes (a kind of bagpipe), bodhrán, and the tin whistle. In this performance, the fiddle is a constant, showing one connection between Celtic and traditional country music; the addition of the harp, whistle, and bodhrán in the middle of the song immediately transforms the sound from country to Celtic.

CELTIC-STYLE JAMMING
Especially in middle, there is lots of activity: multiple versions of the melody in the fiddle and tin whistle, intricate accompaniments in the other instruments. Often one instrument will detour briefly from the melody, then join back in.

PENTATONIC MELODY
"Cotton-Eyed Joe" is a melody constructed from a pentatonic scale. This suggests a common heritage with the minstrel show music heard much earlier.

COMMON GROUND
It's clear that Skaggs and the Chieftains fit well together because there is so much common ground. The series of reel-like dance tunes are equally at home on both sides of the Atlantic; the fiddle is primary in both Celtic and country music; and the high spirits reverberate from both traditions. The performance suggests a reunion of sorts: two long-separated traditions rediscover their common heritage.

Listen to this selection in CourseMate.

with the addition of the Irish instruments. The ease with which the American and Irish musicians work together and their obvious pleasure in their collaborative music making ("that was hot!") highlights the close connection between traditional country music and Irish music, which are different branches of the same musical family.

Ethno-Techno and a Cross-Cultural Synthesis

The music of Afro-Celt Sound System is the product of two remarkable fusions: first, the fusion of Celtic music with the music of west Africa, and second, the fusion of these traditional musics with cutting-edge techno.

Afro-Celt Sound System was the inspiration of Simon Emmerson, a Grammy-nominated producer, guitarist, and programmer. The idea of combining African and Celtic music had taken root several years earlier, and in his work on Senegalese vocalist Baaba Maal's first album, he recruited an Irish musician for one of the tracks. In 1995, he brought together a diverse group of musicians—Celtic musicians from Ireland and Brittany, including multi-instrumentalist James McNally and Breton harpist Myrdhin; West African musicians such as Masamba Diop, a master of the talking drum; and contemporary musicians/programmers like Martin Russell for an appearance at the 1995 WOMAD festival and a recording session.

LISTENING CUE • **"Whirl-y-reel 1 (Beard and Sandals Mix)" (1996),** Emmerson, McNally. Afro-Celt Sound System.

STYLE African/Celtic/techno fusion • **FORM** Multisectional: A reel melody is heard twice, preceded and followed by instruments playing melodic fragments.

Listen For . . .

INSTRUMENTATION
Celtic harp, uilleann pipes, low whistle, bodhrán, kora, talking drums, guitars, keyboards, synthesized drum and keyboard sounds

RHYTHM
Sixteen-beat rhythm with strong beat marking at a fast tempo and extensive syncopation. Melodic figures in reel move in step with faster rhythm; solo episodes have fast rhythms and numerous pauses.

MELODY
Mainly extensive repetition of small melodic cells, usually scale fragments; reel tune is active, instrumental-style melody with short phrases

HARMONY
Unchanged throughout, except for a contrasting section in the reel

TEXTURE
Multiple layers of percussion and melodic instruments; heterophony (different versions of melody heard simultaneously) in reel and elsewhere

Remember . . .

OLD AND NEW
Instrumental sounds combine modern electronics with centuries-old instruments from two cultures.

AFRICAN AND CELTIC
Percussion and melody instruments from both cultures: talking drums/bodhrán, kora (guitar-like instrument) and Celtic harp

CHANCE TO JAM
Much of the track consists of various instrumentalists inventing melodies and rhythms over a relentlessly energetic groove.

MUSIC TO MOVE TO
Fusion of contemporary electronica and a traditional dance tune invites vigorous movement.

Listen to this selection in CourseMate.

McNally, who has worked with many leading contemporary acts, including U2, the Pogues, Sinead O'Connor, and Peter Gabriel, described the approach of Afro-Celts like this: "[W]e try to cross-pollinate and also use electronica to allow people to actually think about their heritage and their culture as something that's not of the past, but still very important and still evolving." We hear one dimension of this cross-pollination in "Whirl-Y-Reel 1," a track from *Sound Magic*.

"Whirly-Y-Reel 1" (there is a "Whirl-Y-Reel 2" on the disc) is a fascinating, joyous fusion of old and new, man and machine, African and Celtic. An electronic dance track runs through the entire song. Other instruments join in and drop out: There are Celtic harp/talking drum jams, pipe and whistle duets that sound centuries old and as new as today, a variety of percussion sounds—some synthetic, others computer generated. What's always present is the great groove.

It is truly a sign of the times that an imaginative producer like Emmerson would combine these two traditions and use electronically generated rhythms as the glue that bonds everything together, and that the group would succeed. Throughout this book, we have traced the American offspring of these two traditions: Celtic music shaped the music of the minstrel show, then old time music and country; African music shaped blues, jazz, R&B and so much more. What American society had kept apart for so much of its history comes together in recordings like these. Musically, at least, the integration is seamless.

UNIT 20

LOOKING BACK, LOOKING AHEAD
A Future World of Music

OUR MINISCULE SAMPLING OF WORLD MUSIC has focused on the two folk traditions that have contributed the most to popular music in the United States, but cross-cultural musical fusions are happening around the world. Unprecedented access to the traditions from virtually every culture has opened the door to literally a world of music, which in turn offers great promise for new directions in twenty-first-century music. Among my hoped-for results of these collaborations are these three:

1. **Successful balancing acts.** India is home to one of the great classical music traditions—one that goes back millennia. It is also home to Bollywood; films produced there often have elaborate song-and-dance numbers that resemble East Indian updates of the production numbers in the Hollywood movie musicals of the 1930s, 1940s, and 1950s. Two of the key creative tensions in world music are finding balance points between old and new and finding common ground when combining different musical traditions. These are in effect the conflicts that country musicians have wrestled with since the 1920s writ large.

   Perhaps the greatest challenge facing collaborators is maintaining authenticity in and awareness of unfamiliar traditions. Fortunately, there are more resources than ever before: an ever-increasing archive of recordings of traditional music, study of these traditions by scholars and enthusiastic performers—as the recent history of the crwth evidences, and venues like WOMAD that bring traditional performers to audiences around the world.

2. **Connecting contemporary "classical" music with a larger audience.** The elevator-trip version of twentieth-century classical music: Classical composers spent the first part of the century creating music that increasingly alienated audiences beyond their immediate circle. They have spent the latter part of the century coming to grips with their cultural isolation; some have tried to recapture a larger audience. This was not always the case. Two centuries ago, what we now call "classical music" spoke the same musical language as the popular music of the time. It was a more elevated level of discourse, but not so different that it was incomprehensible to lay listeners. And even the "advanced" music of the early twentieth century has entered popular culture: Igor Stravinsky's *The Rite of Spring* provided part of the soundtrack for Walt Disney's *Fantasia*.

   The most "popular" classical music of the late twentieth century has come from minimalist composers such as Philip Glass, who has toured with his own "band," the Philip Glass Ensemble. Unlike mid-century avant-garde classical music, which was completely detached from contemporaneous popular music, there is a sense of connection between the music of Glass and other minimalist composers and rock-era music—rock and minimalism are more like points on a continuum rather than music on opposite sides of a canyon. And in general, the classical music composed since 1970 has been much more accessible than the music of the previous generation. But this has not resulted in increased recognition: Bach, Mozart, Beethoven, and even Stravinsky and the American composer Aaron Copland are far more familiar names to a mass audience than any living composer.

   Global fusions may create a path for reintegration of contemporary classical music into mainstream culture. The music of the Chinese-American composer Tan Dun exemplifies this possibility. His soundtrack for the 2000 film *Crouching Tiger, Hidden Dragon* mixes East and West, as evidenced in the use of western and Chinese traditional instruments. The soundtrack won an Academy Award for Best Original Score and a Grammy for

Best Soundtrack Album. Moreover, the haunting music at the end of the film was remixed and released as the popular song "A Love Before Time" in both Mandarin and English, and the film score was also adapted into a cello concerto.

Stronger connections between "classical" and "popular" musicians would be mutually beneficial. The popular music of George Gershwin was informed by his concert music; George Martin's thorough knowledge of classical music was indispensable to the success of the Beatles.

3. **Using technology to address the language problem.** There is no question that the language barrier turns songs from another culture into purely musical experiences. Compare your experience with "Ae-Ae" or the beginning of "Diamonds on the Soles of Her Shoes" to the rest of Simon's song if you speak English but no African languages. Is it too much to dream that artificial intelligence programs and audio software will not someday provide concurrent translations or even remakes of a track in other languages without the need to re-record the vocal track? It is hard to imagine any other development that would do more to bring the music of a culture to a wider audience.

Some or even all of these possibilities may never be realized. However, the one certainty is that musicians with open ears and open minds are listening more widely than ever before: Iarla O'Lionaird, the traditional Irish singer in Afro-Celt Sound System, is a fan of the Icelandic electronic star Björk, and Yo-Yo Ma, the featured performer on Tan Dun's film score, formed the Silk Road Ensemble, to promote collaboration among artists and others for the music and culture along the Silk Road, the old trade routes between Europe and Asia.

• • • •

OUTRO

Around the time that Radiohead began work on their first post-EMI/Capitol album, lead singer Thom Yorke told *Time* magazine, "I like the people at our record company, but the time is at hand when you have to ask why anyone needs one. And, yes, it probably would give us some perverse pleasure to say 'F___ you' to this decaying business model."

Shortly before they completed work on their new album, Radiohead decided to answer—at least for themselves—Yorke's question about the need for a record company. They reserved the domain name "inrainbows.com"—*In Rainbows* was the album title—and offered the album, which they had produced at their own expense, exclusively as a digital download for two months: from October 10 to December 10, 2007. Those who downloaded the album chose how much they wanted to pay for it: Nothing was an option. Reports vary on what percentage actually paid for it and how much they earned, but Warner Chappell, Radiohead's music publisher, reported a year later that the group had made more from their self-released digital version of the album than they had from the sales of *Hail to the Thief*, their previous album.

Radiohead's bold move shocked music industry executives. One producer told *Time,* "Radiohead is the best band in the world; if you can pay whatever you want for music by the best band in the world, why would you pay $13 dollars or $.99 cents for music by somebody less talented? Once you open that door and start giving music away legally, I'm not sure there's any going back."

Radiohead's pay-what-you-want marketing is not for everyone; the group is one of the few acts that have earned sufficient stature to make this kind of offer and expect something in return. And the group also offered an $80 discbox through their website and began selling physical CDs shortly after discontinuing the online downloads, making arrangements with an array of distributors and record companies throughout the world. But the mere fact that an act as important as Radiohead would—and could—undertake a marketing strategy that challenges the current business model does not portend well for the future of the music industry.

Early in 2011, blogger Michael DeGusta, in an article entitled "The REAL Death of the Music Industry," published a revised version of a chart that showed the revenue derived from recorded music sold in the United States between 1973 and 2009 and accounted for by the RIAA (Record Industry Association of America). Among the conclusions drawn from his analysis: a 64 percent drop in revenue from its 1999 peak, and a 45 percent drop from 1973, when adjusted for inflation.

It can be argued that the steep decline in revenues during the 2000s does not signal the death of the music industry so much as a long-awaited market correction. The album as the all-but-universal unit of sales for all types of recorded music is a rock-era development; before the 1960s, singles were far more popular than albums in popular music. From this broader perspective, digital downloads can be understood as a legal means of restoring consumer choice: Buy the entire album or just the tracks you want. Indeed, some who grew up during the era of album dominance regard peer-to-peer sites and online delivery as payback for an industry that they feel had gouged consumers for decades.

For decades, the record industry has been the heart of the popular music business. Does its precipitous decline truly signal the end of the record industry or simply the death of the business model that has been in place for almost half a century? And further, is the decline of the record industry as we have known it symptomatic of a larger malaise that touches every aspect of popular music? We explore these questions in three stages through a brief overview of the music industry in the early twenty-first century, with particular focus on the Internet and its impact on popular music; a review of long-term musical trends in twentieth-century popular music, to provide historical perspective; and a series of discussion points about future directions in popular music, where readers can bring to bear their own experiences, observations, and opinions.

Digital Technology and the Music Industry in the Early Twenty-First Century

The twenty-first century has begun with the music industry in flux. The rapid development of digital technologies and their increasing affordability has democratized every aspect of the music business: creation, production, dissemination, and consumption. In the process, these technologies have made the world of music a true global village, where almost anyone with a computer of some kind, a microphone and/or video camera, and Internet access can create and share music.

Consolidation of the Majors and Rise of Indies

The democratization of the creation, production, and dissemination of music has provided a paradigm-shifting counterpoint to the continuing consolidation of the record industry. In 1980, there were six major record labels: Columbia, RCA, EMI, Polygram, MCA, and WCI. Collectively, they sold about four-fifths of the recordings released that year. By 2005, there were four majors. Seagram acquired MCA in 1995 and Polygram in 1998; they became the Universal Music Group. Columbia (bought by Sony) and RCA (bought by BMG) merged in 2003. An attempted merger between EMI and Warner in 2000 was called off; it may still happen. The four companies continue to control a decided majority of recorded music, although they market it under numerous labels. In 2005, about 82 percent of the recordings sold in the United States came from one of these majors.

The **majors** are as international as the music they sell. Currently, three of the four companies have headquarters outside the United States. Their operations have been similarly diverse. They have served, in effect, as large holding companies, providing administrative structure for numerous smaller labels targeted to specific markets. As a result, the recording industry has continued to diversify.

What the majors lack is the flexibility or the mind-set to respond to variation and change. This has opened the door for independent labels, and even independent artists, to market quickly and specifically, using all available resources. Computers and the Internet enable them to do so at a fraction of conventional marketing costs. The use of a website for promotion, distribution, and online delivery eliminates upfront production expenses, such as pressing a large quantity of CDs, and the need for middlemen and conventional channels of distribution. At the same time, it makes music immediately available to a global audience. Because of these technological advances, artists and entrepreneurs have been able to create their own independent labels—including **netlabels** that deliver music only online, launch personal websites, start online artist cooperatives, and establish interest groups. All of this has enabled artists and labels to extend the sense of personal connection to a potentially much wider audience and return to the artists a much bigger chunk of a smaller pie.

Although different in kind, the revolution precipitated by the commoditization of digital technology and growth of the Internet has been as far-reaching as the tech-fueled revolutions of the 1920s and 1960s. These earlier revolutions aided the two major transformations in twentieth-century popular music: the new popular song and jazz of the early Modern Era and the rock revolution. Popular music in the early twenty-first century has experienced a different kind of transformation.

Popular Music in the Early Twentieth Century: The Search for a New Sound

Each year, at the end of November, *Billboard* compiles "year-end" lists for each of its charts. Using an inverted point system—for example, on a Top 100 chart, 1 point for each week at No. 100, 100 points for each week at No. 1—the journal produces rankings based on chart position for the previous 12 months. In the early twenty-first century, the charts have been remarkably diverse: rappers and pop stars competed for position with country stars and multiple generations of rockers. Even pre-rock pop singers like Tony Bennett and their contemporary counterparts like Diana Krall and Michael Buble have outsold the vast majority of contemporary acts.

An annual survey sponsored by the RIAA—offers further evidence of the diversity of the popular music scene. A research firm gathers data about consumer taste in recorded music, broken down by genre, format, age, and distribution channel, via a survey of more than a thousand past-month music buyers. Genre distribution is determined by asking buyers to identify the genre(s) of their purchases. It is at best an imperfect system. "Rock"

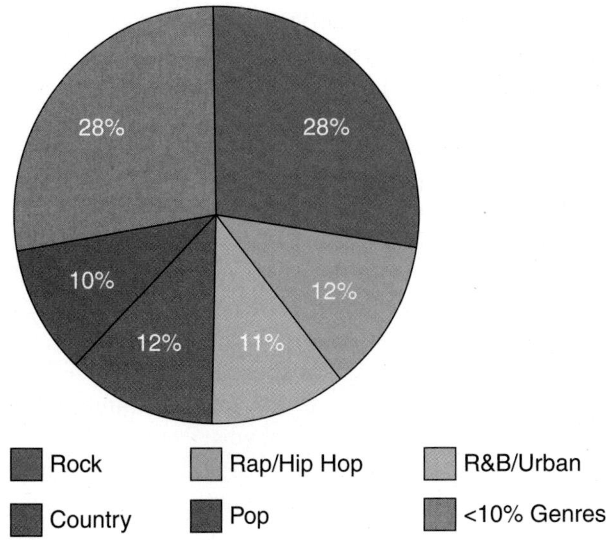

is clearly a grab bag of many substyles, and the "other" category, which amounts to about seven percent, is truly eclectic, including everything from big band and Broadway shows to electronic, emo, and ethnic. The chart above shows those genres that have averaged more than 10 percent market share between 2000 and 2008. These results generally corroborate the artist distribution on *Billboard*'s comprehensive album and year-end charts.

The most striking feature of these charts is what's *not* present. There is no new style that has captured even 10 percent of the market. All of the style families with substantial market share have been active for decades: rap/hip hop, the most recent, dates back to 1979. The various electronic substyles and the numerous world music fusions attract dedicated followings, but they remain niche markets with relatively little crossover to a more mainstream audience. This lack of innovation stands in stark contrast to the 1920s, when the jazzy foxtrot song took over the market, and the 1960s, when rock became the dominant sound.

Why did no new style ascend to a preeminent position in the 2000s? Two evolutionary trends that spanned the entire twentieth century suggest an answer. The first was the shift from melody to rhythm. Around the turn of the twentieth century, the most popular songs were tuneful melodies in waltz rhythm, such as "Take Me Out to the Ball Game." The identity of the song was located almost exclusively in the melody; melodies were coherent enough that they could be sung meaningfully without accompaniment. By contrast, there was little or no rhythmic interest or complexity and the setting was not an integral part of the song.

The songs of the Modern Era also had tuneful melodies, but much of their appeal typically came from the interplay between the rhythm of the melody and the foxtrot or swing rhythm supporting it. Syncopation and other forms of rhythmic play were common in the melody as composed and in the performers' interpretations of the melody, as we heard in songs from "Charleston" to "Chattanooga Choo Choo."

With the ascendancy of rock in the 1960s, the balance between melodic and rhythmic interest swung even more toward rhythm. Embedding the identity of a song exclusively in the melody was now just a relatively infrequent option rather than a requirement. More often, melodic fragments, distributed among the musicians, simply rode the groove, as we heard in the music of James Brown, Bob Dylan, and the Rolling Stones. Even in more tuneful rock and R&B, the most memorable melodic material tends to be repeated melodic hooks, as we heard in songs by the Beatles and Motown acts, rather than riffs that develop into longer phrases. At the same time, rhythm in rock was often more active, denser, and more prominent than in modern-era music.

This shift from melody to rhythm reached its end with rap and techno, which typically have, at most, isolated and repetitive melodic fragments and active and prominent rhythms. Thus, in less than a century popular music morphed from styles in which melody was the almost exclusive source of interest and identity, and rhythms were simple and in the background, to styles in which rhythm was a dominant feature and melody was fragmentary or nonexistent. Given the central role of melody in popular music throughout its history, it's not surprising that the marginal place of melody in techno and rap have resulted in modest market share.

The other long-range trend, the progression of style beats, has also reached an evolutionary endpoint. Recall that style beats provided the rhythmic foundations for four generations of popular music: They became dominant or widely used at approximately 20-year intervals. A two-beat rhythm supported the foxtrot songs beginning in the late 1910s, through the 1920s and beyond. The four-beat rhythm of jazz went mainstream during the swing era; in the late 1930s and early 1940s, it was swing versus sweet. The eight-beat rhythm of rock surfaced in the latter half of the 1950s and became the rhythmic signature of rock in the 1960s. Sixteen-beat rhythms moved from R&B, jazz fusion, and Brazilian music to the disco in the late 1970s, and then into much of the new music of the 1980s, including rap, electronica, and much rock and R&B.

Close observers of the evolution of twentieth-century popular music around 1990 would have predicted that thirty-two-beat rhythms would surface in a dance-oriented genre around the middle of the decade. In fact that occurred, at least to some extent: One can hear occasional machine gun–like electronic percussion sounds in dance music. But this hyperactive rhythm did not become the rhythmic foundation for a new style because it couldn't. At even a slow dance tempo, the thirty-two-beat rhythm is too fast to sing or rap to—consider the speed of a rapper's delivery, and double that.

A different rhythmic foundation—a new style beat—is not a necessary precondition for innovation in popular music. And the new style beat was far from the only significant change. But throughout the twentieth century, it has been the most pervasive and differentiating musical feature of a new style. The vast majority of 1960s rock tracks had a rock beat, and the popular music before rock did not. We know now that further development along this evolutionary path did not occur, for sound musical reasons. So paradigm-shifting innovation must come from another direction.

The nineteenth century saw the birth of American popular music, the development of a distinctively American genre in minstrelsy, the rapid growth of a music industry as stage entertainment and music publishing flourished, and the invention of sound recording. Still, a listener brought from 1800 to 1900 would find much that is familiar in waltz songs like "After the Ball." By contrast, a listener from 1900 would almost certainly be perplexed by the sounds and rhythms of contemporary popular music.

Those contemplating the future of popular music may ponder the question: Will popular music in the twenty-first century develop more as it did in the nineteenth century, with a relentless stream of technological innovations and growth in business, but with little substantive musical change; as it did in the twentieth century, when popular music evolved rapidly and in tandem with technological breakthroughs, continued growth of the music ecosystem, and deep penetration into popular culture; or in a way quite different from either?

Point/Counterpoint

In this outro, I have tried to make the case that popular music is at a point of reckoning—that its continuing evolution and innovation have ground to a halt—and have supported my argument by briefly surveying the patterns that emerge from the music discussed in the text. But there's a lot of music, and especially recent music, that could not be included, and much more that I'm not even aware of: for critic Robert Christgau, listening to music was almost a full-time job for years, and he was able only to cover a small slice of what's out there.

If the course for which you've used this text has been successful for you, you will be a better listener because you'll hear more of what's going on in a track, and you'll have a historical framework for all of the music that you listen to.

So my challenge to you is to challenge my assessment of the state of popular music. Is there music out there that was not covered in the text that is truly innovative? If so, what is the nature of the innovation? Is real innovation even necessary or desirable, or will popular music remain interesting through the infusion of elements from new sound sources or other elements, or music from other cultures, much as the black and white folk elements gave minstrelsy a sound different from the parlor songs of the early nineteenth century? Or will popular music develop in an entirely new direction that's only hinted at by some of today's music? Your responses may not only make you a prophet but also a more astute observer of and participant in today's music.

GLOSSARY

***a cappella*:** Vocal music without instrumental accompaniment.

accent: A musical event that stands out from its neighbors because of a change in one or more musical elements. The most common sources of accent are intensity (the event is louder), duration (longer), density (the event contains more parts), or pitch (higher or lower).

acoustic recording: An early recording process in which sound vibrations were transferred directly to the recording medium (cylinder or disc) by means of a large horn or cone. In 1925 it was replaced by electric recording.

Afropop: A fusion of West African and pop music.

alternative: A term to describe a family of rock-related, punk-inspired styles that began in the early eighties and continues into the twenty-first century.

ambient music: Atmospheric music which emphasizes texture over rhythm: a kind of electronica.

amplifier: A piece of equipment that can increase the strength of an electric signal.

animal dance: A popular dance which emerged in the early 1900s which was adapted or borrowed from a black folk dance.

AOR (album-oriented radio): A type of FM radio format that emphasized a restricted playlist.

arpeggio: A chord whose pitches are performed one after the other instead of simultaneously. Also called broken chord.

art rock: A rock substyle that sought to elevate rock from teen entertainment to artistic statement, often by drawing on or reworking classical compositions (e.g., Emerson, Lake, and Palmer's version of Mussorgsky's Pictures at an Exhibition). Art rock was often distinguished by the use of electronic effects and mood music-like textures far removed from the propulsive rhythms of early rock.

audio CD: An information storage medium in which lasers read digital data stored on a disc.

backbeat: A percussive accent occurring regularly on the second beat of beat pairs: 1 2 1 2 or 1 2 3 4.

bajo sexto: Oversized Mexican twelve-string guitar that typically served as a bass instrument in small groups.

beat: (1) The rhythmic quality of a piece of music that invites a physical response ("that song has a good beat"). (2) The (usually) regular marking of time at walking/dancing/moving speed (usually between 72 and 144 beats per second). (3) The rhythmic foundation of a style or substyle, distinguished by the consistent use of regular rhythms and rhythmic patterns: a two-beat, a rock beat, a shuffle beat.

beguine: In American popular music, an Americanized form of the Cuban rumba. It has a similar rhythmic feel but lacks the clave rhythm heard in authentic Afro-Cuban music.

big-band swing: Swing-era or swing-style music performed by a big band.

blackface: Minstrel show practice in which white and (later) black performers applied burnt cork to darken their complexion

bluegrass: An updated version of country's old-time string band music. Bluegrass developed in the late 1940s under the guidance of mandolinist Bill Monroe.

boogie-woogie: A blues piano style characterized by repetitive bass figures, usually in a shuffle rhythm.

bop (bebop): A jazz style that developed in the 1940s, characterized by fast tempos, irregular streams of notes, and considerable rhythmic conflict.

bossa nova: A samba-based, jazz-influenced Brazilian popular-song style that became popular in the United States in the early 1960s.

break dancing: A vigorous dance form associated with hip-hop music and culture.

British Invasion: An influx of British bands in the early 60s whose styles borrowed from American pop, rock and roll, rhythm and blues, and early blues and who, in turn, were to have a profound influence in the emergence of rock.

broadside: A topical text sung to a well-known tune. Broadsides were, in effect, an urban folk music with printed words.

bugalú: A blend of Latin music and rhythm and blues.

burlesque: In a minstrel show, humorous parodies of cultivated material.

cakewalk: A dance fad of the 1890s; also the music to accompany the dance.

call-and-response: A rapid exchange, usually of rifts, between two different timbres: solo voice and guitar; solo voice and choir; or saxophones and trumpets.

Charleston: The most popular of the vigorous new dances of the early 1920s.

chord: A group of pitches considered as a single unit. The notes of a chord may be played simultaneously, or they may be played in a series as an arpeggio.

chord progression: A sequence of chords. Many of the chord progressions in popular music follow well-used patterns, such as the chord progressions for "Heart and Soul" and "La Bemba."

chorus (refrain): (1) A large singing group. (2) In verse/chorus and rock songs, that part of a song in which both melody and lyrics are repeated. (3) In blues and Tin Pan Alley songs, one statement of the melody.

classic blues: The popular blues style of the 1920s, which typically featured a woman singing the blues (e.g., Bessie Smith) accompanied by one or more jazz musicians.

clave rhythm: The characteristic rhythm of Afro-Cuban music. It can be represented as: //X x x X x x X x // x x X x X x x x //. The x's indicate an eight-beat rhythm; X's are accented notes. To create a reverse clave rhythm, switch the two measures.

claves: Pair of cylindrical wooden sticks that are tapped together

collective improvisation: An improvisational context in which more than one performer is improvising a melody-like line. Collective improvisation is standard practice in New Orleans jazz, free jazz, and much rock-era jazz fusion.

commercial blues: Blues which is performed by professional musicians, is published, and recorded.

comping: In bop jazz style, chordal accompaniment played in rhythmically irregular or unpredictable patterns.

concept album: A rock-era album which represented a unified artistic vision rather than a compilation of a group or individual's songs.

concert band: A band (woodwinds, brass, and percussion instruments) that performs in a concertlike setting (seated onstage, in front of an audience) rather than while marching.

country blues: A family of African American folk blues styles that flourished in the rural South. Country blues differs from commercial blues mainly in its accompanying instrument-usually acoustic guitar-and its tendency toward less regular forms.

country music: A music genre which emerged out of the commercialization, broadcasting, and recording of southern folk music.

country rock: Music combining a strong honky-tonk two-beat with a clear, simple rock rhythm.

cover version: Recording of a song by an act other than the first to record it

crooning: A relaxed, intimate style of singing.

cross-marketing: The practice of using media in tandem so that each helps promote the other. The practice began in the early 1970s, when rock bands toured to promote a newly released recording. Robert Stigwood, producer of Saturday Night Fever, was the first to adapt this promotional strategy to film in a big way by using songs from the soundtrack to spark interest in the film.

dance-oriented rock (DOR): A term coined by Robert Christgau to describe an array of musical styles which emerged in the 1980s, specifically synthesis of the post-punk and post-disco sounds.

deconstruction: Construction of a song out of several components, which can be digitally modified, added to, and otherwise manipulated to create other versions of the song.

deep blues: Early acoustic blues originating from the Mississippi and surrounding areas.

disco: A dance music that rose to popularity in the midseventies. Disco songs typically had a relentless beat; a complex rhythmic texture, usually with a 16-beat rhythm; and rich orchestration, typically an augmented rhythm section with horns and strings.

doo-wop: A pop-oriented R&B genre that typically featured remakes of popular standards or pop-style originals sung by black vocal groups. Doo-wop died out in the early 1960s with the rise of the girl groups and Motown.

downtown Latin style: A watered-down version of Afro-Cuban music intended for the white American market.

duration: The length in time of a musical event.

dynamics: Levels or changes in intensity. The dynamic level of a Ramones song is very loud.

electric recording: A recording procedure developed in the 1920s that converts sound into an electric signal before recording and the converts the electric signal back into sound for playback. With its far superior sound quality, it immediately made acoustic recording obsolete.

electric steel guitar: Invented in the early 1930s, it soon replaced the dobro as the instrument of choice for lap guitarists.

electronica: The umbrella term for a large and varied family of musical styles: house, techno, trance, ambient, jungle, drum & bass, industrial dance, and many more.

endman: A comic in a minstrel troupe. Minstrel performers sat in a semicircle on-stage; an endman sat at one end or the other.

folk music: Music made by a group of people (e.g., Cajuns, Navahos, or whites from rural Appalachia), mostly without formal musical training, primarily for their own amusement or for the amusement of others in the group. Within the group, folk music is transmitted orally. Within the popular tradition, folk music has also referred to folksongs sung by commercial musicians (e.g., the Kingston Trio) or music with elements of folk style (e.g., the folk rock of the late 1960s).

form: The organization of a musical work in time.

four-beat rhythm: A rhythmic foundation in which each beat receives equal emphasis; the common rhythmic basis for jazz.

foxtrot: A popular social dance of the 1920s and 30s that introduced a clearly black beat into mainstream culture.

front line: The horns (or other melody-line instruments, such as the vibraphone) in a jazz combo. The term comes from the position of the horn players on the bandstand: they stand in a line in front of the rhythm instruments.

funk: An R&B-derived style that developed in the 1970s, primarily under the guidance of George Clinton. It is characterized mainly by dense textures (bands may include eight or more musicians) and complex, often 16-beat rhythms.

gangsta rap: A form of rap which emerged in the late 80s and expressed the violence of inner-city life.

genre: Stylistic category.

glam (glitter) rock: A rock style of the early 1970s in which theatrical elements—makeup, outlandish dress—were prominent. David Bowie, in his various incarnations, is considered by many to be the major figure in glam rock.

gospel: A family of religious music styles: there is white and black gospel music. Black gospel music has had the more profound influence on popular music by far. Created around 1930 by Thomas Dorsey and others, gospel has influenced popular singing, especially rhythm and blues, since the early 1950s.

griot: In West African culture, the tribe's healer (witch doctor), historian (preserver of its history in his songs), and, along with the master drummer, most important musician.

grunge: A style of rock music which emerged in the late 80s which fused punk disaffection with the power and distortion of heavy metal.

habanera: A dance created in Cuba during the early nineteenth century that became popular in both Europe and South America. Its characteristic rhythm resurfaced in the Argentine tango and the cakewalk.

harmonics: Sound created on a stringed instrument by depressing the string only partway at certain points, creating higher-pitched sounds with a distinctive ring

harmony: Chords and the study of chord progressions.

headbanging: An high-energy, sometime violent, dance which evolved around heavy metal.

heavy metal: A hard rock style that developed in the early 1970s, featuring often ear-splitting volume; heavy use of distortion; simplified chord progressions and melodies; lyrics that reflect adolescent, often male preoccupations; and elaborate stage shows.

heavy metal: Heavily distorted alternative rock of the 1980s, characterized by both power and defiance.

hip-hop: A term used to describe the African American culture from which rap emerged. Its artistic expressions include not only rap but also break dancing and graffiti.

hokum: A upbeat blues style that emerged between the first and second world wars.

honky-tonk: Country music appropriate for a noisy, working-class bar or club.

house music: An early techno style based originally in Chicago; it was a low-budget continuation of disco.

improvisation: The act of creating music spontaneously rather than performing a previously learned song the same way every time. Improvisation is one of the key elements in jazz. It gives musicians the opportunity to express inspirations and react to situations; requires virtuosity, melodic inventiveness, personality, and the ability to swing.

inflection: Moment-to-moment changes in dynamic level. Aretha Franklin sings in a highly inflected style.

instrumentation: Literally, the instruments chosen to perform a particular score; broadly, the instrumental and vocal accompaniment for a recording.

intensity: The degree of loudness of a musical sound.

interlocutor: The straight man in a minstrel show. The interlocutor would sit in the middle of the semicircle and ask questions of the endmen, who would give comic replies.

interpolation: The insertion of a song into a musical comedy for which it was not written. Interpolation was common in the early years of musical comedy, when producers would insert a song into a show simply because it was a hit.

jazz: A group of popular related styles primarily for listening. Jazz is usually distinguished from the other popular music of an era by greater rhythmic freedom (more syncopation and/or less-insistent beat keeping), extensive improvisation, and more-adventurous harmony. There are two families of jazz styles: those based on a four-beat rhythm and those based on a rock or 16-beat rhythm.

jump band: In the late 1940s, a small band-rhythm section plus a few horns that played a rhythm-and-blues style influenced by big-band swing and electric blues. Saxophonist/vocalist Louis Jordan was a key performer in this style.

Lollapalooza: A music festival during the 90s which featured alternative bands.

loop: A short sound file that can be repeated or combined with other loops to create a background for a song.

mainstream: Prevailing styles.

majors: Major record labels.

mambo: First twentieth-century Latin dance fads to develop on American soil; it merged authentic Afro-Cuban son with big-band horns and riffs

march: Music composed in regularly accented, usually duple meter that is appropriate to accompany marching; a composition in the style of march music.

measure (bar): A consistent grouping of beats. A waltz has measures containing three beats; a march has measures with two beats. Also called bar.

medley: A group of songs connected by musical interludes.

melody: The most musically interesting part of a musical texture. The melody is typically distinguished from other parts by the interest and individuality of its contour and rhythm.

melody: The most musically interesting part of a musical texture. The melody is typically distinguished from other parts by the interest and individuality of its contour and rhythm.

mento: The Jamaican popular music of the early 1950s.

microphone: A device that converts sound waves into an electric signal. The microphone has been in use in popular music since the 1920s.

MIDI (Musical Instrument Digital Interface): A protocol that enables digital devices such as instruments and computers to communicate.

minstrel show: A form of stage entertainment distinguished by cruel parodies of African Americans. Minstrelsy was popular from the early 1840s to the end of the nineteenth century.

mix: A series of songs or dance tracks seamlessly connected by a disc jockey.

modal harmony: Chords built from modal scales, rather than major and minor scales. Modal scales are common in British folk music.

montuno: In Afro-Cuban music, a syncopated accompanying figure, usually played on the piano, that is repeated indefinitely.

Motown sound: A set of stylistic features heard in sixties Motown recordings: melodic saturation, a good mellow beat, a broad spectrum of sound and a predictable format.

MTV: A cable network which began broadcasting music videos in 1981.

multitrack recording: The process of recording each part of a performance separately, then mixing them into a complete performance. The Beatles, along with their producer George Martin, were among the first to take full advantage of multitrack recording techniques.

***musique concrète*:** Music created by used prerecorded sounds.

netlabels: Independent labels that deliver music only online, launch personal websites, start online artist cooperatives, and establish interest groups.

New Orleans jazz: Style of jazz performance based on the early bands that performed in and around New Orleans; revived in the late 1940s, it is based on collective improvisation and quick tempos. The front-line instruments usually include cornet or trumpet, clarinet, and trombone, with a rhythm section usually including banjo, tuba, and sometimes piano. Also called Dixieland jazz.

new wave: The "back to basics" movement within rock beginning in the late 1970s, featuring simplified instrumentation and basic chords and melodies. An early new wave band was the Talking Heads.

no wave: Post-punk substyle, characterized by the music of Sonic Youth.

obbligato: A second melody playing under the main melody.

olio: The second section of a minstrel show-the variety portion that featured a wide range of unrelated acts, much like the later vaudeville shows.

operetta: A light, often humorous, form of opera.

overdubbing: The process of recording an additional part onto an existing recording.

parlor song: A song to be sung at home in the parlor, like Stephen Foster's "Beautiful Dreamer," popular through most of the nineteenth century. Also called home songs and piano bench music.

parlor song: A song to be sung at home in the parlor, like Stephen Foster's "Beautiful Dreamer," popular through most of the nineteenth century. Also called home songs and piano bench music.

patriotic song: A song with a patriotic theme.

payola scandal: The practice of record companies' bribing disk jockeys to secure airplay for their records.

performance style: The way musicians sing and play their instruments

Philadelphia sound: An early 70s style which revised, expanded upon, and modernized the Motwon sound.

piano rag: A marchlike, syncopated composition for the piano.

pitch: The relative highness or lowness of a musical sound, determined by the frequency with which it vibrates.

popular music: Music that appeals to a mass audience, is intended to have wide appeal, and has a sound and a style distinct from classical or folk music.

psychedelic rock (acid rock): A rock substyle defined not by a musical feature but simply by the music's ability to evoke or enhance the drug experience.

punk: A rock style that emerged in the late 1970s characterized musically by relatively simple instrumentation, rhythms, and production. The Ramones and the Sex Pistols were among the best-known punk bands.

queercore: A movement which reacted against mainstream gay and lesbian views and musically centered around punk and industrial rock.

race record: A term that came into use in the early 1920s to describe recordings by African American artists intended for sale primarily in the African American community.

race record: A term that came into use in the early 1920s to describe recordings by African American artists intended for sale primarily in the African American community.

ragtime: A popular style at the turn of the twentieth century that mixed European forms, harmony, and textures with African-inspired syncopation. Ragtime began as a piano music, but soon the term was applied to any music-song and dance as well as piano music-that had some syncopation.

rap: A musical style of the 1980s and '90s characterized by a rhymed text spoken in a heightened voice over a repetitive, mostly rhythmic accompaniment.

rave: A huge dance party conducted in a large space: outdoors, an abandoned warehouse, or even a large club. Ecstasy and other "designer" drugs were very much part of the scene; they suppressed the need to eat or sleep.

reggae: The most widely known Jamaican popular music, it has a distinctive, intoxicating rhythm. It emerged around 1970 in the music of Jimmy Cliff, Bob Marley, and others.

reverse clave rhythm: A version of the clave rhythm, in which the second half of the pattern comes first.

revue: A type of stage entertainment popular in the first third of the century. Revues were topical; they often lampooned prominent public figures. They had a flimsy plot, designed to link—however loosely—a series of songs, dance numbers, and comedy routines.

rhythm: The time dimension of music. The cumulative result of musical events as they happen over time.

rhythm and blues (R&B): A term used since the midforties to describe African American popular styles, especially those influenced by blues and/or dance music.

rhythm section: The part of a musical group that supplies the rhythmic and harmonic foundation of a performance. Usually includes at least one chord instrument (guitar, piano, or keyboard), a bass instrument, and a percussion instrument (typically the drum set).

riff: A short (two to seven pitches), rhythmically interesting melodic idea.

riot grrrl: A 90s militant feminist movement which supported post-punk bands.

rock beat: Eight evenly spaced sounds per measure (or two per beat) over a strong backbeat.

rock steady: Ska's evolution in the latter half of the sixties, in which musicians added a backbeat layer over the afterbeats

rockabilly: According to Carl Perkins, a country take on rhythm and blues, performed mainly by white Southerners, that combined elements of country music with rock and roll. Rockabilly was most popular in the midfifties.

salsa: A popular dance oriented music which developed out of a fusion of Cuban, Puerto Rican, and Latin American musical styles.

sample: A small sound file. There are two basic kinds of samples in common use. One is the recorded sound of a voice or group of voices, an instrument (such as a grand piano) or group of instruments (a violin section), or some other sound. This sound can then be activated through another device. The other main kind of sampling involves lifting short excerpts from existing recordings to use in a new recording, much like a visual artist will use found objects to create a collage or assemblage. It has been a staple of rap background tracks since the technology became available in the mideighties.

sequencer: A device that enables a person to assemble a sound file track by track. Using a sequencer that can store eight tracks, a person can re-create the sound of a band: one track for the bass, another for the rhythm guitar, and so on.

set: A group of songs performed by a band or presented by a disc jockey. Popular and jazz musicians play a set of songs, then take an extended break. A DJ may mix songs into a set that provides continuous music for a half hour or more.

singer-songwriter: A term that came into use around 1970 to describe songwriters who performed their own music. The music of singer-songwriters was generally characterized by an emphasis on melody, a folklike accompaniment, and a relatively low dynamic level.

sixteen-beat rhythm: A style beat in which the fastest rhythmic layer moves four times the speed of the beat: 4 times per beat $\times$ 4 beats $=$ 16-beat rhythm. First popularized in disco and funk, it has been the most widely used style beat since the early 1980s.

ska: The dominant Jamaican popular music through the first part of the 1960s. The most distinctive feature of ska is a strong afterbeat: a strong, crisp chunk on the latter part of each beat.

song interpretation: A rendition of a song which emphasizes a performer's unique understanding and emotions.

song plugger: A publishing-house pianist who could play a new song for a professional singer or a prospective customer.

songster: A book containing the lyrics of popular songs.

soul: A term used widely in the 1960s by both white and black Americans to describe popular music by African Americans, particularly music, like that of James Brown, marginally influenced by pop or white rock styles.

sound collage: A compositional technique created by Granmaster Flash in which sound clips of recorded material are cut and pasted together.

speakeasy: Prohibition-era club that required a softly spoken password for admission.

standard: A song that remains popular well after its initial appearance; songs that live on in recordings, films, and live performances.

stride piano: An offshoot of ragtime that typically featured a more complex bass/chord accompaniment and elaborate figuration in the melody.

style: The set of those common features found in the music of a time, place, culture, or individual.

style beat: A distinctive beat which is associated with the music of a particular era.

surf music: A regional rock from California notable for high-register close harmony vocals and innovative guitar effects.

swing: Rhythmic play over a four-beat rhythm

syncopation: Accents that come between the beats of a regular rhythm, rather than with them.

synthesizer: A family of electronic instruments in which sounds are produced electronically, either by generating a waveform within the machine or by digitally recording acoustic sounds (e.g., the tones of a piano). Most, but not all, synthesizers are operated by a keyboard.

Tambo and Bones: Nicknames for the endmen in a minstrel show, so called because one usually played a tambourine and the other a pair of bones.

techno: Post-disco dance music in which most or all of the sounds are electronically generated.

tejano: Hybrid blending Mexican music with outside influences.

tempo: The speed of the beat.

texture: The relationship of the parts in a musical performance.

thumb-brush style: An early country guitar style in which the performer plays the melody on the lower strings and, between melody notes, brushes the chords on the upper strings. It was first popularized by Maybelle Carter.

timbre: The distinctive tone quality of a voice or an instrument.

Tin Pan Alley: A nickname for a section of East 28th Street in New York City, where many music publishers had their offices. Also, the styles of the songs created in the first half of the century for these publishers: a Tin Pan Alley song refers to songs by Irving Berlin, George Gershwin, and their contemporaries.

toasting: The practice developed by Jamaican disc jockeys of delivering a steady stream of patter. Much of it was topical, even personal: they would pick out, and sometimes pick on, people in the crowd that had gathered around. Toasting is a direct forerunner of rap: both initially featured topical, humorous commentary over pre-existing music.

torch song: A song about unrequited or lost love.

traditional country vocal: A singing style characterized by a flat, sometime nasal sound with little inflection. (a straight tone)

trio: One of the two main sections of a march, in a different key

triplet: Rhythmic pattern that divides each beat into three equal parts

tropical Latin: A kind of rock distinguished by a large number of percussive intruments and a clave-like rhythm.

tumbao: A syncopated bass pattern characteristic of Afro-Cuban music.

twelve-bar blues form: The most widely used form for one chorus of a blues song. It is defined principally by its chord progression, which features I, IV, and V in a consistent pattern over twelve bars: I(1), I(3) / IV(5), I (7) / V(9), I(11). The 12-bar blues form is used in both vocal and instrumental songs. In sung 12-bar blues songs, the typical lyric is a rhymed couplet, with the first line repeated.

two-beat rhythm: The division of the measure into two primary beats or accents; the rhythmic basis of the fox trot and other early syncopated instrumental styles.

unison: Two performers playing the same pitch.

uptown Latin style: The sound of authentic Afro-Cuban music in the 1940s and '50s.

vaudeville: A form of stage entertainment popular from the 1880s to about 1930. It consisted of a series of acts: singers, dancers, novelty performers, and comics. It differed from the revue and musical comedy in that there was no attempt to link vaudeville acts into a dramatically coherent whole.

verse/chorus form: The most popular song form of the late nineteenth century. The verse tells a story in several stages (this section is strophic, i.e., different words are set to the same melody), whereas the chorus, which comes at the end of each verse, repeats both words and melody to reinforce the main message of the song. In early verse/chorus songs, the chorus was often sung by a small group, usually a quartet.

vibrato: Subtle alteration of the pitch of a note.

walkaround: The conclusion of a minstrel show, featuring the entire troupe in a grand finale of song and dance.

waltz song: A type of song popular around 1900 in which a flowing melody is supported by a simple, waltz-time accompaniment.

western swing: A swing style of country music which emerged in the Southwest in the 1930s.

INDEX

Note: Entries in quotes indicate song titles. Entries in italics indicate albums, plays, movies, or books.

F

R

S

T